Bk of North
dividend plus
460

WITHDRAWN

THE WORLD OF PSYCHOLOGY

THE WORLD OF PSYCHOLOGY

Edited with Introductions by

G. B. LEVITAS

I

THE WORLDS OF PERCEPTION

MAN AND HIS EMOTIONS

George Braziller   New York

Copyright © 1963, by G. B. Levitas

Published simultaneously in Canada by Ambassador Books, Ltd., Toronto

All rights reserved.
For information, address the publisher,
George Braziller, Inc.
One Park Avenue, New York 10016

Library of Congress Catalog Card Number:
62-18229
First Printing March, 1963
Second Printing September, 1963
Third Printing April, 1964
Fourth Printing May, 1965

Printed in the United States of America

67457

ACKNOWLEDGMENTS

The editor and publisher have made every effort to determine and credit the holders of copyright of the selections in this book. Any errors or omissions may be rectified in future volumes. The editor and publisher wish to thank the following for permission to reprint the material included in this anthology:

George Allen and Unwin Ltd.—for "Beyond Good and Evil" from *The Philosophy of Nietzsche,* tr. by Helen Zimmern.

American Psychological Association—for "Emotional Expression in Chinese Literature" by Otto Klineberg, *Journal of Abnormal and Social Psychology,* Vol. 33, No. 4 (1938), pp. 517-20. By permission of Otto Klineberg;—for "Value and Need as Organizing Factors in Perception" by Jerome S. Bruner and Cecile C. Goodman, *Journal of Abnormal and Social Psychology,* Vol. 42 (1947), pp. 33-44. By permission of Jerome S. Bruner.

The American Sociological Association and Erich Fromm—for his "Individual and Social Origins of Neurosis" from *American Sociological Review,* Vol. 9 (1944), pp. 380-384. By permission of the author.

The Art Journal—for "Art and Reality" by Margaret Mead from *College Art Journal,* Vol. 2, No. 4 (1943), pp. 119-121. By permission of the author.

The Association for Childhood Education International (Washington, D.C.)—for "Fear" by Harold Ellis Jones and Mary Cover Jones from *Childhood Education,* November, 1928, Vol. 5, No. 3. Reprinted by permission of the Association for Childhood Education International.

Balliere, Tindall & Cox Ltd. and Johann Ambrosius Barth and Dr. T. Schmidt-Kraepelin—for *Lectures on Clinical Psychiatry* by Emil Kraepelin, tr. by T. Johnstone. Originally published by Johann Ambrosius Barth as *Introduction to the Psychiatric Clinic.*

Barron's Educational Series, Inc.—for *Emile,* Vol. I, by Jean Jacques Rousseau, tr. by Rosalie Feltenstein.

Basic Books, Inc.—for "Dostoevsky and Parricide" and "Humour" from *The Collected Papers of Sigmund Freud,* Vol. 5, ed. by Ernest Jones. By permission of Basic Books, Inc.

ACKNOWLEDGMENTS

G. Bell and Sons, Ltd.—for *Moral Duties* by Cicero, tr. by Cyrus Edmonds. (Included in Bohn's Classical Library, published by G. Bell and Sons, Ltd.)

George Braziller, Inc. and W. H. Allen Ltd. and The Pegasus Press—for *Owls Do Cry* by Janet Frame © Janet Frame 1960;—and for *Myth and Guilt* by Theodor Reik © Theodor Reik 1957.

Burns and Oates Ltd. and the Newman Press—for *The Complete Works of St. John of the Cross*. Tr. from the critical ed. of P. Silverio de Santa Teresa, C.D., and ed. by E. Allison Peers, Vol. III.

Cornelia James Cannon—for "What Strong Emotions Do to Us" by Walter B. Cannon, *Harper's Magazine*, 1922, No. 145, pp. 234-241.

Chatto & Windus Ltd. and Mrs. Montague—for "Action" from *Action and Other Stories* by C. E. Montague. Copyright owned by Mrs. M. Montague.

City Lights Books—for "Howl for Carl Solomon" from *Howl and Other Poems* by Allen Ginsberg © 1956 and 1959 by Allen Ginsberg.

Clarendon Press, Oxford—for *De Anima* and *Parva Naturalia* from *The Oxford Translation of Aristotle* by permission of the Clarendon Press;—and for *Conditioned Reflexes* by Ivan Pavlov, tr. and ed. by G. V. Anrep.

Duke University Press—for "Apparitions: Two Theories" by H. H. Price from *Journal of Parapsychology*, Vol. 24, June, 1960, pp. 110-128. By permission of the *Journal of Parapsychology* and the author.

E. P. Dutton & Co., Inc.—for *We* by Eugene Zamiatin, tr. by Gregory Zillzboorg. Copyright, 1924, by E. P. Dutton & Co., Inc. Renewal, 1952, by Gregory Zilboorg. Dutton Paperback. Reprinted by permission of the publisher.

The Free Press of Glencoe, Inc.—for "The Commercial Artist" by Mason Griff from *Identity and Anxiety*, ed. by Stein, Vidich and White. © 1960 by The Free Press, a Corporation.

Grune and Stratton, Inc.—for "Self-Actualization: a Study in Psychological Health" by A. H. Maslow, from *Symposia on Topical Issues*, ed. by W. Wolff, Vol. I, "Values in Personality Research." By permission of A. H. Maslow.

Harper and Row, Publishers—and Chatto and Windus Ltd. for "The Claxtons" from *Brief Candles* by Aldous Huxley. Copyright 1929 by Aldous Huxley. Reprinted by permission of Harper and Row, Publishers, and the author.

The Hogarth Press Ltd.—for "Death of Hamlet's Father" from *Essays in Applied Psychoanalysis* by Ernest Jones;—and for "Dostoevsky and Parricide" and "Humour" from the Standard Edition of the *Complete Psychological Works of Sigmund Freud*, ed. by James Strachey, Vol. XXI.

Houghton Mifflin Company and Russell and Volkening, Inc.—for "Eli, the Fanatic" from *Goodbye, Columbus* by Philip Roth. Copyright © 1957, 1959 by Philip Roth;—and The Cresset Press Ltd. for *The Heart Is a Lonely Hunter* by Carson McCullers. Copyright 1940 by Carson McCullers. By permission of the author.

Humanities Press Inc. and Routledge & Kegan Paul Ltd.—for *Practice and Theory of Individual Psychology* by Alfred Adler, tr. by P. Radin.

Peter H. Knapp—for his "The Ear, Listening and Hearing" from *Journal of American Psychoanalytic Society*, published by The American Psychoanalytic Association, Vol. I, No. 4, pp. 672-689.

Alfred A. Knopf, Inc.—for "Saint Manuel Bueno, Martyr" by Miguel de Unamuno from *Spanish Stories and Tales* ed. by Harriet de Onis. Copyright 1954 by Alfred A. Knopf, Inc. Reprinted by permission of Alfred A. Knopf, Inc.

Libra Publishers, Inc.—for "An Existential View of a Man Suffering from Chronic Schizophrenia" by Maurice Vaisberg from *The Journal of Existential Psychiatry*, Winter-Spring, 1961, No. 4, pp. 543-547. Reprinted by permission of Libra Publishers, Inc.

ACKNOWLEDGMENTS

The Macmillan Company and William Heinemann Ltd.—for *The Gambler* by Fëdor Dostoevsky, tr. by Constance Garnett. First published in 1914 by William Heinemann Ltd.; and The Macmillan Co. of Canada Ltd., Macmillan and Co. Ltd. and Bertha Georgie Yeats—for "Sailing to Byzantium" from *Collected Poems of W. B. Yeats*. Copyright 1928 by The Macmillan Company. Copyright 1956 by Bertha Georgie Yeats.

Judith Merril—for her "Dead Center." Copyright 1954 by Fantasy House, Inc.; originally appeared in *Magazine of Fantasy and Science Fiction*.

National Psychological Association for Psychoanalysis, Inc.—for "Psychoanalytic Observations on Olfaction" by George G. Wayne and Arthur A. Clinco from *Psychoanalysis and The Psychoanalytic Review*, Vol. 46, No. 4, Winter, 1959, pp. 64-74. Reprinted through the courtesy of the editors and publisher, National Psychological Association for Psychoanalysis, Inc.

New Directions, Publishers—for "Intimacy" and "Childhood of a Leader" from *Intimacy and Other Stories* by Jean-Paul Sartre, tr. by Lloyd Alexander. Copyright 1948 by New Directions. Reprinted by permission of New Directions, Publishers.

W. W. Norton & Co., Inc.—for *Childhood and Society* by Erik H. Erikson. Copyright 1950 by W. W. Norton & Co., Inc. By permission of W. W. Norton & Co., Inc.

Psychoanalytic Quarterly, Inc.—for "Psychology of Time Perception" by Edmund Bergler and Géza Róheim from *The Psychoanalytic Quarterly*, Vol. XV, No. 2, pp. 190-206;—and H. Robert Blank for his "Dreams of the Blind" from *Psychoanalytic Quarterly*, Vol. XXVII, No. 2, pp. 158-174.

Random House, Inc. and Chatto and Windus Ltd.—for "Swann's Way" from *Remembrance of Things Past* by Marcel Proust, tr. by C. K. Scott Moncrieff. Copyright 1928 and renewed 1956 by The Modern Library, Inc.;—for *Basic Psychiatry* by Edward A. Strecker. Copyright 1952 by Edward A. Strecker;—for "The Horla" from *The Best Stories of Guy de Maupassant*;—and for *Against the Grain* by J. K. Huysmans.

Schocken Books, Inc.—for "The Hunter Gracchus" and "A Little Fable" from *The Great Wall of China* by Franz Kafka. Copyright 1936, 1937 by Heinr. Mercy Sohn, Prague. Copyright 1946, 1948 by Schocken Books, Inc. Tr. by Willa and Edwin Muir.

University of Chicago Press—for "Two Types of Jewish Mothers" by Martha Wolfenstein from *Childhood in Contemporary Cultures*, ed. by Margaret Mead and Martha Wolfenstein. Copyright 1955 by The University of Chicago © The University of Chicago, 1955. All rights reserved. Copyright 1955 under the International Copyright Union. Reprinted by permission of the University of Chicago Press.

The Viking Press and William Heinemann Ltd. and Laurence Pollinger Ltd. on behalf of the author—for "The End of the Party" from *Twenty-One Stories* by Graham Greene. Copyright 1947 by Graham Greene; and Laurence Pollinger Ltd., the Estate of the late Frieda Lawrence and William Heinemann Ltd.—for "Odour of Chrysanthemums" from *The Complete Short Stories of D. H. Lawrence*. All rights reserved. Reprinted by permission of The Viking Press.

World Publishing Co.—for *Face of the Deep* by Jacob Twersky. Copyright 1953 by Jacob Twersky; and Brandt and Brandt—for "Silent Snow, Secret Snow" from *The Collected Short Stories of Conrad Aiken*. Copyright 1932 by Conrad Aiken, Copyright © 1960 by Conrad Aiken; and The Dreiser Trust—for "Hands" from *Chains* by Theodore Dreiser. Copyright 1927 by Theodore Dreiser. Copyright renewed 1955 by Helen R. Dreiser.

Yale University Press, Inc.—for *Psychology and Religion* by **C. G. Jung.** © 1938 by Yale University Press, Inc. Yale Paperbound. All rights reserved.

PREFACE

THE RELATIONSHIP between literature and psychology is an intimate one—and if psychology has done much to clarify some literary problems, literature in its turn has offered its insights to the psychologist. In this book, we have tried to bring together some of the psychological literature of the past century, its sources in classical philosophy and pertinent fiction. In so doing, we have included the findings of both the rational and analytic schools. Occasionally, the fiction emerges as a case study. Equally often, however, we can perceive the Janus-face of the relationship: the fiction itself offers us a profound psychological knowledge that transcends our intellectual awareness of meaning and offers us an emotional experience of truth that is more vital and compelling than any psychological study-in-depth could hope to be.

A long time ago, Aristotle gave the world the concept of catharsis when he recognized the object of art to be the release of tension. Aristotle assumed that the explicit events of the tragedy provided the source of release, and in framing his theory he raised many important questions about the nature of art which have not yet been fully answered. Until Sigmund Freud rocked us into awareness of the role played by the unconscious in shaping our literature, the field of literary criticism remained relatively static. Freud recognized that art served to transform the fearsome visions of our dreams into an aesthetically satisfying and emotionally reassuring form. He introduced psychological tools into the literary world and turned his own talents to analysis of fiction.

Freud's analyses, as well as those of psychologically oriented critics who followed him, have often been attacked—purportedly because they have replaced aesthetic criticism with psychological reductionism. But such attacks have little basis in fact. Psychological analysis of fiction serves not to narrow fiction and force it down the neck of the Freudian bottle but rather to broaden the base of literary criticism. The psychologists have concerned themselves not only with the exposure of the inner conflict. They have brought a profound understanding to aesthetic problems, they have attempted to deal with the old Aristotelian concepts of death and stasis in art in terms of form as well as content. The tendency to attach psychological labels to aesthetic events has not blurred our aesthetic vision but rather has served to illuminate both the nature of man and of his works.

In organizing this book we arranged our material in a fairly traditional manner. We look at man first in terms of his senses, then his emotions, and finally in terms of his personality and social role. Theoretical and factual material appears first and is followed by fictional. But we hope that the reader will browse through this book, reading, perhaps, the fiction first and the psychology afterward, or sandwiching fiction between psychology and the short editorial notes that provide a brief guide to each section. In this way, he will be able to see the stories not merely as examples of a particular mode of thinking or as the source of a particular theory. He will learn that some of his cherished notions regarding the psychology of the handicapped, the mentally ill, and those "gifted" with extrasensory perception are flatly contradicted by psychological findings. And he will also learn that psychology and literature are not implacable enemies; that each in its own way may complement the other; and that both are finally, different expressions of that marvelous and miserable creature: the human being.

I would like to thank Dr. Robert Popkin and Dr. Milton Handler for their kindness in helping me with this volume. I would also like to express my sincere appreciation to Liselotte Bendix, the librarian at the New York Psychoanalytic Institute who aided me in my search for material by leading me safely through the maze of psychological literature to those subjects in which I was interested. I wish to thank Kim Cohen and George Brantl whose constructive criticisms and suggestions were invaluable to me in the compilation of this book.

Finally, I want to express my appreciation to my family whose forbearance made this book possible.

CONTENTS

Preface   vii

BOOK ONE   THE WORLDS OF PERCEPTION

     I.   The World of the Child   3

JEAN JACQUES ROUSSEAU—*Emile*   4
JEAN PIAGET—*Intellectual Evolution from Childhood to Adult Life*   6
JUDITH MERRIL—*Dead Center*   18

     II.   The Worlds of the Blind and the Deaf   41

H. ROBERT BLANK—*Dreams of the Blind*   43
PETER HOBART KNAPP—*The Ear, Listening and Hearing*   56
WILLIAM JAMES—*The Absence of Certain Sensory Experiences in the Deaf*   71
JACOB TWERSKY—*The Face of the Deep*   77
JONATHAN SWIFT—*On His Deafness*   97
CARSON MCCULLERS—*The Heart Is a Lonely Hunter*   97

     III.   The Worlds of Smell and Taste   128

ARISTOTLE—*On the Soul*   129
GEORGE G. WAYNE and ARTHUR A. CLINCO—*Psychoanalytic Observations on Olfaction*   131
J. K. HUYSMANS—*Against the Grain*   141

MARCEL PROUST—*Swann's Way* 150
O. HENRY—*The Furnished Room* 154

IV. The World as We See It and the World as It Is . . . 160

FRANCIS BACON—*Idols of Perception* 161
JEROME S. BRUNER and CECILE C. GOODMAN—*Value and Need as Organizing Factors in Perception* 168
LEWIS CARROLL—*The Gardener's Song* 179
THOMAS HARDY—*The Three Strangers* 181

V. The Sixth Sense . . . 200

ARISTOTLE—*On Prophetic Dreams* 202
H. H. PRICE—*Apparitions: Two Theories* 206
DANIEL DEFOE—*The Apparition of Mrs. Veal* 222

BOOK TWO MAN AND HIS EMOTIONS . . . 231

I. The Expression of Emotions . . . 233

WALTER B. CANNON—*What Strong Emotions Do to Us* . . . 235
HAROLD E. JONES and MARY COVER JONES—*Maturation and Emotion—Fear of Snakes* 244
ERNEST JONES—*Fear, Guilt and Hate* 251
ERNEST JONES—*Jealousy* 265
SIGMUND FREUD—*Humour* 279
OTTO KLINEBERG—*Emotional Expression in Chinese Literature* 284
RYUNOSUKE AKUTAGAWA—*The Handkerchief* 288
JONATHAN SWIFT—*To Mr. DeLaney* 295
WILLIAM BLAKE—*A Poison Tree* 295
ROBERT BROWNING—*Soliloquy of the Spanish Cloister* . . . 296
GRAHAM GREENE—*The End of the Party* 298
D. H. LAWRENCE—*Odour of Chrysanthemums* 305
SAMUEL L. CLEMENS—*Cannibalism in the Cars* 322

II. Psychoses: Schizophrenia and Manic-Depressive Psychoses	330
ERIK H. ERIKSON—*Early Ego Failure: Jean*	332
EMIL KRAEPELIN—*Lectures on Clinical Psychiatry*	342
CONRAD AIKEN—*Silent Snow, Secret Snow*	387
JANET FRAME—*Owls Do Cry*	402
GUY DE MAUPASSANT—*The Horla*	419
III. Neuroses	440
A. Hysteria and Anxiety	442
EDWARD A. STRECKER—*"Functional" Sickness*	442
ERICH FROMM—*Individual and Social Origins of Neurosis*	475
EDGAR ALLAN POE—*William Wilson*	481
THEODORE DREISER—*The Hand*	497
B. Obsessions and Compulsions	513
GORDIN RAF—*A Case of Kleptomania*	513
SIGMUND FREUD—*Dostoevsky and Parricide*	520
ALAN NELSON—*The Shopdropper*	535
FËDOR DOSTOEVSKY—*The Gambler*	543

BOOK ONE

THE WORLDS OF PERCEPTION

The study of human perception is basic to any understanding of the human mind. How man perceives the world about him has bearing not only upon his sensual life but upon his intellectual evolution as well. Yet the part played by each sense organ in creating for every human being a viable picture of his environment is little understood by most persons. Through his varying modes of perception, man finds and interprets his world.

I

THE WORLD OF THE CHILD

If we could thrust ourselves into the mind of a child to recapture even fleetingly his clear-eyed vision of the world, what would we experience? We would find a new sense of time—the imperative NOW—more fluid than our segmented, restricted adult clock-time, less subject to past and future. Our emotions, in maturity concealed, would bubble to the surface of awareness. The shades and shadows that condition our adult existence would be washed away by the light of wholeness with which the child views the universe.

This freshness of vision is more than a property of childhood; it is the essence of innocence itself. Once mature, we lose the ability to see unqualified wholes and replace it with the equivocating complexity of adult vision. The white hero and the black villain fuse to become the vacillating gray man. Expressions of love and hatred, so ready to erupt into consciousness in childhood, appear in the adult only in dreams or in times of extreme emotional stress.

Rousseau's singular concern with the preservation of this childlike quality can be seen in everything he wrote. He equated his "noble savage" with a child, but he was cognizant that survival in the adult world was dependent upon the development of complexity. His educational program for Émile recognized the necessity for man to evolve psychologically as he does physically from a one-celled being to a multi-faceted organism. Yet Rousseau wistfully hoped to maintain at least a thread of innocence in the complex web of adult life.

Like all children, the child in Judith Merril's story is aware of only one need—the need for love. This awareness is simple, direct, unquestioning. When his love is threatened, he takes the only step he can—but because there is an abyss between him and the adult world around him, his innocence leads to tragedy.

JEAN JACQUES ROUSSEAU/Émile: The Child's View of History

ALTHOUGH MEMORY and reasoning are essentially two different faculties, yet the one does not really develop except with the other. Before the age of reason, the child does not receive ideas, but images; and there is this difference between the one and the other, that images are only absolute depictions of tangible objects, and that ideas are notions about objects, determined by certain relationships. An image can be alone in the mind which conceives it; but every idea presupposes others. When one imagines, one does nothing but see; when one conceives, one compares. Our sensations are purely passive, while all our perceptions or ideas spring from an active principal which judges. That will be demonstrated in the following.

I say, then, that children, not being capable of judgment, have no true memory. They retain sounds, faces, sensations, rarely ideas, more rarely their connections. In arguing against me that they do learn a few elements of geometry, people think to prove a case against me; but quite the contrary, it is in my favor that it is proved. It shows that, far from knowing how to reason by themselves, they do not even know how to retain another's reasoning; for if you follow these little geometricians in their method, you see at once that they have retained the exact impression of only the figure and the terms of the demonstration. At the slightest objection, they are at a loss; turn the figure upside down, they are at a loss. All their knowledge is in sensation; nothing has passed into the understanding. Their memory itself is hardly more perfect than the other faculties, since it is almost always necessary, when they are grown-up, that they learn again the things for which they learned the words in childhood.

I am, however, far from thinking that children have no kind of reasoning power. On the contrary, I see that they reason very well about everything with which they are acquainted and which is connected with their present, tangible interest. But it is about their knowledge that one is deceived, by lending them what they do not have, and by making them reason about that which they do not know how to understand. One is again deceived in wishing to make them attentive to considerations which touch them in no way, such as that of their interest in the future, of their happiness when they are men, of the esteem which people will have for them when they are grown-up; speeches which, made to beings lacking all foresight, signify absolutely nothing for them.

By a still more ridiculous error, they are made to study

history; it is imagined that history is within their grasp because it is only a collection of facts. But what is meant by this word "facts"? Is it thought that the connections which determine historical facts are so easy to grasp that the ideas about them are formed effortlessly in children's minds? Is it thought that the true knowledge of events is separable from that of their causes, from that of their effects, and that history has so little to do with morality that one can know the one without the other? If you see in men's actions only outward and purely external movements, what do you learn from history? Absolutely nothing; and this study, stripped of all interest, gives you no more pleasure than instruction. If you wish to appreciate these actions in terms of their moral connections, try to make these connections understandable to your pupils, and you will see then if history is appropriate to their age.

Readers, always remember that he who speaks to you is neither a sage nor a philosopher, but a simple man, a friend of the truth, without party, without system; a solitary, who, living little with men, has less occasion to be imbued with their prejudices, and more time to reflect upon what strikes him when he has dealings with them. My reasons are less founded upon principles than upon facts; and I think I cannot better place you in a position to judge it than by often giving you some example of the observations which suggested them to me.

I had gone to spend a few days in the country at the home of a devoted mother who took great care of her children and of their education. One morning when I was present at the lessons of the elder, his tutor, who had instructed him very well in ancient history, taking up that of Alexander, lit upon the famous draught of Philip the physician, which had been illustrated, and was surely well worth the trouble. The tutor, an estimable man, made several reflections upon Alexander's daring, which did not please me, but which I refrained from disputing, so as not to discredit him in his pupil's mind. At dinner, according to French custom, they did not fail to have the little fellow babble away a great deal. The natural vivacity of his age and the expectation of certain applause made him give out with a thousand foolishnesses, in the midst of which there appeared from time to time a few fortunate words which caused the rest to be forgotten. Finally came the story of Philip the physician. He told it very clearly and with much grace. After the usual tribute of compliments which the mother demanded and the son expected, they argued about what he had said. The greatest number criticized Alexander's temerity; some, following the tutor's example, admired his firmness, his courage, which made me understand that none of those who were present saw what constituted the true beauty of this draught. "As for me,"

I said to them, "it seems to me that if there is the least courage, the least firmness in Alexander's action, it is nothing but folly." Then everyone joined together, and agreed that it was folly. I was going to answer and to get excited, when a woman who was next to me, and who had not opened her mouth, leaned toward my ear, and said in a low voice, "Be quiet, Jean-Jacques, they will not understand you." I looked at her, I was impressed, and I was silent.

After dinner, suspecting, because of several indications, that my young doctor had understood nothing at all of the story which he had told so well, I took him by the hand, took a turn about the park with him, and having questioned him at my ease, I found that he admired more than anyone the vaunted courage of Alexander. But do you know where he saw this courage? Only in swallowing in a single gulp a bad-tasting drink, without hesitating, without showing the slightest repugnance. The poor child, who had been made to take medicine not a fortnight ago, and who had taken it only with infinite trouble, still had its bad taste in his mouth. Death, poisoning, did not enter his mind except as unpleasant sensations, and he did not conceive, as far as he was concerned, of any other poison but senna. However, it must be declared that the hero's firmness had made a great impression upon his young heart, and that at the first medicine he had to swallow, he had quite resolved to be an Alexander. Without going into explanations which were clearly beyond his reach, I confirmed him in these praiseworthy intentions, and I returned, laughing to myself at the lofty wisdom of fathers and teachers, who think of teaching history to children.

JEAN PIAGET/Intellectual Evolution from Childhood to Adult Life*

1. Introduction

THE SUBJECT of our investigations is intellectual evolution—that is, the development of knowledge and of its different modes, the genesis of the forms of thought, of their adaptation to experience, and the rules which they obey.

In its point of departure this evolution raises a problem

---

* Reprinted from Jean Piaget, *Factors Determining Human Behavior* by Edgar Douglas Adrian and others. Copyright 1937 by the President and Fellows of Harvard College. By permission of Harvard University Press.

which is essentially biological; the relationship between understanding or perception and its objects is a particular case of adaptation—that is, a combination of assimilation and accommodation—which unites the organism with its external environment. The first question which the theory of the development of . . . understanding must investigate is how this relationship results from biological organization and adaptation. For example, it is impossible to determine how the elementary forms of spatial perception are evolved without seeing how they are related to the mode of inheritance of the organs of perception and of equilibrium, and to the different modes of organic adaptation.

But in the last analysis the evolution of individual thought is closely enmeshed in collective systems of knowledge, especially in those great systems of rational collaboration which deductive and experimental science has produced. The genetic theory of knowledge must therefore reach out into an historico-critical analysis of scientific thought, and also into genetic logic. For instance, to understand the evolution of the idea of space in the mind of a child, it is not enough to know how this idea is first born. One must also determine how the so-called "displacement groups" which form it follow one another in succession from the motor level to that of the most abstract conceptions; one must establish the respective parts of the scheme of logic and of the intuition in this formation; one must define exactly the relationship between the ideas of space and those of time, object, number, movement, speed, etc. In short, truly to understand the psychological aspect of the development of space, one must attack all the problems which this idea and related ideas suggest in the realm of mathematics and physics; but not from a point of view which is purely reflective and abstract, rather from one which is genetic and experimental. A comparative analysis must intervene between the psychological development of thought and the history of science.

The psychology of intellectual evolution leans therefore upon the biological theories of adaptation, the psychological theories of understanding, the sociological theories of signs and norms (the rules of socialized thought), the history of science, and upon comparative logic. One can then consider this special branch of psychology as a genetic theory of knowledge, a broad theory which must borrow its elements from a very great number of fields of research, thus partially synthesizing them, but withal an exact and well-defined theory, which has its own method, namely, the envisaging of intellectual realities only from the point of view of their development and genetic construction.

In fact, the best method for the psychological theory of the development of . . . understanding will always be the analysis of the intellectual evolution of the child. The thought of the child alone constitutes a continuous process which by a normal evolution links the initial sensory-motor adaptations to the socialized and scientific forms of understanding. In so far as the development of individual thought from birth to adult life can be observed directly and by experiment, and in so far as it is also open to the influences which various adult social groups have on the formation of the reason, this development forms an ideal field on which to set up all the biological, psychological, sociological, and logical problems of understanding in order to examine their genetic construction. A genetic and experimental epistemology is thus conceivable as a special branch of psychology.

We should like in what follows to give an example of this method and its results in studying—on the three planes of sensory-motor activity, egocentric thought, and rational thought—the genesis of some of those ideas of conservation (continuity) which play such a great role in scientific thought. As we trace this growth we shall also have the opportunity of following, on these three successive levels, the steps of one of the most important processes in the development of thought, namely, the passage from egocentric perception and thought to objective reasoning.

For the following hypotheses may be made in this matter. At the beginning of mental life, the world appears to the child as a series of pictures which are centered about activity and lack any intrinsic stability. The absence of permanent objects and of the objective organization of space seems thus to go hand in hand with a radical and unconscious egocentricity, so that the subject does not consider himself as one thing among many, but only conceives of things in relation to his own actions. Yet at the other extremity of the development the universe is considered as being formed of permanent objects whose movements take place in a space independent of us, and whose many relationships form a series of invariables which prolong the conservation of the object itself; invariables of number, quantity, matter, weight, etc. One may therefore say then that, in so far as egocentricity is reduced by the co-ordination of the individual point of view with other possible ones, the co-ordination which explains this reduction explains also the formation of logical instruments of conservation (ideas of "groups," systems of relations, etc.) and the formation of invariables in the world of reality (ideas of the permanence of the object, of quantities, weights, etc.) .

II. Sensory-Motor Intelligence

Even in the most elementary sensory-motor activities with which the intellectual development of the child begins, it is possible to discern certain of the processes of conservation. Because of the final richness of these processes, as well as their initial limitation, it is necessary to analyze them in detail.

It is evident that the reflex mechanisms (for example sucking), the habits grafted on these reflexes (thumb sucking, etc.), or the more complex "circular reactions" which tend to reproduce an interesting result (to swing suspended toys, etc.) all lead essentially to repetition, and consequently imply a tendency toward persistence. On the one side these factors assume that movements are so organized that they are always capable of returning to their point of departure. From the point of view of space, these motor units form what the geometricians call "displacement groups," closed systems of operations which tend to continuance. On the other side, the elementary psychological activity which is characteristic of them is essentially an "assimilation" of external realities, so that these realities are not considered as entities in themselves, but only as functional elements (things are conceived merely as something to be sucked, something to be swung or handled, etc.). Now this assimilation is also a factor in conservation, since it implies a certain practical recognition and a certain identifying generalization based on habitual repetition. Thus, when the baby of five or six months sees his usual rattle, or even a new plaything, dangling before him, he will swing it at once, assimilating it (by an assimilation which reproduces, recognizes, and generalizes) into the scheme of objects to be swung.

But, if these elementary sensory-motor organizations thus introduce from the very start a certain permanence into the primitive universe by constructing space in practical "groups" and by an assimilation of the things perceived into schemes of action, this conservation and this permanence emanate from the subject himself, and hence begin by presenting a purely egocentric character. In other words, there is not yet any conservation of objects as such, nor any permanence in the external world, not even in the space which forms its framework.

First of all, as far as objects are concerned, it is easy to establish the fact that, although the baby is capable of recognizing differences in things at a very early age, almost to the end of his first year he behaves as if the objects which disappeared from his field perception momentarily ceased to exist. For instance, between the ages of five and eight months, when the child already knows enough to seize any solid objects which he sees, one has only to cover them with a cloth, or place a screen in front of them at the moment when the baby's hand is directed towards them, and he will give up looking for them and immediately lose his interest. I have even observed this in systematically hiding the bottle when my six-months-old son was about to take it. But one can see a still more curious reaction around nine or ten months, when the child is capable of seeking the object behind the screen and the notion of real exterior permanence begins to put in an appearance. For example, when the baby is placed between two pillows and he has succeeded in finding an object hidden under the right one, the object can be taken from his hands and placed under the left pillow before his very eyes, but he will look for it under the right pillow where he has already found it once before, as if the permanence of the objective were connected with the success of the former action, and not with a system of external displacements in space.

In short, the primitive world is not made up of permanent objects with autonomous trajectories, but of moving perceptive pictures which return periodically into non-existence and come back again as the functional result of the proper action. It is easy to prove still more clearly that this world is centered in the activity of the self by an analysis of the egocentric character of space which determines its configuration.

If the movements of the child are immediately capable of organization into "groups," closed and reversible systems, those "groups" are in the beginning centered entirely on the subject himself, and afford no room for any objective spatial construction. The clearest example of these egocentric "groups" is seen in the way in which a baby, before nine or ten months, rotates objects, a movement which finally forms the idea of the "wrong side" of objects. Everyone has observed a child handling things and turning them over and over to explore their various sides. Now do these rotary movements give way immediately to the formation of objective groups? A very simple experiment shows us that this is not so. One has only to give a five- or six-months-old baby his bottle with the nipple away from him, and turn it around slowly before his very eyes. If the child can see a bit of the rubber nipple at the other end of the bottle, he immediately turns the object around, but if he doesn't see the nipple, he doesn't even attempt to turn it, but sucks the wrong end! A series of other experiments with other "displacement groups" has shown the same centering on the subject and not on the object.

How then is the baby going to construct a world of permanent objects situated in a real space, and thus escape from his primitive egocentric universe? It is the work of the sensory-motor or practical intelligence, which precedes language, to set up a system of relations to co-ordinate the series of various perspectives which the baby has and thus cause him to locate himself among objects instead of illusively bringing them to him.

In other words, as the activity of the baby develops and

the casual, temporal, and spatial sequences which this activity creates become more complex, objects are detached more and more from the action itself, and the body of the subject becomes one element among others in an ordered ensemble. Thus a total reversal of perspective takes place, which marks the beginning of the objectification of the external world, and of the idea of its permanence. The interplay of practical relationships in the world of reality teaches the child to shift the center of space and its objects from his action to himself, and thus locate himself at the middle point of this world which is being born. In this way the permanence of objects appears as the product of this formation of objective "groups" of displacements, and these groups themselves depend for their creation upon the way in which the sensory-motor or practical intelligence allows the child to free himself from his initial egocentricity and gives him power to act on things, thanks to a system of co-ordinated relationships.

But, if the co-ordination of practical relationships leads to a first victory over egocentricity and to the beginning of the objective idea of conservation, this external permanence remains limited to the plane of action and immediate perception, and cannot extend at once to the level of conceptual representation in general. In fact, it is in a sense an "ontological egocentricity" from which the practical intelligence delivers the individual, and not social and representative egocentricity, which will remain very important even after the appearance of language, and all through infancy. In other words, the co-ordination of practical relationships teaches the child that his body is one thing among many, and that he is thus part of a world of stable objects, whereas at the beginning the baby saw only a world of inconsistent pictures gravitating about his own activity. But the sensory-motor intelligence is not enough to teach the child that the perspective he has of this world is not absolute but relative, and must be co-ordinated with the perspectives of other people to attain a general and truly objective picture of reality.

III. Egocentric Thought

Just at the moment when the practical world of which we have been speaking has been created, the child comes into possession of language, and henceforth is called upon to adapt himself to the thoughts of others as well as to the external material world. Now on this new plane of thought which the social world creates, the child finds difficulties similar to those he has already overcome on the plane of the practical universe, and so he passes through stages similar to those of his escape from initial egocentricity and his progressive co-ordination. Hence the principles of conservation remain unchanged, only this time they are on the plane of abstract concepts. Although the child admits the permanence of concrete objects in the world of immediate experience, he really has no idea of the conservation of matter, weight, or movement, nor even any conception of logical or numerical groups. If he fails, it is because he lacks the intellectual instrument with which to construct the "invariables of groups" which are formed by physical realities. This instrument is called "the logic of relations" by the logicians, and is really the tool of co-ordination par excellence, both from the social and from the rational point of view. It is created only as it succeeds in stemming the egocentricity which constantly opposes it.

In order to make the link between the ontological egocentricity of the first sensory-motor stage and the social and logical egocentricity of the beginnings of conceptual thought perfectly clear, let us briefly turn again to the example of space. We have already seen that on the practical plane the child of two or three years is capable of using a certain number of "groups" of displacements: he knows how to turn an object over, to hide it behind one screen, or a series of two, and find it in the right place, etc. But what will happen when it is a question not only of acting upon the object, but of imagining distant objects, and of co-ordinating the perspective of different observers?

One of our assistants, Mlle. E. Meyer, has investigated this in the following experiment: the child is placed opposite a small model of three mountains, and given a certain number of colored pictures of these mountains; he is then asked which of the pictures show the mountains from the positions occupied successively by a doll on the mountains in the model. The function of age in the development of these reactions is very clear. The little ones do not understand that the observer sees the same mountains quite differently from various points of view, and hence they consider their own perspective absolute. But the older ones gradually discover the relativity necessary to objectivity, after a number of systematic errors due to the difficulty of co-ordinating the relationships in question. Here then on this social and logical plane of the co-ordination of perspectives we have a passing from egocentricity to an objective "group" of changes, exactly parallel to the passage one has observed on the sensory-motor level in the relationships between the baby and the objects handled, only this time the necessity of considering the point of view of other people has created a new difficulty.

Now this process also influences very closely the idea of the conservation or continuity of the mechanical and physical characteristics of objects as well as of their spatial peculiarities. In fact, since the child considers a mountain as being just what it appears to be in his own perspective, it could not possibly have either form or stable dimensions—that is, no "invariables of groups" are constructed. That is actually what observation shows to be true. I have been able to determine in experimenting on my own children, by going about real mountains with them, that at about four or five years of age they still considered the apparent changes due to our own changes of position as quite real. For every mountain they admitted the existence of changes of form and dimensions absolutely contrary to the idea of the permanence of objects. It would be easy to generalize these results for all objects in distant space (stars, clouds, etc.).

But we must show how this preoccupation with the problem of the proper perspective—that is to say, of "immediate experience" as opposed to experience based on rational deduction—hinders the mind from co-ordinating relationships, and finally forming ideas of the permanence of matter, weight, movement, etc. It is clear that every principle of conservation implies a system of relationships which explains real permanence through apparent change. Now in so far as the mind is dominated by "immediate experience," it is not capable of recognizing this relativity, nor the "invariables" which it implies.

Here is an example dealing with the ideas of the conservation of matter and weight. We show children of different ages two paste balls of the same dimensions and weight. Then we change the shape of one of them to a cylinder (a sausage), and we ask if the two objects still have the same weight. Now the little ones think that the weight of the cylinder is less than that of the ball (because a ball appears to concentrate more matter in itself than an elongated cylinder), and they even state that the quantity of paste has diminished because of the change in form! But the older ones believe in the conservation of weight and matter; and between the two one finds a stage at which children think that weight alone varies with form, matter remaining constant.

In the same way, one of our pupils, Mlle. B. Inhelder, has shown that sugar dissolved in a glass of water is not conserved, in the minds of young children: the level which rises at the immersion of the sugar is considered as being lowered as before, after the sugar is dissolved; the sugar is conceived of as gradually vanishing, and even the sweet taste, which is all that remains of the dissolved piece, is supposed to disappear after several hours. But older children, by a series of steps it is useless to describe here, succeed in attaining the idea of the conservation of the sugar, its weight, and even the volume it occupied in the liquid. Some even go so far as to construct a kind of crude atomic theory, like that which the pre-Socratic physicists had, to account for these phenomena.

It is the same *a fortiori* in the case of more subtle ideas, such as that of the conservation of movement, or the principle of inertia. It is, indeed, easy to show that the physics of the child begins by being impregnated with an animistic dynamism, which is the direct opposite of the idea of inertia. Things are endowed with active forces, spontaneous and untransmittable, formed on the model of voluntary muscular activity. Later, before arriving at more mechanistic ideas, the child passes through an intermediate period which recalls in many respects the physics of Aristotle. Thus the trajectory of a projectile is explained, not by the conservation of the impulse received, but by an $αντιπερίστασις$ in the real sense of the word, the projectile being pushed by the air it displaces in its progress. The clouds move in the same way, by the wind which their displacement arouses, etc.

It seems to us easy to show that all these ideas which are so contrary to the ideas of conservation are explained by the same causes, by an egocentric relationship, not yet reciprocal or rational, between the subject and the objects of the external world. On the one hand, objects are assimilated to the Ego, and conceived on the model of its own activity. Hence the anthropocentric ideas of force, weight, etc., which are common in the physics of the little ones. On the other hand, experience remains "immediate," dominated by a series of successive impressions which have not yet been co-ordinated. It is not formed by that logic of relationships which alone will impress upon it an objective form by co-ordinating the many relationships which are perceived or conceived. Thus, in the case of the pellets which change their form, the child does not succeed in freeing his judgment from the illusions caused by habitual perceptions (we know the point at which the evaluations of weight are dependent on factors of form), [in order] that he may co-ordinate the relationships into a coherent ensemble which can support the deduction of real permanence. In short, the absence of permanence is the result of the preeminence of immediate experience over rational deduction, and immediate experience is the ensemble of subjective impressions, successively registered and not yet co-ordinated into a system of relationships which encloses the subject in an objective world.

IV. Rational Co-ordination

We saw first of all how the sensory-motor co-ordinations led the child from an unstable world centered about his own activity to an idea of the permanence of objects, based on the formation of "displacement groups" which ordered space into an objective practical universe. On the other hand, we have just established the fact that when thought and abstract concepts are imposed on this sensory-motor world, egocentricity reappears on this new plane, and the world of concepts also begins to be centered in the Ego, and is thus stripped of the basic permanence which reason demands. How is the child to surmount this second group of obstacles and reach the idea of rational permanence?

The process of reasoning on this plane of conceptual thought is exactly the same as on the sensory-motor level, with this difference, that it is a question henceforth of the co-ordination of the perspectives of different individuals, as well as the co-ordination of the different aspects of individual experience. This social co-ordination, which adds a new dimension to those which are already a part of rational co-ordination, creates in the intellectual realm what one might call "logic," in contrast to the sensory-motor or practical intelligence, which makes only perceptions and motions into systems. Logic is then the "group" of operations which co-ordinates the inter-individual relationships with the intra-individual ones into a system capable of assuring the permanence which is necessary to the invariables of experience.

The essence of rational co-ordination is then to be sought in the "logic of relations"—that is, in this fundamental group of operations which assures the reciprocity of individual perspectives and the relativity of the facts of experience. To refer again to the example of space, on which we have already insisted, it is the logic of relations which makes the child come gradually to understand, between seven and eleven years, that the left and the right are not absolute, but that his own left corresponds to the right of an individual opposite him, and that an object between two others is at one and the same time at the left of the first and the right of the third. It is then the logic of relationships which permits the formation of the idea of a conceptual space by the co-ordination of the different perspectives possible, and which also allows the imposition of this upon practical space, whose relationships, however well co-ordinated they may be among themselves, are always limited to one's own perspective.

Now this logic of relations, which thus maintains on the level of thought the "groups" of operations outlined by sensory-motor intelligence, and which gradually eliminates intellectual egocentricity, finally succeeds, in the realm we are trying to analyze here, in forming invariables which represent for the reasoning mind so many principles of permanence applicable to the physical world.

In the field of the permanence of quantity, for instance, it is easy to show how the grouping of relationships involves in each case the construction of formal invariables, which, when applied to reality, correct the illusions of non-permanence which we have just described in the "immediate experience" of infancy. In her investigations into the genesis of the ideas of quantity and number, our assistant, Mlle. A. Szeminska, brought to light a number of facts which made this change clear. Here are some of them.

When one fills a large glass with some continuous substance, such as colored water, or a discontinuous one, such as beads, and then separates these into two or four small glasses, or into some narrow and elongated or short and fat ones, etc., the quantities appear to increase or diminish for the child below seven years of age according to whether the subject considers the level of the substance in the receptacles, their size, or their number. Moreover, when one makes two groups correspond piece by piece (for example, the beads in two rectilinear rows), the child considers at first that the two quantities are equal; but this is only an illusion, because one has only to place the elements in one of these groups nearer or farther apart (to put the beads in a heap, or make one row longer and more widely spaced than the other) and the two quantities are no longer considered as equal; a row of ten beads is conceived as increasing in number if they are spaced more widely, and a pile is considered as containing more or fewer beads according to whether one heaps it up or spreads it out before the eyes of the child, etc.

In short, before the age of six or seven there is no idea of the permanence of continuous quantities, nor of discontinuous groups, nor any necessary equivalence between two groups which correspond piece by piece, etc., whatever the active operations may be which the subject himself performs in the course of the experiments. For this reason up to this age the child has not yet formed any idea of cardinal or ordinal numbers which are capable of indefinite extension; nor has he yet elaborated any idea of classes of things in extension, which depends upon the inclusion of parts in a permanent whole. The essential forms which number and logical class give to the mind are thus, after all, bound up closely with the processes of conservation, and one might say in general that if the thought of the child remains prelogical during infancy, it is because of the lack of these very principles of permanence.

Now how does the child proceed from this pre-logical state to the discovery of the permanence of groups and quantities? By the co-ordination of the relationships involved; that is, by those operations of "multiplication of relations" which are essential to the logic of relationships. As soon as he ceases to envisage as separate unities the level, size, and number of the columns of liquid, the length of the rows, and the space between the objects, etc., the child succeeds in co-ordinating these relationships, in understanding their relative positions in a system of independent variables, and thus he forms units which are capable of permanence. It is therefore the logic of relationships which transforms immediate experience, with its illusions of perception, into a rational system, the changes of which depend on necessary invariables. It would be easy to show that the idea of the permanence of matter, weight, and movement, which we were speaking of above, is the result of similar processes. In the thought of the child, as in the evolution of the sciences, rational permanence always results from the union of a deduction based on the co-ordination of relationships with an experience similarly formed; and every invariable implies a "group" which creates it—that is, a system of related and reversible changes.

But you will say that the problem is not yet solved, that there still remains the question of how this "logic of relations" which explains the genesis of the principles of conservation and of the "invariables of groups" is itself originated. Now it is first necessary to understand the epistemological character of what we call the egocentricity of the child (that is, a quite unconscious and natural illusion of perspective, which precedes moral egoism and conscious egocentricity). Then one will understand that this process of co-ordination, at once social and intellectual, by which the child escapes from his self-centered point of view to find his place among other people, is actually the rational instrument which makes up this logic of relations. For, in any field, the faculty of knowing is a process of co-ordination in which the ego is subordinated to some objective system of references, and the logic of relationships is nothing but a tool and a result of this co-ordination; a tool in that it guides the ego in its escape from itself, and a result since it is a grouping of systematic operations and an ensemble of successive invariables.

In conclusion, one sees how the genetic analysis of any aspect of the thought of a child necessarily corresponds to the analysis of scientific thought. Indeed, the effort by which the child, by means of that social and rational instrument which the logic of relationships gives him, escapes from his egocentricity and creates a universe is the very beginning of that ever-present gigantic effort of science to free man from himself by putting him within the relativity of the objective world.

JUDITH MERRIL/Dead Center

THEY GAVE HIM sweet ices, and kissed him all round, and the Important People who had come to dinner all smiled in a special way as his mother took him from the living room and led him down the hall to his own bedroom.

"Great kid you got there," they said to Jock, his father, and "Serious little bugger, isn't he?" Jock didn't say anything, but Toby knew he would be grinning, looking pleased and embarrassed. Then their voices changed, and that meant they had begun to talk about the important events for which the important people had come.

In his own room, Toby wriggled his toes between crisp sheets, and breathed in the powder-and-perfume smell of his mother as she bent over him for a last hurried goodnight kiss. There was no use asking for a story tonight. Toby lay still and waited while she closed the door behind her and went off to the party, click-tap, tip-clack, hurrying on her high silver heels. She had heard the voices change back there too, and she didn't want to miss anything. Toby got up and opened his door just a crack, and set himself down in back of it, and listened.

In the big square living room, against the abstract patterns of gray and vermilion and chartreuse, the men and women moved in easy patterns of familiar acts. Coffee, brandy, cigarette, cigar. Find your partner, choose your seat. Jock sprawled with perfect relaxed contentment on the low couch with the deep red corduroy cover. Tim O'Heyer balanced nervously on the edge of the same couch, wreathed in cigar smoke, small and dark and alert. Gordon Kimberly dwarfed the big easy chair with the bulking importance of him. Ben Stein, shaggy and rumpled as ever, was running a hand through his hair till it too stood on end. He was leaning against a window frame, one hand on the back of the straight chair in which his wife Sue sat, erect and neat and proper and chic, dressed in smart black that set off perfectly her precise blonde beauty. Mrs. Kimberly, just enough overstuffed so that her pearls gave the appearance of *actually* choking her, was the only stranger to the house. She was standing near the doorway, politely admiring Toby's personal art gallery, as Allie Madero valiantly strove to explain each minor masterpiece.

Ruth Kruger stood still a moment, surveying her room and her guests. Eight of them, herself included, and all Very Important People. In the familiar comfort of her own living room, the idea made her giggle. Allie and Mrs. Kimberly both turned to her, questioning. She laughed and shrugged, helpless to explain, and they all went across the room to join the others.

"Guts," O'Heyer said through the cloud of smoke. "How do you do it, Jock? Walk out of a setup like this into ... God knows what?"

"Luck," Jock corrected him. "A setup like this helps. I'm the world's pampered darling and I know it."

"Faith is what he means," Ben put in. "He just gets by believing that last year's luck is going to hold up. So it does."

"Depends on what you mean by *luck*. If you think of it as a vector sum composed of predictive powers and personal ability and accurate information and ..."

"Charm and nerve and ..."

"Guts," Tim said again, interrupting the interrupter.

"All right, all of them," Ben agreed. "*Luck* is as good a word as any to cover the combination."

"We're all lucky people." That was Allie, drifting into range, with Ruth behind him. "We just happened to get born at the right time with the right dream. Any one of us, fifty years ago, would have been called a wild-eyed visiona—"

"Any one of us," Kimberly said heavily, "fifty years ago, would have had a different dream—in time with the times."

Jock smiled, and let them talk, not joining in much. He listened to philosophy and compliments and speculations and comments, and lay sprawled across the comfortable couch in his own living room, with his wife's hand under his own, consciously letting his mind play back and forth between the two lives he lived: this, here ... and the perfect mathematic bleakness of the metal beast that would be his home in three days' time.

He squeezed his wife's hand, and she turned and looked at him, and there was no doubt a man could have about what the world held in store.

When they had all gone, Jock walked down the hall and picked up the little boy asleep on the floor, and put him back into his bed. Toby woke up long enough to grab his father's hand and ask earnestly, out of the point in the conversation where sleep had overcome him:

"Daddy, if the universe hasn't got any ends to it, how can you tell where you are?"

"Me?" Jock asked. "I'm right next to the middle of it."

"How do you know?"

His father tapped him lightly on the chest.

"Because that's where the middle is." Jock smiled and stood up. "Go to sleep, champ. Good night."

And Toby slept, while the universe revolved in all its mystery about the small center Jock Kruger had assigned to it.

"Scared?" she asked, much later, in the spaceless silence of their bedroom.

He had to think about it before he could answer. "I guess not. I guess I think I ought to be, but I'm not. I don't think I'd do it at all if I wasn't sure." He was almost asleep, when the thought hit him, and he jerked awake and saw she was sure enough lying wide-eyed and sleepless beside him. "Baby!" he said, and it was almost an accusation. "Baby, you're not scared, are you?"

"Not if you're not," she said. But they never could lie to each other.

Toby sat on the platform, next to his grandmother. They were in the second row, right in back of his mother and father, so it was all right for him to wriggle a little bit, or whisper. They couldn't hear much of the speeches back there, and what they did hear mostly didn't make sense to Toby. But every now and then Grandma would grab his hand right all of a sudden, and he understood what the whole thing was about: it was because Daddy was going away again.

His Grandma's hand was very white, with little red and tan dots in it, and big blue veins that stood out higher than the wrinkles in her skin, whenever she grabbed at his hand. Later, walking over to the towering skyscraping rocket, he held his mother's hand; it was smooth and cool and tan, all one color, and she didn't grasp at him the way Grandma did. Later still, his father's two hands, picking him up to kiss, were bigger and darker tan than his mother's, not so smooth and the fingers were stronger, but so strong it hurt sometimes.

They took him up in an elevator, and showed him all around the inside of the rocket, where Daddy would sit, and where all the food was stored, for emergency, they said, and the radio and everything. Then it was time to say goodbye.

Daddy was laughing at first, and Toby tried to laugh, too, but he didn't really want Daddy to go away. Daddy kissed him, and he felt like crying because it was scratchy against Daddy's cheek, and the strong fingers were hurting him now. Then Daddy stopped laughing and looked at him very seriously. "You take care of your mother, now," Daddy told him. "You're a big boy this time."

"Okay," Toby said. Last time Daddy went away in a rocket, he was not-quite-four, and they teased him with the poem in the book that said, James James Morrison Morrison Weatherby

George Dupree, Took great care of his mother, though he was only three.... So Toby didn't much like Daddy saying that now, because he knew they didn't really mean it.

"Okay," he said, and then because he was angry, he said, "Only she's supposed to take care of me, isn't she?"

Daddy and Mommy both laughed, and so did the two men who were standing there waiting for Daddy to get done saying goodbye to him. He wriggled, and Daddy put him down.

"I'll bring you a piece of the moon, son," Daddy said, and Toby said, "All right, fine." He reached for his mother's hand, but he found himself hanging onto Grandma instead, because Mommy and Daddy were kissing each other, and both of them had forgotten all about him.

He thought they were never going to get done kissing.

Ruth Kruger stood in the glass control booth with her son on one side of her, and Gordon Kimberly breathing heavily on the other side. Something's wrong, she thought, this time something's wrong. And then, swiftly, I mustn't think that way!

Jealous? she taunted herself. Do you want something to be wrong, just because this one isn't all yours, because Argent did some of it?

But if anything is wrong, she prayed, let it be now, right away, so he can't go. If anything's wrong let it be in the firing gear or the ... what? Even now, it was too late. The beast was too big and too delicate and too precise. If something went wrong, even now, it was too late. It was ...

You didn't finish that thought. Not if you were Ruth Kruger, and your husband was Jock Kruger, and nobody knew but the two of you how much of the courage that had gone twice round the moon, and was about to land on it, was yours. When a man knows his wife's faith is unshakeable, he can't help coming back. (But: "Baby! You're not scared, are you?")

Twice around the moon, and they called him Jumping Jock. There was never a doubt in anyone's mind who'd pilot the KIM-5, the bulky beautiful beast out there today. Kruger and Kimberly, O'Heyer and Stein. It was a combo. It won every time. Every time. Nothing to doubt. No room for doubt.

"Minus five ..." someone said into a mike, and there was perfect quiet all around. "Four ... three ..."

(But he held me too tight, and he laughed too loud ...)

"... two ... one ..."

(Only because he thought I was scared, she answered herself.)

"... Mar—"

You didn't even hear the whole word, because the thunder-drumming roar of the beast itself split your ears.

Ringing quiet came down and she caught up Toby, held him tight, tight . . .

"Perfect!" Gordon Kimberly sighed. "Perfect!"

So if anything was wrong, it hadn't showed up yet.

She put Toby down, then took his hand. "Come on," she said. "I'll buy you an ice-cream soda." He grinned at her. He'd been looking very strange all day, but now he looked real again. His hair had got messed up when she grabbed him.

"We're having cocktails for the press in the conference room," Kimberly said. "I think we could find something Toby would like."

"Wel-l-l-l . . ." She didn't want a cocktail, and she didn't want to talk to the press. "I think maybe we'll beg off this time . . ."

"I think there might be some disappointment—" the man started; then Tim O'Heyer came dashing up.

"Come on, baby," he said. "Your old man told me to take personal charge while he was gone." He leered. On him it looked cute. She laughed. Then she looked down at Toby. "What would you rather, Tobe? Want to go out by ourselves, or go to the party?"

"I don't care." he said.

Tim took the boy's hand. "What we were thinking of was having a kind of party here, and then I think they're going to bring some dinner in, and anybody who wants to can stay up till your Daddy gets to the moon. That'll be pretty late. I guess you wouldn't want to stay up late like that, would you?"

Somebody else talking to Toby like that would be all wrong, but Tim was a friend, Toby's friend too. Ruth still didn't want to go to the party, but she remembered now that there had been plans for something like that all along, and since Toby was beginning to look eager, and it was important to keep the press on their side . . .

"You win, O'Heyer," she said. "Will somebody please send out for an ice-cream soda? Cherry syrup, I think it is this week . . ." She looked inquiringly at her son. ". . . and . . . strawberry ice cream?"

Tim shuddered. Toby nodded. Ruth smiled, and they all went in to the party.

"Well, young man!" Toby thought the redheaded man in the brown suit was probably what they called a reporter, but he wasn't sure. "How about it? You going along next time?"

"I don't know," Toby said politely. "I guess not."

"Don't you want to be a famous flier like your Daddy?" a strange woman in an evening gown asked him.

"I don't know," he muttered, and looked around for his mother, but he couldn't see her.

They kept asking him questions like that, about whether he wanted to go to the moon. Daddy said he was too little. You'd think all these people would know that much.

Jock Kruger came up swiftly out of dizzying darkness into isolation and clarity. As soon as he could move his head, before he fully remembered why, he began checking the dials and meters and flashing lights on the banked panel in front of him. He was fully aware of the ship, of its needs and strains and motion, before he came to complete consciousness of himself, his weightless body, his purpose, or his memories.

But he was aware of himself as a part of the ship before he remembered his name, so that by the time he knew he had a face and hands and innards, these parts were already occupied with feeding the beast's human brain a carefully prepared stimulant out of a nippled flask fastened in front of his head.

He pressed a button under his index finger in the arm rest of the couch that held him strapped to safety.

"Hi," he said. "Is anybody up besides me?" He pressed the button under his middle finger and waited. Not for long.

"Thank God!" a voice crackled out of the loudspeaker. "You really conked out this time, Jock. Nothing wrong?"

"Not so I'd know it. You want . . . How long was I out?"

"Twenty-three minutes, eighteen seconds, takeoff to reception. Yeah. Give us a log reading."

Methodically, in order, he read off the pointers and numbers on the control panel, the colors and codes and swinging needles and quiet ones that told him how each muscle and nerve and vital organ of the great beast was taking the trip. He did it slowly and with total concentration. Then, when he was all done, there was nothing else to do except sit back and start wondering about that big blackout.

It shouldn't have happened. It never happened before. There was nothing in the compendium of information he'd just sent back to Earth to account for it.

A different ship, different . . . different men. Two and a half years different. Years of easy living and . . . growing old? Too old for this game?

Twenty-three minutes!

Last time it was under ten. The first time maybe 90 seconds more. It didn't matter, of course, not at takeoff. There was nothing for him to do then. Nothing now. Nothing for four more hours. He was there to put the beast back down on . . .

He grinned, and felt like Jock Kruger again. Identity returned complete. This time he was there to put the beast down where no man or beast had ever been before. This time they were going to the moon.

Ruth Kruger sipped at a cocktail and murmured responses to the admiring, the curious, the envious, the hopeful, and the hate-full ones who spoke to her. She was waiting for something, and after an unmeasurable stretch of time, Allie Madero brought it to her.

First a big smile seeking her out across the room, so she knew it had come. Then a low-voiced confirmation.

"Wasn't it . . . an awfully long time?" she asked. She hadn't been watching the clock, on purpose, but she was sure it was longer than it should have been.

Allie stopped smiling. "Twenty-three," she said.

Ruth gasped. "What . . . ?"

"You figure it. I can't."

"There's nothing in the ship. I mean nothing was changed that would account for it." She shook her head slowly. This time she didn't know the ship well enough to talk like that. There could be something. Oh, Jock! "I don't know," she said. "Too many people worked on that thing. I . . ."

"Mrs. Kruger!" It was the redheaded reporter, the obnoxious one. "We just got the report on the blackout. I'd like a statement from you, if you don't mind, as designer of the ship—"

"I am not the designer of this ship," she said coldly.

"You worked on the design, didn't you?"

"Yes."

"Well, then, to the best of your knowledge . . . ?"

"To the best of my knowledge, there is no change in design to account for Mr. Kruger's prolonged unconciousness. Had there been any such prognosis, the press would have been informed."

"Mrs. Kruger, I'd like to ask you whether you feel that the innovations made by Mr. Argent could—"

"Aw, lay off, will you?" Allie broke in, trying to be casual and kidding about it; but behind her own flaming cheeks, Ruth was aware of her friend's matching anger. "How much do you want to milk this for, anyhow? So the guy conked out an extra ten minutes. If you want somebody to crucify for it, why don't you pick on one of us who doesn't happen to be married to him?" She turned to Ruth before the man could answer. "Where's Toby? He's probably about ready to bust from cookies and carbonation."

"He's in the lounge," the reporter put in. "Or he was a few minutes—"

Ruth and Allie started off without waiting for the rest. The redhead had been talking to the kid. No telling how many of them were on top of him now.

"I thought Tim was with him," Ruth said hastily, then she thought of something, and turned back long enough to say: "For the record, Mr. . . . uh . . . I know of no criticism that can be made of any of the work done by Mr. Argent." Then she went to find her son.

There was nothing to do and nothing to see except the instrument meters and dials to check and log and check and log again. Radio stations all around Earth were beamed on him. He could have kibitzed his way to the moon, but he didn't want to. He was thinking.

Thinking back, and forward, and right in this moment. Thinking of the instant's stiffness of Ruth's body when she said she wasn't scared, and the rambling big house on the hill, and Toby politely agreeing when he offered to bring him back a piece of the moon.

Thinking of Toby growing up some day, and how little he really knew about his son, and what would they do, Toby and Ruth, if anything . . .

He'd never thought that way before. He'd never thought anything except to know he'd come back, because he couldn't stay away. It was always that simple. He couldn't stay away now, either. That hadn't changed. But as he sat there, silent and useless for the time, it occurred to him that he'd left something out of his calculations. Luck, they'd been talking about. Yes, he'd had luck. But—what was it Sue had said about a vector sum?—there was more to figure in than your own reflexes and the beast's strength. There was the outside. Space . . . environment . . . God . . . destiny. What difference does it make what name you give it?

He couldn't stay away . . . but maybe he could be kept away.

He'd never thought that way before.

"You tired, honey?"

"No," he said. "I'm just sick of this party. I want to go home."

"It'll be over pretty soon, Tobe. I think as long as we stayed this long, we better wait for . . . for the end of the party."

"It's a silly party. You said you'd buy me an ice-cream soda."

"I did, darling," she said patiently. "At least, if I didn't buy it, I got it for you. You had it, didn't you?"

"Yes, but you said we'd go out and have one."

"Look. Why don't you just put your head down on my lap and..."

"I'm no baby! Anyhow I'm not tired."

"All right. We'll go pretty soon. You just sit here on the couch, and you don't have to talk to anybody if you don't feel like it. I'll tell you what. I'll go find you a magazine or a book or something to look at, and—"

"I don't want a magazine. I want my own book with the pirates in it."

"You just stay put a minute, so I can find you. I'll bring you something."

She got up and went out to the other part of the building where the officers were, and collected an assortment of leaflets and folders with shiny bright pictures of mail rockets and freight transports and jets and visionary moon rocket designs, and took them back to the little lounge where she'd left him.

She looked at the clock on the way. Twenty-seven more minutes. There was no reason to believe that anything was wrong.

They were falling now. A man's body is not equipped to sense direction toward or from, up or down, without the help of landmarks or gravity. But the body of the beast was designed to know such things; and Kruger, at the nerve center, knew everything the beast knew.

Ship is extension of self, and self is—extension or limitation?—of ship. If Jock Kruger is the center of the universe—remember the late night after the party, and picking Toby off the floor?—then ship is extension of self, and the man is the brain of the beast. But if ship is universe—certainly continuum; that's universe, isn't it?—then the weakling man-thing in the couch is a limiting condition of the universe. A human brake. He was there to make it stop when it didn't "want" to.

Suppose it wouldn't stop? Suppose it had decided to be a self-determined, free-willed universe?

Jock grinned, and started setting controls. His time was coming. It was measurable in minutes, and then in seconds ... now!

His hand reached for the firing lever (but what was she scared of?), groped, and touched, hesitated, clasped, and pulled.

Grown-up parties at home were fun. But other places, like this one, they were silly. Toby half-woke-up on the way home, enough to realize his Uncle Tim was driving them, and they weren't in their own car. He was sitting on the front seat next to his mother, with his head against her side, and her arm around him. He tried to come all the way awake, to listen to what they were saying, but they weren't talking, so he started to go back to sleep.

Then Uncle Tim said, "For God's sake, Ruth, he's safe, and whatever happened certainly wasn't your fault. He's got enough supplies to hold out till . . ."

"Shh!" his mother said sharply, and then, whispering, "I know."

Now he remembered.
"Mommy . . ."
"Yes, hon?"
"Did Daddy go to the moon all right?"
"Y . . . yes, dear."
Her voice was funny.
"Where is it?"
"Where's what?"
"The moon."
"Oh. We can't see it now, darling. It's around the other side of the earth."
"Well, when is he going to come back?"
Silence.
"Mommy . . . when?"
"As soon as . . . just as soon as he can, darling. Now go to sleep."

And now the moon was up, high in the sky, a gilded football dangling from Somebody's black serge lapel. When she was a little girl, she used to say she loved the man in the moon, and now the man in the moon loved her too, but if she was a little girl still, somebody would tuck her into bed, and pat her head and tell her to go to sleep, and she would sleep as easy, breathe as as soft, as Toby did. . . .

But she wasn't a little girl, she was all grown up, and she married the man, the man in the moon, and sleep could come and sleep could go, but sleep could never stay with her while the moonwash swept the window panes.

She stood at the open window and wrote a letter in her mind and sent it up the path of light to the man in the moon. It said:

"Dear Jock: Tim says it wasn't my fault, and I can't explain it even to him. I'm sorry, darling. Please to stay alive till we can get to you. Faithfully yours, Cassandra."

The glasses and ashes and litter and spilled drinks had all been cleared away. The table top gleamed in polished stripes of light and dark, where the light came through the louvered plastic of the wall. The big chairs were empty, waiting, and at each place, arranged with the precision of a formal dinner-setting, was the inevitable pad of yellow paper, two freshly-sharpened pencils, a small neat pile of typed white sheets of paper, a small glass ashtray and a shining empty water glass. Down the center of the table, spaced for comfort, three crystal pitchers of ice and water stood in perfect alignment.

Ruth was the first one there. She stood in front of a chair, fingering the little stack of paper on which someone (Allie? She'd have had to be up early to get it done so quickly) had tabulated the details of yesterday's events. "To refresh your memory," was how they always put it.

She poured a glass of water, and guiltily replaced the pitcher on the exact spot where it had been; lit a cigarette, and stared with dismay at the burnt match marring the cleanliness of the little ashtray; pulled her chair in beneath her and winced at the screech of the wooden leg across the floor.

Get it over with! She picked up the typed pages, and glanced at them. Two at the bottom were headed "Recommendations of U.S. Rocket Corps to Facilitate Construction of KIM-VIII." That could wait. The three top sheets she'd better get through while she was still alone.

She read slowly and carefully, trying to memorize each sentence, so that when the time came to talk, she could think of what had happened this way, from outside, instead of remembering how it had been for her.

There was nothing in the report that she didn't already know.

Jock Kruger had set out in the KIM-VII at 5:39 P.M., C.S.T. just at sunset. First report after recovery from blackout came at 6:02-plus. First log readings gave no reason to anticipate any difficulty. Subsequent reports and radioed log readings were, for Kruger, unusually terse and formal, and surprisingly infrequent; but earth-to-ship contact at twenty-minute intervals had been acknowledged. No reason to believe Kruger was having trouble at any time during the trip.

At 11:54, an attempt to call the ship went unanswered for 56 seconds. The radioman here described Kruger's voice as "irritable" when the reply finally came, but all he said was, "Sorry. I was firing the first brake." Then a string of figures, and a quick log reading—everthing just what you'd expect.

Earth acknowledged, and waited.

Eighteen seconds later:

"Second brake." More figures. Again, everything as it should be. But twenty seconds after that call was completed:

"This is Kruger. Anything wrong with the dope I gave you?"

"Earth to Kruger. Everthing okay in our book. Trouble?"

"Track me, boy. I'm off."

"You want a course correction?"

"I can figure it quicker here. I'll keep talking as I go. Stop me if I'm wrong by your book." More figures, and Kruger's calculations coincided perfectly with the swift work done at the base. Both sides came to the same conclusion, and both sides knew what it meant. The man in the beast fired once more, and once again, and made a landing.

There was no reason to believe that either ship or pilot had been hurt. There was no way of finding out. By the best calculations, they were five degrees of arc around onto the dark side. And there was no possibility at all, after that second corrective firing, that Kruger had enough fuel left to take off again. The last thing Earth had heard, before the edge of the moon cut off Kruger's radio, was:

"Sorry, boys. I guess I fouled up this time. Looks like you'll have to come and . . ."

One by one, they filled the seats: Gordon Kimberly at one end, and the Colonel at the other; Tim O'Heyer to one side of Kimberly, and Ruth at the other; Allie, with her pad and pencil poised, alongside Tim; the Colonel's aide next down the line, with his little silent stenotype in front of him; the Steins across from him, next to Ruth. With a minimum of formality, Kimberly opened the meeting and introduced Col. Swenson.

The Colonel cleared his throat. "I'd like to make something clear," he said. "Right from the start, I want to make this clear. I'm here to help. Not to get in the way. My presence does not indicate any—criticism on the part of the Armed Services. We are entirely satisfied with the work you people have been doing." He cleared his throat again, and Kimberly put in:

"You saw our plans, I believe, Colonel. Everything was checked and approved by your outfit ahead of time."

"Exactly. We had no criticism then, and we have none now. The rocket program is what's important. Getting Kruger back is important, not just for ordinary humanitarian reasons—pardon me, Mrs. Kruger, if I'm too blunt—but for the sake of the whole program. Public opinion, for one thing. That's your line, isn't it, Mr. O'Heyer? And then, we have to find out what happened!

"I came down here today to offer any help we can give you on the relief ship, and to make a suggestion to facilitate matters."

He paused deliberately this time.

"Go ahead, Colonel," Tim said. "We're listening."

"Briefly, the proposal is that you all accept temporary commissions while the project is going on. Part of that report in front of you embodies the details of the plan. I hope you'll find it acceptable. You all know there is a great deal of—necessary, I'm afraid—red tape, you'd call it, and 'going through channels,' and such in the Services. It makes cooperation between civilian and military groups difficult. If we can all get together as one outfit 'for the duration,' so to speak . . ."

This time nobody jumped into the silence. The Colonel cleared his throat once more.

"Perhaps you'd best read the full report before we discuss it any further. I brought the matter up now just to—to let you know the attitude with which we are submitting the proposal to you . . ."

"Thank you Colonel." O'Heyer saved him. "I've already had a chance to look at the report. Don't know that anyone else has, except of course Miss Madero. But I personally, at least, appreciate your attitude. And I think I can speak for Mr. Kimberly too. . . ."

He looked sideways at his boss; Gordon nodded.

"What I'd like to suggest now," O'Heyer went on, "since I've seen the report already, and I believe everyone else would like to have a chance to bone up some—perhaps you'd like to have a first-hand look at some of our plant, Colonel? I could take you around a bit. . . ."

"Thank you. I would like to." The officer stood up, his gold Rocket Corps uniform blazing in the louvered light. "If I may say so, Mr. O'Heyer, you seem remarkably sensible, for a—well, a publicity man."

"That's all right, Colonel." Tim laughed easily. "I don't even think it's a dirty word. You seem like an all-right guy yourself—for an officer, that is."

They all laughed then, and Tim led the blaze of glory out of the room while the rest of them settled down to studying the R.C. proposals. When they had all finished, Kimberly spoke slowly, voicing the general reaction:

"I hate to admit it, but it makes sense."

"They're being pretty decent about it, aren't they?" Ben said. "Putting it to us as a proposal instead of pulling a lot of weight."

He nodded. "I've had a little contact with this man Swenson before. He's a good man to work with. It . . . makes sense, that's all."

"On paper, anyhow," Sue put in.

"Well, Ruth . . ." the big man turned to her, waiting. "You haven't said anything."

"I . . . it seems all right to me," she said, and added: "Frankly, Gordon, I don't know that I ought to speak at all. I'm not quite sure why I'm here."

Allie looked up sharply, questioning, from her notes; Sue pushed back her chair and half-stood. "My God, you're not going to back out on us now?"

"I . . . look, you all know I didn't do any of the real work on the last one. It was Andy Argent's job, and a good one. I've got Toby to think about, and . . ."

"Kid, we need you," Sue protested. "Argent can't do this one; this is going to be another Three, only more so. Unmanned, remote-control stuff, and no returning atmosphere-landing problems. This is up your alley. It's . . ." She sank back; there was nothing else to say.

"That's true, Ruth." Tim had come back in during the last outburst. Now he sat down. "Speed is what counts, gal. That's why we're letting the gold braid in on the job—we are, aren't we?" Kimberly nodded; Tim went on: "With you on the job, we've got a working team. With somebody new—well, you know what a ruckus we had until Sue got used to Argent's blueprints, and how Ben's pencil notes used to drive Andy wild. And we can't even use him this time. It's not his field. He did do a good job, but we'd have to start in with somebody new all over again . . ." He broke off, and looked at Kimberly.

"I hope you'll decide to work with us, Ruth," he said simply.

"If . . . obviously, if it's the best way to get it done quick, I will," she said. "Twenty-eight hours a day if you like."

Tim grinned. "I guess we can let the braid back in now . . . ?" He got up and went to the door.

Another Three, only more so . . . Sue's words danced in her mind while the Colonel and the Colonel's aide marched in, and took their places, while voices murmured politely exchanging good will.

Another Three—the first ship she had designed for Kimberly. The ship that made her rich and famous, but that was nothing, because it was the ship that brought Jock to her, that made him write the letter, that made her meet him, that led to the Five and Six and now . . .

"I've got some ideas for a manned ship," he'd written. "If we could get together to discuss it some time . . ."

". . . pleasure to know you'll be working with us, Mrs. Kruger." She shook her head sharply, and located in time and place.

"Thank you, Colonel. I want to do what I can, of course . . ."

James James Morrison's mother put on a golden gown . . .

Toby knew the whole thing, almost, by heart. The little boy in the poem told his mother not to go down to the end of the town, wherever that was, unless she took him along. And she said she wouldn't, but she put on that golden gown and went, and thought she'd be back in time for tea. Only she wasn't. She never came back at all. Last seen wandering vaguely . . . King John said he was sorry . . .

Who's King John? And what time is tea?

Toby sat quietly beside his mother on the front seat of the car, and looked obliquely at the golden uniform she wore, and could not find a way to ask the questions in his mind.

Where was James James's father? Why did James James have to be the one to keep his mother from going down to the end of the town?

"Are you in the Army now, Mommy?" he asked.

"Well . . . sort of. But not for long, darling. Just till Daddy comes home."

"When is Daddy coming home?"

"Soon. Soon, I hope. Not too long."

She didn't sound right. Her voice had a cracking sound like Grandma's, and other old ladies. She didn't look right, either, in that golden-gown uniform. When she kissed him goodbye in front of the school, she didn't feel right. She didn't even smell the same as she used to.

"Bye, boy. See you tonight." she said—the same words she always said, but they sounded different.

"Bye." He walked up the driveway and up the front steps and down the corridor and into the pretty-painted room where his teacher was waiting. Miss Callahan was nice. Today she was too nice. The other kids teased him, and called him teacher's pet. At lunch time he went back in the room before anybody else did, and made pictures all over the floor with the colored chalk. It was the worst thing he could think of to do. Miss Callahan made him wash it all up, and she wasn't nice any more for the rest of the afternoon.

When he went out front after school, he couldn't see the car anywhere. It was true then. His mother had put on that golden gown, and now she was gone. Then he saw Grandma waving to him out of her car, and he remembered Mommy had said Grandma would come and get him. He got in the car, and she grabbed at him like she always did. He pulled away.

"Is Daddy home yet?" he asked.

Grandma started the car. "Not yet," she said, and she was crying. He didn't dare ask about Mommy after that, but she wasn't home when they got there. It was a long time after that till dinner was ready.

She came home for dinner, though.

"You have to allow for the human factor. . . ."

Nobody had said it to her, of course. Nobody would. She wondered how much tougher it made the job for everybody, having her around. She wondered how she'd stay sane, if she didn't have the job to do.

Thank God Toby was in school now! She couldn't do it, if it meant leaving him with someone else all day—even his grandmother. As it was, having the old lady in the house so much was nerve-racking.

I ought to ask her if she'd like to sleep here for a while, Ruth thought, and shivered. Dinner time was enough.

Anyhow, Toby liked having her there, and that's what counted.

I'll have to go in and see his teacher. Tomorrow, she thought. I've got to make time for it tomorrow. Let her know . . . but of course she knew. Jock Kruger's family's affairs were hardly private. Just the same, I better talk to her. . . .

Ruth got out of bed and stood at the window, waiting for the moon. Another ten minutes, fifteen, twenty maybe, and it would edge over the hills on the other side of town. The white hands on the clock said 2:40. She had to get some sleep. She couldn't stand here waiting for the moon. Get to sleep now, before it comes up. That's better. . . .

Oh, Jock!

". . . the human factor . . ." They didn't know. She wanted to go tell them all, find somebody right away, and shout it. "It's not his fault. I did it!"

"You're not scared, are you, baby?"

Oh, no! No, no! Don't be silly. Who, me? Just stiff and trembling. The cold, you know . . . ?

Stop that!

She stood at the window, waiting for the moon, the man, the man in the moon.

Human factor . . . well, there wouldn't be a human factor in this one. If she went out to the field on takeoff day and told KIM-VIII she was scared, it wouldn't matter at all.

Thank God I can do something, at least!

Abruptly, she closed the blind, so she wouldn't know when it came, and pulled out the envelope she'd brought home; switched on the bed light, and unfolded the first blueprints.

It was all familiar. Just small changes here and there. Otherwise, it was the Three all over again—the first unmanned ship to be landed successfully on the moon surface. The only important difference was that this one had to have some fancy gadgetry on the landing mech. Stein had given her the orbit calcs today. The rest of the job was hers and Sue's: design and production. Between them, they could do it. What they needed was a goldberg that would take the thing once around low enough to contact Jock, if . . . to contact him, that's all. Then back again, prepared for him to take over the landing by remote, according to instructions, if he wanted to. If he could. If his radio was working. If . . .

Twice around, and then down where they figured he was, if he hadn't tried to bring it down himself.

It was complicated, but only quantitatively. Nothing basically new, or untried. And no human factors to be allowed for, once it was off the ground.

She fell asleep, finally, with the light still on, and the blind drawn, and the blueprints spread out on the floor next to the bed.

Every day, she drove him to school, dressed in her golden gown. And every afternoon, he waited, telling himself she was sure to come home.

That was a very silly little poem, and he wasn't three, he was six now.

But it was a long time since Daddy went away.

"I'd rather not," she said stiffly.

"I'm sorry, Ruth, I know—well, I don't know, but I can imagine how you feel. I hate to ask it, but if you can do it at all . . . just be there and look confident, and . . . you know."

Look confident! I couldn't do it for Jock, she thought; why should I do it for them? But of course that was silly. They didn't know her the way Jock did. They couldn't read her smiles, or sense a barely present stiffness, or know anything except what she chose to show on the front of her face.

"Look confident? What difference does it make, Tim? If the thing works, they'll all know soon enough. If . . ."

She stopped.

"All right, I'll be blunt. If it doesn't work, it's going to make a hell of a difference what the public feeling was at the time it went off. If we have to try again. If—damn it, you want it straight, all right! If we can't save Jock, we're not going to give up the whole thing! We're not going to let space travel wait another half century while the psychological effects wear off. And Jock wouldn't want us to! Don't forget that. It was his dream, too. It was yours, once upon a time. If . . ."

"All right!" She was startled by her voice. She was screaming, or almost.

"All right," she said bitterly, more quietly. "If you think I'll be holding up progress for fifty years by not dragging Toby along to a launching, I'll come."

"Oh, Ruth, I'm sorry. No, it's not that important. And I had no business talking that way. But listen, babe, you used to understand this—the way I feel, the way Jock fel—feels. Even a guy like Kimberly. You used to feel it too. Look: the single item of you showing your face at the takeoff doesn't amount to much. Neither does one ounce of fuel. But either one could be the little bit that makes the difference. Kid, we got to put everything we've got behind it this time."

"All right," she said again. "I told you I'd come."

"You do understand, don't you?" he pleaded.

"I don't know, Tim. I'm not sure I do. But you're right. I would have, once. Maybe—I don't know. It's different for a woman, I guess. But I'll come. Don't worry about it."

She turned and started out.

"Thanks, Ruth. And I am sorry. Uh—want me to come and pick you up?"

She nodded. "Thanks." She was glad she wouldn't have to drive.

He kept waiting for a chance to ask her. He couldn't do it in the house before they left, because right after she told him where they were going, she went to get dressed in her golden uniform, and he had to stay with Grandma all the time.

Then Mr. O'Heyer came with the car, and he couldn't ask because, even though he sat up front with Mommy, Mr. O'Heyer was there too.

When they got to the launching field, there were people around all the time. Once he tried to get her off by himself, but all she did was think he had to go to the bathroom. Then, bit by bit, he didn't have to ask, because he could tell from the way they were all talking, and the way the cameras were all pointed at her all the time, like they had been at Daddy the other time.

Then there was the speeches part again, and this time she got up and talked, so that settled it.

He was glad he hadn't asked. They probably all thought he knew. Maybe they'd even told him, and he'd forgotten, like he sometimes did. "Mommy," he listened to himself in his mind, "Mommy, are you going to the moon too?" Wouldn't that sound silly!

She'd come back for him, he told himself. The other times,

when Daddy went some place—like when they first came here to live, and Daddy went first, then Mommy, and then they came back to get him, and some other time, he didn't remember just what—but when Daddy went away, Mommy always went to stay with him, and then they always came to get him too.

It wasn't any different from Mommy going back to be with Daddy at a party or something, instead of staying in his room to talk to him when she put him to bed. It didn't feel any worse than that, he told himself.

Only he didn't believe himself.

She never did tell me! I wouldn't of forgotten that! She should of told me!

She did not want to make a speech. Nobody had warned her that she would be called upon to make a speech. It was bad enough trying to answer reporters coherently. She stood up and went forward to the microphone dutifully, and shook hands with the President of the United States, and tried to look confident. She opened her mouth and nothing came out.

"Thank you," she said finally, though she didn't know just what for. "You've all been very kind." She turned to the mike, and spoke directly into it. "I feel that a good deal of honor is being accorded me today which is not rightfully mine. We gave ourselves a two-month limit to complete a job, and the fact that it was finished inside of six weeks instead . . ."

She had to stop because everybody was cheering, and they wouldn't have heard her.

". . . that fact is not something for which the designer of a ship can be thanked. The credit is due to all the people at Kimberly who worked so hard, and to the Rocket Corps personnel who helped so much. I think . . ."

This time she paused to find the right words. It had suddenly become very important to level with the crowd, to tell them what she honestly felt.

"I think it is I who should be doing the thanking. I happen to be a designer of rockets, but much more importantly, to me, I am Jock Kruger's wife. So I want to thank everyone who helped..."

Grandma's hand tightened around his, and then pulled away to get a handkerchief, because she was crying. Right up here on the platform! Then he realized what Mommy had just said. She said that being Jock Kruger's wife was more important to her than anything else.

It was funny that Grandma should feel bad about that. Everybody else seemed to think it was a right thing to say, the way they were yelling and clapping and shouting. It occurred to Toby with a small shock of surprise that maybe Grandma sometimes felt bad about things the same way he did.

He was sort of sorry he wouldn't have much chance to find out more about that.

She broke away from the reporters and V.I.P.'s, and went and got Toby, and asked him did he want to look inside the rocket before it left.

He nodded. He was certainly being quiet today. Poor kid —he must be pretty mixed up about the whole thing by now.

She tried to figure out what was going on inside the small brown head, but all she could think of was how much like Jock he looked today.

She took him up the elevator inside the rocket. There wasn't much room to move around, of course, but they'd rigged it so that all the big shots who were there could have a look. She was a little startled to see the President and her mother-in-law come up together in the next elevator, but between trying to answer Toby's questions, and trying to brush off reporters, she didn't have much time to be concerned about such oddities.

She had never seen Toby so intent on anything. He wanted to know everything. Where's this, and what's that for? And where are you going to sit, Mommy?

"I'm not, hon. You know that. There isn't room in this rocket for . . ."

"Mrs. Kruger, pardon me, but . . ."

"Just a minute, please."

"Oh, I'm sorry."

"What was it you wanted to know now, Tobe?" There were too many people; there was too much talk. She felt slightly dizzy. "Look, hon, I want to go on down." It was hard to talk. She saw Mrs. Kruger on the ramp, and called her, and left Toby with her. Down at the bottom, she saw Sue Stein, and asked her if she'd go take over with Toby and try to answer his questions.

"Sure. Feeling rocky, kid?"

"Kind of." She tried to smile.

"You better go lie down. Maybe Allie can get something for you. I saw her over there. . . ." She waved a vague hand. "You look like hell, kid. Better lie down." Then she rushed off.

He got away from Grandma when Sue Stein came and said Mother wanted her to show him everything. Then he said he was tired and got away from her. He could find his Grandma all right, he said.

He'd found the spot he wanted. He could just about wriggle into it, he thought.

The loudspeaker crackled over her head. Five minutes now.

The other women who'd been fixing their hair and brightening their lipstick snapped their bags shut and took a last look and ran out, to find places where they could see everything. Ruth stretched out on the couch and closed her eyes. Five minutes now, by herself, to get used to the idea that the job was done.

She had done everything she could do, including coming here today. There was nothing further she could do. From now on, or in five minutes' time, it was out of anyone's hands, but—Whose? And Jock's, of course. Once the relief rocket got there, it was up to him.

If it got there.

If he was there for it to get to.

The way they had worked it, there was a chance at least they'd know the answer in an hour's time. If the rocket made its orbit once, and only once, it would mean he was alive and well and in control of his own ship, with the radio working, and . . .

And if it made a second orbit, there was still hope. It might mean nothing worse than that his radio was out. But that way they would have to wait . . .

God! It could take months, if the calculations as to where he'd come down were not quite right. If . . . if a million little things that would make it harder to get the fuel from one rocket to the other.

But if they only saw one orbit . . .

For the first time, she let herself, forced herself to, consider the possibility that Jock was dead. That he would not come back.

He's not dead, she thought. I'd know it if he was. Like I knew something was wrong last time. Like I'd know it now if . . .

"Sixty seconds before zero," said the speaker.

But there is! She sat bolt upright, not tired or dizzy any more. Now she had faced it, she didn't feel confused. There was something . . . something dreadfully wrong . . .

She ran out, and as she came on to the open field, the speaker was saying, "Fifty-one."

She ran to the edge of the crowd, and couldn't get through, and had to run, keep running, around the edges, to find the aisle between the cords.

Stop it! she screamed, but not out loud, because she had to use all her breath for running.

And while she ran, she tried to think.

"Minus forty-seven."

She couldn't make them stop without a reason. They'd think she was hysterical . . .

". . . forty-five . . ."

Maybe she was, at that. Coolly, her mind considered the idea and rejected it. No; there was a problem that hadn't been solved, a question she hadn't answered.

But what problem? What . . .

"Minus forty."

She dashed down between the ropes, toward the control booth. The guard stepped forward, then recognized her, and stepped back. The corridor between the packed crowds went on forever.

"Minus thirty-nine . . . eight . . . thirty-seven."

She stopped outside the door of Control, and tried to think, think, think! What was it? What could she tell them? How could she convince them? She knew, but they'd want to know what, why . . .

You just didn't change plans at a moment like this.

But if they fired the rocket before she figured it out, before she remembered the problem, and then found an answer, it was as good as murdering Jock. They could never get another one up quickly enough if anything went wrong this time.

She pushed open the door.

"Stop!" she said. "Listen, you've got to stop. Wait! There's something . . ."

Tim O'Heyer came and took her arm, and smiled and said something. Something soothing.

"Minus nineteen," somebody said into a microphone, quietly.

She kept trying to explain, and Tim kept talking at her, and when she tried to pull away she realized that hand on her arm wasn't just there to comfort her. He was keeping her from making trouble. He . . .

Oh, God! If there was just some way to make them understand! If she could only remember what was wrong . . .

"Minus three . . . two . . ."

It was no use.

She stopped fighting, caught her breath, stood still, and saw Tim's approving smile, as the word and the flare went off together:

"Mark!"

Then, in a dead calm, she looked around and saw Sue.

"Where's Toby?" she asked.

She was looking in the reserved grandstand seats for Mrs. Kruger, when she heard the crowd sigh, and looked up and saw it happening.

The crash fire did not damage the inside of the rocket at all. The cause of the crash was self-evident, as soon at they found Toby Kruger's body wedged into the empty space between the outer hull of the third stage, and the inner hull of the second.

The headlines were not as bad as might have been expected. Whether it was the tired and unholy calm on Ruth Kruger's face that restrained them, or Tim O'Heyer's emergency-reserve supply of Irish whisky that convinced them, the newsmen took it easy on the story. All America couldn't attend the funeral, but a representative hundred thousand citizens mobbed the streets when the boy was buried; the other hundred and eighty million saw the ceremonies more intimately on their TV sets.

Nobody who heard the quiet words spoken over the fresh grave—a historic piece of poetry to which the author, O'Heyer, could never sign his name—nobody who heard that simple speech remained entirely unmoved. Just where or when or with whom the movement started is still not known; probably it began spontaneously in a thousand different homes during the brief ceremony; maybe O'Heyer had something to do with that part of it, too. Whichever way, the money started coming in, by wire, twenty minutes afterwards; and by the end of the week "Bring Jock Back" was denting more paychecks than the numbers racket and the nylon industry combined.

The KIM-IX was finished in a month. They didn't have Ruth Kruger to design this time, but they didn't need her: the KIM-VIII plans were still good. O'Heyer managed to keep the sleeping-pill story down to a tiny back-page notice in most of the papers, and the funeral was not televised.

Later, they brought back the perfectly preserved, emaciated body of Jock Kruger, and laid him to rest next to his wife and son. He had been a good pilot and an ingenious man. The moon couldn't kill him; it took starvation to do that.

They made an international shrine of the house, and the garden where the three graves lay.

Now they are talking of making an interplanetary shrine of the lonely rocket on the wrong side of the moon.

II

THE WORLDS
OF THE BLIND AND
THE DEAF

The man who can see supposes blindness, of all handicaps, as the most terrible. His projections of his own fear of darkness, which he may equate with death or fears of castration, result in his pitying the blind man. But he may also stand in awe of the blind man's ability to compensate for his handicap—to "see" without vision. This seemingly uncanny ability has been exaggerated in fiction in which the blind man may become all-powerful or omniscient. It is easy to see why the blind man, conceived as one of the living dead, should arouse such feelings of pity and terror on the part of the seeing.

Everything that has been discovered about the psychology of the blind, however, contradicts the popular opinion. The blind man is simply a man without eyes. If he happens to possess a "haptic" or nonvisual mind—in other words, if he thinks without visual imagery—he may find adjustment to his blindness less difficult. If, however, like most men, he is accustomed to framing his ideas in pictures, he will never lose his craving for sight. The "haptic" blind man may adjust to sightlessness so completely that he will refuse to see even when the functional cause of his blindness is removed. The "optic" blind, on the other hand, will desire sight—even if he has never possessed it and has no knowledge of its nature.

Jacob Twersky's sensitive probing into the minds of two young blind boys is an explicit statement of normalcy. Both these boys crave sight, and both have adjusted to their blindness in terms of their own fairly normal personalities. One, the more visually oriented, struggles against the dependency of his blindness and structures his world as if he could see. The other, whose images are rarely visual, is more bitter about his handicap yet, in *the end, more accepting of it: he marries a blind girl and uses his handicap as a crutch.*

Unlike the blind man, the deaf man often makes a more limited adjustment to his handicap. If he is born deaf and thus mute, society regards him as little more than an animal. But even if deafness occurs after speech is assured, the deaf man seems to suffer far more emotional disorders than does any other handicapped person. Part of the difficulty undoubtedly arises from his normal appearance. We can never see deafness as we can often see the mutilated eyes of the blind, and we thus tend to misinterpret lack of response in the deaf as stupidity or coldness. We can never imagine deafness, as we can blindness, because we have no way to shut our ears and share the totally silent world in which even the sounds of one's own body are stilled. If the deaf man is also mute, he cannot communicate with us without great difficulty. Lacking speech, the mute represents to us that animal element of man as he was before he achieved language and socialization. He is a reminder of the unconscious and instinctual that we try to repress in our waking life, but that haunts us at times of stress and fills our dream world with terror.

Isolated first by his handicap and secondly by the community, the deaf man far more than the blind suffers from a bitter sense of alienation. He is also subject to other physical difficulties such as pain, giddiness, a loss of his sense of orientation. Under all of these pressures, it is not surprising to find a high incidence of emotional disorders among the deaf.

The alienation of the deaf man from society, his inability to orient himself—to know who he is—symbolizes for many writers their own relationship to the world around them. The terrors of the essential loneliness of man can thus become crystallized in the portrait of a deaf-mute. Carson McCullers' mute is the quintessence of all her lost and lonely characters. Her symbolic use of deafness to embody the condition of man without communication, her prediction of death or madness for them have profound implications for all those who share her tragic view of the human condition.

H. ROBERT BLANK/Dreams of the Blind

THIS PAPER is a sequel to my review of the psychic problems of the blind *(1)*. Although the psychoanalytic items are scant, there exists a considerable literature[1] on dreaming among the blind, beginning, as far as scientific investigation is concerned, with the work of Heermann *(9)* in 1838. Most of the contributions are by psychologists, educators, and blind autobiographers, and consist chiefly of phenomenological and comparative studies, almost devoid of psychoanalytic or even psychodynamic insight. The most striking exception is the unpublished M.A. thesis by McCartney *(15)*, himself blinded at seventeen months of age, written in 1913. The work reveals a uniquely thorough grasp of psychoanalytic principles and a rigorous testing of these principles by the data provided by hundreds of dreams, including one hundred seventy-seven of the author's own. Several of the latter are circumspectly but convincingly analyzed. McCartney's research confirmed Freudian dream theory, e.g., 'dreams of flying and of falling have a sexual significance, though they may be initiated by somatic stimuli'; 'nightmare is of sexual origin'; and 'the blind differ little from the sighted with respect to dreams of the dead, and . . . such dreams often represent wish fulfilment'. He was also in advance of his time in his awareness of the distorting influences of stereotypical and magical thinking, warning against the attribution to the blind of special psychic powers or liabilities unless these could be demonstrated scientifically.

The congenitally blind do not have visual dreams. This will surprise only those who believe in a racial unconscious, hereditary transmission of memories, or other Lamarckian concepts. We must, moreover, include in the category of the congenitally blind, for the purposes of our study, almost all adults who have lost their vision before the age of five. Heermann, in 1838, reported that none of fourteen sightless persons who became blind prior to age five had visual dreams; one of four who were blinded between five and seven had visual dreams; and the thirty-five who lost their sight after seven all retained visual imagery in their dreams. From his study of many aged blind, Heermann concluded that those blinded in adulthood tended to retain their visual imagery longer

---

[1] The most complete bibliography and guide to the literature on blindness is Helga Lende's *Books About the Blind,* published by the American Foundation for the Blind, New York City, 1953. The annotations are especially valuable inasmuch as most of the items are unavailable or available only in a few specialized libraries.

than those blinded nearer the period five to seven years of age.[2]

Jastrow (*12*) in 1900 independently arrived at the same conclusions from his study of the dreams of fifty-eight sightless subjects. 'The period from the fifth to the seventh year is thus indicated as the critical one. Before this age the visual center is undergoing its elementary education, its life is closely dependent upon the constant food supply of sensations; and when these are cut off by blindness, it degenerates and decays. If sight is lost after the seventh year, the sight center can, in spite of the loss, maintain its function, and the dreams of such an individual may be hardly distinguishable from those of a seeing person.'

McCartney confirmed Heermann's and Jastrow's conclusions but cited several cases blinded before three years of age who retained visual imagery into adulthood, which he attributed to exceptional 'precocity' of development of the 'visual center'. Unlike Jastrow and most of his successors (who believed dreams were meaningless manifestations of automatic brain activity), McCartney did not allow his research into dream phenomenology to obscure his awareness of his subjects' need to relate their dreams to their daily problems of living and inner conflicts. Bolli (*2*) agreed with Jastrow except that he defined the critical period as four to six years of age rather than five to seven. My own experience leads me to accept the ages five to seven as the critical period, which is also the period of cerebral structural maturation, the completion of early childhood ego development, and the beginning of latency.

There seem to be fewer exceptions to the lower limit (those blinded before age five who retain visual imagery into adulthood) than to the upper limit. There exists, that is, a definite tendency for visual imagery to deteriorate in waking memory and in dreams in those blinded even as late as nine or ten. The reasons have to do with tremendous individual differences with respect to unconscious conflicts, ego capacities such as memory, talents, and educational experiences. Of particular relevance here is the subject of 'sensory typing', i.e., the classification of people into sensory types based on the predominance of one sensory modality over the others in the individual's ego functions. A thirty-year-old alert and intelligent teacher, musician by avocation, was blinded at age eight. In spite of excellent memory, going back to his third year and including the events of his illness and blinding, he can summon only the vaguest visual memories or images,

---

[2] In one of Heermann's elderly subjects, dream vision was retained for fifty-two years, in another for fifty-four years before fading away. His work is not only a pioneer contribution to psychology and clinical medicine but also to neuropathology: e.g., his observations on optic nerve degeneration in the blind.

and has no dream vision in his fairly frequent and quite vivid dreams. He had demonstrated great musical interest and ability in infancy, and he talked precociously. It is tempting to think of this man as an auditory rather than visual type, and to regard this as a factor in the almost complete disappearance of his visual memory.[3]

The term, congenitally blind, therefore includes, unless otherwise indicated, those born sightless and those blinded in childhood who have lost their dream vision. Except for the absence of vision the dreams of the congenitally blind are fundamentally the same as those of the seeing; this applies to the manifest elements and the dream work, and, transcending the proved and fancied phenomenological differences is the fact that dreams of the blind can be interpreted by psychoanalytic methods in the same way as those of the seeing. In the dreams of the seeing there frequently occur nonvisual sensory, cognitive, and intellectual elements. Occasional dreams in the seeing consist only of a nonvisual element or two, e.g., a dream consisting only of a speech or a smell. A seeing patient of mine dreamed of the number 5. How did you dream it, did you see it or hear it? 'No, I just know I dreamed about it.' This type of immediate response, 'I just knew it,' is more frequently heard from the congenitally blind than from the seeing or the adventitiously blind. Further questioning may or may not disclose auditory, tactile, or other sensory elements.

What is the relative incidence of the nonvisual sensory perceptions in the dreams of the congenitally blind? There is almost universal agreement that hearing ranks first, tactile and kinesthetic next, with gustatory and olfactory unusual, and specific temperature perceptions rare. In my own cases taste and smell have been reported relatively more frequently in dreams than in those reported by others; yet their incidence is surprisingly low in view of the importance in waking life of smell and taste for so many congenitally blind. For example, a blind man who could not recall gustatory or olfactory sensations in his dreams stated that smell was second in importance only to hearing in identifying people and locale (hence valuable in communication and motility in addition to direct libidinal gratification). Elinor Deutsch (3), blind since birth except for light perception, contributes an instructive phenomenological analysis (in addition to some psychoanalytically oriented observations) of her many vivid dreams. 'The imagery found in the writer's dreams is entirely auditory, kinesthetic, static, and tactile. The sense of hearing plays the most

---

[3] The problems of scoptophilia-exhibitionism as factors in the retention or fading of visual memory in the adventitiously blind will be treated in a paper devoted to perception, frustration, and ego development.

important part while the other three sense modalities seem to be of about equal moment. Gustatory and olfactory imagery have never played any part. She often carries on long coherent conversations and actually hears what is being said to her instead of merely knowing it by some sort of intuition as seems so often to be the case in dreams. Voices are reconstructed quite perfectly, having all their usual inflections.' Actual conversations and secondary elaboration are much more prominent dream elements among the congenitally blind than those having visual dreams.

Deutsch's remarks contain certain implications which are worthy of being posited as warnings to less experienced workers with the blind. The first is the glib use by the blind child or adult of a vocabulary referring to vision and the visual qualities of objects. Sometimes this is a relatively superficial veneer. Too frequently, however, it is not just a matter of unrealistic terminology but an indication of impaired reality testing with a tendency to deny the blindness. That one is dealing with an ego defect will usually be confirmed by the presence of impaired school, work, or social performance.

The second caveat involves the need rigorously to differentiate clarity of image from libidinal hypercathexis when one is confronted by a 'vivid' dream. This has not been explicitly defined by any of the writers debating whether the blind have dreams more, less, or just as vivid as the seeing. So many dreams reported by intelligent, articulate, and imaginative people seem to abound with sensory images, but investigation reveals much more verbalism, imagination, and affect than sensory perception. The problem is best exemplified by Helen Keller's accounts of her dreams *(14, 12)*.

CASE I

A thirteen-year-old congenitally blind girl, in treatment because of a phobia associated with the conviction her mother would desert her, reported the following dream and her immediate associations. 'Mrs. Jones was in an elevator going up in a high building. The elevator got stuck just before it reached the eighth floor. Was that funny! I woke up scared. She is the woman I told you about who has seven children. She isn't afraid to let me hold her baby and feed her.' A week earlier the patient had expressed contempt and resentment against some of the mothers in the block who were afraid to trust her with their babies.

Asked how she knew it was Mrs. Jones who was in the elevator with her, Mary replied, 'I just knew it, I know what an elevator is like.' Asked to be more specific about her recognitions, she said, 'I don't have to see it; I can hear it and feel it [patient carves out an elevator shaft in the air with both hands], I just know what it is.' She then described the 'funny' feeling, i.e., anxiety expressed chiefly by abdominal sensations. In questioning her about another dream, Mary had stated, 'Naturally I couldn't see him, but I can smell him a mile away.' It is significant to note that, 'Naturally, I couldn't see . . .' represents a frank acceptance of blindness in contrast to 'I don't have to see . . .' which avoids the acknowledgment of blindness. Unlike the content of the unreported dream which did not particularly involve conflict over blindness, the reported dream is replete with this conflict which we had only begun to approach, namely blindness as punishment for masturbation, fear of not marrying and not getting a baby because of blindness, the marked ambivalence to mother, etc.

CASE II

A sixty-year-old congenitally blind man whom I was treating for a depressive hypochondriacal espisode, but who presented no major illness of any kind, reported, 'I had a dream she came into the room bringing me a dish of gefüllte fish. Isn't that silly?'. How did you know it was she [the shop supervisor]? 'Maybe you'd expect me to see her? Know? I just knew it. The gefüllte fish [grinning]! I don't have to tell you about that.' He was telling me good-naturedly that he knew what I had in mind: it was silly of me to expect a congenitally blind man to see. The joke about the gefüllte fish [no one has to see to enjoy it] screened his reluctance to talk about his sexual longings for the supervisor which was later confirmed.

CASE III

Mr. A, a thirty-year-old congenitally blind teacher of the blind, who came to this country from his distant home for postgraduate study, was one of a group of blind people, not in treatment, who agreed to coöperate by discussing his dreams for research purposes.[4] He reported the following dream: 'I was going up to heaven and St. Peter barred me at the gates, telling me to go down below. I argued with him, feeling I was being treated unjustly, until he said, "All your friends are down there"; whereupon I said, "If that is the case it's fine," and I went down below.' The effect throughout this dream was appropriate to the manifest content, the dreamer finally feeling good about joining his friends. The dream made no sense to him except that he was very much interested in discussing philosophical and religious questions with

---

[4] I am continuing this line of investigation in order to get more case material on dreams of the blind, particularly the congenitally blind, and to clarify certain problems in perception relating to ego differentiation.

friends and colleagues who often argued about 'material versus spiritual' values. When I learned he had the dream two weeks after arriving in this country I ventured the interpretation that he had been more anxious than he thought about leaving his home and religion for material satisfaction. One would feel safer having the protection of one's parents and a belief in God. The patient readily confirmed this. He had actually given up the religion of his family and was content with the pleasures of the mind and body. With regard to vision, he stated, 'I never dreamed I could see. I have no idea of what seeing is like. In my experience with many blind people, some of them told me they had seeing dreams, but in each case I learned that they had some vision before they were blind or they were just using words. Many of them are very intelligent, do a lot of reading [Braille], and use words and descriptions which give the impression they can see. They fool themselves too.'

Of the three cases presented, only Case III provides us with a dream far more characteristic of the blind than the seeing. The typical features are the prominence of heard speeches and conversations, secondary elaboration in the dream work, and undisguised or poorly disguised superego elements. Von Schumann *(16)* stresses the conspicuousness of manifest guilt feelings in the dreams of several blind analysands.[5] Isakower's *(11)* brief preliminary study on the spoken word in dreams is also relevant, but the psychoanalytic appraisal of these typical phenomena will be considered in the next section.

Acquired Blindness

The blind who have had vision beyond the seventh year of life have conscious and unconscious visual memories, and their dreams are essentially the same as those of the seeing. Of greater psychoanalytic interest, however, is the way in which vision and the eyes are utilized and disguised by the individual dreamer. I have frequently encountered frankly wish-fulfilling dreams of seeing, or dreams containing such elements, among the blind who are actively coping with their conflicts about blindness; rarely, among the blind disabled by such conflicts and having strong needs to deny their blindness. Among the latter one usually finds infrequent dreaming as well as great resistance to talking about

[5] Von Schumann analyzes the dreams of the Iliad and Odyssey and concludes that Homer was blinded early in childhood. The Homeric dreams are predominantly auditory with visual elements obscure or shadowy. This is characteristic of the actual vision of those with little more than light perception. The dreams of ancient Greek drama and those on the tablets of the Temple of Epidaurus are by contrast predominantly visual.

their blindness. To talk about and to dream about their blindness seems painful. In their somatic complaints too, as well as in their dreams, there occur frequent displacements from the eyes.

Deutsch (3) examined a large number of blind children who were in a boarding school. A twelve-year-old girl, she says, '... dreamed that all the girls in the school except one whom she could not identify gained their sight and went home. After the others had gone, this girl also obtained her vision and returned to her home, and "there weren't any more schools for the blind." This theme with some variations was found to occur rather frequently in the dreams of the girls attending the state school for the blind. It may be of significance to note that none of the children attending the Chicago Public Schools and living at home dreamed that they acquired their vision.' This is as striking a confirmation as I have ever seen of my often expressed belief that the blind child is more threatened by separation from home than by blindness. The implications for the education and total treatment of the blind child are obvious.

CASE IV

A sixty-eight-year-old resident of a large home for the blind had never fully resigned himself to living there or the reality of his blindness of twenty years duration. I was treating him because of his hostile withdrawal from group activities, multiple somatic complaints, and his noisy recalcitrance about routines. He reported the following dream: 'I saw Mrs. Jones [the director of the home] come into my room with a big scissors to cut off my balls. I woke up screaming.' The day preceding the dream, the director had to refuse his clamorous insistence for another ophthalmological examination. He had had faint and varying light perception for many years, but ophthalmologists had repeatedly told him that there was no hope for restoration of vision. During a previous disturbed episode he had shouted, 'She doesn't want me to see, when will she be satisfied—when my eyeballs are gone?'. This man was not usually paranoid. During periods when he was quiet, dejected, self-derogatory, and masochistic he asked, 'Why did God do this to me? What have I done to deserve this fate?'.

A much younger man, not as disturbed, had a similar dream in which being castrated was more tolerable than being blind. Both men reacted to blindness as the worst possible thing that could happen to anyone and saw no hope in living as a blind man. Both recoiled from associating with other blind people.

The dream of being castrated as a reaction to the painful reality of blindness is somehow reminiscent of an occasional occurrence in psychoanalysis, namely, the frank dream of incest as a reaction to the emergence of 'dangerous' transference feelings. While the two situations are not quite analogous, in both the *remote* intrapsychic danger is defensively substituted for the unbearable present reality.

CASE V

A thirty-five-year-old blind veteran, who is working and successfully rearing a family, reports: 'I dream a lot about the battles I was in. I see the thing just the way it happened, every detail. Even some of the battles I heard about and wasn't in. I also have dreams in which I clearly see my child and other people that I never saw. The strangest thing is that in the middle of the dream I say to myself, "Don't be a jerk, you can't see." ' This reminder in the dream that he is only dreaming and should not take his seeing too seriously I have encountered in two other blind veterans who, characteristically, are also active, productive people with strong superegos. The battle dreams reported are not the classic battle dreams; they are not anxiety dreams. I regard them primarily as wish-fulfilling dreams—taking the dreamer back to the time when he was intact and functioning with his eyes—of persons who are more or less successfully dealing with their reality problems, and who want to be accepted as equals by the seeing.[6]

The blind dreamer's knowledge that he is really blind while he is having a wish-fulfilling visual dream was recently impressively reported by Furness *(6)*, a chemist blinded during World War I by a munitions blast.

> Although the blind sleeper 'sees' in his dreams, it is curious that in most dreams he knows very definitely at the time that he is really blind. 'I was in my old college laboratory when I saw a young lady, unfortunately blind, so I thought, in obvious difficulties as regards her whereabouts. I immediately went to help her, and led her through the intricacies of the passages, but all the time I knew I was blind, and could think how strange it was that I could act as escort.' Many similar dreams have come to me, and scores have been reported.

Another remarkable feature concerning the dreams of the blind is the frequency with which the 'flying' dream occurs. The sensation of floating through the air is very common. One blind man I know experiences this sensation in seventy percent of his dreams. For this I have no explantion to offer, but in this case, too, all objects are usually perfectly visible.

Those of us who become blind in adulthood seem to have

---

[6] This veteran reported another interesting visual phenomenon: 'Most of the time [when awake] I see a most beautiful combination of colors, masses of red, orange, yellow. That was the last thing I ever saw. When that shell burst I saw it, the next thing I knew I was awake in a hospital, blind.'

four distinct types of dreams—namely, those in which we 'see' perfectly, those in which we 'see' but are conscious all the time of being blind, those in which objects are blurred, and those in which impressions come to us, as in waking hours, through the intermediary of senses other than that of sight. It is the experience of some that dreams of the fourth class gradually take first place as time passes and the stock of remembered images gradually fails.

The significance of active visual dreaming is more complex than the manifest wish fulfilment, 'I can see, and my potency is restored.' Almost every blind patient referred to me, regardless of psychiatric diagnosis, was initially disabled: unproductive in work or in school, with definite constriction of his ego, and narcissistic preoccupations.[7] Just as the seeing, with such problems, these patients seldom dreamed or reported dreams. Their waking fantasies were similarly impaired, and they strongly resisted freely expressing their thoughts and feelings. Clinical improvement was distinguished by freer communication, widening of interests, and a richer fantasy and dream life. Visual elements were frequently reported with astonishment: '. . . for the first time since . . .'; or '. . . for the first time in years.' Such changes were noted in several cases in which there was also an intensification of complaints and of anxiety. As a rule, therefore, visual dreaming of the blind is indicative of the blind dreamer's attempting to solve his reality problems. His libido is directed toward object relationships rather than withdrawal into narcissism. He wants acceptance by the seeing; he seeks to increase his capacity to tolerate the anxiety of his frustration and reactive hostility. These dreams are affirmations of equality (identification) with the seeing and attempts to communicate (object relationship) with them. Kanzer's paper (*13*) on the communicative function of the dream would receive particular support from the visual dreams of the blind.[8]

That the dreamer knows in his dream that he is blind, and admonishes or disparages himself, often with direct speech, represents the superego: 'What are you doing engaging in such childish nonsense, such impossible (sexual) activity with your eyes, when you have so many duties to perform?'. I have never encountered a superego dream of this type reported by a person who was not coping with the difficult problems of living which confront every blind person, most often in the face of blandishments that foster regressive dependence and acting out. Notable in this connection

---

[7] In my cases, this applied to the congenitally blind as well. It is easy to understand that a psychiatrist without wide experience with blind people, and without having treated such patients for prolonged periods, could have the conviction that the blind rarely dream.

[8] This discussion does not pertain to isolated visual dreams, e.g., the nightmare in Case IV.

is society's willingness to condone such regression in the blind.⁹ The blind have actually to cope with great sexual frustration due in large measure to factors out of their control. Where obstacles to their freedom of movement and social contact have been eliminated I have observed that blind men have no difficulty in obtaining sexual partners among seeing as well as blind women. The problem is more serious for the single blind woman whose range and choice is more limited. These considerations are almost didactically presented in many dreams of the blind.

Another determinant of the prominent superego element in the manifest dream is the real dependence of the blind person on *seeing and speaking* companions, guides, and others, a condition likely to re-establish and prolong repressed infantile conflicts concerning the powerful giving and frustrating parent, or a favored sibling. Ambivalence and reactive guilt characterizing these conflicts become displaced to the powerful judging, seeing world as a whole, a stereotype which is enhanced by the frustrations experienced by the active blind individual in his daily contacts with the seeing. The net result is an accumulation of unresolved conflict at the day's end which provides a formidable *Tagesrest*. This is given a relatively more prominent representation in the manifest dream than the more deeply repressed, disguised, and distorted elements.

That an overload of reality problems in a dreamer's life does find expression in the dream work was explicitly formulated by Freud (5) in his distinction between 'dreams from below' and those 'from above.' The former are determined primarily by strong unconscious wishes which gain representation in the day's residue. 'They may be regarded as inroads of the repressed into waking life. Dreams from above correspond to thoughts or intentions of the day before, which have contrived during the night to obtain reinforcement from repressed material which is debarred from the ego. When this is so, analysis as a rule disregards this unconscious ally and succeeds in inserting the latent dream-thoughts into the complex of waking thought. This distinction calls for no modification in the theory of dreams.' The visual and nonvisual (Case III) superego dreams are typically dreams from above, and in analyzing them one can profitably take Freud's advice and concentrate on helping the patient understand the sources and degree

---

⁹ Erotic acting out by many blind veterans, as attempted compensation for self-depreciation, (blindness equals castration), during the early weeks of their rehabilitation is reported by Gowman (7). One should however not overlook that the war blind are a selected group of young physically and sexually active men. Gowman also describes how the seeing tolerate the deviant behavior of the blind because the stereotype of the blind is inevitably considered defective or queer. I would add the more important unconscious wish to permit the blind the gratifications for which they have been 'castrated'.

of anxiety produced by his reality problems and his real relationships.

Dreams of the Deaf Blind

Of historical and current clinical interest are the classic reports of Howe (*10*) on Laura D. Bridgman (1829-1889), corroborated by Hall's work (*8*) with her, Jastrow (*12*) referring at length to both Howe's and Hall's observations. Howe and Bridgman are immortalized in literature by Dickens (*4*). Howe demonstrated for the first time that a blind deaf-mute (Laura's case was further complicated by an almost complete loss of olfaction) could learn to speak and be educated to the degree of being capable of abstract thinking. Howe was very much interested in Laura's dreams. For this she was an ideal subject as she dreamed practically every night. She had many nightmares, and recalled a good deal of their content. The quality of Howe's intuitive thinking is perhaps best demonstrated in his comments on Laura's dreams.

> Further inquiry, when she is more capable of talking on intellectual subjects, may change this opinion; but now it seems to me that her dreams are only the spontaneous production of sensations similar to those which she experiences while awake (whether preceded or accompanied by any cerebral action, cannot be known). She often relates her dreams, and says, 'I dreamed to talk' with a person, 'to walk with one,' etc. If asked whether she talked with her mouth, she says, 'No,' very emphatically; 'I do not dream to talk with mouth; I dream to talk with fingers.' Neither does she ever dream of seeing persons, but only of meeting them in her usual way. She came to me the other morning with a disturbed look, and said, 'I cried much in the night because I did dream you said good-bye to go away over the water.' In a word, her dreams seem, as ours do, to be the result of the spontaneous activity of the different mental faculties producing sensations similar in kind to our waking ones, but without order or congruity, because uncontrolled by the will.
>
> She sometimes is frightened in her dreams, and awakes in great terror, and says she dreamed there were animals in the room which would hurt her. She has still much fear of animals, and can hardly be induced to touch the quiet and harmless house dog.

The disturbing effect upon awakening of unpleasant or frightening dreams tends to be greater and more prolonged among the blind, especially in childhood, because they do not have the immediate restorative influence of testing reality provided by visual perception. The conviction, 'It was only a dream,' is, I believe, more difficult for a blind person to attain than it is for the seeing, and this difficulty is aggravated when the sensorium is further deprived of hearing, and communication is blocked by muteness. I have the impression that waking up in general is a slower process, the more limited the sensory apparatus, and that hypnopompic phenomena are more common among the blind than the seeing—an impression requiring more factual corroboration than is now available.

A great deal of dreaming both as to frequency and duration, with a high incidence of anxiety in dreams, characterizes the blind deaf-mute throughout childhood with a later tapering off of violently disturbing dreams. This is a less evident trend the later in life the disabilities occur. Helen Keller's accounts of her dreaming provide examples of these qualities for which some elements may be accounted.

First, there is the dreamer's actual helplessness, and his exaggerated fantasied helplessness due to severe frustrations of external and internal origin. Among the internal frustrations I would rank those stemming directly from muteness ahead of those attributable to blindness or deafness. By frustrations directly imposed by muteness, I refer to the motility and tension discharge functions of the vocal apparatus, which is not to underestimate the more obvious frustrations due to difficulty in communication. If this hypothesis is valid, it becomes doubly imperative to preserve and further to develop speech among those who become deaf in childhood. Efficient techniques are now readily available.

Second, the blind deaf-mute, dreaming for example of a frightening animal, cannot see or hear the animal from a distance which would provide the chance to run away, cry for help, etc. The animal is either felt directly or 'known' to be present, with an imminence of attack which includes all the physiological reactions of anxiety. The high incidence of frightening animals in these dreams I assume to be projections by the ego of the helpless child of secondarily erotized oral aggressive impulses. Oral fixation with prolonged dependence on parental figures is inevitable, with few or no outlets for the discharge of instinctual tension during the phallic phase. The frustration of motility, communication, and other ego functions augments reactive hostility to a degree that makes oral sadistic regression and projection inevitable. Without benefit of psychoanalytic or modern pedagogic theory, Howe intuitively knew this and provided the eager Laura a regimen of physical activities, including long hikes, swimming, and horseback riding, which would earn the respect of any athlete.

Summary

The congenitally blind and, with few exceptions, those blinded before the age of five do not have visual dreams, the predominant sensory modality being hearing. Those blinded later than age seven tend to retain visual memory and visual dream imagery. The phenomenological differences between the dreams of the blind and the seeing are not fundamental. They require no revision of the psychoanalytic theory of dreams. The typical dream of the blind is a dream 'from above,' one that is determined primarily by serious reality problems and it usually contains some prominent spoken statement, or other superego elements more closely related to the day's residue than to deeply repressed conflicts. Five dreams of the blind are presented chiefly to illustrate their variety and the relationship of the dream to the psychic problems of the blind dreamer, especially the problems concerning his blindness. The outstanding contributions in the literature on dreams of the blind are reviewed.

References

1. BLANK, H. ROBERT: *Psychoanalysis and Blindness.* This QUARTERLY, XXVI, 1957, pp. 1-24.
2. BOLLI, LUCIEN: *Le Reve et les aveugles.* J. de Psychologie, XXIX, 1932, pp. 20-73 and pp. 258-309.
3. DEUTSCH, ELINOR: *The Dream Imagery of the Blind.* Psa. Rev., XV, 1928, pp. 288-293.
4. DICKENS, CHARLES: *American Notes and Pictures from Italy.* New York: E. P. Dutton & Co., 1921, pp. 30-44.
5. FREUD: *Remarks Upon the Theory and Practice of Dream Interpretation.* Coll. Papers, V, pp. 136-149.
6. FURNESS, REX: *Dreams Without Sight.* The Beacon, V, No. 58, 1921, p. 16.
7. GOWAN, ALAN G.: *The War Blind in American Social Structure.* New York: American Foundation for the Blind, 1957. Rev. in This QUARTERLY, XXVII, 1958, pp. 117-118.
8. HALL, GRANVILLE STANLEY: *Aspects of German Culture.* Boston: James R. Osgood & Co., 1881, pp. 268-271.
9. HEERMANN, G.: *Beobachtungen und Betrachtungen über die Träume der Blinden. Ein Beitrag zur Physiologie und Psychologie der Sinne.* Monatschrift für Medizin, Augenheilkunde und Chirurgie, I, 1838, pp. 116-180.
10. HOWE, SAMUEL GRIDLEY: *Education of Laura D. Bridgman.* This is a collection of excerpts from Howe's yearly reports to the Trustees of the Perkins Institution, covering the years 1837 to 1846, plus some of his notes posthumously collected. This work, out of print, is available at The American Foundation for the Blind, New York City, and The Perkins Institution, Boston, Mass.
11. ISAKOWER, OTTO.: *Spoken Words in Dreams.* This QUARTERLY, XXIII, 1954, pp. 1-6.

12. JASTROW, JOSEPH: *Fact and Fable in Psychology.* Boston and New York: Houghton Mifflin Co., 1900, pp. 337-370. This contains Helen Keller's description of her dreams when she was twenty years old.
13. KANZER, MARK: *The Communicative Function of the Dream.* Int. J. of Psa., XXXVI, 1955, pp. 1-7.
14. KELLER, HELEN: *The World I Live In.* New York: The Century Co., 1908.
15. MC CARTNEY, FRED MORTON: *A Comparative Study of Dreams of the Blind and of the Sighted with Special Reference to Freud's Theory.* An unpublished Master of Arts Thesis, Department of Philosophy, Indiana University, Bloomington, 1913. Available at The American Foundation for the Blind, New York City.
16. VON SCHUMANN, HANS-JOACHIM: *Phänomenologische und phychoanalytische Untersuchung der Homerischen Träume.* Acta Psychotherapeutica Psychosomatica et Orthopaedagogica, III, No. 3, 1935, pp. 205-219.

PETER HOBART KNAPP/The Ear, Listening and Hearing

THE EAR, in psychodynamic investigation, is a silent area. Meticulously studied by the experimentalist, the auditory mechanism has received little attention from the psychoanalyst, although he depends on it daily. Perhaps this fact reflects a general tendency—to "view" the world in terms of our most useful perceptive tool, vision. In any dictionary of phrases, synonyms or quotations, optical references outnumber acoustic ones about four to one. Schilder's volume on the body image (27) scarcely refers to the ear. Psychoanalysts have written a great deal about language, a certain amount about sounds, including music; but there are few references to the actual acoustic apparatus, except for the studies of Abraham (1), Jones (13), and Isakower (12). This paper is an effort to extend their reports. It will discuss the role played in psychic life by the ear, as a part of the body and as a perceptual instrument.

I

My starting point was work with deafened patients (15). Gross physical damage is often inconspicuous in deafness. That fact, a source of chagrin to those who feel very crippled, can lead in others to an apparent lack of any concern with the ears as such. At a deeper level, of course, the failure of function creates feelings of mutilation, of having inferior, "bad ears." Hard-of-hearing patients may have a special sensitivity, beyond that fostered by cultural inertia, to wearing the badge of invalidism, a hearing aid, inserted in the opening of their faulty part. Along with special, personal defensive attitudes, there is usually some sign of the anxiety one would expect from any lesion—concern over sensations around the ear, drainage from it, or noises in it. One boy, aged fourteen who had chronic perforations of both drums, thought that there was a great hole extending through his entire head; he was literally afraid of things going in one ear and out the other. Such reactions to invalidism and impaired bodily integrity are revealing—but complex. Deafness, in particular, leads to verbal isolation and loss of the many noises of the world. It raises broad problems of language and sound, which this paper can only touch on as they interweave with the specific problems of the ear.

By their very distortions deaf patients emphasize one thing, that is, how little attention we pay, when there is no damage, to the ear. Expressionless, static, beyond our immediate gaze—unlike the face, torso or limbs—it is somewhat like the back of the head. Out of sight, it stays out of mind—in the periphery of our body scheme.

Yet even there it remains constant, and useful. Though they are not blatant the ear has its own meanings. Some of these are the general meanings of orifice and appendage. A receptive passage, which can be stimulated or penetrated, it may be discovered by the infant with apparent pleasure according to Levine (18), even before the genitalia, as early as the third month of life. In later development it may be an obvious substitute for the vagina, either in fact or fantasy. Abraham (1) describes a man who got frank erotic pleasure from using it in this sense. He mentions that children, by sticking objects into the ear or otherwise manipulating it, may create erotic or anxious feelings which can recur later, masked, in states of chronic itching or otalgia. I have seen two women in whom obvious genital conflicts and partial frigidity were accompanied by troublesome otitis externa. They felt disgust for the ear. In other women there is little trace of such conflict, and it becomes a favorite site for adornment. Earrings, in our culture, are small, gemlike, worn only by women, and epitomize femininity. In Shakespeare's simile, Juliet "hangs upon the cheek of night, like a rich jewel in an Ethiop's ear."

The vagina obviously leads to the womb. Mrs. Rank (24) reports a child who had hysterical deafness, and was filled with ideas of violent impregnation, expressed at one point by a dream of someone blowing into her ear.

In addition to the genital, other receptive passages may be represented. The ear, which in childhood listened to anal sounds, may stand for that area in adult language. Slang tells us that "he doesn't know his ear from his elbow," or orders him to "blow it out your ear"—clear substitution for more pungent profanity. Perhaps a substitutive concern enters into the scrubbing, in this civilization, of the small boy's ear. In common phraseology we may "eat 'till it comes out the ears." Or we may simply get, and retain, "an earfull." Finally the ear may become a mouth and "drink in sound." The wish to receive words is common to many individuals, not least those in psychotherapy. They may demand verbal activity from the therapist, regardless of what is said; in short, they want to be fed through the ear.

Those symbolic relationships in myth and literature are clearly elaborated by Ernest Jones in his paper, "The Madonna's Conception Through The Ear" (13). He points to the abundant representations in early Christian writings and in medieval art of the idea that Jesus was conceived by the entrance of the Holy Spirit, usually pictured as a bird, into Mary's ear. The legend is common to other cultures: Maya, mother of the Mongolian savior was impregnated by the ear, and that method of conception was ascribed to the sacred Egyptian crocodile. The mode of birth stays vague in the Christian version; in others it takes place through the mouth; in still others the ear serves as portal of exit, too, as it did for Rabelais' Gargantua. The widest equivalence of the ear, Jones feels, is to the lower gastrointestinal passage. He mentions early paintings of the devil, and references in Indian epic poetry to the sea serpent, each of whom ingested victims through the mouth and eliminated them indifferently through cloaca, or ear, or both. In these myths Jones sees the receptive ear serving as a displacement from the foul anal region, which helps to make the carnal act pure and modest. He compares it to the displacement from below of touching impulses in the child, first to the nostril, and then to the ear—which in our thought receives clean wind, intangible sound, and the abstract Word.

Similar fantasies may appear in the clinic. A young man, who had had fifteen operations between the ages of two and eighteen for bilateral mastoid infection denied his deep dread of attack and mutilation; he spoke of fearing his penis was too big, and claimed to be unconcerned about the marked scarring around his ears. When he was fifteen, he saw a disturbed patient in the hospital held down while a lumbar puncture was done. The boy returned to his home where there were some baby chicks, and at night began to hear a noise near his ears like "canary birds." These sounds, which went away if he focused attention on them, gradually faded out, but recurred later when his masculine resources were put under strain. He recognized them as illusory, and as different from true tinnitus, which he occasionally had. They seemed to represent the idea of a small creature actually inside, or penetrating his ear, a fantasy very close to the Madonna myth.

Another man, fifty-four years old, a plumbing salesman, once enuretic, later an inventor of a "drip-proof" faucet, came to the clinic because of lifetime concern about his ears, which had changed to near panic following instrumentation of his Eustachian tubes two years ago. He traced all his difficulties to an apparent memory from the age of five, of putting three peas into his right ear, and having a doctor attempt to remove them, only to push one through the drum. From then on, although audiograms showed residual hearing, he felt himself to be totally deaf on that side. He hid his defect, even from his domineering wife, never cupped his ear or turned his head toward a speaker, and felt crippled—"like having only one leg." He prided himself on exceptionally keen hearing in the left ear, though it made him "guilty," and he constantly dreaded losing it, too. At the same time there was a persistent feeling, enhanced by frequent colds, that there was something in his bad ear. After a bloody surgical removal of a urethral stone at age forty-six, he developed a swelling in his nose, which culminated, when he was fifty-two, in removal of a bloody nasal polyp. A month later he got some water in his good ear and became terrified when he "couldn't get it out." A doctor tried to dilate his Eustachian tube with a bougie. The patient recalled him "shoving it in," and could "feel the crushing and cracking." He developed transient deafness, accompanied by some paranoid attitudes toward the physician, and the thought that his "ears had been plugged, as if someone had put something in them." During psychotherapy his acute distress subsided. He lost some of his fears of total deafness; at the same time he felt the bone in his nose was "growing back," and he continued to ruminate about the mysterious, threatening events going on inside the passages of his head.

This patient illustrates the persistent fantasy of the ear as a container, which can be penetrated to result in a growth. But also he had the opposite idea, of a keen ear. Anxiety over losing this hung over his lifelong compromise—in which he felt that one ear was damaged, the other intact, one passive and filled up, the other active and grasping.

The latter aspect of the ear, as well as the former, is important. The ear is more than just a receptive opening. It is also a protuberance, which can be valued like other bodily projections as a symbol of strength. We speak of "pricking up our ears," like the animals for whom they are such vital tools. Ears are wiggled by youths with pride, boxed by parents in anger, and in the vernacular they are "pinned back" to denote stinging defeat. One adolescent gang used to initiate new members by holding them down and biting the ear. Precise ritual often surrounds the ceremony of ear-piercing in primitive tribes. Among them earrings may be more than just small baubles, exclusively feminine. Throughout history earrings have been almost universally worn, and by both sexes. They are used not only as adornments, but to increase the size of the ear lobe. The Masai wear ear plugs four and a half inches in diameter, weighing almost three pounds, in order to stretch their ears. According to Murdock (20) the ruling class of Incas were called *orejones*—"big ears"—by the Spaniards because of their "characteristic practice of piercing the ears for an ornamental plug and enlarging the hole until the lobes hung nearly to the shoulder." Hopi girls wear small turquoise earrings beneath an appropriate "whorl of hair over each ear, supposedly symbolic of the squash blossom" (20); the men may wear gigantic earrings, apparently in an effort to represent their own genital equipment.

Again clinical data corroborates. A patient who occasionally scratched his ears remembered from boyhood the fear that his ear lobes were too large, like his father's. He also recalled the same fear about his nose, and the carping mother's claim that his father's nose had grown bulbous and ugly as a result of nose-picking. An example in reverse is that of a disorganized, frightened girl who was finally able, after prolonged psychiatric treatment, to overcome her dread and envy, and establish a satisfactory sexual relationship with a man; the therapist suspected he must be somehow maimed or incomplete. Indeed, he was; he had one missing ear. The phallic significance of the ear reflected itself in the threat of a five-year-old girl to her younger brother: "I'll cut off your ears and then you'll be deaf."

The phallus may remain, but grow and become ludicrous, as happened to Pinnochio, who tried in vain to hide his huge donkey's ears under a cap. In Greek legend, Midas preferred the sensual and obvious music of Pan to the divine Apollo's lyre, and further, refused to listen to the pronouncement that Apollo had won a contest between the two musicians. He, too, was given a pair of donkey's ears, which he struggled to conceal under a turban —until the rushes learned his secret and whispered it eternally. Their voices punished him, not for his earlier greed, but for abuse of his ears, which had heard too avidly the sounds of Pan and failed to listen to the authority of the Gods.

Many of those elements emerged in the psychoanalytic treatment of an intelligent young veteran. He had no acoustic symptoms but obsessional conflicts over following his father, a Southern judge, into the practice of law. He expressed vividly the desire to be filled up by words through the ear, the mouth, the stomach or a "hole in the head." During interpretations he would often lie quietly, confessing that he paid little attention to them but enjoyed the daydream of the analyst's voice entering his ear. Once he said, "I want to put my fingers on your lips and feel the words, and taste them and get them in through the ears; I want to suck you dry." When less favorably disposed he resolved to close his ears, or wear ear muffs. He was extremely sensitive to noise, had repeated fantasies of being overheard, and guilty feelings over listening himself. These stemmed from an intense childhood curiosity, which had been particularly aroused by one period spent in a bedroom adjoining the parents. He could recall eavesdropping on noises from the bathroom, but became anxious and got intensification of mild visual symptoms at the thought that he must have listened to the sounds of intercourse also. One day he overheard the analyst on the telephone, became anxious and gave a burst of acoustic associations, oscillating between peaceful ones—lulling voices at bedtime, the sound of the ocean in sea shells—and more vigorous ones, listening outside a privy for excretory noises, hearing the tramp of marching feet. He ended with a fantasy—"I'd like to be in your ear or in the telephone receiver, then I'd hear a lot." At the age of eight he had had a vivid ether dream when his ear was lanced, during which he heard music, which later he sang. Singing was one of the few accomplishments that gave him satisfaction. Sound often meant power to him. He had a fantasy of playing a trumpet with such force that it uncoiled and stood out straight, blowing forth a "big fart of a sound." He recalled his father roaring at their colored servants, and he had wanted the father's "big voice." He had one particularly vivid dream in which he saw a girl playing the "biggest organ in the world." Its deep tones drowned out a group of cackling women, who reminded him of his mother, sarcastic, devaluating and shrill. The organ seemed to represent the power he attributed to his father, which he wanted to control or get through his ear. When memories of sexual play with his sister began to emerge, he began without noticing it to put his finger in his ear. At times he devaluated the analyst, calling him a fat empty horn into which he poured words that were never heard. At other times there were opposite attitudes. He spoke with anxiety of the therapist—"listening with those big hairy ears." Early in the treatment he saw a young man who resembled a series of brother figures. He became obsessed with the youth's ears, and recalled the sudden impulse to bite them off. This was followed in due course by the directly expressed nuclear fantasy of devouring the prized genital which he felt he lacked.

Thus the ears can become symbolically bisexual. As jutting projections they signify power. When they are lost, the individual becomes also "dumb," helpless and crippled. As a receptive orifice, they may call up even greater dangers of attack, penetration, poisoning, such as happened to Hamlet's father. My impression is that when we think of our body image the orifice predominates. It seems to play a complementary role to the voice, which is felt at unconscious levels to be a projection and extension of oneself. The plumbing salesman, mentioned earlier, often expressed his anxiety in terms of speech. He was afraid that his words would not carry to his customers, and at times, in terror, he would be unable to hear himself speak. In everyday terms, a voice may "blast," "bend" or "chew off" the passive ear. Possibly that is one reason why loss of the ear is thought of as less sweeping and drastic than the loss of the eye—sort of castration in a minor key. In literature there is no deaf Oedipus. Nevertheless fears, and wishes, connected with mutilation may definitely center in the ear. They may be greater the more an individual depends on that organ. I have seen two prospective analysts who had transient morbid anxieties over ear disease, which in their fantasy would leave them deaf, and shorn of patients.

Of course, in this respect the ear does not differ from other projections and orifices, which can acquire similar meanings—as Hart has shown for the eye (10), and Saul for the nose (25). So far, we have established that the ear can substitute for other areas of the body chiefly by the accident of shape. But there have been hints that it substitutes in a special way, as a particular kind of phallus or womb, depending on its unique acoustic functions. These we must now examine.

II

The physiology of hearing will only be mentioned to indicate its complexity and sensitivity. Harris (9) points out that the inner ear can be activated by amounts of energy almost as infinitesimal as those which will stimulate the retina—equivalent to "about the weight of a mosquito's wing, dead or alive." Yet like the eye, the ear can stand enormous energy intensities, at least briefly. It is even more acute than the eye in detecting time intervals (9); and despite its lack of a peripheral focusing apparatus like the visual one, it has a remarkable ability to pick out sound patterns against a chaotic background of noise. Hence there are great capacities for active discrimination as well as passive reception. Psychologically, it may be useful to distinguish, in a rough way, the concept listening, which indicates a definite, usually voluntary effort to apprehend acoustically, from the more comprehensive term hearing, defined as the mere reception of stimuli over auditory pathways. Successful listening presupposes hearing and precedes understanding. As an active function, we may consider listening first, under three headings: language, special skills, and curiosity.

Language is obviously profoundly influenced by the acoustic sense. The exact part played in the mysterious birth of speech, the relation of auditory perception to identification and character formation, the interaction between sound and symbol in the development of language, are unsolved questions, beyond our present scope. We may simply say, clinically, that accurate function of the ear is enormously important for communication. There is an automatic auditory regulation of our own speech. In the presence of noise a speaker talks louder in order to hear himself. If we introduce extraneous words into his ear, speech becomes difficult. If we feed back to him, a fraction of a second later, his own words —as Funkenstein (8) and others are now doing experimentally— it becomes almost impossible. Disruption of language patterns occurs, often accompanied by stammering and anxiety.

Failure of acoustic perception can cause similar difficulties. They may result from actual faulty hearing, as in the deaf child, who becomes "mute" unless he gets special treatment. Or the cause may be only an inability to listen, which at times leads to a variety of distortions, from major neurotic or psychotic forms of hearing loss, through a gamut of minor failure to comprehend. A woman obsessed with guilt because of syphilis was wheeled into staff conference and asked whether she objected to appearing before so many doctors. She replied: "What did you say about a blood test?" Such slips of the ear, the active substitution of one word for another to suit an unconscious purpose, are analogous to, though less common than slips of the tongue.

A particular connection is that between word and command. The prohibitions of the adult may become the "voice of conscience." Freud (7) assigned a special place to the "auditory lobe" in his early blueprints of the psychic organism. Amplifying this concept, Isakower (12) refers to the "auditory sphere" as the "nucleus of the superego." Briefly, he argues: we learn from language, which reaches us through the auditory "sphere," that is, the entire acoustic apparatus, from end organ to psychic representation. Through it we take in the speech and ultimately the attitudes of the environment, to create an inner observing and criticizing institution. Thus the auditory mechanism keeps us oriented in the world of conduct, as the adjacent and embryologically similar vestibular apparatus does in the world of space.

Common speech reflects this connection. When a child is told to "listen to his elders," he is expected to heed, and obey. A "hearing" is a review by a tribunal; to "turn a deaf ear" is to ignore an ethical claim or a threat. A four-year-old girl announced that she was going to pull off her ears—"so I won't have to hear the grownups and do what they say." In psychoanalysis we may see the process of listening, and absorbing words, repeated. Patients often report talking or arguing with the therapist, recalling a crucial phrase, a key interpretation. In short the analyst is introjected and becomes the "auxiliary superego," speaking inside the patient. At times this speech can have an almost hallucinatory intensity. Usually, however, as is the case with many schizophrenic "voices," actual sound is insignificant or absent from the fantasy. It is the idea, the linguistic content, which is important. The new slogans of the analytic experience, replacing old shiboleths, flash into the mind like unheard messages. Gradually they lead to pervasive "insights," which can hardly be verbalized at all.

This very development points out a certain artificiality in Isakower's conception. In the construction of our inner controls the important agent is language as a symbolic process. Heiders (11) has shown that linguistic development takes place even in the absence of all hearing. Furthermore other media convey commands, the raised finger to a child, a traffic light to an adult. The congenitally deaf do not have congenital atrophy of conscience. Although the ears contribute to superego formation, they are not its sole architect.

Words also translate more of reality than its prohibitions. And listening brings us more than words. Britton (3) reports that deaf children, particularly those deafened from birth, seem to have impaired gestalt discrimination and reduced ability to draw human figures—possibly because of inadequate perceptual contact with the earliest environment and inadequate stimulation by their first love objects. The basic contribution, beyond that of words, which audition makes to ego development remains obscure. It is clear, however, that the ears help develop many *special skills*, which are important in everyday functioning. They may be vital, under primitive conditions of life, or when vision has failed, or in particular branches of work—mechanics, medicine, and above all music. Again our words may identify the part with the talent. We say of the virtuoso that he has a "fine ear."

The use of listening in the service of *curiosity* is thoroughly familiar to the psychoanalyst. "Little Pitchers have big ears." The excitement caused by overhearing parental intercourse, excremental acts, or other forbidden events, the conscious struggle to find out by the ears what is going on between adults, the consequent guilt, the repressions and elaborations in fantasy, are almost universally important. Ferenczi (4) points out how obscene words, which normally are subjected to repressive forces, retain a powerful buried emotional force. They continue to have a "peculiar power of compelling the hearer to imagine the object it denotes, the sexual organ or function." Hearing them often produces the same agitation that originally accompanied overhearing actual forbidden speech or events. A patient, who wanted "an ear" into which to pour troubles, who had particularly sensitive acoustic perceptions and concern with voice, and in whose life primal events had played an outstanding part, reported a shocklike reaction on hearing any "dirty" word. When forced at the age of twenty-five to sleep in the same room with both parents, one of whom was dying, this patient became obsessed with morbid acoustic fantasies during the night—and in that setting developed malignant disease of the throat.

The instinctual stimulation from noise or sounds is in essence the same as that resulting from crucial visual stimuli, though audible impressions are more likely to come from the nocturnal world. "The day has eyes; the night has ears." The very vagueness of the unseen noises and verbal innuendo which the ears can detect may throw some light on the auditory vigilance of the paranoid patient. He is alert to all sorts of peripheral clues, as well absorbed by vivid inner dialogues. These two facts together might account for the unexplained susceptibility of this type of patient to auditory, rather than visual, hallucinations.

The act of listening, then, contributes to superego and ego functions and to instinctual gratification. It remains subordinate to the main sensory representative of reality, vision, but extends its bounds. We keep an "eye to the future" to make our major plans, but have our "ear to the ground" to detect nuances and reverberations. The ear can function as a tentacle, plucking pearls from the sea of words and exploring depths that vision does not reach.

III

The ear also serves as a more passive vehicle. We offer it as such when we "lend an ear," and we suffer it as such when our ears are filled or "split" by noise. In metaphor, verbal seeds can germinate and grow in it. To "whisper a word" to someone can signify implanting an idea—or, in slang "putting a bug in his ear." We hear much that we don't, or won't, listen to; and fertilization can take place in a near-virginal state of unawareness. That human fact has assisted the propaganda methods of the police state and the modern advertising industry.

Actually, we have a magnificent ability not to listen. Consider, for example, our performance at a large party, where we talk with one person, and block out the surrounding din. Schilder (26) quotes experiments showing that when the third temporal convolution was anesthetized subjects complained of hearing too many spontaneous sounds. This work suggests central suppressor areas which prevent our being overwhelmed by noise. Regardless of the exact neural basis, such a mechanism exists. Only with its aid could the sense of hearing be at once so acute and so selective. Otherwise we would live in bedlam. In contrast to kinesthetic and visceral perceptions, auditory stimuli, like visual ones, come in a constant flow from the outside world. Yet unlike the eyes, the ears never close.

Most of our life we spend unaware, or only partially so, of innumerable sounds. If we do notice them, precise knowledge may not be in the foreground but rather elements of feeling. Ramsdell (23) believes that the most vital function of the ear is to provide an affective link with the world by bringing us an emotionally charged wealth of sound. The exact feelings evoked by different sounds, and the deeper significance of acoustic stimuli, are problems which can only be hinted at here. In childhood, noises are intimately linked with sexual events, toilet training, feeding, and with the attitudes of crucial persons: soothing cadences of the mother may contrast with the father's booming tones. Kohut and Levarie (16) base a theory of music upon their belief that the deepest of all reactions to noise is fearful. They speculate that the frightening sounds of the world crowd in on the infant, torn from his uterine haven; "unorganized sound symbolizes primitive dread of destruction," which later is overcome by the activity of listening in the music lover (16). The problem may be even more complex. There is definite evidence, quoted by Sontag (28), that responses to sound can be observed in utero in the last few months of pregnancy. Possibly there are extremely profound reflex interactions between the acoustic sense and its anatomical neighbor, the vestibular, and other rhythmic patterns from the earliest phases of life.

For present purposes, the point is that hearing can serve, *par excellence,* as an emotional instrument. To "play by ear" means to rely not on precise rules, but on affect and intuition. The feelings aroused by sound are instantaneous. When we hear a foghorn, a brass band, laughter, wind, rain, the bustle and hum of a city—or its muted counterpart in a snow fall—each of us may react differently at any moment, but we feel. A thunder clap shows as well as a symphony the impact of sound. In its total absence we speak of "dead" silence. Its presence is like the background music at a moving picture, largely unnoticed but leaving overtones of feeling. In respect to crude sound, hearing is similar to the sense of smell, which Brill (2) describes as largely repressed in civilized man, yet retaining its powerful early affective bonds.

Auditory repression is particularly important in sleep. The ears never close, and sleeping would be impossible if we did not stop listening to all that came through them. The sudden obliteration of sound is characteristic of falling asleep, just as sudden awareness of it may signalize awakening, often with a start. Some acoustic impulses may penetrate into the sleeping state—coming from beyond the bed, unlike visceral and tactile sensations, yet persisting throughout the night, unlike visual stimuli. There are even indications that the meaning of the stimulus may be important. Electroencephalographically it can be shown that long before a sound is loud enough fully to wake a subject, it may affect his brain waves, moving them toward a lighter level of sleep (14). It is a common belief that the mother has particular alertness to her child's cry, the sleeping soldier to a warning of attack. Burdach showed over one hundred years ago, Freud (6) says, that meaningful auditory stimuli, such as the sound of one's own name, would be selectively reacted to by a subject asleep. Fox (5) has reviewed some of the efforts to get educational and therapeutic (17) results by bombarding a sleeper with verbal stimuli through the night. Exactly what penetrates, and at what levels of electrical brain activity, remains to be shown. The deepest stages of sleep may be impervious to almost all stimuli, but we know that through the night the depth of sleep ebbs and flows many times (14).

Occasionally exogenous sounds force their way into our dreaming activity, which may then culminate in waking—for example, in the familiar alarm-clock dream. Usually, however, dreams are soundless. They resemble silent movies. Scenes change, animation occurs, but seldom are there sharp sensory impressions, particularly acoustic ones. Communication takes place, but we do not often hear the voices of dream figures. To test this point, a crude survey was made of over three hundred dreams of six patients under intensive observation. Clear sound percepts were reported in only 6 per cent of these dreams—the range being from zero to 14 per cent among different patients. The lawyer who heard the "biggest organ in the world" has already been mentioned. Another patient had only one "sound dream"—of a horrible train wreck, which mangled a young girl; the associations led to her intense fears of intercourse and pregnancy. Further study of such vivid sensory impressions in dreams might prove revealing, for they may offer clues to significant emotional patterns.

For the most part we slumber, and dream, in relative silence. There are even evidences of specific defenses against sound during sleep. Freud (6) reports them clearly in his dream "The Pope is dead"—a puzzling, nonvisual language fragment, recalled on awakening in his Tyrolese vacation resort. It only fell into place later in the day when his wife asked him if he had not been disturbed by the dreadful tolling of the bells in the small hours of the morning.

A parallel, though more mundane, example occurred in my own experience. The offending stimulus in this case was a noisy, and costly, oil burner, prone to rumble on through the winter nights. In a pleasant dream I was asking a group of men if they had seen a cartoon in yesterday's newspaper. They laughed uproariously, though silently. I felt witty and triumphant, and only much later, after waking, did I recall that there really had been a cartoon. It concerned the painful theme of heating cost, and pictured a householder gazing with consternation out of a vast modern glass window at a truck delivering oil to his home. The dream, provoked by the sound of the furnace, had turned this unhappy motif to triumph and effectively silenced the raucous intrusion.

Metaphorically it could be said that in sleep we are genuinely blind but only hysterically deaf. Perhaps this fact has a special importance in childhood development. So much happens when little ones are asleep. True, if events take place early enough in life, there may not be the great gap between waking and sleeping mentation that develops later. Sometimes, also, they are not asleep but only seem to be. What distortions, however, may not occur when they actually are—what access to the facts of adult love and hate, which later may emerge in a fashion that seems "uncanny"— what fusions of real events with those from dreams. One patient now in analysis has been able to reconstruct the oedipal period, spent in a bedroom off the parental sleeping porch. There are memories of hearing the father urinating, and even one of an odd episode of psychogenic paralysis in this traumatic situation—but none of strictly sexual sounds. Instead there is a recollection of a terrifying nightmare about a huge snake outside the window and of cowering under the covers at the foot of the bed to avoid it. Perhaps in addition to repression of actual memories as we usually understand it, there was repression of the events *in statu nascendi*, mediated by the defenses against sound in sleep. Possibly in a less literal sense than Shakespeare meant when he wrote "Hamlet," nocturnal sounds may be experienced as "poison in the ear."

IV

Regardless of these speculations, it has been found that the ears, as a vehicle both for language and for affectively tinged sound, may be specifically sensitized in certain individuals, who later develop hysterical deafness (15). In less flagrant cases acoustic experience obviously makes an important contribution to character formation. One final possibility should also be mentioned, namely that unconscious attitudes centered in the ear may actually alter its physiology. The pathogenesis of certain ear disorders remains a riddle. Lewis (19) in a recent review mentions evidence that emotional factors may serve as an activating agent in otosclerosis, and that certain cases of middle-ear disease and deafness may be due to an allergic process, also present in the nose. In the past few years I have seen a half a dozen cases, in whom isolation, concern with communication, as well as frequent "colds," and in one instance, unusual auditory hallucinations, long preceded demonstrable and definite disease of the ear. Passe (21, 22) in England has called attention to the sympathetic nervous supply of the internal auditory artery and has suggested that vasospasm may be etiologically important in some types of inner ear pathology. In a series of 110 cases, he has reported that localized sympathectomy has helped cases of Meniere's disease, intractable tinnitus, and nerve deafness. Although this evidence needs verification, it suggests what we might expect, that emotional investment of an important organ could conceivably carry with it the capacity for physiologic change and contribute to physical disease.

In *summary*, the ear, often an unobtrusive part of our body scheme, plays a definite role in psychic life. As an orifice and appendage, it may readily substitute for anatomically similar areas—the vagina, anus, or mouth, on the one hand, the phallus on the other. Its symbolic role is in turn influenced by its special functions—reception of sound and perception of words. It may serve passively as a funnel through which we are fed important instinctual stimuli, often strongly and deeply repressed, particularly during sleep. It may function actively as a probe, a weapon, or a sensitive antenna, with which we extend the boundaries of the visible world and grasp important data for the formation of ego and superego.

Bibliography

1. Abraham, K. The ear and auditory passage as erotogenic zones. In *Selected Papers on Psycho-Analysis*. London: Hogarth Press, 1927.

2. Brill, A. A. The sense of smell in the neuroses and psychoses. *Psychoanal. Quart., 1*:1, 1932.
3. Britton, M. Personal communication from the Devereux Schools, summarizing doctorate thesis.
4. Ferenczi, S. On obscene words. In *Contributions to Psychoanalysis*. Boston: R. C. Badger, 1916.
5. Fox, B. H. and Robbins, J. S. The retention of material presented during sleep. *J. Exper. Psychol., 43*:75, 1952.
6. Freud, S. The interpretation of dreams. In *The Basic Writings of Sigmund Freud*. New York: Modern Library, 1938.
7. Freud, S. *The Ego and the Id*. London: Hogarth Press, 1935.
8. Funkenstein, D. Personal communication.
9. Harris, J. D. *Some Relations Between Vision and Audition*. Springfield, Ill.: Charles C. Thomas, 1950.
10. Hart, H. H. The eye in symbol and symptom. *Psychoanal. Rev., 36*:1, 1949.
11. Heiders, F. and Heiders, G. M. Studies in the psychology of deafness. *Psychol. Monogr., 53*, 1941.
12. Isakower, O. On the exceptional position of the auditory sphere. *Internat. J. Psycho-Anal., 20*:340, 1939.
13. Jones, E. The madonna's conception through the ear. *Essays in Applied Psychoanalysis*, 2. London: Hogarth Press, 1951.
14. Kleitman, H. *Sleep and Wakefulness*. Chicago: University of Chicago Press, 1939.
15. Knapp, P. H. Emotional aspects of hearing loss. *Psychosom. Med., 10*:203, 1948.
16. Kohut, H. and Levarie, S. On the enjoyment of listening to music. *Psychoanal. Quart., 29*:64, 1950.
17. Leshan, L. The breaking of a habit by suggestion during sleep. *J. Abnorm. Psychol., 37*:406, 1942.
18. Levine, M. I. Pediatric observations on the masturbation in children. In *The Psychoanalytic Study of the Child*, 4. New York: International Universities Press, 1951.
19. Lewis, D. K. Medical progress: deafness. *New Eng. J. Med., 243*:699, 1950.
20. Murdock, G. P. *Our Primitive Contemporaries*. New York: Macmillan, 1934.
21. Passe, E. G. Sympathectomy in relation to Meniere's Disease, nerve deafness, and tinnitus. *Proc. Royal Soc. Med., 44*:760, 1951.
22. Passe, E. G. and Seymour, J. S. Meniere's syndrome: successful treatment by surgery on the sympathetic. *Brit. Med., J., 11*: 812, 1948.
23. Ramsdell, D. A. *The Psychology of the Hard of Hearing and*

the Deafened Adult in Hearing and Deafness. H. Davis, Ed. New York: Murray Hill Books, 1947.
24. Rank, B. Where child analysis stands today. *Am. Imago, 3,* 1942.
25. Saul, L. Feminine significance of the nose. *Psychoanal. Quart.,* 27:51, 1948.
26. Schilder, P. *Mind Perception and Thought.* New York: Columbia University Press, 1942.
27. Schilder, P. *The Image and Appearance of the Human Body.* New York: International Universities Press, 1951.
28. Sontag, L. W. Synopsis of Psychosomatic Diagnosis and Treatment. Chapter 2. Dunbar, F., Ed. Saint Louis: C. V. Mosby, 1948.

WILLIAM JAMES/The Absence of Certain Sensory Experiences in the Deaf

So FAR as I can make out, the immunity from dizziness which is characteristic of deaf-mutes has never been remarked or commented on before, even at asylums. Another illustration of how few facts "experience" will discover unless some prior interest, born of theory, is already awakened in the mind.

The modern theory, that the semicircular canals are unconnected with the sense of hearing, but serve to convey to us the feeling of movement of our head through space, a feeling which, when very intensely excited, passes into that of vertigo or dizziness, is well known. It occurred to me that deaf-mute asylums ought to offer some corroboration of the theory in question, if a true one. Among their inmates must certainly be a considerable number in whom either the labyrinths or the auditory nerves in their totality have been destroyed by the same causes that produced the deafness. We ought therefore to expect, if the semicircular canals be really the starting-points of the sensation of dizziness, to find, on examining a large number of deaf-mutes, a certain proportion of them who are completely insusceptible of that affection, and others who enjoy immunity in a less complete degree.

The number of deaf-mutes who have been examined to test this suggestion is in all 519. Of these 186 are reported as totally insusceptible of being made dizzy by whirling rapidly round with the head in any position whatever. Nearly 200 students and instructors in Harvard College were examined for purposes of comparison, and but a single one remained exempt from the vertigo. Of the deaf-mutes, 134 are set down as dizzy in a very slight degree; while 199 were normally, and in a few cases abnormally, sensitive.

The surmise with which I started is thus proved, and the theory that the semicircular canals are organs of equilibrium receives renewed corroboration.

Of course the cases observed represent every kind of ear disease, and it is impossible to analyze them so as to show why exemption from vertigo should be associated with the deafness in one case and in another not. "Congenital" mutes are found in all three classes, and so are "semi-mutes," so that the age at which the deafness comes on has nothing to do with it. The diseases which are the most fertile causes of deafness, meningitis, scarlet fever, typhoid fever, etc., are as apt to leave the patient's sensibility to vertigo normal as they are to abolish it.

The cases from which the above aggregate conclusions are drawn are from several distinct sources: the Hartford Asylum; the National College at Washington, and its primary department; the Horace Mann School in Boston; the Clarke Institution at Northampton; the Indiana Institution; the answers to a printed circular I distributed, and a number of separate voluntary reports I received. In tabular form the statistics run as shown in the following table, which lists the responses from all sources.

Institution	Not dizzy	Slightly	Dizzy
National College	18	5	38
Its Primary Department	11	1	19
Hartford	49	49	57
Boston	45	20	4
Northampton	35	30	20
Indiana	6	6	4
Circulars	28	19	46
Various	4	4	11
Total	196	134	199

As regards the accuracy of the reports, there is this to be said. Among normal people it is well known how individuals differ in their sensitiveness to whirling about or swinging. The cases marked "slight" may possibly therefore fall within the normal limits. It is more probable however that the majority of them represent a more or less abnormally reduced susceptibility. In the cases I myself examined, every one where the presence of vertigo was at all doubtful was recorded as "slight," so as not to overload the column of figures favorable to my hypotheses. In the Harvard College records, in which each man inscribed his own result, the expressions "slightly" and "somewhat" occur, but they do so very few times indeed. Where the vertigo was slight, it has often happened that a deaf-mute examined one day or by one person was reported "not dizzy," whilst another day or another examiner caused the case to be recorded either as "slightly dizzy" or as "dizzy." I am disposed to think that both normal and abnormal subjects differ somewhat in their sensibility to vertigo from one day to another. Lowenfeld says that this is markedly the case with the vertigo induced by galvanic currents across the head.

A certain lack of rigorous accuracy in individual instances ought then to throw no discredit whatever on the main result of the investigation, which is that disease of the internal ear is likely to confer immunity from dizziness. Nobody could possibly confound the extreme cases, nor could any difference of opinion arise concerning them. We see on the one hand an affection which may nauseate the patient or make it impossible for him to stand on his feet at all; on the other, absolute and total indifference to the whirling in every respect whatsoever.

As regards the method of examination, active spinning about on the feet with the head successively upright, bent forward, and inclined on one shoulder is of course the simplest way of testing the matter. The eyes must be closed to eliminate optical vertigo pure and simple, but opened when the spinning is over, so that the patient may have every advantage for walking straight. Except in the Boston and Northampton Schools this was the method generally used. It is likely to give an unduly small number of total exemptions, from the fact that if the whirling has been long and violent, some feeling of confusion will remain for a few moments as a consequence of head congestion, and some irregularity of gait as a consequence of involuntary continuance of muscular vertigo —it probably figures in many of the cases marked "slight."

The muscular vertigo may be entirely eliminated by passive rotation. The children of the Boston and Northampton Schools were seated on a square board, each angle whereof had a rope affixed to it. The ropes were kept parallel up to a height above the head of the inmate by a cross-shaped brace of wood which kept them asunder at that point. Above the cross-brace they rapidly converged to the point of suspension of the apparatus. The apparatus is rotated by the examiner's hands till the ropes above the brace are tightly twisted. The child is then seated on the board, with closed eyes, and head in any position desired, and the torsion of the ropes is left to work its effects freely. These consist in a rapid revolution of the whole apparatus, including its inmate. The moment the speed of rotation slackens, the examiner stops the rotation, and sets the child, who has been instructed previously, to open his eyes and walk as straight as possible toward a distant point on the floor. I examined all the Northampton children myself in this way, and (with my brother's assistance) repeated thus the examinations made of the children of the Horace Mann School by their teachers a year before. The Harvard students were also examined in this way.

It is difficult to be sure, in many of the cases marked "slightly dizzy," whether the sensation experienced by the subject was a mild degree of true vertigo, or a slight confusion arising from the effects of centrifugal movement of the intracranial fluids and viscera. That changes of intracranial pressure will give rise to dizziness by directly influencing the brain independently of the semicircular canals is evident from the number of subjects who are of reduced sensibility as respects dizziness from whirling, but who say that they feel dizzy when their head is suddenly raised from a bent position, or when they get up after stooping to the ground. In reply to a question in the circular, "Do you ever experience dizziness under any other circumstances?" (than whirling) two of the "not dizzy" class, six of the "slightly dizzy" class, and five of the "dizzy" class speak of experiencing this feeling.

In view of the great probability that seasickness is due to an over-excitement of the organs of vertigo, propagated to the cerebellum or whatever other "centers" of nausea there may be, I inquired of many deaf-mutes whether they had been exposed to rough weather at sea and suffered in the usual way. The majority, of course, had not been exposed. Fifteen of the "not dizzy" or "scarcely dizzy" classes had been exposed, and of these not one had been seasick. This, it is true, is negative evidence, and might easily be upset by two or three cases of exemption from dizziness with susceptibility to seasickness.

Perhaps the most interesting of all the results to which our inquiries have led is the following. A certain number of non-dizzy deaf-mutes when plunged under water seem to be affected by an indescribable alarm and bewilderment, which only ceases when they find their heads above the surface. Everyone who has lost himself in the woods, or wakened in the darkness of the night to find the relation of his bed's position relatively to the doors and windows of his room forgotten knows the altogether peculiar discomfort and anxiety of such "disorientation" in the horizontal plane. In ordinary life, however, the sense of what is the vertical direction is never lost. Even with eyes closed, and the "static" sense, as Brewer calls it, of the semicircular canals lost, gravity exerts its never-ceasing influence on our limbs, and tells us where the ground is and where the zenith, no matter what our movements may be. "So shakes the magnet, and so stands the pole." Helmholtz, who wrote his Optics before the semicircular canal sense was discovered, ascribes much of the seasick vertigo to the sufferer's sense of the direction of gravity being thrown out of gear: "One feels the traction of gravity (on board ship) now apparently to the right, now to the left, now forwards and now backwards, because one is no longer able to find (with his eyes) the direction of the vertical. Only after long practice, as I can myself testify, does one come to use gravity as an exclusive means of orientation, and only then does the vertigo cease."

But imagine a person without even the sense of gravity to guide him, and the "disorientation" ought to be complete—a sort of bewilderment concerning his relations to his environment in all three dimensions will ensue, to which ordinary life offers absolutely no parallel. Now this case seems realized when a non-dizzy deaf-mute dives under water with his eyes closed. He hears nothing (except perhaps subjective roaring); sees nothing; his semicircular canal sense tells him nothing of motion up or down, right or left, or round about; the water presses on his skin equally in each direction; he is literally cut off from all knowledge of their relations to outer space, and ought to suffer the maximum possible degree of bewilderment to which in his mundane life a creature can attain.

I have received information bearing on this point, and distinct enough to be quoted, from thirty-three cases in all. Curious exceptions occur which I cannot understand, and which I will presently state. Meanwhile here are some extracts from my correspondents' replies which show the condition above described to be no fiction. Prof. Samuel Porter of the College at Washington, from whom I have derived most of my information on this point, says, "I am told it is the case with some deaf-mutes that they sometimes find a difficulty in rising after a dive from uncertainty as to up and down."

> L. G. writes:
> A year after I lost my hearing, on a day when the sun was shining brightly, I dove from a high place, and immediately after entering the water had no knowledge of locality. In what direction the top was I could not determine, and it was the same as respects the bottom. I endured agonies in searching for the surface. At last, when I had given up all hope, my head was fortunately at the surface, and I was soon master of the situation. I was told that I had been swimming on the surface with the back of my head sometimes out of water, and at other times completely immersed. For years I could not summon up courage to dive again. I never feel at my ease under water.

W. H. writes:
Since I became deaf it has been difficult to control myself under water ... When I undertake to dive into the water I immediately lose all control over my movements, and cannot tell which way is up or which is down.... Once I struck against something, but I am not able to say whether it was the bottom of the river or the steep rocks near the shore.

A. S. L.:
If I get my head under water it is impossible for me to tell which is the top or bottom of the river or pond, and there is a great roaring and buzzing in my head.

G. M. T.:
Before I lost my hearing I was a good diver, but after that time I could never trust my head under water.

M. C.:
Difficult to swim or dive without being frightened terribly. ... I generally close eyes till under water, then open them till top is reached. If eyes are kept closed I become confused.

J. L. H.:
It is very seldom that any deaf-mute can escape drowning when his head has got under water. Persons with such heads as mine are rendered unable to come out of the water in the right direction.

J. C. B.:
Dare not go under water at all unless by day and with eyes open.... Must keep the eyes open. Impossible to swim in the dark.

C. S. D.:
Can't dive at all. As soon as water gets in my eyes, I can't get them open; get confused, and do not know whether I am standing on my head or my feet.

JACOB TWERSKY/The Face of The Deep

JOE BERKOWITZ

PHIL AND I are on the sand by the sea, Phil reading to himself and I stretched on my back. I have to keep my arm over my eyes or else the strong sun will make them tear and hurt; how strange that useless eyes should still have to be taken care of, should still be living parts of you as easily irritated and hurt as any useful part!

Through the arm that protects them my eyes seem to see again, to take in my surroundings. There is Phil—leaning on his stomach and elbows, an absorbed expression on his face, as he reads the glossy pages on the sand before him. Strands of light brown hair stiff with salt water fall over his serious face, and he pushes them back impatiently, as he used to do long ago, when I could see. And now I seem to see the children I can hear about me: children running, the white under parts of their feet twinkling in the sun; children digging, the sun pouncing on blond hair. When I myself was a child in that long ago time I collected shells on the beach and held them up to the sun, pink, indigo and iridescent shells.

Through my arm I also seem to see the browned fat women and fat men, sitting and lying and eating; and a young slender woman with white round arms stepping out of the water, droplets shimmering on her like jewels; and a man with every muscle and sinew of his body clearly revealed, and with a face like mine, but with eyes able to see, standing on the wet hard shoulder of the beach, the foaming sparkling water breaking at his feet, standing quietly and looking out toward the hazy blue line where sky and water meet. And I seem to see a white gull in marvelously free flight, and a bright green boat with brown sails, a boat bouncing on waves that rise up spuming and tumble forward still spuming. And there, on the water, is a woman swimming, her gleaming arm raised for the next stroke.

I smell oil and hot dogs and hard-boiled eggs, brine and kelp. I hear the babble of voices punctuated by the shrill children. I hear the breakers sounding like cymbal crashes; a fierce intensifying roll followed by a retreating, softer, more sibilant roll; then the onrushing fierce roll again. I seem to feel the spinning of the earth. I feel the yielding sand and the caressing air and warmth.

But I cannot see, not a damn rotten thing.

Last winter I was thirteen, the age at which Jewish boys have their bar mitzvah, the rite whereby they become full-fledged

Jews. Mama objected to a bar mitzvah for me, saying it would exhaust me to learn the necessary speech and special prayers by heart, and to undergo the strain of standing before everyone in the synagogue. She said it was stuff and nonsense anyway. I didn't care whether the food I ate was kosher or not, didn't wear a head covering, except at Grandpa's and the synagogue, and wasn't restricted in any of the ways of orthodox Jews, for I felt such restrictions were not too important to God. Mama had always said so. But a bar mitzvah, I felt, was important to God. And there were also other reasons why I wanted it.

"If I could see, you wouldn't make such a fuss over it," I said to Mama. "Phil had it."

"Grandpa put the idea into your head."

"I want it for other reasons, too."

"There's no harm in it, Jenny," Papa said.

"You just don't want your old father to be disappointed," Mama told him. "You don't care how much of a strain Joey will have to submit to, just to please that pestering old man."

"Aw, boloney," I said. "You never let me do anything I want to. I'm going to have a bar mitzvah, do you hear?"

And so Grandpa taught me the Hebrew prayers to God and the Yiddish speech of thanks to my parents for rearing me to be a Jew. Once, during the Christmas vacation, we continued to sit behind the counter in his store after we had finished the lesson. He seemed to be thinking, and I sat waiting for him to speak or rise. He would lock up and take me home soon. The radiator hissed, and in the street, in the rain, cars going through puddles hissed too, dragging long trailing hisses after them.

"Have you wondered why you must thank your parents for rearing you to be a Jew, when they taught you practically nothing about Judaism?"

"I just thought it was part of the ceremony."

"That sounds cynical, Yusselleh, but I know you don't mean it so. I agree with you that some ceremonies or parts of them aren't very important, but this one is—all of it, as you really know. Yusselleh, it's because of your parents that you are a Jew, and so it's right to thank them. Every Jew should ask himself: What is a Jew? An old complex question. Tell me—what is a Jew?"

"It's like being Irish or anything else, I guess, only it's also like being Catholic or Protestant. I guess I just think of them like that, only I'm mixed up because Jews aren't liked often, and there are pogroms and things like that."

"A Jew is different, or at least others say he's different. The different are rarely welcomed," Grandpa said.

I thought of my blindness and how that made me different,

but I felt more strongly than ever that I would not be blind much longer.

"Jewishness is something your parents gave you simply by being your parents. You understand, Yusselleh? Born a Jew you're always a Jew, and everybody knows it. Your mama and papa are Jews, whether they believe in Judaism or not. That doesn't mean that Jews are a race, either. They are of all races, of all nationalities, of all types. It hurts not to be able to make it clear to you."

His chair creaked. The emotion I sensed in him made me tense with listening.

"Many Jews have suffered and died because of the ideals they prized, though they did no one harm. Many others have been tormented and killed, merely because they were born Jews. All your ancestors were Jews, Yusselleh."

The emotion in his voice made me hear the plaintive tones of Cantor Rosenblatt. Grandpa put his arm about me and I could feel more fully the emotion in him. Somehow my eyes grew wet.

"You must know the truth, Yusselleh. And you must be proud to be a Jew, for the Jewish people as a whole have always stood on the side of right."

I was afraid at the bar mitzvah, thinking of the people who would stare at me, but I was determined not to disgrace Grandpa by showing my fear or letting my fear make me forget the words I had learned by heart. Grandpa led me up to the altar, and the rabbi put my hand on the Holy Scroll, the Torah. In the stillness, Mama sobbed. I kept my eyes open consciously. I stood completely erect. My voice filled the stillness.

In the evening, Papa was in his office putting his equipment in order. I walked from the living room through the waiting room into his office and closed the door. I smelled the gas burner and Papa's cigar.

"I want to talk to you."

"So serious, Joey. You look as serious as at the bar mitzvah. What is it, son?"

"Don't orthodox Jews believe you're a man at thirteen?"

"I suppose so. You certainly are. Really, I was very proud of you today."

"I want to know when I'm going to see again."

He had hemmed and hawed whenever I had asked the question before. Now I was set on having a definite answer. Of course I would see again some time, but I wanted to know when. Even if it were a couple of years yet before my eyes were right for operating on, I could wait pretty patiently as long as I knew approximately how long it would be. But if it were many years, naturally it would be tougher, though not so tough as not knowing at all and always expecting to see soon.

"I don't know," Papa said.

(Last time I asked him he had said: "Soon. I don't know exactly when, but soon. Meantime you must keep up your educaation at your school.")

"You must know."

"I don't, son."

"But you're a doctor. Not an eye doctor, but you know something about eyes, and you know what the eye doctors say."

He came up to me, stood silently before me without touching me. The gas burner hissed, and the water on top of it bubbled. Papa was boiling needles or something. I could hear Ann at the piano in the living room, and I could hear Mama walk about upstairs. The water boiled over, sizzling on the burner, but Papa did not move.

"Sometimes I think I'll never see again. I have to know."

He sobbed, wrenching up the sobs from deep inside. I had never heard him weep before. I ran from him and his answer, ran upstairs and threw myself on my bed. It was from that moment on, I think, that I stopped believing in God.

On returning to school I did my damnedest to make the track team, practicing the dashes and jumps, till I hated everything connected with the sport. I became the team's youngest and hardest-working member. It was never fun, but victory was always sweet.

I concentrated on dressing neatly, on eating neatly, even insisting on cutting my own meat and through practice learning to do it without touching any of the food with my hands. I walked quickly, and held my head as if I could see. I concentrated on appearing sighted at everything I did. Whatever I liked to do, or felt I had to do, I would do as well as anyone—better.

Crossing streets alone and without a cane was something I had to try, for if I could do it I would feel less blind. And it was not an impossible thing, because there were a few fellows at school who did it.

One evening I decided to make my attempt at getting over a large, busy crossing. I was not with any of the blind fellows who regularly crossed by themselves; I was out on pass with some boys who could see a bit. We had been at a restaurant and were now wandering through the streets, eating peanuts. I threw my shells at parked cars whose presence I could easily feel as we drew near them. The boys were talking about girls, which ones at school they would like to lay. Sometimes, alone in the bathroom or at night when everyone was asleep, I masturbated, imagining I was with a girl and picturing her in detail. The girl could always see, because it did not seem right that I should be with her if she were blind. If in class a blind girl made me think about her because of her scent or rustling clothes, I would make believe she could see. But as we walked along that evening I hardly listened to the boys' talk. I could not take part in it anyway, because they were older than I and would laugh at me for being a snotty kid. Besides, I was thinking of the crossing I wanted to make by myself. I threw the shells hard at the cars.

We came to the avenue on which the school is located. It always seemed more like a busy highway because of the few people around, and the heavy traffic. We had to cross it now because we had to be back at school in a few minutes. We would cross it and head down six blocks to the school. Once across the avenue, the other crossings, over side streets with little traffic, would be nothing. Crossing the avenue was the real test. If I could do it, then I would be started as a blind person who could cross streets regularly by himself. We stood waiting, the boys watching for the light to change.

I stiffened, listening to the traffic. I pictured the cars as mechanical monsters with nothing human about them. One of them had made me blind. Another might injure me further or kill me. Every nerve in me was taut, but when I spoke it was somehow almost calmly.

"You guys go ahead. I'll catch up with you. I want to cross by myself. I have to start some time."

"You're nuts," Johnnie said. "Why cross by yourself if you got us here?"

"I want to. What do you care?"

"We're responsible for you," Al said. "We'd never get another pass from Rogers if anything happened to you."

"He even lets some guys who can't see at all go out by themselves," I said.

"They're not kids," Al said. "Come on. We have the light."

"I'm crossing by myself. Why don't you guys mind your own business?"

"He's right about having to start some time," Ernie said. Ernie was a ringleader at school. "I've seen blinks crossing bigger streets than this."

"This crazy little blink's too young yet," Johnnie said.

"What is this?" I said. "I know what I'm doing. Who are you to tell me what to do?"

"Let's see if he's got guts or is just blowing off," Ernie said.

"But we're responsible for him," Al said.

"Where did you get that?" Ernie said. "What are we supposed to do, carry the blinks who get a pass the same time we do? Let him go ahead and cross by himself if he wants to."

"The hell with him," Al said. "We'll be late if we don't hurry up."

"Look, kid," Johnnie said, "if you get scared, just call out and we'll come back for you."

"You're on your own, kid," Ernie said. "We'll be on the other side waiting for you. We won't call to you or anything. No calling to him, hear?"

They had to wait for the light again, stood there with Johnnie still arguing with Ernie.

"You can't just follow us across, you know," Ernie said. "You have to wait for the next time the cars stop. Jesus, I don't know if I'd have the guts to do it with my eyes closed. This ought to be interesting."

"For crying out tears," Al said, "Come on. We'll be late."

"What if we are a few minutes late?" Ernie said. "They're not going to shoot us. Okay, kid—we'll be waiting for you."

They went across, Johnnie still arguing. The traffic started again. I was alone. I listened for the cars to stop, readying myself to move quickly, but not to run, because it had been while running that I had been blinded. The gas fumes seemed to burn my lungs. The roll of the cars was a roar in my ears.

The roar before me ceased. Motors hummed, at any moment liable to roar again. Straight ahead the road was clear. If I moved in a straight line, didn't veer into the cross-traffic, I would be all right. But I couldn't get started. I was too tight to move. The roar before me released itself again. I wanted to die because of the shame I felt. The boys had seen me fail. Yell, and they would come and help me over, but I would get myself killed rather than do that. They were yelling, but I didn't answer, didn't understand what they were yelling.

The roar ceased again. Because I was desperate I could take off. I walked rapidly and shakily. Hot exhaust was in the cold night air. The asphalt felt like ice. I thought I would slip. I thought I would stiffen in the middle of the crossing and not be able to go on. My stomach felt as if I were falling. Hot radiator breath from a waiting car was on my tight face. How long would the cars wait? No crossing had ever seemed anywhere near so long. I would be hit, I would be hit! My toe struck the curb. Ernie pounded me on the back. I felt like throwing up, but I smiled.

I got as many passes as I could and practiced crossing and finding stores that I might want to get to. Once, as I crossed, the cars started up when I was only halfway over, I froze. I tried to shout, but couldn't. I lost all sense of direction, didn't know from which direction sounds were coming. The cars seemed to be circling me, making the circles ever smaller. I considered leaping up and forward, hoping to land on a runningboard and that way get out of the maelstrom. But luckily I remained frozen in panic. Suddenly it was still, and forgetting about not running at a crossing, I charged, crashed into a lamp post before I could stop myself, and hugged the post while my forehead bled.

Rain, with its curtaining sound, made the going tougher. Snow was even worse, for it deadened sounds, and on the deserted avenue filled in the gutters of the side streets. There were no stepdowns when you came to side streets, so you could not tell how many blocks you covered by counting the crossings. Once I became lost on my way back to school. The snow was so deep and the wind howled so, that I could hardly hear. When I had been walking a long time and still could not find the fence of the school, I knew I was lost, especially since I could not hear a single car, which meant I had wandered off the avenue. I was down some side street, but which one? I might be in the middle of a road where a car, because I could not hear, could sneak up on me. I searched wildly for a building or tree or post. I trembled with cold and fear. I might be going around in circles. But I found the side of a house. I could not go in and ask where I was. I started off, hoping I was heading for the avenue. I felt wretched, but also proud because I was not asking anyone's help. I followed a hedge. I came to the end of a block, but did not think I was at the avenue yet because I heard nothing. There were bound to be some cars on the avenue. I went on slowly, and because the snow was not churned up underfoot I was sure I was not crossing the avenue. I came to another hedge and followed it, too, and because I heard a car up ahead, I turned left at the end of the hedge. I reached the school fence. The familiar touch of it filled me with pride and confidence in myself.

When I was on the street alone, and people offered me help, I was not rude enough to refuse, but as they guided me across I inwardly resented them. When I was out with Ken, however, or with someone else totally blind, I was glad of the help of strangers because I could not risk getting anyone hurt besides myself.

Alone, I sometimes felt that I wanted to get hurt, killed maybe. I had many opportunities, because not many people helped me, perhaps because I don't often look blind. But perhaps it really wasn't very dangerous, as I became better and better at it. But I'm still afraid when I go alone.

Mama didn't know I went on the street alone. Even when I began coming home alone, she didn't guess, believing that someone from school took me to the bus and put me on it so that she or

Papa or Phil could meet me at the terminal in Paterson. Even that was bad enough. Actually I crossed many streets in Trenton to get to the bus, though at the bus I did ask people for help in order to know if I boarded the right one. Poor dear Mama. When she found out about it, she became ill. I had to make all kinds of promises which I knew I wouldn't keep.

I feel Mama's pain, but what can I do? I could act like an invalid, but that's just not in me.

If I had to go on the streets alone, Papa wanted me at least to carry a cane. People would know I was blind and help me. But I did not want to announce to everybody that I was blind, did not want help, except when absolutely necessary. But Papa couldn't understand.

Papa has changed since that night I ran from his sobs that told me I would never see again. His calmness is often so strained it makes me jittery. He has taken to being extremely careful in talking to me, fearing he will say something about which I am touchy. It only makes me more touchy as I feel his fear. And he is always harping on how important it is for me to succeed at school, and afterward at college, as if I didn't know that myself. The harping makes me more tense. He is not himself any more. I don't feel toward him the way I used to.

I don't like to be near him, though at school sometimes I still miss him. If only he could be himself with me again!

Even little Ann has learned to be ill at ease with me.

Old Phil understands, though. When I began traveling the way I do, he was afraid for me, naturally, but he knew I had to do it.

No one, however, could have been more afraid than I myself. Sometimes at night I started out of sleep, thinking I was in the middle of a crossing. I would grab the cold metal of the bed and hold on tight, till I stopped trembling.

I kept to myself a good deal at school. I wasn't a regular guy, even though I sneaked smokes with some of the fellows in the incinerator building. If caught, we could have been suspended from school, for smoking was not permitted except in the smoking room, and that was only for teachers. But regular guy or not, usually no one bothered me, because I was good in track and always ready to fight. Some fellows, though, called me a little Jew in a tone that made me boil. The times it happened I tore into whoever was doing the calling, no matter how much bigger and stronger than I they were, and no matter how beat up I got.

Ken, however, was not just one of the guys, and I liked being with him when I wanted company. The school bought Ken his clothes, but so rarely that what he wore was usually patched and too tight, so I gave him some of mine. Mama's approval made me ask if I could bring him home for a weekend, and she said of course. But Ken in the house, just the sight of him, made Mama fluttery and overtalkative, though every time she fed him all he could hold, she did not talk. Ken was uncomfortable, naturally, and I could not stand it. Still, he wanted to come again, as though discomfort were not too high a price to pay, and he kept asking me the following weeks if he could come, but I kept telling him Mama wasn't feeling well, till he stopped asking.

At school when I could be by myself I liked to sit in the arbor with a book, or just doing nothing—liked the scents of wild grape and laurel, the sleepy stillness with voices in the background, the echoing call of a jay. In rain I liked to stand under the arcade, under the roll of it on the huge stone umbrella, and breathe in the sharpened smells of earth and grass. When snow was new I liked the feel of fragile flakes and a handful packed cold and hard.

I pick up a handful of sand. It's granular and warm. Snow is far away. I let the sand sift through my fingers. Phil turns a page. I'd like to go in the water again, but I never ask him to do anything he doesn't want to do. Luckily, we pretty nearly always want to do the same thing at the same time.

If I can't go into the water now, I'd like to read—I'm tired of just lying here. But I couldn't read out here with all these people around, couldn't make a spectacle of myself. At school the teachers make me read aloud to visitors because I read as well as any sighted person reads print. I hate the teachers and visitors at such times, but just the same it makes me feel good to show that I can read well. Still, I'd never think of reading anywhere in public on my own initiative. It's better not to let strangers know you're blind.

I read everything I can literally lay my hands on when I'm by myself or among people who know me. When I read in bed, of course I can go on reading after Mama comes in and clicks off the light, but Phil has to put his book away. He says I'm lucky. At home I get books in the mail from a public braille library, and when I finish them Phil and I carry the bulky volumes back to the post office. Much of what I read I don't understand, but I can remember at least some of it, and long after I've read something I can think back and understand better. The braille books smell of glue and some of shellac. When I think of a word I often picture in my mind how it feels in braille, how it looks in print, the location of the keys on the typewriter that are used to write it. When you read braille it makes a slithering sound as your fingers pass quickly over the paper and dots, but you don't notice the sound often, thinking only of what you read, not even feeling the coldness of your hands on a winter night. I'm reading *Crime and Punishment* at home. I wish I could have brought it and read it here.

Phil closes his book with a little thud. "Damn interesting —the pituitary of the frog."

That's the kind of stuff he reads most of the time, or at least something scientific. He has a little lab in the cellar.

"Want me to read to you?"

"Not on the pituitary of the frog."

"You know what I mean, jughead."

He has a book of stories with him. He read to me on the way down here on the bus—read low so as not to attract attention to us because he knows how I feel about such things. We took a long trip because we wanted to get to a beach where we could build a fire. We'll build one later, and cook the stuff we brought along.

"I don't want to hear any stories now."

"Let's go in, then."

We stand up and walk over the hot sand among the people. My elbow just touches Phil and that's guidance enough. I don't take his arm any more except when crossing a street.

"What were you thinking about when I was reading?" Phil asks.

"Nothing in particular."

"Just generalizing, huh? The great mind at work again."

"Yeah. I've just about figured out what you can do with the pituitary of the frog."

The sand grows cooler under my feet. At the water's edge we stop; just stand. There are no other people near.

"I guess you do think more than most people," Phil says. "I guess you have to think when you have nothing else to do."

"I can sleep."

"Keep your shirt on. I didn't say blindness makes you think. You're always so damn touchy. I said you think. Of course, there are all kinds of blind people. It could just as easily have been me who had that accident."

"What's this! I didn't say a thing. It's you who's been thinking. Frog pituitary must sure be stimulating."

He shoves me and I make believe he's shoved me hard and start falling toward the water, then I start rushing into it and he catches up to me. It's damn cold. We rush ahead. The water sucks out, charges in, throwing us back. We sputter and laugh and go on. We start to swim, Phil calling to me above the noise of the breakers, guiding me with his call, "Joe. Here Joe." I can just hear him over the raucous water. But soon we are beyond the breakers, where I can hear him clearly, and where the water becomes less convulsed the farther we swim on. "That's far enough," Phil says. I turn on my back in the rocking water. I picture a vast expanse of sky. I feel relaxed and happy. I dive under, my blood rushing faster as it gets colder. I come up, and Phil calls to me. I duck him and he comes up under me and pulls me down.

Coming in, I lose Phil crossing the outer breakers, can't hear him at all. Nor can I hear a guiding sound from shore. The crashing water drowns all sound. I strike out hard. My panic grows. I seem to be whirling in the pommeling water. This time it'll happen; it'll be the end of me. How heavy my arms and legs are! I thrash about, swallowing brine. "Joe." I heard it faintly, or did I hear it at all? "Joe." It's Phil, all right. I feel a glow of warmth and a new strength. Phil keeps calling breathlessly. We swim in side by side.

"You can stand now," Phil says. He takes my hand hard, holds it as we walk in the water. I feel heavy and dizzy. Over the crashes I hear voices on the beach.

"You swam away from me," Phil says. "You sure gave me a scare. You put on a burst of speed."

"I'll stick closer to you next time."

I squeeze Phil's hand.

We come out on the sand. We're still holding hands.

"The lifeguard's motioning to us. What the hell does he want?"

I pull my hand away. I guess I wasn't thinking of people seeing us when I let Phil take my hand.

"I guess he saw you leading me in. I guess that's how he noticed us."

"Here he comes. Take it easy, Joe. It's nothing."

"Is he blind?" the guard says.

I despise people who, instead of addressing me when I'm concerned, speak to the person with me when they think or know I'm blind.

"Yeh, he's blind," Phil says.

"I can swim as well as anybody," I say.

"You stay near him all the time?" the guard says.

"Yes," Phil says.

"Okay," the guard says. "Just be careful."

Phil and I walk up the beach to our spot.

"What a stupid bugger!" I say.

"He could've been stupider. He was all right, in fact. You're so damn touchy."

"Phil, I was kind of scared out there. I don't want to think about it, and maybe I won't if we go in again right away. I mean, after we rest a while. If you feel like it."

"Sure. The water's swell today."

We rest and go in again, and afterward, when the sun is less warm, when people are leaving, we walk along the beach to the part where fires are permissible. Here there are dunes of sand and smaller ones of seaweed. We go over them and around them. There are pines and brush behind the beach. We gather brush and driftwood, make a pyramid, and Phil sets it on fire. From our knapsacks we take out our messkits and food. Phil takes care of the potatoes and coffee. I fry the hamburger, slipping it into the pan from the wax paper, setting the pan on rocks over the fire, testing the meat with a fork till I feel it's done. I'm damn hungry.

The sun's warmth disappears completely by the time we eat, and I'm glad I have my shirt and pants on. The tang of the sea gives added flavor to the food. The fire crackles and soughs, has a bittersweet aroma reminiscent of cold mornings. The pines and brush stir and creak. The water crashes and gurgles, sometimes ripples with the sound of a kitten lapping up milk.

Phil and I are the only people here. Phil lights a cigarette, gives me the pack and matches. I put a cigarette between my lips, strike a match that I cup against the wind. I take hold of the middle of the cigarette with my left hand, bring the right with the match in it toward my left hand. Any jerk can bring one hand toward the other. The cigarette gets in the way and is lit. The The fellows at school taught me to light a cigarette this way. The cigarette tastes good, feels good. Some sighted idiot wrote a story which I read in which he said that a blind person probably wouldn't enjoy smoking because he couldn't see the smoke. Phil is sitting quietly, perhaps watching the fire or the water or the sky. I wish I could.

But with Phil I feel less blind than with anyone else. Because of him this summer and the other summers have been swell: jaunts like this, and workouts in the park on the parallel bars and gym horses, and just being with him all the time.

"Hi, Phil."

Phil grunts.

If it weren't for Phil, I couldn't stay home all summer. Mama would get on my nerves. I'd go to that camp for blind kids Ken goes to. And if it weren't for me, old Phil would just stay in his lab or hang around the house, reading. He likes jaunts and things like that, but he needs someone to spur him on a little. We're a team, Phil and I. Together we can do anything. But Mama doesn't think so, is always worried about me, is plenty worried now, I bet.

"We better start for home," I say.

"There's lots of time," Phil says.

"Mama's probably worried herself into a fit."

"She'll have to learn not to—that's all."

NARRATOR

Paul Berkowitz's uncles and cousins worked in the silk factories during his high-school days in Paterson; and summers, as soon as school let out, he worked with them, contributing to the savings initiated by his father and some of the relatives for his professional education. They wanted the bright, earnest boy to be a doctor, and though, in imitation of one of the non-contributing uncles, Paul sometimes claimed that the family only desired a bourgeois ornament, he always dreamed, after the choice had been made for him, of outstanding service and recognition in medicine.

Following the pre-medical course in New York City, he tried to get into a medical school in the metropolitan area, but none would accept him, in spite of his excellent grades. He went to Syracuse. There, just as he had submitted to his family's choice of a profession and found it exactly what he wanted, he submitted to Jenny's decision to marry and again found it exactly what he wanted.

Joe's blindness brought Paul even closer to Jenny. He discovered great strength in himself, and felt that with her to think of he could endure anything. He had gainsaid her only once—in regard to a knowledge of Judaism for the boys, since they would be Jews whether they liked it or not—but now, for her sake as well as for Joe's, of course, he had to gainsay her frequently.

In Paul's opinion, blindness was a frightful limitation, but one of the ophthalmologists who examined Joe sent Paul some factual pamphlets which revised his opinion. The blindness could not be altered—Joe's optic nerve was severed. Still, he could help Joe adjust to it as successfully as possible.

But poor Jenny, reeling under the blow that chance had dealt Joe, wouldn't or couldn't see it. She wanted only the restoration of his vision, as though Paul and everyone else did not want the same. He was patient; the more effort he expended the closer he felt to her.

Jenny began recovering. She paid some attention to her looks, had people over to the house occasionally, and sometimes of an evening went out with Paul. She also had Phil and Ann to fuss over. But Paul was afraid that not till Joe proved a success, as a lawyer perhaps, and was married to some decent girl who would lead him about and take care of him, would Jenny's pain be effectively lessened. In the meantime, Paul would have to console her and divert her mind the best he could.

There were also the friends and relatives of the family, maudlin people, save for Paul's wise old father, whose gushing pity and imprudent exclamations had to be checked. The maid had to be instructed, as well as visiting patients who encountered Joe, to behave as if nothing were wrong. Ann, as she grew older, offered a problem, too. She imitated Jenny in acting as if Joe were something fragile, crying out when he seemed about to bump into anything. In Phil, however, whose intuition if not understanding was marvelous, Paul found an ally.

Paul discussed things with Joe, too, though less freely. After the bar mitzvah the boy grew more sensitive than ever, perhaps because he realized he would never see again, and Paul in talking to him had to guard his every word and tone. Incredibly mature beyond his years in some respects, as though blindness had made him grow up in a hurry, he was immature and foolish in other ways. A stubborn boy, always able to get his way by scolding or pleading or brooding, but with a sharp inquisitive mind and a memory that seemed to forget nothing. Ashamed of his blindness, yet also beginning to be proud of it, as though saying, "I can do these things even if I am blind, which means I'm a better man than you." Joe would succeed; if other blind people could do it, Paul knew that Joe would do it.

How brave he was to ask about his eyes after the bar mitzvah! That handsome, strong-faced boy whom he yearned to embrace; that boy so beloved, yet seeming a stranger as he demanded the truth. And Paul's strength that snapped, and baby Joey, a big boy now, running upstairs. But Jenny was up there and would hear him and see the torment in his face. He pulled himself together and went up to Joe and Jenny.

After that day, Joe became obsessed with independence, dangerously so.

"You must be careful, son. What if something happened to you?"

"You mean, what if I get hit again by a car? Why don't you say what you mean?"

"What's wrong with carrying a cane, Joe?"

"I'm not a decrepit old blind man."

"Won't you think of your mother?"

"I won't grope. I can't! I'm not going to be seen with a cane."

Joe walked away.

Jenny's intuition told her of Joe's danger. She confronted Paul with what she felt. He denied that Joe crossed streets alone. She begged Joe not to cross alone. Joe thought that she had found out definitely and his answer confirmed her feelings.

There was nothing for Paul to do but console Jenny and keep trying to put some sense into Joe and hope that luck would protect him till he outgrew his stupidity. He had faith that Joe's will power and courage and ability would lead him to success.

Paul had that to hope for. He also had his work, even if it hardly approached the work he had once dreamed of. And there was Jenny, and the other children.

You accepted things you couldn't do anything about. . . .

KEN WERNER

I pick up a sheet of aluminum from the pile to my left, put the sheet in the jig, pull the lever of the power press. A crunching bang, and the various holes are punched out in the sheet, the first step in forming it into a chassis for some special kind of radio set. I take the punched-out sheet from the machine, put it to my right, pick up a fresh sheet, put it into the jig, pull the lever.

The crunching bang, so close to me, gives me the willies sometimes, but it's not dangerous work, as long as you don't pull the lever till you know where your left hand is. A blind guy at a machine like this is actually less likely to get hurt than a sighted guy, because he's had practice all along in being careful about not hurting any part of his body. Quite a few blinks are doing this kind of work in different plants, and doing it as well as anybody. I guess that's why I didn't have much trouble getting this job when I applied here.

From eight in the morning till six in the evening I'm at this machine, five days a week, and there's also half a day on Saturday. Real good money, though; Rosie and I are saving quite a bit. Hell, there's no telling when this'll end and I'll be back at film-rolling or something that pays even less. The savings are going to come in mighty handy, some day. I guess the war, whatever it's about, is a good thing, but it's sure a hell of a thing when a guy can get a good job only when other guys are always trying to keep themselves from getting killed.

When my back hurts from sitting on the high stool and leaning toward the machine, I stand up till my feet hurt. I'm standing now. My feet feel the floor throbbing to the motions of the machines about me. I'll be through soon. It's pretty damn hot. You always sweat in the warmth here, but today especially, because it's such a hot day, I stink of sweat. The other workers about me stink, too. And there are smells of grease and oil and hot metal shavings. And there are the metal screechings and crunchings and grindings. You get used to the noise, except near quitting-time. It's pretty bad now.

But tomorrow's Saturday; after the half-day of work I'll go straight home and just sleep or loll around the rest of the day. I guess I've always been a guy who really knows how to take it easy when he can. I haven't had much time for it, though, since marrying Rosie. But it's been okay; it's been swell. A guy is glad to knock himself out for someone like Rosie. Poor kid—her stomach's been bothering her lately. Nothing to worry about, though; it's just an upset stomach—sure. She says she's been to the doctor, so I guess she'll be over it soon.

Jesus, the last half-hour of the work is always the longest. I stop feeding and working the machine for a second, and touch my watch. I got a good ten minutes yet. I start working again.

Yeah, I'll get me some sleep tomorrow. Last Saturday, though, I didn't get much. Little Mary was five years old and we had a party in the afternoon. She's five years old already—can you beat it! I've got a child five years old. Helen Goshenko rounded up some of the kids Mary has got friendly with on the street. There was a cake and candles and all. When Mary blew out the candles, Rosie said, "Did you blow them all out?" "Yes, Mama, all the candles are out," Mary said. The kids Helen had brought up were pretty quiet for kids long after that. I guess it was clear to them that Rosie was really blind. Will our little Mary and Frankie ever be ashamed of us because we're blind? But they understand a hell of a lot, much more than most grownups.

A couple of days before the party I went with Hank, after work, to get Mary a present. While I was at it, I got Frankie one too, even though it wasn't his party that was coming up. And I also got Rosie a present. Last Saturday was a good day on the whole, even if I didn't get much sleep.

Hank and I are pretty good friends. He's a blink, but he can see a little. He does soldering work here—pretty simple soldering, but he has a tough time and may get fired any day. The trouble is, he tries to use his eyes and can't get far that way. If he soldered like a blink, learned to do it by feeling through the soldering iron, he'd be all right. Hell, I've done some pretty good soldering myself at home. Got a cheap soldering iron and fixed a lamp and a toaster and some other things for Rosie. And I know a blind ham-radio operator, who's always improving his rig, who can solder anything, no matter how small and complex. Yeah, Hank's little sight often gives him a lot of trouble. I sure hope they don't fire him. Maybe they can find some job for him here that won't let the little sight he has get in the way.

There's one more blind guy here, a total blink like myself. He's damn good—inspects parts, feeling if they match the master parts he compares them to. We three hang out together, not that we haven't made other friends here, but we just feel closer to each other than to the sighted guys. We go to lunch together, and sometimes have a beer after work. I've known them about a year—good guys who don't take any crap from anybody.

A year—sometimes it seems I've been at this job many years. The motions of operating this machine seem almost natural motions by now. Maybe I could even go through them in my sleep.

One day one of the blinks I was working with at film-rolling told me in the dark room that he had tried to get a job in a war plant that had already hired two blind men, but it wouldn't take him on. He was from Brooklyn, and he had heard about this plant at an organization for the blind there. I decided to try this plant myself, figuring that maybe they just hadn't liked this guy's looks, though he seemed okay enough to me. I went to the plant, made a specific proposal on what kind of work I felt I could do, and maybe it was that, or just that they had had a change of heart about taking on another blink, that made them give me this job.

Man, it's good not to be cooped up in that dark room any more, but right now I wouldn't mind saying good-by forever to this place, too.

It's knock-off time. Voices become clear in the stillness of the stopped machines. The noise will start up soon again when the next shift takes over.

I go to the locker room for my cane. Nothing else, because it was so warm this morning I didn't wear a jacket. I've just got on a polo shirt and an old pair of pants. In the locker room I tie my shoelaces. I always kind of feel unbalanced, walking, when they are too loose. I run my pocket comb through my hair. My legs and arms feel trembly. Sounds still seem peculiar because I haven't got used to the stillness yet. The place is full of flat, tired voices. Hank comes over and asks about a beer. I say not today; I'm too damn tired, and I'm in a hurry to find out how Rosie is feeling.

I get me a coke in the lobby of the plant on my way out. I stand before the vending machine and drink the coke out of the paper cup. Its coldness feels good in my hand and feels good going down, but it tastes a little like soap. I finish it, though, because of its coldness, and walk out into the heat.

The subway train I get on, am pushed on, in fact, in the stream of others getting on, is packed solid. I stand, bodies tight against me. I can't take a deep breath, my body is so pressed against. I'm pouring sweat. I smell the sweat of the others and I smell bad mouths and an odor like rotting hard-boiled eggs. Well, what can you do?

The train pulls into my stop and I go up into the street. A sprinkler must've passed here not long ago, because there's a smell of wet dust. I go to the corner for the bus that'll complete my trip home. I wait, mopping my face or leaning on my cane. Here comes the bus, snorting and sneezing as it stops. Someone helps me on it. I drop in the fare. Someone gets up and gives me a seat. I can tell it's a man who's sitting next to me. I ask him to please tell me when we get to the street I want. I sit back and feel dead to the world.

I'm practically asleep as the man tells me we've reached my street. I feel kind of dizzy as I get off, and I'm damn eager to get home, but I stop in at the candy store for a quart of ice cream. Strawberry—that's the kind Rosie and the kids like best.

I'm entering my house now. There's a pretty awful stench on the ground floor. Shrimp don't taste too bad, but they sure stink cooking. I start up the stairs. We'll have fish, too, of course, since it's Friday, but I hope it won't be anything too smelly. I stop at my door, dig into my pocket for my key, but Rosie must've been listening for me because she opens the door. We kiss. Jesus, I feel better already.

"Have you been all right, Rosie? Your stomach still bothering you?"

"It's all right, honey. What have you got there? Ice cream! You're the most thoughtful husband in the world."

She takes the cold package and my cane from me. The kids have come up and I bend down to them.

"Ken, you go ahead and wash and sit down to eat," Rosie commands.

The kids follow me to the bathroom. I close the door on them, but as I start to wash, I open it again and talk to them. The water runs; the kids in their high voices compete with each other to see who can tell me more of what they've been doing; Rosie makes the silverware ring as she handles it in the kitchen. I breathe in the smell of the dissolving Camay soap on my face and hands. I smell the fried sole from the kitchen. Man, I'm hungry!

It's later in the evening. The kids are asleep. Rosie and I are on the sofa in the living room. There's a mystery program on the radio. I like mysteries, but now I'm so tired I'm half-asleep in the corner of the sofa where I sit sprawled back. I've lost the thread of the story; I guess I don't much care now. Maybe I'll go to bed. Friday is the toughest day, because you feel the tiredness of the whole week. During the week I'm sometimes still pretty lively at night—go to the Amalgam or do some repair work around the flat—but come Friday night, I'm dead. There's a babble from the street; people are probably on the stoops because it's got cooler. Rosie ought to go down; she hardly gets any air. Her breathing sounds far away, though she's sitting next to me. I'm falling asleep. I ought to go to bed, take a shower and go to bed, but I don't feel like stirring. I doze off, then start awake. Rosie was up and is sitting down again. She turned the radio off and I guess I woke because it got quieter.

"Don't you want to hear the radio?"

"I thought you were asleep, honey."

"No. Just taking it easy."

"My poor baby works so hard."

I put my arm about her.

"Ken, if you feel all right, I'd like to tell you something."

"I'm fine. It's you that's not been feeling well. You're sure you're okay now?"

"Ken, I have to tell you. I ought to wait till tomorrow when you'll be rested up, but I can't wait any longer."

"Tell me what? What are you afraid of?"

"You'll be angry with me."

"Me! Angry with my little Rosie! Come, tell me this dreadful thing you've done. Whom have you murdered? Confess, my daughter."

"You're not funny. You know I don't like you to talk like that."

"Okay, okay. What do you want to tell me?"

"We're going to have a baby."

"You're sure?"

"Yes."

"Jesus!"

I get up, move away from her, stand near the window. Maybe I suspected this, but still it's like suddenly bumping your head hard against something. I had wanted us to have Mary, but we hadn't planned on Frankie, and of course not on this one. Sure I love Frankie as much as Mary, if not more, and I'll love this one, too, but I have to think of taking care of them. If this job lasts forever, it'll be okay, but how do I know when it'll end? You have to consider such things before having babies, only Rosie just thinks of religion. How many times have I argued with her that we can't afford so much religion? Watching the cycle is good enough, she says. Jesus, I'm only twenty-four, and soon I'll have four people besides myself to take care of. Can you beat it? It's my fault, too, huh? Well, what am I supposed to do, use a window that slams hard?

"Ken."

She's just been sitting on the sofa where I left her. Now she thinks I've thought it through and got rid of my steam, so she's calling me to come to her and rejoice because we're going to have another baby.

"Don't you understand what it means to be blind?" I say thickly. "Haven't you talked to enough people at the Amalgam to realize how tough it is for the blind to get jobs? I may be out on my ear any day. Just because I've had jobs up till now doesn't mean I'll get another. We've just been damn lucky so far. You and your religion. What the hell are you, a saint or something?"

"It's on its way now, Ken. What good does all this do?"

Maybe stinking Fred Harris was right. She'll have a dozen, just like he told the guys at the Amalgam.

"It's not just the one that's coming now. That's bad enough, but there'll be others, too. You get more religious all the time. I just can't figure you out. You think there'll always be a war on so that they'll be forced to hire blinks for good jobs?"

She cries. Mary calls "Mama." I guess Frankie has been wakened, too, and will be yowling soon. "Mama," Mary calls. "Go to sleep," I shout. Frankie starts yowling.

I sort of feel like laughing, burned-up though I am. Could it be that in a way deep down I want this new one that's coming? It would mean one more person who would be real close to me, and who else could be that way except my own family? Maybe. But we just can't afford it.

Rosie goes out of the room. I hear her calming the kids down. Her voice is still tearful. I drop down on the sofa.

Poor Rosie. It's she who really works hard, and the new baby will mean even more work for her. Poor Rosie, I ought to know by now I can't change her. There's nothing to do.

It's still in the apartment, now. She has calmed the kids and must be crying silently. She'll come in soon to have it out with me, because that's the way she is, but she'll cry by herself first, because she never cries before me when she can help it.

"Rosie."

She comes in and I get up.

"Do you feel all right, Rosie? You better sit down."

"Oh, honey, I know how you feel, but we just can't have God against us."

"It'll be all right."

"Of course it will. You're not angry with me any more?"

"I guess I never really can be."

JONATHAN SWIFT/On His Deafness

DEAF, GIDDY, helpless, left alone
To all my friends a burthen grown
No more I hear my church's bell
Than if it rang out for my knell:
At thunder now no more I start
Than at the rumbling of a cart:
Nay, what's incredible, alack!
I hardly hear a woman's clack.

CARSON McCULLERS/The Heart is a Lonely Hunter

IN THE town there were two mutes, and they were always together. Early every morning they would come out from the house where they lived and walk arm in arm down the street to work. The two friends were very different. The one who always steered the way was an obese and dreamy Greek. In the summer he would come out wearing a yellow or green polo shirt stuffed sloppily into his trousers in front and hanging loose behind. When it was colder he wore over this a shapeless gray sweater. His face was round and oily, with half-closed eyelids and lips that curved in a gentle, stupid smile. The other mute was tall. His eyes had a quick, intelligent expression. He was always immaculate and very soberly dressed.

Every morning the two friends walked silently together until they reached the main street of the town. Then when they came to a certain fruit and candy store they paused for a moment on the sidewalk outside. The Greek, Spiros Antonapoulos, worked for his cousin, who owned this fruit store. His job was to make candies and sweets, uncrate the fruits, and to keep the place clean. The thin mute, John Singer, nearly always put his hand on his friend's arm and looked for a second into his face before leaving him. Then after this good-bye Singer crossed the street and walked on alone to the jewelry store where he worked as a silverware engraver.

In the late afternoon the friends would meet again. Singer came back to the fruit store and waited until Antonapoulos was ready to go home. The Greek would be lazily unpacking a case of peaches or melons, or perhaps looking at the funny paper in the kitchen behind the store where he cooked. Before their departure Antonapoulous always opened a paper sack he kept hidden during the day on one of the kitchen shelves. Inside were stored various bits of food he had collected—a piece of fruit, samples of candy, or the butt-end of a liverwurst. Usually before leaving Antonapoulos waddled gently to the glassed case in the front of the store where some meats and cheeses were kept. He glided open the back of the case and his fat hand groped lovingly for some particular dainty inside which he had wanted. Sometimes his cousin who owned the place did not see him. But if he noticed he stared at his cousin with a warning in his tight, pale face. Sadly Antonapoulos would shuffle the morsel from one corner of the case to the other. During these times Singer stood very straight with his hands in his pockets and looked in another direction. He did not like to watch this little scene between the two Greeks. For, excepting drinking and a certain solitary secret pleasure, Antonapoulos loved to eat more than anything else in the world.

In the dusk the two mutes walked slowly home together. At home Singer was always talking to Antonapoulos. His hands shaped the words in a swift series of designs. His face was eager and his gray-green eyes sparkled brightly. With his thin, strong hands he told Antonapoulos all that had happened during the day.

Antonapoulos sat back lazily and looked at Singer. It was seldom that he ever moved his hands to speak at all—and then it was to say that he wanted to eat or to sleep or to drink. These three things he always said with the same vague, fumbling signs. At night, if he were not too drunk, he would kneel down before his bed and pray awhile. Then his plump hands shaped the words 'Holy Jesus,' or 'God,' or 'Darling Mary.' These were the only words Antonapoulos ever said. Singer never knew just how much his friend understood of all the things he told him. But it did not matter.

They shared the upstairs of a small house near the business section of the town. There were two rooms. On the oil stove in the kitchen Antonapoulos cooked all of their meals. There were straight, plain kitchen chairs for Singer and an overstuffed sofa for Antonapoulos. The bedroom was furnished mainly with a large double bed covered with an eiderdown comfort for the big Greek and a narrow iron cot for Singer.

Dinner always took a long time, because Antonapoulos loved food and he was very slow. After they had eaten, the big Greek would lie back on his sofa and slowly lick over each one of his teeth with his tongue, either from a certain delicacy or because he did not wish to lose the savor of the meal—while Singer washed the dishes.

Sometimes in the evening the mutes would play chess. Singer had always greatly enjoyed this game, and years before he had tried to teach it to Antonapoulos. At first his friend could not be interested in the reasons for moving the various pieces about on the board. Then Singer began to keep a bottle of something good under the table to be taken out after each lesson. The Greek never got on to the erratic movements of the knights and the sweeping mobility of the queens, but he learned to make a few set, opening moves. He preferred the white pieces and would not play if the black men were given him. After the first moves Singer worked out the game by himself while his friend looked on drowsily. If Singer made brilliant attacks on his own men so that in the end the black king was killed, Antonapoulos was always very proud and pleased.

The two mutes had no other friends, and except when they worked they were alone together. Each day was very much like any other day, because they were alone so much that nothing ever disturbed them. Once a week they would go to the library for Singer to withdraw a mystery book and on Friday night they attended a movie. Then on payday they always went to the ten-cent photograph shop above the Army and Navy Store so that Antonapoulos could have his picture taken. These were the only places where they made customary visits. There were many parts in the town that they had never even seen.

The town was in the middle of the deep South. The summers were long and the months of winter cold were very few. Nearly always the sky was a glassy, brilliant azure and the sun burned down riotously bright. Then the light, chill rains of November would come, and perhaps later there would be frost and some short months of cold. The winters were changeable, but the summers always were burning hot. The town was a fairly large one. On the main street there were several blocks of two- and three-story shops and business offices. But the largest buildings in the town were the factories, which employed a large percentage of the population. These cotton mills were big and flourishing and most of the workers in the town were very poor. Often in the faces along the streets there was the desperate look of hunger and of loneliness.

But the two mutes were not lonely at all. At home they were content to eat and drink, and Singer would talk with his hands eagerly to his friend about all that was in his mind. So the years passed in this quiet way until Singer reached the age of thirty-two and had been in the town with Antonapoulos for ten years.

Then one day the Greek became ill. He sat up in bed with his hands on his fat stomach and big, oily tears rolled down his cheeks. Singer went to see his friend's cousin who owned the fruit store, and also he arranged for leave from his own work. The doctor made out a diet for Antonapoulos and said that he could drink no more wine. Singer rigidly enforced the doctor's orders. All day he sat by his friend's bed and did what he could to make the time pass quickly, but Antonapoulos only looked at him angrily from the corners of his eyes and would not be amused.

The Greek was very fretful, and kept finding fault with the fruit drinks and food that Singer prepared for him. Constantly he made his friend help him out of bed so that he could pray. His huge buttocks would sag down over his plump little feet when he kneeled. He fumbled with his hands to say 'Darling Mary' and then held to the small brass cross tied to his neck with a dirty string. His big eyes would wall up to the ceiling with a look of fear in them, and afterward he was very sulky and would not let his friend speak to him.

Singer was patient and did all that he could. He drew little pictures, and once he made a sketch of his friend to amuse him. This picture hurt the big Greek's feelings, and he refused to be reconciled until Singer had made his face very young and handsome and colored his hair bright yellow and his eyes china blue. And then he tried not to show his pleasure.

Singer nursed his friend so carefully that after a week Antonapoulos was able to return to his work. But from that time on there was a difference in their way of life. Trouble came to the two friends.

Antonapoulos was not ill any more, but a change had come in him. He was irritable and no longer content to spend the evenings quietly in their home. When he would wish to go out Singer followed along close behind him. Antonapoulos would go into a restaurant, and while they sat at the table he slyly put lumps of sugar, or a peppershaker, or pieces of silverware in his pocket. Singer always paid for what he took and there was no disturbance. At home he scolded Antonapoulos, but the big Greek only looked at him with a bland smile.

The months went on and these habits of Antonapoulos grew worse. One day at noon he walked calmly out of the fruit store of his cousin and urinated in public against the wall of the First National Bank Building across the street. At times he would meet people on the sidewalk whose faces did not please him, and he would bump into these persons and push at them with his elbows and stomach. He walked into a store one day and hauled out a floor lamp without paying for it, and another time he tried to take an electric train he had seen in a showcase.

For Singer this was a time of great distress. He was continually marching Antonapoulos down to the courthouse during lunch hour to settle these infringements of the law. Singer became very familiar with the procedure of the courts and he was in a constant state of agitation. The money he had saved in the bank was spent for bail and fines. All of his efforts and money were used to keep his friend out of jail because of such charges as theft, committing public indecencies, and assault and battery.

The Greek cousin for whom Antonapoulos worked did not enter into these troubles at all. Charles Parker (for that was the name this cousin had taken) let Antonapoulos stay on at the store, but he watched him always with his pale, tight face and he made no effort to help him. Singer had a strange feeling about Charles Parker. He began to dislike him.

Singer lived in continual turmoil and worry. But Antonapoulos was always bland, and no matter what happened the gentle, flaccid smile was still on his face. In all the years before it had seemed to Singer that there was something very subtle and wise in this smile of his friend. He had never known just how much Antonapoulos understood and what he was thinking. Now in the big Greek's expression Singer thought that he could detect something sly and joking. He would shake his friend by the shoulders until he was very tired and explain things over and over with his hands. But nothing did any good.

All of Singer's money was gone and he had to borrow from the jeweler for whom he worked. On one occasion he was unable to pay bail for his friend and Antonapoulos spent the night in jail. When Singer came to get him out the next day he was very sulky. He did not want to leave. He had enjoyed his dinner of sowbelly and cornbread with syrup poured over it. And the new sleeping arrangements and his cellmates pleased him.

They had lived so much alone that Singer had no one to help him in his distress. Antonapoulos let nothing disturb him or cure him of his habits. At home he sometimes cooked the new dish he had eaten in the jail, and on the streets there was never any knowing just what he would do.

And then the final trouble came to Singer.

One afternoon he had come to meet Antonapoulos at the fruit store when Charles Parker handed him a letter. The letter explained that Charles Parker had made arrangements for his cousin to be taken to the state insane asylum two hundred miles away. Charles Parker had used his influence in the town and the details were already settled. Antonapoulos was to leave and to be admitted into the asylum the next week.

Singer read the letter several times, and for a while he could not think. Charles Parker was talking to him across the counter, but he did not even try to read his lips and understand. At last Singer wrote on the little pad he always carried in his pocket:

You cannot do this. Antonapoulos must stay with me.

Charles Parker shook his head excitedly. He did not know much American. 'None of your business,' he kept saying over and over.

Singer knew that everything was finished. The Greek was afraid that some day he might be responsible for his cousin. Charles Parker did not know much about the American language —but he understood the American dollar very well, and he had used his money and influence to admit his cousin to the asylum without delay.

There was nothing Singer could do.

The next week was full of feverish activity. He talked and talked. And although his hands never paused to rest he could not tell all that he had to say. He wanted to talk to Antonapoulos of all the thoughts that had ever been in his mind and heart, but there was not time. His gray eyes glittered and his quick, intelligent face expressed great strain. Antonapoulos watched him drowsily, and his friend did not know just what he really understood.

Then came the day when Antonapoulos must leave. Singer brought out his own suitcase and very carefully packed the best of their joint possessions. Antonapoulos made himself a lunch to eat during the journey. In the late afternoon they walked arm in arm down the street for the last time together. It was a chilly afternoon in late November, and little huffs of breath showed in the air before them.

Charles Parker was to travel with his cousin, but he stood apart from them at the station. Antonapoulos crowded into the bus and settled himself with elaborate preparations on one of the front seats. Singer watched him from the window and his hands began desperately to talk for the last time with his friend. But Antonapoulos was so busy checking over the various items in his lunch box that for a while he paid no attention. Just before the bus pulled away from the curb he turned to Singer and his smile was very bland and remote—as though already they were many miles apart.

The weeks that followed did not seem real at all. All day Singer worked over his bench in the back of the jewelry store, and then at night he returned to the house alone. More than anything he wanted to sleep. As soon as he came home from work he would lie on his cot and try to doze awhile. Dreams came to him when he lay there half-asleep. And in all of them Antonapoulos was there. His hands would jerk nervously, for in his dreams he was talking to his friend and Antonapoulos was watching him.

Singer tried to think of the time before he had ever known his friend. He tried to recount to himself certain things that had happened when he was young. But none of these things he tried to remember seemed real.

There was one particular fact that he remembered, but it was not at all important to him. Singer recalled that, although he had been deaf since he was an infant, he had not always been a real mute. He was left an orphan very young and placed in an institution for the deaf. He had learned to talk with his hands and to read. Before he was nine years old he could talk with one hand in the American way—and also could employ both of his hands after the method of Europeans. He had learned to follow the movements of people's lips and to understand what they said. Then finally he had been taught to speak.

At the school he was thought very intelligent. He learned the lessons before the rest of the pupils. But he could never become used to speaking with his lips. It was not natural to him, and his tongue felt like a whale in his mouth. From the blank expression on people's faces to whom he talked in this way he felt that his voice must be like the sound of some animal or that there was something disgusting in his speech. It was painful for him to try to talk with his mouth, but his hands were always ready to shape the words he wished to say. When he was twenty-two he had come South to this town from Chicago and he met Antonapoulos immediately. Since that time he had never spoken with his mouth again, because with his friend there was no need for this.

Nothing seemed real except the ten years with Antonapoulos. In his half-dreams he saw his friend very vividly, and when he awakened a great aching loneliness would be in him. Occasionally he would pack up a box for Antonapoulos, but he never received any reply. And so the months passed in this empty, dreaming way.

In the spring a change came over Singer. He could not sleep and his body was very restless. At evening he would walk monotonously around the room, unable to work off a new feeling of energy. If he rested at all it was only during a few hours before dawn—then he would drop bluntly into a sleep that lasted until the morning light struck suddenly beneath his opening eyelids like a scimitar.

He began spending his evenings walking around the town. He could no longer stand the rooms where Antonapoulos had lived, and he rented a place in a shambling boarding-house not far from the center of the town.

He ate his meals at a restaurant only two blocks away. This restaurant was at the very end of the long main street, and the name of the place was the New York Café. The first day he glanced over the menu quickly and wrote a short note and handed it to the proprietor.

> Each morning for breakfast I want an egg, toast, and coffee $0.15
> For lunch I want soup (any kind), a meat sandwich, and milk— $0.25
> Please bring me at dinner three vegetables (any kind but cabbage), fish or meat, and a glass of beer— $0.35
> Thank you.

The proprietor read the note and gave him an alert, tactful glance. He was a hard man of middle height, with a beard so dark and heavy that the lower part of his face looked as though it were molded of iron. He usually stood in the corner by the cash register, his arms folded over his chest, quietly observing all that went on around him. Singer came to know this man's face very well, for he ate at one of his tables three times a day.

Each evening the mute walked alone for hours in the street. Sometimes the nights were cold with the sharp, wet winds of March and it would be raining heavily. But to him this did not matter. His gait was agitated and he always kept his hands stuffed tight into the pockets of his trousers. Then as the weeks passed the days grew warm and languorous. His agitation gave way gradually to exhaustion and there was a look about him of deep calm. In his face there came to be a brooding peace that is seen most often in the faces of the very sorrowful or the very wise. But still he wandered through the streets of the town, always silent and alone. . . .

The town had not known a winter as cold as this one for years. Frost formed on the windowpanes and whitened the roofs of houses. The winter afternoons glowed with a hazy lemon light and shadows were a delicate blue. A thin coat of ice crusted the puddles in the streets, and it was said on the day after Christmas that only ten miles to the north there was a light fall of snow.

A change came over Singer. Often he went out for the long walks that had occupied him during the months when Antonapoulos was first gone. These walks extended for miles in every direction and covered the whole of the town. He rambled through the dense neighborhoods along the river that were more squalid than ever since the mills had been slack this winter. In many eyes there was a look of somber loneliness. Now that people were forced to be idle, a certain restlessness could be felt. There was a fervid outbreak of new beliefs. A young man who had worked at the dye vats in a mill claimed suddenly that a great holy power had come in him. He said it was his duty to deliver a new set of commandments from the Lord. The young man set up a tabernacle and hundreds of people came each night to roll on the ground and shake each other, for they believed that they were in the presence of something more than human. There was murder, too. A woman who could not make enough to eat believed that a foreman had cheated on her work tokens and she stabbed him in the throat. A family of Negroes moved into the end house on one of the most dismal streets, and this caused so much indignation that the house was burned and the black man beaten by his neighbors. But these were incidents. Nothing had really changed. The strike that was talked about never came off because they could not get together. All was the same as before. Even on the coldest nights the Sunny Dixie Show was open. The people dreamed and fought and slept as much as ever. And by habit they shortened their thoughts so that they would not wander out into the darkness beyond tomorrow.

Singer walked through the scattered odorous parts of town where the Negroes crowded together. There was more gaiety and violence here. Often the fine, sharp smell of gin lingered in the alleys. Warm, sleepy firelight colored the windows. Meetings were held in the churches almost every night. Comfortable little houses set off in plots of brown grass—Singer walked in these parts also. Here the children were huskier and more friendly to strangers. He roamed through the neighborhoods of the rich. There were houses, very grand and old, with white columns and intricate fences of wrought iron. He walked past the big brick houses where automobiles honked in the driveways and where the plumes of smoke rolled lavishly from chimneys. And out to the very edges of the roads that led from the town to general stores where farmers came on Saturday nights and sat around the stove. He wandered often about the four main business blocks that were brightly lighted and then through the black, deserted alleys behind. There was no part of the town that Singer did not know. He watched the yellow squares of light reflect from a thousand windows. The winter nights were beautiful. The sky was a cold azure and the stars were very bright.

Often it happened now that he would be spoken to and

stopped during these walks. All kinds of people became acquainted with him. If the person who spoke to him was a stranger, Singer presented his card so that his silence would be understood. He came to be known through all the town. He walked with his shoulders very straight and kept his hands always stuffed down into his pockets. His gray eyes seemed to take in everything around him, and in his face there was still the look of peace that is seen most often in those who are very wise or very sorrowful. He was always glad to stop with anyone wishing his company. For after all he was only walking and going nowhere.

Now it came about that various rumors started in the town concerning the mute. In the years before with Antonapoulos they had walked back and forth to work, but except for this they were always alone together in their rooms. No one had bothered about them then—and if they were observed it was the big Greek on whom attention was focused. The Singer of those years was forgotten.

So the rumors about the mute were rich and varied. The Jews said that he was a Jew. The merchants along the main street claimed he received a large legacy and was a very rich man. It was whispered in one browbeaten textile union that the mute was an organizer for the C.I.O. A lone Turk who had roamed into the town years ago and who languished with his family behind the little store where they sold linens claimed passionately to his wife that the mute was Turkish. He said that when he spoke his language the mute understood. And as he claimed this his voice grew warm and he forgot to squabble with his children and he was full of plans and activity. One old man from the country said that the mute had come from somewhere near his home and that the mute's father had the finest tobacco crop in all the country. All these things were said about him.

Antonapoulos! Within Singer there was always the memory of his friend. At night when he closed his eyes the Greek's face was there in the darkness—round and oily, with a wise and gentle smile. In his dreams they were always together.

It was more than a year now since his friend had gone away. This year seemed neither long nor short. Rather it was removed from the ordinary sense of time—as when one is drunk or half-asleep. Behind each hour there was always his friend. And this buried life with Antonapoulos changed and developed as did the happenings around him. During the first few months he had thought most of the terrible weeks before Antonapoulos was taken away—of the trouble that followed his illness, of the summons for arrest, and the misery in trying to control the whims of his friend.

He thought of times in the past when he and Antonapoulos had been unhappy. There was one recollection, far in the past, that came back to him several times.

They never had no friends. Sometimes they would meet other mutes—there were three of them with whom they became acquainted during the ten years. But something always happened. One moved to another state the week after they met him. Another was married and had six children and did not talk with his hands. But it was their relation with the third of these acquaintances that Singer remembered when his friend was gone.

The mute's name was Carl. He was a sallow young man who worked in one of the mills. His eyes were pale yellow and his teeth so brittle and transparent that they seemed pale and yellow also. In his blue overalls that hung limp over his skinny little body he was like a blue-and-yellow rag doll.

They invited him to dinner and arranged to meet him beforehand at the store where Antonapoulos worked. The Greek was still busy when they arrived. He was finishing a batch of caramel fudge in the cooking room at the back of the store. The fudge lay golden and glossy over the long marble-topped table. The air was warm and rich with sweet smells. Antonapoulos seemed pleased to have Carl watch him as he glided the knife down the warm candy and cut it into squares. He offered their new friend a corner of the fudge on the edge of his greased knife, and showed him the trick that he always performed for anyone when he wished to be liked. He pointed to a vat of syrup boiling on the stove and fanned his face and squinted his eyes to show how hot it was. Then he wet his hand in a pot of cold water, plunged it into the boiling syrup, and swiftly put it back into the water again. His eyes bulged and he rolled out his tongue as though he were in great agony. He even wrung his hand and hopped on one foot so that the building shook. Then he smiled suddenly and held out his hand to show that it was a joke and hit Carl on the shoulder.

It was a pale winter evening, and their breath clouded in the cold air as they walked with their arms interlocked down the street. Singer was in the middle and he left them on the sidewalk twice while he went into stores to shop. Carl and Antonapoulos carried the sacks of groceries, and Singer held to their arms tightly and smiled all the way home. Their rooms were cozy and he moved happily about, making conversation with Carl. After the meal the two of them talked while Antonapoulos watched with a slow smile. Often the big Greek would lumber to the closet and pour out drinks of gin. Carl sat by the window, only drinking when Antonapoulos pushed the glass into his face, and then taking solemn little sips. Singer could not ever remember his friend so cordial to a stranger before, and he thought ahead with pleasure to the time when Carl would visit them often.

Midnight had passed when the thing happened that ruined the festive party. Antonapoulos returned from one of his trips to the closet and his face had a glowering look. He sat on his bed and began to stare repeatedly at their new friend with expressions of offense and great disgust. Singer tried to make eager conversation to hide this strange behavior, but the Greek was persistent. Carl huddled in a chair, nursing his bony knees, fascinated and bewildered by the grimaces of the big Greek. His face was flushed and he swallowed timidly. Singer could ignore the situation no longer, so at last he asked Antonapoulos if his stomach pained him or if he perhaps felt bad and wished to go to sleep. Antonapoulos shook his head. He pointed to Carl and began to make all the gestures of obscenity which he knew. The disgust on his face was terrible to see. Carl was small with fear. At last the big Greek ground his teeth and rose from his chair. Hurriedly Carl picked up his cap and left the room. Singer followed him down the stairs. He did not know how to explain his friend to this stranger. Carl stood hunched in the doorway downstairs, limp, with his peaked cap pulled down over his face. At last they shook hands and Carl went away.

Antonapoulos let him know that while they were not noticing, their guest had gone into closet and drunk up all the gin. No amount of persuasion could convince Antonapoulos that it was he himself who had finished the bottle. The big Greek sat up in bed and his round face was dismal and reproachful. Large tears trickled slowly down to the neck of his undershirt and he could not be comforted. At last he went to sleep, but Singer was awake in the dark a long time. They never saw Carl again.

Then years later there was the time Antonapoulos took the rent money from the vase on the mantelpiece and spent it all on the slot machines. And the summer afternoon Antonapoulos went downstairs naked to get the paper. He suffered so from the summer heat. They bought an electric refrigerator on the installment plan, and Antonapoulos would suck the cubes of ice constantly and even let a few of them melt in the bed with him as he slept. And the time Antonapoulos got drunk and threw a bowl of macaroni in his face.

Those ugly memories wove through his thoughts during the first months like bad threads through a carpet. And then they were gone. All the times that they had been unhappy were forgotten. For as the year went on his thoughts of his friend spiraled deeper until he dwelt only with the Antonapoulos whom he alone could know.

This was the friend to whom he told all that was in his heart. This was the Antonapoulos who no one knew was wise but him. As the year passed his friend seemed to grow larger in his mind, and his face looked out in a very grave and subtle way from the darkness at night. The memories of his friend changed in his mind so that he remembered nothing that was wrong or foolish—only the wise and good.

He saw Antonapoulos sitting in a large chair before him. He sat tranquil and unmoving. His round face was inscrutable. His mouth was wise and smiling. And his eyes were profound. He watched the things that were said to him. And in his wisdom he understood.

This was the Antonapoulos who now was always in his thoughts. This was the friend to whom he wanted to tell things that had come about. For something had happened in this year. He had been left in an alien land. Alone. He had opened his eyes and around him there was much he could not understand. He was bewildered.

He watched the words shape on their lips.

We Negroes want a chance to be free at last. And freedom is only the right to contribute. We want to serve and to share, to labor and in turn consume that which is due to us. But you are the only white man I have ever encountered who realizes this terrible need of my people.

You see, Mister Singer? I got this music in me all the time. I got to be a real musician. Maybe I don't know anything now, but I will when I'm twenty. See, Mister Singer? And then I mean to travel in a foreign country where there's snow.

Let's finish up the bottle. I want a small one. For we were thinking of freedom. That's the word like a worm in my brain. Yes? No? How much? How little? The word is a signal for piracy and theft and cunning. We'll be free and the smartest will then be able to enslave the others. But! But there is another meaning to the word. Of all words this one is the most dangerous. We who know must be wary. The word makes us feel good—in fact the word is a great ideal. But it's with this ideal that the spiders spin their ugliest webs for us.

The last one rubbed his nose. He did not come often and he did not say much. He asked questions.

The four people had been coming to his rooms now for more than seven months. They never came together—always alone. And invariably he met them at the door with a cordial smile. The want for Antonapoulos was always with him—just as it had been the first months after his friend had gone—and it was better to be with any person than to be too long alone. It was like the time years ago when he had made a pledge to Antonapoulos (and even written it on a paper and tacked it on the wall above his bed)—a pledge that he would give up cigarettes, beer, and meat for one month. The first days had been very bad. He could not rest or be still. He visited Antanopoulos so much at the fruit store that Charles Parker was unpleasant to him. When he had finished all the engraving on hand he would dawdle around the front of the store with the watchmaker and the salesgirl or wander out to some soda fountain to drink a Coca-Cola. In those days being near any stranger was better than thinking alone about the cigarettes and beer and meat that he wanted.

At first he had not understood the four people at all. They talked and they talked—and as the months went on they talked more and more. He became so used to their lips that he understood each word they said. And then after a while he knew what each one of them would say before he began, because the meaning was always the same.

His hands were a torment to him. They would not rest. They twitched in his sleep, and sometimes he awoke to find them shaping the words in his dreams before his face. He did not like to look at his hands or to think about them. They were slender and brown and very strong. In the years before he had always tended them with care. In the winter he used oil to prevent chapping, and he kept the cuticles pushed down and his nails always filed to the shape of his finger-tips. He had loved to wash and tend his hands. But now he only scrubbed them roughly with a brush two times a day and stuffed them back into his pockets.

When he walked up and down the floor of his room he would crack the joints of his fingers and jerk at them until they ached. Or he would strike the palm of one hand with the fist of the other. And then sometimes when he was alone and his thoughts were with his friend his hands would begin to shape the words before he knew about it. Then when he realized he was like a man caught talking aloud to himself. It was almost as though he had done some moral wrong. The shame and the sorrow mixed together and he doubled his hands and put them behind him. But they would not let him rest.

Singer stood in the street before the house where he and Antonapoulos had lived. The late afternoon was smoky and gray. In the west there were streaks of cold yellow and rose. A ragged winter sparrow flew in patterns against the smoky sky and at last came to light on a gable of the house. The street was deserted.

His eyes were fixed on a window on the right side of the

second story. This was their front room, and behind was the big kitchen where Antonapoulos had cooked all their meals. Through the lighted window he watched a woman move back and forth across the room. She was large and vague against the light and she wore an apron. A man sat with the evening newspaper in his hand. A child with a slice of bread came to the window and pressed his nose against the pane. Singer saw the room just as he had left it—with the large bed for Antonapoulos and the iron cot for himself, the big overstuffed sofa and the camp chair. The broken sugar bowl used for an ash tray, the damp spot on the ceiling where the roof leaked, the laundry box in the corner. On late afternoons like this there would be no light in the kitchen except the glow from the oil-burners of the big stove. Antonapoulos always turned the wicks so that only a ragged fringe of gold and blue could be seen inside each burner. The room was warm and full of the good smells from the supper. Antonapoulos tasted the dishes with his wooden spoon and they drank glasses of red wine. On the linoleum rug before the stove the flames from the burners made luminous reflections—five little golden lanterns. As the milky twilight grew darker these little lanterns were more intense, so that when at last the night had come they burned with vivid purity. Supper was always ready by that time and they would turn on the light and draw their chairs to the table.

Singer looked down at the dark front door. He thought of them going out together in the morning and coming home at night. There was the broken place in the pavement where Antonapoulos had stumbled once and hurt his elbow. There was the mailbox where their bill from the light company came each month. He could feel the warm touch of his friend's arm against his fingers.

The street was dark now. He looked up at the window once more and he saw the strange woman and the man and the child in a group together. The emptiness spread in him. All was gone. Antonapoulos was away; he was not here to remember. The thoughts of his friend were somewhere else. Singer shut his eyes and tried to think of the asylum and the room that Antonapoulos was in tonight. He remembered the narrow white beds and the old men playing slapjack in the corner. He held his eyes shut tight, but that room would not become clear in his mind. The emptiness was very deep inside him, and after a while he glanced up at the window once more and started down the dark sidewalk where they had walked together so many times.

It was Saturday night. The main street was thick with people. Shivering Negroes in overalls loitered before the windows of the ten-cent store. Families stood in line before the ticket box of the movie and young boys and girls stared at the posters on display outside. The traffic from the automobiles was so dangerous that he had to wait a long time before crossing the street.

He passed the fruit store. The fruits were beautiful inside the windows—bananas, oranges, alligator pears, bright little cumquats, and even a few pineapples. But Charles Parker waited on a customer inside. The face of Charles Parker was very ugly to him. Several times when Charles Parker was away he had entered the store and stood around a long while. He had even gone to the kitchen in the back where Antonapoulos made the candies. But he never went into the store while Charles Parker was inside. They had both taken care to avoid each other since that day when Antonapoulos left on the bus. When they met in the street they always turned away without nodding. Once when he had wanted to send his friend a jar of his favorite tupelo honey he had ordered it from Charles Parker by mail so as not to be obliged to meet him.

Singer stood before the window and watched the cousin of his friend wait on a group of customers. Business was always good on Saturday night. Antonapoulos sometimes had to work as late as ten o'clock. The big automatic popcorn popper was near the door. A clerk shoved in a measure of kernels and the corn whirled inside the case like giant flakes of snow. The smell from the store was warm and familiar. Peanut hulls were trampled on the floor.

Singer passed on down the street. He had to weave his way carefully in the crowds to keep from being jostled. The streets were strung with red and green electric lights because of the holidays. People stood in laughing groups with their arms about each other. Young fathers nursed cold and crying babies on their shoulders. A Salvation Army girl in her red-and-blue bonnet tinkled a bell on the corner, and when she looked at Singer he felt obliged to drop a coin into the pot beside her. There were beggars, both Negro and white, who held out caps or crusty hands. The neon advertisements cast an orange glow on the faces of the crowd.

He reached the corner where he and Antonapoulos had once seen a mad dog on an August afternoon. Then he passed the room above the Army and Navy Store where Antonapoulos had had his picture taken every pay-day. He carried many of the photographs in his pocket now. He turned west toward the river. Once they had taken a picnic lunch and crossed the bridge and eaten in a field on the other side.

Singer walked along the main street for about an hour. In all the crowd he seemed the only one alone. At last he took out his watch and turned toward the house where he lived. Perhaps one of the people would come this evening to his room. He hoped so.

He mailed Antonapoulos a large box of presents for Christmas. Also he presented gifts to each of the four people and to Mrs. Kelly. For all of them together he had bought a radio and put it on the table by the window. Doctor Copeland did not notice the radio. Biff Brannon noticed it immediately and raised his eyebrows. Jake Blount kept it turned on all the time he was there, at the same station, and as he talked he seemed to be shouting above the music, for the veins stood out on his forehead. Mick Kelly did not understand when she saw the radio. Her face was very red and she asked him over and over if it was really his and whether she could listen. She worked with a dial for several minutes before she got it to the place that suited her. She sat leaning forward in her chair with her hands on her knees, her mouth open and a pulse beating very fast in her temple. She seemed to listen all over to whatever it was she heard. She sat there the whole afternoon, and when she grinned at him once her eyes were wet and she rubbed them with her fists. She asked him if she could come in and listen sometimes when he was at work and he nodded yes. So for the next few days whenever he opened the door he found her by the radio. Her hand raked through her short rumpled hair and there was a look in her face he had never seen before.

One night soon after Christmas all four of the people chanced to visit him at the same time. This had never happened before. Singer moved about the room with smiles and refreshments and did his best in the way of politeness to make his guests comfortable. But something was wrong.

Doctor Copeland would not sit down. He stood in the doorway, hat in hand, and only bowed coldly to the others. They looked at him as though they wondered why he was there. Jake Blount opened the beers he had brought with him and the foam spilled down on his shirtfront. Mick Kelly listened to the music from the radio. Biff Brannon sat on the bed, his knees crossed, his eyes scanning the group before him and then becoming narrow and fixed.

Singer was bewildered. Always each of them had so much to say. Yet now that they were together they were silent. When they came in he had expected an outburst of some kind. In a vague way he had expected this to be the end of something. But in the room there was only a feeling of strain. His hands worked nervously as though they were pulling things unseen from the air and binding them together.

Jake Blount stood beside Doctor Copeland. 'I know your face. We run into each other once before—on the steps outside.'

Doctor Copeland moved his tongue precisely as though he clipped out his words with scissors. 'I was not aware that we were acquainted,' he said. Then his stiff body seemed to shrink. He stepped back until he was just outside the threshold of the room.

Biff Brannon smoked his cigarette composedly. The smoke lay in thin blue layers across the room. He turned to Mick and when he looked at her a blush reddened his face. He half-closed his eyes and in a moment his face was bloodless once more. 'And how are you getting on with your business now?'

'What business?' Mick asked suspiciously.

'Just the business of living,' he said. 'School—and so forth.'

'O.K., I reckon,' she said.

Each one of them looked at Singer as though in expectation. He was puzzled. He offered refreshments and smiled.

Jake rubbed his lips with the palm of his hand. He left off trying to make conversation with Doctor Copeland and sat down on the bed beside Biff. 'You know who it is that used to write those bloody warnings in red chalk on the fences and walls around the mills?'

'No,' Biff said. 'What bloody warnings?'

'Mostly from the Old Testament. I been wondering about that for a long time.'

Each person addressed his words mainly to the mute. Their thoughts seemed to converge in him as the spokes of a wheel lead to the center hub.

'The cold has been very unusual,' Biff said finally. 'The other day I was looking through some old records and I found that in the year 1919 the thermometer got down to ten degress Fahrenheit. It was only sixteen degrees this morning, and that's the coldest since the big freeze that year.'

'There were icicles hanging off the roof of the coal house this morning,' Mick said.

'We didn't take in enough money last week to meet the payroll,' Jake said.

They discussed the weather some more. Each one seemed to be waiting for the others to go. Then on an impulse they all rose to leave at the same time. Doctor Copeland went first and the others followed him immediately. When they were gone Singer stood alone in the room, and as he did not understand the situation he wanted to forget it. He decided to write to Antonapoulos that night.

The fact that Antonapoulos could not read did not prevent Singer from writing to him. He had always known that his friend was unable to make out the meaning of words on paper, but as the months went by he began to imagine that perhaps he had been mistaken, that perhaps Antonapoulos only kept his knowledge of letters a secret from everyone. Also, it was possible there might be a deaf-mute at the asylum who could read his letters and then explain them to his friend. He thought of several justifications for his letters, for he always felt a great need to write to his friend when he was bewildered or sad. Once written, however, these letters were never mailed. He cut out the comic strips from the morning and evening papers and sent them to his friend each Sunday. And every month he mailed a postal money order. But the long letters he wrote to Antonapoulos accumulated in his pockets until he would destroy them.

When the four people had gone, Singer slipped on his warm gray overcoat and his gray felt hat and left his room. He always wrote his letters at the store. Also, he had promised to deliver a certain piece of work the next morning, and he wanted to finish it now so that there would be no question of delay. The night was sharp and frosty. The moon was full and rimmed with a golden light. The rooftops were black against the starlit sky. As he walked he thought of ways to begin his letter, but he had already reached the store before the first sentence was clear in his mind. He let himself into the dark store with his key and switched on the front lights.

He worked at the very end of the store. A cloth curtain separated his place from the rest of the shop so that it was like a small private room. Besides his workbench and chair there was a heavy safe in the corner, a lavatory with a greenish mirror, and shelves full of boxes and worn-out clocks. Singer rolled up the top of his bench and removed from its felt case the silver platter he had promised to have ready. Although the store was cold he took off his coat and turned up the blue-striped cuffs of his shirt so that they would not get in his way.

For a long time he worked at the monogram in the center of the platter. With delicate, concentrated strokes he guided the scriver on the silver. As he worked his eyes held a curiously penetrating look of hunger. He was thinking of his letter to his friend Antonapoulos. Midnight had passed before the work was finished. When he put the platter away his forehead was damp with excitement. He cleared his bench and began to write. He loved to shape words with a pen on paper and he formed the letters with as much care as if the paper had been a plate of silver.

My Only Friend:
    I see from our magazine that the Society meets this year at a convention in Macon. They will have speakers and a four-course banquet. I imagine it. Remember we always planned to attend one of the conventions but we never did. I wish now that we had. I wish we were going to this one and I have imagined how it would be.

But of course I could never go without you. They will come from many states and they will all be full of words and long dreams from the heart. There is also to be a special service at one of the churches and some kind of a contest with a gold medal for the prize. I write that I imagine all this. I both do and do not. My hands have been still so long that it is difficult to remember how it is. And when I imagine the convention I think of all the guests being like you, my Friend.

I stood before our home the other day. Other people live in it now. Do you remember the big oak tree in front? The branches were cut back so as not to interfere with the telephone wires and the tree died. The limbs are rotten and there is a hollow place in the trunk. Also, the cat here at the store (the one you used to stroke and fondle) ate something poisonous and died. It was very sad.

Singer held the pen poised above the paper. He sat for a long while, erect and tense, without continuing the letter. Then he stood up and lighted himself a cigarette. The room was cold and the air had a sour stale odor—the mixed smells of kerosene and silver polish and tobacco. He put on his overcoat and muffler and began writing again with slow determination.

You remember the four people I told you about when I was there. I drew their pictures for you, the black man, the young girl, the one with the mustache, and the man who owns the New York Café. There are some things I should like to tell you about them but how to put them in words I am not sure.

They are all very busy people. In fact they are so busy that it will be hard for you to picture them. I do not mean that they work at their jobs all day and night but that they have much business in their minds always that does not let them rest. They come up to my room and talk to me until I do not understand how a person can open and shut his or her mouth so much without being weary. (However, the New York Café owner is different—he is not just like the others. He has a very black beard so that he has to shave twice daily, and he owns one of these electric razors. He watches. The others all have something they hate. And they all have something they love more than eating or sleeping or wine or friendly company. That is why they are always so busy.)

The one with the mustache I think is crazy. Sometimes he speaks his words very clear like my teacher long ago at the school. Other times he speaks such a language that I cannot follow. Sometimes he is dressed in a plain suit, and the next time he will be black with dirt and smelling bad and in the overalls he wears to work. He will shake his fist and say ugly drunken words that I would not wish you to know about. He thinks he and I have a secret together but I do not know what it is. And let me write you something hard to believe. He can drink three pints of Happy Days whiskey and still talk and walk on his feet and not wish for the bed. You will not believe this but it is true.

I rent my room from the girl's mother for $16 per month. The girl used to dress in short trousers like a boy but now she wears a blue skirt and a blouse. She is not yet a young lady. I like her to come and see me. She comes all the time now that I have a radio for them. She likes music. I wish I knew what it is she hears. She knows I am deaf but she thinks I know about music.

The black man is sick with consumption but there is not a good hospital for him to go to here because he is black. He is a doctor and he works more than anyone I have ever seen. He does not talk like a black man at all. Other Negroes I find it hard to understand because their tongues do not move enough for the words. This black man frightens me sometimes. His eyes are hot and bright. He asked me to a party and I went. He has many books. However, he does not own any mystery books. He does not drink or eat meat or attend the movies.

Yah Freedom and pirates. Yah Capital and Democrats, says the ugly one with the mustache. Then he contradicts himself and says, Freedom is the greatest of all ideals. I just got to get a chance to write this music in me and be a musician. I got to have a chance, says the girl. We are not allowed to serve, says the black Doctor. That is the Godlike need of my people. Aha, says the owner of the New York Café. He is a thoughtful one.

That is the way they talk when they come to my room. Those words in their heart do not let them rest, so they are always very busy. Then you would think when they are together they would be like those of the Society who meet at the convention in Macon this week. But that is not so. They all came to my room at the same time today. They sat like they were from different cities. They were even rude, and you know how I have always said that to be rude and not attend to the feelings of others is wrong. So it was like that. I do not understand, so I write it to you because I think you will understand. I have queer feelings. But I have written of this matter enough and I know you are weary of it. I am also.

It has been five months and twenty-one days now. All of that time I have been alone without you. The only thing I can imagine is when I will be with you again. If I cannot come to you soon I do not know what.

Singer put his head down on the bench and rested. The smell and the feel of the slick wood against his cheek reminded him of his schooldays. His eyes closed and he felt sick. There was only the face of Antonapoulos in his mind, and his longing for his friend was so sharp that he held his breath. After some time Singer sat up and reached for his pen.

The gift I ordered for you did not come in time for the Christmas box. I expect it shortly. I believe you will like it and be amused. I think of us always and remember everything. I long for the food you used to make. At the New York Café it is much worse than it used to be. I found a cooked fly in my soup not long ago. It was mixed with the vegetables and the noodles like letters. But that is nothing. The way I need you is a loneliness I cannot bear. Soon I will come again. My vacation is not due for six months more but I think I can arrange it before then. I think I will have to. I am not meant to be alone and without you who understand.

          Always,
          JOHN SINGER

It was two o'clock in the morning before he was home again. The big, crowded house was in darkness, but he felt his way carefully up three flights of stairs and did not stumble. He took from his pockets the cards he carried about with him, his watch, and his fountain pen. Then he folded his clothes neatly over the back of his chair. His gray-flannel pajamas were warm and soft. Almost as soon as he pulled the blankets to his chin he was asleep.

Out of the blackness of sleep a dream formed. There were dull yellow lanterns lighting up a dark flight of stone steps. Antonapoulos knelt at the top of these steps. He was naked and he fumbled with something that he held above his head and gazed at it as though in prayer. He himself knelt halfway down the steps. He was naked and cold and he could not take his eyes from Antonapoulos and the thing he held above him. Behind him on the ground he felt the one with the mustache and the girl and the black man and the last one. They knelt naked and he felt their eyes on him. And behind them there were uncounted crowds of kneeling people in the darkness. His own hands were huge windmills and he stared fascinated at the unknown thing that Antonapoulos held. The yellow lanterns swayed to and fro in the darkness and all else was motionless. Then suddenly there was a ferment. In the upheaval the steps collapsed and he felt himself falling downward. He awoke with a jerk. The early light whitened the window. He felt afraid.

Such a long time had passed that something might have happened to his friend. Because Antonapoulos did not write to him he would not know. Perhaps his friend had fallen and hurt himself. He felt such an urge to be with him once more that he would arrange it at any cost—and immediately.

In the post-office that morning he found a notice in his box that a package had come for him. It was the gift he had ordered for Christmas that did not arrive in time. The gift was a very fine one. He had bought it on the installment plan to be paid for over a period of two years. The gift was a moving-picture machine for private use, with a half-dozen of the Mickey Mouse and Popeye comedies that Antonapoulos enjoyed.

Singer was the last to reach the store that morning. He handed the jeweler for whom he worked a formal written request for leave on Friday and Saturday. And although there were four weddings on hand that week, the jeweler nodded that he could go.

He did not let anyone know of the trip beforehand, but on leaving he tacked a note to his door saying that he would be absent for several days because of business. He traveled at night, and the train reached the place of his destination just as the red winter dawn was breaking.

In the afternoon, a little before time for the visiting hour, he went out to the asylum. His arms were loaded with the parts of the moving-picture machine and the basket of fruit he carried his friend. He went immediately to the ward where he had visited Antonapoulos before.

The corridor, the door, the rows of beds were just as he remembered them. He stood at the threshold and looked eagerly for his friend. But he saw at once that though all the chairs were occupied. Antonapoulos was not there.

Singer put down his packages and wrote at the bottom of one of his cards, 'Where is Spiros Antonapoulos?' A nurse came into the room and he handed her the card. She did not understand. She shook her head and raised her shoulders. He went out into the corridor and handed the card to everyone he met. Nobody knew. There was such a panic in him that he began motioning with his hands. At last he met an interne in a white coat. He plucked at the interne's elbow and gave him the card. The interne read it carefully and then guided him through several halls. They came to a small room where a young woman sat at a desk before some papers. She read the card and then looked through some files in a drawer.

Tears of nervousness and fear swam in Singer's eyes. The young woman began deliberately to write on a pad of paper, and he could not restrain himself from twisting around to see immediately what was being written about his friend.

> *Mr. Antonapoulos has been transferred to the infirmary. He is ill with nephritis. I will have someone show you the way.*

On the way through the corridors he stopped to pick up the packages he had left at the door of the ward. The basket of fruit had been stolen, but the other boxes were intact. He followed the interne out of the building and across a plot of grass to the infirmary.

Antonapoulos! When they reached the proper ward he saw him at the first glance. His bed was placed in the middle of the room and he was sitting propped with pillows. He wore a scarlet dressing-gown and green silk pajamas and a turquoise ring. His skin was a pale yellow color, his eyes very dreamy and dark. His black hair was touched at the temples with silver. He was knitting. His fat fingers worked with the long ivory needles very slowly. At first he did not see his friend. Then when Singer stood before him he smiled serenely, without surprise, and held out his jeweled hand.

A feeling of shyness and restraint such as he had never known before came over Singer. He sat down by the bed and folded his hands on the edge of the counterpane. His eyes did not leave the face of his friend and he was deathly pale. The splendor of his friend's raiment startled him. On various occasions he had sent him each article of the outfit, but he had not imagined how they would look when all combined. Antonapoulos was more enormous than he had remembered. The great pulpy folds of his abdomen showed beneath his silk pajamas. His head was immense against the white pillow. The placid composure of his face was so profound that he seemed hardly to be aware that Singer was with him.

Singer raised his hands timidly and began to speak. His strong, skilled fingers shaped the signs with loving precision. He spoke of the cold and of the long months alone. He mentioned old memories, the cat that had died, the store, the place where he lived. At each pause Antonapoulos nodded graciously. He spoke of the four people and the long visits to his room. The eyes of his friend were moist and dark, and in them he saw the little rectangled pictures of himself that he had watched a thousand times. The warm blood flowed back to his face and his hands quickened. He spoke at length of the black man and the one with the jerking mustache and the girl. The designs of his hands shaped faster and faster. Antonapoulos nodded with slow gravity. Eagerly Singer leaned closer and he breathed with long, deep breaths and in his eyes there were bright tears.

Then suddenly Antonapoulos made a slow circle in the air with his plump forefinger. His finger circled toward Singer and at last he poked his friend in the stomach. The big Greek's smile grew very broad and he stuck out his fat, pink tongue. Singer laughed and his hands shaped the words with wild speed. His shoulders shook with laughter and his head hung backward. Why he laughed he did not know. Antonapoulos rolled his eyes. Singer continued to laugh riotously until his breath was gone and his fingers trembled. He grasped the arm of his friend and tried to steady himself. His laughs came slow and painfully like hiccoughs.

Antonapoulos was the first to compose himself. His fat little feet had untucked the cover at the bottom of the bed. His smile faded and he kicked contemptuously at the blanket. Singer hastened to put things right, but Antonapoulos frowned and held up his finger regally to a nurse who was passing through the ward. When she had straightened the bed to his liking the big Greek inclined his head so deliberately that the gesture seemed one of benediction rather than a simple nod of thanks. Then he turned gravely to his friend again.

As Singer talked he did not realize how the time had passed. Only when a nurse brought Antonapoulos his supper on a tray did he realize that it was late. The lights in the ward were turned on and outside the windows it was almost dark. The other patients had trays of supper before them also. They had put down their work (some of them wove baskets, others did leatherwork or knitted) and they were eating listlessly. Beside Antonapoulos they all seemed very sick and colorless. Most of them needed a haircut and they wore seedy gray nightshirts slit down the back. They stared at the two mutes with wonder.

Antonapoulos lifted the cover from his dish and inspected the food carefully. There was fish and some vegetables. He picked up the fish and held it to the light in the palm of his hand for a thorough examination. Then he ate with relish. During supper he began to point out the various people in the room. He pointed to one man in the corner and made faces of disgust. The man snarled at him. He pointed to a young boy and smiled and nodded and waved his plump hand. Singer was too happy to feel embarrassment. He picked up the packages from the floor and laid them on the bed to distract his friend. Antonapoulos took off the wrappings, but the machine did not interest him at all. He turned back to his supper.

Singer handed the nurse a note explaining about the movie. She called an interne and then they brought in a doctor. As the three of them consulted they looked curiously at Singer. The news reached the patients and they propped up on their elbows excitedly. Only Antonapoulos was not disturbed.

Singer had practiced with the movie beforehand. He set up the screen so that it could be watched by all the patients. Then he worked with the projector and the film. The nurse took out the supper trays and the lights in the ward were turned off. A Mickey Mouse comedy flashed on the screen.

Singer watched his friend. At first Antonapoulos was startled. He heaved himself up for a better view and would have risen from the bed if the nurse had not restrained him. Then he watched with a beaming smile. Singer could see the other patients calling out to each other and laughing. Nurses and orderlies came in from the hall and the whole ward was in commotion. When the Mickey Mouse was finished Singer put on a Popeye film. Then at the conclusion of this film he felt that the entertainment had lasted long enough for the first time. He switched on the light and the ward settled down again. As the interne put the machine under his friend's bed he saw Antonapoulos slyly cut his eyes across the ward to be certain that each person realized that the machine was his.

Singer began to talk with his hands again. He knew that he would soon be asked to leave, but the thoughts he had stored in his mind were too big to be said in a short time. He talked with frantic haste. In the ward there was an old man whose head shook with palsy and who picked feebly at his eyebrows. He envied the old man because he lived with Antonapoulos day after day. Singer would have exchanged places with him joyfully.

His friend fumbled for something in his bosom. It was the little brass cross that he had always worn. The dirty string had been replaced by a red ribbon. Singer thought of the dream and he told that, also, to his friend. In his haste the signs sometimes became blurred and he had to shake his hands and begin all over. Antonapoulos watched him with his dark, drowsy eyes. Sitting motionless in his bright, rich garments he seemed like some wise king from a legend.

The interne in charge of the ward allowed Singer to stay for an hour past the visiting time. Then at last he held out his thin, hairy wrist and showed him his watch. The patients were settled for sleep. Singer's hand faltered. He grasped his friend by the arm and looked intently into his eyes as he used to do each morning when they parted for work. Finally Singer backed himself out of the room. At the doorway his hands signed a broken farewell and then clenched into fists.

During the moonlit January nights Singer continued to walk about the streets of the town each evening when he was not engaged. The rumors about him grew bolder. An old Negro woman told hundreds of people that he knew the ways of spirits come back from the dead. A certain piece-worker claimed that he had worked with the mute at another mill somewhere else in the state—and the tales he told were unique. The rich thought that he was rich and the poor considered him a poor man like themselves. And as there was no way to disprove these rumors they grew marvelous and very real. Each man described the mute as he wished him to be. . . .

The time had come for Singer to go to Antonapoulos again. The journey was a long one. For, although the distance between them was something less than two hundred miles, the train meandered to points far out of the way and stopped for long hours at certain stations during the night. Singer would leave the town in the afternoon and travel all through the night and until the early morning of the next day. As usual, he was ready far in advance. He planned to have a full week with his friend this visit. His clothes had been sent to the cleaner's, his hat blocked, and his bags were in readiness. The gifts he would carry were wrapped in colored tissue paper—and in addition there was a deluxe basket of fruits done up in cellophane and a crate of late-shipped strawberries. On the morning before his departure Singer cleaned his room. In his ice box he found a bit of left-over goose liver and took it out to the alley for the neighborhood cat. On his door he tacked the same sign he had posted there before, stating that he would be absent for several days on business. During all these preparations he moved about leisurely with two vivid spots of color on his cheekbones. His face was very solemn.

Then at last the hour for departure was at hand. He stood on the platform, burdened with his suitcases and gifts, and watched the train roll in on the station tracks. He found himself a seat in the day coach and hoisted his luggage on the rack above his head. The car was crowded, for the most part with mothers and children. The green plush seats had a grimy smell. The windows of the car were dirty and the rice thrown at some recent bridal pair lay scattered on the floor. Singer smiled cordially to his fellow-travelers and leaned back in his seat. He closed his eyes. The lashes made a dark, curved fringe above the hollows of his cheeks. His right hand moved nervously inside his pocket.

For a while his thoughts lingered in the town he was leaving behind him. He saw Mick and Doctor Copeland and Jake Blount and Biff Brannon. The faces crowded in on him out of the darkness so that he felt smothered. He thought of the quarrel between Blount and the Negro. The nature of this quarrel was hopelessly confused in his mind—but each of them had on several occasions broken out into a bitter tirade against the other, the absent one. He had agreed with each of them in turn, though what it was they wanted him to sanction he did not know. And Mick—her face was urgent and she said a good deal that he did not understand in the least. And then Biff Brannon at the New York Café. Brannon with his dark, iron-like jaw and his watchful eyes. And strangers who followed him about the streets and buttonholed him for unexplainable reasons. The Turk at the linen shop who flung his hands up in his face and babbled with his tongue to make words the shape of which Singer had never imagined before. A certain mill foreman and an old black woman. A businessman on the main street and an urchin who solicited soldiers for a whorehouse near the river. Singer wriggled his shoulders uneasily. The train rocked with a smooth, easy motion. His head nodded to rest on his shoulder and for a short while he slept.

When he opened his eyes again the town was far behind him. The town was forgotten. Outside the dirty window there was the brilliant midsummer countryside. The sun slanted in strong, bronze-colored rays over the green fields of the new cotton. There were acres of tobacco, the plants heavy and green like some monstrous jungle weed. The orchards of peaches with the lush fruit weighting down the dwarfed trees. There were miles of pastures and tens of miles of wasted, washed-out land abandoned to the hardier weeds. The train cut through deep green pine forests where the ground was covered with the slick brown needles and the tops of the trees stretched up virgin and tall into the sky. And farther, a long way south of the town, the cypress swamps—with the gnarled roots of the trees writhing down into the brackish waters, where the gray, tattered moss trailed from the branches, where tropical water flowers blossomed in dankness and gloom. Then out again into the open beneath the sun and the indigo-blue sky.

Singer sat solemn and timid, his face turned fully toward the window. The great sweeps of space and the hard, elemental coloring almost blinded him. This kaleidoscopic variety of scene, this abundance of growth and color, seemed somehow connected with his friend. His thoughts were with Antonapoulos. The bliss of their reunion almost stifled him. His nose was pinched and he breathed with quick, short breaths through his slightly open mouth.

Antonapoulos would be glad to see him. He would enjoy the fresh fruits and the presents. By now he would be out of the sick ward and able to go on an excursion to the movies, and afterward to the hotel where they had eaten dinner on the first visit. Singer had written many letters to Antonapoulos, but he had not posted them. He surrendered himself wholly to thoughts of his friend.

The half-year since he had last been with him seemed neither a long nor a short span of time. Behind each waking moment there had always been his friend. And this submerged communion with Antonapoulos had grown and changed as though they were together in the flesh. Sometimes he thought of Antonapoulos with awe and self-abasement, sometimes with pride—always with love unchecked by criticism, freed of will. When he dreamed at night the face of his friend was always before him, massive and gentle. And in his waking thoughts they were eternally united.

The summer evening came slowly. The sun sank down behind a ragged line of trees in the distance and the sky paled. The twilight was languid and soft. There was a white full moon, and low purple clouds lay over the horizon. The earth, the trees, the unpainted rural dwellings darkened slowly. At intervals mild summer lightning quivered in the air. Singer watched all of this intently until at last the night had come, and his own face was reflected in the glass before him.

Children staggered up and down the aisle of the car with dripping paper cups of water. An old man in overalls who had the seat before Singer drank whiskey from time to time from a Coca-Cola bottle. Between swallows he plugged the bottle carefully with a wad of paper. A little girl on the right combed her hair with a sticky red lollipop. Shoeboxes were opened and trays of supper were brought in from the dining-car. Singer did not eat. He leaned back in his seat and kept desultory account of all that went on around him. At last the car settled down. Children lay on the broad plush seats and slept, while men and women doubled up with their pillows and rested as best they could.

Singer did not sleep. He pressed his face close against the glass and strained to see into the night. The darkness was heavy and velvety. Sometimes there was a patch of moonlight or the flicker of a lantern from the window of some house along the way. From the moon he saw that the train had turned from its southward course and was headed toward the east. The eagerness he felt was so keen that his nose was too pinched to breathe through and his cheeks were scarlet. He sat there, his face pressed close against the cold, sooty glass of the window, through most of the long night journey.

The train was more than an hour late, and the fresh, bright summer morning was well under way when they arrived. Singer went immediately to the hotel, a very good hotel where he had made reservations in advance. He unpacked his bags and arranged the presents he would take to Antonapoulos on the bed. From the menu the bellboy brought him he selected a luxurious breakfast— broiled bluefish, hominy, French toast, and hot black coffee. After breakfast he rested before the electric fan in his underwear. At noon he began to dress. He bathed and shaved and laid out fresh linen and his best seersucker suit. At three o'clock the hospital was open for visiting hours. It was Tuesday and the eighteenth of July.

At the asylum he sought Antonapoulos first in the sick ward where he had been confined before. But at the doorway of the room he saw immediately that his friend was not there. Next he found his way through the corridors to the office where he had been taken the time before. He had his question already written on one of the cards he carried about with him. The person behind the desk was not the same as the one who had been there before. He was a young man, almost a boy, with a half-formed, immature face and a lank mop of hair. Singer handed him the card and stood quietly, his arms heaped with packages, his weight resting on his heels.

The young man shook his head. He leaned over the desk and scribbled loosely on a pad of paper. Singer read what he had written and the spots of color drained from his cheekbones instantly. He looked at the note a long time, his eyes cut sideways and his head bowed. For it was written there that Antonapoulos was dead.

On the way back to the hotel he was careful not to crush the fruit he had brought with him. He took the packages up to his room and then wandered down to the lobby. Behind a potted palm tree there was a slot machine. He inserted a nickel but when he tried to pull the lever he found that the machine was jammed. Over this incident he made a great to-do. He cornered the clerk and furiously demonstrated what had happened. His face was deathly pale and he was so beside himself that tears rolled down the ridges of his nose. He flailed his hands and even stamped once with his long, narrow, elegantly shoed foot on the plush carpet. Nor was he satisfied when his coin was refunded, but insisted on checking out immediately. He packed his bag and was obliged to work energetically to make it close again. For in addition to the articles he had brought with him he carried away three towels, two cakes of soap, a pen and a bottle of ink, a roll of toilet paper, and a Holy Bible. He paid his bill and walked to the railway station to put his belongings in custody. The train did not leave until nine in the evening and he had the empty afternoon before him.

This town was smaller than the one in which he lived. The business streets intersected to form the shape of a cross. The stores had a countrified look; there were harnesses and sacks of feed in half of the display windows. Singer walked listlessly along the sidewalks. His throat felt swollen and he wanted to swallow but was unable to do so. To relieve this strangled feeling he bought a drink in one of the drugstores. He idled in the barber shop and purchased a few trifles at the ten-cent store. He looked no one full in the face and his head drooped down to one side like a sick animal's.

The afternoon was almost ended when a strange thing happened to Singer. He had been walking slowly and irregularly along the curb of the street. The sky was overcast and the air humid. Singer did not raise his head, but as he passed the town pool room he caught a sidewise glance of something that disturbed him. He passed the pool room and then stopped in the middle of the street. Listlessly he retraced his steps and stood before the open door of the place. There were three mutes inside and they were talking with their hands together. All three of them were coatless. They wore bowler hats and bright ties. Each of them held a glass of beer in his left hand. There was a certain brotherly resemblance between them.

Singer went inside. For a moment he had trouble taking his hand from his pocket. Then clumsily he formed a word of greeting. He was clapped on the shoulder. A cold drink was ordered. They surrounded him and the fingers of their hands shot out like pistons as they questioned him.

He told his own name and the name of the town where he lived. After that he could think of nothing else to tell about himself. He asked if they knew Spiros Antonapoulos. They did not know him. Singer stood with his hands dangling loose. His head was still inclined to one side and his glance was oblique. He was so listless and cold that the three mutes in the bowler hats looked at him queerly. After a while they left him out of their conversation. And when they had paid for the rounds of beers and were ready to depart they did not suggest that he join them.

Although Singer had been adrift on the streets for half a day he almost missed his train. It was not clear to him how this happened or how he had spent the hours before. He reached the station two minutes before the train pulled out, and barely had time to drag his luggage aboard and find a seat. The car he chose was almost empty. When he was settled he opened the crate of strawberries and picked them over with finicky care. The berries were of a giant size, large as walnuts and in full-blown ripeness. The green leaves at the top of the rich-colored fruit were like tiny bouquets. Singer put a berry in his mouth and though the juice had a lush, wild sweetness there was already a subtle flavor of decay. He ate until his palate was dulled by the taste and then rewrapped the crate and placed it on the rack above him. At midnight he drew the windowshade and lay down on the seat. He was curled in a ball, his coat pulled over his face and head. In this position he lay in a stupor of half-sleep for about twelve hours. The conductor had to shake him when they arrived.

Singer left his luggage in the middle of the station floor. Then he walked to the shop. He greeted the jeweler for whom he worked with a listless turn of his hand. When he went out again there was something heavy in his pocket. For a while he rambled with bent head along the streets. But the unrefracted brilliance of the sun, the humid heat, oppressed him. He returned to his room with swollen eyes and an aching head. After resting he drank a glass of iced coffee and smoked a cigarette. Then when he had washed the ash tray and the glass he brought out a pistol from his pocket and put a bullet in his chest.

III

THE WORLDS OF SMELL AND TASTE

Rousseau called smell the "sense of the imagination." The idea was not original with him; Aristotle long ago recognized the emotional nature of the olfactory and associated senses. Embedded in Aristotle's description is the realization that the development of reason in man is coincident with a decline in the utilization of the senses of smell and taste as ways of understanding the world. Comparison of the human with the animal brain shows the alteration in physiological form; the portion of the brain which controls smell and taste has diminished as the symbolic centers have grown. Thinking has replaced smell and taste as our chief intellectual tool.

Unlike all other animals, humans have lost the ability both to smell and taste danger. Unlike the rat whose tongue may, in some mysterious way, directly inform him of the presence of poison in his food, the human confronted by a new taste is totally dependent upon his reason to differentiate what is safe from what is not.

The role played by the olfactory senses must therefore be discovered not in man's rational life, but in his emotional existence. Smell and taste provide a tangible gateway into his unconscious and thus into his past. Huysmans recognized the evocative powers of these senses and their ability to arouse violent imagery. Proust was keenly aware of the effect of taste as a conjurer of the past. And O. Henry allows his hero to become a victim of the emotions he has stirred up by his sense of smell.

ARISTOTLE/On the Soul*

SMELL AND its object are much less easy to determine than what we have hitherto discussed; the distinguishing characteristic of the object of smell is less obvious than those of sound or colour. The ground of this is that our power of smell is less discriminating and in general inferior to that of many species of animals; men have a poor sense of smell and our apprehension of its proper objects is inseparably bound up with and so confused by pleasure and pain, which shows that in us the organ is inaccurate. It is probable that there is a parallel failure in the perception of colour by animals that have hard eyes: probably they discriminate differences of colour only by the presence or absence of what excites fear, and that it is thus that human beings distinguish smells. It seems that there is an analogy between smell and taste, and that the species of tastes run parallel to those of smells—the only difference being that our sense of taste is more discriminating than our sense of smell, because the former is a modification of touch, which reaches in man the maximum of discriminative accuracy. While in respect of all the other senses we fall below many species of animals, in respect of touch we far excel all other species in exactness of discrimination. That is why man is the most intelligent of all animals. This is confirmed by the fact that it is to differences in the organ of touch and to nothing else that the differences between man and man in respect of natural endowment are due; men whose flesh is hard are ill-endowed by nature, men whose flesh is soft, well-endowed.

As flavours may be divided into (*a*) sweet, (*b*) bitter, so with smells. In some things the flavour and the smell have the same quality, i.e. both are sweet, or both bitter, in others they diverge. Similarly a smell, like a flavour, may be pungent, astringent, acid, or succulent. But, as we said, because smells are much less easy to discriminate than flavours, the names of these varieties are applied to smells only metaphorically; for example 'sweet' is extended from the taste to the smell of saffron or honey, 'pungent' to that of thyme, and so on.[1]

In the same sense in which hearing has for its object both the audible and the inaudible, sight both the visible and the invisible, smell has for its object both the odorous and the inodorous. 'Inodorous' may be either (*a*) what has no smell at all, or (*b*)

---

* Aristotle, *De Anima*, ii.9.421^a–422^a (tr. J. A. Smith).
[1] Because of the felt likeness between the respective smells and the really sweet or pungent tastes of the same herbs, &c.

what has a small or feeble smell. The same ambiguity lurks in the word 'tasteless.'

Smelling, like the operation of the senses previously examined, takes place through a medium, i.e. through air or water—I add water, because water-animals too (both sanguineous and non-sanguineous) seem to smell just as much as land-animals; at any rate some of them make directly for their food from a distance if it has any scent. That is why the following facts constitute a problem for us. All animals smell in the same way, but man smells only when he inhales; if he exhales or holds his breath, he ceases to smell, no difference being made whether the odorous object is distant or near, or even placed inside the nose and actually on the wall of the nostril; it is a disability common to all the senses not to perceive what is in immediate contact with the organ of sense, but our failure to apprehend what is odorous without the help of inhalation is peculiar (the fact is obvious on making the experiment). Now since bloodless animals do not breathe, they must, it might be argued, have some novel sense not reckoned among the usual five. Our reply must be that this is impossible, since it is scent that is perceived; a sense that apprehends what is odorous and what has a good or bad odour cannot be anything but smell. Further, they are observed to be deleteriously affected by the same strong odours as man is, e.g. bitumen, sulphur, and the like. These animals must be able to smell without being able to breathe. The probable explanation is that in man the organ of smell has a certain superiority over that in all other animals just as his eyes have over those of hard-eyed animals. Man's eyes have in the eyelids a kind of shelter or envelope, which must be shifted or drawn back in order that we may see, while hard-eyed animals have nothing of the kind, but at once see whatever presents itself in the transparent medium. Similarly in certain species of animals the organ of smell is like the eye of hard-eyed animals, uncurtained, while in others which take in air it probably has a curtain over it, which is drawn back in inhalation, owing to the dilating of the veins or pores. That explains also why such animals cannot smell under water; to smell they must first inhale, and that they cannot do under water.

Smells come from what is dry as flavours from what is moist. Consequently the organ of smell is potentially dry.

GEORGE G. WAYNE and ARTHUR A. CLINCO/Psychoanalytic Observations on Olfaction

1

IN OUR culture, a certain forbidden quality is associated with the whole idea of smells and smelling. At the same time, we are constantly confronted with olfactory provocation.

This general cultural ambivalence toward smelling is in many ways reminiscent of the behavior of a person with a dirt phobia. He is so preoccupied with avoiding dirt that he is everlastingly searching it out in order to evade it. In effect, he always seeks what he professes to despise the most, and out of this circular pattern he manages to satisfy both his unconscious and his conscious striving.

It may well be that this is precisely what we as a culture are doing with smells. We live in a deodorized and reodorized culture. Whole new industries have come into being by exploiting our conflicts and our confusions concerning smells. While on the one hand, these arbiters of olfaction supply us with devices for eliminating smells of all varieties ranging from mildly unpleasant to disgusting, another segment of this industry concentrates on substituting one odor for another—assuming, apparently, that there is an absolute point of reference to indicate which smells must go and which are acceptable replacements. Still another segment among the merchants of smell devotes itself to producing smells that can be merchandised, ranging from clean and wholesome odors to exotically stimulating and exciting ones.

In truth, smell is omnipresent in our culture. Hardly an hour of radio or television transpires without mention of it, and it pervades the advertising columns of our mass magazines. It would be hard to find a home without deodorants standing by on closet shelves and perfumes on duty on every dressing table. Olfaction, in brief, pervades many aspects of domestic life, religious ritual, social intercourse, and—recently—commercial enterprise.

We have undertaken this exploration of olfaction on the premise that the tyranny of the unconscious denies many people the pregenital satisfaction of olfaction. We note that there are enormous variations in individual response to smells—even to smells which are socially acceptable. These variations run from complete anosmia to hyperosmia, and, in our opinion, they can be accounted for only in part by the fact that in the human being the olfactory apparatus is to some extent atrophied.

Despite this apparent denial of smell, it is our impression that olfactory sensitivity is far greater than is commonly supposed, and that olfactory phenomena figure more importantly in human functioning than is generally recognized. It may be that we analysts, too, have been partially victimized by the social taboo concerning smell, and, as a result of our own olfactory repression, have overlooked clinical evidence that might be significant.

This belief that the entire phenomena of perceiving and responding to smells should be re-examined in a psychoanalytical orientation, provided the point of departure for this paper.

II

The psychoanalytic contributions to the subject of olfaction, to date, have been sparse but significant. For the most part, they relate olfactory manifestations to anal sexuality and coprophilia. Freud[2] for example, has explained that fetishism depends upon a repressed coprophilic smell desire, the smell of the object apparently serving unconsciously as a determinant in the choice of the fetish. Alexander,[1] in a case he studied, connects transvestitism with a gratification of anal eroticism. Wilson[3] in a study of transvestitism published in 1948 elaborates on its connection with olfactory repression, tacitly accepting its anal basis. An earlier paper published in 1941 by the same author,[4] while it does not deal explicitly with the anal basis of olfactory repression, contains, in our opinion, some exceedingly stimulating insights on the subject. Here clinical data is presented to document Wilson's thesis that "the psychological component of the hay fever symptom is a result of unsuccessful olfactory repression."

The patients on whom the Wilson study was based had been reared in a climate of repression of sexual curiosity. Simultaneously they had been encouraged to olfactory indulgence. This led to conflict-laden olfactory perceptiveness and to symptom formation. When the pregenital gratifications of olfaction catalyzed the superego prohibitions, the hay fever symptoms served as an effective block to these forbidden olfactory sensations. The hay fever symptoms, in effect, accomplished intermittently what a total psychological anosmia accomplishes continuously.

His thesis implies that when the olfactory repression is satisfactory, it is possible for the patient to function symptom-free, provided he is not exposed to physical catalysts so potent as to produce hay fever symptoms.

On the basis of our own extensive observations concerning

olfaction, we suggest that it is possible for some people to subject themselves to almost no olfactory repression, and still to attain relatively conflict-free adjustment.

Whether or not an individual retains his pristine olfactory sensitivity without atoning for this gratification in terms of psychopathology depends, of course, on the emotional and psychological climate in which his infantile and adult sexuality unfolds. For such people—those who need not penalize themselves for exercising their sense of smell—that sense can be used as fully as the neural apparatus allows. Its use can be as serviceable and as untrammelled as it was, presumably, for primitive man. It can be used perceptively to prepare the individual for motor responses. And it can be used for sheer sensual gratification.

III

Our object in this paper is to explore the oral basis of olfaction and its various clinical manifestations, as a supplement to the already existing anal thesis.

The sense of smell and the sense of touch are fundamental to survival in sub-human species. Animals depend on these senses to find food, to avoid danger, and to mate and reproduce.

Evolution has resulted in extensive neuro-anatomical modifications, and the olfactory apparatus in man has undergone a great deal of change. Archaic olfactory areas of the brain, which were once large and dominant, have diminished in size and become overlaid with more recently developed cortical structures, the neopallium. Yet there is no reason to believe—nor are there any scientific studies to indicate—that the archipallium is any less significant in human functioning than in the functioning of sub-human species. The difference, it seems to us, is not that man's sense of smell is less acute or less important to him, but that it plays a different role for him—a role shot through with the complexities of psycho-physiologic functioning which is characteristic of the human species.

The human infant uses his sense of smell more instinctually than the adult. It is available for use immediately at birth; it does not need to wait for further neuro-anatomical maturation in order to begin to experience.

The responses to smell—along with the tactile responses—are among the infant's earliest experiences. His earliest gratifications have, among their components, the smell of the mother's breasts and of milk. It is probable that the rooting reflex in the infant—that is, the food-finding reflex—which is stimulated by tactile sensations is also facilitated by smell sensations.

Not only does the infant react to the mother through smell perceptions but some of the earliest reactions of the mother toward the infant are also based on her response to smell. The odor of the infant's excretions and vomitus may, for example, produce reactions of disgust and rejection. Thus, both infantile gratification and infantile frustration, at a very early level, are intimately bound to olfaction, instinctually and experientially.

It seems to us a plausible speculation that olfactory sensory deprivation in early infancy may be quite significant. The experiments which are currently being carried out with respect to general sensory deprivation in adults suggests that unless there is adequate sensory input, psycho-physiologic functioning begins to deteriorate. Quite possibly this may also hold true for infants; and, since olfaction and tactility are the dominant senses in infancy, deprivation in these two areas might be particularly damaging. For example, it may be that bottle feeding deprives the infant of the sort of olfactory and tactile sensations which are ordinarily provided by the mother, and which contribute to optimal infantile adjustment. The deprived infant's attempt at self-cure by playing with its own feces, serves among other things to gratify its olfactory needs. We feel that research in this area might prove fruitful.

On the basis of our clinical experience, we believe that as the individual matures, olfaction is crowded out by the more "intellectual" sense modalities. But the olfactory function, as an experience, persists, as does its link to ancient memories having vast emotional reverberations. Perhaps the intimate neural connection of olfaction with areas in the brain that regulate viscero-motor expressions of various emotions, endows that particular sense with greater affectivity. In any event, this relatively obscure and overlooked sense can exert strong influences in the individual's emotional life. The popular stereotypes of advertising—men falling in love with women because of their alluring perfume, or women succumbing to men because of their virile shaving lotion—are, despite their exaggerations, evocative for all of us. It is not unusual for analysts to hear patients relate how they are won over in their love lives by odors both natural and synthetic.

Anthropologists have suggested that man has sloughed off his olfactory sense in the process of acculturation. What was once a vital instrument for survival—directing and warning primitive man—has now deteriorated to an instrument for irrelevant and obtuse titillation through the double-jointed vocabulary of advertising. The pattern is echoed in individual development; we see the primitive infant more dependent upon olfaction and making more direct use of it than does the acculturated adult. In short, the suppressive and repressive forces of civilization, directed so insistently against instinctual expression, seem to have caught the olfactory sense in its restraining grip. Yet, despite the subtle pressures against olfaction, it does continue as a dominant element in human functioning at all age levels—sometimes in socially acceptable ways, often in hidden and neurotically symptomatic ways.

IV

We should like to discuss several olfactory dreams, culled from many such dreams recorded by the authors in the course of treating approximately 75 patients. This material has been accumulated over a span of years during which we have been concerned with this subject.

Prompted by this specific interest, it has been our practice, in the course of the therapeutic process, to be particularly alert to any allusion or nuance in the patients' verbalizations which suggested an olfactory experience. All such references were followed through by specific questioning which brought to light many olfactory dreams as well as other associations concerning smells that might otherwise have escaped attention.

Of the patients whose olfactory dreams were noted by us, approximately two-third suffered from depressive reactions. The remaining third manifested psychosomatic disorders (hay fever, asthma, gastrointestinal syndromes), hypochondriacal reactions, and schizophrenia in remission from psychosis.

It is particularly significant that these dreams were, for the most part, experienced and related when a depressive affect was clinically felt.

A patient nearing the termination of his analysis reported the following dream fragment:

> I found myself going down a deep circular staircase into a subterranean sewer. I was confronted by a dark, unpleasant odor of sewer gas, and at the bottom there were many large, dead rats. I could smell the foul odor of rotting carcasses.

At the time he reported the dream, the patient was mildly depressed—a reaction which followed his initial sense of elation when he had first been told that he was approaching the end of formal treatment. He felt, "perhaps I ought to be a permanent patient." His depression persisted for several weeks, duplicating the condition for which he had originally sought treatment. But this depression was terminated rather abuptly by the dream, which was described as "horrifying, so that it was a relief to awaken."

From the totality of his verbal production in reacting to

the dream, some associations which seemed particularly meaningful were:

> I felt like I was buried and smothering . . . Everything seemed over for me, and I could smell death . . . I remember my grief when my wife had a miscarriage . . . We were happy when she finally had a healthy infant . . . I recall how amusing I thought it was when he would nurse with such enthusiasm that he would soil his diapers . . . I loved the smell of the baby anyway . . . No odors seemed to discommode him when it was feeding time.

The dream was a deeply regressive experience, as death dreams so frequently are. On the basis of the patient's associations to the dream, evaluated in the perspective of his total history, the latent content of the dream became apparent. It was the patient's way of combating the threat he felt at the prospect of separation from the analyst. In response to that threat, he sought the security and satisfaction of the archaic pregenital pleasures, where olfactory experiences are so important. It is significant, in this respect, that in reacting verbally to the dream the patient dwelt on memories of his son as an infant which were primarily olfactory.

The dream also served in a restitutional way. The patient seemed to equate the analyst, who was "abandoning" him, with his wife, who had miscarried—that is, abandoned or killed—a child. Against both of them he felt a great unconscious anger, reinforced by a pervasive and enduring anger stemming from infantile frustrations suffered at the hands of his mother. The guilt engendered by this anger invited the punishing experience of the dream, nightmarish and horrifying and close enough in meaning to consciousness to fail to safeguard sleep.

The regressive quality and hidden oral satisfaction in the dream were quickly apparent to the patient, with minimal intervention from the analyst. He smiled knowingly as he spoke of infants and nursing and olfactory memories, accepting them as evidences of his own regressive quest for the touch and smell of mother and milk. It seemed plausible that a real regression in his waking life would no longer be necessary.

The following dream was related by a 26-year-old woman who entered treatment because of recurrent depressions and intermittent anosmia which did not have an organic basis. Both symptoms had become worse since a recent marriage.

> I was in church kneeling at the altar, looking at the Virgin holding the Christ Child. An incense burner sent smoke curling around the figure and I could smell a sweet odor that strangely ex-

cited me. Mother Superior was nearby and her scowl made me feel like a dog, and that I ought not to be there. As I walked out, I became aware of body odors coming from the people in the pews and I was glad to get into the fresh air. Yet I seemed to want to go back inside, but I was afraid of the Mother Superior. She might kick me out this time.

The dream practically summarizes the genetic-dynamic story of the patient's life. Her mother was a rejecting, disappointed, compulsively clean, haughty woman whose husband was a passive and weak man. She had resented having even the one child, although, in the course of an interview, she had said very righteously, "But I did my level best and even nursed her for the first six months. Only rarely did I burden my mother with the child."

The patient's depression seemed to have its roots in early oral-olfactory frustrations. One can visualize the infant greedily clinging to the primitive sucking and olfactory pleasures, niggardly offered and always on the verge of being withdrawn. The intermittent anosmia, which had developed during puberty, also had its roots in these early oral frustrations. It served as a defense against trying to get too close—close enough to smell and taste and feel how good the warm milk and flesh can be, for such pleasures are too exciting and are doomed to be thwarted anyway.

The patient's associations were laden with olfactory memories and preoccupations:

> My husband's body odor excites me so much that I become anxious and frightened. His scent makes me salivate and I immediately think of sucking his penis. He pushes me away when I try and I feel dirty and smelly and my sense of smell disappears . . . I always wear panties and perfume when I go to bed, because I'm afraid I really have B.O. and my husband will surely kick me out if he discovers it . . . My mother always tells me how she can smell a menstruating woman, unless she uses a deodorant . . . She always made me feel smelly, like a salivating dog in hot weather.

The immediate origin of the dream seemed to be her husband's most recent disappointment with her sporadic unresponsiveness to coitus. This time he had said half in anger, half in jest: "Why don't you just pack your perfumes and panties and go back to mama!"

The patient's demeanor in analysis—cold and distant, with just occasional tentative frightened attempts at letting down this barrier—reflected her characteristic way of relating.

The church and the figure of the Virgin and Child wreathed

in sweet-scented smoke from the incense burner brought forth pleasant, early recollections of occasions spent with her maternal grandparents. They were Italian immigrants whose early struggles had made it difficult to devote themselves to their children, but belatedly they had lavished affection on their grandchildren. The patient recalled the satisfying odors of cooking in the house, the comfort of being held and rocked in the lap of her stout, bosomy grandmother, and the many family friends who came to visit and fuss over her. "If it weren't for grandmother, I would have rotted a long time ago," she said.

The dream material was worked with during several sessions and both the depression and the anosmia disappeared temporarily. We surmise that the regressive olfactory satisfaction contained in the dream was in itself reassuring. It was further supported by the analyst's warm comments that not all people were like the patient's rejecting, depriving mother, and that she must give them a chance to prove their feelings toward her. She said wryly, "I think I'll take the chance and smell my husband tonight and let him smell me, too, without perfume."

The dream also provided the patient with restitutive punishment for the archaic hostility toward her rejecting mother. This discharge of guilt obviously aided in the resolution of the depressive episode.

The third case we have selected for presentation was a 31-year-old woman who had been hospitalized for four months for a schizo-affective illness, with predominantly depressive affect and an abundance of paranoid reaction. She suffered many olfactory hallucinations during her psychosis. She insisted that sour, foul-smelling gases emanated from her insides and came out through her mouth and her vagina. She complained that she was being given food that was poisoned, and that what she had eaten was making her insides decay. This hallucination was so persistent that while she was hospitalized it was necessary to resort to tube feeding to maintain her nutrition.

After a period of treatment, she experienced a remission from her psychosis, and continued in psychotherapy as an outpatient. During a subsequent period of depression, non-psychotic in nature, she reported the following dream:

> I saw a strange, pale, scrawny, bird-like creature limping jerkily about in a barnyard, like it was lost. One of its legs seemed broken. Its eyes were full of fear and its beak was wide open, as if it were starving. Its feathers were all burned off, and I could actually smell the odor of burning flesh and feathers. It was a nasty sensa-

tion. There were other animals there, maybe cows and pigs, but I wasn't sure.

The patient's relationship to her mother had been a classic schizophrenogenic one, stemming back to intense oral and olfactory deprivation and fears which had their roots in infancy. She feared and hated her mother, yet constantly sought her out. In short, she could live neither with her nor without her.

Recollections of her mother and of childhood experiences figured importantly in her associations to the dream—associations which were remarkably insightful, for she lived close to her unconscious.

She identified herself immediately as that strange, lost, crippled hungry creature in the dream. "I saw a miscarriage once, and it reminded me of that," she said. The smell of burning feathers brought back many olfactory memories, the most revealing being her memories of drinking boiled milk as a child. She spoke of ". . . that nasty skin on top of it, and the unpleasant burned taste. But after my skin allergy cleared up, I drank regular milk again and it was good." It seemed that the deprivations she experienced in infancy recurred in suggestive fragments throughout her childhood and drinking "regular milk" was associated with the restorative comfort of a "cleared-up skin."

The dream was the therapist's clue to reassure the patient that she was not a cripple, nor did she need to retreat to the fetal stage to survive. She responded well, and the depression soon lifted. The dream provided her with a deeply regressive satisfaction, and served as restitutional punishment for a hostile superego. At the same time, the therapist's work gave strength to her faltering ego.

It might be pointed out that while it is possible for olfactory dreams to serve a constructive function for the patient, the same does not seem to be true for olfactory hallucinations such as this patient experienced during her earlier psychotic stage. In that condition, patients do not seem to have enough ego-integrative capacity to benefit from the regressive gratification provided by these olfactory experiences.

V

We find that olfactory manifestations occur more commonly in clinical practice than is generally supposed. To us, the presence of olfactory dreams and olfactory hallucinations bespeaks intense regression and early oral fixation. Needless to say, during subsequent phases of individual psychosexual development, olfactory manifestations assume more complex psychological connections.

But the relationship between these olfactory experiences and early orality seems of paramount significance.

Olfaction begins with the first breath and cry, fusing with the tactile-kinesthetic components to give rise to the snout orientation of the infant, blindly smelling and clinging to the breast. And the experiences of the infant during this early, vulnerable, needful phase key his later orientation toward olfaction. Throughout our investigation, we observed that many of the classic wishes and fears of the orally oriented person were revealed in the olfactory material produced by patients in the process of treatment.

We were particularly interested in the fact that the olfactory dream seemed to occur in conjunction with a depressive affect. The deeply regressive meaning of such a dream provided the analyst with a specific clue to the intense oral need of the patient. At the same time, the dream served as a regressive gratification and a restitutive punishment for the patient. This suggests that if such dreams are properly interpreted by the therapist, they can be utilized to facilitate the dissolution of a depression.

Beyond this specific implication, our findings suggest that there exists a close similarity in libidinal organization among the depressions, hypochondriacal states, certain psychosomatic syndromes (i.e., hay fever, asthma) and schizophrenic reactions. The main differences must be looked for in the organization and functioning of the ego-superego complex, and it is suggested that this might be a fruitful field for further investigation.

References

1. Alexander, F. *Psychoanalysis of the Total Personality*. Baltimore: Nervous & Mental Disease Publishing Co., 1930. (Monograph 52, p. 128.)
2. Freud, S. Three Contributions To The Theory of Sex. *The Basic Writings of Sigmund Freud*. New York: The Modern Library, Random House, 1938.
3. Wilson, G. W. A further Contribution To The Study of Olfactory Repression With Particular Reference To Transvestitism. *Psychoanalytic Quarterly*, Vol. XVII, No. 3, 1948.
4. ———. A Study of Structural and Instinctive Conflicts in Cases of Hay Fever. *Psychosomatic Medicine*, Vol. III, No. 1, 1941.

J. K. HUYSMANS/Against the Grain

IN THE course of that singular malady which plays such havoc with races of exhausted vitality, sudden intervals of calm succeed the crises. Without being able to explain the reason, Des Esseintes awoke quite strong and well one fine morning; no more hacking cough, no more wedges driven with a hammer into the back of the neck, but an ineffable sensation of well-being and a delightful clearness of brain, while his thoughts became cheerful; and instead of being opaque and dull, grew bright and iridescent, like brilliantly colored soap bubbles.

This lasted some days; then in a moment, one afternoon, hallucinations of the sense of smell appeared.

His room was strong of frangipane. He looked to see if perhaps there was a bottle of the perfume lying about anywhere uncorked; but there was no such thing in the place. He visited his working room and then the dining room; the smell was there too.

He rang for his servant. "Don't you smell something?" he asked, but the man, after sniffing the air, declared he noticed nothing. Doubt was impossible; the nervous derangement was come again, taking the form of a fresh delusion of the senses.

Wearied by the persistency of this imaginary aroma, he resolved to plunge himself in a bath of real perfumes, hoping that his nasal homeopathy might cure him or, at any rate, moderate the force of the overpowering frangipane.

He betook himself to his study. There, beside an ancient font that served him as a hand washbasin, under a long looking glass in a frame of wrought iron that held imprisoned like a well-head silvered by the moonlight the pale surface of the mirror, bottles of all sizes and shapes were ranged in rows on ivory shelves.

He placed them on a table and divided them into two series —first, the simple perfumes, extracts and distilled waters; secondly, composite scents, such as are described under the generic name of *bouquets*.

He buried himself in an armchair and began to think.

Years ago he had trained himself as an expert in the science of perfumes; he held that the sense of smell was qualified to experience pleasures equal to those pertaining to the ear and the eye, each of the five senses being capable, by dint of a natural aptitude supplemented by an erudite education, of receiving novel impressions, magnifying these tenfold, coordinating them, combining them into the whole that constitutes a work of art. It was not, in fact, he argued, more abnormal that an art should exist of disengaging odoriferous fluids than that other arts should whose function is to set up sonorous waves to strike the ear or variously colored rays to impinge on the retina of the eyes; only, just as no one, without a special faculty of intuition developed by study, can distinguish a picture by a great master from a worthless daub, a *motif* of Beethoven from a tune by Clapisson, so no one, without a preliminary initiation, can avoid confounding at the first sniff a *bouquet* created by a great artist with a potpourri compounded by a manufacturer for sale in grocers' shops and fancy bazaars.

In this art of perfumes, one peculiarity had more than all others fascinated him, *viz.*, the precision with which it can artificially imitate the real article.

Hardly ever, indeed, are scents actually produced from the flowers whose name they bear; the artist who should be bold enough to borrow his element from Nature alone would obtain only a half-and-half-result, unconvincing, lacking in style and elegance, the fact being that the essence obtained by distillation from the flowers themselves could at the best present but a far-off, vulgarized analogy with the real aroma of the living and growing flower, shredding its fragrant effluvia in the open air.

So, with the one exception of the jasmine, which admits of no imitation, no counterfeit, no copy, which refuses even any approximation, all flowers are perfectly represented by combinations of alcoholates and essences, extracting from the model its inmost individuality while adding that something, that heightened tone, that heady savor, that rare touch which makes a work of art.

In one word, in perfumery the artist completes and consummates the original natural odor, which he cuts, so to speak, and mounts as a jeweler improves and brings out the water of a precious stone.

Little by little, the arcana of this art, the most neglected of all, had been revealed to Des Esseintes, who could now decipher its language—a diction as varied, as subtle as that of literature itself, a style of unprecedented conciseness under its apparent vagueness and uncertainty.

To reach this end, he had, first of all, been obliged to master the grammar, to understand the syntax of odors, to grasp the rules that govern them; then, once familiarized with this dialect, to study and compare the works of the divers masters of the craft, the Atkinsons and Lubins, the Chardins and Violets, the Legrands and Piesses, to analyze the construction of their sentences, to weigh the proportion of their words and the disposition of their periods.

Next, in this idiom of essences, it was for experience to come to the assistance of theories too often incomplete and commonplace.

The classic art of perfumery was, in truth, little diversified, almost colorless, uniformly run in a mold first shaped by old-world chemists; it was in its dotage, hidebound in its ancient alembics, when the Romantic epoch dawned and took its part in modifying, in rejuvenating it, in making it more malleable and more supple.

Its history followed step by step that of the French language. The Louis XIII style, perfumed and full-flavored, compounded of elements costly at that date, of iris powder, musk, civet, myrtle water, already known by the name of Angels' Water, barely sufficed to express the rude graces, the rather crude tints of the time which certain sonnets of Saint-Amand's have preserved for us. Later on, with the introduction of myrrh, frankincense, the mystic scents, powerful and austere, the pomp and stateliness of the *Grand Siècle,* the redundancy and artificiality of the orator's art, the full, sustained, wordy style of Bossuet and the great preachers became almost possible; later on again, the well-worn, sophisticated graces of French society under Louis XV found a readier interpretation of their charm in the frangipane and *maréchale,* which offered in their way the very synthesis of the period. Then, finally, after the indifference and incuriousness of the First Empire, which used eau de Cologne and preparations of rosemary to excess, perfumery ran for inspiration, in the train of Victor Hugo and Gautier, to the lands of the sun; it created Oriental essences, *selams* overpowering with their spicy odors; invented new savors; tried and approved old tones and shades now rediscovered, which it made more complex, more subtle, more choice; definitely repudiating once for all the voluntary decrepitude to which the art had been reduced by the Malesherbes, the Andrieux, the Baour-Lormians, the vulgar distillers of its poetry.

Nor had the language of perfumes remained stationary since the epoch of 1830. Again it had progressed and following the march of the century had advanced side by side with the other arts. It, too, had complied with the whims of amateurs and artists, flying for motives to China and Japan, inventing scented albums, imitating the flowery nosegays of Takeoka; by a mingling of lavender and clove obtaining the perfume Rondeletia; by a union of patchouli and camphor, the singular aroma of India ink; by compounding citron, clove and neroli (essence of orange blossoms), the odor, the Hovenia of Japan.

Des Esseintes studied, analyzed the soul of these fluids, expounded these texts; he took a delight, for his own personal satisfaction, in playing the part of psychologist, in unmounting and remounting the machinery of a work, in unscrewing the separate pieces forming the structure of a complex odor, and by long practice of this sort, his sense of smell had arrived at the certainty of an almost infallible touch.

Just as a wine merchant knows the vintage by imbibing a single drop; as a hop dealer, the instant he sniffs at a bag, can there and then name its precise quality and price; as a Chinese trader can declare at once the place of origin of the teas he examines, say on what farms of the Bohea mountains, in what Buddhist monasteries, each specimen was grown, and the date at which its leaves were gathered, can state precisely the degree of heat used and the effect produced by its contact with plum blossom, with the aglaia, with the olea fragrance, with all or any of the perfumes employed to modify its flavor, to give it an added piquancy, to brighten up its rather dry savor with a whiff of fresh and alien flowers; even so could Des Esseintes, by the merest sniff at a scent, detail instantly the doses of its composition, explain the psychology of its blending; all but quote the name of the particular artist who wrote it and impressed on it, the personal mark of his style.

Needless to say, he possessed a collection of all the products used by perfume makers; he had even some of the true Balm of Mecca, a very great rarity, to be procured only in certain regions of Arabia Petræa and guarded as a monopoly of the Grand Turk.

Seated now in his study at his working table, he was pondering the creation of a new *bouquet*, and had reached that moment of hesitation so familiar to authors who, after months of idleness, are preparing to start upon a fresh piece of work.

Like Balzac, who was haunted by an imperious craving to blacken reams of paper by way of getting his hand in, Des Esseintes felt the necessity of recovering his old cunning by dint of executing some task of minor importance. He determined to make heliotrope, and measured out the proper quantities from phials of almond and vanilla; then he changed his mind and resolved to try sweet-pea.

The phrases, the processes had escaped his memory. So he made experiments. No doubt in the fragrance of that flower, orange blossom was the dominant factor; he tried a number of combinations and ended by getting the right tone by blending the orange with the tuberose and rose, binding the three together with a drop of vanilla.

All his uncertainties vanished; a fever of eagerness stirred him, he was ready to set to work in earnest. He compounded a fresh brew of tea, adding a mixture of cassia and iris; then, sure of himself, he resolved to march boldly forward, to strike a thundering note, the overmastering crash of which should bury the whisper of that insinuating frangipane which still stealthily impregnated the room.

He handled amber; Tonquin musk, with its overpowering scent; patchouli, the most pronounced of all vegetable perfumes, whose blossom, in the natural state, gives off an odor compounded of wet wood and rusty iron. Do what he would, the associations of the eighteenth century haunted him, gowns with paniers and furbelows hovered before his eyes; memories of Boucher's "Venus," all flesh, without bones, stuffed with pink cotton-wool, besieged him; recollections of the novel *Thémidore* and the exquisite Rosette with skirts high lifted in a fire-red despair, pursued him. In a rage, he sprang up and, to shake himself free from the obsession, sniffed in with all his might that unadulterated essence of spikenard that is so dear to Easterners and so disagreeable to Europeans, by reason of its overstrong savor of valerian. He staggered under the violence of the shock; as if crushed under the blow of a mallet, the delicate fibrils of the dainty scent disappeared. He took advantage of the moment's respite to escape from the dead centuries, the old-time emanations, to enter, as he had been used to do in other days, on creations less limited in scope and more modern in fashion.

Of old, he had loved to soothe his spirit with harmonies in perfumery; he would use effects analogous to those of the poets, would adopt, in a measure, the admirable metrical scheme characterizing certain pieces of Baudelaire's, for instance *"l'Irréparable"* and *"le Balcon,"* where the last of the five lines composing the strophe is the echo of the first, returning like a refrain to drown the soul in infinite depths of melancholy and languor.

He wandered, lost in the dreams these aromatic stanzas called up in his brain, till suddenly recalled to his starting point, to the original *motif* of his meditations, by the recurrence of the initial theme, reappearing at studied intervals in the fragrant orchestration of the poem.

For the actual moment, he was fain to roam in freedom amid a landscape full of surprises and changes, and he began by a simple phrase—ample, sonorous, at once opening a view over an immense stretch of country.

With the help of his vaporizers, he injected into the room an essence composed of ambrosia, Mitcham lavender, sweetpea, compound *bouquet*—an essence which, if distilled by a true artist, well deserves the name bestowed on it of "extract of meadow flowers"; then, into this meadow, he introduced a carefully modulated infusion of tuberose, orange and almond blossom, and instantly artificial lilacs came into being, while lindens swayed in the breeze, shedding on the ground about them their pale emanations, mimicked by the London extract of tilia.

This scene, once arranged in a few imposing lines, melting to the horizon under his closed eyes, he insinuated a light rain of human, not to say half feline, essences, smacking of the petticoat, announcing woman powdered and painted—the stephanotis, the ayapana, the opoponax, the chypre, the champaka, the sarcanthus, over which he superimposed a dash of seringa, to suggest, amid the factitious life of make-up and make-belief which they evoked, a natural flower of hearty, uncontrolled laughter, of the joys of existence in the eye of the sun.

Then he let these fragant waves escape by a ventilator, keeping only the country scent, which he renewed and reinforced, strengthening the dose so as to force it to recur like the burden of a song at the end of each strophe.

Little by little, the feminine aroma disappeared, the country was left without inhabitants. Then, on the enchanted horizon, rose a row of factories whose tall chimneys flamed at their tops like so many bowls of punch.

A breath as of manufactories, of chemical works now floated on the breeze which he raised by waving fans, though Nature still continued to sweeten with her fragrant emanations this foulness of the atmosphere.

Des Esseintes proceeded to turn about and warm between his hands a ball of styrax, and a very curious odor filled the room, a smell at once repugnant and exquisite, blending the delicious scent of the jonquil with the filthy stench of gutta-percha and coal tar. He disinfected his hands, shut away his resin in a box hermetically sealed, and the stinking factories vanished in their turn. Then, he tossed amid the revivified vapors of lindens and meadow-grass some drops of "new-mown hay," and on the magic spot, instantly bared of its lilacs, rose mounds of hay, bringing with them a new season, scattering their delicate odors reminiscent of high summer.

Last of all, when he had sufficiently savored the sight, he hurriedly scattered about exotic perfumes, exhausted his vaporizers, concentrated his strongest essences, gave the rein to all his balms, and lo! the stifling closeness of the room was filled with an atmosphere, maddening and sublime, breathing powerful influences, impregnating with raging alchoholates an artificial breeze —an atmosphere unnatural, yet delightful, paradoxical in its union of the all-spice of the Tropics, the pungent savors of the sandalwood of China and the hediosmia of Japan with native odors of jasmine, hawthorn and vervain, forcing, to grow together, in despite of seasons and climates, trees of diverse essences, flowers of colors and fragrance the most opposite, creating by the blending and shock of all these tones one common perfume, unknown, unforeseen, extraordinary, wherein reappeared at intervals as a persistent refrain, the decorative phrase of the opening, the odor of the broad meadows breathed over by the lilacs and the lindens.

Suddenly a sharp agony assailed him; it felt as though a center-bit were boring into his temples. He opened his eyes, to find himself once more in the middle of his study, seated before his working table; he got up and walked painfully, half stunned, to the window, which he threw part open. A current of fresh air sweetened the stifling atmosphere that enveloped him; he marched up and down the room to recover the proper use of his limbs, going to and fro, his eyes fixed on the ceiling on which crabs and seaweed powdered with sea salt stood out in relief from a grained background, yellow as the sand of a beach. A similar design decorated the plinths bordering the panels, which in their turn were covered with Japanese crape, a watery green in color and slightly waved to imitate the ripple of a wind-blown river, while down the gentle current floated a rose leaf round which frolicked a swarm of little fishes dashed in with two strokes of the pen.

But his eyes were still heavy; he left off pacing the short length of floor between the font and the bath and leaned his elbows on the windowsill. Presently his dizziness ceased, and after carefully recorking the bottles of scents and essences, he seized the opportunity to tidy his apparatus for making up the face—his paints and powders and the like. He had not touched these things since his arrival at Fontenay, and he was almost astonished now at the sight of this collection once visited by so many women. One on top of the other, phials and porcelain pots littered the table in confusion. Here was a china box, of the green sort, containing *schnouda,* that marvelous white cream which, once spread on the cheeks, changes under the influence of the air to a tender pink, then to a scarlet so natural that it gives an absolutely convincing illusion of a complexion mantled with red blood; there, jars incrusted with mother-o'-pearl held Japanese gold and Athens green, colored like the wing of the cantharides beetle, golds and greens that blend into a deep purple directly they are moistened; beside pots full of filbert paste, of *serkis* of the harem, of emulsions of Cashmere lilies, of lotions of strawberry and elderflower for the skin, beside little phials of solutions of India ink and rosewater for the eyes, lay a host of different instruments, of mother-o'-pearl, of ivory and of silver, mixed up with dainty brushes for the teeth and gums—pincers, scissors, strigils, stumps, crimpers, powder puffs, backscratchers, patches and files.

He handled all this elaborate apparatus, bought in former days to please a mistress who found an ineffable pleasure in certain aromatics and certain balms, an ill-balanced, nerve-ridden woman, who loved to have her nipples macerated in scents, but who only really experienced a genuine and over-mastering ecstasy when her head was tickled with a comb and she could, in the act of being caressed by a lover, breathe the smell of chimney soot, of wet plaster from a house building in rainy weather, or of dust churned up by the heavy thunder drops of a summer storm.

He pondered these recollections, recalling particularly an afternoon spent, partly for want of anything better to do, partly out of curiosity, in this woman's company at her sister's house at Pantin, the memory of which stirred in his breast a whole forgotten world of long-ago thoughts and old-time scents. While the two women were chattering and showing each other their frocks, he had gone to the window and, through the dusty panes, had looked out on the long, muddy street and heard its pavements echo under the incessant beat of heavy boots trampling through the puddles.

The scene, now far away in the past, suddenly stood out before him with extraordinary vividness. Pantin lay there in front of his eyes, bustling and alive, imaged in the green, dead water of the mirror into which his eyes involuntarily gazed. A hallucination carried him far away from Fontenay; the looking glass reproduced for him the same reflections the street had once presented to his bodily eye, and buried in a dream, he said over the ingenious, melancholy yet consoling, anthem he had noted down on that former occasion on getting back to Paris:

"Yes, the time of the great rains is come; behold, the gutter-pipes vomit their drippings onto the pavements, with a song of many waters, and the horse-dung lies fermenting in the puddles that fill the holes in the macadam with a coffee-colored fluid; everywhere, for the humble wayfarer, are foot-baths full to overflowing.

"Under the lowering sky, in the dull air, the walls of the houses drip black sweat and the cellar-openings stink; loathing of life is strong within the soul and the spleen is a torment to the flesh; the seeds of filthiness that every man has in his heart begin to bud; cravings for foul pleasures trouble the austerest and in the brain of respectable folks criminal desires spring up.

"And yet, there I am, warming myself before a blazing fire, while a basket of blowing flowers on a table fills the room with a sweet savor of benzoin, geranium and bent-grass. In mid November, it is still springtime at Pantin, in the Rue de Paris, and I find myself laughing in my sleeve to think of the timorous family parties that, in order to avoid the approach of winter, fly to Antibes or Cannes as fast as steam will take them.

"Inclement Nature goes for nothing in this strange phenomenon; it is to industry, to commerce, and that alone, be it said, that Pantin owes this artificial spring.

"The truth is, these flowers are of lustring, mounted on

brass-wire, and the springlike fragrance floating in through the cracks of the window frame, is exhaled by the neighboring factories where Pinaud and Saint-James make their perfumes.

"For the artisan exhausted by the hard labor of the workshops, for the small clerk, alas! only too often a father, the illusion of a breath or two of good air is a possibility—thanks to these manufacturers.

"Indeed, out of this scarcely believable illusion of the country may be developed a quite rational medical treatment. Fast livers affected by chest complaints who are now carted off to the South mostly die, broken down by the rupture of all their habits of life, by the homesick craving to return to the Parisian pleasures that have brought them to this pass by their excess. Here, in an artificial climate, heated and regulated by stoves, libertine recollections will return, gently and harmlessly, along with the languishing feminine emanations given off by scent factories. In lieu of the deadly dreariness of provincial existence, the physician can by this device supply his patient platonically with the longed-for atmosphere of Parisian boudoirs, of Parisian haunts of pleasure.

"In the majority of cases, all that will be required to complete the cure is for the sick man to possess a little touch of imagination.

"Now, seeing that, in these times of ours, there is no single thing really genuine to be found; seeing that the wine we drink and the liberty we acclaim are equally adulterate and derisory; considering how remarkable a dose of credulity it takes to suppose the governing classes to deserve respect and the lower to be worthy either of relief or commiseration, it appears to me," concluded Des Esseintes, "neither more absurd nor more insane to demand of my neighbor a sum total of illusion barely equal to that he expends every day in his life for quite idiotic objects, that he may successfully persuade himself that the town of Pantin is an artificial Nice, a factitious Menton."

"All of which," he exclaimed, rudely interrupted in his reflections by a sudden failure of all his bodily powers, "does not alter the fact that I must beware of these delicious and abominable experiments that are killing me." He heaved a sigh: "Well, well, more pleasures to moderate, more precautions to take," and he retired for refuge to his study, thinking in this way to escape more easily from the haunting influence of the perfumes.

He threw the window wide open, delighted to enjoy an air bath; but next moment, the wind seemed to bring with it a vague breath of essence of bergamot, mingled with a smell of jasmine, cassia and rosewater. He shuddered, asking himself if he was not surely under the tyranny of one of those possessions by the devil that the priests used to exorcise in the Middle Ages. Soon the odor changed and altered, however. An uncertain savor of tincture of tolu, balm of Peru, saffron, blended together by a few drops of amber and musk, now floated in from the sleeping village at the bottom of the hill; then, suddenly, in an instant, the metamorphosis was wrought, the scent of frangipane, of which his nostrils had caught the elements and were so familiar with the analysis, filled all the air from the valley of Fontenay away to the Fort, assailing his exhausted sense of smell, shaking afresh his shattered nerves, prostrating him to such a degree that he fell swooning and half dying across the windowsill.

MARCEL PROUST/Swann's Way

AND so it was that, for a long time afterwards, when I lay awake at night and revived old memories of Combray, I saw no more of it than this sort of luminous panel, sharply defined against a vague and shadowy background, like the panels which a Bengal fire or some electric sign will illuminate and dissect from the front of a building the other parts of which remain plunged in darkness: broad enough at its base, the little parlour, the dining-room, the alluring shadows of the path along which would come M. Swann, the unconscious author of my sufferings, the hall through which I would journey to the first step of that staircase, so hard to climb, which constituted, all by itself, the tapering 'elevation' of an irregular pyramid; and, at the summit, my bedroom, with the little passage through whose glazed door Mamma would enter; in a word, seen always at the same evening hour, isolated from all its possible surroundings, detached and solitary against its shadowy background, the bare minimum of scenery necessary (like the setting one sees printed at the head of an old play, for its performance in the provinces) to the drama of my undressing, as though all Combray had consisted of but two floors joined by a slender staircase, and as though there had been no time there but seven o'clock at night. I must own that I could have assured any questioner that Combray did include other scenes and did exist at other hours than these. But since the facts which I should then have recalled would have been prompted only by an exercise of the will, by my intellectual memory, and since the pictures which that kind of memory shews us of the past preserve

SMELL AND TASTE / *Marcel Proust*

nothing of the past itself, I should never have had any wish to ponder over this residue of Combray. To me it was in reality all dead.

Permanently dead? Very possibly.

There is a large element of hazard in these matters, and a second hazard, that of our own death, often prevents us from awaiting for any length of time the favours of the first.

I feel that there is much to be said for the Celtic belief that the souls of those whom we have lost are held captive in some inferior being, in an animal, in a plant, in some inanimate object, and so effectively lost to us until the day (which to many never comes) when we happen to pass by the tree or to obtain possession of the object which forms their prison. Then they start and tremble, they call us by our name, and as soon as we have recognised their voice the spell is broken. We have delivered them: they have overcome death and return to share our life.

And so it is with our own past. It is a labour in vain to attempt to recapture it: all the efforts of our intellect must prove futile. The past is hidden somewhere outside the realm, beyond the reach of intellect, in some material object (in the sensation which that material object will give us) which we do not suspect. And as for that object, it depends on chance whether we come upon it or not before we ourselves must die.

Many years had elapsed during which nothing of Combray, save what was comprised in the theatre and the drama of my going to bed there, had any existence for me, when one day in winter, as I came home, my mother, seeing that I was cold, offered me some tea, a thing I did not ordinarily take. I declined at first, and then, for no particular reason, changed my mind. She sent out for one of those short, plump little cakes called 'petites madeleines,' which look as though they had been moulded in the fluted scallop of a pilgrim's shell. And soon, mechanically, weary after a dull day with the prospect of a depressing morrow, I raised to my lips a spoonful of the tea in which I had soaked a morsel of the cake. No sooner had the warm liquid, and the crumbs with it, touched my palate than a shudder ran through my whole body, and I stopped, intent upon the extraordinary changes that were taking place. An exquisite pleasure had invaded my senses, but individual, detached, with no suggestion of its origin. And at once the vicissitudes of life had become indifferent to me, its disasters innocuous, its brevity illusory—this new sensation having had on me the effect which love has of filling me with a precious essence; or rather this essence was not in me, it was myself. I had ceased now to feel mediocre, accidental, mortal. Whence could it have come to me, this all-powerful joy? I was conscious that it was connected with the taste of tea and cake, but that it infinitely transcended those savours, could not, indeed, be of the same nature as theirs. Whence did it come? What did it signify? How could I seize upon and define it?

I drink a second mouthful, in which I find nothing more than in the first, a third, which gives me rather less than the second. It is time to stop; the potion is losing its magic. It is plain that the object of my quest, the truth, lies not in the cup but in myself. The tea has called up in me, but does not itself understand, and can only repeat indefinitely, with a gradual loss of strength, the same testimony; which I, too, cannot interpret, though I hope at least to be able to call upon the tea for it again and to find it there presently, intact and at my disposal, for my final enlightenment. I put down my cup and examine my own mind. It is for it to discover the truth. But how? What an abyss of uncertainty whenever the mind feels that some part of it has strayed beyond its own borders; when it, the seeker, is at once the dark region through which it must go seeking, where all its equipment will avail it nothing. Seek? More than that: create. It is face to face with something which does not so far exist, to which it alone can give reality and substance, which it alone can bring into the light of day.

And I begin again to ask myself what it could have been, this unremembered state which brought with it no logical proof of its existence, but only the sense that it was a happy, that it was a real state in whose presence other states of consciousness melted and vanished. I decide to attempt to make it reappear. I retrace my thoughts to the moment at which I drank the first spoonful of tea. I find again the same state, illumined by no fresh light. I compel my mind to make one further effort, to follow and recapture once again the fleeting sensation. And that nothing may interrupt it in its course I shut out every obstacle, every extraneous idea, I stop my ears and inhibit all attention to the sounds which come from the next room. And then, feeling that my mind is growing fatigued without having any success to report, I compel it for a change to enjoy that distraction which I have just denied it, to think of other things, to rest and refresh itself before the supreme attempt. And then for the second time I clear an empty space in front of it. I place in position before my mind's eye the still recent taste of that first mouthful, and I feel something start within me, something that leaves its resting-place and attempts to rise, something that has been embedded like an anchor at a great depth; I do not know yet what it is, but I can feel it mounting slowly; I can measure the resistance, I can hear the echo of great spaces traversed.

Undoubtedly what is thus palpitating in the depths of my being must be the image, the visual memory which, being linked to that taste, has tried to follow it into my conscious mind. But its struggles are too far off, too much confused; scarcely can I perceive the colourless reflection in which are blended the uncapturable whirling medley of radiant hues, and I cannot distinguish its form, cannot invite it, as the one possible interpreter, to translate to me the evidence of its contemporary, its inseparable paramour, the taste of cake soaked in tea; cannot ask it to inform me what special circumstance is in question, of what period in my past life.

Will it ultimately reach the clear surface of my consciousness, this memory, this old, dead moment which the magnetism of an identical moment has travelled so far to importune, to disturb, to raise up out of the very depths of my being? I cannot tell. Now that I feel nothing, it has stopped, has perhaps gone down again into its darkness, from which who can say whether it will ever rise? Ten times over I must essay the task, must lean down over the abyss. And each time the natural laziness which deters us from every difficult enterprise, every work of importance, has urged me to leave the thing alone, to drink my tea and to think merely of the worries of today and of my hopes for tomorrow, which let themselves be pondered over without effort or distress of mind.

And suddenly the memory returns. The taste was that of the little crumb of madeleine which on Sunday mornings at Combray (because on those mornings I did not go out before church-time), when I went to say good day to her in her bedroom, my aunt Léonie used to give me, dipping it first in her own cup of real or of lime-flower tea. The sight of the little madeleine had recalled nothing to my mind before I tasted it; perhaps because I had so often seen such things in the interval, without tasting them, on the trays in pastry-cooks' windows, that their image had dissociated itself from those Combray days to take its place among others more recent; perhaps because of those memories, so long abandoned and put out of mind, nothing now survived, everything was scattered, the forms of things, including that of the little scallop-shell of pastry, so richly sensual under its severe, religious folds, were either obliterated or had been so long dormant as to have lost the power of expansion which would have allowed them to resume their place in my consciousness. But when from a long-distant past nothing subsists, after the people are dead, after the things are broken and scattered, still, alone, more fragile, but with more vitality, more unsubstantial, more persistent, more faithful, the smell and taste of things remain poised a long time, like souls, ready to remind us, waiting and hoping for their moment, amid the ruins of all the rest; and bear unfaltering, in the tiny and almost impalpable drop of their essence, the vast structure of recollection.

And once I had recognised the taste of the crumb of madeleine soaked in her decoction of lime-flowers which my aunt used to give me (although I did not yet know and must long postpone the discovery of why this memory made me so happy) immediately the old grey house upon the street, where her room was, rose up like the scenery of a theatre to attach itself to the little pavilion, opening on to the garden, which had been built out behind it for my parents (the isolated panel which until that moment had been all that I could see); and with the house the town, from morning to night and in all weathers, the Square where I was sent before luncheon, the streets along which I used to run errands, the country roads we took when it was fine. And just as the Japanese amuse themselves by filling a porcelain bowl with water and steeping in it little crumbs of paper which until then are without character or form, but, the moment they become wet, stretch themselves and bend, take on colour and distinctive shape, become flowers or houses or people, permanent and recognisable, so in that moment all the flowers in our garden and in M. Swann's park, and the water-lilies on the Vivonne and the good folk of the village and their little dwellings and the parish church and the whole of Combray and of its surroundings taking their proper shapes and growing solid, sprang into being, town and gardens alike, from my cup of tea.

O. HENRY/The Furnished Room

RESTLESS, SHIFTING, fugacious as time is a certain vast bulk of the population of the red brick district of the lower West Side. Homeless, they have a hundred homes. They flit from furnished room to furnished room, transients forever—transients in abode, transients in heart and mind. They sing "Home, Sweet Home" in ragtime; they carry their *lares et penates* in a bandbox; their vine is entwined about a picture hat; a rubber plant is their fig tree.

Hence the houses of this district, having had a thousand dwellers, should have a thousand tales to tell, mostly dull ones, no doubt; but it would be strange if there could not be found a ghost or two in the wake of all these vagrant guests.

One evening after dark a young man prowled among these crumbling red mansions, ringing their bells. At the twelfth he rested his lean hand-baggage upon the step and wiped the dust from his hatband and forehead. The bell sounded faint and far away in some remote, hollow depths.

To the door of this, the twelfth house whose bell he had rung, came a housekeeper who made him think of an unwholesome, surfeited worm that had eaten its nut to a hollow shell and now sought to fill the vacancy with edible lodgers.

He asked if there was a room to let.

"Come in," said the housekeeper. Her voice came from her throat; her throat seemed lined with fur. "I have the third-floor back, vacant since a week back. Should you wish to look at it?"

The young man followed her up the stairs. A faint light from no particular source mitigated the shadows of the halls. They trod noiselessly upon a stair carpet that its own loom would have forsworn. It seemed to have become vegetable; to have degenerated in that rank, sunless air to lush lichen or spreading moss that grew in patches to the stair-case and was viscid under the foot like organic matter. At each turn of the stairs were vacant niches in the wall. Perhaps plants had once been set within them. If so they had died in that foul and tainted air. It may be that statues of the saints had stood there, but it was not difficult to conceive that imps and devils had dragged them forth in the darkness and down to the unholy depths of some furnished pit below.

"This is the room," said the housekeeper, from her furry throat. "It's a nice room. It ain't often vacant. I had some most elegant people in it last summer—no trouble at all, and paid in advance to the minute. The water's at the end of the hall. Sprowls and Mooney kept it three months. They done a vaudeville sketch. Miss B'retta Sprowls—you may have heard of her—Oh, that was just the stage names—right there over the dresser is where the marriage certificate hung, framed. The gas is here, and you see there is plenty of closet room. It's a room everybody likes. It never stays idle long."

"Do you have many theatrical people rooming here?" asked the young man.

"They comes and goes. A good proportion of my lodgers is connected with the theatres. Yes, sir, this is the theatrical district. Actor people never stays long anywhere. I get my share. Yes, they comes and they goes."

He engaged the room, paying for a week in advance. He was tired, he said, and would take possession at once. He counted out the money. The room had been made ready, she said, even to towels and water. As the housekeeper moved away he put, for the thousandth time, the question that he carried at the end of his tongue.

"A young girl—Miss Vashner—Miss Eloise Vashner—do you remember such a one among your lodgers? She would be singing on the stage, most likely. A fair girl, of medium height and slender, with reddish, gold hair and a dark mole near her left eyebrow."

"No, I don't remember the name. Them stage people has names they change as often as their rooms. They comes and they goes. No, I don't call that one to mind."

No. Always no. Five months of ceaseless interrogation and the inevitable negative. So much time spent by day in questioning managers, agents, schools and choruses; by night among the audiences of theatres from all-star casts down to music halls so low that he dreaded to find what he most hoped for. He who had loved her best had tried to find her. He was sure that since her disappearance from home this great, water-girt city held her somewhere, but it was like a monstrous quicksand, shifting its particles constantly, with no foundation, its upper granules of to-day buried to-morrow in ooze and slime.

The furnished room received its latest guest with a first glow of pseudo-hospitality, a hectic, haggard, perfunctory welcome like the specious smile of a demirep. The sophistical comfort came in reflected gleams from the decayed furniture, the ragged brocade upholstery of a couch and two chairs, a foot-wide cheap pier glass between the two windows, from one or two gilt picture frames and a brass bedstead in a corner.

The guest reclined, inert, upon a chair, while the room, confused in speech as though it were an apartment in Babel, tried to discourse to him of its divers tenantry.

A polychromatic rug like some brilliant-flowered, retangular, tropical islet lay surrounded by a billowy sea of soiled matting. Upon the gay-papered wall were those pictures that pursue the homeless one from house to house—The Huguenot Lovers, The First Quarrel, The Wedding Breakfast, Psyche at the Fountain. The mantel's chastely severe outline was inglorioulsy veiled behind some pert drapery drawn rakishly askew like the sashes of the Amazonian ballet. Upon it was some desolate flotsam cast aside by the room's marooned when a lucky sail had borne them to a fresh port—a trifling vase or two, pictures of actresses, a medicine bottle, some stray cards out of a deck.

One by one, as the characters of a cryptograph become explicit, the little signs left by the furnished room's procession of guests developed a significance. The threadbare space in the rug in front of the dresser told that lovely women had marched in the throng. The tiny fingerprints on the wall spoke of little prisoners trying to feel their way to sun and air. A splattered stain, raying like the shadow of a bursting bomb, witnessed where a hurled glass or bottle had splintered with its contents against the wall. Across the pier glass had been scrawled with a diamond in staggering letters the name "Marie." It seemed that the succession of dwellers in the furnished room had turned in fury—perhaps tempted beyond forbearance by its garish coldness—and wreaked upon it their passions. The furniture was chipped and bruised; the couch, distorted by bursting springs, seemed a horrible monster that had been slain during the stress of some grotesque convulsion. Some more potent upheaval had cloven a great slice from the marble mantel. Each plank in the floor owned its particular cant and shriek as from a separate and individual agony. It seemed incredible that all this malice and injury had been wrought upon the room by those who had called it for a time their home; and yet it may have been the cheated home instinct surviving blindly, the resentful rage at false household gods that had kindled their wrath. A hut that is our own we can sweep and adorn and cherish.

The young tenant in the chair allowed these thoughts to file, soft-shod, through his mind, while there drifted into the room furnished sounds and furnished scents. He heard in one room a tittering and incontinent, slack laughter; in others the monologue of a scold, the rattling of dice, a lullaby, and one crying dully; above him a banjo tinkled with spirit. Doors banged somewhere; the elevated trains roared intermittently; a cat yowled miserably upon a back fence. And he breathed the breath of the house—a dank savor rather than a smell—a cold, musty effluvium as from underground vaults mingled with the reeking exhalations of linoleum and mildewed and rotten woodwork.

Then suddenly, as he rested there, the room was filled with the strong, sweet odor of mignonette. It came as upon a single buffet of wind with such sureness and fragrance and emphasis that it almost seemed a living visitant. And the man cried aloud: "What, dear?" as if he had been called, and sprang up and faced about. The rich odor clung to him and wrapped him around. He reached out his arms for it, all his senses for the time confused and commingled. How could one be peremptorily called by an odor? Surely it must have been a sound. But, was it not the sound that had touched, that had caressed him?

"She has been in this room," he cried, and he sprang to wrest from it a token, for he knew he would recognize the smallest thing that had belonged to her or that she had touched. This enveloping scent of mignonette, the odor that she had loved and made her own—whence came it?

The room had been but carelessly set in order. Scattered upon the flimsy dresser scarf were half a dozen hairpins—those discreet, indistinguishable friends of womankind, feminine of gender, infinite mood and uncommunicative of tense. These he ignored, conscious of their triumphant lack of identity. Ransacking the drawers of the dresser he came upon a discarded, tiny, ragged handkerchief. He pressed it to his face. It was racy and insolent with heliotrope; he hurled it to the floor. In another drawer he found odd buttons, a theatre programme, a pawnbroker's card, two lost marshmallows, a book on the divination of dreams. In the last was a woman's black satin hair bow, which halted him, poised between ice and fire. But the black satin hair bow also is femininity's demure, impersonal common ornament and tells no tales.

And then he traversed the room like a hound on the scent, skimming the walls, considering the corners of the bulging matting on his hands and knees, rummaging mantel and tables, the curtains and hangings, the drunken cabinet in the corner, for a visible sign, unable to perceive that she was there beside, around, against, within, above him, clinging to him, wooing him, calling him so poignantly through the finer senses that even his grosser ones became cognizant of the call. Once again he answered loudly: "Yes, dear!" and turned, wild-eyed, to gaze on vacancy, for he could not yet discern form and color and love and outstretched arms in the odor of mignonette. Oh, God! whence that odor, and since when have odors had a voice to call? Thus he groped.

He burrowed in crevices and corners, and found corks and cigarettes. These he passed in passive contempt. But once he found in a fold of the matting a half-smoked cigar, and this he ground beneath his heel with a green and trenchant oath. He sifted the room from end to end. He found dreary and ignoble small records of many a peripatetic tenant; but of her whom he sought, and who may have lodged there, and whose spirit seemed to hover there, he found no trace.

And then he thought of the housekeeper.

He ran from the haunted room downstairs and to a door that showed a crack of light. She came out to his knock. He smothered his excitement as best he could.

"Will you tell me, madam," he besought her, "who occupied the room I have before I came?"

"Yes, sir. I can tell you again. 'Twas Sprowls and Mooney, as I said. Miss B'retta Sprowls it was in the theatres, but Missis Mooney she was. My house is well known for respectability. The marriage certificate hung, framed, on a nail over—"

"What kind of a lady was Miss Sprowls—in looks, I mean?"

"Why, black-haired, sir, short, and stout, with a comical face. They left a week ago Tuesday."

"And before they occupied it?"

"Why, there was a single gentleman connected with the draying business. He left owing me a week. Before him was Missis Crowder and her two children, that stayed four months; and back of them was old Mr. Doyle, whose sons paid for him. He kept the room six months. That goes back a year, sir, and further I do not remember."

He thanked her and crept back to his room. The room was dead. The essence that had vivified it was gone. The perfume of mignonette had departed. In its place was the old, stale odor of mouldy house furniture, of atmosphere in storage.

The ebbing of his hope drained his faith. He sat staring at the yellow, swinging gaslight. Soon he walked to the bed and began to tear the sheets into strips. With the blade of his knife he drove them tightly into every crevice around windows and door. When all was snug and taut he turned out the light, turned the gas full on again and laid himself gratefully upon the bed.

It was Mrs. McCool's night to go with the can for beer. So she fetched it and sat with Mrs. Purdy in one of those subterranean retreats where housekeepers foregather and the worm dieth seldom.

"I rented out my third-floor-back this evening," said Mrs. Purdy, across a fine circle of foam. "A young man took it. He went up to bed two hours ago."

"Now, did ye, Mrs. Purdy, ma'am?" said Mrs. McCool, with intense admiration. "You do be a wonder for rentin' rooms of that kind. And did ye tell him, then?" she concluded in a husky whisper laden with mystery.

"Rooms," said Mrs. Purdy, in her furriest tones, "are furnished for to rent. I did not tell him, Mrs. McCool."

" 'Tis right ye are, ma'am; 'tis by renting rooms we kape alive. Ye have the rale sense for business, ma'am. There be many people will rayjict the rentin' of a room if they be tould a suicide has been after dyin' in the bed of it."

"As you say, we has our living to be making," remarked Mrs. Purdy.

"Yis, ma'am; 'tis true. 'Tis just one wake ago this day I helped ye lay out the third-floor-back. A pretty slip of a colleen she was to be killin' herself wid the gas—a swate little face she had, Mrs. Purdy, ma'am."

"She'd a-been called handsome, as you say," said Mrs. Purdy, assenting but critical, "but for that mole she had a'growin' by her left eyebrow. Do fill up your glass again, Mrs. McCool."

IV

THE WORLD AS WE SEE IT AND THE WORLD AS IT IS

  The human being's reaction to the world about him is at first very simple. As he matures, however, his perception comes to be dependent on many factors: his background and language, temperament and role, physical and emotional condition. The reality of what he sees depends upon the way in which he interprets phenomena. A cup standing on a table has a very real existence; it can be measured, touched, filled with water and used for drinking. It has a definite physical reality. How we feel about the cup, however—its psychic reality—will depend on who we are, what we are, and how we are feeling. For one person, the cup may signify the presence of a lover, or it may mean that the maid has been sloppy, or that a neighbor has returned a cup of sugar she borrowed last week. It may arouse no emotion at all, but it may also be the trigger for an emotional upheaval. Which cup then, is the real cup?

  The question of reality, of how much we can depend upon our senses, is raised most frequently in the courtroom. There phenomenal reality is the only reality, and the power of psychic events is recognized only where there is a question of insanity. The fact that we see what we want to see or what we think we should see is neatly illustrated by Thomas Hardy in his ironic tale, and it is amusingly underscored by Lewis Carroll's verse in which the difference between an object and its observer is dependent upon the preoccupation of the observer.

FRANCIS BACON / Idols of Perception*

WE HAVE no sound notions either in logic or physics; substance, quality, action, passion, and existence are not clear notions; much less weight, levity, density, tenuity, moisture, dryness, generation, corruption, attraction, repulsion, element, matter, form, and the like. They are all fantastical and ill-defined.

The notions of less abstract natures, as man, dog, dove, and the immediate perceptions of sense, as heat, cold, white, black, do not deceive us materially, yet even these are sometimes confused by the mutability of matter and the intermixture of things. All the rest which men have hitherto employed are errors, and improperly abstracted and deduced from things.

There is the same degree of licentiousness and error in forming axioms as in abstracting notions, and that in the first principles, which depend on common induction; still more is this the case in axioms and inferior propositions derived from things. . . .

The idols and false notions which have already preoccupied the human understanding, and are deeply rooted in it, not only so beset men's minds that they become difficult of access, but even when access is obtained will again meet and trouble us in the instauration of the sciences, unless mankind when forewarned guard themselves with all possible care against them.

Four species of idols beset the human mind, to which (for distinction's sake) we have assigned names, calling the first Idols of the Tribe, the second Idols of the Den, the third Idols of the Market, the fourth Idols of the Theatre.

The formation of notions and axioms on the foundation of true induction is the only fitting remedy by which we can ward off and expel these idols. It is, however, of great service to point them out; for the doctrine of idols bears the same relation to the interpretation of nature as that of the confutation of sophisms does to common logic.

The idols of the tribe are inherent in human nature and the very tribe or race of man; for man's sense is falsely asserted to be the standard of things; on the contrary, all the perceptions both of the senses and the mind bear reference to man and not to the universe, and the human mind resembles those uneven mirrors which impart their own properties to different objects, from which rays are emitted and distort and disfigure them.

* Reprinted from Francis Bacon, *Novum Organum*.

The idols of the den are those of each individual; for everybody (in addition to the errors common to the race of man) has his own individual den or cavern, which intercepts and corrupts the light of nature, either from his own peculiar and singular disposition, or from his education and intercourse with others, or from his reading, and the authority acquired by those whom he reverences and admires, or from the different impressions produced on the mind, as it happens to be preoccupied and predisposed, or equable and tranquil, and the like; so that the spirit of man (according to its several dispositions), is variable, confused, and as it were actuated by chance; and Heraclitus said well that men search for knowledge in lesser worlds, and not in the greater or common world.

There are also idols formed by the reciprocal intercourse and society of man with man, which we call idols of the market, from the commerce and association of men with each other; for men converse by means of language, but words are formed at the will of the generality, and there arises from a bad and unapt formation of words a wonderful obstruction to the mind. Nor can the definitions and explanations with which learned men are wont to guard and protect themselves in some instances afford a complete remedy—words still manifestly force the understanding, throw everything into confusion, and lead mankind into vain and innumerable controversies and fallacies.

Lastly, there are idols which have crept into men's minds from the various dogmas of peculiar systems of philosophy, and also from the perverted rules of demonstration, and these we denominate idols of the theatre: for we regard all the systems of philosophy hitherto received or imagined, as so many plays brought out and performed, creating fictitious and theatrical worlds. Nor do we speak only of the present systems, or of the philosophy and sects of the ancients, since numerous other plays of a similar nature can be still composed and made to agree with each other, the causes of the most opposite errors being generally the same. Nor, again, do we allude merely to general systems, but also to many elements and axioms of sciences which have become inveterate by tradition, implicit credence, and neglect. We must, however, discuss each species of idols more fully and distinctly in order to guard the human understanding against them.

The human understanding, from its peculiar nature, easily supposes a greater degree of order and equality in things than it really finds; and although many things in nature be *sui generis* and most irregular, will yet invent parallels and conjugates and relatives, where no such thing is. Hence the fiction, that all celestial bodies move in perfect circles, thus rejecting entirely spiral and serpentine lines (except as explanatory terms). Hence also the element of fire is introduced with its peculiar orbit, to keep square with those other three which are objects of our senses. The relative rarity of the elements (as they are called) is arbitrarily made to vary in tenfold progression, with many other dreams of the like nature. Nor is this folly confined to theories, but it is to be met with even in simple notions.

The human understanding, when any proposition has been once laid down (either from general admission and belief, or from the pleasure it affords), forces everything else to add fresh support and confirmation; and although most cogent and abundant instances may exist to the contrary, yet either does not observe or despises them, or gets rid of and rejects them by some distinction, with violent and injurious prejudice, rather than sacrifice the authority of its first conclusions. It was well answered by him who was shown in a temple the votive tablets suspended by such as had escaped the peril of shipwreck, and was pressed as to whether he would then recognize the power of the gods, by an inquiry. But where are the portraits of those who have perished in spite of their vows? All superstition is much the same, whether it be that of astrology, dreams, omens, retributive judgment, or the like, in all of which the deluded believers observe events which are fulfilled, but neglect and pass over their failure, though it be much more common. But this evil insinuates itself still more craftily in philosophy and the sciences, in which a settled maxim vitiates and governs every other circumstance, though the latter be much more worthy of confidence. Besides, even in the absence of that eagerness and want of thought (which we have mentioned), it is the peculiar and perpetual error of the human understanding to be more moved and excited by affirmatives than negatives, whereas it ought duly and regularly to be impartial; nay, in establishing any true axiom the negative instance is the most powerful.

The human understanding is most excited by that which strikes and enters the mind at once and suddenly, and by which the imagination is immediately filled and inflated. It then begins almost imperceptibly to conceive and suppose that everything is similar to the few objects which have taken possession of the mind, while it is very slow and unfit for the transition to the remote and heterogeneous instances by which axioms are tried as by fire, unless the office be imposed upon it by severe regulations and a powerful authority.

The human understanding is active and cannot halt or rest, but even, though without effect, still presses forward. Thus we canot conceive of any end or external boundary of the world, and it seems necessarily to occur to us that there must be something beyond. Nor can we imagine how eternity has flowed on down to the present day, since the usually received distinction of an infinity, a parte ante and a parte post, cannot hold good; for it would thence follow that one infinity is greater than another, and also that infinity is wasting away and tending to an end. There is the same difficulty in considering the infinite divisibility of lines, arising from the weakness of our minds, which weakness interferes to still greater disadvantage with the discovery of causes; for although the greatest generalities in nature must be positive, just as they are found, and in fact not causable, yet the human understanding, incapable of resting, seeks for something more intelligible. Thus, however, while aiming at further progress, it falls back to what is actually less advanced, namely, final causes; for they are clearly more allied to man's own nature, than the system of the universe, and from this source they have wonderfully corrupted philosophy. But he would be an unskilful and shallow philosopher who should seek for causes in the greatest generalities, and not be anxious to discover them in subordinate objects.

The human understanding resembles not a dry light, but admits a tincture of the will and passions, which generate their own system accordingly; for man always believes more readily that which he prefers. He, therefore, rejects difficulties for want of patience in investigation; sobriety, because it limits his hope; the depths of nature, from superstition; the light of experiment, from arrogance and pride, lest his mind should appear to be occupied with common and varying objects; paradoxes, from a fear of the opinion of the vulgar; in short, his feelings imbue and corrupt his understanding in innumerable and sometimes imperceptible ways.

But by far the greatest impediment and aberration of the human understanding proceeds from the dulness, incompetence, and errors of the senses; since whatever strikes the senses preponderates over everything, however, superior, which does not immediately strike them. Hence contemplation mostly ceases with sight, and a very scanty, or perhaps no regard is paid to invisible objects. The entire operation, therefore, of spirits inclosed in tangible bodies is concealed, and escapes us. All that more delicate change of formation in the parts of coarser substances (vulgarly called alteration, but in fact a change of position in the smallest particles) is equally unknown; and yet, unless the two matters we have mentioned be explored and brought to light, no great effect can be produced in nature. Again, the very nature of common air, and all bodies of less density (of which there are many) is almost unknown; for the senses are weak and erring, nor can instruments be of great use in extending their sphere or acuteness—all the better interpretations of nature are worked out by instances, and fit and apt experiments, where the senses only judge of the experiment, the experiment of nature and the thing itself.

The human understanding is, by its own nature, prone to abstraction, and supposes that which is fluctuating to be fixed. But it is better to dissect than abstract nature: such was the method employed by the school of Democritus, which made greater progress in penetrating nature than the rest. It is best to consider matter, its conformation, and the changes of that conformation, its own action, and the law of this action or motion; for forms are a mere fiction of the human mind, unless you will call the laws of action by that name.

Such are the idols of the tribe, which arise either from the uniformity of the constitution of man's spirit, or its prejudices, or its limited faculties or restless agitation, or from the interference of the passions, or the incompetence of the senses, or the mode of their impressions.

The idols of the den derive their origin from the peculiar nature of each individual's mind and body, and also from education, habit, and accident; and although they be various and manifold, yet we will treat of some that require the greatest caution, and exert the greatest power in polluting the understanding. . . .

The idols of the market are the most troublesome of all, those namely which have entwined themselves round the understanding from the associations of words and names. For men imagine that their reason governs words, while, in fact, words react upon the understanding; and this has rendered philosophy and the sciences sophistical and inactive. Words are generally formed in a popular sense, and define things by those broad lines which are most obvious to the vulgar mind; but when a more acute understanding or more diligent observation is anxious to vary those lines, and to adapt them more accurately to nature, words oppose it. Hence the great and solemn disputes of learned men often terminate in controversies about words and names, in regard to which it would be better (imitating the caution of mathematicians) to proceed more advisedly in the first instance, and to bring such disputes to a regular issue by definitions. Such definitions, however, cannot remedy the evil in natural and material objects, because they consist themselves of words, and these words produce others; so that we must necessarily have recourse to particular instances, and their regular series and arrangement, as we shall mention when we come to the mode and scheme of determining notions and axioms.

The idols imposed upon the understanding by words are of two kinds. They are either the names of things which have no existence (for as some objects are from inattention left without a name, so names are formed by fanciful imaginations which are without an object), or they are the names of actual objects, but confused, badly defined, and hastily and irregularly abstracted from things. Fortune, the *primum mobile*, the planetary orbits, the element of fire, and the like fictions, which owe their birth to futile and false theories, are instances of the first kind. And this species of idols is removed with greater facility, because it can be exterminated by the constant refutation or the desuetude of the theories themselves. The others, which are created by vicious and unskilful abstraction, are intricate and deeply rooted. Take some word, for instance, as "moist," and let us examine how far the different significations of this word are consistent. It will be found that the word "moist" is nothing but a confused sign of different actions admitted of no settled and defined uniformity. For it means that which easily diffuses itself over another body; that which is indeterminable and cannot be brought to a consistency; that which yields easily in every direction; that which is easily divided and dispersed; that which is easily united and collected; that which easily flows and is put in motion; that which easily adheres to, and wets another body; that which is easily reduced to a liquid state though previously solid. When, therefore, you come to predicate or impose this name, in one sense flame is moist, in another glass is moist; so that it is quite clear that this notion is hastily abstracted from water only, and common ordinary liquors, without any due verification of it.

There are, however, different degrees of distortion and mistake in words. One of the least faulty classes is that of the names of substances, particularly of the less abstract and more defined species (those then of chalk and mud are good, of earth bad); words signifying actions are more faulty, as to generate, to corrupt, to change; but the most faulty are those denoting qualities (except the immediate objects of sense), as heavy, light, rare, dense. Yet in all of these there must be some notions a little better than others, in proportion as a greater or less number of things come before the senses.

The idols of the theatre are not innate, nor do they introduce themselves secretly into the understanding, but they are manifestly instilled and cherished by the fictions of theories and depraved rules of demonstration. To attempt, however, or undertake their confutation would not be consistent with our declarations. For since we neither agree in our principles nor our demonstrations, all argument is out of the question. And it is fortunate that the ancients are left in possession of their honors. We detract nothing from them, seeing our whole doctrine relates only to the path to be pursued. The lame (as they say) in the path outstrip the swift who wander from it, and it is clear that the very skill and swiftness of him who runs not in the right direction must increase his aberration.

Our method of discovering the sciences is such as to leave little to the acuteness and strength of wit, and indeed rather to level wit and intellect. For as in the drawing of a straight line, or accurate circle by the hand, much depends on its steadiness and practice, but if a ruler or compass be employed there is little occasion for either; so it is with our method. Although, however, we enter into no individual confutations, yet a little must be said, first, of the sects and general divisions of these species of theories; secondly, something further to show that there are external signs of their weakness; and, lastly, we must consider the causes of so great a misfortune, and so long and general a unanimity in error, that we may thus render the access to truth less difficult, and that the human understanding may the more readily be purified, and brought to dismiss its idols.

The idols of the theatre, or of theories, are numerous, and may, and perhaps will, be still more so. For unless men's minds had been now occupied for many ages in religious and theological considerations, and civil governments (especially monarchies), had been averse to novelties of that nature even in theory (so that men must apply to them with some risk and injury to their own fortunes, and not only without reward, but subject to contumely and envy), there is no doubt that many other sects of philosophers and theorists would have been introduced, like those which formerly flourished in such diversified abundance among the Greeks. For as many imaginary theories of the heavens can be deduced from the phenomena of the sky, so it is even more easy to found many dogmas upon the phenomena of philosophy—and the plot of this our theatre resembles those of the poetical, where the plots which are invented for the stage are more consistent, elegant, and pleasurable than those taken from real history.

In general, men take for the groundwork of their philosophy either too much from a few topics, or too little from many; in either case their philosophy is founded on too narrow a basis of experiment and natural history, and decides on too scanty grounds. For the theoretic philosopher seizes various common circumstances by experiment, without reducing them to certainty or examining and frequently considering them, and relies for the rest upon meditation and the activity of his wit.

There are other philosophers who have diligently and accurately attended to a few experiments, and have thence presumed to deduce and invent systems of philosophy, forming everything to conformity with them.

A third set, from their faith and religious veneration,

introduce theology and traditions; the absurdity of some among them having proceeded so far as to seek and derive the sciences from spirits and genii. There are, therefore, three sources of error and three species of false philosophy; the sophistic, empiric, and superstitious.

JEROME S. BRUNER and CECILE C. GOODMAN / Value and Need as Organizing Factors in Perception

THROUGHOUT THE history of modern psychology, until very recent times, perception has been treated as though the perceiver were a passive recording instrument of rather complex design. One might, in most experiments, describe him in much the same graphical terms as one uses to describe the latest piece of recording apparatus obtainable from Stoelting or the American Optical Company. Such psychology, practiced as it were *in vitro*, has fallen short of clarifying the nature of *perception* in everyday life much as did the old nerve-muscle psychophysiology fall short of explaining *behavior* in everyday life. Both have been monumentally useful—in their place. The names of Weber, Fechner, Wundt, Titchener, Hecht, and Crozier are safely ensconced in any respectable psychological hall of fame. But their work, like the work of the nerve-muscle men, is only a beginning.

For, as Professor Thurstone (13) has put it, "In these days when we insist so frequently on the interdependence of all aspects of personality, it would be difficult to maintain that any of these functions, such as perception, is isolated from the rest of the dynamical system that constitutes the person." The problem is, indeed, to understand how the process of perception is affected by other concurrent mental functions and how these functions in their turn are affected by the operation of perceptual processes. Given a dark room and a highly motivated subject, one has no difficulty in demonstrating Korte's Laws of phenomenal movement. Lead the subject from the dark room to the market place and then find out what it is he sees moving and under what conditions, and Korte's Laws, though still valid, describe the situation about as well as the Laws of Color Mixture describe one's feelings before an El Greco canvas.

The discrepancy between the dark room and the market

place we have in the past found it convenient to dismiss by invoking various *dei ex machina:* Attention, Apperception, *Unbewusster Schluss, Einstellung,* Preparatory Set, etc. Like the vengeful and unannounced step-brother from Australia in the poorer murder mysteries, they turn up at the crucial juncture to do the dirty work. Though such constructs are useful, perception itself must remain the primary focus. To shift attention away from it by invoking poorly understood intervening variables does little service. What we must study before invoking such variables are the variations perception itself undergoes when one is hungry, in love, in pain, or solving a problem. These variations are as much a part of the psychology of perception as Korte's Laws.

It is the contention of this paper that such perceptual phenomena are as scientifically measurable in terms of appropriate metrics as such more hallowed phenomena as flicker fusion, constancy, or tonal attributes. But let us pause first to construct a sketchy terminology. Let us, in what ensues, distinguish heuristically between two types of perceptual determinants. These we shall call *autochthonous* and *behavioral.* Under the former we group those properties of the nervous system, highly predictable, which account for phenomena like simple pair formation, closure, and contrast, or at another level, tonal masking, difference and summation tones, flicker fusion, paradoxical cold, and binaural beats. Given ideal "dark-room" conditions and no compelling distractions, the "average" organism responds to set physical stimuli in these relatively fixed ways. Autochthonous determinants, in brief, reflect directly the *characteristic* electrochemical properties of sensory end organs and nervous tissue.

Under the category of *behavioral* determinants we group those active, adaptive functions of the organism which lead to the governance and control of all higher-level functions, including perception: the laws of learning and motivation, such personality dynamics as repression, the operation of quasi-temperamental characteristics like introversion and extroversion, social needs and attitudes, and so on. Underlying these behavioral determinants, doubtless, are a host of physiological mechanisms. But we can hardly wait until we understand these before tackling experimentally the role of behavioral determinants in perception. The physiology of Weber's Law is still more or less obscure, yet the enunciation of it has been recognizably useful—even to the physiologist for whom it has been a challenge to discovery.

There exists a fruitful if slim body of literature on behavioral factors in perception. Where does one go from here? Two approaches are open. Armed with our slender reed of empirical proof, we can set about the task of systematization, indulging in

S-R's, topology, or psychoanalytic constructs to suit the taste. There is already one brilliant theoretical structure to account for many of the facts we have been discussing, presented in Egon Brunswik's *Wahrnehmung und Gegenstandswelt* (2). Or we may go on to the empirical demonstration of general hypotheses concerning the relation of behavior dynamics and perception. Both are indispensable activities. The present paper, however, is concerned mainly with empirical hypotheses. But certain minimum systematic assumptions must first be made clear to bring these hypotheses into clear focus.

The organism exists in a world of more or less ambiguously organized sensory stimulation. What the organism sees, what is *actually there* perceptually represents some sort of compromise between what is presented by autochthonous processes and what is selected by behavioral ones. Such selection, we know, is determined not only by learning, as already indicated, but also by motivational factors such as have been indicated for hunger by Sanford (10, 11) and Levine, Chein, and Murphy (7). The selective processes in perception we shall refer to as a *perceptual hypothesis*, using the term, with Krech (5), to denote a systematic response tendency. Such an hypothesis may be set into operation by a need, by the requirements of learning a task, or by any internally or externally imposed demands on the organism. If a given perceptual hypothesis is rewarded by leading to food, water, love, fame, or what not, it will become *fixated;* and the experimental literature, notably the work of Ellson (3) and Leeper (6), indicates that the fixation of "sensory conditioning" is very resistant to extinction. As fixation takes place, the perceptual hypothesis grows stronger not only in the sense of growing more frequent in the presence of certain types of stimulation, but also more perceptually *accentuated*. Perceptual objects which are habitually selected become more vivid, have greater clarity or greater brightness or greater apparent size.

Two other systematic matters must concern us before we turn to the experiments. One has to do with perceptual *compromise,* the other with perceptual *equivocality*. Frequently, alternative hypotheses operate: a quick glimpse of a man in gray on a European battlefield may leave us in doubt as to whether he is a civilian or a Wehrmacht infantryman. Almost inevitably one or the other hypothesis prevails, and the field is perceived as either one or the other. But in spite of the dominance of a single hypothesis in perception, *compromise* also occurs. Using Ansbacher's experiments (1) as an example, a group of small paper squares is seen both in terms of number and in terms of value as stamps. What results, if you will, is a perception of "number-value." We know precious little about such perceptual compromises, although we shall be discussing experiments demonstrating their operation.

As for *equivocality,* or ambiguity in the perceptual field, it has generally been supposed that the greater the equivocality the greater the chance for behavioral factors in perception to operate, all other things being equal. Sherif (12) chose the autokinetic phenomenon to work with for this reason. Proshansky and Murphy (9) worked close to threshold illumination with similar intent. Within broad limits, which we shall discuss, the generalization is valid, in so far as equivocality reduces the organizing capacity of autochthonous perceptual determinants. How important this generalization is we, who think so exclusively in terms of the well-controlled dark-room experiment, often forget. For in everyday life, perception is, by and large, a series of quick looks, glances, inattentive listenings, furtive touches. Save for what is at the very focus of interested attention, the world of sense is more equivocal than our textbook writers seem to think.

Empirical Hypotheses

We may turn now to the experiments with which this paper is primarily concerned. Three general hypotheses, growing out of the systematic principles just presented, are under consideration.

1. *The greater the social value of an object, the more will it be susceptible to organization by behavioral determinants.* It will be *selected* perceptually from among alternative perceptual objects, will become *fixated* as a perceptual response tendency, and will become perceptually *accentuated.*

2. *The greater the individual need for a socially valued object, the more marked will be the operation of behavioral determinants.*

3. *Perceptual equivocality will facilitate the operation of behavioral determinants only in so far as equivocality reduces the operation of autochthonous determinants without reducing the effectiveness of behavioral determinants.*

In the experiments reported here, only one aspect of behavioral determination will be treated, what we have called *accentuation*—the tendency for sought-after perceptual objects to become more vivid. Perceptual selectivity and fixation have already been demonstrated in other experiments, though they remain poorly systematized. For purposes of economy of exposition we omit consideration of them here, though they constitute important variables in the broader research project of which the present experiments are a part.

The Subjects and the Apparatus

The subjects were 30 ten-year-old children of normal intelligence, divisible according to certain characteristics to be discussed shortly into three groups, two experimental and one control. The apparatus consisted of a rectangular wooden box (9"x9"x18") at one end of which was a 5" square ground-glass screen and a knob at its lower right-hand corner. At the center of the ground-glass screen was an almost circular patch of light (16.2 app. ft. cdls.) cast upon the back of the screen by a 60-watt incandescent light shining through an iris diaphragm which could be varied in diameter from $\frac{1}{8}$" to 2" by turning the knob on the front end of the box. All that was visible to the subject was the box with its ground-glass screen and the circle of light whose diameter he could change by turning the knob. The circle was not truly round, containing the familiar nine elliptoid sides found in the Bausch & Lomb iris diaphragm. It was so close to round, however, that subjects had no difficulty making the subjective equations required of them.

Subjects individually sat in a chair in front of the screen on the box with the light circle slightly below eye level. The box rested on a table behind which sat the experimenter. The child was told that this was a game, and that he was to make the circle of light on the box the same size as various objects he was shown or told about. Before beginning judgments, each child, with no urging, was encouraged to see how large and small the circle of light could be made.

The two experimental groups received the same treatment. Two series were run for these groups, comprising 20 of the children in all. First the child was asked to estimate the sizes of coins from a penny through a half dollar from memory. He did the first in ascending order of value, then in descending order, always making two judgments for each coin named, one from the open, the other from the closed position of the iris diaphragm. Four judgments were made for each coin by each child. No inkling was given the child as to how "close" he had come.

Following the memory series, and using the same order of presentation, a similar series was then run with coins present. Coins, individually, were held close to the center of the palm of the left hand, at a level with the light circle and six inches to its left. The subjects took as much time as suited them.

A control group of ten subjects followed a procedure identical with the one just described. Instead of coins, medium gray cardboard discs of identical size were employed. No mention of money was made to this group.

Results

Let us compare the difference between judgments of size of coins and identically sized cardboard discs. Two things can be noted in Figure 1, which presents judgments of experimentals and controls with coins present. First off, coins, socially valued objects, are judged larger in size than gray discs. Secondly, the greater the value of the coin, the greater is the deviation of *apparent* size from *actual* size. The exception to this generalization is the half dollar, overestimation of which falls off below that of a quarter. By way of the sheerest guess one might explain this reversal of the curve

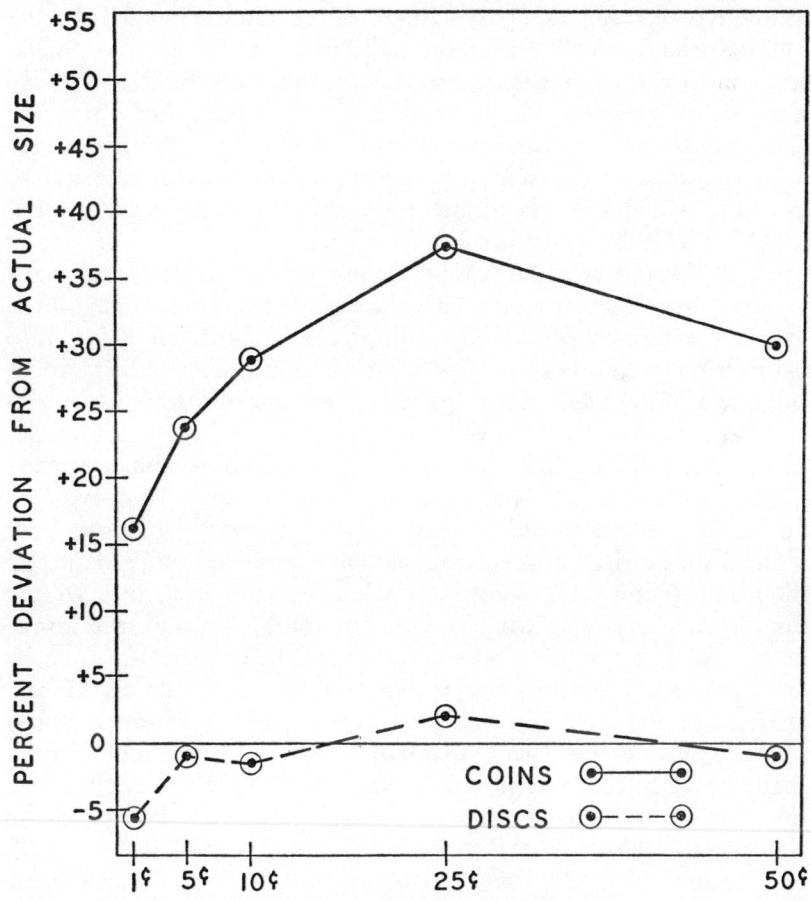

Fig. 1. *Size estimations of coins and discs of same size made by ten-year-olds. (Method of average error.)*

in terms of the lesser reality-value of a half dollar as compared with a quarter for the ten-year-old. A half dollar at that age is, so to speak, almost too valuable to be real! More likely there is some simple autochthonous reason for the reversal. Yet, no such reversal is found in curves plotted for adults.

The difference between experimentals and controls is, of course, highly significant. The variance in overestimation in the experimental groups introduced by using coins of different value is similarly significant. Our results, as handled by the Postman-Bruner (8) adaptation of the analysis of variance to psychophysical data, show that variances due to coin value and due to using discs *versus* coins yield F-scores convertible to P-values of less than .01.

So much for the first hypothesis, that socially valued objects are susceptible to behavioral determinants in proportion to their value. Consider now the second hypothesis, that the greater the subjective need for a socially valued object, the greater will be the role of behavioral determinants of perception. In the second experimental variation, the experimental group was divided into two component groups. One we call the *rich* group, the other the *poor* group, each comprising ten subjects. Well-to-do subjects were drawn from a progressive school in the Boston area, catering to the sons and daughters of prosperous business and professional people. The poor subjects came from a settlement house in one of Boston's slum areas. The reasonable assumption is made that poor children have a greater subjective need for money than rich ones. When the figures presented in Figure 1 are broken down into scores for rich and poor groups, a striking difference will be noted (Figure 2). The poor group overestimates the size of coins considerably more than does the rich. Again there are some irregularities in the curves. The drop-off for the half dollar we have already sought to explain. As for the dip in the rich group's curve at a dime, the explanation is problematical. All curves which we have plotted for adults—and by now we have collected more than two thousand judgments—show this dip. Perhaps it is due to the discrepancy between the relative size and value of the dime, perhaps to some inherent characteristic of the coin itself.

The difference between rich and poor is highly significant, analysis of variance showing that the source of variance is significant beyond the P level of .01. Our second hypothesis cannot, then, be rejected. It is notable too that the interaction between the parameters of economic status and value of coins yields an F-score convertible to a P-value between .05 and .01 which leads to a secondary hypothesis: given perceptual objects of the same class but varying in value, the effect of need for that class of objects will be to accentuate the most valuable objects most, the least valuable least, etc.

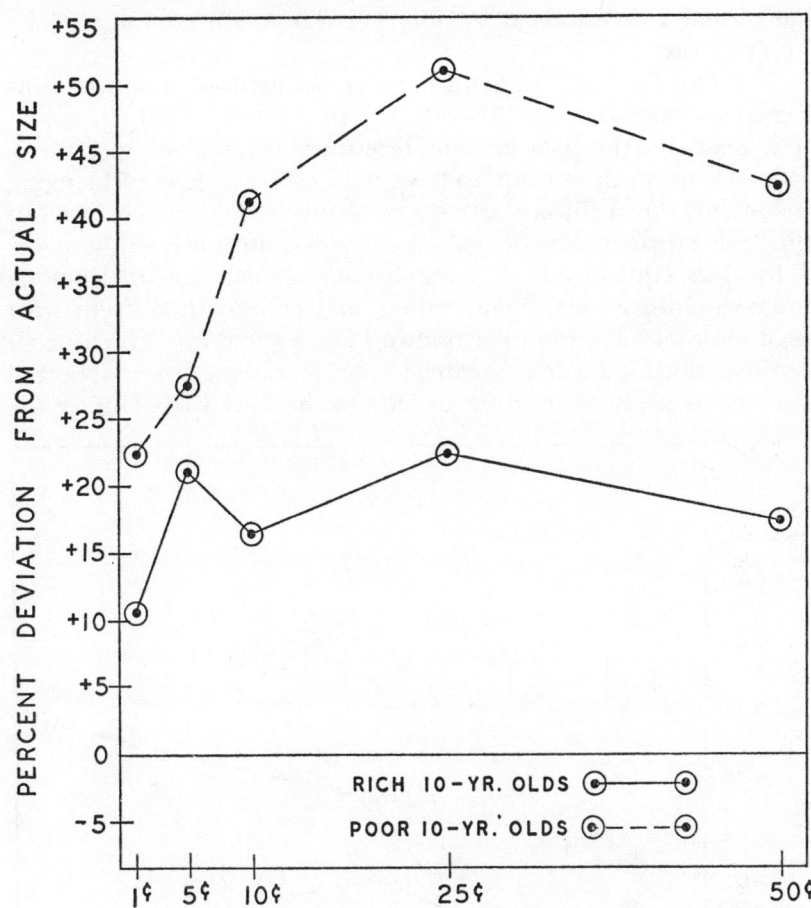

Fig. 2. *Size estimations of coins made by well-to-do and poor ten-year-olds. (Method of average error.)*

What of ambiguity or perceptual equivocality? We have arbitrarily assumed that a situation in which one is judging size from memory is more "equivocal" than one in which the object being judged is in clear view six inches away from the test patch. The assumption is open to serious question, but let us examine what follows from it experimentally. Compare first the judgments of the rich group under conditions like those described: with coin present as compared with coin as a mere memory image. The curves are in Figure 3. It would seem that, for all values below a quarter, equivocality has the effect of making judgments conform more to actual size, aiding, in other words, the operation of autochthonous determinants. For values over a quarter, equivocality favors behavioral factors, making apparent size diverge still more from actual size. For the rich group, with coin *present*, a half dollar is overjudged by 17.4 per cent; with coin *absent*, by 34.7 per cent.

This finding is difficult to interpret by itself. Consider now Figure 4, showing the discrepancy in "absent" and "present" judgments for the poor group. Here there is no crossing. Equivocality seems, in this group, to have the exclusive effect of bringing judgments down toward actual size. Equivocality even brings out the "dime dip" in the poor group. How account for the difference? Why does equivocality liberate behavioral determinants among the rich children for higher values, and depress these factors for poor children? We can offer nothing but a guess, one which needs confirmation by further research. Some years ago, Oeser[1] reported that in his study of children in Dundee he found the fantasy life

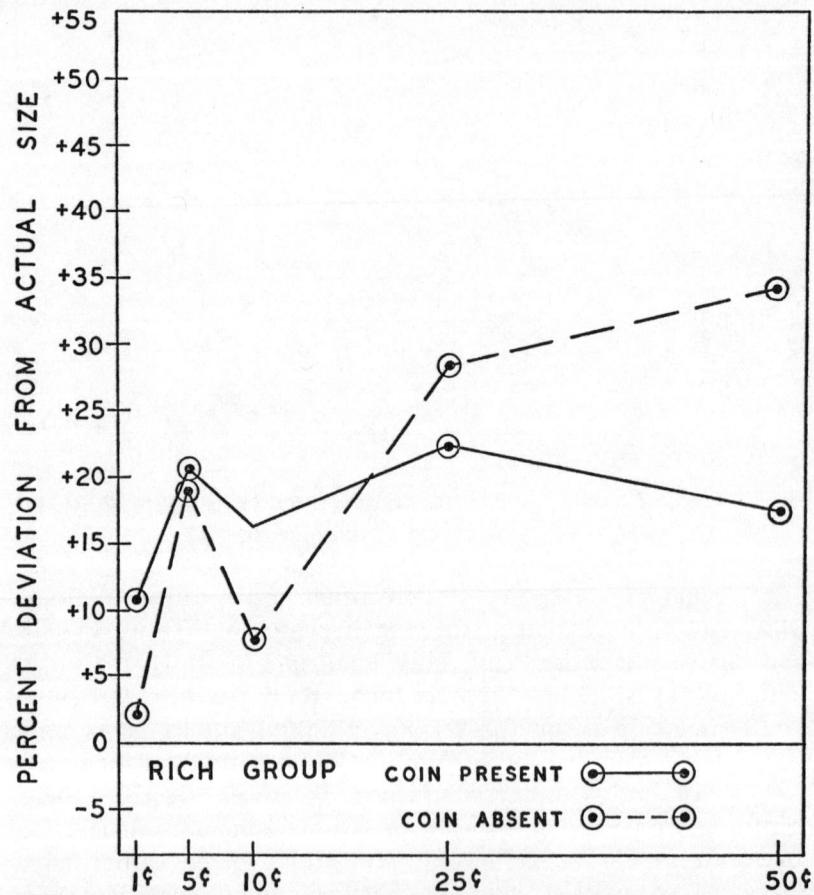

Fig. 3. *Size estimations of coins with coins present and from memory by well-to-do ten-year-olds. (Method of average error.)*

[1] Oeser, O. A. Personal communication, 1939.

of the children of the unemployed strikingly choked off. Asked what they would like to be when grown, normal children of employed parents gave such glamorous replies as cowboy or film star, while children of the unemployed named the rather lowly occupations traditionally followed by members of their class. In the figures just presented, it is our contention that we are witnessing the same phenomenon. In the case of the poor children, judging coin size from memory, a weakened fantasy is substituted for the compelling presence of a valued coin, while among rich children equivocality has the effect of liberating strong and active fantasy.

Are any other explanations available to account for the shape of the curves we have been concerned with here? Weber's Law would predict in all cases a straight line plot parallel to the axis representing actual size. DL should be a constant fraction of

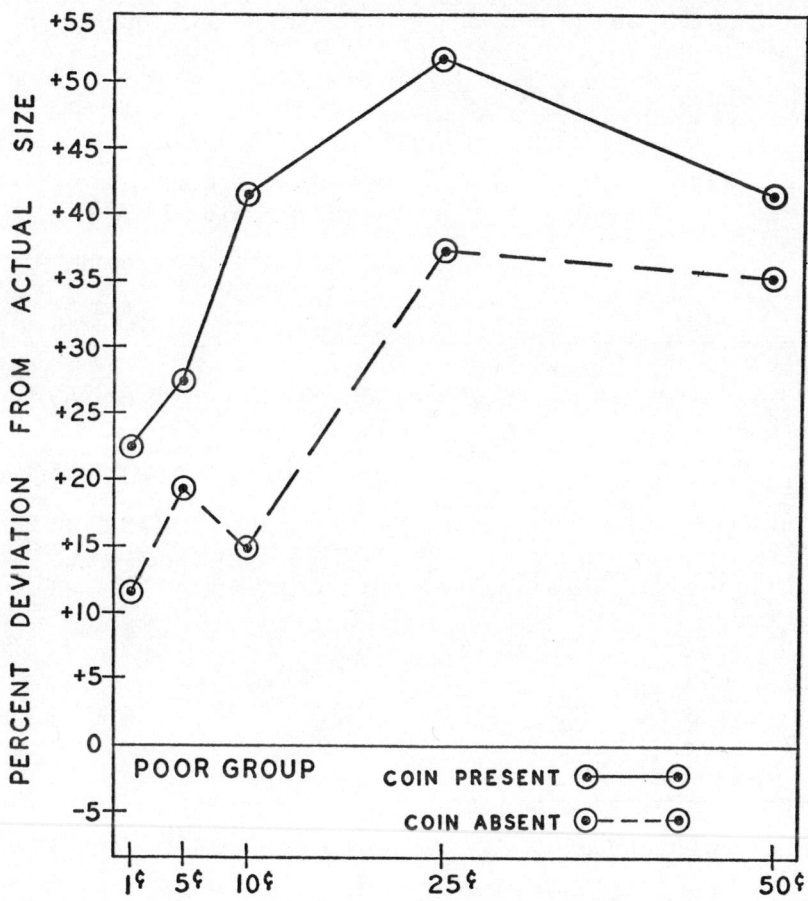

Fig. 4. *Size estimations of coins with coins present and from memory by poor ten-year-olds. (Method of average error.)*

the stimulus, whatever its magnitude. If one were to treat the slope of the curves by reference to Hollingworth's (4) central-tendency effect, one should find a negative rather than a positive slope. All values smaller than the center of the series should appear larger in size; all larger than the center of the series, smaller. Assuming that the Hollingworth effect is mediated by autochthonous factors, then it represents one more autochthonous factor outweighed by the behavioral determinants discussed in the course of this paper.

In conclusion, only one point need be reiterated. For too long now, perception has been virtually the exclusive domain of the Experimental psychologists with a capital E. If we are to reach an understanding of the way in which perception works in everyday life, we social psychologists and students of personality will have to join with the experimental psychologists and reexplore much of this ancient field of perception whose laws for too long have been taken for granted.

Table

PERCENTAGE DEVIATION FROM ACTUAL SIZE OF JUDGMENTS OF COINS AND DISCS UNDER VARIOUS CONDITIONS

Group and Condition	Penny	Nickel	Dime	Quarter	Half Dollar	Number Judgments per Coin
20 0's coin present	16.5	23.9	29.1	37.0	29.6	80
20 0's coin absent	7.2	19.6	11.6	32.8	35.8	80
10 0's disc present	—5.4	—.9	—1.5	1.8	—.8	40
10 rich 0's coin present	10.3	20.4	16.3	22.4	17.4	40
10 rich 0's coin absent	2.6	19.8	7.8	28.3	34.7	40
10 poor 0's coin present	22.7	27.3	41.8	51.6	42.0	40
10 poor 0's coin absent	11.8	19.4	15.4	37.3	36.9	40

Bibliography

1. Ansbacher, H. Perception of number as affected by the monetary value of the objects. *Arch. Psychol.*, 1937, No. 215.

2. Brunswik, E. *Wahrnehmung und Gegenstandswelt.* Vienna, 1934.
3. Ellson, D. G. Experimental extinction of an hallucination produced by sensory conditioning. *J. exp. Psychol.*, 1941, 28: 350-361.
4. Hollingworth, H. L. The inaccuracy of movement. *Arch. Psychol.*, 1909, No. 13.
5. Krechevsky, I. "Hypothesis" versus "chance" in the pre-solution period in sensory discrimination learning. *Univ. Calif. Publ. Psychol.*, 1932, 6:27-44.
6. Leeper, R. A study of a neglected portion of the field of learning—the development of sensory organization. *J. genet. Psychol.*, 1935, 46:41-75.
7. Levine, R., Chein, I., and Murphy, G. The relation of the intensity of a need to the amount of perceptual distortion: a preliminary report. *J. Psychol.*, 1942, 13:283-293.
8. Postman, L., and Bruner, J. S. The reliability of constant errors in psychophysical measurement. *J. Psychol.*, 1946, 21:293-299.
9. Proshansky, H., and Murphy, G. The effects of reward and punishment on perception. *J. Psychol.*, 1942, 13:295-305.
10. Sanford, R. N. The effect of abstinence from food upon imaginal processes: a preliminary experiment. *J. Psychol.*, 1936, 2:129-136.
11. ———. The effect of abstinence from food upon imaginal processes: a further experiment. *J. Psychol.*, 1937, 3:145-159.
12. Sherif, M. A study in some social factors in perception. *Arch. Psychol.*, 1935, No. 187.
13. Thurstone, L. L. *A factorial study of perception.* Chicago: Univ. Chicago Press, 1944.

LEWIS CARROLL/The Gardener's Song

HE THOUGHT he saw an Elephant
That practised on a fife:
He looked again, and found it was
A letter from his wife
"At length I realise," he said
"The bitterness of life!"

He thought he saw a Buffalo
Upon the chimney-piece

He looked again, and found it was
    His sister's husband's niece
"Unless you leave this house," he said
    "I'll call for the police."

He thought he saw a Rattlesnake
    That questioned him in Greek
He looked again, and found it was
    The Middle of Next Week
"The one thing I regret," he said,
    "Is that it cannot speak!"

He thought he saw a Banker's Clerk
    Descending from the bus
He looked again, and found it was
    A Hippopotamus
"If this should stay to dine," he said
    "There won't be much for us!"

He thought he saw a Kangaroo
    That worked a coffee mill:
He looked again and found it was
    A Vegetable Pill
"Were I to swallow this," he said,
    "I should be very ill!"

He thought he saw a Coach-and-Four
    That stood beside his bed
He looked again, and found it was
    A Bear without a Head
"Poor thing," he said, "Poor silly thing
    It's waiting to be fed!"

He thought he saw an Albatross
    That fluttered round the lamp
He looked again, and found it was
    A Penny-Postage-Stamp
"You'd best be getting home," he said,
    "The nights are very damp!"

He thought he saw a Garden-Door
    That opened with a key
He looked again, and found it was
    A Double Rule of three
"And all its mystery," he said
    "Is clear as day to me!"

> He thought he saw an Argument
> That proved he was the Pope
> He looked again, and found it was
> A Bar of Mottled Soap
> "A fact so dread," he faintly said
> "Extinguishes all hope!"

THOMAS HARDY/The Three Strangers

AMONG THE few features of agricultural England which retain an appearance but little modified by the lapse of centuries may be reckoned the high, grassy and furzy downs, coombs, or ewe-leases, as they are indifferently called, that fill a large area of certain counties in the south and southwest. If any mark of human occupation is met with hereon, it usually takes the form of the solitary cottage of some shepherd.

Fifty years ago such a lonely cottage stood on such a down, and may possibly be standing there now. In spite of its loneliness, however, the spot, by actual measurement, was not more than five miles from a county-town. Yet that affected it little. Five miles of irregular upland, during the long inimical seasons, with their sleets, snows, rains, and mists, afford withdrawing space enough to isolate a Timon or a Nebuchadnezzar; much less, in fair weather, to please that less repellent tribe, the poets, philosophers, artists, and others who "conceive and meditate of pleasant things."

Some old earthen camp or barrow, some clump of trees, at least some starved fragment of ancient hedge is usually taken advantage of in the erection of these forlorn dwellings. But, in the present case, such a kind of shelter had been disregarded. Higher Crowstairs, as the house was called, stood quite detached and undefended. The only reason for its precise situation seemed to be the crossing of two footpaths at right angles hard by, which may have crossed there and thus for a good five hundred years. Hence the house was exposed to the elements on all sides. But, though the wind up here blew unmistakably when it did blow, and the rain hit hard whenever it fell, the various weathers of the winter season were not quite so formidable on the coomb as they were imagined to be by dwellers on low ground. The raw rimes were not so pernicious as in the hollows, and the frosts were scarcely so severe. When the shepherd and his family who tenanted the house were pitied for their sufferings from the exposure, they said that upon the whole they were less inconvenienced by "wuzzes and flames" (hoarses and phlegms) than when they had lived by the stream of a snug neighbouring valley.

The night of March 28, 182—, was precisely one of the nights that were wont to call forth these expressions of commiseration. The level rainstorm smote walls, slopes, and hedges like the clothyard shafts of Senlac and Crecy. Such sheep and outdoor animals as had no shelter stood with their buttocks to the winds; while the tails of little birds trying to roost on some scraggy thorn were blown inside-out like umbrellas. The gable-end of the cottage was stained with wet, and the eavesdroppings flapped against the wall. Yet never was commiseration for the shepherd more misplaced. For that cheerful rustic was entertaining a large party in glorification of the christening of his second girl.

The guests had arrived before the rain began to fall, and they were all now assembled in the chief or living room of the dwelling. A glance into the apartment at eight o'clock on this eventful evening would have resulted in the opinion that it was as cosy and comfortable a nook as could be wished for in boisterous weather. The calling of its inhabitant was proclaimed by a number of highly polished sheep crooks without stems that were hung ornamentally over the fireplace, the curl of each shining crook varying from the antiquated type engraved in the patriarchal pictures of old family Bibles to the most approved fashion of the last local sheep-fair. The room was lighted by half a dozen candles having wicks only a trifle smaller than the grease which enveloped them, in candlesticks that were never used but at high-days, holy-days, and family feasts. The lights were scattered about the room, two of them standing on the chimney piece. This position of candles was in itself significant. Candles on the chimney piece always meant a party.

On the hearth, in front of a back-brand to give substance, blazed a fire of thorns, that crackled "like the laughter of the fool."

Nineteen persons were gathered here. Of these, five women, wearing gowns of various bright hues, sat in chairs along the wall; girls shy and not shy filled the window-bench; four men, including Charley Jake the hedge-carpenter, Elijah New the parish-clerk, and John Pitcher, a neighboring dairyman, the shepherd's father-in-law, lolled in the settle; a young man and maid, who were blushing over tentative *pourparlers* on a life-companionship, sat beneath the corner-cupboard; and an elderly engaged man of fifty or upward moved restlessly about from spots where his betrothed was not to the spot where she was. Enjoyment was pretty general, and so much the more prevailed in being unhampered by conventional restrictions. Absolute confidence in each other's good opinion begat perfect ease, while the finishing stroke of manner, amounting to a truly princely serenity, was lent to the majority by the absence of any expression or trait denoting that they wished to get on in the world, enlarge their minds, or do any eclipsing thing whatever—which nowadays so generally nips the bloom and *bonhomie* of all except the two extremes of the social scale.

Shepherd Fennel had married well, his wife being a dairyman's daughter from a vale at a distance, who brought fifty guineas in her pocket—and kept them there, till they should be required for ministering to the needs of a coming family. This frugal woman had been somewhat exercised as to the character that should be given to the gathering. A sit-still party had its advantages; but an undisturbed position of ease in chairs and settles was apt to lead on the men to such an unconscionable deal of toping that they would sometimes fairly drink the house dry. A dancing-party was the alternative; but this, while avoiding the foregoing objection on the score of good drink, had a counterbalancing disadvantage in the matter of good victuals, the ravenous appetites engendered by the exercise causing immense havoc in the buttery. Shepherdess Fennel fell back upon the intermediate plan of mingling short dances with short periods of talk and singing, so as to hinder any ungovernable rage in either. But this scheme was entirely confined to her own gentle mind: the shepherd himself was in the mood to exhibit the most reckless phases of hospitality.

The fiddler was a boy of those parts, about twelve years of age, who had a wonderful dexterity in jigs and reels, though his fingers were so small and short as to necessitate a constant shifting for the high notes, from which he scrambled back to the first position with sounds not of unmixed purity of tone. At seven the shrill tweedle-dee of this youngster had begun, accompanied by a booming ground-bass from Elijah New, the parish-clerk, who had thoughtfully brought with him his favorite musical instrument, the serpent. Dancing was instantaneous, Mrs. Fennel privately enjoining the players on no account to let the dance exceed the length of a quarter of an hour.

But Elijah and the boy, in the excitement of their position, quite forgot the injunction. Moreover, Oliver Giles, a man of seventeen, one of the dancers, who was enamored of his partner, a fair girl of thirty-three rolling years, had recklessly handed a new crown-piece to the musicians, as a bribe to keep going as long as they had muscle and wind. Mrs. Fennel, seeing the steam begin to generate on the countenances of her guests, crossed over and touched the fiddler's elbow and put her hand on the serpent's mouth. But they took no notice, and fearing she might lose her character of genial hostess if she were to interfere too markedly, she retired and sat down helpless. And so the dance whizzed on with cumulative fury, the performers moving in their planet-like courses, direct and retrograde, from apogee to perigee, till the hand of the well-kicked clock at the bottom of the room had traveled over the circumference of an hour.

While these cheerful events were in course of enactment within Fennel's pastoral dwelling, an incident having considerable bearing on the party had occurred in the gloomy night without. Mrs. Fennel's concern about the growing fierceness of the dance corresponded in point of time with the ascent of a human figure to the solitary hill of Higher Crowstairs from the direction of the distant town. This personage strode on through the rain without a pause, following the little-worn path which, further on in its course, skirted the shepherd's cottage.

It was nearly the time of full moon, and on this account, though the sky was lined with a uniform sheet of dripping cloud, ordinary objects out of doors were readily visible. The sad, wan light revealed the lonely pedestrian to be a man of supple frame; his gait suggested that he had somewhat passed the period of perfect and instinctive agility, though not so far as to be otherwise than rapid of motion when occasion required. At a rough guess, he might have been about forty years of age. He appeared tall, but a recruiting sergeant, or other person accustomed to the judging of men's heights by the eye, would have discerned that this was chiefly owing to his gauntness, and that he was not more than five-feet-eight or nine.

Notwithstanding the regularity of his tread, there was caution in it, as in that of one who mentally feels his way; and despite the fact that it was not a black coat nor a dark garment of any sort that he wore, there was something about him which suggested that he naturally belonged to the black-coated tribes of men. His clothes were of fustian, and his boots hobnailed, yet in his progress he showed not the mud-accustomed bearing of hobnailed and fustianed peasantry.

By the time that he had arrived abreast of the shepherd's premises the rain came down, or rather came along, with yet more determined violence. The outskirts of the little settlement partially broke the force of wind and rain, and this induced him to stand still. The most salient of the shepherd's domestic erections was an empty sty at the forward corner of his hedgeless garden, for in these latitudes the principle of masking the homelier features of your establishment by a conventional frontage was unknown. The traveler's eye was attracted to this small building by the pallid shine of the wet slates that covered it. He turned aside, and, finding it empty, stood under the pent-roof for shelter.

While he stood, the boom of the serpent within the adjacent house, and the lesser strains of the fiddler, reached the spot as an accompaniment to the surging hiss of the flying rain on the sod, its louder beating on the cabbage-leaves of the garden, on the eight or ten beehives just discernible by the path, and its dripping from the eaves into a row of buckets and pans that had been placed under the walls of the cottage. For at Higher Crowstairs, as at all such elevated domiciles, the grand difficulty of housekeeping was an insufficiency of water; and a casual rainfall was utilized by turning out, as catchers, every utensil that the house contained. Some queer stories might be told of the contrivances for economy in suds and dishwaters that are absolutely necessitated in upland habitations during the droughts of summer. But at this season there were no such exigencies; a mere acceptance of what the skies bestowed was sufficient for an abundant store.

At last the notes of the serpent ceased and the house was silent. This cessation of activity aroused the solitary pedestrian from the reverie into which he had elapsed, and, emerging from the shed, with an apparently new intention, he walked up the path to the house-door. Arrived here, his first act was to kneel down on a large stone beside the row of vessels, and to drink a copious draught from one of them. Having quenched his thirst, he rose and lifted his hand to knock, but paused with his eye upon the panel. Since the dark surface of the wood revealed absolutely nothing, it was evident that he must be mentally looking through the door, as if he wished to measure thereby all the possibilities that a house of this sort might include, and how they might bear upon the question of his entry.

In his indecision he turned and surveyed the scene around. Not a soul was anywhere visible. The garden path stretched downward from his feet, gleaming like the track of a snail; the roof of the little well (mostly dry), the well-cover, the top rail of the garden-gate, were varnished with the same dull liquid glaze; while, far away in the vale, a faint whiteness of more than usual extent showed that the rivers were high in the meads. Beyond all this winked a few bleared lamplights through the beating drops—lights that denoted the situation of the county-town from which he had appeared to come. The absence of all notes of life in that direction seemed to clinch his intentions, and he knocked at the door.

Within, a desultory chat had taken the place of movement and musical sound. The hedge-carpenter was suggesting a song to the company, which nobody just then was inclined to undertake, so that the knock afforded a not unwelcome diversion.

"Walk in!" said the shepherd, promptly.

The latch clicked upward, and out of the night our pedestrian appeared upon the door-mat. The shepherd arose, snuffed two of the nearest candles, and turned to look at him.

Their light disclosed that the stranger was dark in complexion and not unprepossessing as to feature. His hat, which for a moment he did not remove, hung low over his eyes, without concealing that they were large, open, and determined, moving with a flash rather than a glance round the room. He seemed pleased with his survey, and, baring his shaggy head, said, in a rich, deep voice: "The rain is so heavy, friends, that I ask leave to come in and rest awhile."

"To be sure, Stranger," said the shepherd. "And faith, you've been lucky in choosing your time, for we are having a bit of a fling for a glad cause—though, to be sure, a man could hardly wish that glad cause to happen more than once a year."

"Nor less," spoke up a woman. "For 'tis best to get your family over and done with, as soon as you can, so as to be all the earlier out of the fag o't."

"And what may be this glad cause?" asked the stranger.

"A birth and christening," said the shepherd.

The stranger hoped his host might not be made unhappy either by too many or too few of such episodes and, being invited by a gesture to a pull at the mug, he readily acquiesced. His manner, which, before entering, had been so dubious, was now altogether that of a careless and candid man.

"Late to be traipsing athwart this coomb—hey?" said the engaged man of fifty.

"Late it is, Master, as you say.—I'll take a seat in the chimney corner, if you have nothing to urge against it, Ma'am; for I am a little moist on the side that was next the rain."

Mrs. Shepherd Fennel assented, and made room for the self-invited comer, who, having got completely inside the chimney corner, stretched out his legs and arms with the expansiveness of a person quite at home.

"Yes, I am rather cracked in the vamp," he said freely, seeing that the eyes of the shepherd's wife fell upon his boots, "and I am not well fitted either. I have had some rough times lately, and have been forced to pick up what I can get in the way of wearing, but I must find a suit better fit for working-days when I reach home."

"One of hereabouts?" she inquired.

"Not quite that—further up the country."

"I thought so. And so be I; and by your tongue you come from my neighborhood."

"But you would hardly have heard of me," he said quickly. "My time would be long before yours, Ma'am, you see."

This testimony to the youthfulness of his hostess had the effect of stopping her cross-examination.

"There is only one thing more wanted to make me happy,"

continued the newcomer, "and that is a little baccy, which I am sorry to say I am out of."

"I'll fill your pipe," said the shepherd.

"I must ask you to lend me a pipe likewise."

"A smoker, and no pipe about 'ee?"

"I have dropped it somewhere on the road."

The shepherd filled and handed him a new clay pipe, saying, as he did so, "Hand me your baccy-box—I'll fill that too, now I am about it."

The man went through the movement of searching his pockets.

"Lost that too?" said his entertainer, with some surprise.

"I am afraid so," said the man with some confusion. "Give it to me in a screw of paper." Lighting his pipe at the candle with a suction that drew the whole flame into the bowl, he resettled himself in the corner and bent his looks upon the faint steam from his damp legs, as if he wished to say no more.

Meanwhile the general body of guests had been taking little notice of this visitor by reason of an absorbing discussion in which they were engaged with the band about a tune for the next dance. The matter being settled, they were about to stand up when an interruption came in the shape of another knock at the door.

At sound of the same the man in the chimney corner took up the poker and began stirring the brands as if doing it thoroughly were the one aim of his existence; and a second time the shepherd said, "Walk in!" In a moment another man stood upon the straw-woven door-mat. He too was a stranger.

This individual was one of a type radically different from the first. There was more of the commonplace in his manner, and a certain jovial cosmopolitanism sat upon his features. He was several years older than the first arrival, his hair being slightly frosted, his eyebrows bristly, and his whiskers cut back from his cheeks. His face was rather full and flabby, and yet it was not altogether a face without power. A few grog-blossoms marked the neighborhood of his nose. He flung back his long drab greatcoat, revealing that beneath it he wore a suit of cinder-gray shade throughout, large heavy seals, of some metal or other that would take a polish, dangling from his fob as his only personal ornament. Shaking the water drops from his low-crowned glazed hat, he said, "I must ask for a few minutes' shelter, comrades, or I shall be wetted to my skin before I get to Casterbridge."

"Make yourself at home, Master," said the shepherd, perhaps a trifle less heartily than on the first occasion. Not that Fennel had the least tinge of niggardliness in his composition; but the room was far from large, spare chairs were not numerous, and damp companions were not altogether desirable at close quarters for the women and girls in their bright-colored gowns.

However, the second comer, after taking off his greatcoat, and hanging his hat on a nail in one of the ceiling-beams as if he had been specially invited to put it there, advanced and sat down at the table. This had been pushed so closely into the chimney corner, to give all available room to the dancers, that its inner edge grazed the elbow of the man who had ensconced himself by the fire; and thus the two strangers were brought into close companionship. They nodded to each other by way of breaking the ice of unacquaintance, and the first stranger handed his neighbor the family mug—a huge vessel of brown ware, having its upper edge worn away like a threshold by the rub of whole generations of thirsty lips that had gone the way of all flesh, and bearing the following inscription burnt upon its rotund side in yellow letters:

THERE IS NO FUN
UNTIL i CUM.

The other man, nothing loth, raised the mug to his lips, and drank on, and on, and on—till a curious blueness overspread the countenance of the shepherd's wife, who had regarded with no little surprise the first stranger's free offer to the second of what did not belong to him to dispense.

"I knew it!" said the toper to the shepherd with much satisfaction. "When I walked up your garden before coming in, and saw the hives all of a row, I said to myself, 'Where there's bees there's honey, and where there's honey there's mead.' But mead of such a truly comfortable sort as this I really didn't expect to meet in my older days." He took yet another pull at the mug, till it assumed an ominous elevation.

"Glad you enjoy it!" said the shepherd warmly.

"It is goodish mead," assented Mrs. Fennel, with an absence of enthusiasm which seemed to say that it was possible to buy praise for one's cellar at too heavy a price. "It is trouble enough to make—and really I hardly think we shall make any more. For honey sells well, and we ourselves can make shift with a drop o' small mead and metheglin for common use from the comb-washings."

"Oh, but you'll never have the heart!" reproachfully cried the stranger in cinder-gray, after taking up the mug a third time and setting it down empty. "I love mead, when 'tis old like this, as I love to go to church o' Sundays, or to relieve the needy any day of the week."

"Ha, ha, ha!" said the man in the chimney corner, who, in

spite of the taciturnity induced by the pipe of tobacco, could not or would not refrain from this slight testimony to his comrade's humor.

Now the old mead of those days, brewed of the purest first-year or maiden honey, four pounds to the gallon—with its due complement of white of eggs, cinnamon, ginger, cloves, mace, rosemary, yeast, and processes of working, bottling, and cellaring—tasted remarkably strong; but it did not taste so strong as it actually was. Hence, presently, the stranger in cinder-gray at the table, moved by its creeping influence, unbuttoned his waistcoat, threw himself back in his chair, spread his legs, and made his presence felt in various ways.

"Well, well, as I say," he resumed, "I am going to Casterbridge, and to Casterbridge I must go. I should have been almost there by this time; but the rain drove me into your dwelling, and I'm not sorry for it."

"You don't live in Casterbridge?" said the shepherd.

"Not as yet; though I shortly mean to move there."

"Going to set up in trade, perhaps?"

"No, no," said the shepherd's wife. "It is easy to see that the gentleman is rich, and don't want to work at anything."

The cinder-gray stranger paused, as if to consider whether he would accept that definition of himself. He presently rejected it by answering, "Rich is not quite the word for me, Dame. I do work, and I must work. And even if I only get to Casterbridge by midnight I must begin work there at eight tomorrow morning. Yes, het or wet, blow or snow, famine or sword, my day's work tomorrow must be done."

"Poor man! Then, in spite o' seeming, you be worse off than we," replied the shepherd's wife.

"'Tis the nature of my trade, men and maidens. 'Tis the nature of my trade more than my poverty.... But really and truly I must up and off, or I shan't get a lodging in the town." However, the speaker did not move, and directly added, "There's time for one more draught of friendship before I go; and I'd perform it at once if the mug were not dry."

"Here's a mug o' small," said Mrs. Fennel. "Small, we call it, though to be sure 'tis only the first wash o' the combs."

"No," said the stranger, disdainfully. "I won't spoil your first kindness by partaking o' your second."

"Certainly not," broke in Fennel. "We don't increase and multiply every day, and I'll fill the mug again." He went away to the dark place under the stairs where the barrel stood. The shepherdess followed him.

"Why should you do this?" she said, reproachfully, as soon

as they were alone. "He's emptied it once, though it held enough for ten people; and now he's not contented wi' the small, but must needs call for more o' the strong! And a stranger unbeknown to any of us. For my part, I don't like the look o' the man at all."

"But he's in the house, my honey; and 'tis a wet night, and a christening. Daze it, what's a cup of mead more or less? There'll be plenty more next bee-burning."

"Very well—this time, then," she answered, looking wistfully at the barrel. "But what is the man's calling, and where is he one of, that he should come in and join us like this?"

"I don't know. I'll ask him again."

The catastrophe of having the mug drained dry at one pull by the stranger in cinder-gray was effectually guarded against this time by Mrs. Fennel. She poured out his allowance in a small cup, keeping the large one at a discreet distance from him. When he had tossed off his portion the shepherd renewed his inquiry about the stranger's occupation.

The latter did not immediately reply, and the man in the chimney corner, with sudden demonstrativeness, said, "Anybody may know my trade—I'm a wheelwright."

"A very good trade for these parts," said the shepherd.

"And anybody may know mine—if they've the sense to find it out," said the stranger in cinder-gray.

"You may generally tell what a man is by his claws," observed the hedge-carpenter, looking at his own hands. "My fingers be as full of thorns as an old pincushion is of pins."

The hands of the man in the chimney corner instinctively sought the shade, and he gazed into the fire as he resumed his pipe. The man at the table took up the hedge-carpenter's remark, and added smartly, "True; but the oddity of my trade is that, instead of setting a mark upon me, it sets a mark upon my customers."

No observation being offered by anybody in elucidation of this enigma, the shepherd's wife once more called for a song. The same obstacles presented themselves as at the former time—one had no voice, another had forgotten the first verse. The stranger at the table, whose soul had now risen to a good working temperature, relieved the difficulty by exclaiming that, to start the company, he would sing himself. Thrusting one thumb into the armhole of his waistcoat, he waved the other hand in the air, and, with an extemporizing gaze at the shining sheep-crooks above the mantelpiece, began:

>O my trade it is the rarest one,
>   Simple shepherds all—
>My trade is a sight to see;

> *For my customers I tie, and take them up on high,*
> *And waft 'em to a far countree!*

The room was silent when he had finished the verse—with one exception, that of the man in the chimney corner, who at the singer's word, "Chorus!" joined him in a deep bass voice of musical relish:

> *And waft 'em to a far countree!*

Oliver Giles, John Pitcher the dairyman, the parish-clerk, the engaged man of fifty, the row of young women against the wall, seemed lost in thought not of the gayest kind. The shepherd looked meditatively on the ground, the shepherdess gazed keenly at the singer, and with some suspicion; she was doubting whether this stranger were merely singing an old song from recollection, or was composing one there and then for the occasion. All were as perplexed at the obscure revelation as the guests at Belshazzar's Feast, except the man in the chimney corner, who quietly said, "Second verse, stranger," and smoked on.

The singer thoroughly moistened himself from his lips inward, and went on with the next stanza as requested:

> *My tools are but common ones,*
>   *Simple shepherds all—*
> *My tools are no sight to see;*
> *A little hempen string, and a post whereon to swing,*
>   *Are implements enough for me!*

Shepherd Fennel glanced round. There was no longer any doubt that the stranger was answering his question rhythmically. The guests one and all started back with suppressed exclamations. The young woman engaged to the man of fifty fainted halfway, and would have proceeded, but finding him wanting an alacrity for catching her she sat down trembling.

"Oh, he's the—!" whispered the people in the background, mentioning the name of an ominous public officer. "He's come to do it! 'Tis to be at Casterbridge jail tomorrow—the man for sheep-stealing—the poor clockmaker we heard of, who used to live away at Shottsford and had no work to do—Timothy Summers, whose family were astarving, and so he went out of Shottsford by the highroad, and took a sheep in open daylight, defying the farmer and the farmer's wife and the farmer's lad, and every man jack among 'em. He" (and they nodded toward the stranger of the deadly trade) "is come from up the country to do it because there's not enough to do in his own county-town, and he's got the place here now our own county-man's dead; he's going to live in the same cottage under the prison wall."

The stranger in cinder-gray took no notice of this whispered string of observations, but again wetted his lips. Seeing that his friend in the chimney corner was the only one who reciprocated his joviality in any way, he held out his cup toward that appreciative comrade, who also held out his own. They clinked together, the eyes of the rest of the room hanging upon the singer's actions. He parted his lips for the third verse; but at that moment another knock was audible upon the door. This time the knock was faint and hesitating.

The company seemed scared; the shepherd looked with consternation toward the entrance, and it was with some effort that he resisted his alarmed wife's deprecatory glance, and uttered for the third time the welcoming words, "Walk in!"

The door was gently opened, and another man stood upon the mat. He, like those who had preceded him, was a stranger. This time it was a short, small personage, of fair complexion, and dressed in a decent suit of dark clothes.

"Can you tell me the way to—?" he began: when, gazing round the room to observe the nature of the company among whom he had fallen, his eyes lighted on the stranger in cinder-gray. It was just at the instant when the latter, who had thrown his mind into his song with such a will that he scarcely heeded the interruption, silenced all whispers and inquiries by bursting into his third verse:

> *Tomorrow is my working day,*
> *   Simple shepherds all—*
> *Tomorrow is a working day for me:*
> *For the farmer's sheep is slain, and the lad who did it ta'en,*
> *And on his soul may God ha' merc-y!*

The stranger in the chimney corner, waving cups with the singer so heartily that his mead splashed over on the hearth, repeated in his bass voice as before:

> *And on his soul may God ha' merc-y!*

All this time the third stranger had been standing in the doorway. Finding now that he did not come forward or go on speaking, the guests particularly regarded him. They noticed to their surprise that he stood before them the picture of abject terror —his knees trembling, his hand shaking so violently that the door-latch by which he supported himself rattled audibly: his white lips were parted, and his eyes fixed on the merry officer of justice in the middle of the room. A moment more and he had turned, closed the door, and fled.

"What a man can it be?" said the shepherd.

The rest, between the awfulness of their late discovery and the odd conduct of this third visitor, looked as if they knew not what to think, and said nothing. Instinctively they withdrew further and further from the grim gentleman in their midst, whom some of them seemed to take for the Prince of Darkness himself, till they formed a remote circle, an empty space of floor being left between them and him—

... *circulas, cujus centrum diabolus.*

The room was so silent—though there were more than twenty people in it—that nothing could be heard but the patter of the rain against the window-shutters, accompanied by the occasional hiss of a stray drop that fell down the chimney into the fire, and the steady puffing of the man in the corner, who had now resumed his pipe of long clay.

The stillness was unexpectedly broken. The distant sound of a gun reverberated through the air—apparently from the direction of the county-town.

"Be jiggered!" cried the stranger who had sung the song, jumping up.

"What does that mean?" asked several.

"A prisoner escaped from the jail—that's what it means."

All listened. The sound was repeated, and none of them spoke but the man in the chimney corner, who said quietly, "I've often been told that in this county they fire a gun at such times; but I never heard it till now."

"I wonder if it is *my* man?" murmured the personage in cinder-gray.

"Surely it is!" said the shepherd involuntarily. "And surely we've zeed him! The little man who looked in at the door by now, and quivered like a leaf when he zeed ye and heard your song!"

"His teeth chattered, and the breath went out of his body," said the dairyman.

"And his heart seemed to sink within him like a stone," said Oliver Giles.

"And he bolted as if he'd been shot at," said the hedge-carpenter.

"True—his teeth chattered, and his heart seemed to sink;

and he bolted as if he'd been shot at," slowly summed up the man in the chimney corner.

"I didn't notice it," remarked the hangman.

"We were all awondering what made him run off in such a fright," faltered one of the women against the wall, "and now 'tis explained!"

The firing of the alarm-gun went on at intervals, low and sullenly, and their suspicions became a certainty. The sinister gentleman in cinder-gray roused himself. "Is there a constable here?" he asked, in thick tones. "If so, let him step forward."

The engaged man of fifty stepped quavering out from the wall, his betrothed beginning to sob on the back of the chair.

"You are a sworn constable?"

"I be, Sir."

"Then pursue the criminal at once, with assistance, and bring him back here. He can't have gone far."

"I will, Sir, I will—when I've got my staff. I'll go home and get it, and come sharp here, and start in a body."

"Staff!—never mind your staff; the man'll be gone!"

"But I can't do nothing without my staff—can I, William, and John, and Charles Jake? No; for there's the king's royal crown apainted on en in yaller and gold, and the lion and the unicorn, so as when I raise en up and hit my prisoner, 'tis made a lawful blow thereby. I wouldn't 'tempt to take up a man without my staff—no, not I. If I hadn't the law to gie me courage, why, instead o' my taking up him he might take up me!"

"Now, I'm a king's man myself, and can give you authority enough for this," said the formidable officer in gray. "Now then, all of ye, be ready. Have ye any lanterns?"

"Yes—have ye any lanterns?—I demand it!" said the constable.

"And the rest of you able-bodied—"

"Able-bodied men—yes—the rest of ye!" said the constable.

"Have you some good stout staves and pitchforks—"

"Staves and pitchforks—in the name o' the law! And take 'em in yer hands and go in quest, and do as we in authority tell ye!"

Thus aroused, the men prepared to give chase. The evidence was, indeed, though circumstantial, so convincing, that but little argument was needed to show the shepherd's guests that after what they had seen it would look very much like connivance if they did not instantly pursue the unhappy third stranger, who could not as yet have gone more than a few hundred yards over such uneven country.

A shepherd is always well provided with lanterns; and,

lighting these hastily, and with hurdle-staves in their hands, they poured out of the door, taking a direction along the crest of the hill, away from the town, the rain having fortunately a little abated.

Disturbed by the noise, possibly by unpleasant dreams of her baptism, the child who had been christened began to cry heart-brokenly in the room overhead. These notes of grief came down through the chinks of the floor to the ears of the women below, who jumped up one by one, and seemed glad of the excuse to ascend and comfort the baby, for the incidents of the last half-hour greatly oppressed them. Thus in the space of two or three minutes the room on the ground-floor was deserted quite.

But it was not for long. Hardly had the sound of footsteps died away when a man returned round the corner of the house from the direction the pursuers had taken. Peeping in at the door, and seeing nobody there, he entered leisurely. It was the stranger of the chimney corner, who had gone out with the rest. The motive of his return was shown by his helping himself to a cut piece of skimmer-cake that lay on a ledge beside where he had sat, and which he had apparently forgotten to take with him. He also poured out half a cup more mead from the quantity that remained, ravenously eating and drinking these as he stood. He had not finished when another figure came in just as quietly—his friend in cinder-gray.

"Oh—you here?" said the latter, smiling. "I thought you had gone to help in the capture." And this speaker also revealed the object of his return by looking solicitously round for the fascinating mug of old mead.

"And I thought you had gone," said the other, continuing his skimmer-cake with some effort.

"Well, on second thoughts, I felt there were enough without me," said the first confidentially, "and such a night as it is, too. Besides, 'tis the business o' the Government to take care of its criminals—not mine."

"True; so it is. And I felt as you did, that there were enough without me."

"I don't want to break my limbs running over the humps and hollows of this wild country."

"Nor I neither, between you and me."

"These shepherd-people are used to it—simpled-minded souls, you know, stirred up to anything in a moment. They'll have him ready for me before the morning, and no trouble to me at all."

"They'll have him, and we shall have saved ourselves all labor in the matter."

"True, true. Well, my way is to Casterbridge; and 'tis as

much as my legs will do to take me that far. Going the same way?"

"No, I am sorry to say! I have to get home over there" (he nodded indefinitely to the right), "and I feel as you do, that it is quite enough for my legs to do before bedtime."

The other had by this time finished the mead in the mug, after which, shaking hands heartily at the door, and wishing each other well, they went their several ways.

In the meantime the company of pursuers had reached the end of the hog's-back elevation which dominated this part of the down. They had decided on no particular plan of action; and, finding that the man of the baleful trade was no longer in their company, they seemed quite unable to form any such plan now. They descended in all directions down the hill, and straightway several of the party fell into the snare set by Nature for all misguided midnight ramblers over this part of the cretaceous formation. The "lanchets," or flint slopes, which belted the escarpment at intervals of a dozen yards, took the less cautious ones unawares, and losing their footing on the rubbly steep they slid sharply downward, the lanterns rolling from their hands to the bottom, and there lying on their sides till the horn was scorched through.

When they had again gathered themselves together, the shepherd, as the man who knew the country best, took the lead, and guided them round these treacherous inclines. The lanterns, which seemed rather to dazzle their eyes and warn the fugitive than to assist them in the exploration, were extinguished, due silence was observed; and in this more rational order they plunged into the vale. It was a grassy, briery, moist defile, affording some shelter to any person who had sought it; but the party perambulated it in vain, and ascended on the other side. Here they wandered apart, and after an interval closed together again to report progress. At the second time of closing in they found themselves near a lonely ash, the single tree on this part of the coomb, probably sown there by a passing bird some fifty years before. And here, standing a little to one side of the trunk, as motionless as the trunk itself appeared the man they were in quest of, his outline being well defined against the sky beyond. The band noiselessly drew up and faced him.

"Your money or your life!" said the constable sternly to the still figure.

"No, no," whispered John Pitcher. " 'Tisn't our side ought to say that. That's the doctrine of vagabonds like him, and we be on the side of the law."

"Well, well," replied the constable, impatiently; "I must say something, mustn't I? and if you had all the weight o' this undertaking upon your mind, perhaps you'd say the wrong thing, too!—Prisoner at the bar, surrender in the name of the Father—the Crown, I mane!"

The man under the tree seemed now to notice them for the first time, and, giving them no opportunity whatever for exhibiting their courage, he strolled slowly toward them. He was, indeed, the little man, the third stranger; but his trepidation had in a great measure gone.

"Well, travelers," he said, "did I hear you speak to me?"

"You did; you've got to come and be our prisoner at once!" said the constable. "We arrest 'ee on the charge of not biding in Casterbridge jail in a decent proper manner to be hung tomorrow morning. Neighbors, do your duty, and seize the culpet!"

On hearing the charge, the man seemed enlightened, and, saying not another word, resigned himself with preternatural civility to the search-party, who, with their staves in their hands, surrounded him on all sides, and marched him back toward the shepherd's cottage.

It was eleven o'clock by the time they arrived. The light shining from the open door, a sound of men's voices within, proclaimed to them as they approached the house that some new events had arisen in their absence. On entering they discovered the shepherd's livingroom to be invaded by two officers from Casterbridge jail, and a well-known magistrate who lived at the nearest country-seat, intelligence of the escape having become generally circulated.

"Gentlemen," said the constable, "I have brought back your man—not without risk and danger; but every one must do his duty! He is inside this circle of able-bodied persons, who have lent me useful aid, considering their ignorance of Crown work.—Men, bring forward your prisoner!" And the third stranger was led to the light.

"Who is this?" said one of the officials.

"The man," said the constable.

"Certainly not," said the turnkey; and the first corroborated his statement.

"But how can it be otherwise?" asked the constable. "Or why was he so terrified at sight o' the singing instrument of the law who sat there?" Here he related the strange behavior of the third stranger on entering the house during the hangman's song.

"Can't understand it," said the officer coolly. "All I know is that it is not the condemned man. He's quite a different character from this one; a gauntish fellow, with dark hair and eyes, rather good-looking, and with a musical bass voice that if you heard it once you'd never mistake as long as you lived."

"Why, souls—'twas the man in the chimney corner!"

"Hey—what?" said the magistrate, coming forward after inquiring particulars from the shepherd in the background. "Haven't you got the man after all?"

"Well, Sir," said the constable, "he's the man we were in search of, that's true; and yet he's not the man we were in search of. For the man we were in search of was not the man we wanted, Sir, if you understand my everyday way; for 'twas the man in the chimney corner!"

"A pretty kettle of fish altogether!" said the magistrate. "You had better start for the other man at once."

The prisoner now spoke for the first time. The mention of the man in the chimney corner seemed to have moved him as nothing else could do. "Sir," he said, stepping forward to the magistrate, "take no more trouble about me. The time is come when I may as well speak. I have done nothing; my crime is that the condemned man is my brother. Early this afternoon I left home at Shottsford to tramp it all the way to Casterbridge jail to bid him farewell. I was benighted, and called here to rest and ask the way. When I opened the door I saw before me the very man, my brother, that I thought to see in the condemned cell at Casterbridge. He was in this chimney corner; and jammed close to him, so that he could not have got out if he had tried, was the executioner who'd come to take his life, singing a song about it and not knowing that it was his victim who was close by, joining in to save appearances. My brother looked a glance of agony at me, and I know he meant, 'Don't reveal what you see; my life depends on it.' I was so terror-stuck that I could hardly stand, and, not knowing what I did, I turned and hurried away."

The narrator's manner and tone had the stamp of truth, and his story made a great impression on all around. "And do you know where your brother is at the present time?" asked the magistrate.

"I do not. I have never seen him since I closed this door."

"I can testify to that, for we've been between ye ever since," said the constable.

"Where does he think to fly to?—what is his occupation?"

"He's a watch-and-clock-maker, Sir."

" 'A said 'a was a wheelwright—a wicked rogue," said the constable.

"The wheels of clocks and watches he meant, no doubt," said Shepherd Fennel. "I thought his hands were palish for's trade."

"Well, it appears to me that nothing can be gained by retaining this poor man in custody," said the magistrate; "your business lies with the other, unquestionably."

And so the little man was released off-hand; but he looked nothing the less sad on that account, it being beyond the power of magistrate or constable to raze out the written troubles in his brain, for they concerned another who he regarded with more solicitude than himself. When this was done, and the man had gone his way, the night was found to be so far advanced that it was deemed useless to renew the search before the next morning.

Next day, accordingly, the quest for the clever sheep-stealer became general and keen, to all appearance at least. But the intended punishment was cruelly disproportioned to the transgression, and the sympathy of a great many country-folk in that district was strongly on the side of the fugitive. Moreover, his marvelous coolness and daring in hob-and-nobbing with the hangman, under the unprecedented circumstances of the shepherd's party, won their admiration. So that it may be questioned if all those who ostensibly made themselves so busy in exploring woods and fields and lanes were quite so thorough when it came to the private examination of their own lofts and outhouses. Stories were afloat of a mysterious figure being occasionally seen in some old overgrown trackway or other, remote from turnpike roads, but when a search was instituted in any of these suspected quarters nobody was found. Thus the days and weeks passed without tidings.

In brief, the bass-voiced man of the chimney corner was never recaptured. Some said that he went across the sea, others that he did not, but buried himself in the depths of a populous city. At any rate, the gentleman in cinder-gray never did his morning's work at Casterbridge, nor met anywhere at all, for business purposes, the genial comrade with whom he had passed an hour of relaxation in the lonely house on the coomb.

The grass has long been green on the graves of Shepherd Fennel and his frugal wife; the guests who made up the christening party have mainly followed their entertainers to the tomb; the baby in whose honor they all had met is a matron in the sere and yellow leaf. But the arrival of the three strangers at the shepherd's that night, and the details connected therewith, is a story as well-known as ever in the country about Higher Crowstairs.

V

THE SIXTH SENSE

From earliest times, examinations of dreams have raised all sorts of speculations regarding the true nature of the human psyche. As the most tangible "proof" of the separation between the spiritual and the physical, dreams were the first phenomena subjected to careful analysis. They are probably the source of our earliest speculations about both telepathy (communication without speech) and psychokinesis (transportation of objects through the use of psychic energy).

The prophetic dream—in which we are given a message about some future event—has its source in the basic emotional needs of human beings. As Aristotle realized long ago, most dreams express the fulfillment of hidden desires. Sigmund Freud added to the idea of the dream as wish fulfillment his theory of psychic determinism. In other words, the analysis of any dream, no matter how chaotic, should show the same forces at work creating the dream as are creating our conscious behavior. Every dream, therefore, including a prophetic dream, could be interpreted through the use of psychoanalytic techniques. If a man dreamed of his brother's death, then there could be no doubt that in some secret corner of his mind, he wholeheartedly desired his brother's death. If the brother lived, then the dream merely expressed a wish fulfillment. If his brother died, then the dream became "prophetic." And if, in his dream, the man foresaw not only his brother's death but the specific manner in which that death occurred, then we must be right in assuming that the dreamer had some information that led him into the uncannily correct prediction. That information, said Freud, was lodged in the dreamer's unconscious: a collection of facts, impressions, and events which, heightened by the emotional intensity of the relationship, might well allow the dreamer to predict the nature of his brother's death.

In writing of telepathy, Freud attempted to use the same scientific objectivity. Like many analysts in close emotional rapport with their patients, Freud had experienced "telepathic" communi-

cations: patients often seemed to know exactly what was in his mind. Freud even advanced the idea that telepathy was, perhaps, the primary mode of communication for man before he developed speech. Indeed, he accepted the fact of telepathy and subjected presumably telepathic events to the same kind of searching analysis that he used in his therapy. The possibility of communication between the unconscious—without the mediation of the symbol-creating ego—was very real to Freud. And he seemed to feel that the mechanism by which such communication was accomplished lay in subliminal perceptions that were stored by the unconscious until some human need dredged them up from their hiding place. In subjecting such phenomena to the cold light of his rational mind, Freud gently removed the problem from the occultists and placed it in the hands of the scientists.

Exactly what he would have said about Daniel Defoe's little story can only be conjectured. However, Professor H. H. Price provides us with an interesting explanation of this kind of hallucination—an explanation in the scientific tradition which reads, nevertheless, as if it were based on "The Apparition of Mrs. Veal."

ARISTOTLE/On Prophetic Dreams*

As to the divination which takes place in sleep, and is said to be based on dreams, we cannot lightly either dismiss it with contempt or give it implicit confidence. The fact that all persons, or many, suppose dreams to possess a special significance, tends to inspire us with belief in it [such divination], as founded on the testimony of experience; and indeed that divination in dreams should, as regards some subjects, be genuine, is not incredible, for it has a show of reason; from which one might form a like opinion also respecting all other dreams. Yet the fact of our seeing no probable cause to account for such divination tends to inspire us with distrust. For, in addition to its further unreasonableness, it is absurd to combine the idea that the sender of such dreams should be God with the fact that those to whom he sends them are not the best and wisest, but merely commonplace persons. If, however, we abstract from the causality of God, none of the other causes assigned appears probable. For that certain persons should have foresight in dreams concerning things destined to take place at the Pillars of Hercules, or on the banks of the Borysthenes, seems to be something to discover the explanation of which surpasses the wit of man. Well then, the dreams in question must be regarded either as *causes,* or as *tokens,* of the events, or else as *coincidences*; either as all, or some, of these, or as one only. I use the word 'cause' in the sense in which the moon is [the cause] of an eclipse of the sun, or in which fatigue is [a cause] of fever; 'token' [in the sense in which] the entrance of a star [into the shadow] is a token of the eclipse, or [in which] roughness of the tongue [is a token] of fever; while by 'coincidence' I mean, for example, the occurrence of an eclipse of the sun while some one is taking a walk; for the walking is neither a token nor a cause of the eclipse, nor the eclipse [a cause or token] of the walking. For this reason no coincidence takes place according to a universal or general rule. Are we then to say that some dreams are causes, others tokens, e.g. of events taking place in the bodily organism? At all events, even scientific physicians tell us that one should pay diligent attention to dreams, and to hold this view is reasonable also for those who are not practitioners, but speculative philosophers. For the movements which occur in the daytime [within the body] are, unless very great and violent, lost sight of in contrast with the waking movements, which are more impressive. In sleep the opposite takes place, for then even trifling movements seem considerable. This is plain in what often happens during

* Aristotle, *Parva Naturalia,* 462^b–464^a (tr. J. I. Beare).

sleep; for example, dreamers fancy that they are affected by thunder and lightning, when in fact there are only faint ringings in their ears; or that they are enjoying honey or other sweet savours, when only a tiny drop of phlegm is flowing down [the oesophagus]; or that they are walking through fire, and feeling intense heat, when there is only a slight warmth affecting certain parts of the body. When they are awakened, these things appear to them in this their true character. But since the beginnings of all events are small, so, it is clear, are those also of the diseases or other affections about to occur in our bodies. In conclusion, it is manifest that these beginnings must be more evident in sleeping than in waking moments.

Nay, indeed, it is not improbable that some of the presentations which come before the mind in sleep may even be causes of the actions cognate to each of them. For as when we are about to act [in waking hours], or are engaged in any course of action, or have already performed certain actions, we often find ourselves concerned with these actions, or performing them, in a vivid dream; the cause whereof is that the dream-movement has had a way paved for it from the original movements set up in the daytime; exactly so, but conversely, it must happen that the movements set up first in sleep should also prove to be starting-points of actions to be performed in the daytime, since the recurrence by day of the thought of these actions also has had its way paved for it in the images before the mind at night. Thus then it is quite conceivable that some dreams may be tokens and causes [of future events].

Most [so-called prophetic] dreams are, however, to be classed as mere coincidences, especially all such as are extravagant, and those in the fulfilment of which the dreamers have no initiative, such as in the case of a sea-fight, or of things taking place far away. As regards these it is natural that the fact should stand as it does whenever a person, on mentioning something, finds the very thing mentioned come to pass. Why, indeed, should this not happen also in sleep? The probability is, rather, that many such things should happen. As, then, one's mentioning a particular person is neither token nor cause of this person's presenting himself, so, in the parallel instance, the dream is, to him who has seen it, neither token nor cause of its [so-called] fulfilment, but a mere coincidence. Hence the fact that many dreams have no 'fulfilment,' for coincidences do not occur according to any universal or general law.

On the whole, forasmuch as certain of the lower animals also dream, it may be concluded that dreams are not sent by God, nor are they designed for this purpose [to reveal the future]. They have a divine aspect, however, for Nature [their cause] is divinely planned, though not itself divine. A special proof [of their not being sent by God] is this: the power of foreseeing the future and of having vivid dreams is found in persons of inferior type, which implies that God does not send their dreams; but merely that all those whose physical temperament is, as it were, garrulous and excitable, see sights of all descriptions; for, inasmuch as they experience many movements of every kind, they just chance to have visions resembling objective facts, their luck in these matters being merely like that of persons who play at even and odd. For the principle which is expressed in the gambler's maxim: 'If you make many throws your luck must change,' holds good in their case also.

That many dreams have no fulfilment is not strange, for it is so too with many bodily symptoms and weather-signs, e.g., those of rain or wind. For if another movement occurs more influential than that from which, while [the event to which it was pointed was] still future, the given token was derived, the event [to which such token pointed] does not take place. So, of the things which ought to be accomplished by human agency, many, though well-planned, are by the operation of other principles more powerful [than man's agency] brought to nought. For, speaking generally, that which *was* about to happen is not in every case what now is *happening*; nor is that which *shall* hereafter *be* identical with that which is now *going to* be. Still, however, we must hold that the beginnings from which, as we said, no consummation follows, are *real* beginnings, and these constitute natural tokens of certain events, even though the events do not come to pass.

As for [prophetic] dreams which involve not such beginnings [sc. of future events] as we have here described, but such as are extravagant in times, or places, or magnitudes; or those involving beginnings which are not extravagant in any of these respects, while yet the persons who see the dream hold not in their own hands the beginnings [of the event to which it points]: unless the foresight which such dreams give is the result of pure coincidence, the following would be a better explanation of it than that proposed by Democritus, who alleges 'images' and 'emanations' as its cause. As, when something has caused motion in water or air, this [the portion moved] moves another [portion of water or air], and, though the cause has ceased to operate, such motion propagates itself to a certain point, though there the prime movement is not present; just so it may well be that a movement and a consequent sense-perception should reach sleeping souls from the objects from which Democritus represents 'images' and 'emanations' as coming; that such movements, in whatever way they arrive, should be more perceptible at night [than by day], because when proceeding thus in the daytime they are more liable to dissolution (since at night the air is less disturbed, there being then less wind); and that they shall be perceived within the body owing to sleep, since persons are more sensitive even to slight sensory movements when asleep than awake. It is these movements then that cause 'presentations,' as a result of which sleepers foresee the future even relatively to such events as those referred to above. These considerations also explain why this experience befalls commonplace persons and not the most intelligent. For it would have regularly occurred both in the daytime and to the wise had it been God who sent it; but, as we have explained the matter, it is quite natural that commonplace persons should be those who have foresight [in dreams]. For the mind of such persons is not given to thinking, but, as it were, derelict, or totally vacant, and, when once set moving, is borne passively on in the direction taken by that which moves it. With regard to the fact that some persons who are liable to derangement have this foresight, its explanation is that their normal mental movements do not impede [the alien movements], but are beaten off by the latter. Therefore it is that they have an especially keen perception of the alien movements.

That certain persons in particular should have vivid dreams, e.g. that familiar friends should thus have foresight in a special degree respecting one another, is due to the fact that such friends are most solicitous on one another's behalf. For as acquaintances in particular recognize and perceive one another a long way off, so also they do as regards the sensory movements respecting one another; for sensory movements which refer to persons familiarly known are themselves more familiar. Atrabilious persons, owing to their impetuosity, are, when they, as it were, shoot from a distance, expert at hitting; while, owing to their mutability, the series of movements deploys quickly before their minds. For even as the insane recite, or con over in thought, the poems of Philaegides, e.g. the Aphrodite, whose parts succeed in order of similitude, just so do they [the 'atrabilious'] go on and on stringing sensory movements together. Moreover, owing to their aforesaid impetuosity, one movement within them is not liable to be knocked out of its course by some other movement.

The most skilful interpreter of dreams is he who has the faculty of observing resemblances. Any one may interpret dreams which are vivid and plain. But, speaking of 'resemblances,' I mean that dream presentations are analogous to the forms reflected in water, as indeed we have already stated. In the latter case, if the motion in the water be great, the reflexion has no resemblance to its original, nor do the forms resemble the real objects. Skilful, indeed, would he be in interpreting such reflexions who could rapidly discern, and at a glance comprehend, the scattered and distorted fragments of such forms, so as to perceive that one of them represents a man, or a horse, or anything whatever. Accordingly, in the other case also, in a similar way, some such thing as this [blurred image] is all that a dream amounts to; for the internal movement effaces the clearness of the dream.

The questions, therefore, which we proposed as to the nature of sleep and the dream, and the cause to which each of them is due, and also as to divination as a result of dreams, in every form of it, have now been discussed.

H. H. PRICE / Apparitions: Two Theories[1]

AN APPARITION may be roughly defined as a visible but non-physical phenomenon closely resembling a particular human being. The human being in question is not necessarily dead. (The assumption that all apparitions are apparitions of the dead is one of the popular misconceptions engendered by the word "ghost.") Certainly there are what one may call "*post mortem* apparitions" however we explain them. But there are also apparitions of the living. That is, cases when the human being whom the apparition resembles is not dead. In some cases an apparition of a living person occurs when he is near the point of death, or is in some other "critical" situation; for instance, he is undergoing some accident at the time (not necessarily a fatal one) or is dangerously ill. But such crisis apparitions, as they are called, are not the only apparitions of the living. There are apparitions of living persons who are in perfectly good health at the time or are in no sort of critical situation at all. Occasionally the person to whom or in whose immediate neighborhood the apparition appears is himself in a critical situation (very ill, or dying, or is threatened by some danger or other, known to him or not) but this is not necessary either. If I may say so, the circumstances in which an apparition occurs need not be in any way lurid or soul-stirring, either on the side of the person appearing or on the side of the percipient, though sometimes they are. Perhaps I should add that in the well-authenticated cases (unlike the fictitious ones) there is no evidence that an apparition ever has physical effects—moves physical objects, opens doors, leaves footprints.

[1] This paper was delivered as part of the Symposium on Incorporeal Personal Agency which was held at the Parapsychology Laboratory of Duke University, June 9-12, 1959.

The most remarkable fact about an apparition is that it can occur at a distance from the place where the person's physical organism is (whether his physical organism is alive or dying or dead). The distance may extend to hundreds or even thousands of miles. In the Bowyer-Bower case, from the 1914 war, an airman was shot down and killed in France. And at about the same time an apparition of him was seen by his half-sister in India.[2] Occasionally, however, the apparition of a person is seen very near the place where the person himself is, so near it that both the apparition and the person himself can be seen by the same percipient at the same time. In another case, a lady called Mrs. Hall was sitting at the dining table having supper with three other people. They saw an apparition of her standing in front of the sideboard a few feet away. Moreover, Mrs. Hall herself saw the apparition.[3] Such a self-apparition is a very curious phenomenon indeed and a very rare one. There are, however, reports of one or two other cases of it.

The popular term "ghost" is misleading in another way. Not only does it imply that all apparitions are apparitions of the dead (it would not make sense to speak of the ghost of a living person); it also tends to suggest that all apparitions are haunting apparitions. A ghost, according to popular ideas, is something which haunts a particular house or town or street; or perhaps it haunts a particular person or family. Now it is true that there are haunting apparitions; that is, there are cases where the same apparition occurs over and over again in the same locality. But it is very far from being true that all apparitions are of this haunting kind. In most of the cases an apparition of someone occurs only once and only for a short period—a few minutes at the most.

I said at the beginning that an apparition is a visible though non-physical entity. But it is convenient to extend this definition a little to cover auditory phenomena as well as visual ones. Thus footsteps may be heard or a sound as of the rustling of clothes, or other sounds (bumps, scraping noises, etc.). Very occasionally an apparition is heard to speak, though I do not know of any case when it says more than a few words. Thus Mr. and Mrs. P. saw an apparition of Mr. P.'s deceased father which uttered the words "Willie, Willie" in a "commanding yet reproachful voice."[4] These sounds are as non-physical as the visible apparition is. Very occasionally there are tactual experiences. In one case a "sharp slap on the back" was felt when there was no physical cause for it. In another, the percipient says, "I heard distinctly the footsteps of the gentleman to whom I was engaged, quickly mounting the stairs

---

[2] Tyrrell, G. N. M. *Apparitions*, revised ed. London: Gerald Duckworth, 1953. (See p. 36.)
[3] *Ibid.*, pp. 129-30.
[4] *Ibid.*, pp. 36-37.

after me; then I as plainly felt him put his arms around my waist."[5]

I also said at the beginning that an apparition closely resembled a particular human being. But this needs to be amplified too. In an apparitional experience the central figure does almost always resemble a particular human being; but the central figure often has appurtenances or accompaniments which are equally apparitional (Tyrrell calls them "additional features"). Thus an apparition of Canon Bourne is seen mounted on his white horse, waving his hat in his hand; and on another occasion he is seen on horseback in a plantation which was physically out of sight from the place where the percipient was.[6] In another case a lady called Mrs. Paquet sees an apparition of her brother, Edmund Dunn, with a rope around his leg which was pulling him over "a low railing or bulwark."[7] In several cases a horse and carriage was seen, as well as the people driving it. It may be noticed too that apparitions are almost invariably clothed. The apparition of Mr. P.'s father, already mentioned, had a peaked cap on its head. The clothes, caps, hats, etc. are as apparitional as the central figure itself and may be counted as "appurtenances or accompaniments" of it. I should add that there are cases—though only very few as far as I know—in which the central figure is an animal and not a human being.

It will be obvious from what I have said already that apparitional phenomena are pretty complex and varied. I doubt whether any satisfactory classification of them is possible in the present stage of investigation. But most psychical researchers, if they were asked to give a list of the main types of apparitions, would probably mention four different types: I will now give this list, which will serve as a kind of summary of what I have so far said, and as a rough survey of the different types of phenomena which a theory of apparitions has to explain.

The list runs as follows:
1. Crisis apparitions of the living.
2. Non-crisis apparitions of the living, including self-apparitions (i.e., cases where someone sees an apparition of himself).
3. Haunting apparitions, which are usually, though not quite always, apparitions of the dead.
4. Non-haunting apparitions of the dead.

In addition, "out-of-the-body" experiences might be included in the list on the ground that these have some connection with apparitional phenomena. Perhaps I should say a word more about out-of-

[5] *Ibid.*, p. 58.
[6] *Ibid.*, pp. 70 and 97.
[7] *Ibid.*, pp. 51-52.

the-body experiences, which I have not previously mentioned. As their name suggests, they are experiences in which someone seems to himself to be outside his body and to be viewing it from a distance, much as if it were the body of someone else.

Usually (though not, I think, invariably) the percipient is in a physiologically abnormal state. For instance, he is under an anaesthetic and is undergoing or about to undergo a surgical operation. Or he is extremely ill and is thought to be dying or even dead, though he recovers afterwards. Or he is in a state of extreme fatigue.

I shall quote a case from the second world war. The narrator was an armored car officer in the British Army. On August 3, 1944, his armored car received a direct hit and blew up. The officer was blown out of the car and over a hedge. He says, "I was conscious of being two persons—one lying on the ground. . . . My clothes on fire and waving my limbs about wildly. . . . The other 'me' was floating up in the air about 20 feet from the ground, from which position I could see not only my other self, but also the hedge and the car. . . . I remember quite distinctly telling myself, 'It's no use gibbering like that—roll over and over to put the flames out.' This my ground-body eventually did. . . . The flames went out, and at this stage I suddenly became one person again."[8]

Another percipient who had a rather similar experience (during an acute attack of gastro-enteritis from which he very nearly died) says that his consciousness was divided into two. One consciousness belonged to himself, and the other to his body. The body-consciousness, he says, appeared to be composite and seemed to be breaking up or disintegrating. This rather suggests the ancient Greek doctrine about the "parts of the soul" which seems so unintelligible to modern philosophers. Perhaps this doctrine had its origin in experiences of this kind. The percipient not only saw his body from outside. He saw other things as well, "not only 'things' at home, but in London and in Scotland; in fact wherever my attention was directed. . . ."[9]

There are other cases where the percipient, once he is "out of his body," makes a kind of excursion and sees or appears to see things which are going on elsewhere. Sometimes the details of what is seen do not correspond to any verifiable physical fact and suggest rather some kind of symbolic dream or vision. In one report, the percipient speaks of "wandering through silent fields of asphodel."

[8] Johnson, R. C. *The Imprisoned Splendour.* London: Hodder & Stoughton, 1953. (See p. 227.)
[9] Tyrrell, G. N. M. *The Personality of Man.* Great Britain: Penguin Books (Pelican Edition), 1948. (See pp. 197-99.)

But the same percipient also had veridical experiences, apparently of a clairvoyant kind, in the course of his out-of-the-body excursions.[10] Again, M. Bertrand, who had an experience of this kind during a climbing expedition in the Alps, saw what was really happening at a distance. "He saw the guide lagging behind and drinking his (M. Bertrand's) bottle of Madeira and steal a leg of his chicken." When charged with these misdeeds afterwards, the guide "fled and spread the rumor that M. Bertrand was a devil and not a man."[11]

These out-of-the-body experiences are connected with apparitional phenomena in the following way. Sometimes the person who has had an out-of-the-body experience reports that he found himself to be "in" another body or quasi-body, closely resembling his physical body, and yet spatially separate from it.[12] And this "other" body seems to have much the same paradoxical qualities as an apparition has. It is a spatial entity with a shape and a size, and its exterior resembles the exterior of his physical body closely. Yet it is not a physical entity. Like an apparition, it is spatial, but not impenetrable. It can pass through physical obstacles without hindrance. Moreover, cases have been reported, though only very rarely, where one person, A, has an out-of-the-body experience, and at the same time another person, B, sees an apparition of him; and it is seen in the place where A, during his out-of-the-body excursions, seems to himself to be. Here it looks as if this "other body" was actually the same as the apparition, and as if the apparition was serving as a "vehicle of consciousness" to the person appearing, much as the physical organism is a "vehicle of consciousness" in normal life.[13] And finally, it is claimed by some people that voluntary out-of-the-body experiences are possible; that his "other" or "second" body can be voluntarily "projected." Obviously, these claims ought to be further investigated.

After this very brief and sketchy survey of the main types of apparitional phenomena, we may turn to two theories which have been suggested to explain them. The first may be called the "Telepathic Theory," the second the "Theory of the Double."

[10] Tyrrell, *Apparitions*, p. 154.
[11] *Ibid.*, pp. 151-52.
[12] It looks as if this happened in the case of the armored car officer mentioned just now (see Footnote 8). This is suggested by his phrase "the other 'me'" which was floating up in the air about twenty feet from the ground; and "my ground body" suggests that it seemed to him that he had another body which was not on the ground.
[13] These are sometimes called "reciprocal cases," a name which implies the correctness of the Telepathic Theory which I am about to discuss. But whatever we call them, it is very desirable that investigators should be on the look-out for further cases of this type. The most celebrated one is the Wilmot case (see Tyrrell's *Apparitions*, pp. 116-17).

The Telepathic Theory of Apparitions

The telepathic theory of apparitions was first proposed in the very early days of the Society for Psychical Research. But much the best and most detailed statement of it is to be found in a brilliant little book called *Apparitions* by the late G.N.M. Tyrrell (originally written in 1943 and republished in 1953). I should like to express my great admiration for Tyrrell's book, and for its distinguished author whom I had the privilege of knowing well for a number of years. There are difficulties in Tyrrell's theory, as we shall see. But it was a most important achievement to formulate the telepathic theory of apparitions so fully and so ingeniously as he did.

The telepathic theory, I suspect, was originally suggested by the study of crisis apparitions. The crisis cases are probably the best documented ones in the records of psychical research and have been more carefully investigated than any others.

Roughly, the theory is this: Some thought or emotion in the mind of a person A, whom we will call the agent, has a telepathic effect upon the mind of another person B, whom we will call the percipient. And this telepathic impression manifests itself to the percipient's consciousness in the form of a visual hallucination, or sometimes an auditory one, or sometimes both. In short, the telepathic impressions he has received cause him to see, or hear, something which is "not physically there." But it would be insisted that his experience is not a purely subjective hallucination. In this important respect (it would be said) apparitional experiences differ from the hallucinations of insane or delirious patients, and from the hallucinations which are produced by drugs such as hashish or mescaline or by hypnotic suggestion. Unlike these, a telepathic hallucination corresponds, sometimes very closely, with some external fact or state of affairs. I have already mentioned the case of Mrs. Paquet, who saw an apparition of her brother, Edmund Dunn, with a rope around his legs pulling him over a railing or bulwark. On the telepathic theory, this was a visual hallucination. But it corresponded very accurately with a fatal accident which had happened to the percipient's brother about six hours earlier, when he was dragged off a tug in Chicago harbor by a rope and was drowned.

To see how very plausible this telepathic theory of apparitions is we must consider some fairly well established points about telepathy in general. It seems pretty clear that telepathy is a two-stage process. In the first stage, a telepathic impression is received at some unconscious level of the percipient's mind; and then secondly, it manifests itself in one way or another to his consciousness. Now it is important to notice that this second state, the stage of manifestation or emergence, may take several different forms. Sometimes the telepathic impression emerges in the form of a dream; sometimes in the form of waking mental imagery, either visual or auditory; sometimes in the form of what is called a "hunch" (that is, an unreasoned belief which suddenly breaks into a person's mind and later turns out to be correct); sometimes in the form of an equally unreasoned impulse to do something (for instance, to go home at once though there is no apparent reason for doing so); sometimes, again, a telepathic impression manifests itself in the form of automatic or semi-automatic bodily behavior (for example as in automatic writing or automatic speech). And finally, if the telepathic theory of apparitions is right, a telepathic impression may manifest itself in the form of a complex visual or auditory hallucination.

Thus an apparition, on this theory, is just the most complete and the most dramatic of all the different ways in which a telepathic impression may manifest itself in consciousness. And so apparitions are brought into line, as it were, with a number of other types of phenomena which are manifestations of telepathy. If there are telepathic dreams, for instance, (as there certainly are) why would these not be telepathic hallucinations too? Indeed, it might be argued that a dream is a kind of hallucination occurring in sleep; or, to put it the other way around, that a hallucination is a kind of partial and waking dream.

So far I have been trying to show how the telepathic theory explains apparitions of the living. What does it say about apparitions of the dead ("ghosts," if you like to call them so)?

Here there is a choice of two alternatives. First, one could suppose that in these cases the telepathic "agent"—the mind from which the telepathic impression is received—is the surviving mind or personality of a deceased human being. Presumably, if he does survive he will remember what he looked like when alive, what sort of clothes he wore, and so on. Some thought or emotion which he has consciously or subconsciously (including this thought about what he looked like when alive) is telepathically conveyed to the percipient and externalizes itself or manifests itself in the percipient's consciousness in the form of a hallucinatory figure resembling what he looked like when alive.

It need not be supposed that the surviving mind of the deceased person is consciously or voluntarily sending a "telepathic message." Perhaps this might happen sometimes. But the source of the telepathic impression might equally well be some kind of brooding memory of his—perhaps even a subconscious one—about some experience he had when he was alive. It may be noticed that haunting apparitions often behave in a rather dreamy and semi-automatic manner (like sleep-walkers, as someone has said) repeating a stereotyped routine of actions over and over again, whenever they appear.

Secondly, if one thinks (as I do not myself) that the possibility of survival can be ruled out on purely *a priori* grounds, one could explain apparitions of the dead by retrocognitive telepathy. One could suppose that the percipient is telepathically affected by a past event, not by a present one; that what he gets his telepathic impression from is not some thought or emotion occurring now in the mind of the late Mr. X, but some thought or emotion which did occur in the mind of Mr. X when he was still alive, perhaps many years ago. There is, of course, evidence that telepathy is to some degree independent of the physical time order and that people can be "telepathically sensitive to" past events (and even to future ones) as well as to events occurring now.

Conceivably there might be some truth in both these explanations; it might be that some apparitions of the dead are caused by contemporary events in the minds of surviving personalities, while others are caused in the "retrocognitive" manner I have just described.

As I have said, the telepathic theory regards an apparition as a telepathically-induced hallucination. But of course it would have to be admitted that an apparition is often a very realistic sort of hallucination, a very lifelike and vivid reproduction of the person from whom the telepathic impression comes; so much so that the percipient is often quite convinced at first that this person is actually present in the flesh before his eyes. (This vivid and lifelike character of apparitions is often emphasized in the narratives.) But we know that hallucinations can be very realistic, quite realistic enough to cause intense surprise and alarm in those who experience them. This is certainly true of some of the "subjective" hallucinations of insane or delirious patients or persons under the influence of drugs. It could also be argued, as I mentioned before, that dreams, after all, are a kind of visual hallucination occurring in sleep, and we know that dreams can be very realistic also.

Perhaps a word more should be said about the term "hallucination" itself, because it may tend to make the layman uncomfortable. He is liable to suppose (wrongly but sometimes unshakeably) that anyone who has a hallucination is *ipso facto* in a morbid condition, mentally or physically—"off his head," or "not in his right mind" either temporarily or permanently. This is not in fact true. Hallucinations do occur occasionally in perfectly normal and healthy people. But I have heard it suggested, and with some plausibility, that this mistaken but widespread assumption makes people reluctant to report apparitional experiences to psychical researchers. Unfortunately parapsychology, like other important activities, does have its "public relations" aspect, and we cannot afford to forget this. It is fairly well known that many psychical researchers nowadays do regard apparitional experiences as telepathic hallucinations, and the term "hallucination" frightens the layman so much that he overlooks the adjective "telepathic" which qualifies it; nor does he notice that a telepathic hallucination (unlike the hallucinations of insanity or delirium, or of drug-addicts) would be a veridical hallucination, corresponding closely with some fact or state of affairs external to the percipient's mind. Perhaps it might be better to use some other word like "vision" instead of "hallucination." A man might be pleased or even proud to think that he had a vision when he would be ashamed or alarmed to think he had had a hallucination.

But when students of psychical research are talking to each other (as we are doing now) the word "hallucination" is much the most convenient to use, and I hope you will allow me to go on using it in my discussions of the telepathic theory.

Let us now consider this theory further. If the theory is correct, we should expect to find that there would be other telepathic hallucinations which are not quite realistic enough to be counted as apparitions, and yet are closely akin to them. And it may be argued that this is what we do find. I will quote a case of Tyrrell's which he calls "The Pillow Case." A lady woke early one morning and saw what appeared to be a half-sheet of notepaper lying on her pillow with the words written on it: 'Elsie was dying last night.' There was only one person to whom the message could refer and it turned out that she had, in fact, died during that night."[14] What the lady saw was not exactly an apparition. But it conveyed much the same information as would have been conveyed if she had seen a full-fledged apparition of the deceased person; only in this case this information was conveyed by means of hallucinatory written words. Mr. W. H. Salter has drawn attention to an intermediate case which he calls "semi-realistic." "An Indian prince . . . saw a portrait of his father, then at the point of death, occupying the space of a real picture in his home bedroom." Again, when a telepathic impression manifests itself in the form of a mental image (as it sometimes does) this image may be "projected" into a crystal into which the percipient is gazing. Such a projected mental image

[14] G. N. M. Tyrrell, *Science and Psychical Phenomena* (New York: Harper & Bros., 1938), p. 24.

would be a kind of half-way house between an ordinary mental image and a full-fledged and fully "realistic" apparition.

I now turn to a problem which appears rather puzzling at first sight but is very easily solved by the telepathic theory. It is rather crudely expressed in the tea-party question "Why do ghosts wear clothes?" But the problem is wider than this. As I have mentioned already, an apparitional figure often has appurtenances or accompaniments of various kinds. Canon Bourne's white horse is an example.[15]

All this is explained quite easily if we suppose that an apparitional experience is a telepathically induced hallucination. These additional details which accompany the central figure are part of the "telepathic message" if one cares to put it so. No one is surprised or puzzled because someone we see in dreams wears clothes, or has a hat in his hand, or is riding a bicycle, or is carrying a suitcase. All this is just part of the dream, like the figure of the person himself. Such a dream might happen to be a telepathic one; and on the theory we are considering, apparitional experiences are closely analogous to telepathic dreams.

TYRRELL ON THE APPARITIONAL DRAMA

This brings us to the most interesting and novel idea in Tyrrell's version of the telepathic theory. He conceives of an apparitional experience as a kind of dramatic performance, something like a short one-act play.[16] "The apparitional drama" is a favorite phrase of his. The stage on which the play is presented consists of the physical surroundings in which the percipient happens to be at the time—for example, the room in which he is sitting. But the play itself is a hallucination or vision. Thus the "apparitional drama" has a curious two-faced character. It is a hallucinatory performance presented on a real stage. We must bear this point in mind, if we are to understand Tyrrell's theory.

What Tyrrell calls the motif or theme of the drama is a rather general idea in the mind of the telepathic agent with strong emotions attached to it. For example, it might be the idea "if only dear old So-and-So could see me now" or "I wish I could be with him now, wherever he is." This idea which the agent has, whether consciously or subconsciously, is telepathically transmitted to the mind of the percipient. But this rather general idea is not enough by itself to constitute the apparitional drama. It is only, so to speak, the outline of the plot. Before the play can be presented, the details of the plot must be thoroughly worked out, with due regard to the stage on which the performance is to take place—the actual

---

[15] See p. 112 [p. 208 of this volume].
[16] Tyrrell, *Apparitions*, pp. 100 *et seq.*

physical position of the furniture in the room, the fact that there is a looking glass over the mantelpiece, the exact place where the percipient happens to be sitting. According to Tyrrell, this involves quite a complicated process of unconscious imaginative construction, the aim of which is to make the hallucination as realistic as possible, to imitate as closely as possible what would happen in physical fact if A were to be physically present in the room where his friend B is at the time. To achieve this aim, the hallucination must be vivid, detailed, and lifelike; and the apparition must fit in with its physical surroundings; for instance, it must stand on the carpet in front of the chair where the percipient is sitting, instead of floating in the air. (Tyrrell admits, however, or indeed insists, that complete success is not always achieved.) Then finally, when the details have been worked out, the drama has to be actually presented in the form of a quite complex hallucination, going on perhaps for several minutes. According to Tyrrell, this work of unconscious dramatic construction is a co-operative effort in which both agent and percipient take part. The agent contributes some of the details, and the percipient contributes others. What the agent looks like in profile, for instance, is something the agent himself does not know at all clearly; but the percipient usually does. Such co-operation between agent and percipient is possible because all this work of imaginative construction goes on in the unconscious level or stratum of the mind, and here there is no clear-cut separation between one person and another, as there is at the conscious level. So both parties can co-operate in planning the apparitional drama. Indeed in Tyrrell's view it is a case of non-separation rather than co-operation.[17]

    I find this notion of an apparitional drama very suggestive. I think that some such process of unconscious dramatic construction must indeed be supposed to go on when we are dreaming (and probably in some forms of mediumship too). A dream really is a kind of hallucinatory drama. And in the case of a telepathic dream, I think we do have to suppose that there is some kind of unconscious co-operation, or non-separation, between the mind of the agent and the mind of the percipient. So if an apparition is something closely analogous to a telepathic dream, as the telepathic theory assumes, it must, I think, be constructed in the sort of way Tyrrell describes.

    But we have still to decide whether the telepathic theory is right at all. Plausible and ingenious as it is, it does have it difficulties, and something must now be said about them.

[17] *Ibid.*, pp. 101-102.

DIFFICULTIES IN THE TELEPATHIC THEORY

The first and most obvious difficulty, as Frederic Myers noticed long ago, is the existence of "collective" cases, where an apparition is seen (or apparitional sounds are heard) by several percipients at the same time. Some apparitions, though not all, seem to be public entities, as ordinary physical objects are. And the notion of a public hallucination is surely a very strange one. If a drunkard sees snakes which are not physically there, we hardly expect that other people in the room will see them too. Of course, we shall have to admit that the publicity of an apparition is a restricted sort of publicity at best. If there are three people in the room, we may find that two of them see the apparition, while the third does not see it at all, though he is looking in the same direction as they are. But the idea that a hallucination (or vision as you like) should have any degree of publicity at all is surely very difficult.

Tyrrell tries to solve this difficulty by means of the notion of dramatic appropriateness. (This is just a further application of his idea of "the apparitional drama.") As we have seen, the underlying aim of all the elaborate process of unconscious dramatic construction postulated by Tyrrell is to make the apparition as realistic and lifelike as possible by fitting it into the actual physical surroundings in which the percipient happens to be at the time. Now those surroundings may happen to include another person. Well, if Mr. Jones, the telepathic agent, was really present in the room in actual physical fact, both the people then would see him. So this second percipient is drawn into the apparitional drama, because it is dramatically appropriate that he should be, just as the chairs and the mirror are "drawn in"—in the way appropriate to them (e.g., in their capacity of physical obstacles, or objects capable of reflecting things). He is drawn into it in the sense that his mind too takes part (unconsciously) in the process by which the apparitional drama is constructed. The result is that both percipients have similar and corresponding hallucinations. We do not have to suppose that literally the same hallucination is experienced by both of them. A has his hallucination of Mr. Jones standing on the hearth rug, and B has his, a similar but slightly different one. But the two hallucinations correspond closely with one another: they fit together perspectively like two views of the same material object seen from different directions. And that is what we must mean (on Tyrrell's theory) by saying that the same apparition is seen by both of them.[18]

Ingenious as this solution is, I cannot but feel, as others

[18] *Ibid.*, pp. 109-110.

have, that there is something artificial and over-complex about it. There is surely something to be said for Myers' view that if an apparition is public to several different percipients, this is good evidence that something is actually present in the place in question, and is not merely hallucinatory.

Moreover, there are cases where Tyrrell's notion of dramatic appropriateness seems not to apply very easily. There are cases where the apparition is seen by the wrong person and is not seen by the right one. I shall mention a case which was reported to me in 1955. During the Second World War a young man, the son of an English father and a French mother, had been dropped by parachute to operate with the French Resistance. He was posted as missing, and for some time after the end of the war nothing at all was heard about him. Naturally, his parents were in a state of acute anxiety. It turned out later that he had been captured by the Gestapo and killed. But before this was known, an apparition of him was seen going up to the door of his parents' house in London. It was not, however, seen by his parents, who were away from home at the time, nor by any member of the household. It was seen, and afterwards carefully described, by someone next door, who had never seen the young man in real life and knew nothing about him.

If this was indeed a case of telepathy, as Tyrrell's theory requires, one would have expected that one or other of the parents would have received the telepathic impression and would have seen the apparition: and if a complete stranger saw it too, he ought to have been someone who was with the parents at the time. The fact that the parents were away from home at the moment should have made no difference. Telepathy, so far as we know, is a purely mind-to-mind relation, and the spatial location of the agent and the percipient makes no difference to it. If so, one would think that the parents would have received the telepathic impression wherever they were.

Moreover, the stranger who did see the apparition had no idea what the young man looked like, and could not therefore have co-operated in producing the apparition in the way Tyrrell's theory requires.

THE DIFFICULTY ABOUT CONSCIOUS APPARITIONS

Moreover, I do not think that Tyrrell's theory applies at all easily to what may be called conscious apparitions. As I have mentioned already, there are some rare cases when the apparition serves as a vehicle of consciousness to the person appearing, just as the physical body does in ordinary life. The kind of thing that happens is this: You see an apparition of Mr. X in your drawing room, and at the same time Mr. X himself has the experience of seeing you and your surroundings, and is able to describe them accurately afterwards even though he had no normal means of acquiring information about them. This is the phenomenon sometimes called bilocation, which literally means "being in two places at once": Mr. X's body is in one place, while his mind or consciousness is in another place perhaps many miles away. It is as if his mind or consciousness had transferred itself to the place where the apparition is. That place has temporarily become the point of view from which he observes things.

This is what I mean by saying that in this special and rare type of case the apparition is a vehicle of consciousness. It is not easy to understand how this can happen if an apparition is something hallucinatory, as Tyrrell thinks it is. A hallucination exists only for the mind which experiences it. How can my hallucination be the vehicle for someone else's consciousness?

Tyrrell tries to explain this type of case in terms of reciprocal telepathy.[19] Mr. X's mind or consciousness is not really in your drawing room, and the place where the apparition of him is located is not really serving as a point of view from which he temporarily observes things. X is having a telepathic hallucination too. He gets his information about your present surroundings from your mind telepathically; and this information manifests itself to his consciousness in the form of a complicated vision or hallucination corresponding more or less accurately with the physical facts about the room, the furniture, and the position of your body in relation to it. At the same time, you have a telepathic hallucination of him, and it appears to you that he is standing on the hearth rug looking at you and your surroundings. I will not venture to say that this very complicated explanation is absolutely impossible, but I do find it almost too complicated to believe.

So much for the telepathic theory of apparitions. It explains many of the facts very well, but there are some which it cannot explain at all easily. I expect that it can get over all the difficulties I have mentioned, but only at the cost of great complication.

So in conclusion it may be worth while to say a few words about another and very different theory, which I shall call the "Theory of the Double."

Statement of the Theory of the Double

The main point of this theory is to maintain that an apparition is an objective entity, though not a physical one. When someone sees an apparition, he is supposed to be seeing the "double" of another person (or in some rare cases, his own double). It is the

[19] *Ibid.*, pp. 116-19.

"double" of a particular person, because it closely resembles the person's body, or at any rate the exterior of his body, and yet it is capable of being at a place which is at a distance (perhaps a very long distance) from the place where his body is at the time.

On this theory the double is supposed to be an objective entity in the sense that it is in no way hallucinatory, as the telepathic theory says it is. It is supposed to be actually there in the place where it is perceived to be, and to have an existence which is independent of the mind (or mind and brain) of the percipient. In this respect, it has the same kind of status as an ordinary material object.

On the other hand, it differs from a material object in having very different causal properties. Although it is a spatial entity, it is not impenetrable; it can pass through physical obstacles, such as walls, without hindrance. And to judge from reports of out-of-the-body experiences, it seems to be able to pass from one place to another without necessarily passing through any intermediate places. In general, it seems to be responsive to the thoughts and wishes (conscious or subconscious) of the person whose double it is. Outwardly, it looks just like a material object. But the causal laws it obeys are not the laws of physics, but the laws of psychology.

This theory is strong where the telepathic theory is weak. It has no difficulty about "collective cases." If an apparition is an objective entity, actually present in a particular place, we would expect that anyone who is appropriately situated and has the appropriate kind of sensitivity would be able to see it.

Nor is there any difficulty about its being perceived by "the wrong person," as there is in the telepathic theory—for example, some indifferent bystander or complete stranger who knows nothing about the person appearing.

And finally, if an apparition is an objective (though nonphysical) entity, there is no reason in principle why it should not sometimes be a vehicle of consciousness for the person appearing.

But the theory of the Double has its difficulties too. How does it answer the popular question "Why do ghosts wear clothes?" which I mentioned before? How does it account for what I called the appurtenances and accompaniments of the apparition: the horses and carriages, the rope which the lady saw round her brother's leg, pulling him over "a railing or bulwark," the hat in Canon Bourne's hand?

So far as I can see, it will have to say that these appurtenances and accompaniments of the apparition are somehow the expressions of the thoughts (conscious or unconscious) of the person appearing; or rather, perhaps, of his thoughts or wishes (conscious or unconscious).

The apparition is clothed, and clothed in a particular way, because the person thinks of himself as being clothed in that way. And similarly he thinks of himself as being in a particular situation at this particular time—on horseback, for instance, or seated in a carriage. We might expect that the thoughts which he has about himself could sometimes be expressed in a symbolic rather than a literal manner (somewhat as thoughts are expressed symbolically in dreams).[20]

So in this theory, these appurtenances and accompaniments of the apparition (including its clothes) will be, so to speak, thoughts made visible. Perhaps we might go further. The same might be true of the Double itself. The person appearing habitually thinks of himself as having a physical body, and a physical body of a particular sort (tall or short, fat or thin, red-haired or dark-haired). Perhaps the Double is just the visible expression of this permanent thought of his about his own body.

This leads to the very curious idea of something which is intermediate between the mental and the physical. The Double, and its appurtenances too, has some of the properties of a material object; as I have said, it is in space, it has a shape and a size, it can move, it is "public" to a number of observers. On the other hand, it has other properties which are psychological rather than physical, because it is a manifestation of the thoughts (or thoughts and wishes) of the person appearing. In this respect it is more like a dream-image. Both in its genesis and in the changes it undergoes, it is subject to psychological causal laws.

This idea of something which is intermediate between the mental and the physical—something which does not quite belong either to the mental or the physical realm, but has some of the properties of both—this is certainly a very strange idea. But strange though it is, I think it may possibly be useful, not only in the theory of apparitions, but in other departments of psychical research as well.

Conclusion

So much for the two theories of apparitions which I wished to discuss, the "Telepathic Theory" and the "Theory of the Double." Neither of them perhaps is perfectly adequate, but both do help us to make sense of a strange group of phenomena which seem at first sight to have "no rhyme or reason about them" and thereby help to make the phenomena themselves more credible. It is possible, of course, that both may be correct. It might be that there are

---

[20] F. W. H. Myers gives a case in which an apparition carried a sheet of music in its hand. It was an apparition of a recently deceased singer in a church choir. (See *Human Personality*. London: Longmans, Green & Co., 1903. P. 46.)

two quite distinct types of apparitions, and that the telepathic theory gives a correct account of one type, and the theory of the double gives a correct account of the other.

On the other hand, it might perhaps be argued that the two theories are not quite so different as they look: and if we use them as starting points for our reflections, if we reconsider old facts in the light of these two theories and look out for new facts to test them, we may eventually be able to think of a new theory which will be better than either of them.

DANIEL DEFOE/The Apparition of Mrs. Veal

A True Relation of the Apparition of Mrs. Veal,
The Next Day After Her Death, to One Mrs. Bargrave,
at Canterbury, the 8th of September, 1705

The Preface

THIS RELATION is matter of fact, and attended with such circumstances as may induce any reasonable man to believe it. It was sent by a gentleman, a justice of peace at Maidstone, in Kent, and a very intelligent person, to his friend in London, as it is here worded; which discourse is attested by a very sober and understanding gentleman, who had it from his kinswoman, who lives in Canterbury, within a few doors of the house in which the within-named Mrs. Bargrave lived; and who he believes to be of so discerning a spirit, as not to be put upon by any fallacy, and who positively assured him that the whole matter as it is related and laid down is really true, and what she herself had in the same words, as near as may be, from Mrs. Bargrave's own mouth, who, she knows, had no reason to invent and publish such a story, or any design to forge and tell a lie, being a woman of much honesty and virtue, and her whole life a course, as it were, of piety. The use which we ought to make of it is to consider that there is a life to come after this, and a just God who will retribute to every one according to the deeds done in the body, and therefore to reflect upon our past course of life we have led in the world; that our time is short and uncertain; and that if we would escape the punishment of the ungodly and receive the reward of the righteous, which is the laying hold of eternal life, we ought, for the time to come to return to God by a speedy repentance, ceasing to do evil, and learning to do well; to seek after God early, if haply He may be found of us, and lead such lives for the future as may be well pleasing in His sight.

A Relation, Etc.

This thing is so rare in all its circumstances, and on so good authority, that my reading and conversation have not given me anything like it. It is fit to gratify the most ingenious and serious inquirer. Mrs. Bargrave is the person to whom Mrs. Veal appeared after her death; she is my intimate friend, and I can avouch for her reputation for these last fifteen or sixteen years, on my own knowledge; and I can confirm the good character she had from her youth to the time of my acquaintance; though since this relation she is calumniated by some people that are friends to the brother of Mrs. Veal who appeared, who think the relation of this appearance to be a reflection, and endeavor what they can to blast Mrs. Bargrave's reputation, and to laugh the story out of countenance. But by the circumstances thereof, and the cheerful disposition of Mrs. Bargrave, notwithstanding the ill-usage of a very wicked husband, there is not the least sign of dejection in her face; nor did I ever hear her let fall a desponding or murmuring expression; nay, not when actually under her husband's barbarity, which I have been witness to, and several other persons of undoubted reputation.

Now you must know Mrs. Veal was a maiden gentlewoman of about thirty years of age, and for some years last past had been troubled with fits, which were perceived coming on her by her going off from her discourses very abruptly to some impertinence. She was maintained by an only brother, and kept his house in Dover. She was a very pious woman, and her brother a very sober man, to all appearance; but now he does all he can to null or quash the story. Mrs. Veal was intimately acquainted with Mrs. Bargrave from her childhood. Mrs. Veal's circumstances were then mean; her father did not take care of his children as he ought, so that they were exposed to hardships; and Mrs. Bargrave in those days had as unkind a father, though she wanted neither for food nor clothing, whilst Mrs. Veal wanted for both, insomuch that she would often say, "Mrs. Bargrave, you are not only the best, but the only friend I have in the world; and no circumstance in life shall ever dissolve my friendship." They would often condole each other's adverse fortunes, and read together Drelincourt *Upon Death,* and other good books; and so, like two Christian friends, they comforted each other under their sorrow.

Some time after Mr. Veal's friends got him a place in the

custom-house at Dover, which occasioned Mrs. Veal, by little and little, to fall off from her intimacy with Mrs. Bargrave, though there never was any such thing as a quarrel; but an indifferency came on by degrees, till at last Mrs. Bargrave had not seen her in two years and a half; though about a twelve-month of the time Mrs. Bargrave had been absent from Dover, and this last half-year had been in Canterbury about two months of the time, dwelling in a house of her own.

In this house, on the 8th of September 1705, she was sitting alone, in the forenoon, thinking over her unfortunate life, and arguing herself into a due resignation to Providence, though her condition seemed hard. "And," said she, "I have been provided for hitherto, and doubt not but I shall be still; and am well satisfied that my afflictions shall end when it is most fit for me;" and then took up her sewing-work, which she had no sooner done but she hears a knocking at the door. She went to see who was there, and this proved to be Mrs. Veal, her old friend, who was in a riding-habit; at that moment of time the clock struck twelve at noon.

"Madam," says Mrs. Bargrave, "I am surprised to see you, you have been so long a stranger," but told her she was glad to see her, and offered to salute her, which Mrs. Veal complied with, till their lips almost touched; and then Mrs. Veal drew her hand across her own eyes and said, "I am not very well," and so waived it. She told Mrs. Bargrave she was going a journey, and had a great mind to see her first. "But," says Mrs. Bargrave, "how came you to take a journey alone? I am amazed at it, because I know you have a good brother." "Oh," says Mrs. Veal, "I gave my brother the slip, and came away, because I had so great a desire to see you before I took my journey." So Mrs. Bargrave went in with her into another room within the first, and Mrs. Veal set her down in an elbow-chair, in which Mrs. Bargrave was sitting when she heard Mrs. Veal knock. Then says Mrs. Veal, "My dear friend, I am come to renew our old friendship again, and beg your pardon for my breach of it; and if you can forgive me, you are the best of women." "Oh," says Mrs. Bargrave, "do not mention such a thing. I have not had an uneasy thought about it; I can easily forgive it." "What did you think of me?" said Mrs Veal. Says Mrs. Bargrave, "I thought you were like the rest of the world, and that prosperity had made you forget yourself and me." Then Mrs. Veal reminded Mrs. Bargrave of the many friendly offices she did in her former days, and much of the conversation they had with each other in the times of their adversity; what books they read, and what comfort in particular they received from Drelincourt's *Book of Death,* which was the best, she said, on that subject ever written. She also mentioned Dr. Sherlock, the two Dutch books which were translated, written upon Death, and several others; but Drelincourt, she said, had the clearest notions of death and of the future state of any who had handled that subject. Then she asked Mrs. Bargrave whether she had Drelincourt. She said, "Yes." Says Mrs. Veal, "Fetch it." And so Mrs. Bargrave goes upstairs and brings it down. Says Mrs. Veal, "Dear Mrs. Bargrave, if the eyes of our faith were as open as the eyes of our body, we should see numbers of angels about us for our guard. The notions we have of heaven now are nothing like to what it is, as Drelincourt says. Therefore be comforted under your afflictions, and believe that the Almighty has a particular regard to you, and that your afflictions are marks of God's favor; and when they have done the business they are sent for, they shall be removed from you. And believe me, my dear friend, believe what I say to you, one minute of future happiness will infinitely reward you for all your sufferings; for I can never believe" (and claps her hands upon her knees with great earnestness, which indeed ran through most of her discourse) "that ever God will suffer you to spend all your days in this afflicted state; but be assured that your afflictions shall leave you, or you them, in a short time." She spake in that pathetical and heavenly manner that Mrs. Bargrave wept several times, she was so deeply affected with it.

Then Mrs. Veal mentioned Dr. Horneck's *Ascetic,* at the end of which he gives an account of the lives of the primitive Christians. Their pattern she recommended to our imitation, and said, "Their conversation was not like this of our age; for now," says she, "there is nothing but frothy, vain discourse, which is far different from theirs. Theirs was to edification, and to build one another up in faith; so that they were not as we are, nor are we as they were; but," said she, "we ought to do as they did. There was a hearty friendship among them; but where is it now to be found?" Says Mrs. Bargrave, "It is hard indeed to find a true friend in these days." Says Mrs. Veal, "Mr. Norris has a fine copy of verses, called *Friendship in Perfection,* which I wonderfully admire. Have you seen the book?" says Mrs. Veal. "No," says Mrs. Bargrave, "but I have the verses of my own writing out." "Have you?" says Mrs. Veal; "then fetch them." Which she did from above-stairs, and offered them to Mrs. Veal to read, who refused, and waived the thing, saying holding down her head would make it ache; and then desired Mrs. Bargrave to read them to her, which she did. As they were admiring *Friendship,* Mrs. Veal said, "Dear Mrs. Bargrave, I shall love you for ever." In these verses there is twice used the word Elysian. "Ah!" says Mrs. Veal, "these poets have such names for heaven!" She would often draw her hand across her own eyes and say, "Mrs. Bargrave, do not you think I am mightily impaired by my fits?" "No," says Mrs. Bargrave, "I think you look as well as ever I knew you."

After all this discourse, which the apparition put in much

finer words than Mrs. Bargrave said she could pretend to, and as much more than she can remember, for it cannot be thought that an hour and three-quarters' conversation could be retained, though the main of it she thinks she does, she said to Mrs. Bargrave she would have her write a letter to her brother, and tell him she would have him give rings to such and such, and that there was a purse of gold in her cabinet, and that she would have two broad pieces given to her cousin Watson.

Talking at this rate, Mrs. Bargrave thought that a fit was coming upon her, and so placed herself in a chair just before her knees, to keep her from falling to the ground, if her fits should occasion it (for the elbow-chair, she thought, would keep her from falling on either side); and to divert Mrs. Veal, as she thought, took hold of her gown-sleeve several times and commended it. Mrs. Veal told her it was a scoured silk, and newly made up. But for all this, Mrs. Veal persisted in her request, and told Mrs. Bargrave that she must not deny her, and she would have her tell her brother all their conversation when she had an opportunity. "Dear Mrs. Veal," said Mrs. Bargrave, "this seems so impertinent that I cannot tell how to comply with it; and what a mortifying story will our conversation be to a young gentleman? Why," says Mrs. Bargrave, "it is much better, methinks, to do it yourself." "No," says Mrs. Veal, "though it seems impertinent to you now, you will see more reason for it hereafter." Mrs. Bargrave then, to satisfy her importunity, was going to fetch a pen and ink, but Mrs. Veal said, "Let it alone now, but do it when I am gone; but you must be sure to do it;" which was one of the last things she enjoined her at parting. So she promised her.

Then Mrs. Veal asked for Mrs. Bargrave's daughter. She said she was not at home, "But if you have a mind to see her," says Mrs. Bargrave, "I'll send for her." "Do," says Mrs. Veal. On which she left her, and went to a neighbor's to see for her; and by the time Mrs. Bargrave was returning, Mrs. Veal was got without the door into the street, in the face of the beast-market, on a Saturday (which is market-day), and stood ready to part, as soon as Mrs. Bargrave came to her. She asked her why she was in such haste. She said she must be going, though perhaps she might not go her journey until Monday; and told Mrs. Bargrave she hoped she should see her again at her cousin Watson's before she went whither she was going. Then she said she would take her leave of her, and walked from Mrs. Bargrave in her view, till a turning interrupted the sight of her, which was three-quarters after one in the afternoon.

Mrs. Veal died the 7th of September, at twelve o'clock at noon, of her fits, and had not above four hours' sense before death, in which time she received the sacrament. The next day after Mrs. Veal's appearing, being Sunday, Mrs. Bargrave was so mightily indisposed with a cold and a sore throat, that she could not go out that day; but on Monday morning she sent a person to Captain Watson's to know if Mrs. Veal was there. They wondered at Mrs. Bargrave's inquiry, and sent her word that she was not there, nor was expected. At this answer, Mrs. Bargrave told the maid she had certainly mistook the name or made some blunder. And though she was ill, she put on her hood, and went herself to Captain Watson's, though she knew none of the family, to see if Mrs. Veal was there or not. They said they wondered at her asking, for that she had not been in town; they were sure, if she had, she would have been there. Says Mrs. Bargrave, "I am sure she was with me on Saturday almost two hours." They said it was impossible; for they must have seen her, if she had. In comes Captain Watson while they are in dispute, and said that Mrs. Veal was certainly dead, and her escutcheons were making. This strangely surprised Mrs. Bargrave, when she sent to the person immediately who had the care of them, and found it true. Then she related the whole story to Captain Watson's family, and what gown she had on, and how striped, and that Mrs. Veal told her it was scoured. Then Mrs. Watson cried out, "You have seen her indeed, for none knew but Mrs. Veal and myself that the gown was scoured." And Mrs. Watson owned that she described the gown exactly; "for," said she, "I helped her to make it up." This Mrs. Watson blazed all about the town, and avouched the demonstration of the truth of Mrs. Bargrave's seeing Mrs. Veal's apparition; and Captain Watson carried two gentlemen immediately to Mrs. Bargrave's house to hear the relation from her own mouth. And when it spread so fast that gentlemen and persons of quality, the judicious and sceptical part of the world, flocked in upon her, it at last became such a task that she was forced to go out of the way; for they were in general extremely well satisfied of the truth of the thing, and plainly saw that Mrs. Bargrave was no hypochondriac, for she always appears with such a cheerful air and pleasing mien, that she has gained the favor and esteem of all the gentry, and it is thought a great favor if they can but get the relation from her own mouth. I should have told you before that Mrs. Veal told Mrs. Bargrave that her sister and brother-in-law were just come down from London to see her. Says Mrs. Bargrave, "How came you to order matters so strangely?" "It could not be helped," said Mrs. Veal. And her brother and sister did come to see her, and entered the town of Dover just as Mrs. Veal was expiring. Mrs. Bargrave asked her whether she would drink some tea. Says Mrs. Veal, "I do not care if I do; but I'll warrant you this mad fellow" (meaning Mrs. Bargrave's husband) "has broken all your trinkets." "But," says Mrs. Bargrave, "I'll get something to drink in for all that." But Mrs. Veal waived it, and said, "It is no matter; let it alone;" and so it passed.

All the time I sat with Mrs. Bargrave, which was some hours, she recollected fresh sayings of Mrs. Veal. And one material thing more she told Mrs. Bargrave—that old Mr. Breton allowed Mrs. Veal ten pounds a year, which was a secret, and unknown to Mrs. Bargrave till Mrs. Veal told it her. Mrs. Bargrave never varies in her story, which puzzles those who doubt of the truth or are unwilling to believe it. A servant in the neighbor's yard adjoining to Mrs. Bargrave's house heard her talking to somebody an hour of the time Mrs. Veal was with her. Mrs. Bargrave went out to her next neighbor's the very moment she parted with Mrs. Veal, and told her what ravishing conversation she had with an old friend, and told the whole of it. Drelincourt's *Book of Death* is, since this happened, bought up strangely. And it is to be observed that, notwithstanding all the trouble and fatigue Mrs. Bargrave has undergone upon this account, she never took the value of a farthing, nor suffered her daughter to take anything of anybody, and therefore can have no interest in telling the story.

But Mr. Veal does what he can to stifle the matter, and said he would see Mrs. Bargrave; but yet it is certain matter of fact that he has been at Captain Watson's since the death of his sister, and yet never went near Mrs. Bargrave; and some of his friends report her to be a liar, and that she knew of Mr. Breton's ten pounds a year. But the person who pretends to say so has the reputation of a notorious liar among persons whom I know to be of undoubted credit. Now, Mr. Veal is more of a gentleman than to say she lies, but says a bad husband has crazed her. But she needs only present herself and it will effectually confute that pretence. Mr. Veal says he asked his sister on her deathbed whether she had a mind to dispose of anything, and she said no. Now, the things which Mrs. Veal's apparition would have disposed of were so trifling, and nothing of justice aimed at in their disposal, that the design of it appears to me to be only in order to make Mrs. Bargrave so to demonstrate the truth of her appearance, as to satisfy the world of the reality thereof as to what she had seen and heard, and to secure her reputation among the reasonable and understanding part of mankind. And then again Mr. Veal owns that there was a purse of gold; but it was not found in her cabinet, but in a comb-box. This looks improbable; for that Mrs. Watson owned that Mrs. Veal was so very careful of the key of the cabinet that she would trust nobody with it; and if so, no doubt she would not trust her gold out of it. And Mrs. Veal's often drawing her hand over her eyes, and asking Mrs. Bargrave whether her fits had not impaired her, looks to me as if she did it on purpose to remind

Mrs. Bargrave of her fits, to prepare her not to think it strange that she should put her upon writing to her brother to dispose of rings and gold, which looks so much like a dying person's request; and it took accordingly with Mrs. Bargrave, as the effects of her fits coming upon her; and was one of the many instances of her wonderful love to her and care of her that she should not be affrighted, which indeed appears in her whole management, particularly in her coming to her in the daytime, waiving the salutation, and when she was alone, and then the manner of her parting to prevent a second attempt to salute her.

Now, why Mr. Veal should think this relation a reflection, as it is plain he does by his endeavoring to stifle it, I cannot imagine, because the generality believe her to be a good spirit, her discourse was so heavenly. Her two great errands were to comfort Mrs. Bargrave in her affliction, and to ask her forgiveness for the breach of friendship, and with a pious discourse to encourage her. So that after all to suppose that Mrs. Bargrave could hatch such an invention as this from Friday noon to Saturday noon, supposing that she knew of Mrs. Veal's death the very first moment, without jumbling circumstances, and without any interest too, she must be more witty, fortunate, and wicked too than any indifferent person, I dare say, will allow. I asked Mrs. Bargrave several times if she was sure she felt the gown. She answered modestly, "If my senses are to be relied on, I am sure of it." I asked her if she heard a sound when she clapped her hands upon her knees. She said she did not remember she did, but said she appeared to be as much a substance as I did, who talked with her. "And I may," said she, "be as soon persuaded that your apparition is talking to me now as that I did not really see her; for I was under no manner of fear, and received her as a friend, and parted with her as such. I would not," says she, "give one farthing to make any one believe it; I have no interest in it. Nothing but trouble is entailed upon me for a long time, for aught I know; and had it not come to light by accident, it would never have been made public." But now she says she will make her own private use of it, and keep herself out of the way as much as she can; and so she has done since. She says she had a gentleman who came thirty miles to her to hear the relation, and that she had told it to a room full of people at a time. Several particular gentlemen have had the story from Mrs. Bargrave's own mouth.

This thing has very much affected me, and I am as well satisfied as I am of the best grounded matter of fact. And why we should dispute matter of fact because we cannot solve things of which we have no certain or demonstrative notions, seems strange to me. Mrs. Bargrave's authority and sincerity alone would have been undoubted in any other case.

BOOK TWO

MAN AND HIS EMOTIONS

Most people think of psychology primarily in terms of emotions and emotional diseases—probably because this is the most dramatic area of psychological knowledge. Yet we know less about the emotions and how they function than about any other area of the mind. Here we can trace some of the arguments that have raged about the source and effect of the various emotions in both the physical and psychic worlds of man.

I

THE EXPRESSION OF EMOTIONS

In attempting to discover the source of the emotions in man, psychologists have been confronted by the same difficulties that have characterized so much of their work in the field: namely, is the source of emotions to be found in the physical or animal nature of man, or is it attributable to the psychic or nonmaterial sphere of human activity?

Do we cry because we are sad, or are we sad because we cry? It would seem that the answer to this question is twofold: we do cry because we are sad, and we are sad because we have the physical ability to cry.

The attempt to track down the source of human emotional behavior in animals has led to an impasse: animals seem to be incapable of the complex emotions as we know them. It is true that we can find something akin to love, fear, and hatred among animals. But the further elaboration of these basic physical reactions into amusement or grief, guilt or shame, is virtually nonexistent.

We have also learned that the ability to feel emotion in certain specific ways alters with growth. Children, for example, with their limited knowledge of the world, are apt to act more like animals in their first reactions to frightening situations. Their response is undifferentiated, intense, and lacks the possibility of social patterning which growth will eventually graft onto it. The fear exhibited by the boy in Graham Greene's story is the same pure fear that sends adrenalin pumping into the heart of an animal and sets it off to run or fight for its life. Without the outlet for the activity set up by fear, however, the body may undergo complex physical changes—and the fear, set up as a tool to preserve life, may in the end lead to death.

The elaboration of emotion into set patterns is, of course, never obvious among animals. Smiles and laughter, the tears that signify emotional turmoil, these exist only among men. And among men, these expressions are universal and have a universal meaning. The elaboration of emotion into certain specific forms seems to be imbedded in the physical and psychological nature of man. Its further specialization, however, may often prove to be culturally conditioned. Thus, kissing (which may have developed from the love bite) as an expression of love may be unknown among cultures in which another form of affection (equally solidly rooted in man's animal past) has been selected as the activity outlet for the emotion in question. Eskimo nose-rubbing can thus replace Western kissing.

These cultural concomitants of emotional expression are the concern of Otto Klineberg who sees in many of our modes of emotional expression the long arm of cultural determinism. Walter B. Cannon, on the other hand, supplies an analysis of the nature of emotion through the study of its physiological manifestations. In Ryunosuke Akutagawa's tale we find the characteristic emotional outlet dammed up by the necessities of culture. Grief is concealed behind a smiling mask—but in the end it is betrayed by the physical need for an appropriate, tension-relieving activity. There is no doubt that we are meant to see both faces in this story. The smiling mask that conceals the grief may have as much to tell us as the quivering fingers that betray it.

Smiling grief, tears of happiness, the hysterical laughter of the frightened—these have given us a clue to the peculiarly ambivalent nature of emotion. One cannot simply love or hate. Indeed, the idea of love could not exist without the possibility of hate. This human paradox is grist to the mill of the practicing psychoanalyst who helps the individual untangle the skeins of love and hate, which all intertwined can lead to emotional disorder. This paradox is also at the source of some of the world's finest literature. D. H. Lawrence was fascinated by the perverse duality which allowed a human to use love to control or destroy the object of his love. Ernest Jones indicates how the intensity of feelings of hate or guilt are conditioned by the intensity of love.

There is little doubt that a freer verbal expression of hostility could reduce the need for physical aggression. William Blake knew this a long time before psychologists "proved" it. But, in general, society frowns upon such expressions as Browning's, and most people are left with the necessity of repressing their anger and hatred. These emerge, however, in our literature and art, in our dreams, in our slips of the tongue, and in our humor. The truth—unpalatable as it may be—must have some means of expression—and humor is the most socially acceptable manner of cloaking unconscious hostility while relieving it.

Thus humor, like tragedy, is a device that lessens our libidinal tension. Imbedded in each quip of Clemens', buried in his sharp irony, is a deep bitterness which is an unconscious awareness of a hostile world. The themes of humor, like the themes of tragedy, can be traced in our dreams. Techniques of humor (condensation, substitution, etc.) are dream techniques. It is the gift that compensates us in some small way for our knowledge of death.

WALTER B. CANNON / What Strong Emotions Do to Us

AN ELEMENT of surprise and mystery accompanies a strong emotional outburst. In times of terror or of intense anger, for example, there is a surging up within us of forces of which in days of calm and comfortable living we have been quite unaware. So powerful may these forces be that their dominance, even though temporary, may be terrifying. They may lead us to acts which we remember with a thrill of self-satisfaction or, on the contrary, with pain and chagrin. Anyone who has been in the grip of great emotional excitement can readily understand deeds of desperate violence, whether good or bad, which may be the natural consequence of such an experience.

The mystery of the origin of our strong emotions has long interested philosophers and naturalists. It was early recognized that they are states which we have in common with subhuman beings. Significantly, Darwin entitled his classic study, *The Expression of the Emotions in Man and Animals*. And he was able to collect a remarkable array of evidence showing that among widely diverse races of mankind, as well as among the higher vertebrates, the same modes of expression were manifested. Baring of the teeth, dilation of the pupils, erection of the hair, growling or snarling, and a menacing approach are so generally the signs of rage and aggressive feeling that they form a common language which animals of very different types clearly understand.

Now the question arises as to why there is so much similarity in the expression of strong emotions in man and the lower animals. We can account for this fact by studies which have revealed that there is an ancient and primitive part of the brain which is the common possession of all vertebrates. Besides this, there is a new and, in the higher animals, a much larger part of the brain which has been gradually developed and which varies in complexity with the ability to make adjustments to novel situations. The cerebral hemispheres represent the new brain. In them occur the processes which are associated with consciousness. It has been shown that the cerebral hemispheres are not at all needed for emotional expression. In the absence of these structures all the varied and intricate activities that indicate rage, for example, will occur quite perfectly. The cat without cerebral hemispheres will snarl, bare its teeth, and show erection of its hairs, quite as the cat does naturally when enraged by a barking dog. From these observations some highly interesting inferences may be drawn.

In the first place, it is probable that in low forms of vertebrates having only the primitive brain, the reactions to circumstances are chiefly of the relatively simple reflex type. These animals have not the facilities for making many new combinations of response to their surroundings. Further, though the addition of the cerebral hemispheres permits the development of a more varied behavior, the persistence in higher animals of the archaic portion of the brain with its ingrained patterns assures fixed and typical reactions when proper occasions arise to call them forth. And again, since the mechanism of these primitive responses lies in a part of the nervous system not concerned with consciousness, we can readily understand how these mechanisms, when brought into action with elemental intensity and power, would seem to have a mysterious origin, would appear like a strange external force sweeping in and seizing control of one's actions. It is most natural that under such circumstances one behaves as if "possessed," and becomes, unless control is exercised, "a slave of passion."

Closely related to the archaic portion of the brain in which the patterns of the strong emotional responses are engraved, is a part of the outreaching nervous system which connects the brain with the viscera. This is the so-called "sympathetic" system. Its strands are widely distributed to the stomach and intestines, to the liver and pancreas and other structures essential for proper digestion, to the heart and all over the body to the muscles in the walls of blood-vessels, to the iris in the eye, to the hair and sweat glands in the skin, and to some of the glands of internal secretion. These last mentioned organs—for example, the adrenal bodies which lie just above the kidneys, and the thyroid gland which lies in the neck—elaborate materials of extraordinary potency which are given off into the blood stream and which have profound effects on the organism. Obviously, if the sympathetic system is brought into action, many changes will occur in structures hidden away from the superficial observer.

The sympathetic, or visceral, part of our nervous organization is often distinguished from the part which controls the muscles attached to the skeleton by being called "involuntary." By taking thought we cannot cause the stomach to contract quickly or slowly or to start or stop its services. The agitated person may, to be sure, say, "Be still, my heart"; but this is an admonition which that organ, fortunately for the continued existence of the individual, does not obey. Indeed, if the multitude of intricate adjustments that are constantly occurring in the organs which operate to digest the food we eat, to store it or distribute it where it is needed, to remove waste, to arrange for growth and repair and the processes of reproduction, had to be looked after by us, consciously, moment by moment, we should be incapable of attending to any affairs outside our own bodies. Luckily, all these visceral functions are managed by automatic devices. The lower animals, and primitive men as well, are quite unaware of what occurs in these hidden parts of the organism. Only by prolonged and painstaking study have the secrets of these internal processes been revealed.

Though the workings of the viscera cannot be directly controlled by act of will, they can be profoundly affected by emotional states. In fact the *sympathetic* nervous system received that name because it is roused to activity in times of intense feeling. Since its filaments are widely distributed to structures having most important offices to perform in the bodily economy, it is clear that the "expression" of strong emotions is much more complex and deep-seated than we might at first think. Many of the alterations that take place under great emotional stress have been recently revealed by physiological study. More of them are sure to be revealed as investigation proceeds. In order to understand the significance of emotional responses it will be important to review briefly what we already know about these visceral aspects.

Fundamental to all our other activities is that of digesting the food we eat, for from that food is derived the energy for the work we do. The stomach and intestines receive the food that is swallowed, transmit it from stage to stage along the alimentary tract, mix it thoroughly with the juices poured out by the digestive glands and, when it has been properly changed for passage through the intestinal wall, the intestinal motions bring it into intimate contact with the absorbing surfaces of that wall. All these processes are completely stopped in states of fear or anger or deep anxiety. The X-rays have permitted us to look into animals while they are digesting. If any great excitement is occasioned, the churning stomach becomes a flabby inactive sac, the kneading intestines cease their motions, and the digestive glands no longer secrete the juices necessary to prepare the food for absorption. Thus, the whole beneficent process is brought to a standstill. This cessation of the digestive activities, first clearly demonstrated on lower animals, has been proved true also of human beings. And it is interesting to note that the workings of the alimentary canal are not only stopped during an outburst of rage, but do not start again for a considerable period after the emotional storm has passed off.

While digestion is not going on and the organs are at rest, only a moderate amount of blood is supplied to them. When examined under these circumstances the alimentary tract may have even a pallid appearance. At the height of digestive activity the conditions are very different. Then the blood-vessels are dilated, and the surfaces are flushed red by the abundance of the blood supply. The same emotional states that stop the processes of digestion alter simultaneously the distribution of blood in the body. The muscles encircling the small arteries in the digestive organs are made to contract, and thus to lessen the size of the channels. Thereby, the delivery of blood to these organs is greatly reduced. The pressure of blood is raised in the arteries all over the body. In the presence of increased arterial pressure the blood-vessels of the brain, the heart and the lungs do not contract. In consequence the blood, which is no longer delivered in great volume to the digestive canal, is transferred to these organs, which are now lavishly provided with this essential fluid. At the same time the heart beats very much more rapidly and, as a result, greatly increases the rate at which the blood circulates through the body.

Incidentally, it may be mentioned that any muscles which are set at work by voluntary act will also be richly supplied with blood. Thus, both the brain which sends forth the nervous impulses and the instruments by which these impulses become effective, the muscles, are especially fortified against failure in case demands for activity are made upon them in an emotional outburst.

The services which the blood performs for active organs are various. It conveys the material which is used by the laboring muscles as a source of energy. The material most readily available for that purpose is the kind of sugar that the blood carries. In order to render this energy available combustion must occur, and for combustion oxygen is required just as it is required for a fire outside the body. The rapidly moving blood becomes loaded with oxygen in the lungs and delivers it to the active organs according to their needs. The products of the burning that takes place in the body, just as in the burning of the same substance outside the body, are water and a gas, carbon dioxide. These waste products the blood transports from where they are produced to where they are discharged—the water to the kidneys, the carbon dioxide to the lungs.

During great muscular activity the amount of carbon dioxide that is discharged by the lungs is commonly six times as much as the amount given off during rest. This means that approximately the same degree of increase of oxygen-delivery to the active organs will be required. We are all aware of the much deeper and more rapid breathing which is automatically required whenever we engage in any vigorous exertion. The air that rushes in and out of the lungs must pass through the narrow tubes of the lungs, the bronchioles. If the muscles in the walls of these tubules contract, the passageway is made still narrower and breathing then becomes difficult. Such is the condition in one kind of asthma. Great emotional excitement has the opposite effect: It causes relaxation of these muscles. A London physician has observed the sudden disappearance of a distressing asthmatic attack in consequence of intense fright. With the widening of the bronchioles there would be a freer movement of the air to and fro, and thus, in case of need, oxygen could be brought more readily to the depths of the lungs and carbon dioxide could be eliminated, even though the production of this gas were multiplied many-fold.

In the liver is stored a reserve of energy-yielding material in the form of glycogen, or animal starch. In times of great excitement this substance is changed to sugar, is set free into the blood stream, and thus is circulated all over the body. The amount of sugar thus liberated for use may be so abundant that it may actually be wasted by passing out of the body through the kidneys. Half the members of a football squad, at the time of the supreme contest of the season, were found to have such an abundance of sugar as a result of their emotional tension.

The discharge of sugar from the liver is a sort of internal secretion—like the secretion of saliva by the salivary glands—with the difference that the substance is given off to the circulating blood instead of being poured out on a body surface. Another organ which has an internal secretion of high potency and which is subject to the control of sympathetic nerves is the inner portion of the adrenal glands. These are small structures, which, as previously mentioned, are found just above the kidneys on either side of the body. The substance which they produce, called adrenin or epinephrin, has the remarkable property of mimicking by chemical action the effects produced by sympathetic nerve impulses. Thus, if it is extracted from the adrenal glands and injected into the blood stream, it will induce a stoppage of all the processes of digestion, it will cause a rise of blood pressure while sending the blood away from the digestive organs to the heart and the central nervous system and the skeletal muscles, it will dilate the bronchioles, and it will liberate sugar from the liver. Besides these effects and others which need not be mentioned, it has the capacity of producing certain striking changes in fatigued muscles and in blood.

As a muscle is more and more used in a routine manner until it is fatigued, it becomes less and less responsive. We are all familiar with the sense of effort which we experience under these conditions. Though a part of our difficulty is doubtless due to disturbances in the controlling nerves, there is good evidence that the inability of the muscles to perform their task is an important element in the complex. For example, in artificial stimulation of muscles by electric shocks it is found that as the muscle shows signs of fatigue the strength of the stimulus required barely to cause contraction must be much increased. If now the muscle is permitted to rest, it regains in time its former responsiveness. An hour or more may have to elapse, however, before complete recovery occurs. It has been discovered that a minute amount of adrenin in the circulating blood will refresh the muscle in an almost miraculous way. Within a few minutes the tired muscle is as ready to respond to stimulation as if it had had a prolonged rest.

A remarkable property of the circulating blood is that of changing from a liquid to a jelly when it comes in contact with an injured surface. This formation of a clot occurs in normal animals whenever the blood-vessels are torn or cut. Thereby the opening in the vessels is sealed and the precious fluid is prevented from being lost. Evidently the more rapidly the process of clotting occurs, the less will be the escape of blood through the break in the channel. Recent studies have shown that a small amount of adrenin set free in the blood stream will induce a more rapid clot formation. And if an animal has been much excited, the time required for coagulation of a given amount of blood may be reduced from about five minutes to a minute or less. Here is an instance of a striking chemical change brought about in the body by emotional conditions which we have been accustomed to regard chiefly in their psychological or subjective aspects. It is probable that other similar effects will be revealed by further investigation—effects which may readily account for tales of surprising "cures" or physical improvements in consequence of an altered mental state.

The question now arises as to the significance of this group of internal changes associated with strong emotional stress. Why should a function so serviceable to bodily maintenance as digestion be stopped? Why should the blood be shifted to the brain and the muscles? What is the reason for liberating sugar from the liver? Is there any meaning in the action of adrenin in refreshing the tired muscles? Are there circumstances in which a more rapid clotting of the blood would be especially valuable to the organism?

If we revert to the point, previously mentioned, that the expression of emotion is ingrained in our nervous system and is always ready to appear at the appropriate time, we get a noteworthy hint regarding the nature of the emotional responses. It is characteristic of these ingrained reactions that they are useful. When we cough we clear a foreign object from the throat, when we vomit we usually prevent the passage of harmful material onward through the digestive tract, when our eyes "water" the tears dilute an irritant substance or help to wash away an intrusive bit of dust. The close association between such automatic acts and their utility has led to the general statement that as a rule reflex behavior is typically purposive—it serves the individual or the race in some beneficial way. In other words, when the right performance is run off without rehearsal or any previous instruction, we are justified in looking for some definite good that may result.

In order to understand the service which may be performed by the bodily changes occurring in great emotional excitement, we must consider the conditions under which such excitement is aroused. And we must not confine our inquiry to human beings, but must extend it to lower animals in which the same changes take place. Furthermore, we must think of animals in their natural existence, surrounded by their enemies, having to fight or escape, and in need of pursuing their prey. If we take these various situations into our survey, we shall have a clearer view of all the elements in the fundamental emotions of fear and rage.

The emotion of fear is typically evoked when a creature is in the presence of danger, and most commonly in natural existence the danger is that of being assailed by a stronger creature. Associated with fear is the impulse to run away, to escape by flight from the presence of the enemy. On the other hand, if escape is impossible and a fight is necessary, the emotion of fear is likely to turn to a fury of aggressive feeling. This attitude also is associated with an impulse—that of attack. Whether an animal is the attacker or the attacked, the pursuer or the pursued, the issue of the struggle which ensues may be life or death. In other words, these emotions and impulses are concerned with the primitive law of self-preservation. Since animals have struggled with each other for existence through myriads of generations, we can perceive that the internal changes which automatically accompany strong emotional stress may have become quite naturally developed in our nervous systems as pattern responses, and may help in some manner to make the strong stronger and the swift swifter and more enduring at times of critical peril.

Either running or fighting for life involves the use of large muscular masses—the great muscles of the thighs, the back and the shoulders—in prolonged and perhaps supreme exertion. With this fact in mind, let us see how the diverse internal alterations, already described, may fit together for the service of the organism as a whole. As previously noted, the laboring muscles require an abundant supply of oxygen—much more than they need when at rest. In emotional excitement the blood, which carries the oxygen from the lungs to all parts of the body, is pressed out of the abdominal organs and into the heart, the lungs, the brain and the active muscles. The processes of digestion cannot continue effectively in the absence of a large delivery of blood; as the blood is removed from the stomach and intestines these organs cease working. In short, digestion is of incidental importance when the body as a whole is endangered. The material which has been stored in the liver in consequence of previous digestion, however, is now called forth. Sugar is released and is carried in the blood stream to be ready at once as a source of muscular energy. The immensely increased work of the muscles is linked with a greatly increased production of carbon dioxide. This must be eliminated at the same time that more oxygen is brought for transport in the blood. The breathing becomes more deep and rapid, and the dilation of the bronchioles that follows sympathetic stimulation renders more facile the tidal flow of air in and out of the lungs. The secretion which is set free from the adrenal glands in emotional excitement can also be given a role to play. In case the struggle or flight is prolonged and fatigue begins to render the muscles less responsive, the secreted adrenin has the effect of restoring their original capacity to do work. And furthermore, if there is fighting, with rupture of blood-vessels, the faster clotting of the blood that accompanies adrenal secretion operates promptly to check bleeding.

The foregoing review of the bodily changes in emotional excitement shows that they can all be reasonably interpreted as a mobilization of the resources of the organism for purposes of special efficiency in a critical struggle. With other conditions equal, doubtless the animal in which these changes appear quickly and thoroughly would have a distinct advantage in a conflict with another animal in which they are tardy and partial in their development. And since the struggles associated with the major emotions of rage and fear often decide the continued existence of the victor and the death of the vanquished, the transmission to offspring of the well-ordered arrangements for rapid assembling of the bodily forces is assured.

The changes which we have detailed are not all that might be mentioned as favorable to effective physical effort. For example, heat is produced by active muscles and must be dissipated if the body temperature is not to reach a fever level. That result is obviated by sweating, for the evaporation of sweat removes heat from the body. The sweating which occurs in strong emotion can be regarded as anticipatory of that function. Again, there is evidence that the thyroid gland, like the adrenal, is subject to sympathetic control, but just what its secretion may do in emergencies has not yet been determined. Enough has been stated, however, to show that the various profound alterations in the bodily economy which attend an outburst of strong feeling are characterized by being highly serviceable in rendering the organism more efficient in physical struggle.

The mobilization of the bodily forces for struggle will occur under great excitement although no muscular effort is undertaken. For example, a careful observation of students subjected to severe examination has proved that they not infrequently have so large an amount of sugar set free in the blood that it escapes through the kidneys. The heart beats rapidly, the blood pressure is elevated, the blood becomes concentrated, indeed, probably all of the organic adjustments preparatory to a fight or a flight are fully elaborated. In the presence of these preparations for action, however, the only physical effort which the students engage in is that of moving the small muscles of the hand and forearm in writing. Many of the worries and anxieties and excitements of civilized life are of this character. The stockbroker watching the ticker may become as much disturbed as if he were confronted by a wild beast. But the situation in which he finds himself usually does not require any exhibition of muscular strength or endurance for which the complex internal rearrangements have been developed. In other words, because of racial habits, established by multitudes of generations of our ancestors who have had to protect themselves and one another against fierce attack, we are today agitated by deep-seated disturbances which are commonly of little service to us. The question arises as to whether such useless and frustrated mobilization of the bodily forces for activity, with no activity ensuing, may not be harmful; whether, to use another figure, getting up steam and letting the engine "race" without doing work is not likely to be damaging. There is some evidence that such is the fact. During our Civil War and, to a much greater degree during recent wars, men broke down with "disorderly action of the heart." This was a condition characterized by a remarkable acceleration of the pulse on the slightest exertion or in the mildest emotional upset. Furthermore, physicians are aware that a large proportion of the cases of disturbed digestion with which they have to deal are what are designated "emotional dyspepsia." We may conceive these derangements of the working of the heart and the stomach as being due to repeated excitements calling upon these organs to prepare for a crisis. Thus a sort of habit is established such that even very trifling worries and anxieties are sufficient to set going the emotional mechanism, or parts of it, when there is no possible use for the changes that occur. Thus an admirable internal arrangement, of highest value to the organism in natural conditions, may become so badly disordered as to be a menace to the welfare of the body as a whole.

From the foregoing facts and considerations there are at least two practical hints that seem reasonable. First, since the bodily changes induced by strong feeling are preparatory for action, it is in accord with ages of past experience to let them be expressed in action. A fit of rage can be turned to good account by the performance of hard labor that needs to be done. Thereby, the emotional preparations have their outlet, the task is accomplished and the body has the benefit of the muscular exercise! Again if irritating conditions develop which cannot be dealt with in a practical manner by doing something, the wise man is he who accepts them philosophically, and, so far as possible, turns his attention to other affairs. Thus the futile emotional disturbance may be aborted. There is no advantage to be gained by letting the body make ready for a supreme effort, when there is no effort whatever to be made. This is, to be sure, often a counsel of unattainable perfection, but there is no doubt that by taking one attitude emotional factors can be emphasized and elaborated to alarming proportions, and by taking another attitude they can often be diverted and minimized to insignificance.

HAROLD E. JONES and MARY COVER JONES/Maturation and Emotion—Fear of Snakes

What Do Children Fear?

As CHILDREN grow older, they begin to show differences in the number and kinds of things of which they are afraid. The only general statement which seems to cover all the cases of fear which we have observed in children is that children tend to be afraid of things that require them to make a sudden and unexpected adjustment. Stimuli which are startlingly strange, which are presented without due preparation, or which are painful or excessively intense, belong in this category. For example, in our study of the reactions of pre-school children to flashlights, darkness, falsefaces, snakes, rabbits, frogs, and the like, it was found that the animal which most often caused fear was the frog, the fear not usually appearing at first sight of the frog, but at sight of the frog suddenly jumping. Likewise, a child was often afraid of a jack-in-the-box. A species of beetle which suddenly snaps up in the air when placed on its back was fairly efficient in arousing alarm, while caterpillars and earthworms produced no more than a mild curiosity in the younger children.

While traces of these childhood fears may last throughout life, affecting adult behavior profoundly, the overt expression of fear is apt to be less marked as childhood is outgrown—partly because the adult meets fewer unfamiliar situations (encounters fewer stimuli for which his action system contains no ready adjustment) and partly because he has learned to mask and repress the more conspicuous symptoms of emotion. From watching individuals of different ages in similar test situations, it is evident that the effectiveness of a stimulus and the type of emotional response are greatly affected by maturity. From the diffuse responsiveness of the infant, to the blunted and inhibited reaction of the blasé adult, the variety of unpredictable behavior in fear-producing situations provides a rich field for research.

How does the sight of a snake affect a baby, a toddler, a youth, a grandfather? A few cases, chosen from our laboratory notes, show an interesting development sequence.

Experiments with Young Children

Experimental Situation. A pen 8 by 10 feet by 6 inches high was built on the nursery floor. Within this a number of blocks and toys were scattered, and two black suitcases were placed flat on the floor near the wall. The suitcases could be opened easily by a child; one contained a familiar mechanical toy, the other contained a snake of a harmless variety (*Spilotes corais*) about six feet in length and slightly under four inches in girth at the middle of the body. When free in the pen, the snake glided actively about, showing a powerful and agile type of movement, and frequently protruding a black forked tongue about an inch in length. If the child did not open the suitcase containing the snake, an observer was able to do so from a concealed position behind a screen, by pulling a string attached to the lid of the case.

Subject 1. Irving, age 1 year 3 months.

Irving sat in the pen, playing idly with the ball and blocks. After being released, the snake glided slowly toward Irving, whipping up his head and deflecting his course when within 12 inches of the infant. Irving watched unconcerned, fixating the snake's head or the middle of his body, and letting his gaze wander frequently to other objects in the pen. The snake furnished only a mild incentive to his attention.

Subject 3. Enid, age 1 year 7 months.

Enid sat passively in the pen, playing with blocks in an unsystematic fashion. The snake was released and moved fairly rapidly about the pen. Enid showed no interest, giving the snake only casual glances and continuing to play with her blocks when it was within two feet of her. When (later) the snake was held by the observer directly in front of her face, she showed no changes in facial expression, but presently reached out her hand and grasped the snake tightly about the neck.

Subject 8. Sol, age 2 years 3 months.

When the snake began moving about the pen, Sol watched closely, holding his ground when the snake came near, but making no effort to touch it. He resisted when an attempt was made to have him pick up the snake (this was the same guarded reaction that he had shown previously with the rabbit and white rat). He stood unmoved when the snake was thrust toward him, and showed no overt response, save an attempt to follow visually, when the head of the animal was swung in front and in back of him, neck writhing and tongue darting. After the snake was returned to the suitcase he went to it again and lifted the lid, looked within and then closed it in a business-like manner.

Subject 11. Laurel, age 3 years 8 months.

Laurel opened the suitcase, picking out two blocks which were lying against the snake's body. The snake was immobile and she evidently had no differential reaction to it. The snake was taken out. Laurel: "I don't want it." Avertive reactions, moved off, then stood up and started to leave the pen, although without apparent stir or excitement. Experimenter: "Let's put him back in the box." Laurel: "I don't want it." Experimenter: "Come and help me put him back." After slight urging she came over and assisted, using both hands in picking up the snake and dropping him quickly when she reached the suitcase.

Subject 12. Edward, age 4 years 2 months.

Edward sat down in the pen and began playing constructively with the blocks. At sight of the snake he asked: "Can it drink water?" Experimenter: "Do you know what it is?" Edward: "It's a fish." He puckered his brows and made slight avertive reactions when the snake was swung within a foot of him, but this was overcome through adaptation in three trials. When encouraged to touch the snake he did so, tentatively, but soon grasped it without hesitation at the neck and body.

Subject 15. Ely, age 6 years 7 months.

On opening the suitcase he smiled and looked within for nearly a minute, making no effort to reach, and dropping the cover quickly when the snake moved. The snake thrust the lid up with his head, and glided out into the room. Ely took up a post of observation outside the pen. Experimenter: "Do you like him?" Ely nodded in the affirmative and smiled. Experimenter: "Touch him like this." Ely very hesitatingly touched his back, and withdrew his hand quickly, later consenting to stroke him. He asked: "Does he have teeth?" a reasonable enough inquiry. When the snake moved in his direction he drew away and looked distressed, but was persuaded to help pick him up and to put him back in the suitcase.

Of 15 children, 7 showed complete absence of fear indications; their age range was from 14 to 27 months, with a median of 20 months. Eight individuals showed "guarded" reactions, 2 of these revealing distinct fear, and 2 showing marked avertive responses when the snake gave the appearance of aggression; the other four being classified as "unafraid but wary." The age range of the "guarded" group was from 26 to 79 months, with a median of 44 months. The only case of a child under three years showing fear was Doris, age 26 months, and her reaction changed markedly the following day, as indicated by the report of the group response:

The suitcase was taken into the nursery when 9 children were present. Most of them recognized it, and one of the older children said, "There's an animal in there." Several of the children moved forward to touch it as soon as the snake was released; Doris who had been afraid the day before now showed no fear, crowding close and attempting to hit the snake's head with a wooden boat. The two oldest children in the group remained cautious: Lawrence, age five years seven months, climbed up on a table, and John, age five years ten months, retained hold of the experimenter's hand, and refused to come near. After a few minutes of play, the experimenter said, "Now everyone has touched it except John and Lawrence." Both of these now came forward and touched the snake's back, social pressure being evidently effective in encouraging a more positive response.

Experiments with Older Children

The following results were obtained in a group of 36 school children, with an age range of from about six to ten years.

The children were sitting on low chairs in a circle about 20 feet in diameter. The experimenter placed the suitcase containing the snake in the middle of the circle, asking, "Who wants to open the suitcase?" Harry, eight years of age, opened it, and took the snake out when requested. The snake glided about the floor, passing between the feet of one of the boys; no disturbance was shown. The experimenter now asked, "Who wants to touch the snake?" holding the snake's head so that the children had to reach past it, and walking slowly around the inside of the circle. The first 11 children touched the snake with no hesitancy. Four boys about ten years of age hesitated, one withdrawing markedly, another falling over backward in his chair. (This was due to an emotional heightening, arising partly from fear and partly from a desire to show off.) Two girls refused to touch the snake, but jumped up and ran around behind the circle, following the experimenter and watching closely. An undercurrent of reassurance was constantly heard, "He won't let it hurt you. Go ahead, touch it, it won't bite."

Only 9 of the 26 children showed definitely resistive behavior, and these were chiefly boys and chiefly the oldest in the group.

Experiments with College Students

How do adults behave, when presented with a similar situation?

In several classes of undergraduate and graduate students, a snake was introduced as "a perfectly harmless animal; the skin of this reptile has a smooth and pleasant feeling, and we guarantee that in touching him no one runs the slightest risk." In some classes the same reptile was used as in the preceding experiments; in others the snake was a boa constrictor, somewhat smaller and of a less "dangerous" appearance than the *Spilotes*. Of about 90 students nearly one-third refused to have the snake brought near; one-third touched him, with obvious hesitation and dislike, while the remainder (including as many women as men) reached forward with apparently complete freedom from any emotional disturbance. Several of the women obviously regarded the presence of a snake in the room as an almost unbearable ordeal, and several of the men solved the problem of emotional conflict by retiring to a neighboring room until the experiment was concluded.

Recommendations for Further Experiments

With some of our adult subjects, we noted that while they stroked the snake in an apparently composed fashion, the subject's face and palms were nevertheless covered with beads of perspiration, indicating a marked degree of emotional tension. With young children such repressions are less likely to occur: The emotion is more superficial, and expresses itself readily and frankly in external symptoms. In studying the elimination of a fear, however, we should bear in mind the possibility that an attitude of tolerance

ERNEST JONES/Fear, Guilt and Hate*

I

ANYONE WHO has seriously tried to unravel the complicated relationships subsisting between any two of these emotional attitudes will agree that the problem is one of exceptional difficulty. I hope, nevertheless, that the considerations to be brought forward here will contribute in some measure in elucidating at least the nature of the complexities in question and thus in furthering the approach to the more fundamental problems that lie behind them. As in our daily analytic practice, and indeed in all forms of scientific investigation, to get problems clearly stated is by no means the least difficult part of the task, nor is it the least important part.

Let us first consider the more purely clinical aspects of these relationships. The heart of the difficulty soon reveals itself. It is that—to speak statically—there exists a curious series of layer formations definitely connected one with the next, the connection being often in the nature of a reaction. This holds good for each of the emotional attitudes in question, so that one may be found at a given level in the mind, another at a deeper level, the former again at a still deeper level, and so on. It is this stratification that makes it so hard to tell which is the primary and which is the secondary of any two groups. To put the matter more dynamically, it is the complex series of interactions among these attitudes that makes it hard to determine chronologically their developmental relationships.

Let me now illustrate these generalities. If we have a patient suffering from any form of fear neurosis, of bound or unbound 'morbid anxiety,' we know from our experience that guilt must surely be present also. It is sometimes easy to demonstrate this, sometimes extremely hard, but we know that if the analysis is consistently pursued this proposition will be proved to be true. I am not maintaining in the abstract that fear cannot exist apart from guilt, but I should certainly maintain that clinically observed fear, a neurosis in which fear is one of the symptoms, always has guilt behind it. As Shakespeare long ago pointed out, 'Thus conscience does make cowards of us all.' Yet the matter is not so simple. It cannot be that an emotional reaction so phylogenetically ancient as fear is can be solely dependent on, or gener-

* Reprinted from Ernest Jones, *Papers on Psychoanalysis* (London: Balliere, Tindall & Cox Ltd., 1937), chap. xxi, 444-59. By permission of Balliere, Tindall & Cox, Ltd., and Beacon Press.

ated by, one so recently acquired as guilt is, one the very existence of which—at all events in a fully developed form—is doubtful in other animals than man. We have here an example of how a biological outlook may serve as a check on clinical investigation and warn us against a possibility of readily going astray. Our scepticism is confirmed by still deeper analytic research, particularly into the earliest stages of infantile development, where we find extensive evidence indicating that the guilt itself proceeds from a yet earlier state of fear. And it is worth while remembering in this connection that the guilt can be extraordinarily deep. A patient may have succeeded so extensively in expressing unconscious guilt conflicts in terms of conscious fear, may be so completely convinced that his difficulties arise from fear and nothing else, that it may in certain cases take years of analysis to make the underlying guilt conscious. Were it not that this procedure does not necessarily in itself solve the therapeutic problem the analyst might well have rested from his labours and felt satisfied that he had found a complete answer to his problem of the genesis of the phobia—namely, that it originated in guilt.

A similar stratification can be observed with hate. This is one of the commonest covers for guilt, and the way in which it functions here is easy to understand. Hatred for someone implies that the other person, through his cruelty or unkindness, is the cause of one's sufferings, that the latter are not self-imposed or in any way one's own fault. All the responsibility for the misery produced by unconscious guilt is thus displaced on to the other, supposedly cruel person, who is therefore heartily hated. The mechanism is, of course, very familiar in the transference situation. We know that behind it there always lies guilt, but further analysis still shows, in my opinion always, that the guilt itself is dependent on a still deeper and quite unconscious layer of hate, one that differs strikingly from the top layer in not being ego-syntonic.

In the last of the three possible combinations, of fear and hate, the same thing is to be observed. Hate, notably in its milder forms of ill-temper, irritability and anger, is commonly enough a cover for, or a defence against, an underlying state of apprehensiveness. This may occur either chronically, as in a disagreeable and irritable character, or acutely, as when a sudden alarm evokes an outburst of anger in place of panic. Yet we have good reason to think that the underlying fear is rarely, if ever, present unless there is a still deeper layer of hate, of the same ego-dystonic type mentioned just above.

In all these three cases, therefore, it is not hard to demonstrate the presence of three layers of which the first and third are of the same nature. In one of the three cases fear constitutes the deepest layer, in the other two hate. But we are here only at the beginning of our problem, for the state of affairs just presented does no more than illustrate the nature of the complexity in it; it tells us nothing about the final chronological or ætiological relationships. For this a deeper analysis is necessary, and this time I shall find it easier to consider each of the three emotional attitudes separately. We may begin with that of hate, for it would appear to be the least complicated of the three.

II

We have seen how various manifestations of the *Hate* impulse can cover both anxiety and guilt, but that there is reason to suppose that in all such cases there is present below these a still deeper layer of hate. It is highly probable that the more superficial one is derived from the latter, so that it might from one point of view be described as a breaking through of what had been repressed. It is, of course, not simply a break through, for there are several notable differences between the two, the aim towards which it is directed, the conditions under which it appears, and so on. Among these the most important doubtless is the relation to the ego. What we have called the superficial—*i.e.*, conscious—layer achieves in most instances, at least at the moment when it is being experienced, an extraordinary degree of ego-syntonicity. There are few emotions in life that can give the subject such intense conviction of being in the right, that carry with them such a complete sense of self-justification, as anger—the acme being reached in what is called righteous indignation. By definition this is quite otherwise with the deeper, unconscious layer of hate. If now we try to reconstruct the precise relationships between the two layers, we shall come to the following conclusions: The primary hate is probably the instinctive response of the infant, usually in the form of rage, to frustration of its wishes, particularly its libidinal wishes. This primary 'reactive' impulse commonly fuses with the sadistic component of the libido to make what we meet with clinically as sadism. In the overcoming of the thwarting object there are therefore two sources of erotic satisfaction, the original, previously thwarted one and the pure sadistic one. Later on, however, this gratification is interfered with by guilt. The secondary, conscious reaction of hate is an attempt to deal with the guilt, or, rather, the impotence it has caused. Its method of revolting against the guilt is to project this outwards, to identify the forbidding agency with another person, who is then identified with the original thwarting person in connection with whom the guilt has been generated to start with. It is in this sense that we can speak of the secondary hate layer as a return of the repressed, but it is strictly conditioned by creating a phantasy of the other person being in the wrong or by manœuvring reality so as to bring this about.

It is curious, and seemingly a paradox, that guilt can be relieved by an exhibition of the very thing—namely, hate—which was the generating occasion of the guilt itself. We are familiar with the talion principle in psychology and with the exactness with which the punishment is made to fit the crime. We have here an example of a very similar principle, which might be termed the *isopathic principle*,[1] according to which the cause cures the effect. If hate causes guilt, then only more hate, or rather hate otherwise exhibited, can remove the guilt. The most remarkable example of it is the idea unconsciously cherished by every neurotic, part illusion, part truth, that love is the only cure for guilt, that only by pursuing (and being allowed to pursue) a sexual goal will he ever be relieved of his suffering. The idea is compounded of a pleonastic platitude ('if I feel free and sanctioned in a sexual situation I shall feel no guilt') and an illusion, that privation or frustration must necessarily signify guiltiness. I may quote another example of this isopathic principle, one also closely connected with the themes here under discussion. In a previous paper, on the Origin and Structure of the Super-Ego, I insisted on the essentially defensive nature of guilt, on its being generated to protect the personality from the privation which this characteristically interprets as frustration (*e.g.*, at the hands of the father). Now clinically in the neuroses, and always in the transference situation, we observe this guilt mainly in the indirect perspective of projection; the prohibiting, condemnatory and thwarting functions of the guilt-arousing agency, the super-ego, are mirrored in the patient's vision of the analyst. More than this, if the self-punishing tendencies are at all highly developed, we may expect to find that the patient will provoke the outer world—*i.e.*, father-substitutes—to inflict punishments on him, and it is easy to see that this is done in order to diminish the sense of guilt; by provoking external punishment the patient saves himself from some of the severity of internal (self-) punishment. We get three layers very alike to the other sets of three mentioned above: first dread of external punishment (*e.g.*, by the father); then guilt and self-punishment to protect the personality from the outer one, the method of religious penance; and finally, the evoking of external punishment, a disguised form of the original one, so as to protect the personality from the severity of the self-punishing tendencies. The father is invoked to

---

[1] At the Congress I used the phrase 'homeopathic principle,' but Dr. Federn has reminded me that homeopathists reserve the term 'isopathy' for the particular part of their principles here concerned.

save the person from the thing that saved him from the father! As in vaccine therapy, the disease is cured by administering a dose of its cause, and, just as there, the success of the cure depends on the dosage of the morbific agency being brought under voluntary control.

The last part of this excursion, which I hope will help us in our further considerations, leads us to the second of our themes, namely *Guilt*. I should expect to find general agreement among analysts in the clinical and analytical observation that the sense of guilt is the most concealed—though not necessarily the deepest —of the three emotional attitudes we are considering. My experience is that human consciousness tolerates either fear or hatred more readily than the sense of guilt. A feeling of inferiority or general unworthiness is the utmost that the majority of patients can achieve in this direction, and from their extreme sensitiveness to the very idea of criticism one can only infer that the risk of really—not merely verbally—admitting that they are in the wrong constitutes a formidable threat to the personality. This intolerability varies a good deal, of course, among different people, and I have very much the impression that one of the chief factors on which the variation depends is the strength of the sadism present. If this observation proves to be correct[2]—that is, that the intolerability of guilt varies directly with the savagery of the sadism present—then one could not fail to connect it with Melanie Klein's opinion that the genesis of the super-ego is to be found in the sadistic rather than in the phallic stage of development. In this connection one must raise the question whether guilt can arise purely as a way of dealing with—a defence against—the primary anxiety of unsatisfied libido or, on the other hand, is it always and inevitably associated with the hate impulse? I should be inclined to answer both these questions in the affirmative, but with the important modification that one is thereby distinguishing two phases in the development of guilt. In the former case it would not really be correct to speak of guilt in the full sense: one needs some such expression as a 'prenefarious' stage of guilt. This must closely resemble the processes of inhibition and renunciation; the formula would appear to be the categorical 'I mustn't because it is intolerable.' It attempts thus to avoid the primary anxiety, but the situation becomes more complicated when an object relationship begins to be set up. Here sadism combined with rage at frustration breaks through, love of the other person[3] conflicts with dread of

[2] Freud has pointed out a similar connection in the case of obsessional neuroses ('Hemmung, Symptom und Angst,' S. 50).
[3] It seems to me highly unlikely that guilt ever appears in relation to an object who is simply hated: ambivalence is an essential condition of guilt.

punishment at his hands (castration and withdrawal of the loved person), and the second stage, that of fully developed guilt, is constituted. Here we may describe the formula as 'I shouldn't because it is wrong and dangerous.' Love, fear and hate[4] are all equally necessary for this consummation, so that it would not be wrong to describe the super-ego as a compound of all three, its peculiarity being the making internal of attitudes previously directed outwards. As was remarked earlier, there is little doubt that the self-punishing function of guilt is destined to protect the individual from the risk of punishment from without, just as it is with religious penance.

It is at this point that we encounter the first of the more ultimate problems. How comes it that the process designed to protect the personality from an impossible situation, which may for present purposes be defined as the fear evoked by hate, becomes itself unendurable? So much so that the individual in self-defence against this salvation reverts to the very attitudes, fear and hate, he was being protected from. How can these be at the same time more intolerable and less intolerable than guilt? It can only be that we are confounding two things under the one term, that of guilt. I suggest that the two things are the two stages indicated above, that of renunciation and that of self-punishment respectively. If so we should expect a certain inverse correlation between the two. There is a great deal of evidence to bear this out, and indeed Reik and Alexander go so far as to see in the self-punishing tendency a device to spare the subject the necessity of renunciation; that is to say, he punishes himself so as to procure for himself the necessary condition for indulgence. It has further to be remembered, as was hinted earlier in this paper, that the secondary appearance of fear and hate is by no means identical with the deeper layers of these. It is in a sense much more artificial: the danger of external punishment to which the subject exposes himself, for instance, is rarely serious, certainly not in comparison with the grim reality that the original danger seems to the unconscious. They are, in other words, much more ego-syntonic than the primary layers, much more under the control and regulation of the ego.

We now have to consider the third and last theme, that of *Fear*.[5] Let us begin by putting the question: does fear (of injury) always signify the idea of retaliation—*i.e.*, does it always imply a previous attitude of hate, or even of guilt as well? Theoretically

---

[4] It is interesting that the word 'innocent' denotes 'not hurting.'
[5] It will be plain that I constantly use the word 'fear' in this paper in the clinical sense of anxiety and apprehension, not necessarily in the biological sense of alertness with its appropriate responses.

there appears no good reason why it should, and with many animals—*e.g.,* rabbits—it would seem a very gratuitous assumption. Nevertheless, if we adhere to our clinical findings, at least in all ages beyond the very earliest infancy, we are bound to admit that we never find the one without the other, so that we have to postulate the presence of hate, and probably also guilt, whenever we come across fear. This is perhaps because pure privation so rapidly comes to signify deprivation and frustration and hence evokes anger and hate. If privation proves too hard to bear and leads to fear we may be sure that in practice both hate and guilt are also present. This clinical observation is, however, no proof that *early* anxiety is secondary to either hate or guilt, as it would often appear to be in the upper layers of the mind. On the contrary, all the evidence, notably that of infant analyses, points to its preceding these.

Coming now to the subject of fear itself, the first problem is to distinguish between fear of an external danger, an event proceeding from without, and fear of an internal danger, one arising from the development of a certain internal situation. There is no doubt that failure adequately to appreciate this distinction has greatly retarded our progress in the past. It has been so illuminatingly drawn by Freud in his 'Hemmung, Symptom und Angst' that I need only refresh your memory by quoting one passage from that work (S. 120): 'Der Angst wurden so im späteren Leben zweierlei Ursprungweisen zugewiesen, die eine ungewollt, automatisch, jedesmal ökonomisch gerechtfertigt, wenn sich eine Gefahrsituation analog jener der Geburt hergestellt hatte, die andere, *vom Ich produzierte,* wenn eine solche Situation nur drohte, um zu ihrer Vermeidung aufzufordern.' ('Thus we attributed two sources of origin to anxiety in later life. One was involuntary, automatic and always due to economic causes and arose whenever a situation analogous to birth had established itself. The other was produced by the ego as soon as a situation of this kind merely threatened to occur, in order that it might be avoided.') Our patients sometimes give us a conscious hint of it in their complaint of being 'afraid of fear,' or 'afraid of being afraid.'

Before inquiring into the nature and function of the fear or anxiety response let us be clear about the nature of the danger. Freud (*op. cit.,* S. 126) gives the name of 'traumatic situation,' characterised by helplessness and completely vague indefiniteness about the object of the dread, to that in which the subject is unable to cope with a mass of over-excitation for which no discharge can be provided. It is evidently the primordial situation, though he thinks it can recur in later life, particularly in the somatic anxiety neurosis. The typical fear in the psychoneuroses, on the other hand, he terms 'a danger situation,' where anxiety is purposively produced by the ego so as to warn the personality of the possible approach of the traumatic situation and the desirability of taking precautions to avoid it. These two evidently correspond to what we have provisionally termed the internal and external dangers respectively. Freud insists that the dread in the psychoneuroses is always dread of an outside intervention, that the libidinal impulse is ultimately a source of danger not in itself but only because of the intervention it may give rise to (*op. cit.*, S. 67). There would appear to be two fundamental ways in which the external danger expresses itself, and we shall see that they both lead to the re-establishment of the primary internal one. Either the object who can provide gratification—*e.g.*, the mother in the boy's case—is withdrawn, or else a parent, there the father, threatens to take away the organ necessary for the obtaining of gratification. In either event the result is the same: in the former a state of privation is set up directly, in the latter indirectly through deprivation. But privation is another name for the original traumatic situation, that of intolerable libidinal tension consequent on the blocking of efferent discharge. We can thus say that the danger to which Freud alludes when speaking of the 'Kastrationsangst des Ichs' (*op. cit.*, S. 40) is that the ego may lose the capacity, or opportunity, for obtaining erotic gratification. The fear is lest the excitation of libido that cannot or is not allowed to obtain gratification may lead to the interference with the libido that can: to put it shortly, the libido that is not ego-syntonic constitutes a danger to the libido that is. This may be expressed clinically as a direct fear of impotence, but the more interesting variety is where the fear is lest the personality itself be lost, lest the loftiest ideals or the most laudable enjoyments be interfered with. Analysis shows that in such cases these always represent *imperfect* sublimations of the incest wishes themselves, for they constitute the kernel of the narcissistic investment of the ego. That is why the danger in question can be equally well described as one to the ego or to the libido; strictly speaking, it is to the ego's possession of libido, to its capacity for achieving libidinal gratification whether of a sensual or of a sublimated kind.

  Now this is exactly what I wished to designate by using the term 'aphánisis.' Some colleagues have expressed surprise that just I, who have always insisted on the concrete nature of the unconscious, notably in connection with symbolism, should now describe part of its content by such an abstract Greek term. My reasons were two. In the first place I find it necessary to insist on the absoluteness of the thing feared, and this thing is something even wider and more complete than castration, if we use this word in its proper sense. The penis can be very extensively renounced by men, even in the unconscious, its place being taken by other erotic zones in exchange, and with women the personal significance of it is almost altogether secondary. The ultimate danger with which we are here concerned is to all possible forms of sexuality, not only to the inaccessible, forbidden ones, but also to the ego-syntonic ones and the sublimations of these. It means total annihilation of the capacity for sexual gratification, direct or indirect, a matter on which we shall again have to lay emphasis when we come to consider the primary traumatic situation. In the second place it is intended to represent an intellectual description on our part of a state of affairs that originally has no ideational counterpart whatever in the child's mind, consciously or unconsciously. It is therefore quite a different thing from an analytic interpretation of the unconscious in the usual sense. In the anxiety neurosis, for instance, there is, according to Freud, an automatic creation of an emotional state of anxiety rather than a state of fear with the idea, either consciously or unconsciously, of any specific danger. Whether this is so there or not—and it seems to me likely enough —we have to admit that it must be so in infancy, at a period that precedes any ideational thought whatever; I refer not merely to the birth situation itself, about which so much is still doubtful, but to many months afterwards when we can observe a state that may be called pre-ideational primal anxiety (*Urangst*). It is only later, when the situation is becoming externalised and the anxiety is created by the ego as a 'signal' (Freud) for warning purposes, that we can speak of ideational fear, one which then usually has a specific reference.

Having cleared some of the ground concerning the 'danger,' we can now pass to closer consideration of the dread itself, and this brings us to the primary 'traumatic situation.' There is little doubt that, as Freud has from the beginning insisted, this early anxiety is quite directly connected with the simple situation of libidinal privation. One says 'connected with,' but the precise nature of the relationship between the two constitutes the second of the more fundamental problems we encounter in the course of the present considerations, and one of the most obscure in the whole field of psycho-analysis. I have for many years expressed the view that Freud's formula of the conversion of repressed libido into anxiety was untenable on both psychological and biological grounds and he has himself recently withdrawn it (*op. cit.*, S. 40), though he still makes a reservation in the case of primal, automatic or objectless anxiety (*op. cit.*, S. 41, 88). The question therefore arises whether the known biological significance of the fear instinct as a defensive response, together with the entirely defensive significance of 'signal' anxiety in the psychoneuroses, should not lead one to attempt the same solution in the case of primal anxiety. The situation itself can be defined: it is that of helplessness in the face of intolerable libidinal tension for which no discharge is available, no relief or gratification of it; Freud speaks of the 'Unbefriedigung, des Anwachsens der Bedürfnisspannung, gegen die er ohnmächtig ist' ('non-gratification, of a growing tension due to need, against which it is helpless') (*op. cit.*, S. 82) and says that the real kernel of the 'danger' is 'das Anwachsen der Erledigung heischenden Reizgrössen' ('an accumulation of amounts of stimulation which require to be disposed of') (*op. cit.*, S. 83). Can we get any further than this? Why is the tension in question intolerable, and in what sense is it alarming? Is the evidently inhibiting effect of the anxiety in some way a defence against whatever is intolerable, or is it a simple, so to speak mechanical, consequence of over-excitation that is blocked? I believe it is both. If we consult the sister science of physiology—and perhaps we are justified in doing so when dealing with such a profound pre-ideational region—we learn that a similar situation there, which can of course be experimentally induced, ends in exhaustion of the stimulation itself; a hungry man ceases to be hungry when food is unobtainable for long, and fasting experts are presumably men who can tolerate the initial stage of excitation and reach that of gastric anæsthesia better than others can. With the libido, however, this would be tantamount to total annihilation of it, and all possibility of erotic functioning would be gone, subjectively for ever. It may be that it is this resulting state of aphánisis, corresponding exactly with that brought about by external danger in the ways described above, against which the primal anxiety constitutes a defence.

There are two other points of view which would appear capable of throwing light on the problem. If we inquire into the constituent phenomena of anxiety we find, as I have described elsewhere in detail,[6] that both the mental and physical ones can be divided into two groups, that of inhibition and that of over-excitation respectively; the contrast between the diminished flow of saliva and the increased flow of urine will serve to illustrate the point. This must have some meaning. A second consideration is afforded by the following suggestion. It continues the train of thought already hinted at, according to which it may be possible to show that even primal anxiety has, if not a purpose in the psychological sense, at least a function to perform. It would not be strange if the ego, in the truly desperate situation in which it finds itself, made every imaginable effort to alleviate it. These

[6] See Chapter XIX.

efforts, I suggest, may be divided into two groups, which overlap the division of the actual phenomena into the two groups mentioned above. They are (1) attempts to isolate the ego from the excitation; these represent the flight aspects of the fear instinct, would if successful bring about a state akin to hysterical anæsthesia, and must be the dawnings of what Freud terms the primal repression (*Urverdrängung*), and (2) attempts to deal more directly with the excitation itself, either by affording limited avenues of discharge or, more aggressively, by damping down the excitation itself. The first of these groups needs no further explanation, but it is necessary to amplify the account of the second one. Many of the over-excitation phenomena—*e.g.*, mental excitement, pollakiuria, etc.—must afford some measure of libidinal discharge, and Freud has suggested (*op. cit.*, S. 129, footnote) that even the paralysis of inhibition may be exploited in a masochistic sense. We are reminded of the circumstance, which has not, I think, been explicitly formulated, that the same is true of all forms of defensive mechanisms. Reik and Alexander have, for instance, forcibly pointed out that guilt has not only the effect of inhibiting the forbidden impulses; it has also invented a special mechanism, that of punishment, whereby they can, at least in some measure, be gratified. In regression, which, as Freud has clearly pointed out, is a form of defence, there occurs a leak on the lowlier but more accessible levels to which the libido has receded. In guilty self-castration itself, the subject obtains the benefit of functioning erotically on the feminine plane. As to the damping-down process, the essence of every inhibition, I regard this as the earliest stage of the renunciation which later on is an essential part of the process whereby the unavailing incest wishes become transformed into more useful psychical activities. The central importance of it in the genesis of the neuroses will presently claim our further attention.

If the conception put forward here is valid we reach the conclusion that what the infant finds so intolerable in the primal 'traumatic' situation, the danger against which it feels so helpless, is the loss of control in respect of libidinal excitation, its incapacity to relieve it and enjoy the relief of it. If the situation is not allayed it can only end in the exhaustion of a temporary aphánisis, one which doubtless signifies a permanent one to the infant. All the complicated measures of defence that compose the material of our study in psycho-analysis are fundamentally endeavours to avoid this consummation. Primary anxiety, no less than the later 'signal' anxiety, belongs essentially to these defensive measures. Repression, which, as Freud has recently pointed out, takes its place in the series of defences, is one of the consequences of anxiety.

III

It remains to co-ordinate the relations subsisting between fear, guilt and hate, and to formulate the generalisations that would appear to emerge from the reflections I have detailed above.

We have observed that two stages can be distinguished in the development of each of these three mental reactions. With fear there is first the primal aphánistic dread arising from the intolerable tension of unrelieved excitation, and, secondly, when this privation has become identified with external frustration, the 'signal' dread of this danger. With hate there is first the anger at frustration, and, secondly, the sadism resulting from the sexualising of the hate impulse. With guilt there is first what we have termed the prenefarious inhibition, the function of which is to assist the early fear reaction and which in effect is hardly to be distinguished from it, and, secondly, the stage of guilt proper, the function of which is to protect against the external dangers.

It will be noticed that only fear and guilt exhibit the phenomenon of inhibition. When this develops further into the renunciation undertaken with the object of deflecting the wishes into more promising directions the outcome may prove satisfactory. Perhaps it is because this element is lacking in the hate-sadism reaction, and also because from its very nature it tends to provoke the external danger still more, that this reaction has such unfortunate consequences both socially and pathologically (obsessional neurosis, paranoia and melancholia). Clinically it commonly appears as the only available alternative to inhibition and guilt, as a defence or protest against them, but the reverse of this may also occur, where inhibition and guilt alternate with each other as a defence against the dangers of sadism.

The critical point in the whole development is evidently that where the internal situation becomes externalised, where privation gets equated to frustration. Just because it is more accessible, more easily influenced, and a welcome aid in the task of obtaining the relief of gratification, the infant must find the situation altered to its advantage, though, it is true, it then encounters old dangers in a new form. In dealing with these the phantasy of the strict parent plays an important and, indeed, indispensable part. The magnification of the external dangers increases the advantages gained by externalising the situation and also, by the development of the super-ego, points the way to coping with the difficulties in their new form. Just as the reactions of adolescence are determined by those of the infantile sexual phase, so must those of the external—*i.e.*, Œdipus—situation of fancy be influenced by those of the preceding internal situation. For instance, the greater the primal anxiety the more will the imago of a strict parent be used in the Œdipus situation; the more sadistic the earlier reaction the more difficult will it be to deal with the guilt of the latter, and so on. We are thus led to lay stress on the importance of the earliest reactions. It was a revelation when Freud established the fundamental truth that all fear is ultimately fear of the parent, all guilt is guilt in respect of the parent, and all hate is hate of the parent. We are beginning to see, however, that even these very early attitudes must themselves have a pre-history, one which in all probability greatly influences them.

To complete the list of our conclusions the considerations should be recalled that were brought forward at the beginning of this paper. There I called attention to the various layers of secondary defence that covered the three attitudes of fear, hate and guilt, and pointed out that the defences themselves constituted a sort of 'return of the repressed.' We have seen how deep must be the primary layers of these three emotional attitudes, and also that two stages can be distinguished in the development of each of them. The relationship of the secondary layers would appear to be somewhat as follows. Any one of these primary attitudes may prove to be unendurable, and so secondary defensive reactions are in turn developed, these being derived, as was just indicated, from one of the other attributes. Thus a secondary hate may be developed as a means of coping with either fear or guilt, a secondary fear attitude ('signal' anxiety) as a means of coping with guilty hate, or rather the dangers that this brings, and occasionally even a secondary guilt as a means of coping with the other two. These secondary reactions are therefore of a regressive nature, and they subserve the same defensive function as all other regressions.

It is worth calling attention to the part played by the libido in connection with the three emotional attitudes in question. Each one of them may become sexualised. With fear there is the masochistic aspect of paralytic inhibition and the somatic discharge in the fear reaction itself, with guilt there is moral masochism, and with hate the development of sadism.

Freud has recently commented on the remarkable fact that we are even yet not in a position to give a satisfactory answer to the apparently simple question of why one person develops a neurosis and another not. I am convinced that when we are able to give a final form to this answer it will prove to lie in the infant's response to the primal 'traumatic' situation, and consequently to the Œdipus danger that later develops out of it. The main conclusion of the present paper is that fear, hate and guilt can all be regarded as reactions to this primal situation, as means of coping with it. The fundamental problem is evidently how to sustain a high degree of libidinal tension without losing control of the situation. If the infant is so helpless as to stand in danger of the spontaneous aphánisis of exhaustion he will resort to desperate measures and will then run the risk of oscillating between two unfavourable reactions. On the one hand he may depend too much on the artificial aphánisis of inhibition, and this will, in its turn, bring with it loss of control over the disturbing wishes through losing possession of them, through disappearance of the wishes themselves. On the other hand, he may pursue the easier path of developing in an excessive degree the defensive reactions of fear, hate and guilt, the path leading surely to neurosis. It would probably be more accurate to say, not that he oscillates between these two ways, but that the former is the primary one and that he is impelled to adopt the latter one only when that fails. This would account for the prominence of the 'all-or-none' reaction so characteristic of severe neuroses and of the demonstrable fear of moderation that neurotics display. To control or guide a wish, or to hold it in suspense when necessary, signifies to a neurotic to admit into play the reaction of guilt which to him appears the only conceivable motive for controlling an impulse. Of this he has a well-founded dread, because he has never learnt to control the inhibiting tendency that constitutes its essence and in which is inherent the danger of artificial aphánisis. The very thing in which he originally sought salvation has become his greatest danger.

If the train of thought here presented is substantiated it must have important bearings on the practical problems of therapeutics. The most difficult aim of therapeutic analysis is to induce toleration, first for the reaction of guilt, then for the hate and fear that underlie it, and the greatest obstacle we encounter is the patient's lack of confidence in the possibility of controlling the originally defensive inhibiting tendency. The battle is half won when he realises that there are other than moral reasons for restraining the gratification of an impulse; it is wholly won when he fully realises that this capacity for restraint, instead of being the danger he has always imagined, is, on the contrary, the only thing that will give him what he seeks, secure possession of his personality, particularly of his libidinal potency, together with self-control in the fullest sense of the word. Then only is he able to deal adequately with reality, both in his own nature and in the outer world.

ERNEST JONES/Jealousy*

IF A FOREIGNER ventures to develop a psychological theme before a French audience, in the land *par excellence* of psychology, he will need to justify himself with more than usual care. What, then, will you think of his audacity when he selects as his theme the one chosen for this lecture? For if there is any of the human sentiments about which the French are supposed to know everything worth knowing, surely it is jealousy. Your poets, writers and psychologists have explored it both intensively and extensively, and their intuitive genius has flashed illumination on its secrets. After what they have written, can anything be said that is not banal? Yet I tell myself that even if I said nothing new I could nevertheless count on your interest. That your interest in the theme is perennial and inexhaustible is shown by the part it plays in your public life. I do not know if anyone has ever calculated what proportion of your theatre is occupied with the theme of jealousy, but it must be greater than that of any other theatre. And what would be the circulation of any newspaper if it excluded *crimes passionels* from its contents? Perhaps some would buy it from curiosity to see what else of interest there could be in the world to fill a whole newspaper. You have even evolved a special jurisprudence in this connection, though I understand it is not actually yet incorporated into your laws.

The theme may therefore be presumed to be interesting to you. But this consideration alone would be a poor excuse for my having chosen it, for it would mean exploiting a ready-made interest. On the contrary I have the high ambition of stimulating in you a new interest in this well-worn theme, and the reason why I dare cherish such an ambition is that, thanks to the new science of psycho-analysis, I have something new to offer you. For the truth is mightier even than national pride. And the truth is that, with all her brilliant contributions to science, especially to that of psychology, France has not a monopoly of knowledge. It happens from time to time that discoveries of great importance are made in other countries, and then France is faced with a somewhat painful situation. Like all great lovers, France prefers to give rather than to receive, and when she is asked to receive knowledge won in a foreign country she consents to do so only after transforming the gift so as to impart to it something of her own peculiar genius.

* Reprinted from Ernest Jones, *Papers on Psychoanalysis* (London: Balliere, Tindall & Cox Ltd., 1937), chap. xxiv, 469-85. By permission of Balliere, Tindall & Cox Ltd., and Beacon Press.

I do not doubt that this will be the case also with psycho-analysis and, indeed, its leading exponent in France, M. le Dr. Laforgue, has already occupied himself with this task by adapting the new knowledge to the characteristic idiom of French thought.

Why psycho-analysis is a discovery of great importance can be told in a word or two. It is because it has shown that what we have hitherto known as our minds is really but the small part of a totality. In the future we shall have to refer to them by the more modest title of conscious mind, realising that this conscious mind is only a relatively small and selected portion of our whole mind, that it is in great part derived from a deeper layer which we now call the unconscious, and that it owes to this its driving force. The nature of this unconscious, absolutely and totally unknown to the conscious mind, has been laid bare to us by Professor Freud, of Vienna, whose genius forged a method for exploring this previously dark and inaccessible territory. To make our understanding of any psychological process complete, therefore, we now have to add to what we may know about it by conscious introspective methods all that can be found out by the psycho-analytic method about its origins, derivations and unconscious associations. This work has not only answered many questions previously obscure, but has made us realise that there is a number of questions which till now we had not even put, because being content with our knowledge we did not know that these questions existed.

Let me at once illustrate this last remark by proceeding to the theme of the lecture itself. So much is known about jealousy, its relation to love and hate, the exact circumstances under which it arises, and so on, that it would be easy to come to the conclusion that everything essential about it is already known. But I can put a number of questions to which I do not think it would be easy to give a really satisfying answer. To begin with, is it really known why some people are more jealous than others, or why women suffer more frequently from this complaint than men? It certainly is not to be correlated simply with the strength or the fidelity of the love: some of the best lovers are rarely jealous, and some of the weakest appear to be more interested in jealousy than in love itself. When men are betrayed is it known why one man proceeds to shoot the woman, another the interloping rival? This certainly does not depend on the external situation, but on something obscure in the psychology of the individual man. Is there any psychological difference between the jealousy of a lover who does not yet know whether his wooing is going to be preferred to his rival's and the jealousy against a rival who later intrudes and threatens to take from him the woman he has already won; or between the jealousy founded on suspicions, often groundless, and the outburst on the occasion of an open betrayal? It is even difficult to say to what extent jealousy is a normal phenomenon, an inevitable accompaniment of love, and if so how this differs in its nature, apart from its external manifestations, from what psychologists call morbid jealousy, a condition which may at times amount to actual insanity.

These few questions alone are enough to remind you that there are many kinds as well as degrees of jealousy, and one is led to ask whether there can be any single underlying principle to account for this variety. I may say at once that in my opinion investigation of the unconscious processes on which all these manifestations depend justifies one in announcing a single key which can unlock all the main secrets. Before disclosing this, however, I propose to lead you first from the manifestations themselves to consideration of the deeper factors concerned, and I will begin with contrasting the more familiar 'normal' jealousy with the extreme forms of insane jealousy; that will give you some idea of the magnitude of our task.

It will be simpler to consider separately the problems in the two sexes and we will start with the classic situation of the eternal triangle, two rivals for a woman's love. My first remark will be one that will astonish those of you who are not acquainted with psycho-analysis. It is that we have the best reasons to conclude that when a man finds himself in this situation it is not for the first time in his life. Every little boy finds himself in the same situation, for he has had two parents of opposite sexes and he cannot escape an attitude of jealousy in his desire for the exclusive possession of his mother's love. This is just as true whether his father is still present or already dead, or even if he is brought up by another woman than his own mother. An emotional attitude towards the father is then developed which contains all the elements present later in the adult situation. They are fear, hostility and guilt. The little child does not, of course, manifest these emotions in the open manner that an adult may, though signs of them often enough leak through to the surface and can be detected by the attentive observer. They soon enter into what we term a state of repression, are buried and forgotten, and usually remain entirely unconscious for the rest of the person's life. They are, however, none the less actively operative for that. We consider that this primal situation is the archetype for all later life, and that on the particular way in which the child deals with it will depend his reactions and behaviour when confronted in later life with all the manifold problems and difficulties that occupy so much of the sphere of love. All the typical attributes of his love-life are thus determined in early infancy. You will agree now that this first conclusion is strange and astonishing, that if it is true it belongs to knowledge that is unrecognised, and probably also that the conclusion is repellent as well as strange. Yet this discovery of Freud's was forestalled nearly two centuries ago, of course by a Frenchman. Diderot, in *Le Neveu de Rameau,* writes of a little boy: 'Si le petit sauvage était abandonné à lui-même, qu'il conserva toute son imbécillité et qu'il réunit au peu de raison de l'enfant au berceau la violence des passions de l'homme de trente ans, il torderait le cou à son père et coucherait avec sa mère.' In these words we have a perfect description of what psycho-analysts call the Œdipus complex.

It is easy to enumerate the elements of which jealousy is made up in the simple situation when a dangerous rival appears. The first sign is fear at the thought of losing the loved object, and this will turn into the pain of grief if she has been lost. Accompanying this is hatred of the rival and perhaps also of the faithless woman. Then, more secret but probably more important than either of the other two elements, there is the wound to self-esteem and self-love, to what in psycho-analysis is called narcissism. I am going to lay a great deal of stress on this element and hope to elucidate it further. In doing so I find support in the words of a great French writer, La Rochefoucauld, who very aptly said: 'Il y a dans la jalousie plus d'amour-propre que d'amour.'[1] Shand, the Scottish psychologist, writes in a similar vein: 'It is due to the desire of self-love to possess certain things exclusively for self . . . that jealousy principally arises.'[2]

This feeling is tantamount to what we call a feeling of inferiority, a sense of diminished worth, and at times the person is aware of a sense of self-criticism as though he were wondering what fault on his part could have led to this state of affairs. This observation is in accord with the results of psycho-analytic investigation, which show that all such feelings of inferiority ultimately proceed from a latent sense of moral inferiority, from the reservoir of guiltiness rarely absent from the unconscious and which many people spend most of their lives in evading. The unconscious guilt is derived from the early reactions to the Œdipus complex in infancy, and the constant fight between it and human desires constitutes the unconscious conflict on the results of which mainly depend an individual's capacity for happiness.

So far the description is readily intelligible: fear or grief, wounded self-esteem and anger. It is all so evident that no need is felt for any special explanation, although I have perhaps already hinted that the full analysis even of this simple situation will prove

[1] La Rochefoucald, 'Maximes,' ccxxiv.
[2] Shand, 'The Foundations of Character,' 1914, p. 258.

it to be more complete than it appears. At all events, it is clarity itself in comparison with the extreme or insane form of jealousy, to which I now invite your attention. Here we see the same elements magnified into a caricature, but with the striking feature added of groundlessness, for it is well known that the most insatiable jealousy may co-exist with absolute fidelity of thought and deed on the part of the loved person. The fear here takes the form of a mad suspiciousness, that overthrows all reason, that finds food in the most innocent trifles, and that distorts, misreads, misjudges evidence to such an extent that no sanity remains. The anger and hatred may culminate, as we know, in savage murder. The wounded narcissism is less in evidence, being evidently protected by the hate which, like most hate, presents itself as righteous. Now in the true delusional type of jealousy, psycho-analysis has made a very remarkable discovery, one, I think, never anticipated before Freud's work on the subject. It has been able to show that the jealousy process is dictated far more by interest in the rival than by interest in the woman—that, in short, it is a perverted expression of a repressed homosexuality. The chain of events that underlies it is as follows: The subject has a strong homosexual tendency which he has repudiated so completely as to bury it in the unconscious—*i.e.*, to make himself quite unaware of its existence. As a reaction to it, or compensation for it, or defence against it—all expressions are equally correct—he has in a forced way tried to love a woman. This has perhaps succeeded for a time until the buried tendency re-asserts itself, often in response to some new stimulation, some change in the environment, or perhaps some diminution in the woman's attractiveness. This type of man, who, incidentally, is often too fond of drink, makes a special appeal to many women, particularly those with a highly developed maternal instinct. They instinctively feel that he needs help and encouragement, and their vanity assures them that they are the destined saviour. Such marriages are, however, built on an insecure foundation, love of the adult type is hardly possible in them, and the *dénouement* we are now concerned with is far from being the only one that can ensue. When the collapse comes the interest in the other man is, in the nature of the case, not allowed to manifest itself in a positive fashion. The resulting symptom of morbid jealousy can be described in many ways, all accurate according to the point of view adopted. One can say that it constitutes a violent repudiation of the homosexuality: it says, in effect, 'No, I do not love that man; on the contrary I detest him.' Or one can say that the man identifies himself with his wife and through her plays, in his imagination, a feminine part with the other man. In other words, he projects on to his wife the desires he has to repudiate in himself. He says: 'It is not I who am in love with that man, it is my wife who is.' His forbidden love for the man comes to expression under the mask of exaggerated love for his wife, if we accept the conventional judgement that jealousy is a measure of love.

The actual manifestations of this delusional jealousy are often so mad and the underlying factors I have just outlined are so foreign to ordinary consciousness that one might well despair of being able to establish a common bond between it and the familiar everyday jealousy to which I first referred. Nevertheless psycho-analysis has been able to show that the factors underlying even ordinary jealousy are more subtle and complex than is generally supposed, and that in their nature they are not so very far removed from those responsible for delusional jealousy. It would indeed be strange if it were otherwise, for it is pretty plain that the extreme form is essentially an exaggeration of the simple one. All the main elements of suspicion, fear, grief, anger and shame are present with both, and it would be unlikely if this unique constellation of emotions that we call jealousy could arise in two entirely separate ways and from two entirely different sources. I can at once point to one psychological mechanism common to the two forms, the one we referred to above under the name of projection. We saw how the masked homosexual projected on to his wife his repressed love for the other man. Now what is very frequent, possibly even universal, in simple jealousy is that the man projects general feelings of infidelity on to the woman, feelings he does not always avow to himself. It is undoubtedly the Don Juans of this world who cannot trust women; they cannot believe in their fidelity because they cannot believe in their own: they project on to them their own faithless and fickle desires. Who was it sang 'La donna è mobile, quant 'è il vento'? Rigoletto's duke, whose only pastime was the pursuit of women. A cynic might say that such men mistrust women because their experience has shown them how easy it is to seduce them, but this logical rationalisation only covers the deeper psychological factors. If, therefore, this particular mechanism of projection can occur in both forms perhaps we shall find that the origins also of the two have more in common than might at first sight appear.

To develop my argument I must next consider some general propositions on the subject of love itself. Here again I am going to be bold and venture to think that it will be possible to say something new about love to, of all audiences in the world, a Parisian one. Now what I have to say is something sad, and that is that there is much less true love in the world than there appears to be, and even much less true passion. Investigation of the deeper layers of the mind teaches one that love and passion can fulfil many other functions than their own, which means that they can be conjured up for other motives than the normal one of love. And it is by no means easy to distinguish what we might thus call secondary love from primary love, especially as they commonly occur together, completely fused with each other. Let us take the case of ordinary politeness, the mildest manifestation there is of affection. We all know the difference here between genuine politeness, what the French so gracefully call *politesse du cœur,* and the artificial mannered politeness. More interesting is the observation that the latter is commonly employed to mask an unfriendly attitude, to cover disdain, suspicion, dislike, apprehension or even hostility. This is notably so with well-bred, well-controlled men, whose first reaction to a threat is an increase of stiff politeness. In one of his poems[3] Rudyard Kipling has wonderfully illustrated this psychological mechanism in reference to the training of self-control that is said to be characteristic of the English ideal; the last two lines are:

'Cock the gun that is not loaded, cook the frozen dynamite—
But oh, beware my country, when my country grows polite!'

What is evidently true of politeness is even truer of more intense grades of affection and of love itself. Often and often rivalry, disaccord, jealousy, and hatred of a degree that would make life together difficult or impossible are dealt with unconsciously by using these emotions to stimulate the exactly contrary one of affection, which is the most obvious mask for them and the most complete defence against them. As a result the hateful emotions are kept at bay, suppressed or even buried in the unconscious. This state of affairs is naturally commonest in family life, where the people concerned are forced to live together; one might say that they have to love each other so as to avoid hating each other. I hope that these remarks do not shock you, nor do I want to be misunderstood as having generalised too extensively. I only wish to remark that there is far more hatred in the unconscious mind than is generally known, and that the most characteristic defence against it is the development of an overcharge of affection, of a greater amount than would otherwise be there. One has to remember that any close contact between human beings brings a restriction of the personality that is apt to breed resentment. It is rare for such close contact to be present without providing numerous reasons for resentment, friction, disagreements, oppositions and so on, all of which are mild expressions for some degree of hatred. What in consciousness is felt as annoyance is in the less

[3] 'Et dona ferentes.'

restrained unconscious already hatred. The question has even been raised whether it is possible for love to exist at all without there being also an accompanying undercurrent of hate, naturally of varying intensity according to the disposition of the person concerned. One could quote many passages from the great writers which would support this supposition. Racine, for example, in his 'Andromaque'[4] makes Hermione say:

'Ah! je l'ay trop aimé pour ne le point haïr.'

In the same play[5] he also indicates the alternative between love and hate in these words of Pyrrhus:

'Songez-y bien: il faut desormais que mon cœur,
S'il n'aime avec transport, haïsse avec fureur.'

One might say that what is meant in this last passage is merely the familiar fact that a person often reacts with hate to disappointed love, as was so well expressed by Congreve in the oft-quoted lines:

'Heaven hath no rage like love to hatred turned,
Nor hell a fury like a woman scorned.'

But this is just what I mean when I speak of the frictions, oppositions and dissatisfactions so rarely separable from love. They all arise from disappointment at the love not proving the perfect ideal they had imagined and expected, with consequent resentment against the person responsible for the disappointment. It is evident that this will be the greater the greater the disproportion between the ideal and the actual. Ultimately, therefore, the resentment depends on the distance of the previous ideal from reality and on the person's capacity to exchange the one for the other; to accept the positive side of what reality offers and to neglect the unobtainable. Of the two the second factor, that of adaptability, is in practice much more important than the first, the loftiness of the ideals. Ideals do not harm so long as one does not expect them to be realised, so long as one does not build on them. Now excessive dependence on ideals for the achievement of happiness is a thing that varies greatly among different people, and, as it underlies the greater part of jealousy, we shall have to inquire more closely into its nature.

This leads us to a second accessory function of love. We

[4] Acte ii., Sc. 1.
[5] Acte i., Sc. 4.

have seen that love can fulfil not only its own proper function, that of bringing happiness by gratifying the instinct of love, but other accessory ones, such as the masking of hate. The second accessory function we are now concerned with is the part it plays in affording reassurance and security about one's self-value, particularly in the erotic sphere. I want to distinguish this sharply from what might be called the normal function of love, and that is not easy because it is often concealed behind this. Let me put the matter another way by differentiating two things that are often confounded, desire and need. One can perhaps see this distinction most readily in such spheres as drinking and smoking or similar indulgences. One man will drink wine because he enjoys the pleasure it adds to his mood—in other words, for a positive reason. Another will drink because without it he is unhappy, unfree in himself, weighed down by what Janet calls 'un sentiment d'incomplétude'—in short, he drinks for a negative reason, because he is dependent on it, cannot do without it, *needs* it. The same is true of love. Normally, a man loves because it expresses his desires, not his needs. He wants, it is true, an external opportunity to express his desire for self-completion in its fullest terms, but he does not feel particularly incomplete without this. It is otherwise with a man who is driven to search for a suitable object in order to relieve his doubts about his own value, to reassure himself about his erotic capacity, to give himself the inner security that he otherwise lacks. To him love is a therapeutic cure for a morbid state of affairs, not simply the fulfilment of desire. The first man has in any case the *internal capacity* for self-expression even when the external opportunity for gratifying it may be absent. But the second man has not this internal capacity of his own accord; he hopes that it will be engendered or bestowed on him by the external opportunity for gratification. He thus becomes dependent on the external opportunity—*i.e.*, on the object of affection—in the same way as a morphinomaniac becomes dependent on his dose. His passion, his craving, his declarations may very well be more vehement than the first man's, but the observant eye can perceive the difference and does not account him a good lover for all his protestations. The most striking feature about his love is that, strictly speaking, it is not love at all, but a craving to be loved. He is not interested in the object of his affection as such, only in her relationship to himself. I am of course describing extreme forms of the type, but I am afraid that attentive observation reveals some degree of this attitude often enough in life. It is this type that is the victim of jealousy, and for that reason we must continue our analysis of the mental state in it.

What, then, is the secret of the doubt, the inferiority, that he seeks to remedy at the woman's hands? The obvious answer is his erotic capacity, but the matter is by no means so simple as this. Closer examination shows that the sense of deficiency is connected with an inner self-dissatisfaction, a self-criticism that betrays some conflict within the self. And actual psycho-analysis of such cases reveals the inner nature of this conflict in the unconscious itself. One can say definitely that all sense of inferiority, mental or physical, is ultimately based on a sentiment of *moral* inferiority, on a sense of guilt of which the person is often entirely unaware. This guiltiness relates fundamentally to the parents; it arises in early childhood in connection with the difficulties in development to which I alluded earlier, and few people get entirely rid of it. Mental health and freedom, with the capacity for happiness that this brings, is essentially dependent on freedom from unconscious guiltiness. With this goes a compensatory self-love. It is the self-love, self-esteem and self-respect that is wounded and damaged by the unconscious guilt, hence the person's sensitiveness to criticism and his constant demand for approval or recognition in various forms. Hence also the unsparing nature of the hatred aroused when one is betrayed; if love is pitiful, self-love is certainly pitiless. La Rochefoucauld[6] justly observed that 'la jalousie est le plus grand de tous les maux, et celui qui fait le moins de pitié aux personnes qui le causent.'

You will say that I am here describing neurotic, and therefore abnormal people, but it is often easier to perceive the nature of the more subtle processes of the normal when they are placed under the magnifying glass of neurosis: in their essence the two are identical. Let us take, therefore, someone suffering in the way I have described and try to ascertain what precisely he is impelled towards. He seeks from the loved woman something vital to him that can be described by many terms, for they are all equivalent in this connection: security (from fear), certainty (from doubt), peace of mind (from the troublings of the unconscious guiltiness), potency, freedom. All these precious gifts are identified with the woman, or, rather, with the assurance of her absolute love for him and fidelity to him. I add here the word fidelity because lack of confidence always sets up a throw-back, what we call a regression, to earlier stages in the development of the love instinct. The two features of this that concern us here are, first, the regression to the childish desire to be loved in place of the desire to love, and, secondly, the insistence on the lowly instinct of possessiveness, and so, on exclusive possession of the object. One begins to see now how feverishly important the woman's fidelity is to such a man. To

[6] La Rochefoucauld, 'Maximes,' mdiii.

lose it is not simply to lose the most desired thing that the world outside can give, it is also to lose the confidence in one's own personality. This is the fear that underlies jealousy. But there is even worse than this. The loss in question risks in such a person exposing the moral inferiority and guiltiness that is the primary cause of the lack of confidence; and this is something that no human being can endure and towards the concealment of which most of our strivings are directed. Unless he rapidly takes steps to protect himself against it, the next stage in the jealousy situation would be shame. To quote again La Rochefoucauld:[7] 'On a honte d'avouer que l'on ait de la jalousie.' Socially also a jealous lover or husband mostly cuts a ridiculous figure. France is perhaps the only civilised country where this is less so and where there is even a certain approval of jealousy if it is cast on a sufficiently tragic scale. Jealous people take full advantage of this. Certainly there would be fewer crimes of passion—*i.e.*, of jealousy—in France were it not that the jealous person has a certain confidence that he can in this way obtain social sympathy and approval and so ease the pangs of shame and guilt that threaten to emerge behind his manifest desires. The psychological process can be described quite simply. The more wicked and dastardly he can make out the conduct of the other persons concerned to be the more is he relieved from responsibility; the onus and odium are on them, not on himself. He has lost what was necessary to his peace of mind, but there is an alternative way open to him to obtain this—namely, by displacing his unconscious dislike and disapproval of himself on to the object of affection. This is one reason why the persistence of the jealous person produces at times an acute impression of someone who actually wants to be assured that the betrayal has taken place. He almost implores the woman to assure him that this is so and is obviously dissatisfied when she denies it, however truthfully. At this stage it is not so much the betrayal that he cannot endure, but the state of uncertainty. In the most classic case in literature, Shakespeare's 'Othello,' we find this vividly expressed:

> 'I had been happy, if the general camp,
> Pioneers and all, had tasted her sweet body,
> So I had nothing known.'

One sees from these considerations that such a man has two alternative and competing ways of attempting to solve his unconscious conflict, or, put in simpler language, of achieving a stable self-confidence. The one is by being assured that he is loved, the other is by finding some justification to hate. The one closed to

[7] La Rochefoucauld, 'Maximes,' cccclxxii.

him is the normal one of loving. Of his two methods certainly the fundamental one, to which he constantly recurs, is the solution by means of being loved, ideally by the woman who most reverses the rôle of the forbidding mother. Unfortunately, however, quite apart from external chances of fate, there is an internal tendency that can interfere seriously with this proposed solution. For there is often a fear of being loved too greatly, a fear of having his personality 'possessed' by the love-object, which really means 'disapproved of.' In this case the cure would be worse than the disease; the very thing that was meant to restore his self-confidence threatens to take away the little he has. There is thus what is called an ambivalent attitude towards the idea of being loved, a craving for it and a dread of it; it represents at once the highest security and the greatest danger. It is this ambivalent attitude that renders the position of such a person so insecure and predisposes him to the pangs of jealousy. If it is not strong then jealousy will not arise unless there is a reasonable cause, but it will then be exaggerated; if it is strong, jealousy will arise in any event, even if imaginary grounds for it have to be invented.

Traces of this ambivalent attitude are common enough and account for the apprehension of marriage and postponement of it that a majority of young men display. It is, as I have just remarked, stronger in those predisposed to jealousy. This did not escape the observation of the master-psychologist, Shakespeare. Othello, at the moment of his elopement, says:

> 'But that I love the gentle Desdemona,
> I would not my unhoused free condition
> Put into circumscription and confine
> For the seas' worth.'

In an interesting sub-variety of the type the apprehension is hidden beneath a compensatory mask of over-confidence. Schnitzler, in his play 'Paracelsus,' has described this type excellently, and has very clearly shown how the concealed lack of confidence with its concomitant jealousy may nevertheless emerge in certain circumstances. In the play these are provided by the hypnotist's revealing the buried thoughts of infidelity in the wife's mind, thoughts which hardly pass a normal range but the knowledge of which is quite enough to disturb the husband's equanimity. The hypnotist, realising the significance of insecurity in this connection, plays on the husband's fears by alternatively arousing and allaying his suspicions until his mental equilibrium quite breaks down. Whereupon he admonishes him on the mistake of being over-confident—*i.e.*, of gratifying his self-love at the expense of love for his wife. We thus see that the insecure attitude under discussion may lurk where it is least expected.

After this excursus into the realm of neurotic jealousy we may now return to the possibility of finding some unitary formula that will unite the extremes of so-called normal jealousy on the one hand and delusional or insane jealousy on the other. I have purposely chosen the neurotic jealousy for our investigation, because it stands midway between these two extremes and shows the characteristics of both: it is both an exaggeration of the normal and an adumbration of the insane. You will remember that the salient feature of the insane type was the projection outwards of repressed homosexual desires. How does this idea agree with the psychology of the other two? Well, when I pointed out that the neurotic man attempts to achieve potency through the method of becoming loved instead of expressing it by the usual way of loving I might just as well have said that he seeks to achieve it by inverting his sex—*i.e.*, his sexual attitude. Naturally this change varies greatly in extent and may be in no wise apparent except to those who know how to appreciate slight indications; it is, for instance, commonly masked by the vehemence of the pleadings and cravings. Nevertheless that is the essence of the change that has taken place in the unconscious. By it is avoided the responsibility of claiming the right to what may be called the primary desires, those pertaining to the person's own sex, for, owing to the incest attachment, these are the most deeply forbidden of all. If this inversion is carried up to a certain point, and responded to—*i.e.*, sanctioned— by the woman, the man acquires all the confidence of which he is capable. If, however, it passes beyond this point, in which case the woman assumes a masculine meaning in the man's eyes (this being often contributed to by his tendency to select women with a somewhat masculine inclination), then fear is aroused, the original fear of deprivation which started the whole difficulty in childhood. His defence against this is flight. The commonest step to be taken first is to develop impulses of infidelity so as to free himself from what he now feels to be a threatening bondage. Much more marital infidelity is of neurotic origin than is generally supposed; it is not a sign of freedom or potency, but quite the reverse. This tendency is in itself one of the factors leading to jealousy, as I explained earlier, for it is often projected on to the wife and she is suspected of impulses which are perhaps being repressed in the man. The further step in the flight is in the homosexual direction. What is the real meaning of this? The ultimate source of the fear and guilt that lie behind all these reactions is the relationship to another potential man and it is derived from the boy's attitude towards his father. So long as there is an unconscious fixation on childish attitudes it is hard for him to picture a woman quite apart from another man to whom she secretly belongs; this is simply another way of saying that he cannot refrain from reproducing the situation of childhood when the woman he loved belonged to another man who was never far away. The homosexual tendency we have noted is really an impulse to placate this 'other man'—*i.e.*, the father—by identifying himself with the woman, by replacing his masculine attitude towards the mother by a feminine one towards the father. In his love life he needs, as I indicated formerly, a certain masculinity in the woman; this is the father she carries about with her. The woman's love protects him from his guilt and the fear of the father. If this love is unsuccessful he has to reproduce a triangular situation, often delusionally, so as to deal along homosexual lines with the father. If the love is less unsuccessful, he is fairly safe until a rival appears on the scene. The situation then becomes intolerable to him. Instead of reacting in a manly way by using his love of the woman to make her happy, and devoting himself to this sole aim, he becomes concerned with the man rather than with the woman, and with her attitude towards him and the other man rather than with her personality itself. He reproaches her with not loving him enough. Psychologically this means a reproach that she no longer by her love protects him from the feared and hated father.

If matters go further he protects himself against his fear and guilt by developing anger. You will remember that I described the three psychological stages in jealousy as consisting first of fear of loss, secondly of shame and wounded self-esteem that is derived from the unconscious guiltiness, and thirdly of anger which protects him against both by justifying his hatred, putting him in the right and thus once more restoring his self-esteem.

Whether this anger will be directed more against the woman or against the man depends on the level to which his psychosexual development has proceeded. If the inhibition is a deep one, so that the homosexual solution has gone far, then he will turn on the woman and in certain cases will even kill her. If he has proceeded further along the normal line of development, his fear of the father is less and his aggressive opposition to him will be allowed to express itself against the rival.

I have for the sake of simplicity considered the psychological problems of jealousy in terms of the man, but there is little to add about the woman's problems because they are essentially of the same order. The source of the conflicts in childhood is the same, as are also the attempted solution by sexual inversion and the consequent dependence on the partner's approval. For both physiological and psychological reasons the woman is normally—*i.e.*, usually—more dependent on this approval than is the man, and this I take to be the essential reason why women are so much more prone to jealousy than men.

I should like now to sum up in a few words the gist of what I have had to say. It is my experience that jealousy is a much less normal phenomenon than is commonly supposed, that for the greater part it rests on an abnormal and neurotic basis. It betokens a failure in the development of the capacity to love, a lack of self-confidence due ultimately to unconscious guiltiness that has not been overcome from childhood days, and an undue dependence on the love object that indicates a tendency in the direction of sex inversion. This last feature becomes plain enough in insane jealousy, but I consider it is present in a milder degree in the other forms also. In short, jealousy is a sign of weakness in love, not of strength; it takes its source in fear, guilt and hate rather than in love.

SIGMUND FREUD / Humour

IN MY volume on *Jokes and their Relation to the Unconscious* (1905c), I in fact considered humour only from the economic point of view. My object was to discover the source of the pleasure obtained from humour, and I think I was able to show that the yield of humorous pleasure arises from an economy in expenditure upon feeling. [*Standard Ed.*, 8, 236.]

There are two ways in which the humorous process can take place. It may take place in regard to a single person, who himself adopts the humorous attitude, while a second person plays the part of the spectator who derives enjoyment from it; or it may take place between two persons, of whom one takes no part at all in the humorous process, but is made the object of humorous contemplation by the other. When, to take the crudest example [ibid., 229], a criminal who was being led out to the gallows on a Monday remarked: 'Well, the week's beginning nicely,' he was producing the humour himself; the humorous process is completed in his own person and obviously affords him a certain sense of satisfaction. I, the non-participating listener, am affected as it were at long-range by this humorous production of the criminal's; I feel, like him, perhaps, the yield of humorous pleasure.

We have an instance of the second way in which humour arises when a writer or a narrator describes the behaviour of real or imaginary people in a humorous manner. There is no need for those people to display any humour themselves; the humorous attitude is solely the business of the person who is taking them as his object; and, as in the former instance, the reader or hearer shares in the enjoyment of the humour. To sum up, then, we can say that the humorous attitude—whatever it may consist in—can be directed either towards the subject's own self or towards other people; it is to be assumed that it brings a yield of pleasure to the person who adopts it, and a similar yield of pleasure falls to the share of the non-participating onlooker.

We shall best understand the genesis of the yield of humorous pleasure if we consider the process in the listener before whom someone else produces humour. He sees this other person in a situation which leads the listener to expect that the other will produce the signs of an affect—that he will get angry, complain, express pain, be frightened or horrified or perhaps even in despair; and the onlooker or listener is prepared to follow his lead and to call up the same emotional impulses in himself. But this emotional expectancy is disappointed; the other person expresses no affect, but makes a jest. The expenditure on feeling that is economized turns into humorous pleasure in the listener.

It is easy to get so far. But we soon tell ourselves that it is the process which takes place in the other person—the 'humorist' —that merits the greater attention. There is no doubt that the essence of humour is that one spares oneself the affects to which the situation would naturally give rise and dismisses the possibility of such expressions of emotion with a jest. As far as this goes, the process in the humorist must tally with the process in the hearer—or, to put it more correctly, the process in the hearer must have copied the one in the humorist. But how does the latter bring about the mental attitude which makes a release of affect superfluous? What are the dynamics of his adoption of the 'humorous attitude'? Clearly, the solution of the problem is to be sought in the humorist; in the hearer we must assume that there is only an echo, a copy, of this unknown process.

It is now time to acquaint ourselves with a few of the characteristics of humour. Like jokes and the comic, humour has something liberating about it; but it also has something of grandeur and elevation, which is lacking in the other two ways of obtaining pleasure from intellectual activity. The grandeur in it clearly lies in the triumph of narcissism, the victorious assertion of the ego's invulnerability. The ego refuses to be distressed by the provocations of reality, to let itself be compelled to suffer. It insists that it cannot be affected by the traumas of the external world; it shows, in fact, that such traumas are no more than occasions for it to gain pleasure. This last feature is a quite essential element of humour. Let us suppose that the criminal who was being led to execution on Monday had said: 'It doesn't worry me. What does it matter, after all, if a fellow like me is hanged? The world won't come to an end because of it.' We should have to admit that such a speech does in fact display the same magnificent superiority over the real situation. It is wise and true; but it does not betray a trace of humour. Indeed, it is based on an appraisal of reality which runs directly counter to the appraisal made by humour. Humour is not resigned; it is rebellious. It signifies not only the triumph of the ego but also of the pleasure principle, which is able here to assert itself against the unkindness of the real circumstances.

These last two features—the rejection of the claims of reality and the putting through of the pleasure principle—bring humour near to the regressive or reactionary processes which engage our attention so extensively in psychopathology. Its fending off of the possibility of suffering places it among the great series of methods which the human mind has constructed in order to evade the compulsion to suffer—a series which begins with neurosis and culminates in madness and which includes intoxication, self-absorption and ecstasy.[1] Thanks to this connection, humour possesses a dignity which is wholly lacking, for instance, in jokes, for jokes either serve simply to obtain a yield of pleasure or place the yield of pleasure that has been obtained in the service of aggression. In what, then, does the humorous attitude consist, an attitude by means of which a person refuses to suffer, emphasizes the invincibility of his ego by the real world, victoriously maintains the pleasure principle—and all this, in contrast to other methods having the same purposes, without overstepping the bounds of mental health? The two achievements seem incompatible.

If we turn to the situation in which one person adopts a humorous attitude towards others, a view which I have already put forward tentatively in my book on jokes will at once suggest itself. This is that the subject is behaving towards them as an adult does towards a child when he recognizes and smiles at the triviality of interests and sufferings which seem so great to it [ibid., 233–4]. Thus the humorist would acquire his superiority by assuming the role of the grown-up and identifying himself to some extent with his father, and reducing the other people to being children. This view probably covers the facts, but it hardly seems a conclusive

[1] [Cf. the subsequent long discussion of these various methods of avoiding pain in Chapter II of *Civilization and its Discontents* (1930a), p. 77 ff. above. But Freud had already pointed out the defensive function of humour in *Jokes* (1905c), Standard Ed., 8, 233.]

one. One asks oneself what it is that makes the humorist arrogate this role to himself.

But we must recall the other, probably more primary and important, situation of humour, in which a person adopts a humorous attitude towards himself in order to ward off possible suffering. Is there any sense in saying that someone is treating himself like a child and is at the same time playing the part of a superior adult towards that child?

This not very plausible idea receives strong support, I think, if we consider what we have learned from pathological observations on the structure of the ego. This ego is not a simple entity. It harbours within it, as its nucleus, a special agency—the super-ego.[2] Sometimes it is merged with the super-ego so that we cannot distinguish between them, whereas in other circumstances it is sharply differentiated from it. Genetically the super-ego is the heir to the parental agency. It often keeps the ego in strict dependence and still really treats it as the parents, or the father, once treated the child, in its early years. We obtain a dynamic explanation of the humorous attitude, therefore, if we assume that it consists in the humorist's having withdrawn the psychical accent from his ego and having transposed it on to his super-ego. To the super-ego, thus inflated, the ego can appear tiny and all its interests trivial; and, with this new distribution of energy, it may become an easy matter for the super-ego to suppress the ego's possibilities of reacting.

In order to remain faithful to our customary phraseology, we shall have to speak, not of transposing the psychical accent, but of displacing large amounts of cathexis. The question then is whether we are entitled to picture extensive displacements like this from one agency of the mental apparatus to another. It looks like a new hypothesis constructed *ad hoc*. Yet we may remind ourselves that we have repeatedly (even though not sufficiently often) taken a factor of this kind into account in our attempts at a metapsychological picture of mental events. Thus, for instance, we supposed that the difference between an ordinary erotic object-cathexis and the state of being in love is that in the latter incomparably more cathexis passes over to the object and that the ego empties itself as it were in favour of the object.[3] In studying some cases of paranoia I was able to establish the fact that ideas of persecution are formed early and exist for a long time without any perceptible effect, until, as the result of some particular precipitat-

---

[2] [It may be remarked that in a footnote at the beginning of Chapter III of *The Ego and the Id* (1923*b*) Freud says that 'the system *Pcpt.-Cs.* alone can be regarded as the nucleus of the ego' *(Standard Ed.*, 19, 28).]

[3] [See Chapter VIII of *Group Psychology* (1921*c*), *Standard Ed.*, 18, 112-13.]

ing event, they receive sufficient amounts of cathexis to cause them to become dominant.[4] The cure, too, of such paranoic attacks would lie not so much in a resolution and correction of the delusional ideas as in a withdrawal from them of the cathexis which has been lent to them. The alternations between melancholia and mania, between a cruel suppression of the ego by the super-ego and a liberation of the ego after that pressure, suggests a shift of cathexis of this kind;[5] such a shift, moreover, would have to be brought in to explain a whole number of phenomena belonging to normal mental life. If this has been done hitherto only to a very limited extent, that is on account of our usual caution—something which deserves only praise. The region in which we feel secure is that of the pathology of mental life; it is here that we make our observations and acquire our convictions. For the present we venture to form a judgement on the normal mind only in so far as we can discern what is normal in the isolations and distortions of the pathological material. When once we have overcome this hesitancy we shall recognize what a large contribution is made to the understanding of mental processes by the static conditions as well as by the dynamic changes in the *quantity* of energic cathexis.

I think, therefore, that the possibility I have suggested here, that in a particular situation the subject suddenly hypercathects his super-ego and then, proceeding from it, alters the reactions of the ego, is one which deserves to be retained. Moreover, what I have suggested about humour finds a remarkable analogy in the kindred field of jokes. As regards the origin of jokes I was led to assume that a preconscious thought is given over for a moment to unconscious revision [ibid., 166]. A joke is thus the contribution made to the comic by the unconscious [ibid., 208]. In just the same way, *humour would be the contribution made to the comic through the agency of the super-ego.*

In other connections we knew the super-ego as a severe master. It will be said that it accords ill with such a character that the super-ego should condescend to enabling the ego to obtain a small yield of pleasure. It is true that humorous pleasure never reaches the intensity of the pleasure in the comic or in jokes, that it never finds vent in hearty laughter. It is also true that, in bringing about the humorous attitude, the super-ego is actually repudiating reality and serving an illusion. But (without rightly knowing why) we regard this less intense pleasure as having a character of very high value; we feel it to be especially liberating and elevating. More-

---

[4] [See Section B of 'Some Neurotic Mechanisms' (1922*b*), *Standard Ed.*, 18, 228-9.]
[5] [See 'Mourning and Melancholia' (1917*e*), *Standard Ed.*, 14, 253-5.]

over, the jest made by humour is not the essential thing. It has only the value of a preliminary. The main thing is the intention which humour carries out, whether it is acting in relation to the self or other people. It means: 'Look! here is the world, which seems so dangerous! It is nothing but a game for children—just worth making a jest about!'

If it is really the super-ego which, in humour, speaks such kindly words of comfort to the intimidated ego, this will teach us that we have still a great deal to learn about the nature of the super-ego. Furthermore, not everyone is capable of the humorous attitude. It is a rare and precious gift, and many people are even without the capacity to enjoy humorous pleasure that is presented to them. And finally, if the super-ego tries, by means of humour, to console the ego and protect it from suffering, this does not contradict its origin in the parental agency.

OTTO KLINEBERG/Emotional Expression in Chinese Literature

THE FACT that the expression of the emotions is at least to some extent patterned by social factors is probably known to all psychologists. Even in our own society there is considerable evidence that this is so. When we turn to the descriptions of other cultures, instances of this patterning occur frequently. One of the most striking examples is the copious shedding of tears by the Andaman Islanders and the Maori of New Zealand when friends meet after an absence, or when two warring parties make peace. Another is the smile with which the Japanese responds to the scolding of his superior, or which accompanies his announcement of the death of his favorite son.

This paper represents part of a more extensive study of emotional expression among the Chinese, an investigation made possible by a Guggenheim Fellowship and a supplementary grant from the Social Science Research Council. Among the various techniques employed, it seemed valuable in the case of a civilization as articulate as the Chinese to examine at least a portion of the Chinese literature for the light it might throw on this problem. There is not much precedent for the reading of novels as a technique of psychological investigation, but in this case it seemed warranted at least as an introduction to more objective methods.

Before turning to the question of the kind of expression

involved, a word should be said as to the related question of the amount of expression which the culture permits. There are, for example, many admonitions—especially to the young girl—not to show emotion too readily. In *Required Studies for Women* we find such warnings as the following: "Do not show your unhappiness easily and do not smile easily"; also, "Do not let your teeth be seen when you smile," that is, your smile must be so circumspect that the teeth do not show. On the other hand, there are many occasions on which the emotion of grief has to be displayed. One piece of advice from the same volume reads, "If your father or mother is sick, do not be far from his or her bed. Do not even take off your girdle. Taste all the medicine yourself. Pray your god for his or her health. If anything unfortunate happens cry bitterly."

The alleged inscrutability of the Chinese, which as a matter of fact has been greatly exaggerated, completely breaks down in the case of grief. Not only is grief expressed, but there is an elaborate set of rules and regulations which insure that it shall be properly expressed. One of the Chinese classics is *The Book of Rites*, a considerable portion of which is devoted to the technique of the mourning ceremonial, with elaborate instructions as to just what procedure should be followed in order that the expression of the grief may be socially acceptable.

The most extreme degree of patterning of emotional expression is found on the Chinese stage, and is illustrated by the following examples from a Chinese *Treatise on Acting*. There is an occasional pattern which does conform closely to our own; for example, "taking the left sleeve with the right hand and raising it to the eyes as if to wipe the tears" is clearly an expression of sorrow. There are others, however, that are not so clear. To "draw one leg up and stand on one foot" means surprise. To "raise one hand as high as the face and fan the face with the sleeve" means anger, as does also to "blow the beard to make it fly up." Joy or satisfaction is represented by stretching "the left arm flatly to the left and the right arm to the right." To "move one hand around in front of the middle of the beard and touch your head with the fingers of the other hand" means sorrow, while to "put the middle part of the beard into the mouth with both hands and bite firmly" indicates that one has come to a decision. To "raise both hands above the head with the palms turned outwards and the fingers pointing up, let the sleeves hang down behind the hands, then walk towards the other person, shake the sleeves over, and let the hands fall" means love.

There were two long novels which were read for this study; one, *The Dream of the Red Chamber*, was read in Chinese, with considerable help from Miss Wu T'ien Min, a graduate student at Yenching University, and the other, *All Men are Brothers*, in Pearl Buck's English translation. These represent two of the three most famous Chinese novels, the third being *The Romance of the Three Kingdoms*. *The Dream of the Red Chamber* is a love story; *All Men are Brothers* is a tale of swashbuckling adventure dealing with the so-called "bandits" who are among the most picturesque figures of Chinese legend and history. Besides these, several modern stories were also consulted.

In some cases the descriptions of emotional expression correspond closely to our own. When we read (D.R.C.), for example, that "everyone trembled with a face the color of clay," there can be little doubt that fear is meant. The same holds for the statement that "every one of his hairs stood on end, and the pimples came out on the skin all over his body" (from "Married Life Awakening the World"). Other descriptions of fear (A.M.B.) are the following: "A cold sweat broke forth on his whole body, and he trembled without ceasing"; "it was as though her two feet were nailed to the ground and she would fain have shrieked but her mouth was like a mute's"; "they stood like death with mouths ajar"; "they were so frightened that their waters and wastes burst out of them." In general, it may be said that fear is expressed in very much the same way in the Chinese literature as in our own. As far as other emotions are concerned, in the sentence, "He gnashed his teeth until they were all but ground to dust," we recognize anger: "He was listless and silent" suggests sorrow; "His face was red and he went creeping alone outside the village" clearly indicates shame. There is no doubt of the frequent similarity between Chinese and Western forms of expression.

There are also differences, however. When we read "They stretched out their tongues" (D.R.C.), most of us would not recognize this description as meaning surprise, except for the context. This phrase as an expression of surprise occurs with great frequency, and it would be easy to give many examples. The sentence "Her eyes grew round and opened wide," would probably suggest to most of us surprise or fear; to the Chinese it usually means anger. This expression, with slight variations, also occurs very often. In the form "He made his two eyes round and stared at him" (A.M.B.), it can mean nothing but anger. "He would fain have swallowed him at a gulp" (A.M.B.) implies hatred; our own "I could eat you up!" has a somewhat different significance. "He scratched his ears and cheeks" would probably suggest embarrassment to us, but in the *Dream of the Red Chamber* it means happiness. "He clapped his hands" (D.R.C.) is likely to mean worry or disappointment.

The case of anger appears to be particularly interesting. We have already noted the expressions connected with "round eyes," "eyes wide open," "staring," etc. We find in addition descriptions like these: "He laughed a great ho-ho," and "He smiled a chill smile," and "He looked at them and he smiled and cursed them" (A.M.B.). Both the laugh and the smile of anger or contempt occur in our own culture, but apparently not nearly so frequently as in China and the Chinese literature. More curious still is the phrase "He was so angry that several times he fainted from his anger" (A.M.B.). This expression occurs frequently. When I showed wonder as to why this should be, Chinese friends said that they in turn could never understand why European women fainted so frequently in the mid-Victorian literature with which they were acquainted. Certainly the delicately nurtured young women of not so long ago did faint with astonishing ease and regularity; there were even etiquette books which taught them how to faint elegantly. Such a custom is certainly no less surprising than that the Chinese should faint in anger. The conclusion seems clear that fainting, like tears, may be conditioned by social custom to appear on widely varying occasions.

Most striking of all perhaps, is the indication in the literature that people may die of anger. "His anger has risen so that he is ill of it and lies upon his bed, and his life cannot be long assured." " 'To-day am I killed by anger' . . . and when he had finished speaking he let his soul go free" (A.M.B.). This phenomenon, incidentally, mysterious though it may sound, is reported as still occurring, and I saw one patient in a hospital in Peiping whose father was said to have died of anger after losing a lawsuit. It is important to note that a death of this kind cannot be explained as due to anything like an apoplectic stroke; it does not occur suddenly as a stroke would. When someone is very angry but is forced to suppress his anger because there is nothing he can do about it, he may become ill, faint many times and take to his bed; death may follow after the lapse of some days or weeks. The only explanation is in terms of suggestion; the belief that people die of anger when they can do nothing about it, may succeed in actually bringing on the death of an impressionable person. There is the parallel case of the Polynesian native who inadvertently eats the tabooed food of the chief, remains perfectly well as long as he does not know it, but may die when he learns what he has done.

These examples indicate that, although there are many similarities between the literary descriptions of the emotions in China and in the West, there are also important differences which must be recognized if Chinese literature is to be read intelligently. When the literary pattern is such that the expression alone is described but not labeled, real misunderstandings may arise. When I first read, for instance, "They stretched out their tongues," I did not know that surprise was meant. Our own literature is of course also rich in these unlabeled expressions. We read, "His jaw dropped"; "He gnashed his teeth"; "His lip curled"; "His eyes almost popped out of his head"; "He clenched his fists," etc., and in each case we know at once what emotion is indicated. These expressions are a part of language and must be learned in order to be understood.

The question arises as to the degree to which these Chinese literary expressions are related to expression in real life. Caution must certainly be exercised in inferring from one to the other. A Chinese reader of our literature, for instance, might conclude that laughter was dangerous to Westerners, in view of the frequency with which he read the expression "I nearly died laughing." I think I may say, however, on the basis of information obtained by methods other than the reading of novels, that the Chinese patterns which I have described do appear not only in the literature but also in real life. I may add that photographs illustrating these literary expressions are judged more easily by Chinese than by American subjects.

It seems to me to be worth while to extend this literary approach to other cultures. In the writings of India, Japan and other peoples of the Near and Far East, material must certainly be available which would further illustrate the extent and the nature of the cultural patterning of emotional expression.

RYUNOSUKE AKUTAGAWA/The Handkerchief

PROFESSOR KINZO HASEGAWA of the Tokyo Imperial University Law School, seated on a cane chair on his veranda, was reading Strindberg's "Dramaturgy."

The Professor's specialty, we all know, is the study of colonial administration. Perhaps the reader finds it strange that he was reading a book of dramatic criticism. But the Professor is known as an educator as well as a scholar, and it has been his policy to look over any book, in or out of his field, that has any influence on the thought or emotion of modern students. For instance, he has read Oscar Wilde's *De Profundis* and *Intentions* for the simple reason that they were widely read among the pupils of a special college of which he is the dean. Therefore, there is nothing strange in finding the Professor perusing a book which treats of the drama and acting of modern Europe. For among the numerous students of the Professor are not only some who write criticism of Ibsen, Strindberg and Maeterlinck, but others who intend to follow in the footsteps of these modern dramatists and make playwriting their life-work.

At the close of each of its witty chapters the Professor would drop the yellow, cloth-bound book on his lap and vaguely look over to the Gifu lantern hanging from the ceiling. Immediately his mind left Strindberg behind. Instead he would be thinking of his wife who had gone with him to buy the lantern. The Professor had married in America, where he was studying. His wife, therefore, is an American. But in the love of Japan and the Japanese she is no different from the Professor. In particular, the intricate art work of Japan has been Mrs. Hasegawa's passion. The Gifu lantern on the veranda is more an expression of Madam's taste than due to the wishes of the Professor.

Whenever he dropped the book the Professor thought of his wife, and the Gifu lantern, and the civilization represented by that lantern. The Professor believes that Japanese civilization has made great progress materially in the past fifty years, but spiritually has remained stagnant: in fact, in some phases, it has retrogressed. What are the means by which contemporary thinkers may help erase this retrogression? The Professor argues that the means must be found in Japan's own *Bushido*. Bushido should not be regarded merely as the narrow morality of an island nation. In fact, it has many elements that correspond to the Christian spirit of the western nations. If a forward impetus were to be given Japanese thinking by the revival of Bushido, it would not only contribute to the spiritual civilization of Japan but would lead to a better understanding between Japan and the western countries. It might even contribute to international peace. The Professor has always wished, in this sense, to become a bridge connecting East and West. That being the case, it was not unpleasant to this man to find in his consciousness the presence of the harmonious trio: his wife, the lantern and the civilization represented by that lantern.

The Professor at last realized that this self-satisfied reverie was keeping him from fully understanding Strindberg. He shook his head irritably and again began patiently to scan the fine print before him. The first thing he read was this:

"When an actor finds a suitable, expressive technique for any common emotional state and wins success by this technique, he will have a tendency to resort to this technique regardless of its suitability to the material at hand, partly because it is easy, partly because it has been successful before: this is mannerism."

The arts, especially the stage, have been a *terra incognita* to the Professor. He could count on the fingers of one hand the number of times he has seen plays in Japan. One of his students once wrote a novel in which the name "Baiko" appeared. The name meant nothing to the Professor's encyclopedic mind. The next time he met the student he put the question:

"Eh, this Baiko, what is that?"

"Baiko, sir? Baiko is an actor attached to the Imperial Theater, and is now appearing as Misao in the tenth play of the Taikoki," answered the student very politely.

The Professor, therefore, had absolutely no critical opinion of his own about the various techniques of theatrical production so provocatively discussed by Strindberg. It kept up a slight interest in him by reminding him of certain plays he had seen abroad. His reading of Strindberg, in fact, was not much different from the reading of Bernard Shaw's plays by a teacher of English in a secondary school in order to collect a few new idioms. However negligible, interest is, nevertheless, an interest.

An unlit Gifu lantern hanging from the ceiling of the veranda and, on the cane chair underneath, Professor Kinzo Hasegawa reading Strindberg's "Dramaturgy"—this is enough to show the reader that this was a long afternoon of a day in early summer. But do not think the Professor was being tormented by boredom. If anybody insists on such a cynical interpretation I can only say he is mistaken. For even the Strindberg the Professor had to abandon. A maid announcing a caller interrupted his pleasant leisure. The world was insistent that the Professor must be kept busy even on such a long summer day.

He put down his book and looked at the small card that the maid had just brought him. On the ivory paper was printed in small letters, "Mrs. Atsuko Nishiyama." The name struck no chord of recognition. As he left the chair, he made a quick roll call of his extensive acquaintance. But no face was remembered that matched the name. Leaving the book on the chair with the card as a marker, the Professor tidied his appearance a little and took another look at the lantern. Often the host keeping a guest waiting is more impatient for the meeting than the waiting guest. It is not necessary to add here, to those who know him, that the Professor's impatience was not on account of the sex of the unknown caller.

Soon the Professor opened the door to the drawing room. Almost at the same time a woman in her forties got up from a chair. The caller was dressed in a tasteful, iron-blue kimono, over which she wore a *haori* of black silk gauze, leaving the cool, diamond-shaped *obi*-brooch of nephrite exposed near the breast. That she wore her hair in a sort of round chignon peculiar to married women, even the Professor, who is careless about these trifles, recognized. She was clearly a "wise mother" type, with the round face and amber-colored skin characteristic of the Japanese. One glance convinced the Professor that he had seen this face before.

"How do you do; I am Hasegawa," he said and bowed amiably, thinking that with that greeting she would have to answer where and when she had met him before.

"I am the mother of Kenichiro Nishiyama," she said in a clear voice and bowed courteously.

Kenichiro Nishiyama was a name quite familiar to the Professor. He was one of those very students who often wrote criticism of Ibsen and Strindberg, though his specialty at the University was German law. He frequented the Professor's home, always full of ideological problems. This spring he had been taken with peritonitis, and the Professor had visited him once or twice at the University Hospital. No wonder I felt I had seen this woman before, the Professor thought. That lively young man with his dark eyebrows and this woman resemble each other amazingly; like two melons, as the Japanese commonly say.

"Oh, Mr. Nishiyama's—yes, of course."

The Professor nodded to himself as he pointed to the chair on the other side of the small table. "Please sit down."

The woman apologized for her sudden call and bowed courteously again before she sat down. As she took the chair she drew out something white from her long sleeve. Recognizing a handkerchief, the Professor recommended the use of the Korean fans on the table and took the chair facing hers.

"This is indeed a beautiful room," she said rather artificially and looked about the room.

"Well, it's large, but we hardly bother with it."

Quite used to these preliminary conversations, the Professor placed the cup of tea, just brought in by the maid, before her and shifted the topic toward the caller.

"How is Mr. Nishiyama? I hope he is better now."

"Well," she stopped for a moment as she modestly folded her hands on her lap, then went on in the same smooth voice. "My visit to you today is really for his sake. I am sorry to say he was not able to pull through; and since he was such a bother to you while he was alive—"

Seeing that the woman did not touch her tea, and interpreting this as her reserve, the Professor had just taken up his teacup. He wanted to put her at ease by setting the example. But before the cup reached his soft mustache the woman's words threatened his ears unexpectedly. Should I drink this or shouldn't I? For one moment this question monopolized the Professor's mind to the complete exclusion of the young man's death. He knew he shouldn't keep the cup in the air for ever. So, with one quick gulp, he drank the tea, and was barely able to bring out in a choking voice, "No, really?"

"He spoke of you so often while in the hospital," she went on. "I presumed to call today, though I know how occupied you are, to offer our thanks as well as to let you know—"

"Oh, not at all."

The Professor deposited the cup and took up a fan with a blue wax finish, while his voice went on thoughtfully:

"I had no idea his condition was so critical. And he was just at the age when we could have expected great things in a few years, too. I neglected the hospital for a while, and so believed that he was quite well by now. Just exactly when was he—?"

"It would be a week ago yesterday."

"Eh—at the hospital, was it?"

"Yes, at the hospital."

"Well, this is most unexpected," he said.

"We should console ourselves," she replied, "knowing all the excellent care he had, but still it is easy to cry over spilt milk when one thinks of all that might have been."

In the course of the conversation the Professor became aware of something surprising. There was no trace in this woman's attitude or manner of the fact that she was talking of her son's death. There were no tears. The voice was calm. There was even a trace of a smile in the corner of her mouth. Anyone seeing her without hearing her words would have thought she was speaking of some ordinary daily happening. This was strange to the Professor.

A long time ago, when the Professor was studying in Berlin, the old Kaiser, Wilhelm I, died. He heard of the death at a café he frequented, but his sense of loss was naturally quite slight. So he returned to his pension at his usual lively gait, his cane under his arm. As soon as he opened the outer door, the two children of the concierge rushed up to him, weeping loudly—the girl of twelve, in her brown jacket, the nine-year-old boy clad in short blue pants. Always very fond of children, the Professor bent down, patting their two heads, earnestly asking, "Why, what's the matter, what's the matter?" Finally he made out what they were saying through their tears: "Grandpapa Emperor died. Grandpapa Emperor died!"

It had been strange to him to find the death of the head of a state so affecting to children. Not only did it make him think of such a question as Royalty and the People; the Westerner's impulsive expression of emotion, which he had so often noted before, renewed the sense of wonder in the Professor, a Japanese and a believer in Bushido. He could never forget the curious, uncomprehending sympathy which he felt on that occasion. Now he was surprised to an equal degree in the opposite direction by the fact that this woman was dry-eyed.

But the first discovery was soon succeeded by a second.

The conversation was proceeding from reminiscences of the deceased to the details of his daily life, back again to general reminiscences. The Professor accidentally dropped the fan on the parquet floor. The conversation, of course, was not so pressing that he could not interrupt it by reaching under the table to pick up the fan, which was lying near the woman's neat, white *tabis*, partly hidden in her slippers.

The Professor's eyes took in the woman's lap, and the folded hands resting on it. That in itself would not be a discovery. But he saw that the hands were trembling violently and, in the effort to suppress the shaking, they clutched the handkerchief so tightly as to nearly tear it. And, finally, he saw that the wrinkled silk handkerchief within her delicate fingers communicated the trembling of her hands, for its embroidered edges were shaking as if fanned by a breeze. The woman had been laughing with her face but weeping with her whole body.

When he picked up the fan and straightened himself, there was a new expression on the Professor's face. A kind of pious sense of guilt that he had seen something he was not supposed to, and a certain satisfaction coming from the consciousness of that feeling, both exaggerated into a slight theatricality—it was a very complex expression.

"No, even a childless person like me can imagine what a terrible lost this has been to you," said the Professor in a low voice, full of emotion, and his eyes looked as if they were gazing at something dazzlingly bright.

"Thank you very much," she said. "But, after all, this is something we cannot bring back."

She made a slight bow; her untroubled face still supporting a gracious smile.

Two hours later, the Professor had had his bath, finished his supper, eaten some cherries for dessert and was again seated luxuriously in the cane chair on the veranda.

The summer's long twilight was still some way off from the oncoming night in this broad, open veranda. The Professor sat in this pleasant afterglow, his knees crossed, his head pressed back on the chair, his eyes placidly contemplating the red tassel on the

Gifu lantern. The Strindberg was in his hand, but he hadn't turned a page since his return, for his mind was full of the gallant demeanor of Mrs. Atsuko Nishiyama.

During supper he had told his wife of the encounter, praising the other's conduct as the expression of the Japanese woman's Bushido. Mrs. Hasegawa, who loved Japan and the Japanese, was naturally sympathetic. The Professor was pleased to find in his wife an enthusiastic listener. The three—his wife, the other woman and the Gifu lantern—had been occupying his consciousness with a certain ethical implication.

For a long time he was immersed in this happy reverie. It presently came to him that he had been requested by a magazine to contribute an article. The magazine was collecting general opinions on morals by various eminent personages under the title of "The Book Addressed to Contemporary Youth." "I could send them an impression based on today's incident," thought the Professor and scratched his head.

The hand with which he scratched his head was the hand that had held the book. The Professor realized he had been neglecting the book and opened it to the page in which the calling card was inserted as a marker. The maid had lit the lantern above his head, which gave him enough light to pick through the fine print of the book. He idly scanned the page, not particularly anxious for the content. Says Strindberg:

"When I was young, the people talked about Mme. Heiberg's Parisian handkerchief. It was a double acting in which, with her face smiling, the hands tear the handkerchief in two. We now call it mannerism."

The Professor lowered the book. It was still open, with the card of Mrs. Atsuko Nishiyama left on the page. But that woman was no longer in the Professor's mind. Neither were Mrs. Hasegawa nor the civilization of Japan. What was left was some indefinable thing that attempted to break the peaceful harmony of the trio. Of course, problems in practical morality are different from the production technique pointed out by Strindberg. But there was something in the hint he had received from the passage that was disturbing to the hitherto comfortably assured mind of the Professor. Bushido, and its mannerism—

The Professor shook his head once or twice as though to drive away the unpleasant thought, then again looked up at the newly lit lantern.

JONATHAN SWIFT/To Mr. Delaney

What humor is, not all the tribe
   Of Logick mongers can describe;
Here only Nature acts her part,
   Unhelpt by practice, books, or art,
For Wit and humor differ quite,
   That gives surprise, and this delight
Humor is oft grotesque and wild,
   Only by affectation spoiled,
'Tis never by invention got
   Men have it when they know it not.

WILLIAM BLAKE/A Poison Tree

I was angry with my friend:
I told my wrath, my wrath did end.
I was angry with my foe:
I told it not, my wrath did grow.

And I water'd it in fears,
Night & morning with my tears;
And I sunned it with smiles,
And with soft deceitful wiles.

And it grew both day and night,
Till it bore an apple bright;
And my foe beheld it shine,
And he knew that it was mine,

And into my garden stole
When the night had veil'd the pole:
In the morning glad I see
My foe outstretch'd beneath the tree.

ROBERT BROWNING / Soliloquy of the Spanish Cloister

I

Gr-r-r—there go, my heart's abhorrence!
 Water your damned flower-pots, do!
If hate killed men, Brother Lawrence,
 God's blood, would not mine kill you!
What? your myrtle-bush wants trimming?
 Oh, that rose has prior claims—
Needs its leaden vase filled brimming?
 Hell dry you up with its flames!

II

At the meal we sit together:
 Salve tibi! I must hear
Wise talk of the kind of weather,
 Sort of season, time of year:
Not a plenteous cork-crop: scarcely
 Dare we hope oak-galls, I doubt:
What's the Latin name for "parsley"?
 What's the Greek name for Swine's Snout?

III

Whew! We'll have our platter burnished,
 Laid with care on our own shelf!
With a fire-new spoon we're furnished,
 And a goblet for ourself,
Rinsed like something sacrificial
 Ere 'tis fit to touch our chaps—
Marked with L. for our initial!
 (He-he! There his lily snaps!)

IV

Saint, forsooth! While brown Dolores
 Squats outside the Convent bank
With Sanchicha, telling stories,
 Steeping tresses in the tank,
Blue-black, lustrous, thick like horsehairs,
 —Can't I see his dead eye glow,
Bright as 'twere a Barbary corsair's?
 (That is, if he'd let it show!)

V

When he finishes refection,
 Knife and fork he never lays
Cross-wise, to my recollection,

      As do I, in Jesu's praise.
I the Trinity illustrate,
      Drinking watered orange-pulp—
In three sips the Arian frustrate;
      While he drains his at one gulp.

VI

Oh, those melons? If he's able
      We're to have a feast! so nice!
One goes to the Abbot's table,
      All of us get each a slice.
How go on your flowers? None double
      Not one fruit-sort can you spy?
Strange!—And I, too, at such trouble,
      Keep them close-nipped on the sly!

VII

There's a great text in Galatians,
      Once you trip on it, entails
Twenty-nine distinct damnations,
      One sure, if another fails:
If I trip him just a-dying,
      Sure of heaven as sure can be,
Spin him round and send him flying
      Off to hell, a Manichee?

VIII

Or, my scrofulous French novel
      On gray paper with blunt type!
Simply glance at it, you grovel
      Hand and foot in Belial's gripe:
If I double down its pages
      At the woful sixteenth print,
When he gathers his greengages,
      Ope a sieve and slip it in't?

IX

Or, there's Satan!—one might venture
      Pledge one's soul to him, yet leave
Such a flaw in the indenture
      As he'd miss till, past retrieve,
Blasted lay that rose-acacia
      We're so proud of! *Hy, Zy, Hine.*
'St, there's Vespers! *Plena gratiâ*
      Ave, Virgo! G-r-r-r—you swine!

GRAHAM GREENE/The End of the Party

PETER MORTON awoke with a start to face the first light. Through the window he could see a bare bough dropping across a frame of silver. Rain tapped against the glass. It was January the fifth.

He looked across a table, on which a night-light had guttered into a pool of water, at the other bed. Francis Morton was still asleep, and Peter lay down again with his eyes on his brother. It amused him to imagine that it was himself whom he watched, the same hair, the same eyes, the same lips and line of cheek. But the thought soon palled, and the mind went back to the fact which lent the day importance. It was the fifth of January. He could hardly believe that a year had passed since Mrs. Henne-Falcon had given her last children's party.

Francis turned suddenly upon his back and threw an arm across his face, blocking his mouth. Peter's heart began to beat fast, not with pleasure now but with uneasiness. He sat up and called across the table, "Wake up." Francis's shoulders shook and he waved a clenched fist in the air, but his eyes remained closed. To Peter Morton the whole room seemed suddenly to darken, and he had the impression of a great bird swooping. He cried again, "Wake up," and once more there was silver light and the touch of rain on the windows. Francis rubbed his eyes. "Did you call out?" he asked.

"You are having a bad dream," Peter said with confidence. Already experience had taught him how far their minds reflected each other. But he was the elder, by a matter of minutes, and that brief extra interval of light, while his brother still struggled in pain and darkness, had given him self-reliance and an instinct of protection towards the other who was afraid of so many things.

"I dreamed that I was dead," Francis said.

"What was it like?" Peter asked with curiosity.

"I can't remember," Francis said, and his eyes turned with relief to the silver of day, as he allowed the fragmentary memories to fade.

"You dreamed of a big bird."

"Did I?" Francis accepted his brother's knowledge without question, and for a little the two lay silent in bed facing each other, the same green eyes, the same nose tilting at the tip, the same firm lips parted, and the same premature modelling of the chin. The fifth of January, Peter thought again, his mind drifting idly from the image of cakes to the prizes which might be won.

Egg-and-spoon races, spearing apples in basins of water, blindman's-buff.

"I don't want to go," Francis said suddenly. "I suppose Joyce will be there . . . Mabel Warren." Hateful to him, the thought of a party shared with those two. They were older than he. Joyce was eleven and Mabel Warren thirteen. Their long pigtails swung superciliously to a masculine stride. Their sex humiliated him, as they watched him fumble with his egg, from under lowered scornful lids. And last year . . . he turned his face away from Peter, his cheeks scarlet.

"What's the matter?" Peter asked.

"Oh, nothing. I don't think I'm well. I've got a cold. I oughtn't to go to the party."

Peter was puzzled. "But, Francis, is it a bad cold?"

"It will be a bad cold if I go to the party. Perhaps I shall die."

"Then you mustn't go," Peter said with decision, prepared to solve all difficulties with one plain sentence, and Francis let his nerves relax in a delicious relief, ready to leave everything to Peter. But though he was grateful he did not turn his face towards his brother. His cheeks still bore the badge of a shameful memory, of the game of hide-and-seek last year in the darkened house, and of how he had screamed when Mabel Warren put her hand suddenly upon his arm. He had not heard her coming. Girls were like that. Their shoes never squeaked. No boards whined under their tread. They slunk like cats on padded claws. When the nurse came in with hot water Francis lay tranquil, leaving everything to Peter. Peter said, "Nurse, Francis has got a cold."

The tall starched woman laid the towels across the cans and said, without turning, "The washing won't be back till tomorrow. You must lend him some of your handkerchiefs."

"But, Nurse," Peter asked, "hadn't he better stay in bed?"

"We'll take him for a good walk this morning," the nurse said. "Wind'll blow away the germs. Get up now, both of you," and she closed the door behind her.

"I'm sorry," Peter said, and then, worried at the sight of a face creased again by misery and foreboding, "Why don't you just stay in bed? I'll tell mother you felt too ill to get up." But such a rebellion against destiny was not in Francis's power. Besides, if he stayed in bed they would come up and tap his chest and put a thermometer in his mouth and look at his tongue, and they would discover that he was malingering. It was true that he felt ill, a sick empty sensation in his stomach and a rapidly beating heart, but he knew that the cause was only fear, fear of the party, fear of being made to hide by himself in the dark, uncompanioned by Peter and with no night-light to make a blessed breach.

"No, I'll get up," he said, and then with sudden desperation, "But I won't go to Mrs. Henne-Falcon's party. I swear on the Bible I won't." Now surely all would be well, he thought. God would not allow him to break so solemn an oath. He would show him a way. There was all the morning before him and all the afternoon until four o'clock. No need to worry now when the grass was still crisp with the early frost. Anything might happen. He might cut himself or break his leg or really catch a bad cold. God would manage somehow.

He had such confidence in God that when at breakfast his mother said, "I hear you have a cold, Francis," he made light of it. "We should have heard more about it," his mother said with irony, "if there was not a party this evening," and Francis smiled uneasily, amazed and daunted by her ignorance of him. His happiness would have lasted longer if, out for a walk that morning, he had not met Joyce. He was alone with his nurse, for Peter had leave to finish a rabbit-hutch in the woodshed. If Peter had been there he would have cared less; the nurse was Peter's nurse also, but now it was as though she were employed only for his sake, because he could not be trusted to go for a walk alone. Joyce was only two years older and she was by herself.

She came striding towards them, pigtails flapping. She glanced scornfully at Francis and spoke with ostentation to the nurse. "Hello, Nurse. Are you bringing Francis to the party this evening? Mabel and I are coming." And she was off again down the street in the direction of Mabel Warren's home, consciously alone and self-sufficient in the long empty road. "Such a nice girl," the nurse said. But Francis was silent, feeling again the jump-jump of his heart, realizing how soon the hour of the party would arrive. God had done nothing for him, and the minutes flew.

They flew too quickly to plan any evasion, or even to prepare his heart for the coming ordeal. Panic nearly overcame him when, all unready, he found himself standing on the door-step, with coat-collar turned up against a cold wind, and the nurse's electric torch making a short luminous trail through the darkness. Behind him were the lights of the hall and the sound of a servant laying the table for dinner, which his mother and father would eat alone. He was nearly overcome by a desire to run back into the house and call out to his mother that he would not go to the party, that he dared not go. They could not make him go. He could almost hear himself saying those final words, breaking down for ever, as he knew instinctively, the barrier of ignorance that saved his mind from his parents' knowledge. "I'm afraid of going. I won't go. I daren't go. They'll make me hide in the dark, and I'm afraid of the dark. I'll scream and scream and scream." He could see the expression of amazement on his mother's face, and then the cold confidence of a grown-up's retort. "Don't be silly. You must go. We've accepted Mrs. Henne-Falcon's invitation."

But they couldn't make him go; hesitating on the door-step while the nurse's feet crunched across the frost-covered grass to the gate, he knew that. He would answer, "You can say I'm ill. I won't go. I'm afraid of the dark." And his mother, "Don't be silly. You know there's nothing to be afraid of in the dark." But he knew the falsity of that reasoning; he knew how they taught also that there was nothing to fear in death, and how fearfully they avoided the idea of it. But they couldn't make him go to the party. "I'll scream. I'll scream."

"Francis, come along." He heard the nurse's voice across the dimly phosphorescent lawn and saw the small yellow circle of her torch wheel from tree to shrub and back to tree again. "I'm coming," he called with despair, leaving the lighted doorway of the house; he couldn't bring himself to lay bare his last secrets and end reserve between his mother and himself, for there was still in the last resort a further appeal possible to Mrs. Henne-Falcon. He comforted himself with that, as he advanced steadily across the hall, very small, towards her enormous bulk. His heart beat unevenly, but he had control now over his voice, as he said with meticulous accent, "Good evening, Mrs. Henne-Falcon. It was very good of you to ask me to your party." With his strained face lifted towards the curve of her breasts, and his polite set speech, he was like an old withered man. For Francis mixed very little with other children. As a twin he was in many ways an only child. To address Peter was to speak to his own image in a mirror, an image a little altered by a flaw in the glass, so as to throw back less a likeness of what he was than of what he wished to be, what he would be without his unreasoning fear of darkness, footsteps of strangers, the flight of bats in dusk-filled gardens.

"Sweet child," said Mrs. Henne-Falcon absent-mindedly, before, with a wave of her arms, as though the children were a flock of chickens, she whirled them into her set programme of entertainments: egg-and-spoon races, three-legged races, the spearing of apples, games which held for Francis nothing worse than humiliation. And in the frequent intervals when nothing was required of him and he could stand alone in corners as far removed as possible from Mabel Warren's scornful gaze, he was able to plan how he might avoid the approaching terror of the dark. He knew there was nothing to fear until after tea, and not until he was sitting down in a pool of yellow radiance cast by the ten candles on Colin Henne-Falcon's birthday cake did he become fully conscious of the imminence of what he feared. Through the confusion of his brain, now assailed suddenly by a dozen contradictory plans, he heard Joyce's high voice down the table. "After tea we are going to play hide-and-seek in the dark."

"Oh, no," Peter said, watching Francis's troubled face with pity and an imperfect understanding, "don't let's. We play that every year."

"But it's in the programme," cried Mabel Warren. "I saw it myself. I looked over Mrs. Henne-Falcon's shoulder. Five o'clock, tea. A quarter to six to half-past, hide-and-seek in the dark. It's all written down in the programme."

Peter did not argue, for if hide-and-seek had been inserted in Mrs. Henne-Falcon's programme, nothing which he could say could avert it. He asked for another piece of birthday cake and sipped his tea slowly. Perhaps it might be possible to delay the game for a quarter of an hour, allow Francis at least a few extra minutes to form a plan, but even in that Peter failed, for children were already leaving the table in twos and threes. It was his third failure, and again, the reflection of an image in another's mind, he saw a great bird darken his brother's face with its wings. But he upbraided himself silently for his folly, and finished his cake encouraged by the memory of that adult refrain, "There's nothing to fear in the dark." The last to leave the table, the brothers came together to the hall to meet the mustering and impatient eyes of Mrs. Henne-Falcon.

"And now," she said, "we will play hide-and-seek in the dark."

Peter watched his brother and saw, as he had expected, the lips tighten. Francis, he knew, had feared this moment from the beginning of the party, had tried to meet it with courage and had abandoned the attempt. He must have prayed desperately for cunning to evade the game, which was now welcomed with cries of excitement by all the other children. "Oh, do let's." "We must pick sides." "Is any of the house out of bounds?" "Where shall home be?"

"I think," said Francis Morton, approaching Mrs. Henne-Falcon, his eyes focused unwaveringly on her exuberant breasts, "it will be no use my playing. My nurse will be calling for me very soon."

"Oh, but your nurse can wait, Francis," said Mrs. Henne-Falcon absent-mindedly, while she clapped her hands together to summon to her side a few children who were already straying up the wide staircase to upper floors. "Your mother will never mind."

That had been the limit of Francis's cunning. He had refused to believe that so well prepared an excuse could fail. All that he could say now, still in the precise tone which other children hated, thinking it a symbol of conceit, was, "I think I had better not play." He stood motionless, retaining, though afraid, unmoved features. But the knowledge of his terror, or the reflection of the terror itself, reached his brother's brain. For the moment, Peter Morton could have cried aloud with the fear of bright lights going out, leaving him alone in an island of dark surrounded by the gentle lapping of strange footsteps. Then he remembered that the fear was not his own, but his brother's. He said impulsively to Mrs. Henne-Falcon, "Please. I don't think Francis should play. The dark makes him jump so." They were the wrong words. Six children began to sing, "Cowardy, cowardy custard," turning torturing faces with the vacancy of wide sunflowers towards Francis Morton.

Without looking at his brother, Francis said, "Of course I will play. I am not afraid. I only thought . . ." But he was already forgotten by his human tormentors and was able in loneliness to contemplate the approach of the spiritual, the more unbounded, torture. The children scrambled round Mrs. Henne-Falcon, their shrill voices pecking at her with questions and suggestions. "Yes, anywhere in the house. We will turn out all the lights. Yes, you can hide in the cupboards. You must stay hidden as long as you can. There will be no home."

Peter, too, stood apart, ashamed of the clumsy manner in which he had tried to help his brother. Now he could feel, creeping in at the corners of his brain, all Francis's resentment of his championing. Several children ran upstairs, and the lights on the top floor went out. Then darkness came down like the wings of a bat and settled on the landing. Others began to put out the lights at the edge of the hall, till the children were all gathered in the central radiance of the chandelier, while the bats squatted round on hooded wings and waited for that, too, to be extinguished.

"You and Francis are on the hiding side," a tall girl said, and then the light was gone, and the carpet wavered under his feet with the sibilance of footfalls, like small cold draughts, creeping away into corners.

"Where's Francis?" he wondered. "If I join him he'll be less frightened of all these sounds." "These sounds" were the casing of silence. The squeak of a loose board, the cautious closing of a cupboard door, the whine of a finger drawn along polished wood.

Peter stood in the centre of the dark deserted floor, not listening but waiting for the idea of his brother's whereabouts to enter his brain. But Francis crouched with fingers on his ears, eyes uselessly closed, mind numbed against impressions, and only a sense of strain could cross the gap of dark. Then a voice called "Coming," and as though his brother's self-possession had been shattered by the sudden cry, Peter Morton jumped with his fear. But it was not his own fear. What in his brother was a burning panic, admitting no ideas except those which added to the flame, was in him an altruistic emotion that left the reason unimpaired. "Where, if I were Francis, should I hide?" Such, roughly, was his thought. And because he was, if not Francis himself, at least a mirror to him, the answer was immediate. "Between the oak bookcase on the left of the study door and the leather settee." Peter Morton was unsurprised by the swiftness of the response. Between the twins there could be no jargon of telepathy. They had been together in the womb, and they could not be parted.

Peter Morton tiptoed towards Francis's hiding place. Occasionally a board rattled, and because he feared to be caught by one of the soft questers through the dark, he bent and untied his laces. A tag struck the floor and the metallic sound set a host of cautious feet moving in his direction. But by that time he was in his stockings and would have laughed inwardly at the pursuit had not the noise of someone stumbling on his abandoned shoes made his heart trip in the reflection of another's surprise. No more boards revealed Peter Morton's progress. On stockinged feet he moved silently and unerringly towards his object. Instinct told him that he was near the wall, and, extending a hand, he laid the fingers across his brother's face.

Francis did not cry out, but the leap of his own heart revealed to Peter a proportion of Francis's terror. "It's all right," he whispered, feeling down the squatting figure until he captured a clenched hand. "It's only me. I'll stay with you." And grasping the other tightly, he listened to the cascade of whispers his utterance had caused to fall. A hand touched the bookcase close to Peter's head and he was aware of how Francis's fear continued in spite of his presence. It was less intense, more bearable, he hoped, but it remained. He knew that it was his brother's fear and not his own that he experienced. The dark to him was only an absence of light; the groping hand that of a familiar child. Patiently he waited to be found.

He did not speak again, for between Francis and himself touch was the most intimate communion. By way of joined hands thought could flow more swiftly than lips could shape themselves round words. He could experience the whole progress of his brother's emotion, from the leap of panic at the unexpected contact to the steady pulse of fear, which now went on and on with the regularity of a heart-beat. Peter Morton thought with intensity, "I am here. You needn't be afraid. The lights will go on again soon. That rustle, that movement is nothing to fear. Only Joyce, only Mabel Warren." He bombarded the drooping form with thoughts of safety, but he was conscious that the fear continued. "They are beginning to whisper together. They are tired of looking for us. The lights will go on soon. We shall have won. Don't be afraid. That was only someone on the stairs. I believe it's Mrs. Henne-Falcon. Listen. They are feeling for the lights." Feet moving on a carpet, hands brushing a wall, a curtain pulled apart, a clicking handle, the opening of a cupboard door. In the case above their heads a loose book shifted under a touch. "Only Joyce, only Mabel Warren, only Mrs. Henne-Falcon," a crescendo of reassuring thought before the chandelier burst, like a fruit tree, into bloom.

The voices of the children rose shrilly into the radiance. "Where's Peter?" "Have you looked upstairs?" "Where's Francis?" but they were silenced again by Mrs. Henne-Falcon's scream. But she was not the first to notice Francis Morton's stillness, where he had collapsed against the wall at the touch of his brother's hand. Peter continued to hold the clenched fingers in an arid and puzzled grief. It was not merely that his brother was dead. His brain, too young to realize the full paradox, yet wondered with an obscure self-pity why it was that the pulse of his brother's fear went on and on, when Francis was now where he had been always told there was no more terror and no more darkness.

D. H. LAWRENCE / Odour of Chrysanthemums

I

THE small locomotive engine, Number 4, came clanking, stumbling down from Selston with seven full wagons. It appeared round the corner with loud threats of speed, but the colt that it startled from among the gorse, which still flickered indistinctly in the raw afternoon, out-distanced it at a canter. A woman, walking up the railway line to Underwood, drew back into the hedge, held her basket aside, and watched the footplate of the engine advancing. The trucks thumped heavily past, one by one, with slow inevitable movement, as she stood insignificantly trapped between the jolting black wagons and the hedge; then they curved away towards the coppice where the withered oak leaves dropped noiselessly, while the birds, pulling at the scarlet hips beside the track, made off into the dusk that had already crept into the spinney. In the open, the smoke from the engine sank and cleaved to the rough grass. The fields were dreary and forsaken, and in the marshy strip that led to the whimsey, a reedy pit-pond, the fowls had already abandoned their run among the alders, to roost in the tarred fowl-house. The pit-bank loomed up beyond the pond, flames like red sores licking its ashy sides, in the afternoon's stagnant light. Just beyond rose the tapering chimneys and the clumsy black headstocks of Brinsley Colliery. The two wheels were spinning fast up against the sky, and the winding engine rapped out its little spasms. The miners were being turned up.

The engine whistled as it came into the wide bay of railway lines beside the colliery, where rows of trucks stood in harbour.

Miners, single, trailing and in groups, passed like shadows diverging home. At the edge of the ribbed level of sidings squat a low cottage, three steps down from the cinder track. A large bony vine clutched at the house, as if to claw down the tiled roof. Round the bricked yard grew a few wintry primroses. Beyond, the long garden sloped down to a bush-covered brook course. There were some twiggy apple trees, winter-crack trees, and ragged cabbages. Beside the path hung dishevelled pink chrysanthemums, like pink cloths hung on bushes. A woman came stooping out of the felt-covered fowl-house, half-way down the garden. She closed and padlocked the door, then drew herself erect, having brushed some bits from her white apron.

She was a tall woman of imperious mien, handsome, with definite black eyebrows. Her smooth black hair was parted exactly. For a few moments she stood steadily watching the miners as they passed along the railway: then she turned towards the brook course. Her face was calm and set, her mouth was closed with disillusionment. After a moment she called:

"John!" There was no answer. She waited, and then said distinctly:

"Where are you?"

"Here!" replied a child's sulky voice from among the bushes. The woman looked piercingly through the dusk.

"Are you at that brook?" she asked sternly.

For answer the child showed himself before the raspberry-canes that rose like whips. He was a small, sturdy boy of five. He stood quite still, defiantly.

"Oh!" said the mother, conciliated. "I thought you were down at that wet brook—and you remember what I told you——"

The boy did not move or answer.

"Come, come on in," she said more gently, "it's getting dark. There's your grandfather's engine coming down the line!"

The lad advanced slowly, with resentful, taciturn movement. He was dressed in trousers and waistcoat of cloth that was too thick and hard for the size of the garments. They were evidently cut down from a man's clothes.

As they went slowly towards the house he tore at the ragged wisps of chrysanthemums and dropped the petals in handfuls among the path.

"Don't do that—it does look nasty," said his mother. He refrained, and she, suddenly pitiful, broke off a twig with three or four wan flowers and held them against her face. When mother and son reached the yard her hand hesitated, and instead of laying the flower aside, she pushed it in her apron-band. The mother and son stood at the foot of the three steps looking across the bay of lines at the passing home of the miners. The trundle of the small train was imminent. Suddenly the engine loomed past the house and came to a stop opposite the gate.

The engine-driver, a short man with round grey beard, leaned out of the cab high above the woman.

"Have you got a cup of tea?" he said in a cheery, hearty fashion.

It was her father. She went in, saying she would mash. Directly, she returned.

"I didn't come to see you on Sunday," began the little grey-bearded man.

"I didn't expect you," said his daughter.

The engine-driver winced; then, reassuming his cheery, airy manner, he said:

"Oh, have you heard then? Well, and what do you think——?"

"I think it is soon enough," she replied.

At her brief censure the little man made an impatient gesture, and said coaxingly, yet with dangerous coldness:

"Well, what's a man to do? It's no sort of life for a man of my years, to sit at my own hearth like a stranger. And if I'm going to marry again it may as well be soon as late—what does it matter to anybody?"

The woman did not reply, but turned and went into the house. The man in the engine-cab stood assertive, till she returned with a cup of tea and a piece of bread and butter on a plate. She went up the steps and stood near the footplate of the hissing engine.

"You needn't 'a' brought me bread an' butter," said her father. "But a cup of tea"—he sipped appreciatively—"it's very nice." He sipped for a moment or two, then: "I hear as Walter's got another bout on," he said.

"When hasn't he?" said the woman bitterly.

"I heerd tell of him in the 'Lord Nelson' braggin' as he was going to spend that b—— afore he went: half a sovereign that was."

"When?" asked the woman.

"A' Sat'day night—I know that's true."

"Very likely," she laughed bitterly. "He gives me twenty-three shillings."

"Aye, it's a nice thing, when a man can do nothing with his money but make a beast of himself!" said the grey-whiskered man. The woman turned her head away. Her father swallowed the last of his tea and handed her the cup.

"Aye," he sighed, wiping his mouth. "It's a settler, it is——"

He put his hand on the lever. The little engine strained and groaned, and the train rumbled towards the crossing. The woman again looked across the metals. Darkness was settling over the spaces of the railway and trucks: the miners, in grey sombre groups, were still passing home. The winding engine pulsed hurriedly, with brief pauses. Elizabeth Bates looked at the dreary flow of men, then she went indoors. Her husband did not come.

The kitchen was small and full of firelight; red coals piled glowing up the chimney mouth. All the life of the room seemed in the white, warm hearth and the steel fender reflecting the red fire. The cloth was laid for tea; cups glinted in the shadows. At the back, where the lowest stairs protruded into the room, the boy sat struggling with a knife and a piece of white wood. He was almost hidden in the shadow. It was half-past four. They had but to await the father's coming to begin tea. As the mother watched her son's sullen little struggle with the wood, she saw herself in his silence and pertinacity; she saw the father in her child's indifference to all but himself. She seemed to be occupied by her husband. He had probably gone past his home, slung past his own door, to drink before he came in, while his dinner spoiled and wasted in waiting. She glanced at the clock, then took the potatoes to strain them in the yard. The garden and fields beyond the brook were closed in uncertain darkness. When she rose with the saucepan, leaving the drain steaming into the night behind her, she saw the yellow lamps were lit along the high road that went up the hill away beyond the space of the railway lines and the field.

Then again she watched the men trooping home, fewer now and fewer.

Indoors the fire was sinking and the room was dark red. The woman put her saucepan on the hob, and set a batter-pudding near the mouth of the oven. Then she stood unmoving. Directly, gratefully, came quick young steps to the door. Someone hung on the latch a moment, then a little girl entered and began pulling off her outdoor things, dragging a mass of curls, just ripening from gold to brown, over her eyes with her hat.

Her mother chid her for coming late from school, and said she would have to keep her at home the dark winter days.

"Why, mother, it's hardly a bit dark yet. The lamp's not lighted, and my father's not home."

"No, he isn't. But it's a quarter to five! Did you see anything of him?"

The child became serious. She looked at her mother with large, wistful blue eyes.

"No, mother, I've never seen him. Why? Has he come up an' gone past, to Old Brinsley? He hasn't, mother, 'cos I never saw him."

"He'd watch that," said the mother bitterly, "he'd take care as you didn't see him. But you may depend upon it, he's seated in the 'Prince o' Wales.' He wouldn't be this late."

The girl looked at her mother piteously.

"Let's have our teas, mother, should we?" said she.

The mother called John to table. She opened the door once more and looked out across the darkness of the lines. All was deserted: she could not hear the winding-engines.

"Perhaps," she said to herself, "he's stopped to get some ripping done."

They sat down to tea. John, at the end of the table near the door, was almost lost in the darkness. Their faces were hidden from each other. The girl crouched against the fender slowly moving a thick piece of bread before the fire. The lad, his face a dusky mark on the shadow, sat watching her who was transfigured in the red glow.

"I do think it's beautiful to look in the fire," said the child.

"Do you?" said her mother. "Why?"

"It's so red, and full of little caves—and it feels so nice, and you can fair smell it."

"It'll want mending directly," replied her mother, "and then if your father comes he'll carry on and say there never is a fire when a man comes home sweating from the pit. A public-house is always warm enough."

There was silence till the boy said complainingly: "Make haste, our Annie."

"Well, I am doing! I can't make the fire do it no faster, can I?"

"She keeps wafflin' it about so's to make 'er slow," grumbled the boy.

"Don't have such an evil imagination, child," replied the mother.

Soon the room was busy in the darkness with the crisp sound of crunching. The mother ate very little. She drank her tea determinedly, and sat thinking. When she rose her anger was evident in the stern unbending of her head. She looked at the pudding in the fender, and broke out:

"It is a scandalous thing as a man can't even come home to his dinner! If it's crozzled up to a cinder I don't see why I should care. Past his very door he goes to get to a public-house, and here I sit with his dinner waiting for him——"

She went out. As she dropped piece after piece of coal on the red fire, the shadows fell on the walls, till the room was almost in total darkness.

"I canna see," grumbled the invisible John. In spite of herself, the mother laughed.

"You know the way to your mouth," she said. She set the dust-pan outside the door. When she came again like a shadow on the hearth, the lad repeated, complaining sulkily:

"I canna see."

"Good gracious!" cried the mother irritably, "you're as bad as your father if it's a bit dusk!"

Nevertheless, she took a paper spill from a sheaf on the mantelpiece and proceeded to light the lamp that hung from the ceiling in the middle of the room. As she reached up, her figure displayed itself just rounding with maternity.

"Oh, mother——!" exclaimed the girl.

"What?" said the woman, suspended in the act of putting the lamp-glass over the flame. The copper reflector shone handsomely on her, as she stood with uplifted arm, turning to face her daughter.

"You've got a flower in your apron!" said the child, in a little rapture at this unusual event.

"Goodness me!" exclaimed the woman, relieved. "One would think the house was afire." She replaced the glass and waited a moment before turning up the wick. A pale shadow was seen floating vaguely on the floor.

"Let me smell!" said the child, still rapturously, coming forward and putting her face to her mother's waist.

"Go along, silly!" said the mother, turning up the lamp. The light revealed their suspense so that the woman felt it almost unbearable. Annie was still bending at her waist. Irritably, the mother took the flowers out from her apron-band.

"Oh, mother—don't take them out!" Annie cried, catching her hand and trying to replace the sprig.

"Such nonsense!" said the mother, turning away. The child put the pale chrysanthemums to her lips, murmuring:

"Don't they smell beautiful!"

Her mother gave a short laugh.

"No," she said, "not to me. It was chrysanthemums when I married him, and chrysanthemums when you were born, and the first time they ever brought him home drunk, he'd got brown chrysanthemums in his button-hole."

She looked at the children. Their eyes and their parted lips were wondering. The mother sat rocking in silence for some time. Then she looked at the clock.

"Twenty minutes to six!" In a tone of fine bitter carelessness she continued: "Eh, he'll not come now till they bring him. There he'll stick! But he needn't come rolling in here in his pit-dirt, for *I* won't wash him. He can lie on the floor—— Eh, what a fool I've been, what a fool! And this is what I came here for, to this dirty hole, rats and all, for him to slink past his very door. Twice last week—he's begun now——"

She silenced herself, and rose to clear the table.

While for an hour or more the children played, subduedly intent, fertile of imagination, united in fear of the mother's wrath, and in dread of their father's home-coming, Mrs. Bates sat in her rocking-chair making a 'singlet' of thick cream-coloured flannel, which gave a dull wounded sound as she tore off the grey edge. She worked at her sewing with energy, listening to the children, and her anger wearied itself, lay down to rest, opening its eyes from time to time and steadily watching, its ears raised to listen. Sometimes even her anger quailed and shrank, and the mother suspended her sewing, tracing the footsteps that thudded along the sleepers outside; she would lift her head sharply to bid the children 'hush', but she recovered herself in time, and the footsteps went past the gate, and the children were not flung out of their playworld.

But at last Annie sighed, and gave in. She glanced at her wagon of slippers, and loathed the game. She turned plaintively to her mother.

"Mother!"—but she was inarticulate.

John crept out like a frog from under the sofa. His mother glanced up.

"Yes," she said, "just look at those shirt-sleeves!"

The boy held them out to survey them, saying nothing. Then somebody called in a hoarse voice away down the line, and suspense bristled in the room, till two people had gone by outside, talking.

"It is time for bed," said the mother.

"My father hasn't come," wailed Annie plaintively. But her mother was primed with courage.

"Never mind. They'll bring him when he does come—like a log." She meant there would be no scene. "And he may sleep on the floor till he wakes himself. I know he'll not go to work to-morrow after this!"

The children had their hands and faces wiped with a flannel. They were very quiet. When they had put on their nightdresses, they said their prayers, the boy mumbling. The mother looked down at them, at the brown silken bush of intertwining curls in the nape of the girl's neck, at the little black head of the lad, and her heart burst with anger at their father, who caused all three such distress. The children hid their faces in her skirts for comfort.

When Mrs. Bates came down, the room was strangely empty, with a tension of expectancy. She took up her sewing and stitched for some time without raising her head. Meantime her anger was tinged with fear.

II

The clock struck eight and she rose suddenly, dropping her sewing on her chair. She went to the stair-foot door, opened it, listening. Then she went out, locking the door behind her.

Something scuffled in the yard, and she started, though she knew it was only the rats with which the place was over-run. The night was very dark. In the great bay of railway lines, bulked with trucks, there was no trace of light, only away back she could see a few yellow lamps at the pit-top, and the red smear of the burning pit-bank on the night. She hurried along the edge of the track, then, crossing the converging lines, came to the stile by the white gates, whence she emerged on the road. Then the fear which had led her shrank. People were walking up to New Brinsley; she saw the lights in the houses; twenty yards farther on were the broad windows of the 'Prince of Wales', very warm and bright, and the loud voices of men could be heard distinctly. What a fool she had been to imagine that anything had happened to him! He was merely drinking over there at the 'Prince of Wales'. She faltered. She had never yet been to fetch him, and she never would go. So she continued her walk towards the long straggling line of houses, standing back on the highway. She entered a passage between the dwellings.

"Mr. Rigley?—Yes! Did you want him? No, he's not in at this minute."

The raw-boned woman leaned forward from her dark scullery and peered at the other, upon whom fell a dim light through the blind of the kitchen window.

"Is it Mrs. Bates?" she asked in a tone tinged with respect.

"Yes. I wondered if your Master was at home. Mine hasn't come yet."

"'Asn't 'e! Oh, Jack's been 'ome an' 'ad 'is dinner an'

gone out. 'E's just gone for 'alf an hour afore bed-time. Did you call at the 'Prince of Wales'?"

"No——"

"No, you didn't like——! It's not very nice." The other woman was indulgent. There was an awkward pause. "Jack never said nothink about—about your Master," she said.

"No!—I expect he's stuck in there!"

Elizabeth Bates said this bitterly, and with recklessness. She knew that the woman across the yard was standing at her door listening, but she did not care. As she turned:

"Stop a minute! I'll just go an' ask Jack if 'e knows anythink," said Mrs. Rigley.

"Oh no—I wouldn't like to put——!"

"Yes, I will, if you'll just step inside an' see as th' childer doesn't come downstairs and set theirselves afire."

Elizabeth Bates, murmuring a remonstrance, stepped inside. The other woman apologised for the state of the room.

The kitchen needed apology. There were little frocks and trousers and childish undergarments on the squab and on the floor, and a litter of playthings everywhere. On the black American cloth of the table were pieces of bread and cake, crusts, slops, and a teapot with cold tea.

"Eh, ours is just as bad," said Elizabeth Bates, looking at the woman, not at the house. Mrs. Rigley put a shawl over her head and hurried out, saying:

"I shanna be a minute."

The other sat, noting with faint disapproval the general untidiness of the room. Then she fell to counting the shoes of various sizes scattered over the floor. There were twelve. She sighed and said to herself: "No wonder!"—glancing at the litter. There came the scratching of two pairs of feet on the yard, and the Rigleys entered. Elizabeth Bates rose. Rigley was a big man, with very large bones. His head looked particularly bony. Across his temple was a blue scar, caused by a wound got in the pit, a wound in which the coal-dust remained blue like tattooing.

" 'Asna 'e come whoam yit?" asked the man, without any form of greeting, but with deference and sympathy. "I couldna say wheer he is—'e's non ower theer!"—he jerked his head to signify the 'Prince of Wales'.

" 'E's 'appen gone up to th' 'Yew'," said Mrs. Rigley.

There was another pause. Rigley had evidently something to get off his mind:

"Ah left 'im finishin' a stint," he began. "Loose-all 'ad bin gone about ten minutes when we com'n away, an' I shouted: 'Are ter comin', Walt?' an' 'e said: 'Go on, Ah shanna be but a'ef a minnit,' so we com'n ter th' bottom, me an' Bowers, thinkin' as 'e wor just behint, an' 'ud come up i' th' next bantle——"

He stood perplexed, as if answering a charge of deserting his mate. Elizabeth Bates, now again certain of disaster, hastened to reassure him:

"I expect 'e's gone up to th' 'Yew Tree', as you say. It's not the first time. I've fretted myself into a fever before now. He'll come home when they carry him."

"Ay, isn't it too bad!" deplored the other woman.

"I'll just step up to Dick's an' see if 'e *is* theer," offered the man, afraid of appearing alarmed, afraid of taking liberties.

"Oh, I wouldn't think of bothering you that far," said Elizabeth Bates, with emphasis, but he knew she was glad of his offer.

As they stumbled up the entry, Elizabeth Bates heard Rigley's wife run across the yard and open her neighbour's door. At this, suddenly all the blood in her body seemed to switch away from her heart.

"Mind!" warned Rigley. "Ah've said many a time as Ah'd fill up them ruts in this entry, sumb'dy 'll be breakin' their legs yit."

She recovered herself and walked quickly along with the miner.

"I don't like leaving the children in bed, and nobody in the house," she said.

"No, you dunna!" he replied courteously. They were soon at the gate of the cottage.

"Well, I shanna be many minnits. Dunna you be frettin' now, 'e'll be all right," said the butty.

"Thank you very much, Mr. Rigley," she replied.

"You're welcome!" he stammered, moving away. "I shanna be many minnits."

The house was quiet. Elizabeth Bates took off her hat and shawl, and rolled back the rug. When she had finished, she sat down. It was a few minutes past nine. She was startled by the rapid chuff of the winding-engine at the pit, and the sharp whirr of the brakes on the rope as it descended. Again she felt the painful sweep of her blood, and she put her hand to her side, saying aloud: "Good gracious!—it's only the nine o'clock deputy going down," rebuking herself.

She sat still, listening. Half an hour of this, and she was wearied out.

"What am I working myself up like this for?" she said pitiably to herself, "I s'll only be doing myself some damage."

She took out her sewing again.

At a quarter to ten there were footsteps. One person! She watched for the door to open. It was an elderly woman, in a black bonnet and a black woollen shawl—his mother. She was about sixty years old, pale, with blue eyes, and her face all wrinkled and lamentable. She shut the door and turned to her daughter-in-law peevishly.

"Eh, Lizzie, whatever shall we do, whatever shall we do!" she cried.

Elizabeth drew back a little, sharply.

"What is it, mother?" she said.

The elder woman seated herself on the sofa.

"I don't know, child, I can't tell you!"—she shook her head slowly. Elizabeth sat watching her, anxious and vexed.

"I don't know," replied the grandmother, sighing very deeply. "There's no end to my troubles, there isn't. The things I've gone through, I'm sure it's enough——!" She wept without wiping her eyes, the tears running.

"But, mother," interrupted Elizabeth, "what do you mean? What is it?"

The grandmother slowly wiped her eyes. The fountains of her tears were stopped by Elizabeth's directness. She wiped her eyes slowly.

"Poor child! Eh, you poor thing!" she moaned. "I don't know what we're going to do, I don't—and you as you are—it's a thing, it is indeed!"

Elizabeth waited.

"Is he dead?" she asked, and at the words her heart swung violently, though she felt a slight flush of shame at the ultimate extravagance of the question. Her words sufficiently frightened the old lady, almost brought her to herself.

"Don't say so, Elizabeth! We'll hope it's not as bad as that; no, may the Lord spare us that, Elizabeth. Jack Rigley came just as I was sittin' down to a glass afore going to bed, an' 'e said: ' 'Appen you'll go down th' line, Mrs. Bates. Walt's had an accident. 'Appen you'll go an' sit wi' 'er till we can get him home.' I hadn't time to ask him a word afore he was gone. An' I put my bonnet on an' come straight down, Lizzie. I thought to myself: 'Eh, that poor blessed child, if anybody should come an' tell her of a sudden, there's no knowin' what'll 'appen to 'er.' You mustn't let it upset you, Lizzie—or you know what to expect. How long is it, six months—or is it five, Lizzie? Ay!"—the old woman shook her head—"time slips on, it slips on! Ay!"

Elizabeth's thoughts were busy elsewhere. If he was killed —would she be able to manage on the little pension and what she could earn?—she counted up rapidly. If he was hurt—they wouldn't take him to the hospital—how tiresome he would be to nurse!—but perhaps she'd be able to get him away from the drink and his hateful ways. She would—while he was ill. The tears offered to come to her eyes at the picture. But what sentimental luxury was this she was beginning? She turned to consider the children. At any rate she was absolutely necessary for them. They were her business.

"Ay!" repeated the old woman, "it seems but a week or two since he brought me his first wages. Ay—he was a good lad, Elizabeth, he was, in his way. I don't know why he got to be such a trouble, I don't. He was a happy lad at home, only full of spirits. But there's no mistake he's been a handful of trouble, he has! I hope the Lord'll spare him to mend his ways. I hope so, I hope so. You've had a sight o' trouble with him, Elizabeth, you have indeed. But he was a jolly enough lad wi' me, he was, I can assure you. I don't know how it is. . . ."

The old woman continued to muse aloud, a monotonous irritating sound, while Elizabeth thought concentratedly, startled once, when she heard the winding-engine chuff quickly, and the brakes skirr with a shriek. Then she heard the engine more slowly, and the brakes made no sound. The old woman did not notice. Elizabeth waited in suspense. The mother-in-law talked, with lapses into silence.

"But he wasn't your son, Lizzie, an' it makes a difference. Whatever he was, I remember him when he was little, an' I learned to understand him and to make allowances. You've got to make allowances for them——"

It was half-past ten, and the old woman was saying: "But it's trouble from beginning to end; you're never too old for trouble, never too old for that——" when the gate banged back, and there were heavy feet on the steps.

"I'll go, Lizzie, let me go," cried the old woman, rising. But Elizabeth was at the door. It was a man in pit-clothes.

"They're bringin' 'im, Missis," he said. Elizabeth's heart halted a moment. Then it surged on again, almost suffocating her.

"Is he—is it bad?" she asked.

The man turned away, looking at the darkness:

"The doctor says 'e'd been dead hours. 'E saw 'im i' th' lamp-cabin."

The old woman, who stood just behind Elizabeth, dropped into a chair, and folded her hands, crying: "Oh, my boy, my boy!"

"Hush!" said Elizabeth, with a sharp twitch of a frown. "Be still, mother, don't waken th' children: I wouldn't have them down for anything!"

The old woman moaned softly, rocking herself. The man was drawing away. Elizabeth took a step forward.

"How was it?" she asked.

"Well, I couldn't say for sure," the man replied, very ill at ease. " 'E wor finishin' a stint an' th' butties 'ad gone, an' a lot o' stuff come down atop 'n 'im."

"And crushed him?" cried the widow, with a shudder.

"No," said the man, "it fell at th' back of 'im. 'E wor under th' face, an' it niver touched 'im. It shut 'im in. It seems 'e wor smothered."

Elizabeth shrank back. She heard the old woman behind her cry:

"What?—what did 'e say it was?"

The man replied, more loudly: "'E wor smothered!"

Then the old woman wailed aloud, and this relieved Elizabeth.

"Oh, mother," she said, putting her hand on the old woman, "don't waken th' children, don't waken th' children."

She wept a little, unknowing, while the old mother rocked herself and moaned. Elizabeth remembered that they were bringing him home, and she must be ready. "They'll lay him in the parlour," she said to herself, standing a moment pale and perplexed.

Then she lighted a candle and went into the tiny room. The air was cold and damp, but she could not make a fire, there was no fireplace. She set down the candle and looked round. The candlelight glittered on the lustre-glasses, on the two vases that held some of the pink chrysanthemums, and on the dark mahogany. There was a cold, deathly smell of chrysanthemums in the room. Elizabeth stood looking at the flowers. She turned away, and calculated whether there would be room to lay him on the floor, between the couch and the chiffonier. She pushed the chairs aside. There would be room to lay him down and to step round him. Then she fetched the old red tablecloth, and another old cloth, spreading them down to save her bit of carpet. She shivered on leaving the parlour; so, from the dresser drawer she took a clean shirt and put it at the fire to air. All the time her mother-in-law was rocking herself in the chair and moaning.

"You'll have to move from there, mother," said Elizabeth. "They'll be bringing him in. Come in the rocker."

The old mother rose mechanically, and seated herself by the fire, continuing to lament. Elizabeth went into the pantry for another candle, and there, in the little pent-house under the naked tiles, she heard them coming. She stood still in the pantry doorway, listening. She heard them pass the end of the house, and come awkwardly down the three steps, a jumble of shuffling footsteps and muttering voices. The old woman was silent. The men were in the yard.

Then Elizabeth heard Matthews, the manager of the pit, say: "You go in first, Jim. Mind!"

The door came open, and the two women saw a collier backing into the room, holding one end of a stretcher, on which they could see the nailed pit-boots of the dead man. The two carriers halted, the man at the head stooping to the lintel of the door.

"Wheer will you have him?" asked the manager, a short, white-bearded man.

Elizabeth roused herself and came from the pantry carrying the unlighted candle.

"In the parlour," she said.

"In there, Jim!" pointed the manager, and the carriers backed round into the tiny room. The coat with which they had covered the body fell off as they awkwardly turned through the two doorways, and the women saw their man, naked to the waist, lying stripped for work. The old woman began to moan in a low voice of horror.

"Lay th' stretcher at th' side," snapped the manager, "an' put 'im on th' cloths. Mind now, mind! Look you now——!"

One of the men had knocked off a vase of chrysanthemums. He stared awkwardly, then they set down the stretcher. Elizabeth did not look at her husband. As soon as she could get in the room, she went and picked up the broken vase and the flowers.

"Wait a minute!" she said.

The three men waited in silence while she mopped up the water with a duster.

"Eh, what a job, what a job, to be sure!" the manager was saying, rubbing his brow with trouble and perplexity. "Never knew such a thing in my life, never! He'd no business to ha' been left. I never knew such a thing in my life! Fell over him clean as a whistle, an' shut him in. Not four foot of space, there wasn't—yet it scarce bruised him."

He looked down at the dead man, lying prone, half naked, all grimed with coal-dust.

" ' 'Sphyxiated', the doctor said. It *is* the most terrible job I've ever known. Seems as if it was done o' purpose. Clean over him, an' shut 'im in, like a mouse-trap"—he made a sharp, descending gesture with his hand.

The colliers standing by jerked aside their heads in hopeless comment.

The horror of the thing bristled upon them all.

Then they heard the girl's voice upstairs calling shrilly: "Mother, mother—who is it? Mother, who is it?"

Elizabeth hurried to the foot of the stairs and opened the door:

"Go to sleep!" she commanded sharply. "What are you shouting about? Go to sleep at once—there's nothing——"

Then she began to mount the stairs. They could hear her on the boards, and on the plaster floor of the little bedroom. They could hear her distinctly:

"What's the matter now?—what's the matter with you, silly thing?"—her voice was much agitated, with an unreal gentleness.

"I thought it was some men come," said the plaintive voice of the child. "Has he come?"

"Yes, they've brought him. There's nothing to make a fuss about. Go to sleep now, like a good child."

They could hear her voice in the bedroom, they waited whilst she covered the children under the bedclothes.

"Is he drunk?" asked the girl, timidly, faintly.

"No! No—he's not! He—he's asleep."

"Is he asleep downstairs?"

"Yes—and don't make a noise."

There was silence for a moment, then the men heard the frightened child again:

"What's that noise?"

"It's nothing, I tell you, what are you bothering for?"

The noise was the grandmother moaning. She was oblivious of everything, sitting on her chair rocking and moaning. The manager put his hand on her arm and bade her "Sh—sh!!"

The old woman opened her eyes and looked at him. She was shocked by this interruption, and seemed to wonder.

"What time is it?" the plaintive thin voice of the child, sinking back unhappily into sleep, asked this last question.

"Ten o'clock," answered the mother more softly. Then she must have bent down and kissed the children.

Matthews beckoned to the men to come away. They put on their caps and took up the stretcher. Stepping over the body, they tiptoed out of the house. None of them spoke till they were far from the wakeful children.

When Elizabeth came down she found her mother alone on the parlour floor, leaning over the dead man, the tears dropping on him.

"We must lay him out," the wife said. She put on the kettle, then returning knelt at the feet, and began to unfasten the knotted leather laces. The room was clammy and dim with only one candle, so that she had to bend her face almost to the floor. At last she got off the heavy boots and put them away.

"You must help me now," she whispered to the old woman. Together they stripped the man.

When they arose, saw him lying in the naïve dignity of death, the women stood arrested in fear and respect. For a few moments they remained still, looking down, the old mother whimpering. Elizabeth felt countermanded. She saw him, how utterly inviolable he lay in himself. She had nothing to do with him. She could not accept it. Stooping, she laid her hand on him, in claim. He was still warm, for the mine was hot where he had died. His mother had his face between her hands, and was murmuring incoherently. The old tears fell in succession as drops from wet leaves; the mother was not weeping, merely her tears flowed. Elizabeth embraced the body of her husband, with cheek and lips. She seemed to be listening, inquiring, trying to get some connection. But she could not. She was driven away. He was impregnable.

She rose, went into the kitchen, where she poured warm water into a bowl, brought soap and flannel and a soft towel.

"I must wash him," she said.

Then the old mother rose stiffly, and watched Elizabeth as she carefully washed his face, carefully brushing the big blond moustache from his mouth with the flannel. She was afraid with a bottomless fear, so she ministered to him. The old woman, jealous, said:

"Let me wipe him!"—and she kneeled on the other side drying slowly as Elizabeth washed, her big black bonnet sometimes brushing the dark head of her daughter-in-law. They worked thus in silence for a long time. They never forgot it was death, and the touch of the man's dead body gave them strange emotions, different in each of the women; a great dread possessed them both, the mother felt the lie was given to her womb, she was denied; the wife felt the utter isolation of the human soul, the child within her was a weight apart from her.

At last it was finished. He was a man of handsome body, and his face showed no traces of drink. He was blond, full-fleshed, with fine limbs. But he was dead.

"Bless him," whispered his mother, looking always at his face, and speaking out of sheer terror. "Dear lad—bless him!" She spoke in a faint, sibilant ecstasy of fear and mother love.

Elizabeth sank down again to the floor, and put her face against his neck, and trembled and shuddered. But she had to draw away again. He was dead, and her living flesh had no place against his. A great dread and weariness held her: she was so unavailing. Her life was gone like this.

"White as milk he is, clear as a twelve-month baby, bless him, the darling!" the old mother murmured to herself. "Not a mark on him, clear and clean and white, beautiful as ever a child was made," she murmured with pride. Elizabeth kept her face hidden.

"He went peaceful, Lizzie—peaceful as sleep. Isn't he beautiful, the lamb? Ay—he must ha' made his peace, Lizzie. 'Appen he made it all right, Lizzie, shut in there. He'd have time. He wouldn't look like this if he hadn't made his peace. The lamb, the dear lamb. Eh, but he had a hearty laugh. I loved to hear it. He had the heartiest laugh, Lizzie, as a lad——"

Elizabeth looked up. The man's mouth was fallen back, slightly open under the cover of the moustache. The eyes, half shut, did not show glazed in the obscurity. Life with its smoky burning gone from him, had left him apart and utterly alien to her. And she knew what a stranger he was to her. In her womb was ice of fear, because of this separate stranger with whom she had been living as one flesh. Was this what it all meant—utter, intact separateness, obscured by heat of living? In dread she turned her face away. The fact was too deadly. There had been nothing between them, and yet they had come together, exchanging their nakedness repeatedly. Each time he had taken her, they had been two isolated beings, far apart as now. He was no more responsible than she. The child was like ice in her womb. For as she looked at the dead man, her mind, cold and detached, said clearly: "Who am I? What have I been doing? I have been fighting a husband who did not exist. *He* existed all the time. What wrong have I done? What was that I have been living with? There lies the reality, this man." And her soul died in her for fear: she knew she had never seen him, he had never seen her, they had met in the dark and had fought in the dark, not knowing whom they met nor whom they fought. And now she saw, and turned silent in seeing. For she had been wrong. She had said he was something he was not; she had felt familiar with him. Whereas he was apart all the while, living as she never lived, feeling as she never felt.

In fear and shame she looked at his naked body, that she had known falsely. And he was the father of her children. Her soul was torn from her body and stood apart. She looked at his naked body and was ashamed, as if she had denied it. After all, it was itself. It seemed awful to her. She looked at his face, and she turned her own face to the wall. For his look was other than hers, his way was not her way. She had denied him what he was—she saw it now. She had refused him as himself. And this had been her life, and his life. She was grateful to death, which restored the truth. And she knew she was not dead.

And all the while her heart was bursting with grief and pity for him. What had he suffered? What stretch of horror for this helpless man! She was rigid with agony. She had not been able to help him. He had been cruelly injured, this naked man, this other being, and she could make no reparation. There were the children—but the children belonged to life. This dead man had nothing to do with them. He and she were only channels through which life had flowed to issue in the children. She was a mother—but how awful she knew it now to have been a wife. And he, dead now, how awful he must have felt it to be a husband. She felt that in the next world he would be a stranger to her. If they met there, in the beyond, they would only be ashamed of what had been before. The children had come, for some mysterious reason, out of both of them. But the children did not unite them. Now he was dead, she knew how eternally he was apart from her, how eternally he had nothing more to do with her. She saw this episode of her life closed. They had denied each other in life. Now he had withdrawn. An anguish came over her. It was finished then: it had become hopeless between them long before he died. Yet he had been her husband. But how little!

"Have you got his shirt, 'Lizabeth?"

Elizabeth turned without answering, though she strove to weep and behave as her mother-in-law expected. But she could not, she was silenced. She went into the kitchen and returned with the garment.

"It is aired," she said, grasping the cotton shirt here and there to try. She was almost ashamed to handle him; what right had she or anyone to lay hands on him; but her touch was humble on his body. It was hard work to clothe him. He was so heavy and inert. A terrible dread gripped her all the while: that he could be so heavy and utterly inert, unresponsive, apart. The horror of the distance between them was almost too much for her—it was so infinite a gap she must look across.

At last it was finished. They covered him with a sheet and left him lying, with his face bound. And she fastened the door of the little parlour, lest the children should see what was lying there. Then, with peace sunk heavy on her heart, she went about making tidy the kitchen. She knew she submitted to life, which was her immediate master. But from death, her ultimate master, she winced with fear and shame.

SAMUEL L. CLEMENS / Cannibalism in the Cars

I VISITED St. Louis lately, and on my way West, after changing cars at Terre Haute, Indiana, a mild, benevolent-looking gentleman of about forty-five, or maybe fifty, came in at one of the way-stations and sat down beside me. We talked together pleasantly on various subjects for an hour, perhaps, and I

* Reprinted from *Sketches New and Old*.

found him exceedingly intelligent and entertaining. When he learned that I was from Washington, he immediately began to ask questions about various public men, and about Congressional affairs; and I saw very shortly that I was conversing with a man who was perfectly familiar with the ins and outs of political life at the Capital, even to the ways and manners, and customs of procedure of Senators and Representatives in the Chambers of the National Legislature. Presently two men halted near us for a single moment, and one said to the other:

"Harris, if you'll do that for me, I'll never forget you, my boy."

My new comrade's eye lighted pleasantly. The words had touched upon a happy memory, I thought. Then his face settled into thoughtfulness—almost into gloom. He turned to me and said, "Let me tell you a story; let me give you a secret chapter of my life—a chapter that has never been referred to by me since its events transpired. Listen patiently, and promise that you will not interrupt me."

I said I would not, and he related the following strange adventure, speaking sometimes with animation, sometimes with melancholy, but always with feeling and earnestness.

The Stranger's Narrative

"On the 19th of December, 1853, I started from St. Louis on the evening train bound for Chicago. There were only twenty-four passengers, all told. There were no ladies and no children. We were in excellent spirits, and pleasant acquaintanceships were soon formed. The journey bade fair to be a happy one; and no individual in the party, I think, had even the vaguest presentiment of the horrors we were soon to undergo.

"At 11 p.m. it began to snow hard. Shortly after leaving the small village of Welden, we entered upon that tremendous prairie solitude that stretches its leagues on leagues of houseless dreariness far away toward the Jubilee Settlements. The winds, unobstructed by trees or hills, or even vagrant rocks, whistled fiercely across the level desert, driving the falling snow before it like spray from the crested waves of a stormy sea. The snow was deepening fast; and we knew, by the diminished speed of the train, that the engine was plowing through it with steadily increasing difficulty. Indeed, it almost came to a dead halt sometimes, in the midst of great drifts that piled themselves like colossal graves across the track. Conversation began to flag. Cheerfulness gave place to grave concern. The possibility of being imprisoned in the snow, on the bleak prairie, fifty miles from any house, presented itself to every mind, and extended its depressing influence over every spirit.

"At two o'clock in the morning I was aroused out of an uneasy slumber by the ceasing of all motion about me. The appalling truth flashed upon me instantly—we were captives in a snow-drift! 'All hands to the rescue!' Every man sprang to obey. Out into the wild night, the pitchy darkness, the billowy snow, the driving storm, every soul leaped, with the consciousness that a moment lost now might bring destruction to us all. Shovels, hands, boards—anything, everything that could displace snow, was brought into instant requisition. It was a weird picture, that small company of frantic men fighting the banking snows, half in the blackest shadow, and half in the angry light of the locomotive's reflector.

"One short hour sufficed to prove the utter uselessness of our efforts. The storm barricaded the track with a dozen drifts while we dug one away. And worse than this, it was discovered that the last grand charge the engine had made upon the enemy had broken the fore-and-aft shaft of the driving wheel! With a free track before us we should still have been helpless. We entered the car wearied with labor, and very sorrowful. We gathered about the stoves, and gravely canvassed our situation. We had no provisions whatever—in this lay our chief distress. We could not freeze, for there was a good supply of wood in the tender. This was our only comfort. The discussion ended at last in accepting the disheartening decision of the conductor, viz., that it would be death for any man to attempt to travel fifty miles on foot through snow like that. We could not send for help, and even if we could it would not come. We must submit, and await, as patiently as we might, succor or starvation! I think the stoutest heart there felt a momentary chill when those words were uttered.

"Within the hour conversation subsided to a low murmur here and there about the car, caught fitfully between the rising and falling of the blast; the lamps grew dim; and the majority of the castaways settled themselves among the flickering shadows to think—to forget the present, if they could—to sleep, if they might.

"The eternal night—it surely seemed eternal to us—wore its lagging hours away at last, and the cold gray dawn broke in the east. As the light grew stronger the passengers began to stir and give signs of life, one after another, and each in turn pushed his slouched hat up from his forehead, stretched his stiffened limbs, and glanced out at the windows upon the cheerless prospect. It was cheerless, indeed!—not a living thing visible anywhere, not a human habitation; nothing but a vast white desert; uplifted sheets of snow drifting hither and thither before the wind—a world of eddying flakes shutting out the firmament above.

"All day we moped about the cars, saying little, thinking much. Another lingering dreary night—and hunger.

"Another dawning—another day of silence, sadness, wasting hunger, hopeless watching for succor that could not come. A night of restless slumber, filled with dreams of feasting—wakings distressed with the gnawings of hunger.

"The fourth day came and went—and the fifth! Five days of dreadful imprisonment! A savage hunger looked out at every eye. There was in it a sign of awful import—the foreshadowing of a something that was vaguely shaping itself in every heart—a something which no tongue dared yet to frame into words.

"The sixth day passed—the seventh dawned upon as gaunt and haggard and hopeless a company of men as ever stood in the shadow of death. It must out now! That thing which had been growing up in every heart was ready to leap from every lip at last! Nature had been taxed to the utmost—she must yield. RICHARD H. GASTON of Minnesota, tall, cadaverous, and pale, rose up. All knew what was coming. All prepared—every emotion, every semblance of excitement was smothered—only a calm, thoughtful seriousness appeared in the eyes that were lately so wild.

" 'Gentlemen: It cannot be delayed longer! The time is at hand! We must determine which of us shall die to furnish food for the rest!'

"MR. JOHN J. WILLIAMS of Illinois rose and said: 'Gentlemen—I nominate the Rev. James Sawyer of Tennessee.'

"MR. WM. R. ADAMS of Indiana said: 'I nominate Mr. Daniel Slote of New York.'

"MR. CHARLES J. LANGDON: 'I nominate Mr. Samuel A. Bowen of St. Louis.'

"MR. SLOTE: 'Gentlemen—I desire to decline in favor of Mr. John A. Van Nostrand, Jun., of New Jersey.'

"MR. GASTON: 'If there be no objection, the gentleman's desire will be acceded to.'

"MR. VAN NOSTRAND objecting, the resignation of Mr. Slote was rejected. The resignations of Messrs. Sawyer and Bowen were also offered, and refused upon the same grounds.

"MR. A. L. BASCOM of Ohio: 'I move that the nominations now close, and that the House proceed to an election by ballot.'

"MR. SAWYER: 'Gentlemen—I protest earnestly against these proceedings. They are, in every way, irregular and unbecoming. I must beg to move that they be dropped at once, and that we elect a chairman of the meeting and proper officers to assist him, and then we can go on with the business before us understandingly.'

"MR. BELL of Iowa: 'Gentlemen—I object. This is no time to stand upon forms and ceremonious observances. For more than seven days we have been without food. Every moment we lose in idle discussion increases our distress. I am satisfied with the nominations that have been made—every gentleman present is, I believe —and I, for one, do not see why we should not proceed at once to elect one or more of them. I wish to offer a resolution—'

"Mr. Gaston: 'It would be objected to, and have to lie over one day under the rules, thus bringing about the very delay you wish to avoid. The gentleman from New Jersey—'

"Mr. Van Nostrand: 'Gentlemen—I am a stranger among you; I have not sought the distinction that has been conferred upon me, and I feel a delicacy—'

"Mr. Morgan of Alabama (interrupting): 'I move the previous question.'

"The motion was carried, and further debate shut off, of course. The motion to elect officers was passed, and under it Mr. Gaston was chosen chairman, Mr. Blake, secretary, Messrs. Holcomb, Dyer, and Baldwin, a committee on nominations, and Mr. R. M. Howland, purveyor, to assist the committee in making selections.

"A recess of half an hour was then taken, and some little caucusing followed. At the sound of the gavel the meeting reassembled, and the committee reported in favor of Messrs. George Ferguson of Kentucky, Lucien Herrman of Louisiana, and W. Messick of Colorado as candidates. The report was accepted.

"Mr. Rogers of Missouri: 'Mr. President—The report being properly before the House now, I move to amend it by substituting for the name of Mr. Herrman that of Mr. Lucius Harris of St. Louis, who is well and honorably known to us all. I do not wish to be understood as casting the least reflection upon the high character and standing of the gentleman from Louisiana—far from it. I respect and esteem him as much as any gentleman here present possibly can; but none of us can be blind to the fact that he has lost more flesh during the week that we have lain here than any among us—none of us can be blind to the fact that the committee has been derelict in its duty, either through negligence or a graver fault, in thus offering for our suffrages a gentleman who, however pure his own motives may be, has really less nutriment in him—'

"The Chair: 'The gentleman from Missouri will take his seat. The Chair cannot allow the integrity of the committee to be questioned save by the regular course, under the rules. What action will the House take upon the gentleman's motion?'

"Mr. Halliday of Virginia: 'I move to further amend the report by substituting Mr. Harvey Davis of Oregon for Mr. Messick. It may be urged by gentlemen that the hardships and privations of a frontier life have rendered Mr. Davis tough; but, gentlemen, is this a time to cavil at toughness? Is this a time to be fastidious concerning trifles? Is this a time to dispute about matters of paltry significance? No, gentlemen, bulk is what we desire—substance, weight, bulk—these are the supreme requisites now—not talent, not genius, not education. I insist upon my motion.'

"Mr. Morgan (excitedly) : 'Mr. Chairman—I do most strenuously object to this amendment. The gentleman from Oregon is old, and furthermore is bulky only in bone—not in flesh. I ask the gentleman from Virginia if it is soup we want instead of solid sustenance? if he would delude us with shadows? if he would mock our suffering with an Oregonian specter? I ask him if he can look upon the anxious faces around him, if he can gaze into our sad eyes, if he can listen to the beating of our expectant hearts, and still thrust this famine-stricken fraud upon us? I ask him if he can think of our desolate state, of our past sorrows, of our dark future, and still unpityingly foist upon us this wreck, this ruin, this tottering swindle, this gnarled and blighted and sapless vagabond from Oregon's inhospitable shores? Never!' [*Applause.*]

"The amendment was put to vote, after a fiery debate, and lost. Mr. Harris was substituted on the first amendment. The balloting then began. Five ballots were held without a choice. On the sixth, Mr. Harris was elected, all voting for him but himself. It was then moved that his election should be ratified by acclamation, which was lost, in consequence of his again voting against himself.

"Mr. Radway moved that the House now take up the remaining candidates, and go into an election for breakfast. This was carried.

"On the first ballot there was a tie, half the members favoring one candidate on account of his youth, and half favoring the other on account of his superior size. The President gave the casting vote for the latter, Mr. Messick. This decision created considerable dissatisfaction among the friends of Mr. Ferguson, the defeated candidate, and there was some talk of demanding a new ballot; but in the midst of it, a motion to adjourn was carried, and the meeting broke up at once.

"The preparations for supper diverted the attention of the Ferguson faction from the discussion of their grievance for a long time, and then, when they would have taken it up again, the happy announcement that Mr. Harris was ready, drove all thought of it to the winds.

"We improvised tables by propping up the backs of carseats, and sat down with hearts full of gratitude to the finest supper that had blessed our vision for seven torturing days. How changed we were from what we had been a few short hours before! Hopeless, sad-eyed misery, hunger, feverish anxiety, desperation, then—thankfulness, serenity, joy too deep for utterance now. That I know was the cheeriest hour of my eventful life. The wind howled, and blew the snow wildly about our prison-house, but they were powerless to distress us any more. I liked Harris. He might have been better done, perhaps, but I am free to say that no man ever agreed with me better than Harris, or afforded me so large a degree of satisfaction. Messick was very well, though rather high-flavored, but for genuine nutritiousness and delicacy of fiber, give me Harris. Messick had his good points—I will not attempt to deny it, nor do I wish to do it—but he was no more fitted for breakfast than a mummy would be, sir—not a bit. Lean?—why, bless me! —and tough? Ah, he was very tough! You could not imagine it—you could never imagine anything like it."

"Do you mean to tell me that—"

"Do not interrupt me, please. After breakfast we elected a man by the name of Walker, from Detroit, for supper. He was very good. I wrote his wife so afterwards. He was worthy of all praise. I shall always remember Walker. He was a little rare, but very good. And then the next morning we had Morgan of Alabama for breakfast. He was one of the finest men I ever sat down to—handsome, educated, refined, spoke several languages fluently—a perfect gentleman—he was a perfect gentleman, and singularly juicy. For supper we had that Oregon patriarch, and he *was* a fraud, there is no question about it—old, scraggy, tough, nobody can picture the reality. I finally said, gentlemen, you can do as you like, but *I* will wait for another election. And Grimes of Illinois said, 'Gentlemen, *I* will wait also. When you elect a man that has *something* to recommend him, I shall be glad to join you again.' It soon became evident that there was general dissatisfaction with Davis of Oregon, and so, to preserve the good-will that had prevailed so pleasantly since we had had Harris, an election was called, and the result of it was that Baker of Georgia was chosen. He was splendid! Well, well—after that we had Doolittle, and Hawkins, and McElroy (there was some complaint about McElroy, because he was uncommonly short and thin), and Penrod, and two Smiths, and Bailey (Bailey had a wooden leg, which was clear loss, but he was otherwise good), and an Indian boy, and an organ-grinder, and a gentleman by the name of Buckminster—a poor stick of a vagabond that wasn't any good for company and no account for breakfast. We were glad we got him elected before relief came."

"And so the blessed relief *did* come at last?"

"Yes, it came one bright, sunny morning, just after election. John Murphy was the choice, and there never was a better,

I am willing to testify; but John Murphy came home with us, in the train that came to succor us, and lived to marry the widow Harris—"

"Relict of—"

"Relict of our first choice. He married her, and is happy and respected and prosperous yet. Ah, it was like a novel, sir—it was like a romance. This is my stopping-place, sir; I must bid you good-by. Any time that you can make it convenient to tarry a day or two with me, I shall be glad to have you. I like you, sir; I have conceived an affection for you. I could like you as well as I liked Harris himself, sir. Good day, sir, and a pleasant journey."

He was gone. I never felt so stunned, so distressed, so bewildered in my life. But in my soul I was glad he was gone. With all his gentleness of manner and his soft voice, I shuddered whenever he turned his hungry eye upon me; and when I heard that I had achieved his perilous affection, and that I stood almost with the late Harris in his esteem, my heart fairly stood still!

I was bewildered beyond description. I did not doubt his word; I could not question a single item in a statement so stamped with the earnestness of truth as his; but its dreadful details overpowered me, and threw my thoughts into hopeless confusion. I saw the conductor looking at me. I said, "Who is that man?"

"He was a member of Congress once, and a good one. But he got caught in a snowdrift in the cars, and like to have been starved to death. He got so frost-bitten and frozen up generally, and used up for want of something to eat, that he was sick and out of his head two or three months afterward. He is all right now, only he is a monomaniac, and when he gets on that old subject he never stops till he has eaten up that car-load of people he talks about. He would have finished the crowd by this time, only he had to get out here. He has got their names as pat as A B C. When he gets them all eat up but himself, he always says: 'Then the hour for the usual election for breakfast having arrived, and there being no opposition, I was duly elected, after which, there being no objections offered, I resigned. Thus I am here.'"

I felt inexpressibly relieved to know that I had only been listening to the harmless vagaries of a madman instead of the genuine experiences of a bloodthirsty cannibal.

II

PSYCHOSES

      Most of us have no conception of the true nature of emotional disorders. The psychoses comprise a specific group of diseases, characterized by the process of disintegration of the personality.

      The schizophrenic exhibits this disintegration in various degrees depending on the nature of his particular form of the illness. Many schizophrenics or schizophrenic types pass their days quietly without ever being confined in mental institutions or having their disease diagnosed. Nevertheless, they are generally thought of as "queer" by their neighbors, and do not seem to be able to make lasting emotional attachments.

      Schizophrenia in its most violent form involves the complete withdrawal of the personality from the real world. Here the sense of awareness of self, the ability to control future acts on the basis of present ones, is completely destroyed. When completely withdrawn, patients may become catatonic—recognition both of the body and the psyche is then gone as well. Besides its physiological manifestations, schizophrenia can be diagnosed by associative tests in which the logical connections between ideas are seen to disappear. Janet Frame's "Owls Do Cry" is a unique literary example of schizophrenic thinking. At times the heroine's thinking is lucid and reasonable; at other times all the connections between sentence and sentence are lost, her paranoic fear emerges, and we can watch her mind shuttle between the real and the unreal.

      Childhood schizophrenia, although it bears the same name, is quite a different disease. The child schizophrenic may be characterized by his lack of ego development. Typically, the child schizophrenic views himself as an extension of the mother. He has no sense of his own boundaries in space, or of the physical presence of other people whom he will frequently treat as objects. Without the development of personality he becomes an automaton, stumbling through life in a secret, inscrutable world that bears no relation to reality. In "Silent Snow, Secret Snow," the process of schizophrenia is described with chilling reality and an immediacy that is terrifying even to an adult who has never questioned his own mental balance. Its child hero, although too old to exhibit the complete lack of ego development that characterizes the youngest schizophrenics, exhibits the same kind of relationship to his mother as does Jean in Erik Erikson's case study. The onset of his disease is rapid; the retreat into a world without ego and without language is complete.

The symptoms of manic depressive psychoses are sometimes confused with those of paranoid schizophrenia but even more often with those arising out of certain functional diseases of the mind. De Maupassant's "The Horla" was composed three years before its author died of paresis—a syphilitic infection of the brain. Yet a psychiatrist not familiar with the physical source of the author's illness could, with honesty, describe the disease pictured in the story as a perfect example of manic-depressive psychosis. The rapid swings in mood from despair to elation are typical of the disease. And the manic periods are characterized by highly integrated activity that is rare or non-existent among schizophrenics.

ERIK H. ERIKSON / Early Ego Failure: Jean*

To COME face to face with a "schizophrenic" child is one of the most awe-inspiring experiences a psychotherapist can have. It is not the bizarreness of the child's behavior which makes the encounter so immediately challenging, but rather the very contrast of that behavior with the appeal of some of these children. Their facial features are often regular and pleasing, their eyes are "soulful" and seem to express deep and desperate experience, paired with a resignation which children should not have. The total impression immediately convinces the observer, often against the better knowledge of previous experience, that the right person and the right therapeutic regime could bring the child back on the road to coherent progress. This conviction has the more or less explicit corollary that the child has been in the wrong hands and, in fact, that he has every reason to mistrust his neglectful and rejecting parents. (We saw how far Indians and whites would go in accusing one another of doing deliberate harm to their children: our occupational prejudice is "the rejecting mother.")

I first saw Jean when she was almost six years old. I did not see her at her best. She had just made a train trip, and my house was strange to her. What glimpses I could catch of her (for she was frantically on the move through garden and house) showed her to be of graceful build, but tense and abrupt in her movements. She had beautiful dark eyes which seemed like peaceful islands within the anxious grimace of her face. She ran through all the rooms of the house, uncovering all the beds she could find, as if she were looking for something. The objects of this search proved to be pillows, which she hugged and talked to in a hoarse whisper and with a hollow laugh.

Yes, Jean was "schizophrenic." Her human relationships were centrifugal, away from people. I had observed this strange phenomenon of a "centrifugal approach," often interpreted as mere lack of contact, years before in the behavior of another little girl who was said to "notice nobody." When that little girl came down a flight of stairs toward me, her glance drifted in an absent way over a series of objects, describing concentric circles around my face. She focused on me negatively, as it were. This flight is the common denominator for a variety of other symptoms, such as the preoccupation with things far away and imagined; the in-

* Reprinted from Erik H. Erikson, *Childhood and Society* (New York: W. W. Norton and Co., Inc., 1950), pp. 169-81.

ability to concentrate on any task at hand; violent objection to all close contact with others unless they fit into some imaginary scheme; and immediate diffused flight from verbal communication, if it happens to become more or less established. Meaning is quickly replaced by parrotlike repetition of stereotyped phrases, accompanied by sounds of disgust and despair.

The observation that Jean, on her mad rush through my house, again and again paused long enough to concentrate her attention and to lavish her affection on bed pillows seemed important to me, for the following reason. Her mother had told me that Jean's extreme disorientation had begun after the mother had become bedridden with tuberculosis. She was permitted to stay at home in her own room, but the child could speak to her only through the doorway of her bedroom, from the arms of a good-natured but "tough" nurse. During this period the mother had the impression that there were things which the child urgently wanted to tell her. The mother regretted at the time that, shortly before her illness, she had let Jean's original nurse, a gentle Mexican girl, leave them. Hedwig, so the mother anxiously noticed from her bed, was always in a hurry, moved the baby about with great energy, and was very emphatic in her disapprovals and warnings. Her favorite remark was, "Ah, baby, you stink!" and her holy war was her effort to keep the creeping infant off the floor so that she would not be contaminated by dirt. If the child were slightly soiled, she scrubbed her "as if she were scrubbing a deck."

When after four months of separation Jean (now thirteen months old) was permitted to re-enter the mother's room, she spoke only in a whisper. "She shrank back from the pattern of the chintz on the armchair and cried. She tried to crawl off the flowered rug and cried all the time, looking very fearful. She was terrified by a large, soft ball rolling on the floor and terrified of paper crackling." These fears spread. First, she did not dare to touch ashtrays and other dirty objects, then she avoided touching or being touched by her elder brother and gradually by most people around her. Although she learned to feed herself and to walk at the normal time, she gradually became sad and silent.

Maybe the child's frantic affection for pillows had to do with that period when she was prevented from approaching her mother's bed. Maybe, for some reason, she had not been able to take the separation, had "adjusted" to it by a permanent pattern of fleeing from all human contact, and was now expressing her affection for the bedridden mother in her love for pillows.

The mother confirmed that the child had a fetish, a small pillow or sheet which she would press over her face when going to sleep. For her part, the mother seemed desirous of making restitution to the child for what she felt she had denied her, not only during those months of illness, but by what now seemed like a general kind of neglect by default. This mother by no means lacked affection for the child, but she felt that she had not given Jean the relaxed affection she needed most *when* she needed it most.

Some such maternal estrangement may be found in every history of infantile schizophrenia. What remains debatable is whether the maternal behavior could possibly be a "cause" for such a radical disturbance in a child's functioning; or whether such children, for some intrinsic and perhaps constitutional reasons, have needs or need stimulations which no mother would understand without professional help—and professional people, until very recently, were utterly unable to spot these children when they were young enough to perhaps be saved with special dosages of well-planned mother love. About this, later.

On the children's part, early oral traumata are often suggested in the history. Take, for example, Jean's feeding history. The mother tried to nurse her for one week but had to give up because of a breast infection. The baby vomited, cried excessively, seemed always hungry. When Jean was ten days old, she began to suffer from thrush, which remained acute for three weeks and persisted as a low-grade infection for the remainder of her first year. Drinking was often painful. At one time during the first half of the first year, an infected layer of skin was removed from the underside of her tongue. Early moving pictures of the little girl show a heavy lower lip and a protruding, hyperactive tongue. No doubt the oral trauma had been severe. It should be noted here that Jean's fetish consisted of a sheet which she made into a ball and pressed against her mouth with one piece between her teeth. Besides these pillows, Jean loved only instruments and machines: egg-beaters, vacuum cleaners, and radiators. She smiled at them, whispered to them, and hugged them, and was impelled by their very presence to a kind of excited dancing—all this, while she remained completely uninterested in people unless they invaded her preoccupations, or unless she wished to invade theirs.

In the mother's early notes there was another item which seemed of great relevance to me. She showed me the statement of a psychologist who, when testing the child at the age of four, noted his impression that "the child had turned against speech." For it seems important to understand that these children repudiate their own organs and functions as hostile and "outside." They have a defective screening system; their sensory contacts fail to master the overpowering impressions as well as the disturbing impulses which intrude themselves upon consciousness. They therefore experience their own organs of contact and communication as enemies, as potential intruders into a body ego which has withdrawn "under the skin." It is for this reason that these children close their eyes and hold their hands over their ears, or hide their whole heads in blankets, in reaction to unsuccessful contacts. Thus, only a carefully dosed and extraordinarily consistent application of maternal encouragement could enable the child's ego to reconquer, as it were, its own organs, and with them to perceive the social environment and to make contact with it more trustingly.

When I saw Jean she had not lived with her parents for many months. Most of the time she appeared not to care. Yet, on the previous Christmas, after attending a party at her parents' house, the child threw all the presents which she had received from her parents on the street outside her foster home, stamped on them, and cried wildly. Maybe she did care. I proposed that the family move together and that, for some extended time, the mother should take over Jean's care under my guidance to be given on regular trips to their home in a college town. This family-treatment plan, I felt, should precede any direct therapy with the child.

When she found herself back within her family, with her mother in constant attendance, Jean expressed appreciation by a determined and goal-directed attempt to restore contact. But these attempts were often too determined and too specific in their goal. She became fascinated with *parts* of people. Her shocked brothers found their penises grabbed—and politely withdrew their sincere wish to co-operate in the treatment plan. Her father found her an enthusiastic attendant at his showers, where she waited for opportunities to grab his genitals. He could not hide, first, his amused consternation, and then his somewhat nervous annoyance. When he was dressed she concentrated on a bump on his hand which she called a "lumpy," and on his cigarettes, which she would tear from his lips and throw out of the window. She knew where people are vulnerable; these children, so vulnerable themselves, are masters at such diagnosis.

Luckily, Jean's greatest "partialistic" interest was in her mother's breasts; luckily, because the mother could indulge this interest for a period. The child would love to sit on the mother's lap and take sly pokes at breasts and nipples. Climbing on the mother, she would say "gloimb you, gloimb you," which apparently meant "climb on you." The mother let her sit on her for hours. The "gloimb you" gradually expanded into singsongs such as this (I quote from the mother's diary).

> Gloimb you, gloimb you, not hurt a chest—not touch a didge—not touch a ban—not touch a dage—not touch a bandage—throw away a chest—hurt a chest.

This apparently meant that the child was preoccupied with the idea that touching her mother's chest-bandage (brassière) might hurt her. We even went so far as to surmise that she communicated an impression according to which she had hurt the mother when she developed "chest trouble" and that she had been banished from her mother's room for this reason. For her talk seemed to indicate that the "throwing away" she referred to really meant that she would be thrown away. It must be understood that the most difficult verbal (and maybe conceptual) feat for these children, even where they have acquired extensive vocabularies, is to differentiate between active and passive, and between "I" and "you": the basic grammar of two-ness. As the game with the mother progressed, Jean could be heard whispering to herself "spank you" or "not pick you finger off." She apparently associated her attacks on penises with those on the mother's breasts, for she would continue, "Brother has a penis. Be gentle. Don't hurt. Don't cut off your nailfingers. Bola. Jean has a bola (vulva)." Gradually she became outspokenly self-punitive and asked to be "thrown away." In solitary games she would go back to her old fears of dirt, and would act as if she were brushing away a cobweb or throwing away something disgusting.

Let us pause here to note that Jean was already describing here the basic cycle of an infantile schizophrenic conflict, which must be analyzed as to content and as to the fate of its ego involvement. There seems to be little doubt that the child, given a chance to communicate with the mother in her own way, referred back to the time, five years earlier, when her mother was ill. These children have an excellent memory—in spots, in vulnerable spots—but their memory does not seem to sustain a continuous sense of identity. Their sayings, like dream images, indicate what they want to talk about, but do not indicate what causal connection is to be communicated. Interpretation must do that. In talking about her mother's illness, then, so we must infer, Jean alluded to the possibility that she had hurt the mother's chest, that as token of her hurt condition the mother had worn a "bandage," and that for that reason the child had been thrown away (not permitted to come and hug her mother). The confusion as to what was hurt, the child's finger or the mother's chest, we may ascribe to semantic difficulties. Adults are of little help in those early stages when they say, "Don't touch it, you will hurt it," and then switch to "Don't touch it, or else you will hurt your fingers." Yet one might say that the confusion of adult dicta here fits only too well that early ego stage when all pain is experienced as "outside," all pleasures as "inside," no matter where its actual source is. Jean may never have outgrown that stage; and yet, there was also the early experience of being abandoned by the mother to a nurse who was a "don't touch" zealot. In retesting the reality of the prohibition, of course, she only had to do what she did to the men in the family. With her mother she was more fortunate. But here an important item enters—namely, the immense self-punitive tendency in these driven children. Their law is "all or none"; they take the dictum, "If thine eye offend thee, pluck it out," literally and quite seriously. Thus it may happen that a little boy in a schizophrenic episode requests his horrified parents in all sincerity to cut off his penis because it is no good.

The mother continued to explain patiently to Jean that the illness had not been her fault. She let Jean sleep with her, let her sit on her lap, and, in general, gave her the attention and consideration for her thought processes and verbal ways usually awarded only to an infant. Jean seemed to begin to believe her. After several months she showed marked improvement. She became more graceful in her movements; her vocabulary increased, or, as one should say in such cases, became apparent, for it is usually there before its presence is suspected. And she played "nurse and baby." She put a little black toy dog to bed and said, "Go to sleep, dog, stay under covers; shut your eyes, have to spank you, dog." Also she began to build long block trains which were "going east." During one of these games she looked her mother in the eyes with one of her rare, completely contact-seeking glances and said, "Not go on long ride on the train sometime." "No," said the mother, "we are going to stay together."

Such improvements seemed most rewarding. They were usually interrupted by crises which led to emergency calls. I would visit the family and talk with everybody until I had ascertained what was going on in all their lives. A whole series of difficulties arose in this one-patient sanitarium. One can live with schizophrenic thought only if one can make a profession out of understanding it. The mother had accepted this task, which demands a particular gift of empathy and at the same time the ability to keep oneself intact. Otherwise one must refute such thinking in order to be protected against it. In each member of the household, then, a glance into Jean's life, characterized as it was by the alternation of naked impulsiveness and desperate self-negation, endangered his own equilibrium and self-esteem. This had to be pointed out repeatedly, because Jean would constantly change the direction of her provocation. And she would withdraw repeatedly for no apparent reason.

The following incident will serve to illustrate the impact of the mother's first attempts to make Jean sleep by herself. Suddenly a pathological attachment to spoons developed, and it assumed such proportions that it led to the first crisis of despair both in Jean and in her parents. Jean would insistently repeat such sentences as "not sleep in the light in Jean's room," "light in the spoon," "incinerator in the spoon," "blankets in the spoon," etc. During dinnertime she would often sit and merely look at the "light in the spoon." Unable to make herself understood, she began to withdraw and to stay in bed for hours and days. Yet she refused to go to sleep at night. The parents put in an emergency call and asked me to try to clear up the matter. When I asked Jean to show me the light in the spoon, she showed me a plug behind a bookcase. Some weeks ago she had broken off one piece of this plug and had caused a short circuit. As I went with her to her room to investigate the electrical appliances there I found that she had a dim bulb in her room with a small spoonlike shade attached to it which was intended to keep the light from shining on her bed. Was that the original "light in the spoon"? Jean indicated it was. Now it became clear. On returning home, Jean had first slept in the mother's bed. Then the mother had slept with her in her bed. Then the mother had slept in her own bed and Jean in hers, the door ajar and the hall light on. Finally the hall light had been turned off and only the light from a small bulb ("the light in the spoon") left in Jean's room. Apparently at night, then, Jean would look at this light as her last consolation—the last "part" of her mother—and endow it with the same partialistic affection and fear which she had demonstrated in relation to her mother's breast, her father's and her brothers' penises, and all the fetishes before. It was at that time that she touched a plug in the living room with those problem fingers of hers, causing a short circuit and making everything dark, including the "light in the spoon." Again she had brought on catastrophe: by touching something she had caused a crisis which threatened to leave her alone in the dark.

The circumstances having been explained all around, the spoon fetish was abandoned, and the course of restoration resumed. However, one could not fail to be impressed with the persistence of the pathogenic pattern and the violence of its eruption, for Jean was now a whole year older (nearly seven). Yet she seemed to begin to feel that her fingers could do no irreparable harm and that she could not only keep them but also use them for learning and for making beautiful things.

First, she became enchanted by the finger play which says that "this little pig does this" and "that little pig does that." She made the little pigs do what she had been doing during the day, namely, "go to market," "go to ten-cent store," "go to escalator," or "cry all the way home." Thus, in referring to the coherent series of her fingers she learned to integrate time and to establish a continuity of the various selves which had done different things at different times. But she could not say, "*I* did this" and "*I* did that." Not that I consider this a problem of mere mental capacity. The ego of schizoid (as well as schizophrenic) people is dominated by the necessity for repeating the testing and integrating experience because of an inadequate sense of the trustworthiness of events at the time when they happen. Jean, then, accomplished such reintegration, together with its communication, by the use of her fingers, which, now permitted, could be readmitted to the body ego. She learned the letters of the alphabet by drawing them with her fingers, after studying them with the help of the Montessori touch method. And she learned to play melodies by scratching a xylophone with her nails. The mother reported:

> Since the time when Jean began to show such a disturbing, because apparently senseless, interest in the xylophone, I have noticed that she is actually playing it with her fingernails. She does it so quietly one cannot distinguish what she is doing. Tonight, however, I discovered that she could play "Water, Water Wild Flower" all the way through. This song requires every note in the scale. I asked for it to be repeated and watched her hand travel up and down the scale. I was amazed and made a big fuss over her, saying it was wonderful. I said, "Let's go downstairs to the others and play it for them." She came down willingly, even self-consciously, and very pleased. She now played it aloud for them, and they were astounded. She then played several other things: "Rain Is Falling Down," "ABCDEFG," etc. We all praised her and she ate it up. She did not want to go upstairs but seemed to want to stay and play on for the audience, a new delightful feeling.

Thus Jean "sublimated" and gained friends; but she also made new enemies, in new ways. For she also used her fingers for poking people and came so near to hurting a visitor's eyes that she had to be energetically stopped. She especially liked to poke her father, obviously as a sequence to her penis- and cigarette-grabbing activities. When, at this point, the father had to go on a trip, she regressed to whining, resumed her sheet fetish (saying "blanket is mended"), spoke only in a soft voice, and ate little, even refusing ice cream. She had again made somebody go away by touching him! She seemed particularly desperate because she had, in fact, begun to respond to her father's devoted efforts to help her.

At the height of this crisis, Jean lay down beside her mother in bed and with desperate crying repeated over and over, "No vulva on Jean, no eggplant, take it off, take it off, no egg in the plant, not plant the seed, cut off your finger, get some scissors, cut it off." This obviously represented the old deep self-punitive reaction.

Jean's mother gave her appropriate explanations concerning her father's "disappearance." She also told Jean that it was not because she had touched herself that her "eggplant" had disappeared; in fact, she still had it, way inside. Jean resumed her play with her fingers. She had to work her way again through previous stages of existence by chanting: "This little girl sleeps in the refrigerator, this little girl sleeps in the vacuum cleaner," etc. Gradually her interest in animals and now also in other children reappeared, and the fingers would represent "this little boy is jumping, this little boy is running . . . is walking . . . is racing," etc. Her interest in fingers then spread to various forms of locomotion both of children and of animals. She learned to read the names of various domestic animals and, again using her fingers, also the days of the week, and adding her toes, numbers up to twenty. At the same time her play on the xylophone began to include more difficult French folk songs, all of which she played with great ease and abandon, knowing always exactly where to find the first note. The pleasure of having the use of her fingers restored can be seen from the mother's report:

> Last Sunday Jean made a painting of a little girl in a yellow dress. At night she went up to the picture on the wall silently and felt of the paint. She paused long over the hands, each of which was bigger than the whole girl, and very carefully done with five fingers each. Then she said, "The hands are nice." I agreed, repeating the words. Then in a minute she said, "The hands are pretty." Again I agreed appreciatively. She retreated to the bed without taking her eyes off the picture as she sat down on the bed, still studying it. Then she burst out loudly, "The hands are *lovely*."

During all this time, Jean had, off and on, played the xylophone and sung songs. Now the parents were fortunate enough to find a piano teacher who based her methods on Jean's auditory gift and ingenuity in imitating. At my next visit, after being taken to my room, I heard somebody practicing some phrases of Beethoven's first sonata, and innocently remarked on the strong and sensitive touch. I thought a gifted adult was playing. To find Jean at the piano was one of the surprises, which are so gripping in work with these cases—and which often prove so misleading, because again and again they make one believe in the child's total progress where one is justified in believing only in isolated advances of individual faculties. This I say with feeling and conviction, for Jean's piano playing, whether it was Beethoven, Haydn, or boogie-woogie, was truly astounding—until she turned against this gift, just as she had "turned against speech," in the words of the first psychologist who had seen her.

This completes one episode in Jean's improvement: her relation to her hands. It also completes the specimen to be reported here as an illustration of the essential ego weakness which causes these children to be swayed at one time by a "drivenness" focused on a part of another person; and at another by cruel self-punitiveness and paralyzing perfectionism. It is not that they fail to be able to learn, to remember, and to excel—usually in some artistic endeavor which reflects the sensory counterpart of their essentially oral fixation. It is that they cannot integrate it all: their ego is impotent.

You will want to know how Jean fared. As the child grew more mature, the discrepancy between her age and her behavior became so marked that associations with children anywhere near her age level were impossible. Other difficulties arose which made at least an interval in a special school mandatory. There she quickly lost what she had gained in the years of her mother's heroic effort. Her treatment has since been resumed under the best residential circumstances and under the guidance of one of the most devoted and most imaginative child psychiatrists in this particular field.

The role which "maternal rejection" or special circumstances of abandonment play in cases such as Jean's is still debatable. I think one should consider that these children may very early and subtly fail to return the mother's glance, smile, and touch; an initial reserve which makes the mother, in turn, unwittingly withdraw. The truism that the original problem is to be found in the mother-child relationship holds only in so far as one considers this relationship an emotional pooling which may multiply well-being in both but which will endanger both partners when the communication becomes jammed or weakened. In those cases of infantile schizophrenia which I have seen, the primary deficiency in "sending power" was in the child; although, of course, the child as a former part of the parent may well share with the parent some frailty of contact and communication which may appear in malignant form in the younger mind and organism, while in the adult it may have found a compensatory expression in superior intellectual or artistic equipment. It may well be that in some cases this equipment can be used to develop in mothers and nurses that surplus of curative and creative effort of which Jean's mother was capable, and which alone may be expected to make up for a deficiency of such magnitude. But only a therapist with faith as well as experience in the matter, and only a sturdy and enlightened mother, should undertake to pioneer on this frontier of human trust.

EMIL KRAEPELIN / Lectures on Clinical Psychiatry

Depressed Stages of Maniacal-Depressive Insanity (Circular Stupor)

GENTLEMEN,—The patient you see before you to-day is a merchant, forty-three years old, who has been in our hospital almost uninterruptedly for about five years. He is strongly built, but badly nourished, and has a pale complexion, and an invalid expression of face. He comes in with short, wearied steps, sits down slowly, and remains sitting in a rather bent position, staring in front of him almost without moving. When questioned, he turns his head a little, and, after a certain pause, answers softly, and in monosyllables, but to the point. We get the impression that speaking gives him a great deal of trouble, his lips moving for a little while before the sound comes out. The patient is clear about time and place, knows the doctors, and says that he has been ill for more than five years, but cannot give any further explanation of this than that his spirits are affected. He says he has no apprehension. He gives short and perfectly relevant answers to questions about his circumstances and past life. He does exercises in arithmetic slowly but correctly, even when they are fairly hard. He writes his name on the blackboard, when asked to do so, with firm though hesitating strokes, after having got up awkwardly. No delusions, particularly ideas of sin, can be made out, the patient only declaring that he is in low spirits, without knowing of any cause for it, except that his illness has lasted so long, and worries him. He hopes, however, to get well again.

As you may see, it is evident that in reality we have to deal with *emotional depression* in this case, as well as in those already discussed. It is true that there are no delusions associated with it here, as there were in the other cases; but let us not be inclined to lay too much stress on this, after having learned by experience how widely delusions may vary in the same illness. On the other hand, it must strike us that this patient is not apprehensive, but only "low spirited," and still more that, unlike the patients already considered, he is apparently unable to move and express himself freely. In those cases there were lively gesticulations, lamentations, and complaints, and a certain necessity of giving vent to the oppression within, while here it is hard to draw any remark from the patient on his mental condition, or on questions of fact. This very circumstance, that the answers come so slowly, even on matters of indifference, shows that in this patient we have not to deal with a fear of expressing himself, but with some general obstacle to utterance in speech. Indeed, not only speech, but *all action of the will is extremely difficult to him*. For three years he has been incapable of getting up from bed, dressing, and occupying himself, and since that time has lain in bed almost without moving. But as he has the most perfect comprehension of his surroundings, and is able to follow difficult trains of thought, the disturbance must be essentially confined to the accomplishment of voluntary movements, or at any rate must find by far its strongest manifestations in this direction. We clearly recognise the pain he takes to act and to comply with our demands, and at the same time the delay and difficulty attending every effort of the will. Under these circumstances, it will be permissible here to speak of an *impediment* of *volition,* in the sense that the transformation of the impulses of the will into action meets with obstacles which cannot be overcome without difficulty, and often not at all by the patient's own strength. This constraint is by far the most obvious clinical feature of the disease, and compared with this, the sad, oppressed mood has but little prominence. No other psychical disturbances can be made out at present.

Having established this, we have got an insight, on several points, into the nature of the disease before us. In the first place, we see that this condition differs from that of our melancholic patients, in a very definite way, through the strong impediment of volition, and the absence of the apprehensive restlessness so clearly marked in them. Experience shows that this condition is very characteristic of an entirely different disease, to which we will give the name of *maniacal-depressive insanity,* for reasons to be discussed immediately. This disease generally runs its course in *a series* of *isolated attacks,* which are not uniform, but present either states of depression of the kind described or characteristic states of excitement, which we will learn to know better later on. The isolated attacks are generally separated by longer or shorter intervals of freedom.

The conclusion we have drawn from our patient's present condition is correct. He first became ill when he was twenty-three years old, and was then depressed, as is generally the case in first attacks; but the depression was followed next year by a state of excitement, which led to his being brought to the asylum. Two years later he married a person very much beneath him, very probably when under slight excitement, but separated from her during the depression which ensued. At the age of thirty-one, probably when again in an excited state, he fell into the hands of an adventuress, who abandoned him when he became depressed again. Indeed, his relations held his depression to be the result of the melancholy experience he had been through. In his thirty-sixth and thirty-seventh years a further and stronger excitement followed, which again made treatment in the asylum necessary.

The patient's father, as well as his two brothers, was a drunkard, while his sister was ill in the same way as himself. He suffered for several years from diabetes insipidus. A doctor advised him, presumably on this account, to take a little wine, as too much water was not good for him. The patient followed this advice, and about five and a half years ago he suddenly fell ill of delirium tremens, immediately followed by a state of excitement, gradually and continually growing worse, which only disappeared slowly after two years. Only a few weeks after his discharge from our hospital, where he was then treated, the extraordinarily severe impediment of volition which you may still observe in a milder form set in rather suddenly. The patient remained motionless in bed, would not eat, was wet and dirty in his habits, could hardly speak, and expressed apprehensive ideas. Thought also seems to have been affected at first, and the patient made no answer, or replied only very slowly, alike to emphatic and to gentle questionings. But there were no actual delusions even then. The patient soon returned to the hospital, but in spite of the most careful nursing, his condition has improved only very slowly and immaterially in the course of the last three years. Yet we may expect that this attack also will end in recovery, like those which have preceded it, if only the patient can live through so severe a disturbance.[1] But it is no less probable that he will again fall ill of attacks of depression or excitement such as he has so often had before.

Fluctuations of *weight* are of special interest in the disease we are now discussing. In the last attack of excitement he had in the hospital our patient lost nearly 13 kilogrammes, and then gained 25 kilogrammes when he became calm. In the first eighteen months of the depression, his weight fell from 91.5 kilogrammes to 56.5 kilogrammes, and has only risen 14 kilogrammes since. These figures show the violent revolutions in the province of general nutrition which take place in diseases of this kind. Little as we are yet able to account for the details of these occurrences, regular and continuous weighings afford us an excellent means of judging of the general state of the disease in this as in most other forms of insanity. A decided increase in the previously reduced weight in maniacal-depressive insanity is the most reliable sign that the attack has passed its worst.

---

[1] Unfortunately, this expectation was not realized. The psychical disturbances still continued, and the patient succumbed to acute phthisis when the depression had lasted three and a half years.

In the light of the case we have just considered the meaning of what follows will, I think, be clearer to you than it formerly was to me. Here is a case of a woman, twenty-three years old, who was admitted only a fortnight ago. The patient, whose mother is mentally rather limited, bore her second child six weeks ago. Seventeen days later she got a great fright from a fire in her room, and she then became apprehensive and restless, saw flames, black birds and dogs, heard whistling and singing, began to pray, screamed out of the window, lamented her sins, promised to be good, and could not sleep. The patient is ill-nourished and anæmic. She sits almost motionless, with her eyes cast down, staring in front of her, and moving her lips slightly now and then. Her expression is strained, and rather apprehensive. When questioned about dates, the place where she is, and the people about her, she either makes no answer at all, or shakes her head, or says in a low, hesitating voice: "I do not know." She nods when I ask her if she is unhappy, and mutters to herself: "There are always so many carriages coming; a great number drive about outside." Now and then she uses isolated, broken expressions, in a tone of lamentation, often repeating them one after the other: "I want to go home, to get out. Alas! alas! only let me go away. I will not let myself be done to death. I cannot stay here. Good heavens! there is poison in the food!" She obeys orders with hesitation, and sometimes resists, but can plainly be influenced by persuasion. When threatened with a needle, she screams and turns away hastily. She generally has to be fed.

On consideration of the want of freedom in our patient's bearing, and the slowness and constraint of her movements, which will only become more active in apprehensive gestures of self-defence, you will clearly see that, in this case, too, we have to deal with an impediment of volition, particularly apparent in the almost entire falling off of utterance in speech and of expressive movement. But it presents a contrast with the previous case in the more definite apprehension, which is far less amenable to persuasion and influence, and also by the severe disturbance of comprehension. The patient has absolutely no clear idea of her position, does not understand what goes on around her, and cannot solve any mental problems. A similar difficulty in thought is associated with the difficulty in the action of the will. You will remember that a disturbance of this kind occurred at the beginning of the last patient's attack, and that it was only later on that it became less and less obvious. This *impediment of cognition,* as we will call it, is in fact a symptom regularly accompanying the state of depression in maniacal-depressive insanity. It is sometimes more, sometimes less clearly defined, and is generally perceived very plainly by the patients themselves.

As the intensity and colouring of the emotional depression may vary very widely in maniacal-depressive insanity, we will conclude, in consideration of the well-defined impediment of volition and cognition, that the case which is before us now belongs to the same group of diseases as the last case. Hence, it would seem probable that similar attacks, and also attacks of excitement, will clearly be noticed sooner or later in our patient. This conclusion is confirmed by the remarkable fact that, although she is so apprehensive, she begins, after a good deal of persuasion, to twist her face into an extraordinary smile. You will understand the meaning of this symptom at once if we glance back into the past. The patient was here four years ago. At that time she had aborted, after having been pregnant by a married man. A few weeks later she became dumb and rigid, expressed ideas of death, saw spirits, grew quite confused, mixed, perplexed, and apprehensive, and refused to eat —in short, a state of impediment of volition and cognition was developed very like the present condition, but even more severe, lasting about seven months. Then, quite suddenly, there was a *complete* change, and the patient became clear and collected, and was in high spirits. Finally, she passed through a very violent state of excitement, which gradually disappeared after nearly six months. During her convalescence, there was slight and transitory emotional depression, but after this the patient became well, and remained so till the beginning of the present attack.

Thus we see that the conclusion drawn from the patient's present condition was correct. The similarity of the two periods of depression of which we know leaves no room for reasonable doubt that they both belong to the same clinical picture of disease. We must indeed notice that both attacks followed a confinement, so that the same cause might have produced the same illness each time. But we saw the same characteristic symptoms of impediment of thought and will in the preceding case, where there had been no confinement, and the subsequent change from depression to excitement, occurring in the same way in both patients, is a fresh proof that our case is one of maniacal-depressive insanity. We will see later on that those representations of disease in which we really have grounds for regarding a confinement as the actual cause present entirely different clinical features. Finally, experience shows that single attacks of maniacal-depressive insanity are very often set free by injurious external influences. We must, therefore, expect our patient's next attack to break out once again without any very tangible cause.

On the strength of these considerations, we may venture to suppose that the patient will often fall ill again in the future course of her life, either of depression, as on this occasion, or of excitement, but that each attack may be expected to end in recovery. In the present attack, this may certainly be expected, yet it is very possible that a slighter state of excitement may first intervene, as has happened before.[2] The smile already mentioned might be the first sign of such a change.

The condition of severe impediment of volition is generally included with some other and outwardly similar states under the name of *stupor*. We may call the form now before us "circular stupor," as maniacal-depressive insanity is often called circular insanity (*folie circulaire*), on account of the cycle of recurrent conditions. The common characteristic of all forms of stupor is the absence of expression in speech or otherwise in response to external influences. Stupor is, however, no uniform condition, much less a separate disease, but a symptom which may arise from very different causes, and therefore may have very different clinical meanings. Even circular stupor meets us in such various forms that it is often difficult to recognise their real agreement. Here you see an innkeeper's wife, aged forty-four, who has been ill for about ten weeks. There has been no insanity in her family, and she has three healthy children. When her husband was obliged to change his inn a little while ago, she began to complain of heaviness in her head, and worried herself groundlessly—*e.g.*, with the idea that the children had no clothes, that everything was torn up, and that the house-moving would be the death of her. She thought she had made her husband unhappy, that the bailiffs were coming, that life was no longer possible at her home, and that everything was going to ruin. At the same time she spoke and ate but little, stared into space, and hardly slept at all. She also took a knife to bed with her at night, and expressed ideas of suicide, so she was brought to the hospital. Here she seemed quite collected and clear about her position, and, in answer to questions, gave a monosyllabic but consecutive account of her circumstances and her illness. For the last three months, she said, she had no rest, and had been absentminded and forgetful; she had such a bad memory. She could not be happy now; everything was spoiled for her, and her work had grown so hard for her that she could not get through with it. The patient spoke little of her own accord, and generally lay still in bed with a downcast expression. She was obliged to think for a disproportionately long time over the answers to simple questions, was not quite clear about the chronological order of her experiences, and hardly knew at all where she was. All her expressions and movements were slow and hesitating, as if she did not quite know what she ought to say and do. She was low-spirited, and in particular cried a great deal when she had visitors.

[2] The patient recovered without any distinct maniacal excitement, after having spent five months in the asylum, and gained 13 kilogrammes in weight. She has been well for two years since then.

She described her complaint as "dejection," and burst into tears whenever it was discussed, without being able to give a more precise account of her condition. The picture the patient now presents still shows substantially the same features: a quiet, oppressed mood, a sad expression, low hesitating speech, and slow, tired movements, while at the same time she is quite collected. But the ideas of sin have grown much stronger. With tears, the patient calls herself the greatest of sinners, because she has brought her husband and children into misfortune; she will certainly be executed. These are the same ideas of sin as we have learned to recognise in melancholia. We might, therefore, be tempted, especially in view of the patient's age, to take the illness for simple climacteric melancholia. But I think that this idea is contradicted by the obvious presence of the impediment of thought and will, which we have observed before, in just the same form, in maniacal-depressive insanity, but not in melancholia. I think that this symptom will justify our regarding the present case as one of the former disease. If this opinion of mine be correct, we need not expect a lingering, uniform course of disease, ending in recovery or in the characteristic state of weakness following melancholia, which has already been briefly described. We may hope for a much shorter duration of the disease, and for complete recovery, as the first attack of maniacal-depressive insanity generally runs a fairly rapid and favourable course. On the other hand, we must certainly be prepared to see it return, either as the same affection or in the form of excitement.

The course of the case until now would certainly tend to show that our conception is correct. The patient's downcast mood disappeared almost entirely after three or four weeks in the asylum. In its place she showed a rather impatient, discontented temper, with frequent smiling, of which we will learn the clinical meaning on a future occasion. The patient was so anxious to go home that her husband thought he ought to humour her homesickness, even against our advice. But her condition grew worse so quickly that she had to be brought back in four days. But probably we will soon effect an improvement even now.[3]

The milder form of impediment of volition seen in this case is noticed by patients themselves as "inability to come to a decision," and meets us as such in the numberless mild cases of maniacal-depressive insanity which never come into an asylum, and indeed, are never recognised as morbid states at all. Then we have the "psychological riddle" that, without any adequate cause, but

---

[3] The patient is still under treatment here, and has substantially improved. Unfortunately, her husband has again jeopardized her recovery by taking her home in the face of medical advice, and a serious attempt at suicide has been the result.

in the opinion of the sufferers and those around them, as the result of some external influence or other, there arise times of complete inability to come to a decision, when every determination of the will costs the greatest effort, which alternate more or less regularly with periods of the most reckless enterprise. It is just these mildest forms of the illness, leading by an infinity of gradations to the severe forms, and the most severe, which show how deeply maniacal-depressive insanity is rooted in the natural disposition of certain individuals. Hence we frequently find it in several members of the same family. Often enough we see nearly a whole lifetime filled with slight attacks, succeeding one another almost uninterruptedly. But just as often the illness only appears a few times, as in the case described, either at a particular period of life, or as the result of some external influence. The attacks usually set in during the years of evolution, or later on at the time of reversion.

Many of the quite slight attacks—which, by the way, may always alternate with the severe—pass off without any treatment. Other cases are sent as "neurasthenia" to different asylums and watering places, or ordered to travel, and the patients then extol, with full conviction, the particular cure they were taking when the improvement or the change to excitement occurred. In all the more serious attacks, however, treatment in an asylum is urgently required, on account of the danger of suicide, which is greatest at the beginning or near the end of an attack, because at those times their indecision does not make the patients incapable of pulling themselves together to act. In the asylum they must be carefully watched, and an intelligent and moderately strict treatment in bed should be carried out. Of drugs, bromides may be used, either alone or in combination with opium or other suitable hypnotics, but too much must not be expected of them. Prolonged warm baths sometimes do good service. Visits from near relations and premature discharge from the asylum are frequent causes of relapses. . . .

Maniacal Excitement

In the course of our lectures hitherto we have considered widely different states of depression. It has been my aim to show you that sad or apprehensive depression permits in itself of no conclusions as to the disease through which it is engendered. It is far more our task to become clear as to the special clinical meaning of this symptom in each separate case. Under some circumstances we can draw important conclusions as to the nature of the underlying disease merely from the kind of depression, from its duration, from its repeated return, from its trifling depth, and so on; but often enough it is the consideration of the other symptoms of disease that will first lead us on the right track. Very similar conditions can, at the first glance, be apparent in the course of very different diseases. But inversely we frequently find that the most differentiated and apparently quite opposite conditions can make their appearance in succession as indications of the same malady. Here there is no question of the connection of different independent diseases, as was formerly often believed to be the case. Apart from the frequency of the phenomenon, this is proved to a certainty by the often extraordinarily rapid transition of the alternating pictures, by the occasional mixing of the separate features, and, lastly, by the similarity of the course and its termination.

The powerfully-built and well-nourished merchant, aged fifty, who is brought before you to-day, enters the room with a rapid step, and greets us in a loud voice; he takes a seat with a courteous bow, and looks about him expectantly and with curiosity. He answers quickly and with assurance as soon as we address him, and gives fluent and pertinent information as to his personal circumstances, as well as concerning his present position. Very soon he not only answers, but also leads the conversation; says jokingly that he is not going to relate everything so glibly, but will make the examination a little more difficult, in order that he may see whether we understand anything ourselves. He explains that he suffers from paralysis, makes quite senseless statements, and adds up incorrectly, but is as happy as a king if you go further into things. If you give him free scope, he talks a great deal and with animation, hardly allowing himself to be interrupted; but he easily loses the thread, forever bringing into his history some new irrelevant details. A short, concise answer cannot be obtained from him; he has always something to add and to exaggerate. During my lecture he, at intervals, frequently asks for "a hearing," but always draws back with a polite bow. He often addresses his discourse to you students, adverts to student life, interpolates verses from student songs, even making up some topical doggerel rhymes himself.

His frame of mind is joyous and exalted; he amuses himself with all sorts of jokes, even tolerably risky ones, makes fun of himself and of others, imitates well-known characters, laughs at his own tricks, which he knows how to put in a quite harmless light. For instance, the last few nights before his admission to the hospital he had gadded about to all sorts of taverns and disreputable houses, had drunk hard everywhere, behaved in the highest degree extravagantly, sprinkled himself from head to foot with water in the market-place, and had driven in a cab from one public-house to another in the neighbouring villages. Finally he smashed the mirror, crockery, and furniture in his own house, so that he had to be brought to the hospital under a strong escort of police. For all that, he observes cutely his wife alone is to blame, for she did not treat him properly, nor had she cooked anything decently for him. As a consequence, he had to go to the public-house, and, besides, he must give people something by which to earn a living. He does not consider himself to be ill, but, he adds with a significant smile, if it will give us pleasure, he will remain with us for awhile. The patient does not present any physical disturbance, except some wounds that he sustained in being conveyed by force to the hospital.

This case appears to us in every respect to be the exact opposite to certain states of depression that we have already learnt to recognise. Comprehension occurs quickly, ideas spring up unhindered, though soon driven out by something new. The spirits are cheerful, actions run untrammelled and without obstacles, without even those which act as a restraint in a normal life. This combination of symptoms of disease, which we frequently meet with in the same form, we designate by the name of *Mania,* or, if the individual disturbances are only slightly developed, as in the present case, by that of *Hypomania.* Our patient is, however, by no means always so considerate and jovially amiable as he is at present. For a time, especially at the beginning, he was quite confused and incoherent in his headlong talk, very irritated by his surroundings, smashed tables, chairs, and windowpanes, poured his soup over his head, and behaved in very disgusting ways. At other times, by teasing and ill-treating the other patients, slandering the attendants, and grumbling and making mischief at every opportunity, he was almost unbearable.

Mania, to a certain degree, is not only a true subversion of states of circular depression, but in itself is nothing but a stage of *maniacal-depressive insanity.* Where we really meet with maniacal excitements we are then able to draw the probable inference, not only that the excitements will recur often during life, but that states of depression of the kind already described will alternate with them. To return to our patient, we can state that he has already been in the asylum seven times. He is illegitimate; his mother died of an apoplectic fit; a sister of hers was insane. The patient had always been considered eccentric, but was sober and industrious. The first attack of the malady occurred in his thirty-seventh year, and exactly resembled the present one. At that time the patient, through the press, suddenly invited the whole "nobility of the place" to a "haute-volee soiree" at a belvedere, drove up to the police-station with the pretext that he had discovered a long-wanted anarchist criminal in the person of a gendarme, and indulged in all manner of practical jokes with the officials. He was at that time supposed to be suffering from general paralysis. The later attacks began with an inclination, for the time being, to extravagant expenditure, alcoholic and sexual excess, as well as every imaginable open misdemeanour; once on admission to the hospital he had all his pockets full of worthless rings, foreign coins, and cheap jewellery, which he had bought up everywhere, as well as numerous pawn-tickets.

At the beginning the attacks lasted from two to three months, and later on about six months. The patient generally soon became composed in the hospital, and scarcely presented even slight disturbances, yet a number of experiments of dismissal turned out badly because he at once began to drink again, and then quickly became re-excited. After recovery, he was, in the intervals, a very sober man, leading an extremely retired life, and on good terms with his wife, whom he tormented and insulted in his excitement. For three months after the last dismissal but one, and for nine months after the last, he was deeply depressed, misanthropic, lay in bed a great deal, and expressed thoughts of suicide, until his mental equilibrium gradually became restored.

The expectation already expressed by us has been verified. Not only have a series of maniacal attacks occurred, but in the course of the year attacks of depression with distinctive features have also made their appearance. Most probably the future will bring a more or less regular return of one or the other of these states.[4] That in the course of time the duration and severity of the attacks have increased, while the intervals have become shorter and shorter, corresponds with the general experience of the disease. The future course will probably involve a gradual aggravation of the behaviour of the attacks, with fluctuations possibly.

As you may have already guessed from the noise outside, the second patient, who now storms into the room, is violently excited. She does not sit down, but walks about quickly, examines briefly what she sees, interferes unceremoniously with the students, and tries to be familiar with them. No sooner is she induced to sit down than she quickly springs up again, flings away her shoes, unties her apron, and begins to sing and dance. The next minute she stops, claps her hands, goes to the blackboard, seizes the chalk, and begins to write her name, but ends with a gigantic flourish which in an instant covers the whole board. She wipes it off perfunctorily with the sponge, again hastily writes some letters of the alphabet, suddenly flings away the chalk over the heads of the audience, seizes the chair, swings it in a circle, and sits down on it with vigour, only to spring up again immediately and repeat the

---

[4] After the setting in of tranquility the patient was at first low-spirited for a long time, and a year later he again became maniacal.

old game in other forms. During the whole time the patient chatters almost incessantly, though the purport of her rapid headlong talk is scarcely intelligible and quite disconnected. On addressing her impressively, one generally obtains a short, sensible answer, to which all kinds of disconnected sentences are, however, immediately joined. Still, one can sometimes follow up her erratic thoughts; they seem to be recollections springing up, fragments of phrases and verses, words and turns that she has heard formerly from her companions, and which she now interlaces into her stream of talk. The patient gives her age and her name, and knows that she is in a "mad-house," but gives quite arbitrary names to other people. She refuses to be led into a connected conversation, but at once digresses, jumps up, addresses one of the students, runs to the window, sings part of a song, and dances about. Her mood is extremely merry; she laughs and titters continuously between her talk, but easily becomes angry on slight provocation, and then breaks out into a torrent of the nastiest abuse, only to become tranquil a minute after with a happy laugh. In spite of her great restlessness, she is tolerably easy to manage, and obeys orders given in a friendly tone, although it must be admitted that she immediately does something else quite different. There is nothing to notice in the physical condition of the delicately-built patient, except a certain amount of anæmia, and an inflammation of the margin of the left eyelid, which she will not allow to be touched.

The extraordinary *mutability of the individual psychical processes* constitutes the characteristic feature of the condition under consideration. These processes are quickly and easily induced, but just as easily supplanted by others. Some accidental attraction at once arrests the attention, but only for the moment; every arising idea or mood, every impulse of the will, is already replaced by another before it is properly carried out. Evidently the patient is wanting in ability to prevent herself from being ruled in thought, mood, and action by the changing influences of the moment, or to work these out to their proper endings. It is in this way that the important symptom of *divertibility* arises—that is to say, increased liability to influence through outward and inward attractions. In the province of comprehension it makes itself perceptible in that it is not impressions of real importance that arrest the attention, but those which, presenting themselves directly, are chosen at haphazard, to be at once replaced, just as accidentally, by others. Thus, in the province of the course of ideas, there arises that phenomenon which we are accustomed to call the "flight of ideas." As the idea of a goal is wanting which gives its fixed direction to healthy thought and at once arrests all side issues, the train of thought is perpetually driven out of its course, while incidental and non-essential ideas, often only awakened through habit of speech or similarity of sound, intrude everywhere. That the succession of thought is not hastened by this, as is generally taken for granted, but that the generation of new ideas often goes on very inadequately and slowly, can easily be proved by suitable experiments. But the designation "flight of ideas" is so far quite appropriate, as, in point of fact, the *duration of the individual idea* appears to be very much shortened; the ideas are "fleeting," and soon fade again before they have actually attained clearness. Hence, as a rule, there exists at the height of such disturbance a more or less pronounced incomplete consciousness.

The divertibility can be recognised in the abrupt *change of colouring* of the frame of mind, which can *change* in a moment from exuberant merriment to angry irritation, as well as to tearful despair. Lastly, in the form taken by expressions of the will, the disturbance shows as motor unrest, as *press of occupation*. There constantly spring up in the patient the most manifold impulses of the will, whose transposition into action is impeded by no checks, but is very soon crossed by new impulses.

Compare this description with the picture of the first patient, and you will easily see that there we were met by the same features that meet us here, only they were in a less aggravated form. There, too, we noticed the divertibility of the train of thought, the change of mood, and the unsteadiness of the will, and the tendency to give way unresistingly to every rising impulse. In both cases we have in reality the same picture of disease, that of *maniacal excitement*. That the differences, so striking at the first glance, are only a question of degree, becomes clear to us when we see the same state develop with growing excitement in the first patient as in the case we are now considering. But, again, our patient has from time to time presented the picture of "hypomania." Certainly that is not true of the present attack, which began pretty suddenly about two months ago, or at least is only true of the first few days. On the other hand, as we had to consider probable after our previous lecture, the patient has already gone through a whole series of maniacal attacks, some of which have passed off wonderfully mildly.

The woman is now thirty-two years of age; her father was very excitable; so also was his brother, who committed suicide; and a cousin of the father was insane. Her sister is feebleminded. The patient's illness began in her fourteenth year with an attack of depression, which was followed two years after by a state of excitement. Two years later another attack of depression came on, with self-accusations and severe impediment of the will. This was followed by an excitement, then again by a depression, and then another excitement. From that time frequent fluctuations between slight depression and hypomaniacal states were observed, but were only recognised as morbid by the mother. The patient led, at that time, an unsettled life, published a notification of marriage, engaged in love affairs without discretion, which were not without results, but had only been considered by her friends as "full of spirits." Once she actually married while in such a state, only to separate again. Thrice the excitement was so strong that the patient had to be temporarily lodged in an asylum. In her states of depression she felt deep repentance for her behaviour during the excitement. Between the attacks long periods intervened, however, in which neither sad nor cheerful moods existed.

The whole development and course of this case is wonderfully diagnostic of maniacal-depressive insanity. The beginning at a youthful age with depressed states of mind, the later vacillation between mania and depression, the occurrence of a single severe attack after numerous slighter ones, which to the unitiated scarcely appear as morbid, we find repeated in the same way innumerable times. We know from experience that patients of that kind are generally descended from families in which attacks of mental derangement have occurred. We may expect that our patient will have a series of different-coloured mild or severe attacks to go through in the future.[5]

The patient who next follows, a sea-captain, aged forty-nine, also begins to speak immediately on his entrance, and introduces himself as "The accused under chief command of Herr Professor General K." He answers the questions put to him promptly, and shows that he is quite clear as to time, residence, and surroundings. Very soon, however, he goes into long-winded, nineteen-to-the-dozen statements, which he suddenly brings to an end with the somewhat surprising remarks, "Either I am well or ill or off my head." To the name Katherine he adds "Kathereinen-Kneipps-Malzkaffee"—"Frohlich Pfalz, Gott erhalts" (Happy Palace, God uphold it!") —"all will be roasted." His comprehension and memory are very good; he makes his statement with a kind of joking minuteness; he came to the hospital on Friday, July 1, at ten minutes to six o'clock. He considers himself well; there was no need to bring him here. He makes derisive remarks about the doctors and the hospital, as well as about himself; he may talk nonsense, but he is clever—more clever than the doctors, who learnt nothing in Heidelberg. When he begins to "thee and thou"

---

[5] After five months' duration of the attack the patient recovered, with great increase of weight, but in the eight years elapsing since then she has again been through numerous slight depressions and excitements.

us, and we express our astonishment, he breaks out into a torrent of abuse, trying always to surpass himself, and ending in shouts of laughter. His mood is exalted and insolent, his behaviour jolly and vigorous; in answering, he holds his hand to his temple as in military salute, speaks loudly and abruptly as if making a military report, but soon relapses into the easy tone of a narrator.

The patient's real condition, as you will have already seen, is likewise one of manaical excitement. The unstable nature of his train of thought, the exalted, changing mood, the motor unrest, and especially the passion for talk, are significant enough. You would also be astonished at his press of occupation in other ways if you saw him in the ward arranging his clothes in ever new and intricate ways, manufacturing a horse, on which he rides, out of his bedding, or an anchor, the emblem of his calling; how he bawls, dances, or sings, and also occasionally destroys what he gets hold of. Our previous conjecture, based on common experience, that the present attack was certainly not the first, proves to be true. The patient came here for the first time eight years ago; since then he has been here eight times. The attack set in each time quite suddenly—the two first after a fall into the water, the second at the burial of his daughter, the later ones without known cause. Each time he at once became very excited, and developed the most senseless delusions—that he was God, Joseph in Egypt, called his companions by the names of princes and emperors, and had to be put into a strait-waistcoat on account of his very violent resistance. The excitement disappeared regularly, however, after from one to two weeks, so that he could soon be let out again.

The last five admissions took place this year. For this reason we kept the patient in the hospital this time after the disappearance of the excitement, and during that time we were able to observe the beginning of two new attacks. We have tried to cut short the last attack by at once giving the patient 12 and then 15 grammes of bromide of sodium daily on the first symptoms of excitement. In point of fact, the attack passed off much more quickly and mildly than the previous ones; perhaps we might venture to hope that the next attack will be longer in coming.[6]

In addition to this, we have employed those remedies which are generally found to be of use in maniacal states—first, rest in bed; but when that was found impracticable, then prolonged warm baths, which we are accustomed, under certain circumstances, to employ, with the best results, for a month at a time, for the half or even for the whole of the day. Doses of hyoscin or sulphonal are often necessary at the commencement to accustom the patients

---

[6] After a very brief excitement four weeks later, also treated with bromide of sodium, the patient remained well for over five months, then had another slight relapse, and has now again been at home for more than four months.

to the baths; but afterwards they stay in the comfortable warm bath, in which they also take their meals and can sometimes amuse and occupy themselves without much resistance. As in this case, it is found that with many patients simple separation from others is an efficient calmative, the employment of which has, however, to be immediately abandoned if and so long as the patients show any inclination to uncleanliness or destruction. Under kindly, quiet, non-exciting treatment, these "delirious" patients are far less troublesome than one usually imagines.

So far we have only considered the states of excitement in our patients. As they generally come under observation, morbid phenomena of that kind are commonly designated simply as "periodic mania." Very marked *low spirits* have, however, been also observed here. Especially after the disappearance of the excitement the patient was often downcast and quiet for days, thought that he had no longer any friends left—it was misery to be in his position. There are also hours intervening in the maniacal excitement when he weeps bitterly and deplores his sad fate, soon to fall back into the old boisterous mood. It appears to me that not only the deep inward relationship of such apparently contradictory states, but also the clinical unity of all those cases, which one generally tries to distinguish as the different forms of simple and periodic mania and of circular insanity, are distinctly marked in these fluctuations, which are hardly ever absent, even in the most hilarious mania. The tendency to repeated relapses, as well as the usually favourable termination of a single attack, is common to all of them, even if the indications are very severe and of very long duration. . . .

Mixed Conditions of Manaical-Depressive Insanity

If the different colouring, severity, and duration of even a single attack of maniacal-depressive insanity can give an extraordinarily varied form to the pictures of disease, this wealth of form will receive yet a substantial increase through the consideration of some further cases. You see before you a man, aged fifty, of uncommonly strong build, but badly nourished, who has been in the hospital for a few weeks. On my addressing him, the patient turns to me and answers questions as to his personal circumstances slowly and with difficulty, but correctly. Sometimes one has to repeat the questions several times, as the patient does not pay attention, but looks around the room, drums on the table with his fingers, suddenly gets up or stretches out his hand to the doctor. He gives the date of his admission quite incorrectly, says he is here, "in the Castle"; it is so beautiful here. He is not ill; he is very well; he is here "to make peace with us all." At this he breaks into a hearty laugh, so that one is not clear as to whether his remark is not intended for a joke. He knows the doctors, but not by name—"You must know that better than I." He does sums sometimes correctly and sometimes incorrectly, usually adding: "That squares wonderfully." As far as one can judge, his general knowledge is good, though the patient very often says: "I must first think"; and he has to be asked the same question several times, until at last, after some wrong answers, he gives the right one. His mood is cheerful and exalted; he sits there with beaming countenance, and often laughs away happily to himself, makes facetious remarks, and begins in a booming voice to sing a song. At the same time his behaviour is almost quiet; the movements are remarkably slow and awkward, but strong; he presses the hand offered to him very hard, and holds it firmly. He says little, breaks off abruptly, and soon comes to a standstill, ending with a laugh. When told to write his name on the blackboard, he draws the separate letters exceedingly slowly, pressing very hard on the board, and then adds a row of other names. On going away, he says good-bye in a loud voice, placing his hand in military fashion to his head. Except for a slight oscillation on shutting the eye, and a rupture in the left groin, the physical examination shows no disturbance worth remarking.

The condition under consideration cannot at first be classified with any of the conditions already considered. On the one hand we are met by symptoms of stupor, dimness of comprehension, forgetfulness, poverty of thought, and clumsiness of expression of the will; on the other hand, a certain divertibility shows itself, with exalted mood and slight motor unrest. Under these circumstances, the question must in the first place be raised whether we may not possibly have to deal with general paralysis, in which similar phenomena can occur. Only, the physical examination has furnished us with no good grounds for such a supposition; neither the pupils, nor the speech, nor the reflexes, nor the sensibility to pain, present the symptoms of general paralysis of the insane. Add to this that the memory also is less disturbed than at first appears, the patient is only stupefied and somewhat confused, so that, as he says himself, he must first consider even with simple answers. But in the end he usually finds the right answer, in contradistinction to the general paralytic, who does not at all notice the uncertainty and contradictions of his statements. That the condition is not be considered as katatonic stupor is obvious. The attention of the patient is easily aroused, but he comprehends with difficulty; his mood is not indifferent or childish, but really cheerful and happy; no negativism, no stereotypism, or automatic obedience appears in his actions, but a singular mixture of constraint and excitement. Finally, the supposition of epileptic stupor, quite apart from the long duration of the condition, will also present difficulties in diagnosis, because the emotional tension and irritability which usually distinguish that state are here completely wanting.

The fact that the patient has already suffered three times from mental derangement shows us the way to the right interpretation of this particular clinical picture. The father and a brother drowned themselves; a sister became insane in her youth. He himself, as a child, suffered from St. Vitus' dance; later on he was always a very quiet, reserved, temperate man, who, since his twenty-fifth year, has lived in happy wedlock, but has no children. He became ill for the first time in his thirty-first year. He was sad, thoughtful, overanxious on account of a tapeworm from which he suffered, and of which one heard now for the first time, and left off working. After a short time he became well again. The second attack set in seven years later with ideas of grandeur. The patient wanted to bring out a new machine, thought he need no longer work, was sexually very excited, and was raving mad and violent towards his wife, so that he had to be put into a strait-waistcoat. He hardly ate or slept at all. Here, in the hospital, where he was brought at once, he was very confused and apprehensive, expressed ideas of persecution, and had to be fed artificially; then be became ill with septic pneumonia, and after four weeks was taken home again by his wife.

The third attack began four years later with melancholia, which was very soon succeeded by wild excitement. It appears that at that time the patient presented in the hospital a similar picture to what he does now—slight restlessness, with cheerful, occasionally irritable mood, and an inclination to funny pranks. Recovery followed after eight months. This time the attack began with sleeplessness, restlessness, and quickly increasing bewilderment. In the beginning the patient also appears to have had singular hallucinations; he heard singing, shouts, saw a red cushion signifying England, a shirt that represented a heart, declared that he was the Son of God, that he would redeem the world, that he could heal all diseases, that he had transformed everything. He mistook people, called the doctor the King of Bavaria, and wanted to embrace and to kiss him, made stupid jokes, and shook hands violently, shook his sheet in other people's faces, but was easily managed, only now and then angrily excited, and always easily quieted with a cigar. Quite transitory and violent weeping and lamenting was observed.

As you will see, the two first attacks were both depressive, the two last expansive. But while in the second attack ideas of grandeur stepped in along with the apprehensive bewilderment, in the present and in the preceding attacks we have a combination of cheerful mood with impediment of thought and action. Thus, in a series of favourably resulting attacks, the clinical course of the malady quite corresponds with that of *maniacal-depressive insanity*. In point of fact, we have to do here with conditions in which the otherwise different attacks of related or successively recurring symptoms of disease *mix with each other* in wonderful ways. While a cheerful frame of mind with facility of expression of the will usually accompanies maniacal-depressive insanity, and impediments of the same go along with a depressive mood, here impediments of thought and action are connected with exaltation. In this way the picture of maniacal stupor is formed, in which the patients are forgetful, intellectually dull, clumsy, taciturn, sometimes almost dumb, but occasionally showing their wanton moods in all manner of tricks, adornments, facetious remarks, and play on words.

Quite another form of these mixed conditions is shown by a farmer of fifty-three years, whom I will now show you. The patient gives coherent information as to his personal circumstances, knows where he is, knows the doctors, but is not quite clear as to time. At first he behaves quietly, but in the course of the conversation becomes more and more excited, begs urgently to be allowed to go home to his wife and children, entreats once more to be pardoned. Can they answer for keeping him always and for ever in the penitentiary? The attendants had said so; he had seen in the crossed spoons that they would shackle him; the five plates on the top of one another had meant that he would go no more to his family—four at home, and one here. He sees very well that they think him incurable, and will not eat another bite. He steals money from his children through his residence here. To-morrow he will certainly be put to death; but why has he not taken heed thereof of what was meant when the cup was broken and the vessel stood in that way on the table? He should have said, "I know not why," and demanded his clothes. In this confused way he talks on, only allowing himself to be interrupted for a short time, to immediately begin his lamentations anew. At the same time he shows active emotional excitement, wrings his hands, wishes to kneel down, groans and weeps aloud. All the same, his expression is not really sad. He looks round him with lively and sparkling eyes, answers questions between whiles quite to the purpose, is ready to make a compact that he will not speak and will eat regularly for eight whole days if he may go home, urging half jokingly that one must give him one's hand on it, but then falls again into his former loquacity. The physical examination shows no deviation from health worth noticing.

The patient's condition, therefore, is one of *depression*. If we ask what this signifies clinically, we shall first think of *melancholia*, as general paralysis is little probable on account of the want of physical disturbances; so also is a state of circular depression, there being full freedom of expression of the will. The only symptoms, perhaps, that do not so entirely fit into the picture of melancholia are the great *loquacity* of the patient, and the ease with which one succeeds in *diverting* him, if only for a time.

If we now look back at the development of the condition, we learn that the patient comes of a healthy family, but has a son who is insane; two other children are healthy. He was in the campaign of 1870, and was a quiet, sober workman, healthy till his forty-third year, when he was treated in this hospital for "melancholia," recovering after a short time. Now for about a year he has again been ill. The illness came on gradually. The patient had groundless anxieties, worked badly, and expressed thoughts of suicide. According to his own account, he did not know in the morning whether he was to go out or whether he was to go in, whether he was to take the manure here or there. At last his wife said: "Now, do go away once and for all." Some days things went well with him, then again he thought he could never any more be happy. Why should he go on living? Often he became excited and angry; subsequently he regretted this.

On admission to the hospital six weeks ago, the patient was in a cheerful mood, showed strong desire for talking, and had no feelings of illness. He said that now he could decide everything easily that had been so very difficult to him before. But next day the picture changed quite suddenly. The patient became forgetful, was only able with difficulty to give the names of his children, showed great apprehension, thought he was condemned to death, slid about the ground on his knees, and refused to eat. But this condition changed quickly also, and now there developed a quite erratic alternation between exalted and apprehensive moods, which sometimes occurred within a few hours.

The apprehensive mood, however, gradually gained the upper hand. Contradictory ideas of sin and persecution sprang up, and disappeared; at the same time the patient, in the way indicated, had the inclination to refer every occurrence in his surroundings to himself. He was especially tormented by the compulsion to add, "I know not why," to all his observations, so as to come to no harm from them. In his "delusions of reference" the great divertibility of the patient showed very distinctly, always allowing him to find out new connections, while the old would be quickly forgotten. Great motor unrest showed during the whole illness, manifesting itself in lively gesticulations, continual wandering about, and particularly in the exceedingly strong desire for talking. In that respect the enhancement of the excitement by speech itself was worthy of notice. As soon as one addressed the patient, his torrent of talk unfailingly quickly rose up, however much he had firmly resolved to remain quiet. Latterly, a more cheerful, hopeful mood has for the time stepped in again.

It is clear from the course of the attack that we have not here to do with a melancholic illness. The *distinct maniacal colouring* of the condition in the first weeks of the present attack, as well as the early appearance of the first attack of the illness, are contradictory to that throughout. At the same time, we see from the statements of the patient that *want of resolution,* which we have learnt to recognise as a symptom of circular depression, was very marked during the first time of the illness. We were also often able without difficulty to show an *impediment of thought.* The condition of the patient, therefore, in the beginning of the present attack showed symptoms already known to us as those of *circular depression*—that is to say, impediment of thought and will; later, from time to time those of *maniacal excitement*—namely, cheerful mood, with desire for talking, though without marked "flight of ideas." Then, after a time of fluctuations backwards and forwards, the sad apprehensive depression again became stronger, while the motor excitement continued. In our opinion, this picture also belongs to the embodiments of maniacal-depressive insanity, and is to be described as a *mixed condition of psycho-motor excitement with psychic depression.* The patient shows us, therefore, as we believe, the very opposite of the picture in the preceding case, in which we could establish cheerful moods side by side with psycho-motor impediment. The grounds for these opinions are drawn chiefly from the marked, if at the same time transitory prominence of the ordinary maniacal and depressive conditions in the same patient in the same or in different attacks, alongside of the mixed states already described.

The value of this interpretation consists in the fact that we gain through it a clear opinion as to the further course of the malady. If we know that conditions of this particular kind only represent maniacal-depressive insanity, we may expect recovery from the present attack, but in all probability a relapse will occur later on in this or in another form of the periodically recurring disease. This tendency to fall each time into mixed conditions of the same nature apparently often exists in the same patient; sometimes, as in our first case, this tendency comes out only later on, yet an ordinary attack may appear, in addition, between several mixed attacks. As a rule, mixed conditions seem to represent rather more severe forms of the disease than simple attacks.[7]

[7] After twenty months' duration of the attack, the patient has quite recovered, with great increase of weight.

In maniacal-depressive insanity we have already been repeatedly met by *delusions,* usually ideas of sin and persecution, more rarely ideas of grandeur. These delusions do not necessarily belong to the indications of the disease. They can be entirely wanting, but can also be so strongly developed that they give a deceptive character to the whole condition. You see here before you a student of music, aged nineteen, who has been ill for about a year. His old father is disabled in consequence of several apoplectic fits; a brother of his became insane. The highly-gifted patient, without any tangible cause, while studying music, became depressed, felt ill at ease, and lonely, made all manner of plans, which he always gave up, for changing his place of residence and his profession, for he could come to no fixed resolutions. During a visit to Munich, he felt as if people in the street had something to say to him, and as if he were talked about everywhere. He heard an offensive remark at an inn at the next table, which he answered rudely. Next day he was seized with the apprehension that his remark might be taken as *lese majeste.* He heard that students asked for him at the door, and he left Munich post-haste with every precautionary measure, because he thought himself accompanied and followed on the way. Since then he overheard people in the street who threatened to shoot him, and to set fire to his house, and on that account he burned no light in his room. In the streets voices pointed out the way he ought to go so as to avoid being shot. Behind doors, windows, hedges, pursuers seemed everywhere to lurk. He also heard long conversations of not very flattering purport as to his person. In consequence of this, he withdrew altogether from society, but yet behaved in such an ordinary way that his relatives, whom he visited, did not notice his delusions. At last the many mocking calls which he heard at every turn provoked the thought of shooting himself.

After about six months he felt more free, "comfortable, enterprising, and cheerful," began to talk a lot, to compose, criticised everything, concocted great schemes, and was insubordinate to his teacher. The voices still continued, and he recognised in them the whisperings of master spirits. Hallucinations of sight now became very marked. The patient saw Beethoven's image radiant with joy at his genius; saw Goethe, whom he had abused, in a threatening attitude; masked old men and ideal female forms floated through his room. He saw lightning and glorious brilliancy of colours, which he interpreted partly as the flowing out of his great genius, partly as attestations of applause from the dead.

He regarded himself as the Messiah, preached openly against prostitution, wished to enter into an ideal connection with a female student of music, whom he sought for in strange houses, composed the "Great Song of Love," and on account of this priceless work was brought to the hospital by those who envied him, as he said.

The patient is quite collected, and gives connected information as to his personal circumstances. He is clear as to time and place, but betrays himself by judging his position falsely, inasmuch as he takes us for hypnotizers, who wish to try experiments with him. He does not look upon himself as ill; at the most as somewhat nervously overexcited. Through diplomatic questions we learn that all people know his thoughts; if he writes, the words are repeated before the door. In the creaking of boards, in the whistle of the train, he hears calls, exhortations, orders, threats. Christ appears to him in the night, or a golden figure as the spirit of his father; coloured signs of special meaning are given through the window. In prolonged conversation the patient very quickly loses the thread, and produces finally a succession of fine phrases, which wind up unexpectedly with some facetious question. His mood is arrogant, conceited, generally condescending, occasionally transitorily irritated or apprehensive. The patient speaks much and willingly, talks aloud to himself, and marches boisterously up and down the ward, interests himself more than is desirable in his fellow-patients, seeking to cheer them and to manage them. He is very busy, too, with letter-writing and composing, but only produces fugitive, carelessly jotted down written work, with numerous marginal notes. Physically, he is well.

The interpretation of this condition is not easy at the first glance. Of the diseases hitherto considered, dementia præcox would perhaps come first and foremost under consideration, especially certain forms of it with which we shall have to deal later on. But the exceedingly fresh, active mood of the patient, his interest in his surroundings, his sociability, and his press of occupation, are decidedly opposed to this supposition. Also, the manifold peculiarities of action and behaviour which we saw stand out so prominently in that disease are entirely wanting. On the other hand, the *divertibility* which is seen in his ever flying off at a tangent and so easily losing the thread of his narratives, in his *cheerfull, arrogant frame of mind, and in his urgent need to be talking and doing,* points to the relationship of the condition with maniacal-depressive insanity. And this opinion would be justified by the joyless, irresolute manifestations, so characteristic of the first stage, passing into the comfortable but active states, so noticeable in the second stage. Hallucinations and delusions are not such essential clinical indications that they would suffice to found another diagnosis, because they could be absent in one attack of the malady and present in another. If our supposition with regard to our patient be right, we are able to predict complete recovery in the near future, though the possibility of a subsequent relapse has to be admitted.[8] . . .

Dementia Præcox

You have before you to-day a strongly-built and well-nourished man, aged twenty-one, who entered the hospital a few weeks ago. He sits quietly looking in front of him, and does not raise his eyes when he is spoken to, but evidently understands all our questions very well, for he answers quite relevantly, though slowly and often only after repeated questioning. From his brief remarks, made in a low tone, we gather that he thinks he is ill, without getting any more precise information about the nature of the illness and its symptoms. The patient attributes his malady to the onanism he has practised since he was ten years old. He thinks he has thus incurred the guilt of a sin against the sixth commandment, has very much reduced his power of working, has made himself feel languid and miserable, and has become a hypochondriac. Thus, as the result of reading certain books, he imagined that he had a rupture and suffered from wasting of the spinal cord, neither of which was the case. He would not associate with his comrades any longer, because he thought they saw the results of his vice and made fun of him. The patient makes all these statements in an indifferent tone, without looking up or troubling about his surroundings. His expression betrays no emotion; he only laughs for a moment now and then. There is occasional wrinkling of the forehead or facial spasm. Round the mouth and nose a fine, changing twitching is constantly observed.

The patient gives us a correct account of his past experiences. His knowledge speaks for the high degree of his education; indeed, he was ready to enter the University a year ago. He also knows where he is and how long he has been here, but he is only very imperfectly acquainted with the names of the people round him, and says that he has never asked about them. He can only give a very meagre account of the general events of the last year. In answer to our questions, he declares that he is ready to remain in the hospital for the present. He would certainly prefer it if he could enter a profession, but he cannot say what he would like to take up. No physical disturbances can be definitely made out, except exaggerated knee-jerks.

At first sight, perhaps, the patient reminds you of the states of depression which we have learned to recognise in former lectures. But on closer examination you will easily understand that, in spite of certain isolated points of resemblance, we have to deal

---

[8] The patient quite recovered, and has now been well for eight years.

here with a disease having features of quite another kind. The patient makes his statements slowly and in monosyllables, not because his wish to answer meets with overpowering hindrances, but because he feels no desire to speak at all. He certainly hears and understands what is said to him very well, but he does not take the trouble to attend to it. He pays no heed, and answers whatever occurs to him without thinking. No visible effort of the will is to be noticed. All his movements are languid and expressionless, but are made without hindrance or trouble. There is no sign of emotional dejection, such as one would expect from the nature of his talk, and the patient remains quite dull throughout, experiencing neither fear nor hope nor desires. He is not at all deeply affected by what goes on before him, although he understands it without actual difficulty. It is all the same to him who appears or disappears where he is, or who talks to him and takes care of him, and he does not even once ask their names.

This peculiar and fundamental want of any *strong feeling of the impressions of life,* with unimpaired ability to understand and to remember, is really the diagnostic symptom of the disease we have before us. It becomes still plainer if we observe the patient for a time, and see that, in spite of his good education, he lies in bed for weeks and months, or sits about without feeling the slightest need of occupation. He broods, staring in front of him with expressionless features, over which a vacant smile occasionally plays, or at the best turns over the leaves of a book for a moment, apparently speechless, and not troubling about anything. Even when he has visitors, he sits without showing any interest, does not ask about what is happening at home, hardly even greets his parents, and goes back indifferently to the ward. He can hardly be induced to write a letter, and says that he has nothing to write about. But he occasionally composes a letter to the doctor, expressing all kinds of distorted, half-formed ideas, with a peculiar and silly play on words, in very fair style, but with little connection. He begs for "a little more *allegro* in the treatment," and "liberationary movement with a view to the widening of the horizon," will *"ergo* extort some wit in lectures," and *"nota bene* for God's sake only does not wish to be combined with the club of the harmless." "Professional work is the balm of life."

These scraps of writing, as well as his statements that he is pondering over the world or putting himself together a moral philosophy, leave no doubt that, besides the emotional barrenness, there is also a high degree of *weakness* of *judgment* and *flightiness,* although the pure memory has suffered little, if at all. We have a *mental and emotional infirmity* to deal with, which reminds us only outwardly of the states of depression previously described. This infirmity is the incurable outcome of a very common history of disease, to which we will provisionally give the name of *Dementia Præcox*.

The development of the illness has been quite gradual. Our patient, whose parents suffered transitorily from "dejection," did not go to school till he was seven years old, as he was a delicate child and spoke badly, but when he did he learned quite well. He was considered to be a reserved and stubborn child. Having practised onanism at a very early age, he became more and more solitary in the last few years, and thought that he was laughed at by his brothers and sisters, and shut out from society because of his ugliness. For this reason he could not bear a looking-glass in his room. After passing the written examination on leaving school, a year ago, he gave up the *viva voce*, because he could not work any longer. He cried a great deal, masturbated much, ran about aimlessly, played in a senseless way on the piano, and began to write observations " 'On the Nerve-play of Life,' which he cannot get on with." He was incapable of any kind of work, even physical, felt "done for," asked for a revolver, ate Swedish matches to destroy himself, and lost all affection for his family. From time to time he became excited and troublesome, and shouted out of the window at night. In the hospital, too, a state of excitement lasting for several days was observed, in which he chattered in a confused way, made faces, ran about at full speed, wrote disconnected scraps of composition, and crossed and recrossed them with flourishes and unmeaning combinations of letters. After this a state of tranquillity ensued, in which he could give absolutely no account of his extraordinary behaviour.[9]

Besides the mental and emotional weakness, we meet with other very significant features in the case before us. The first of these is the silly, vacant *laugh,* which is constantly observed in dementia præcox. There is no joyous humour corresponding to this laugh; indeed, some patients complain that they cannot help laughing, without feeling at all inclined to laugh. Other important symptoms are *making faces* or grimacing, and the fine muscular twitching in the face which is also very characteristic of dementia præcox. Then we must notice the tendency to peculiar, distorted turns of speech—*senseless playing with syllables and words*—as it often assumes very extraordinary forms in this disease. Lastly, I may call your attention to the fact that, when you offer him your hand, the patient does not grasp it, but only *stretches his own hand out stiffly to meet it.* Here we have the first sign of a disturbance which is often developed in dementia præcox in the most astounding way.

As the illness developed quite gradually, it is hardly pos-

---

[9] The patient afterwards returned to the care of his family unchanged. He has now been in an asylum again for three and a half years, dull and demented.

sible to fix on any particular point of time as the beginning. In such cases, the change which is taking place is easily referred to some culpable looseness of morality, which it is sought to combat by educational means. Onanism in particular, which is very common in our patients, is usually held to be the source of the disease, so that cases of this kind were formerly spoken of as the insanity of onanism. I am nevertheless inclined to see in onanism a symptom, rather than the cause, of the disease. We often see the whole severe mental and physical condition arise, without any striking degree of onanism, and we also know degenerate onanists who present quite different symptoms. Hence there cannot well be any question of a regular causal connection between onanism and dementia præcox. Besides, the disease is just as common among women, in whom the weakening effect of onanism must be much slighter. Lastly, it is to be observed that the disease often sets in quite suddenly, another circumstance not exactly adapted to confirm the supposition of its onanistic origin.

Dementia Præcox often begins with a state of depression, which at first may easily be confused with the kinds of depression already described. As an example of this, I will show you a day-labourer, aged twenty-two, who first came into the hospital three years ago. He belongs, it is said, to a healthy family, and did well at school. A few weeks before his admission he had some attacks of apprehension, and then became disturbed, ill-balanced and absent-minded, stared in front of him, spoke in a confused way, and expressed vague ideas of sin and persecution. On admission, he gave hesitating, broken answers, did sums and obeyed orders, but did not know where he was. He hardly spoke at all of his own accord, or at most muttered a few almost incomprehensible words: there was war; he could not eat, lived by the word of God; there was a raven at the window that wished to eat his flesh, and so on. Although he understood what was said to him quite well, and even let his attention be easily diverted, he did not trouble at all about his surroundings, had no desire to make himself clear about his position, and expressed neither apprehension nor desires. He generally lay in bed with a rigid, vacant expression, but often got up to kneel down or go about slowly. All his movements showed a certain constraint and want of freedom. His limbs remained for some time in the position in which you placed them. If you raised your arms quickly in front of him, he imitated the movement, and he also clapped his hands when it was done before him. These phenomena, called respectively *flexibilitas cerea,* "*waxen flexibility,*" or catalepsy in the one case, and *echopraxis* in the other, are familiar to us from experiments in hypnotism. They are always symptoms of a peculiar disturbance of volition, of which we include the various manifestations under the name of *automatic obedience.* Inequality of the pupils is also to be noticed in our patient, and I must mention the occurrence of an attack of unconsciousness, with twitching in the arms.

The patient's condition improved in the course of the next few months. He became clearer, his behaviour was more natural, and he had a distinct feeling of illness, but he remained strikingly dull, apathetic, and devoid of ideas. Nevertheless, he found employment outside, and only came back to the hospital a year ago. He had thrown himself in front of a train, losing his right foot and breaking his left arm. This time he was collected and clear about his surroundings, and showed considerable knowledge of geography and arithmetic, but spoke to none of his own accord, and lay in bed dully, with a vacant expression, without occupying himself or paying attention to what went on around him. He alleged as the reason for his attempted suicide that he was ill; his brain had burst out a year before. Since then he could not think by himself; others knew his thoughts, spoke about them, and heard if he read the newspaper.

The patient is still in the same condition to-day. He stares apathetically in front of him, does not glance round at his surroundings, although they are strange to him, and does not look up when he is spoken to. Yet it is possible to get a few relevant answers by questioning him urgently. He knows where he is, can tell the year and month and the names of the doctors, does simple sums, and can repeat the names of some towns and rivers, but at the same time he calls himself Wilhelm Rex, the son of the German Emperor. He does not worry about his position, and says he is willing to stay here, as his brain is injured and the veins are burst. The waxen flexibility and echopraxis can still be made out clearly. When told to give his hand, he stretches it out stiffly, without grasping.

You will understand at once that we have a *state of dementia*[10] before us, in which the faculty of comprehension and the recollection of knowledge previously acquired are much less affected than the judgment, and especially than the emotional impulses and the acts of volition which stand in closest relation to those impulses. The disease thus delineated agrees to a great extent with the case which was last described, in spite of the different development of the illness. The complete loss of mental activity, and of interest in particular, and the failure of every impulse to energy, are such characteristic and fundamental indications that they give a very definite stamp to the condition in both cases. Together with the weakness of judgment, they are invariable and permanent fundamental features of dementia præcox, accompany-

---

[10] The patient has now spent five years in a nursing asylum, and has become quite affected and demented.

ing the whole evolution of the disease. Compared with these, all other disturbances, however prominent they may be in individual cases, must be regarded as merely transitory, and therefore not absolutely diagnostic, features. This holds good, for instance, of delusions and hallucinations; which are very frequently present, but may be developed in very different degrees or be altogether absent, or disappear, without the fundamental features of the disease or its course and issue being in any way affected. Yet we may consider it a rule that states of depression which are accompanied *at the very beginning* by vivid hallucinations or confused delusions usually form the prelude to dementia præcox. Fluctuations in spirits are always only of a fugitive kind in this disease, and therefore cannot be made use of for the diagnosis. At the very onset, indeed, we often observe states of lively apprehension or sad depression, but generally we can soon satisfy ourselves that the affections of the emotions really disappear very quickly, even when the external signs of them continue for some time longer.

Looking at the strongly-built postman, aged thirty-five, who stands before you now, you will hardly believe that a few days ago this man not only tried to make away with himself, but also wished to persuade his wife to die with him. He had been cut down insensible from the water-pipe a few days before. The patient is pale, and his general nutrition is much impaired. He is quite collected, knows where he is, understands his position, and gives relevant and connected answers to questions. He says that he has been ill for five weeks. He suffered from headaches, and thought that his comrades talked about little failings of which he had been guilty in former places. He heard someone say, "We'll catch you; we'll pull your little shirt off." There was also a great deal that he did not understand; there was telephoning into his ear. Then he hanged himself because of the voices. Later on he began to work again, but was still apprehensive. He was afraid he had passed false money and would go to prison for it, was confused in his head, and asked his wife to shoot herself with him, as she would be left in misfortune if he went to prison. He could not sleep or eat, and kept on reproaching himself. He saw a head, of which he was afraid at first, on the ceiling; then, with his eyes shut, he saw two tables, of which one was split, and on them a house with windows and an arch.

The patient relates all these experiences smilingly and with an affected way of speaking. He gives no further thought to his attempted suicide, or to his having been brought to the asylum. He offers his hand in a stiff, spread-out way, shows well-marked catalepsy and echopraxis, which also takes the form of echolalia, when he repeats words shouted to him immediately, sometimes distorting them. For the first part of his stay in the asylum he lay in bed almost all day, often with his eyes closed and without moving, not even stirring when he was spoken to or even pricked with a needle. As he sometimes related, he heard voices which said all manner of things before him or called them to him. He told in a whisper how he had seen a blue heart up above, and behind it quivering sunshine and another blue heart, "a little woman's heart." He also saw flashes of lightning and a comet with a long tail. The sun rose on the wrong side.

It is also to be noticed that for the last few days the patient has suddenly refused to eat, without any cause, so that it has been necessary to feed him artificially. He declined the suggestion that he should write to his wife, on the ground that he had more important things to do. He did not wish for a visit from her: "it would really not be worth while." When told to show his tongue, he opened his mouth, but rolled back his tongue with all his strength against his soft palate. Once, for a short time, he suddenly became blindly violent against his surroundings, without being able to give any account of his reasons afterwards. The only physical symptom worth noticing is a great increase in the knee-jerks.

It cannot have escaped you that the same fundamental symptoms of emotional dulness, absence of independent impulses of the will, and increased susceptibility of the will to influence, which have already struck us in the cases previously described, are to be found again in this description. And there are just as many details, such as the hallucinations and the extraordinary way of giving the hand, to support the conclusion that the present case is also one of dementia præcox, which we drew from the emotional dulness and the automatic obedience. Finally, we must take a number of disturbances, which we shall have to consider more exactly at the earliest opportunity—the patient's senseless resistance to receiving food, to showing his tongue, and to writing letters, and also his stuporose behaviour—in the same sense. We therefore come to the conclusion that in reality the case now before us most probably belongs to the same disease as the two cases previously described.

In those cases, however, we had to deal with diseases of several years' standing, which had resulted in a condition of incurable mental infirmity. Experience shows that this is by far the most frequent result of dementia præcox. The importance of our diagnosis would therefore consist in this: that we are now able, at the very beginning of the illness, to predict its resulting in a characteristic state of feebleness, in the same way as we arrived at certain probable conclusions about the further course of the disease in circular stupor. The prognosis, however, is really by no means simple. Whether dementia præcox is susceptible of a complete and permanent recovery answering to the strict demands of science is still very doubtful, if not impossible to decide. But improvements are not at all unusual, which in practice may be considered equivalent to cures. In these cases the patients suffer a certain impairment of their mental and emotional activity and of their power of action, and other slight remains of the symptoms of the disease may perhaps be recognised, yet they may be fully capable of filling their old place in simple relations. It is a more serious matter that in most of these cases the improvement is only *temporary,* and that such patients are in great danger of relapsing sooner or later, without any particular cause, and then generally suffer more serious injury from their illness. We had to record such an improvement in our second case, though it is true that it did not go very far. It was followed by a relapse. In the case of our third patient also we may hope for the disappearance of the present symptoms, but we must be prepared for their return in an even more serious form.[11]

Katatonic Stupor

The cases that I have to place before you to-day are peculiar. First of all, you see a servant-girl, aged twenty-four, upon whose features and frame traces of great emaciation can be plainly seen. In spite of this, the patient is in continual movement, going a few steps forwards, and then back again; she plaits her hair, only to unloose it the next minute. On attempting to stop her movement, we meet with unexpectedly strong resistance; if I place myself in front of her with my arms spread out in order to stop her, if she cannot push me on one side, she suddenly turns and slips through under my arms, so as to continue her way. If one takes firm hold of her, she distorts her usually rigid, expressionless features with deplorable weeping, that only ceases so soon as one lets her have her own way. We notice besides that she holds a crushed piece of bread spasmodically clasped in the fingers of the left hand, which she absolutely will not allow to be forced from her. The patient does not trouble in the least about her surroundings so long as you leave her alone. If you prick her in the forehead with a needle, she scarcely winces or turns away, and leaves the needle quietly sticking there without letting it disturb her restless, beast-of-prey-like

[11] The patient, having made an extraordinary recovery physically, but with no proper understanding of his ailment, was discharged from the asylum after he had been there for three months. He has now been at home for four years and nine months, apparently cured.

wandering backwards and forwards. To questions she answers almost nothing, at the most shaking her head. But from time to time she wails: "O dear God! O dear God! O dear mother! O dear mother!" always repeating uniformly the same phrases. If you try to grasp her hand she draws it away very suddenly, and at last, if she can no longer avoid you, begins to roll it up in her apron. Orders are of no use; on the contrary, she resists in everything you try to do with her. But when she quickly hides her hand directly one speaks of taking away the bread, it becomes evident that she understands what is happening around her.

In this clinical picture two new symptoms of disease stand out with great clearness—namely, *stereotypism* and *negativism*. The first, a kind of instinctive inclination to purposeless repetition of the same expressions of the will, shows itself in the untiring running backwards and forwards, in the lacing of the hands in the hair, in the holding fast the bit of bread, and in the uniform expressions of speech. The negativism, a senseless resistance against every outward influence, we recognise in the "mutacismus"—*i.e.*, forced dumbness—as well as in the whole persistent obstinacy of the patient.

In addition, these characteristics have come forward many times in very similar forms in her ordinary behaviour. For a long time the patient would take no nourishment, so that mechanical feeding had to be temporarily resorted to. It is true that she asked for water, "and cakes with it"; then, as soon as it was brought, would not take it. But now she lets her food stand beside her, and after a little time begins to swallow it greedily, but stops at once if you try to persuade her. Otherwise, she eats double and treble quantities, and also, very dexterously and unscrupulously, takes food away from the other patients.

There is little to be learnt from her broken sentences of what is passing in her mind. She certainly sometimes calls the doctor "Herr Doktor!" and knows the names of all the attendants, but appears to have delusions of all sorts, and prays that she may be able to stay one night longer. "Grant me yet one night before the many, many fires of the whole world, before the great Judgment Seat, before the many men." She was tormented by "scythes." "Let me go, the many heads and the many arms. Must I carry the whole world, the whole earth?" Whether the patient really experienced lively dread it is hard to decide. Threats make no impression upon her. Sometimes she twists her usually rigid features into a slight smile. Of physical disturbances there are to be noticed increased excitability of the facials, very active knee-jerks, and a bluish-red discoloration of the hands and feet.

So far as it is possible to form an opinion from these observations, it would appear that the patient's comprehension is comparatively little disturbed, while confused delusions and perhaps illusions persist. In the emotional province a certain fear exists, but it can scarcely be very active, while in the province of action we meet with the phenomena of stereotypism and negativism in their fullest development. This diseased condition, which is distinguished from all those we have previously considered by these last two prominent characteristics, is known as *katatonic stupor*. The term "stupor" serves here for a state bearing only a quite superficial resemblance to the circular stupor already described.

Some thirty years ago a disease was described by *Kahlbaum* as *katatonia,* or "insanity of rigidity," of which the most prominent symptom is a stiffness in the muscles, which would only be increased by outward interference. The disease should run through a series of different evolutions, and end at last in recovery or dementia. In the main, Kahlbaum's long-contested description has proved to be right, although I have to assume that the descriptions of disease summed up by him as katatonia are only special forms of dementia præcox. At all events, in katatonia also, disturbances of the emotional province and of action control the condition, while comprehension and memory suffer little in proportion. But then we meet with the katatonic symptoms—negativism, stereotypism, more especially the automatic obedience already described, the strange behaviour, and the sudden onset of senseless impulses—in all gradations in the different forms of dementia præcox. Indications of the same kind were also present in the cases already discussed.

In our present case the development of the disease goes back only about sixteen weeks. The patient has no heredity, and had always been quiet and respectable. Some months previously she went into service, and there became ill. She left off working, wept and groaned a great deal, sat mute, and did not sleep. Then she became apprehensive. Now she would be tortured: the murderers would come with scythes; she sang songs from the hymn-book; she clung to her mother, and smiled from time to time. Once she sprang out of the window, another time down from a tolerably high rock, but without seriously hurting herself. On admission to the hospital four weeks ago, she behaved frivolously, answered only to pressing interrogation, but then correctly. She was clear as to place and time, said herself that she was ill mentally, declared that she had heard voices that always scolded her the whole time they were speaking; the Saviour had allowed her to fall. The recognition of colour and numbers was quickly made out, as well as the solution of simple sums; also, in contrast to the condition found in circular stupor, the movements showed no kind of impediment. The patient presented echolalia and catalepsy; further, we were struck by the grimacing movements of the muscles of the mouth. Negativism made itself apparent, in that the patient, who had been led into the room resisting, when told to go would not leave, but held back, only to decide on going when told to remain.

The stupor which you have before you is only a stage of the course of the disease in katatonia. Its beginning reminds us distinctly of the states that we discussed in our last lecture. In the same way the termination can be a similar one. Sometimes, however, the stupor passes imperceptibly into confirmed imbecility. The patients may perhaps become a little more manageable and active, but they still remain wanting in ideas, and dull and slow, and also retain permanently many of the prominent features of the disease—illusions, confused hallucinations, stereotypism in deportment and behaviour, negativism, and automatic obedience. The stupor, nevertheless, can also form the transition to states of quite other kinds, or it can disappear, only to reappear.[12]

The next patient whom I will bring before you to-day is a merchant, aged twenty-six, who comes into the room under guidance, with closed eyes, hanging head, and shuffling gait, and at the earliest opportunity sinks limply into a chair. On being spoken to, his pale, expressionless features do not show any animation; the patient does not reply to questions or obey orders. If you stick a needle into his forehead or his nose, or touch the cornea, there follows at most a slight blinking or flushing, without any attempt at defence. But during this the patient quite unexpectedly breaks into a slight laugh. If you raise his arm in the air, it falls down as if palsied, and remains in the same position that it took accidentally. After much persuasion the patient at last opens his eyes; he now also gives his hand, advancing it by jerks with stiff angular movements, and remains like that. If you bend his head back, he stays in this uncomfortable position, and his leg, which I have raised up, he also keeps stiffly stretched in the air. By degrees one succeeds in calling forth still further signs of automatic obedience. The patient raises his arms if anyone does it in front of him, and imitates pushing and turning movements, whirling his fists with great exactness and rapidity. On the other hand, he does not utter a word, presses his lips together when he ought to show his tongue, cannot be induced to write, and apart from sudden, repeated grins, remains quite mute, but repeats some words shouted out loud to him with his mouth closed. He at once obeys the order to go.

The characteristic *disturbance of will* that forms a mixture

---

[12] After ten months' residence at the asylum the patient was able to return to her family. She was physically healthy and capable of work, but wanting in ideas, unintelligent, dull and inaccessible, and still showed affected movements. At home she works, but lives in seclusion, and associates with no one.

of automatic obedience and negativism is, above all, obvious in this patient also. In a quite inexplicable manner the patient allows himself on the one hand to be influenced without will of his own, while, again, on the other hand, he suppresses the natural impulse of the will or that introduced from without. This contrast is best illustrated by his mimicry of speech with his mouth shut. As the result of his negativism, the patient has not for a long time opened his mouth in trying to speak, but yet he cannot quite withstand the impulse to imitate what is said before him. From this we recognise clearly that negativism and automatic obedience are psychological, but not clinical, contrasts. Indeed, both disturbances not only come forward in the same patients at the same time, but they also very easily change into one another, so that you are never quite sure whether at a given moment you will meet with the one or with the other in a given patient. Sometimes also, through various suggestive means, you can at once lead over the one into the other.

As it would appear, both are only an expression of the fact that the control of that deliberation, conscious of an end, over the impulse of the will is lost, so that now impulse and counter-impulse of inner or outer origin determine irregularly the subsequent action. Thus, at least to a certain extent, one would understand that the patients, even if their deliberation is not affected in itself, involuntarily first follow that impulse which presents itself to them, only persistently to answer it in the most stubborn way with the counter-impulse, or to repeat some senseless action or other innumerable times, in every case without any regard for their own weal or woe. It is clear that such a loss of connection between thoughts and actions, which perhaps rests on the profound destruction of the sensory life, must quite rob the action of that inner unity and logical accuracy which we regard as the issue of healthy mental personality. By this means, even in the slighter forms of dementia præcox, the proceedings and behaviour of the patients keep up their incomprehensibility and their confusing tendency to jump from one thing to another.

No one defined colouring of mood is to be observed in our patient. On the contrary, he is completely dull emotionally, shows no interest in what goes on around him, not even on the visits of his nearest relations, in whom he shows no interest, and to whom he speaks not a word; he has no wishes, and does not care about anything. At the same time it can be seen from his occasional utterances that he is clear as to his situation, knows the people about him, and takes in what one says to him. Here again we find the same grouping of the disturbances in the order in which we were able to place them in the cases of dementia præcox already discussed.

This conception is also in accordance with the previous history of the patient. His father was temporarily insane, and could not on that account finish his college course. The patient himself learnt with difficulty, after having struggled through typhus in his youth; was easily excited, anxious, and inclined to hypochondriacal broodings. He fell ill six months ago. As the result of differences of opinion as to plans of marriage, he became anxious, believed himself to be mocked by everyone, was afraid of coming into contact with the public prosecutor, and finally, because he looked upon his life as threatened, sprang out of the window one night in his shirt, fracturing his *os calcis*. On admittance, the patient was decidedly dull; he declared himself quite ready to remain in the hospital, although he was not insane, but only suffered from delusions. He had thought he would be murdered; everything appeared to him so changed; voices spoke to him about all sorts of family affairs; catalepsy, echolalia and echopraxis were very marked. There was no demonstration of physical disturbances except an old scar on the head and a newly-formed callus on the foot.

In the further course of the illness the patient's want of judgment, as well as his emotional dulness, became more and more marked. He thought that the meat placed before him to eat was human flesh; everything in the newspapers was about himself; the assassination of the Empress of Austria and the Peace Conference had to do with him; his mother wanted to murder him; he was the worst man alive. The doctor he designated as the German Emperor, who had dyed his beard; another gentleman as Christ—all in quite an indifferent tone of voice, without a trace of emotion. Sometimes he said senseless rhymes to himself—"Nem, bem, kem, dem, schem, rem"—over and over again, or he repeated this incomprehensible sentence: "One for all, and all for one, and two for all, and three for all, here and there everywhere, and 'Almightiness,' and 'Almightiness,' and 'Almightiness,' " and so on. Gradually he became more and more quiet, and gave up speaking and eating, hid himself under the bedclothes, took up extremely uncomfortable attitudes, and allowed the saliva to run out of his mouth; he has only latterly become rather more active again.

A whole series of disturbances recur here with which we are already familiar: the illusions, the strange hallucinations, the dulness, the refusal of food, the twaddling speech, with play on words and stereotyped repetition. Through other symptoms, such as the hiding, the strange attitudes, and the slobbering, which are likewise frequent in dementia præcox, the description of katatonic stupor becomes still more complete. As to the future course of the case, the same will hold good as in that of the first patient; probably the disturbances, now so well defined, will gradually clear up, while a more or less high grade of mental enfeeblement may remain.[13]

The woman, aged twenty-eight, whom I will now show you is perhaps calculated to give you an idea of the further development of these cases. The patient has no heredity, married seven years ago, and has had four children. Headache, loss of appetite, and depression appeared at the first confinement, but only for some months. The same slight disturbances were noticed after the subsequent confinements also, a new and graver symptom showing itself after the last. The patient gave up working, ideas of persecution made their appearance, and she thought someone wanted to kill her by poisoning her food. She became indifferent, capricious, resistive, much reduced in physical health, and ate little. At the same time, she remained quite collected, and understood what was said to her.

On admission, nine months after the last confinement, the patient was mentally inaccessible, discontented, and fretful; desired to go home again at once; gave no information as to her condition, because she said she was not ill, and could work; did not trouble about her surroundings or employ herself. One gathered from her occasional utterances, as well as from her letters, which only contained in endless repetition the entreaty to be fetched away, that she was clear as to where she was; she also did simple sums very slowly, but correctly. A test of her knowledge and memory was impossible, as she did not answer questions directed to that end. In any case, an extraordinary poverty of thought existed. Delusions were not prominent, except perhaps single complaints that she appears to have been sold, and that people were angry with her; hallucinations were absent. In the emotional province, except for an irritable, peevish character, complete vacuity existed. The patient sat there apathetic and dull; she allowed no emotion to be perceived either at the Christmas festival or with visitors, not saying a word to them, while she devoured greedily the sweetmeats they had brought with them. All attempts to get on friendly terms with her she met with obstinate resistance. She remained nearly always mute, frequently refused food, would not remain in bed at night, refused to work, would take no medicine, often made herself dirty, neglecting the calls of nature, and so on.

As you may see, the patient now sits with bent head, holding herself crouched up. On being spoken to she does not look up, but now and then throws a furtive glance around her if anything

[13] The patient improved somewhat, but was twaddling and imbecile. He gained 24 kilogrammes in weight, and was taken home into family custody. Later on he went to a nursing asylum, where he died after the whole illness had lasted five years.

striking occurs. On shaking hands she does not give her hand, and if you grasp it you feel the arm become rigid. If you raise her head, it immediately goes down again; if you try to bend it down or to incline it sideways, it springs back again in the opposite direction; if, however, you put her leg on a chair, the patient allows it to remain in this uncomfortable position, a sign that indications of catalepsy also exist, side by side with negativism, which have occasionally been seen at other times. The features are rigid, like a mask; the lips slightly stretched out like a snout, a sign which Kahlbaum has designated as "snout cramp." Sometimes also slight tremors are seen round the mouth. After urgent and repeated orders to get up, the patient begins to rise slowly and jerkily, only suddenly to sit down again. It can be seen clearly on this and on numberless other occasions how the original impulse subsequently becomes thwarted through a counter-impulse. The patient cannot be persuaded to write on the blackboard. Lastly, the lively exaggerations of the knee-jerks, the mechanical excitability of the facials, strong idio-muscular swellings on tapping the muscles, the somewhat puffy face and the extremely poor action of the heart, are also noteworthy.

The *diagnosis of katatonia,* in face of the results of the examination submitted to us, cannot be doubted. Probably it is already a question of a final stage of dementia, which is hardly now capable of more extensive improvement[14]—so, at least, the marked signs of a far-advanced mental weakness indicate. The long duration of the illness also points to the fact that we have no longer to deal with a fresh example of disease still in a state of fusion. It certainly appears, up till now, as if a certain improvement has occurred after each separate attack of the disease, but yet on the whole a gradual downward progress of the malady has taken place. Finally, it is a very important experience that *childbirth* has always worked unfavourably. This corresponds entirely with our former observations, which frequently show us a connection of the disease in women with the process of reproduction. In such cases, the very great revolutions in the economy of the body probably play a significant causative part. . . .

Paranoidal Forms of Dementia Præcox

The merchant, aged twenty-five, whom you see before you to-day, has made himself conspicuous by putting leaves and ferns into his buttonhole. He takes a seat with a certain amount of ceremony, and gives positive, concise, and generally relevant an-

---

[14] The patient remained for five years in an asylum, quite imbecile, mute, negative, affected, at times excited, and died of phthisis.

swers to our questions. We learn that he was admitted to the hospital a year ago, that he afterwards spent six weeks at home, and that he has now been here again for six months. The patient makes no explicit statements about the nature of the disturbances which appeared, but he admits, when he is asked about it, that he did not speak for some time, he does not know why. But he remembers most of the details of what he has been through. Although he knows where he is, he mistakes the people about him, calls us by wrong names, and takes us for merchants. While he is more or less indifferent at first, taking very little interest in us and looking round with a conceited expression, he gradually becomes rather excited, grows rude, irritable, and threatening, and breaks out into an incoherent flood of words, in which there is a quite senseless play on syllables—"Macbeth—mach'ins Bett," "Irr ich mich nicht—Klinik," "je suis—Jesus," and so on.

At the same time, the patient intimates that he is the German Emperor, and that the Grand Duke is his father-in-law; he has been promised the Grand Duke's daughter since 1871. He is studying astronomy here. He denies that he has hallucinations. He declines to obey orders, but after some persuasion he finally stretches out his hand stiffly to shake hands. The patient is divertible; he often breaks off in his talk, and he intersperses it with curious snorting noises. His mood is changeable, but on the whole very much exalted. Often, more especially when he makes his jesting play on words, the patient bursts into a tittering laugh. His behaviour shows no marked excitement. His deportment is pompous and affected.

The diagnosis will have to rest principally on the peculiar aberrations in the patient's actions—the *mannerisms*, the *play on words*, the signs of *negativism*, and also on his *emotional indifference*, while he is yet quite collected. The patient does not consider himself ill, but stays here without making any resistance, does not worry at all, forms no plans for the future, and expresses no desires. We know this picture well already as a form in which *dementia præcox* appears. What seems strange about the condition is the absence of strong excitement on the one hand, and on the other the delusionary mistaking of people and the ideas of grandeur quite quietly expressed. But you will see at once, when we follow out the development of the case, that these deviations from the appearances discussed in an earlier lecture do not essentially affect the clinical interpretation of the patient's condition.

The patient is said to belong to a healthy family. He was clever at school, was always serious and conscientious, and served as a one-year's conscript. So far back as three years ago he complained of being shaky and excited, and no longer able to work as he had once done. Then, after he had been particularly active and enterprising for some time, marked depression of spirits set in fifteen months ago. The patient became sleepless, and complained of pains in the back of his head. He felt stupid and unfit for work, took no pleasure in his business, played apathetically with his fingers, lay in bed all day, and thought that he had abused his principal's confidence and embezzled. In this way he came to the hospital. Here he showed a striking conjunction of emotional dulness with good comprehension and perfect lucidity. Very soon he sank into a stupor, became dumb, showed signs of automatic obedience alternating with negativism, and masturbated very much. He was afraid that the French were coming, and that the knife would be whetted and people made away with, heard threatening voices, felt electricity in bed, wished to die, and ate hardly anything. He was perfectly indifferent when he was visited. It was only quite slowly that he became a little more active, got out of bed, and followed the doctor in his shirt, without speaking, or at the most murmured in a low tone to himself, or occasionally uttered irrelevant expressions, as to the meaning of which nothing could be learned from him.

In this condition he was taken home by his relations. There, too, he was almost dumb, and ate little, but jumped into a carriage one day, saying, "I drive a cab." He drove a little way, got out, and remained standing on the same spot for an hour and a quarter. During the next few days he suddenly became excited, clapped his hands, stamped with his feet, threw himself about, spoke quite incoherently in a loud voice about princesses, the Grand Duke, pardon, beheading, and the like, and laughed a great deal to himself. As he then became violent and broke windows, he was brought back to the hospital. Here he was very irritable and disobliging, gave senseless, irrelevant answers to questions, expressed disconnected ideas of grandeur, mistook people, and spoke and behaved affectedly. In speech and writing he plainly showed confusion of speech with playing on words. Thus he wrote in a letter, "$2 \times 4 = 8$, that is the day of the Lord come to pass; good mine to bad man is bad; bad wicked mine d'or to good man better as first recovery; I B flat in A—Saucier, you got—Minister—Mercier." When shown a knife, he answered, "Knife, razor, Barber of Bagdad, Salem aleikum." On seeing a gold piece, "Louis d'or, Napoleon, Empress Eugénie, la France, Spain, thither will we go." He often spoke out of the window, and said he was talking to spirits or acting a play. His sleep was very much disturbed. The physical examination showed no abnormalities worth noticing, but great dermatography and mechanical excitability of the facials. His weight had increased considerably.

The patient was originally supposed to be suffering from maniacal-depressive insanity. His previous history and the alternation of excited and depressed moods seemed greatly to favour this view. But in the further course of the case *katatonic* symptoms came out prominently during both the stuporose and the excited periods—negativism, mannerisms, automatic obedience, and confusion of speech. The diagnosis we derived from the clinical condition is thus fully confirmed by the whole development of the disease until now. It is true that divertibility and quibbling, as we see them here, are generally considered to be symptoms of mania. I may, however, point out that in maniacal cases it is only in the very worst states of excitement that the incoherence reaches as high a degree as it did here, where rationality was fully maintained and the excitement was comparatively slight. Under these circumstances, we must certainly adhere to the diagnosis of katatonia, and may therefore suppose that considerable improvement in the patient's condition is still possible, but that even in the most favourable event a certain degree of dulness and want of freedom will probably remain in the spheres of emotion and action.[15]

At first sight, the mechanic, aged forty-three, who takes his place before us now, seems to present much the same features as the last patient. He is slightly built, shows a certain formal politeness, and answers all our questions about his personal circumstances quickly and correctly. He is clear about time, knows where he is, knows the doctor, does sums quite well, and possesses a fair amount of general knowledge. His mood is conceited, and a superior smile plays over his features. When asked what he is doing here, he suddenly comes out with a whole flood of the most fantastic ideas, which he utters with great fluency, paying absolutely no attention to objections. He has been brought here to have his mental condition observed, through the Black League. He is not ill, though potash, arsenic, prussic acid, sulphuric acid, and other poisons have been put into his food. He has been put under excommunication, inflicted by means of a mirror. In this mirror the spirit appears, through which men may communicate with spirits. There is such a mirror in every house where there is a member of the Black League; even priests have it in the monstrance. The members of the League devour the born and unborn fruit of the womb, and make offerings of blood. "With these gifts, they inflict the excommunication, under the simultaneous stipulation if what they seek by their offerings is not granted, they stake their personal freedom. By offerings of dead life, it is understood that one is declared to be dead, but is not dead. Man need not die at all; there are thousands who are only said to be dead, but

[15] When the patient had been eight months in the asylum, we were able to discharge him substantially improved. He was not very accessible, but fairly intelligent and free from delusions. Now, six years later, he is actively engaged in his business, but is shy, 'does not get on with people,' shows marked catalepsy, and expresses hypochondriacal delusions.

are still alive and devour human flesh." "There are women, particularly Jesuits, who even sit on thrones, who are territorial princes, and others who are in high positions in the Government —Ministers, for instance. They make the sacrifice of uncleanness, and let themselves be defiled by beasts, even in church. There are even beasts which take the form of men. The worst of this evil dates from Chamisso; that is seen in the very name, 'Shame-is-so'!"

He goes on in this confused way. Whatever subject is mentioned he immediately tacks on his monstrous delusions. Napoleon was used for uncleanness by Catherine I in Russia. He got the testicles and penis of new-born children to eat, and so was turned into a hermaphrodite who could let himself be used by men, brought down misfortune on his head, and is now inspector of a penitentiary. He has been given sweat-powder and cats' dung himself in his food, and has had his heart, liver, lungs, and testicles taken out. Parson Kneipp is enthroned as Germania on the Niederwald Monument; Germania has a brother in the High Street at Freiburg. "That is the real 'Heit,' which is derived from heathendom [heidenthum]; he calls that truth [wahrheit]; he is not a real heathen at all."

All these things are very fluently alleged by the patient as quiet self-evident matters of fact. When cross-questioned, he goes into details at once, explaining his statements with more and more monstrous assertions. But as soon as he sees that his word is doubted he becomes extremely irritated, and breaks out into a flood of abuse, saying that his questioner is also one of the hired assassins and a swindler and a hermaphrodite, and he can only be quieted with difficulty. Echolalia, echopraxis, and catalepsy exist in the patient. The knee-jerks are much exaggerated, and the outspread fingers tremble, but no other physical disturbances can be made out.

The clinical interpretation of this highly fantastic condition presents some difficulty at first. However, the senselessness and incoherence of the delusions, expressed with a complete absence of emotion, show that we have to deal with a state of mental *weakness*. The automatic obedience, the confusion and indecency of the patient's talk, and the quite senseless playing with assonances, remind us of what we have observed before in cases of *dementia præcox*. We also met with entirely similar disturbances in our last patient.

If we look back to the development of the illness, we find that a sister of the patient was idiotic, and that he led a frivolous life himself, separated from his wife, entered into brief relations with other women, and served several terms of penal servitude for theft, forgery, and fraud. The first traces of disease appeared in the **convict prison four years ago, in** the form of hallucinations of hearing. The patient heard himself admired by his fellow-convicts for his blooming appearance, or threatened with arrest. The inspectors whispered, "Be quiet; there he goes; he has heard again. Good God! what ears the fellow has!" People called out his first name and talked about him. Then hallucinations of taste appeared, and he mistook people, and only six months later more and more senseless ideas of grandeur and persecution gradually developed. These often changed and assumed new features, but gradually they took the forms still existing, while the earlier ideas disappeared. States of lively excitement, with a tendency to violence, were repeatedly observed.

The patient has been in the hospital for three months. He generally keeps quite quiet, associates little with the other patients, does not occupy himself, lives for the day alone, is in a cheerful mood, says he is comfortable, greets the doctors in a rather formal way, and expresses no delusions of his own accord. But as soon as you get into conversation with him you find yourself under a shower of delusionary talk, consistent only in the main features. The patient gets increasingly excited, and more and more incoherent and irritated, but is friendly again next time he meets you, however abusive and threatening he may have been. He speaks in affected High German.

The beginning of this course of disease, with the rather quickly-developed hallucinations, would agree quite well with our previous observations in cases of dementia præcox. We may add that the outbreak of the disease in prison is no unusual occurrence. The great majority of "prison psychoses," or at least of those forms of them which run a lengthy course, belong to the province of dementia præcox. But we have never yet met with the luxuriant production of such extraordinary and constantly-changing delusions. For this reason the case before us bears a quite peculiar stamp, which formerly induced me to set this group of observations to a certain extent apart, under the name of "Dementia Paranoides." I think I may say from my experience that such cases usually present almost exactly the same features for dozens of years, and neither recover nor become more mentally dull.[16] The delusions remain permanently active; and new and extraordinary forms are always succeeding one another. At the same time, there are hallucinations of hearing and often of sight also, and particularly a most remarkable change in the physical condition and the course of thought. In the sphere of the emotions, *irritability* may be observed, with complete indifference to the natural relations of life. Patients have a tendency to outbursts of loquacity, without

---

[16] The patient has been in a nursing asylum for four years unchanged. He expresses confused and changeable delusions, and is at times very much excited; but in the intervals he is quite collected and orderly in his behaviour.

feeling the need of occupation or purposeful striving for the improvement of their position, and without any thought for the future.

This *emotional enfeeblement,* in conjunction with the symptoms previously described, leads us to assume that this condition may be closely allied to dementia præcox, in spite of many individual points of difference. Up to the present, I have not been able to discover any sharp division between the two clinical conditions; indeed, there seem to be many transitional forms. If we bear in mind that in dementia præcox and maniacal-depressive insanity delusions in particular may either be wholly absent or may take on the most various forms of development, we will hardly have sufficient reason, considering the similarity of the disturbances in feeling and action, fundamentally to separate the forms described here from the various other forms of dementia præcox.

The question is rather more difficult in another fairly large group of cases. The widow, aged thirty-five, whom I will now bring before you, may serve as an example of these. The patient gives full information about her life in answer to our questions, knows where she is, can tell the date and the year, and gives proof of satisfactory school knowledge. It is noteworthy that she does not look at her questioner, and speaks in a low and peculiar, sugary, affected tone. When you touch on her illness, she is reserved at first, and says that she is quite well, but she soon begins to express a number of remarkable *ideas of persecution.* For many years she has heard voices, which insult her and cast suspicion on her chastity. They mention a number of names she knows, and tell her she will be stripped and abused. The voices are very distinct, and, in her opinion, they must be carried by a telescope or a machine from her home. Her thoughts are dictated to her; she is obliged to think them, and hears them repeated after her. She is interrupted in her work, and has all kinds of uncomfortable sensations in her body, to which something is "done." In particular, her "mother parts" are turned inside out, and people send a pain through her back, lay ice-water on her heart, squeeze her neck, injure her spine, and violate her. There are also hallucinations of sight—black figures and the altered appearance of people—but these are far less frequent. She cannot exactly say who carries on all the influencing, or for what object it is done. Sometimes it is the people from her home, and sometimes the doctors of an asylum where she was before who have taken something out of her body.

The patient makes these extraordinary complaints without showing much emotion. She cries a little, but then describes her morbid experiences again with secret satisfaction and even with an erotic bias. She demands her discharge, but is easily consoled, and does not trouble at all about her position and her future. Her use of numerous strained and hardly intelligible phrases is very striking. She is ill-treated "flail-wise," "utterance-wise," "terror-wise"; she is "a picture of misery in angel's form," and "a defrauded mamma and housewife of sense of order." They have "altered her form of emotion." She is "persecuted by a secret insect from the District Office." She gives her hand in a spread-out way, and is cataleptic and echopractic. There are no indications of physical disturbances of any clinical importance.

The symptoms last mentioned will suggest the idea that the case belongs to the group constituted by the forms of dementia præcox. But the long and unvarying persistence of the same delusions is very much opposed to what has been described hitherto. The patient's father was rather excitable, and a brother had convulsions as a child. Her former history shows that she has been ill for nearly ten years. The disease developed gradually. About a year after the death of her husband, by whom she has two children, she became apprehensive, slept badly, heard loud talking in her room at night, and thought that she was being robbed of her means and persecuted by people from Frankfort, where she had formerly lived. Four years ago she spent a year in an asylum. She thought she found the "Frankforters" there, noticed poison in the food, heard voices, and felt influences. After her discharge she brought accusations against the doctors of having mutilated her while she was there. She now thought them to be her persecutors, and openly abused the public authorities for failing to protect her, so she had to be admitted to this hospital two months ago. Here she made the same complaints day after day, without showing much excitement, and wrote long-winded letters full of senseless and unvarying abuse about the persecution from which she suffered, to her relations, the asylum doctors, and the authorities. She did not occupy herself in any way, held no intercourse with her fellow-patients, and avoided every attempt to influence her.

Cases of this kind are very common. As a rule, the permanent delusions are thought to be of the greatest importance in their clinical interpretation, and for that reason they are generally classed under the head of Paranoia. To me, however, the patient's *peculiar feeble-mindedness,* which corresponds exactly to what is seen in dementia præcox, seems to be decisive of the diagnosis. The emotional dulness and loss of mental activity, the signs of automatic obedience and negativism, the mannerisms in the patient's behaviour, and the affected turns of speech, are symptoms with which we are well acquainted in that disease. There, too, we so often meet with the obstinate delusions of hearing, and even more with the delusion of influences on the body and on thought, that we can only look on the greater development of these disturbances here as a matter of degree, and not as an essential deviation from the ordinary features of dementia præcox.

The condition before us differs from paranoia in some very essential respects. The delusions are quite without sense from first to last, and are not worked out in the mind. The patient feels no need at all to raise objections and refute them, or to get a clear idea of the personality, motives, and procedure of her persecutors. Important details such as their personality are altered by her quite unconsciously. There is a transformation of the delusions, but no extension of them, and they do not develop into a completed view of the world, but remain fantastic and only loosely coherent fancies. Here hallucinations of the most different kinds play a predominant part all the time, while in paranoia we saw that the delusions were almost exclusively connected with real experiences mistakenly worked out. I wish to lay special stress on the development of the ideas of being physically influenced—the so-called "delusion of physical persecution"—and more especially on the disturbances of volition manifested in the stiff and affected movements, the automatic obedience, the coining of new words, and the constraint of thought, which, as far as I can see, are quite foreign to paranoia in our sense of the word. Lastly, as years go on, the purport of the delusions loses its influence on action fairly quickly, and the patients become dull and indifferent.[17] Very often the delusions are simply forgotten. The final condition may then be simple feeble-mindedness, which we see in other cases also as the outcome of dementia præcox. This result is never seen in real paranoia. It is from observations of this kind, more especially, that I am convinced that even those forms of feeble-mindedness which take their course with permanent delusions must not be called paranoia, but are more correctly to be brought under the head of dementia præcox. Where and when the limits of this over-extensive province are to be fixed the future alone can show.

CONRAD AIKEN / Silent Snow, Secret Snow

I

JUST WHY it should have happened, or why it should have happened just when it did, he could not, of course, possibly have said; nor perhaps could it even have occurred to him to ask. The thing was above all secret, something to be preciously

[17] The patient has been about five years in a nursing asylum. She is twaddling, affected, and negativistic, and still expresses her old ideas of being influenced.

concealed from Mother and Father; and to that very fact it owed an enormous part of its deliciousness. It was like a peculiarly beautiful trinket to be carried unmentioned in one's trouser-pocket— a rare stamp, an old coin, a few tiny gold links found trodden out of shape on the path in the park, a pebble of carnelian, a sea shell distinguishable from all others by an unusual spot or stripe—and, as if it were anyone of these, he carried around with him everywhere a warm and persistent and increasingly beautiful sense of possession. Nor was it only a sense of possession—it was also a sense of protection. It was as if, in some delightful way, his secret gave him a fortress, a wall behind which he could retreat into heavenly seclusion. This was almost the first thing he had noticed about it —apart from the oddness of the thing itself—and it was this that now again, for the fiftieth time, occurred to him, as he sat in the little schoolroom. It was the half hour for geography. Miss Buell was revolving with one finger, slowly, a huge terrestrial globe which had been placed on her desk. The green and yellow continents passed and repassed, questions were asked and answered, and now the little girl in front of him, Deirdre, who had a funny little constellation of freckles on the back of her neck, exactly like the Big Dipper, was standing up and telling Miss Buell that the equator was the line that ran around the middle.

Miss Buell's face, which was old and grayish and kindly, with gray stiff curls beside the cheeks, and eyes that swam very brightly, like little minnows, behind thick glasses, wrinkled itself into a complication of amusements.

"Ah! I see. The earth is wearing a belt, or a sash. Or someone drew a line round it!"

"Oh, no—not that—I mean—"

In the general laughter, he did not share, or only a very little. He was thinking about the Arctic and Antarctic regions, which of course, on the globe, were white. Miss Buell was now telling them about the tropics, the jungles, the steamy heat of equatorial swamps, where the birds and butterflies, and even the snakes, were like living jewels. As he listened to these things, he was already, with a pleasant sense of half-effort, putting his secret between himself and the words. Was it really an effort at all? For effort implied something voluntary, and perhaps even something one did not especially want; whereas this was distinctly pleasant, and came almost of its own accord. All he needed to do was to think of that morning, the first one, and then of all the others—

But it was all so absurdly simple! It had amounted to so little. It was nothing, just an idea—and just why it should have become so wonderful, so permanent, was a mystery—a very pleasant one, to be sure, but also, in an amusing way, foolish. However, without ceasing to listen to Miss Buell, who had now moved up to the north temperate zone, he deliberately invited his memory of the first morning. It was only a moment or two after he had waked up—or perhaps the moment itself. But was there, to be exact, an exact moment? Was one awake all at once? or was it gradual? Anyway, it was after he had stretched a lazy hand up towards the headrail, and yawned, and then relaxed again among his warm covers, all the more grateful on a December morning, that the thing had happened. Suddenly, for no reason, he had thought of the postman, he remembered the postman. Perhaps there was nothing so odd in that. After all, he heard the postman almost every morning in his life—his heavy boots could be heard clumping round the corner at the top of the little cobbled hill-street, and then, progressively nearer, progressively louder, the double knock at each door, the crossing and recrossings of the street, till finally the clumsy steps came stumbling across to the very door, and the tremendous knock came which shook the house itself.

(Miss Buell was saying "Vast wheat-growing areas in North America and Siberia."

Deirdre had for the moment placed her left hand across the back of her neck.)

But on this particular morning, the first morning, as he lay there with his eyes closed, he had for some reason waited for the postman. He wanted to hear him come round the corner. And that was precisely the joke—he never did. He never came. He never had come—round the corner—again. For when at last the steps were heard, they had already, he was quite sure, come a little down the hill, to the first house; and even so, the steps were curiously different—they were softer, they had a new secrecy about them, they were muffled and indistinct; and while the rhythm of them was the same, it now said a new thing—it said peace, it said remoteness, it said cold, it said sleep. And he had understood the situation at once—nothing could have seemed simpler—there had been snow in the night, such as all winter he had been longing for; and it was this which had rendered the postman's first footsteps inaudible, and the later ones faint. Of course! How lovely! And even now it must be snowing—it was going to be a snowy day—the long white ragged lines were drifting and sifting across the street, across the faces of the old houses, whispering and hushing, making little triangles of white in the corners between cobblestones, seething a little when the wind blew them over the ground to a drifted corner; and so it would be all day, getting deeper and deeper and silenter and silenter.

(Miss Buell was saying "Land of perpetual snow.")

All this time, of course (while he lay in bed), he had kept

his eyes closed, listening to the nearer progress of the postman, the muffled footsteps thumping and slipping on the snow-sheathed cobbles; and all the other sounds—the double knocks, a frosty far-off voice or two, a bell ringing thinly and softly as if under a sheet of ice—had the same slightly abstracted quality, as if removed by one degree from actuality—as if everything in the world had been insulated by snow. But when at last, pleased, he opened his eyes, and turned them towards the window, to see for himself this long-desired and now so clearly imagined miracle—what he saw instead was brilliant sunlight on a roof; and when, astonished, he jumped out of bed and stared down into the street, expecting to see the cobbles obliterated by the snow, he saw nothing but the bare bright cobbles themselves.

Queer, the effect this extraordinary surprise had had upon him—all the following morning he had kept with him a sense as of snow falling about him, a secret screen of new snow between himself and the world. If he had not dreamed such a thing—and how could he have dreamed it while awake?—how else could one explain it? In any case, the delusion had been so vivid as to affect his entire behavior. He could not now remember whether it was on the first or the second morning—or was it even the third?—that his mother had drawn attention to some oddness in his manner.

"But my darling—" she had said at the breakfast table, "what has come over you? You don't seem to be listening. . . ."

And how often that very thing had happened since!

(Miss Buell was now asking if anyone knew the difference between the North Pole and the Magnetic Pole. Deirdre was holding up her flickering brown hand, and he could see the four white dimples that marked the knuckles.)

Perhaps it hadn't been either the second or third morning —or even the fourth or fifth. How could he be sure? How could he be sure just when the delicious progress had become clear? Just when it had really begun? The intervals weren't very precise. . . . All he now knew was, that at some point or other—perhaps the second day, perhaps the sixth—he had noticed that the presence of the snow was a little more insistent, the sound of it clearer; and, conversely, the sound of the postman's footsteps more indistinct. Not only could he not hear the steps come round the corner, he could not even hear them at the first house. It was below the first house that he heard them; and then, a few days later, it was below the second house that he heard them; and a few days later again, below the third. Gradually, gradually, the snow was becoming heavier, the sound of its seething louder, the cobblestones more and more muffled. When he found, each morning, on going to the window, after the ritual of listening, that the roofs and cobbles were as bare as ever, it made no difference. This was, after all, only what he had expected. It was even what pleased him, what rewarded him: the thing was his own, belonged to no one else. No one else knew about it, not even his mother and father. There, outside, were the bare cobbles; and here, inside, was the snow. Snow growing heavier each day, muffling the world, hiding the ugly, and deadening increasingly—above all—the steps of the postman.

"But my darling—" she had said at the luncheon table, "what has come over you? You don't seem to listen when people speak to you. That's the third time I've asked you to pass your plate. . . ."

How was one to explain this to Mother? or to Father? There was, of course, nothing to be done about it: nothing. All one could do was to laugh embarrassedly, pretend to be a little ashamed, apologize, and take a sudden and somewhat disingenuous interest in what was being done or said. The cat had stayed out all night. He had a curious swelling on his left cheek—perhaps somebody had kicked him, or a stone had struck him. Mrs. Kempton was or was not coming to tea. The house was going to be house cleaned, or "turned out," on Wednesday instead of Friday. A new lamp was provided, for his evening work—perhaps it was eye-strain which accounted for this new and so peculiar vagueness of his—Mother was looking at him with amusement as she said this, but with something else as well. A new lamp? A new lamp. Yes Mother, No Mother, Yes Mother. School is going very well. The geometry is very easy. The history is very dull. The geography is very interesting—particularly when it takes one to the North Pole. Why the North Pole? Oh, well, it would be fun to be an explorer. Another Peary or Scott or Shackleton. And then abruptly he found his interest in the talk at an end, stared at the pudding on his plate, listened, waited, and began once more—ah how heavenly, too, the first beginnings—to hear or feel—for could he actually hear it?—the silent snow, the secret snow.

(Miss Buell was telling them about the search for the Northwest Passage, about Hendrik Hudson, the Half Moon.)

This had been, indeed, the only distressing feature of the new experience: the fact that it so increasingly had brought him into a kind of mute misunderstanding, or even conflict, with his father and mother. It was as if he were trying to lead a double life. On the one hand he had to be Paul Hasleman, and keep up the appearance of being that person—dress, wash, and answer intelligently when spoken to; on the other, he had to explore this new world which had been opened to him. Nor could there be the slightest doubt—not the slightest—that the new world was the profounder and more wonderful of the two. It was irresistible. It was miraculous. Its beauty was simply beyond anything—beyond speech as beyond thought—utterly incommunicable. But how then, between the two worlds, of which he was thus constantly aware, was he to keep a balance? One must get up, one must go to breakfast, one must talk with Mother, go to school, do one's lessons—and, in all this, try not to appear too much of a fool. But if all the while one was also trying to extract the full deliciousness of another and quite separate existence, one which could not easily (if at all) be spoken of—how was one to manage? How was one to explain? Would it be safe to explain? Would it be absurd? Would it merely mean that he would get into some obscure kind of trouble?

These thoughts came and went, came and went, as softly and secretly as the snow; they were not precisely a disturbance, perhaps they were even a pleasure; he liked to have them; their presence was something almost palpable, something he could stroke with his hand, without closing his eyes, and without ceasing to see Miss Buell and the school-room and the globe and the freckles on Deirdre's neck; nevertheless he did in a sense cease to see, or to see the obvious external world, and substituted for this vision the vision of snow, the sound of snow, and the slow, almost soundless, approach of the postman. Yesterday, it had been only at the sixth house that the postman had become audible; the snow was deeper now, it was falling more swiftly and heavily, the sound of its seething was more distinct, more soothing, more persistent. And this morning, it had been—as nearly as he could figure—just above the seventh house—perhaps only a step or two above; at most, he had heard two or three footsteps before the knock had sounded. ... And with each such narrowing of the sphere, each nearer approach of the limit at which the postman was first audible, it was odd how sharply was increased the amount of illusion which had to be carried into the ordinary business of daily life. Each day, it was harder to get out of bed, to go to the window, to look out at the—as always—perfectly empty and snowless street. Each day it was more difficult to go through the perfunctory motions of greeting Mother and Father at breakfast, to reply to their questions, to put his books together and go to school. And at school, how extraordinarily hard to conduct with success simultaneously the public life and the life that was secret. There were times when he longed—positively ached—to tell everyone about it—to burst out with it—only to be checked almost at once by a far-off feeling as of some faint absurdity which was inherent in it—but was it absurd?—and more importantly by a sense of mysterious power in his very secrecy. Yes: it must be kept secret. That, more and more, became clear. At whatever cost to himself, whatever pain to others—

(Miss Buell looked straight at him, smiling, and said, "Perhaps we'll ask Paul. I'm sure Paul will come out of his daydream long enough to be able to tell us. Won't you, Paul?" He rose slowly from his chair, resting one hand on the brightly varnished desk, and deliberately stared through the snow towards the blackboard. It was an effort, but it was amusing to make it. "Yes," he said slowly, "it was what we now call the Hudson River. This he thought to be the Northwest Passage. He was disappointed." He sat down again, and as he did so Deirdre half turned in her chair and gave him a shy smile of approval and admiration.)

At whatever pain to others.

This part of it was very puzzling, very puzzling. Mother was very nice, and so was Father. Yes, that was all true enough. He wanted to be nice to them, to tell them everything—and yet, was it really wrong of him to want to have a secret place of his own?

At bedtime, the night before, Mother had said, "If this goes on, my lad, we'll have to see a doctor, we will! We can't have our boy—" But what was it she had said? "Live in another world"? "Live so far away"? The word "far" had been in it, he was sure, and then Mother had taken up a magazine again and laughed a little, but with an expression which wasn't mirthful. He had felt sorry for her. . . .

The bell rang for dismissal. The sound came to him through long curved parallels of falling snow. He saw Deirdre rise, and had himself risen almost as soon—but not quite as soon—as she.

II

On the walk homeward, which was timeless, it pleased him to see through the accompaniment, or counterpoint, of snow, the items of mere externality on his way. There were many kinds of bricks in the sidewalks, and laid in many kinds of patterns. The garden walls too were various, some of wooden palings, some of plaster, some of stone. Twigs of bushes leaned over the walls; the little hard green winter-buds of lilac, on gray stems, sheathed and fat; other branches very thin and fine and black and desiccated. Dirty sparrows huddled in the bushes, as dull in color as dead fruit left in leafless trees. A single starling creaked on a weather vane. In the gutter, beside a drain, was a scrap of torn and dirty newspaper, caught in a little delta of filth: the word ECZEMA appeared in large capitals, and below it was a letter from Mrs. Amelia D. Cravath, 2100 Pine Street, Fort Worth, Texas, to the effect that after being a sufferer for years she had been cured by Caley's Ointment. In the little delta, beside the fan-shaped and deeply runneled continent of brown mud, were lost twigs, descended from their parent trees, dead matches, a rusty horsechestnut burr, a small concentration of sparkling gravel on the lip of the sewer, a fragment of eggshell, a streak of yellow sawdust which had been wet and was now dry and congealed, a brown pebble, and a broken feather. Further on was a cement sidewalk, ruled into geometrical parallelograms, with a brass inlay at one end commemorating the contractors who had laid it, and, halfway across, an irregular and random series of dog-tracks, immortalized in synthetic stone. He knew these well, and always stepped on them; to cover the little hollows with his own foot had always been a queer pleasure; today he did it once more, but perfunctorily, and detachedly, all the while thinking of something else. That was a dog, a long time ago, who had made a mistake and walked on the cement while it was still wet. He had probably wagged his tail, but that hadn't been recorded. Now, Paul Hasleman, aged twelve, on his way home from school, crossed the same river, which in the meantime had frozen into rock. Homeward through the snow falling in bright sunshine. Homeward?

Then came the gateway with the two posts surmounted by egg-shaped stones which had been cunningly balanced on their ends, as if by Columbus, and mortared in the very act of balance: a source of perpetual wonder. On the brick wall just beyond, the letter H had been stenciled, presumably for some purpose. H? H.

The green hydrant, with a little green-painted chain attached to the brass screw-cap.

The elm tree, with the great gray wound in the bark, kidney-shaped, into which he always put his hand—to feel the cold but living wood. The injury, he had been sure, was due to the gnawings of a tethered horse. But now it deserved only passing palm, a merely tolerant eye. There were more important things. Miracles. Beyond the thoughts of trees, mere elms. Beyond the thoughts of sidewalks, mere stone, mere brick, mere cement. Beyond the thoughts even of his own shoes, which trod these sidewalks obediently, bearing a burden—far above—of elaborate mystery. He watched them. They were not very well polished; he had neglected them, for a very good reason: they were one of the many parts of the increasing difficulty of the daily return to daily life, the morning struggle. To get up, having at last opened one's eyes, to go to the window, and discover no snow, to wash, to dress, to descend the curving stairs to breakfast—

At whatever pain to others, nevertheless, one must persevere in severance, since the incommunicability of the experience demanded it. It was desirable of course to be kind to Mother and Father, especially as they seemed to be worried, but it was also desirable to be resolute. If they should decide—as appeared likely —to consult the doctor, Doctor Howells, and have Paul inspected, his heart listened to through a kind of dictaphone, his lungs, his stomach—well, that was all right. He would go through with it. He would give them answer for question, too—perhaps such answers as they hadn't expected? No. That would never do. For the secret world must, at all costs, be preserved.

The bird-house in the apple-tree was empty—it was the wrong time of the year for wrens. The little round black door had lost its pleasure. The wrens were enjoying other houses, other nests, remoter trees. But this too was a notion which he only vaguely and grazingly entertained—as if, for the moment, he merely touched an edge of it; there was something further on, which was already assuming a sharper importance; something which already teased at the corners of his eyes, teasing also at the corner of his mind. It was funny to think that he so wanted this, so awaited it—and yet found himself enjoying this momentary dalliance with the bird-house, as if for a quite deliberate postponement and enhancement of the approaching pleasure. He was aware of his delay, of his smiling and detached and now almost uncomprehending gaze at the little bird-house; he knew what he was going to look at next: it was his own little cobbled hill-street, his own house, the little river at the bottom of the hill, the grocer's shop with the cardboard man in the window—and now, thinking of all this, he turned his head, still smiling, and looking quickly right and left through the snow-laden sunlight.

And the mist of snow, as he had foreseen, was still on it—a ghost of snow falling in the bright sunlight, softly and steadily floating and turning and pausing, soundlessly meeting the snow that covered, as with a transparent mirage, the bare bright cobbles. He loved it—he stood still and loved it. Its beauty was paralyzing—beyond all words, all experience, all dream. No fairy-story he had ever read could be compared with it—none had ever given him this extraordinary combination of ethereal loveliness with a something else, unnameable, which was just faintly and deliciously terrifying. What was this thing? As he thought of it, he looked upward toward his own bedroom window, which was open—and it was as if he looked straight into the room and saw himself lying half awake in his bed. There he was—at this very instant he was still perhaps actually there—more truly there than standing here at the edge of the cobbled hill-street, with one hand lifted to shade his eyes against the snow-sun. Had he indeed ever left his room, in all this time? since that very first morning? Was the whole progress still being enacted there, was it still the same morning, and himself not yet wholly awake? And even now, had the postman not yet come round the corner? . . .

This idea amused him, and automatically, as he thought of it, he turned his head and looked toward the top of the hill. There was, of course, nothing there—nothing and no one. The street was empty and quiet. And all the more because of its emptiness it occurred to him to count the houses—a thing which, oddly enough, he hadn't before thought of doing. Of course, he had known there weren't many—many, that is, on his own side of the street, which were the ones that figured in the postman's progress—but nevertheless it came to him as something of a shock to find that there were precisely *six*, above his own house—his own house was the seventh.

Six!

Astonished, he looked at his own house—looked at the door, on which was the number thirteen—and then realized that the whole thing was exactly and logically and absurdly what he ought to have known. Just the same, the realization gave him abruptly, and even a little frighteningly, a sense of hurry. He was being hurried—he was being rushed. For—he knit his brows—he couldn't be mistaken—it was just above the *seventh* house, his *own* house, that the postman had first been audible this very morning. But in that case—in that case—did it mean that tomorrow he would hear nothing? The knock he had heard must have been the knock of their own door. Did it mean—and this was an idea which gave him a really extraordinary feeling of surprise—that he would never hear the postman again?—that tomorrow morning the postman would already have passed the house, in a snow by then so deep as to render his footsteps completely inaudible? That he would have made his approach down the snow-filled street so soundlessly, so secretly, that he, Paul Hasleman, there lying in bed, would not have waked in time, or, waking, would have heard nothing?

But how could that be? Unless even the knocker should be muffled in the snow—frozen tight, perhaps? . . . But in that case—

A vague feeling of disappointment came over him; a vague sadness, as if he felt himself deprived of something which he had long looked forward to, something much prized. After all this, all this beautiful progress, the slow delicious advance of the postman through the silent and secret snow, the knock creeping closer each day, and the footsteps nearer, and audible compass of the world thus daily narrowed, narrowed, narrowed, as the snow soothingly and beautifully encroached and deepened, after all this, was he to be defrauded of the one thing he had so wanted—to be able to count, as it were, the last two or three solemn footsteps, as they finally approached his own door? Was it all going to happen, at the end, so suddenly? or indeed, had it already happened? with no slow and subtle gradations of menace, in which he could luxuriate?

He gazed upward again, toward his own window which

flashed in the sun: and this time almost with a feeling that it would be better if he *were* still in bed, in that room; for in that case this must still be the first morning, and there would be six more mornings to come—or, for that matter, seven or eight or nine—how could he be sure?—or even more.

III

After supper, the inquisition began. He stood before the doctor, under the lamp, and submitted silently to the usual thumpings and tappings.

"Now will you please say 'Ah!'?"

"Ah!"

"Now again please, if you don't mind."

"Ah!"

"Say it slowly, and hold it if you can—"

"Ah-h-h-h-h-h—"

"Good."

How silly all this was. As if it had anything to do with his throat! Or his heart or lungs!

Relaxing his mouth, of which the corners, after all this absurd stretching, felt uncomfortable, he avoided the doctor's eyes, and stared towards the fireplace, past his mother's feet (in gray slippers) which projected from the green chair, and his father's feet (in brown slippers) which stood neatly side by side on the hearth rug.

"Hm. There is certainly nothing wrong there. . . ."

He felt the doctor's eyes fixed upon him, and, as if merely to be polite, returned the look, but with a feeling of justifiable evasiveness.

"Now, young man, tell me—do you feel all right?"

"Yes, sir, quite all right."

"No headaches? no dizziness?"

"No, I don't think so."

"Let me see. Let's get a book, if you don't mind—yes, thank you, that will do splendidly—and now, Paul, if you'll just read it, holding it as you would normally hold it—"

He took the book and read:

"And another praise have I to tell for this city our mother, the gift of a great god, a glory of the land most high; the might of horses, the might of young horses, the might of the sea. . . . For thou, son of Cronus, our lord Poseidon, hast throned herein this pride, since in these roads first thou didst show forth the curb that cures the rage of steeds. And the shapely oar, apt to man's hands, hath a wondrous speed on the brine, following the hundred-footed

Nereids. . . . O land that art praised above all lands, now is it for thee to make those bright praises seen in deeds."

He stopped, tentatively, and lowered the heavy book.

"No—as I thought—there is certainly no superficial sign of eye-strain."

Silence thronged the room, and he was aware of the focused scrutiny of the three people who confronted him. . . .

"We could have his eyes examined—but I believe it is something else."

"What could it be?" This was his father's voice.

"It's only this curious absent-minded—" This was his mother's voice.

In the presence of the doctor, they both seemed irritatingly apologetic.

"I believe it is something else. Now Paul—I would like very much to ask you a question or two. You will answer them, won't you—you know I'm an old, old friend of yours, eh? That's right! . . ."

His back was thumped twice by the doctor's fat fist—then the doctor was grinning at him with false amiability, while with one fingernail he was scratching the top button of his waistcoat. Beyond the doctor's shoulder was the fire, the fingers of flame making light prestidigitation against the sooty fireback, the soft sound of their random flutter the only sound.

"I would like to know—is there anything that worries you?"

The doctor was again smiling, his eyelids low against the little black pupils, in each of which was a tiny white bead of light. Why answer him? why answer him at all? "At whatever pain to others"—but it was all a nuisance, this necessity for resistance, this necessity for attention: it was as if one had been stood up on a brilliantly lighted stage, under a great round blaze of spotlight; as if one were merely a trained seal, or a performing dog, or a fish, dipped out of an aquarium and held up by the tail. It would serve them right if he were merely to bark or growl. And meanwhile, to miss these last few precious hours, these hours of which every minute was more beautiful than the last, more menacing? He still looked, as if from a great distance, at the beads of light in the doctor's eyes, at the fixed false smile, and then, beyond, once more at his mother's slippers, his father's slippers, and soft flutter of the fire. Even here, even amongst these hostile presences, and in this arranged light, he could see the snow, he could hear it—it was in the corners of the room, where the shadow was deepest, under the sofa, behind the half-opened door which led to the dining room. It was gentler here, softer, its seethe the quietest of whispers, as if, in deference to a drawing room, it had quite deliberately put on its "manners"; it kept itself out of sight, obliterated itself, but distinctly with an air of saying, "Ah, but just wait! Wait till we are alone together! Then I will begin to tell you something new! Something white! something cold! something sleepy! something of cease, and peace, and the long bright curve of space! Tell them to go away. Banish them. Refuse to speak. Leave them, go upstairs to your room, turn out the light and get into bed—I will go with you, I will be waiting for you, I will tell you a better story than Little Kay of the Skates, or The Snow Ghost—I will surround your bed, I will close the windows, pile a deep drift against the door, so that none will ever again be able to enter. Speak to them! . . ." It seemed as if the little hissing voice came from a slow white spiral of falling flakes in the corner by the front window—but he could not be sure. He felt himself smiling, then, and said to the doctor, but without looking beyond him still—

"Oh, no, I think not—"

"But are you sure, my boy?"

His father's voice came softly and coldly then—the familiar voice of silken warning. . . .

"You needn't answer at once, Paul—remember we're trying to help you—think it over and be quite sure, won't you?"

He felt himself smiling again, at the notion of being quite sure. What a joke! As if he weren't so sure that reassurance was no longer necessary, and all this cross-examination a ridiculous farce, a grotesque parody! What could they know about it? These gross intelligences, these humdrum minds so bound to the usual, the ordinary? Impossible to tell them about it! Why, even now, even now, with the proof so abundant, so formidable, so imminent, so appallingly present here in this very room, could they believe it?—could even his mother believe it? No—it was only too plain that if anything were said about it, the merest hint given, they would be incredulous—they would laugh—they would say "Absurd!" think things about him which weren't true. . . .

"Why no, I'm not worried—why should I be?"

He looked then straight at the doctor's low-lidded eyes, looked from one of them to the other, from one bead of light to the other, and gave a little laugh.

The doctor seemed to be disconcerted by this. He drew back in his chair, resting a fat white hand on either knee. The smile faded slowly from his face.

"Well, Paul!" he said, and paused gravely, "I'm afraid you don't take this quite seriously enough. I think you perhaps don't quite realize—don't quite realize—" He took a deep quick breath, and turned, as if helplessly, at a loss for words, to the others. But Mother and Father were both silent—no help was forthcoming.

"You must surely know, be aware, that you have not been quite yourself, of late? don't you know that? . . ."

It was amusing to watch the doctor's renewed attempt at a smile, a queer disorganized look, as of confidential embarrassment.

"I feel all right, sir," he said, and again gave the little laugh.

"And we're trying to help you." The doctor's tone sharpened.

"Yes sir, I know. But why? I'm all right. I'm just *thinking*, that's all."

His mother made a quick movement forward, resting a hand on the back of the doctor's chair.

"Thinking?" she said. "But my dear, about what?"

This was a direct challenge—and would have to be directly met. But before he met it, he looked again into the corner by the door, as if for reassurance. He smiled again at what he saw, at what he heard. The little spiral was still there, still softly whirling, like the ghost of a white kitten chasing the ghost of a white tail, and making as it did so the faintest of whispers. It was all right! If only he could remain firm, everything was going to be all right.

"Oh, about anything, about nothing—*you* know the way you do!"

"You mean—day-dreaming?"

"Oh, no—thinking!"

"But thinking about *what*?"

"Anything."

He laughed a third time—but this time, happening to glance upward towards his mother's face, he was appalled at the effect his laughter seemed to have upon her. Her mouth had opened in an expression of horror. . . . This was too bad! Unfortunate! He had known it would cause pain, of course—but he hadn't expected it to be quite so bad as this. Perhaps—perhaps if he just gave them a tiny gleaming hint—?

"About the snow," he said.

"What on earth!" This was his father's voice. The brown slippers came a step nearer on the hearth rug.

"But my dear, what do you mean?" This was his mother's voice.

The doctor merely stared.

"Just *snow*, that's all. I like to think about it."

"Tell us about it, my boy."

"But that's all it is. There's nothing to tell. *You* know what snow is?"

This he said almost angrily, for he felt they were trying to corner him. He turned sideways so as no longer to face the doctor, and the better to see the inch of blackness between the windowsill and the lowered curtain—the cold inch of beckoning and delicious night. At once he felt better, more assured.

"Mother—can I go to bed, now, please? I've got a headache."

"But I thought you said—"

"It's just come. It's all these questions—! Can I, Mother?"

"You can go as soon as the doctor has finished."

"Don't you think this thing ought to be gone into thoroughly, and now?" This was Father's voice. The brown slippers again came a step nearer, the voice was the well-known "punishment" voice, resonant and cruel.

"Oh, what's the use, Norman—"

Quite suddenly, everyone was silent. And without precisely facing them, nevertheless he was aware that all three of them were watching him with an extraordinary intensity—staring hard at him—as if he had done something monstrous, or was himself some kind of monster. He could hear the soft irregular flutter of the flames; the cluck-click-cluck-click of the clock; far and faint, two sudden spurts of laughter from the kitchen, as quickly cut off as begun; a murmur of water in the pipes; and then, the silence seemed to deepen, to spread out, to become worldlong and worldwide, to become timeless and shapeless, and to center inevitably and rightly, with a slow and sleepy but enormous concentration of all power, on the beginning of a new sound. What this new sound was going to be, he knew perfectly well. It might begin with a hiss, but it would end with a roar—there was no time to lose—he must escape. It mustn't happen here—

Without another word, he turned and ran up the stairs.

IV

Not a moment too soon. The darkness was coming in long white waves. A prolonged sibilance filled the night—a great seamless seethe of wild influence went abruptly across it— a cold low humming shook the windows. He shut the door and flung off his clothes in the dark. The bare black floor was like a little raft tossed in waves of snow, almost overwhelmed, washed under whitely, up again, smothered in curled billows of feather. The snow was laughing: it spoke from all sides at once: it pressed closer to him as he ran and jumped exulting into his bed.

"Listen to us!" it said. "Listen! We have come to tell you the story we told you about. You remember? Lie down. Shut your eyes, now—you will no longer see much—in this white darkness who could see, or want to see? We will take the place of everything. . . . Listen—"

A beautiful varying dance of snow began at the front of the

room, came forward and then retreated, flattened out toward the floor, then rose fountain-like to the ceiling, swayed, recruited itself from a new stream of flakes which poured laughing in through the humming window, advanced again, lifted long white arms. It said peace, it said remoteness, it said cold—it said—

But then a gash of horrible light fell brutally across the room from the opening door—the snow drew back hissing—something alien had come into the room—something hostile. This thing rushed at him, clutched at him, shook him—and he was not merely horrified, he was filled with such a loathing as he had never known. What was this? this cruel disturbance? this act of anger and hate? It was as if he had to reach up a hand toward another world for any understanding of it—an effort of which he was only barely capable. But of that other world he still remembered just enough to know the exorcising words. They tore themselves from his other life suddenly—

"Mother! Mother! Go away! I hate you!"

And with that effort, everything was solved, everything became all right: the seamless hiss advanced once more, the long white wavering lines rose and fell like enormous whispering seawaves, the whisper becoming louder, the laughter more numerous.

"Listen!" it said. "We'll tell you the last, the most beautiful and secret story—shut your eyes—it is a very small story—a story that gets smaller and smaller—it comes inward instead of opening like a flower—it is a flower becoming a seed—a little cold seed —do you hear? we are leaning closer to you—"

The hiss was now becoming a roar—the whole world was a vast moving screen of snow—but even now it said peace, it said remoteness, it said cold, it said sleep.

JANET FRAME/Owls Do Cry

AND DAPHNE lived there alone for many years. It is quiet in the mountain room. Will Toby come or Francie or Chicks, or the mother and father who are set like sculpture, in the same place for ever, with their lives growing up through their body like grass through an ageing monument of stone? Who will come, into the quiet?

Someone stirs in the next room, and sings to curse the west wind and all men, and it is Mona with the olive skin and dark hair and brown eyes like darkened beer. She wants her child back to look at and feed and teach to hate, and sing to,

> —Like this, she says, with my ukelele or guitar in my hand, now what shall I sing. Ah!
>> Sunny Australian sweetheart,
>> I'm in love with you.
>
> —And then the rollicking one, my child, that your father, curse him, sang
>> I'm a rambler, I'm a gambler, I'm a long way from home
>> And if you don't like me then leave me alone.
>> I eat when I'm hungry and I drink when I'm dry,
>> And if moonshine don't kill me, I'll live till I die.

And then, in case her child that she holds now in her arms to sing to and teach to hate, may be left hungry, she thinks of its food and tells from the side of the mountain to the world, not of milk flowing rich and yellow, crusted with love, from the breast or the cow's teat when the new calf butts and dances, hornless and still wet from birth: but

> *cheese blisters,* how to mix them, how to cook them, and
> —Do you know cheese blisters, Mona cries. Do you *know* them? They crackle and are salt, like blood, mixed with cheese that is old soured milk, skim milk, blue and deprived, the dregs of love. Do you know cheese blisters? Do you *know* them? Is there anyone there to answer me?

Daphne, in the next room, does not answer, for she waits for Toby to come, or Francie, or Chicks with a little pocket of wheat to share and share alike. Ah, there is a footstep outside the door, the eyes of the world look through the hole in the door, the key turns in the lock and here is a member of the white tribe, the chief perhaps, come to say why and where and how.

> And then,
> —Now. Where are you? the chief said. Do you know now where you are? You have been sick for a long time. What month and year is it? Or what day? Do you know your name?
>
> And then,
> —Why are you here? Do you know why you are here?

And all the time Flora Norris stood beside him, her hands clasped behind her back, her face cut through with the wire from the dream nasturtium, her lips pressed close to imprison the hallucinatory kiss of thirty years ago.

> —Tell him, Daphne, she said, unclasping her ringless antiseptic hands and uniting them in front, beneath her breast.
> —Don't be afraid. Talk to him.

Daphne sat in the corner upon her straw mattress, her legs covered with a piece of torn blanket, her nightie, striped and oblong on her like a faded peppermint stick.

—Tell him, Daphne, urged Flora Norris again.

Daphne said nothing. Inside herself she thought,

They are mad. They are frauds. They are thieves who sneak through the night and day of their lives, exchanging their counterfeit whys and hows and wheres, like fake diamonds and gold, to zip them inside their leather human brain till the next raid and violence of exchanging, when they jingle their clay and glass baubles, untouched by sun, in their hands, and cry out,

—Who'll buy our answers, genuine treasure, who'll buy?

They are frauds, for the real how and where and who and why are in the circle of toi-toi, with the beautiful ledger writing and the book thrown away that told of Tom Thumb sitting in the horse's ear; and the sun shining through the sacrificial fire, to make real diamonds and gold. And we sat, didn't we, Toby, Chicks and Francie, as the world sits in the morning, unafraid, touching how and why and where, the wonder currency that I take with me, slipped in the lining of my heart, to hide it because I know. And Toby carries it backward and forward across continents and seas and does not understand it though it glitters and strikes part of the fire in him; and Chicks is afraid, and covers it with a washing-machine and refrigerator, and a space-heater behind glass.

Everything behind glass is valuable.

So Daphne thought and did not speak, and the chief of the white tribe, who wore spectacles, and carried in his pocket the sprout of a rubber tree to listen at the underground door of the heart and its beating of secret, walked forward and smiled encouragingly, saying

—Now now, Daphne, speak to me, like a good girl. We are going to make you better after all this time. You'll be home soon.

And still Daphne did not speak, so the chief tried a different subject, forgetting how and why and where, but a question, all the same.

—How are your bowels, he said. And your water?

Flora Norris moved impatiently and pulled hold of Daphne's shoulders,

—Can't you understand? she said. You're being spoken to.

And then Daphne moved and slapped the face of Flora Norris, digging her hands in the barbed wire, yet feeling for one instant the velvet and warmth of the dream nasturtium; and turning to the white chief she pushed him back to the door so that, almost toppling, he cried out a protesting

—Now now, my dear.

And with a sideways glance at Flora Norris, a curious look at the new flower growing on her right cheek, he whispered, pointing to Daphne,

—She's dangerous. Give her a sedative.
Flora Norris, recovered and withered, said swiftly,
—Certainly doctor.

And both left the room, locking the door, and peeping finally with the eyes of the world, through the hole in the door, to see if any evidence of storm remained in the small mountain room.

And after they had gone Daphne crept to the door, and poking her finger through the hole, waited there, many hours it seemed, for someone to come and hang upon her finger, a gentian or snowberry or a penny orange, or one stalk of snowgrass plucked from as high as larks fly to sing.

In the morning at six o'clock, half-dark for autumn, the nurse gave Daphne clothes, a pair of long grey woollen socks like Christmas and the fireplace and Toby crying because he was sick and couldn't look inside to see the presents; he was in bed, kept there until the doctor came to write his code writing in the black book and order the new bottle of pills; in bed, with a clean pillowcase and the only clean sheet, otherwise the doctor would notice, and ring up the health inspector from the corner telephone box where a man in a crimson coat and felt slippers, tore the directory in half, twice, to become the champion of the world, champion at tearing things to pieces. There are so many possible champions, you would think there is room for all people to be one and wear a medal and carry a certificate, rolled up, to be unrolled and the fancy writing pointed to with pride. And when the health inspector came he would have the family turned out of their home to sit in the gutter, with a penny box of matches to sell in the driving snow, and no one buying them, and the whole family, mother and father and Francie and Toby and Daphne and Chicks looking up at the lights in the rich people's houses, and seeing their feasts on the table, the white tablecloth and the candles lit upon the cake.

Yes, a pair of long woollen socks; and a pair of pants. Only
—There's a pants for you, the maori nurse said. And a striped blue smock, galatea, and a grey jersey.
—Put these on, Daphne. You're to get up.

And there was a yard full of people hopping and skipping and dancing and crying and laughing fighting and screaming and dead. Daphne sat in the corner by the wall. There were nails growing, like flowers, out of the top of the wall, except they were no colour and there to hurt if you tried to climb over.

Daphne sat all morning in the corner, and spoke to no one, only stared at the people hopping and skipping and dancing and crying and laughing and screaming and fighting and dead.

There were two girls, young, but ageless now, twins, toothless, crawling their sixteen years back and forth across the grey crater, their sun-stained faces fixed toward nothing, unless to the time after the Bomb and the emptiness; their throats gurgling and choking with the speech of idiocy; and their big brown eyes full of gentleness. Barbara and Leila. All day performing their dress and undress, submitting their clothes and body each to the other, crooning and wailing their animal vision of domesticity and doom. And the maori nurse watching, fat and smiling, her legs wide, her large feet cramped in the once white, now yellow, shoes; the cigarettes in her pocket, and the matches and keys; or frowning and calling in the mellow voice,
—Lavatory ladies,
grabbing the necks of the grey jerseys and the people inside them, dragging them to the door, pushing them inside; then, bawling at them, mocking them, happy with them, dressing them as a child will dress a world of witless blinking dolls that are wound for nothing save crying mama mama, and wetting; and walking half a dozen steps at a time, without direction or meaning; and the maori nurse with creek-water eyes and paddle-flat nose, thinking
—I'll have a hundred babies for my granny to look after, eh, up north in the sun.

And so passed one morning and every morning and day but the people growing gentle and together, like old bulbs without promise of bloom, thrown to the rubbish heap and sinking in the filth and blindness to sprout a separate community of dark, touching tendril and root to yet invisible colour of maimed flowers, narcissus, daffodil, tulip, and crocus-leaf stained with blade of snow.

And the night. The dormitory, and the rigid, afraid and wandering people, knowing the mountain outside and the wild storms there, huddling into their bedclothes, all of them; save Florence, sitting up to comb her hair called argent, hidden all day with the red and blue handkerchief tied across it; Florence talking, like a spell, of the places up north, and of herself being an orphan alone there, working at two years of age in the city pubs, filling the beer for the wild and bearded men; two years old, catching the tram to the city, struggling through the crowd, but travelling free because she was Florence, two years old, working as barmaid in the pub. And Florence, stroking the spell from her hair waist-long and called argent, is believed and loved and none laugh at her or contradict her dream; nor the dream of any, save the ungentle and aggressive, who wear their dream closer, the gentleness inside to the heart to keep it warm but not sharing. *And the grey crater of the long-dead mad lies empty enough to be filled with many truths together....*

The year of Christmas and picnic was a confused and strange time, not like any other time of Christmas or picnic; first, the colour of both was a white of death, the cottonwool of pretended birth, and the star of manuka fixed nowhere for any world to follow. And the same year, in winter-time, there was a dance, where the men from their side of the mountain were encouraged to rejoice with the women from *their* side of the mountain, while the chief and Flora Norris and Sister Dulling watched, saying,

—Dance, dance. Get up and dance. What do you think we put on a dance for if you don't dance?

So the patients danced, being told to, and the women were dressed like real ladies in the same bright picnic frocks, though this was June, with the night set on the windowpanes before sundown, and the plaster walls of the rooms lined with drops of water, or

damp,

as Flora Norris called it.

—Look, Doctor, the rooms are damp. We must have them seen to.

And the chief nodded and replied that certainly he would have it seen to, or make a note of it, or refer it to someone who would refer it to the proper quarter.

Most certainly.

Yes, it was June that they danced, when in the world, as you know who live there, young ladies are being measured and fitted for their coming-out dresses; and choosing their long gloves; and between talk of swot and the music master, preparing to attend their first real ball, and be presented to the Bishop or the Governor-General, or the local member of parliament, or whoever has what is called dignity and standing in the community. Ah, June is a romantic time, no matter how cold the park seats or the sand dunes and the lupins, or the garden, that has no summerhouse now, but a little green gnome, giving no shade or sympathy.

Now, all day the men in the mountain world prepared for the dance of the evening. Most of them had a bath, queueing outside the bathroom and being warned not to waste the water; others were bathed by force, with the attendant hopping them in and out, quickly, to put clean clothes on them and make them smell sweeter than they smell every other day, working in the garden and on the farm with the cows and pigs, or shovelling coal, or sorting the dirty laundry. When the canteen opened at one o'clock those who could free themselves from their work were there to buy hair-oil and hair-cream, or perhaps a new tie, the cheating type that you pin on and do not have to struggle with; or a new handkerchief, or a pen to put in their pocket, displaying it there, as if they worked in an office, and were not patients. So that when the time came for the dance that was held from six o'clock until ten o'clock, the band arrived from town, sleek, and in evening dress, sitting on the stage, waiting, whispering together, smiling, amused. And there were the women sitting on the long forms against one wall, and the men on the long forms against the other wall, with the powdered floor between, and the smell everywhere of perfume and talcum powder and hair-oil, while the nurses and Flora Norris and the bigger chiefs sat on red velvet chairs, watching and pointing.

When the first dance began, the nurses walked up and down the wall on the women's side, and the attendants on the men's, saying,

—Dance. Dance. Go on, get up and dance!

So they danced, being told to, like real ladies and gentlemen, except the men sweated and smelt and held too closely and the women forgot to listen to the orchestra so that people had their feet trodden on, and no one apologised but laughed instead and said,

—It serves you right.

So they danced or walked or hopped or twirled round and round in the same place, and though it was a joking time, with a fine supper afterwards, no one will deny that inside was crying and confusion. The bandsmen kept darting to the back of the stage for a drink of whisky, and returning full of laughter, to play more vigorously their tango or foxtrot, while the pianist jigged up and down at the piano, playing hot rhythm.

At ten o'clock sharp the people were stripped of their finery and thrust back into the ashes, and no woman left a pink and dainty slipper of satin or glass lying on the dance floor, for the prince to find, nor was there any prince. The room was left empty and stuffy and smelling of tobacco.

—Open a window, for goodness' sake, said Flora Norris.

No, there was no magic slipper lying anywhere on the floor. If there had been, imagine the excitement, with Flora Norris and Sister Dulling and the nurses arguing to say,

—It's mine, it's mine, it fits me well,

and not knowing that to walk in its glitter they would need to hack their heel of reason till the blood flowed and they cried out with the torture of it.

The day after the strange time and the sitting among the dry beans in the ashes, counting two and two make five, a nurse peeped through the door of Daphne's mountain room, and seeing Daphne safe on the straw mattress, opened the door,

—Daphne, she said.

She was the maori nurse, with a bag of toffees in her pocket. She gave Daphne a toffee.

—Here. Catch. Come with me, Daphne, the matron wants you.

She took Daphne to the office where the matron sat at her desk, busy with charts and books and half-opened parcels.

—Ah, Daphne dear.

The matron drew from the corner a screen that slipped along on wheels and had a pattern on it of roses and rose leaves, two roses to each flap of screen.

—For greater privacy, explained Flora Norris. You wait there, nurse, in case I need you.

Flora Norris seemed to want everything very private. She put out her hand and touched Daphne on the shoulder. The girl shivered and drew back nearer the door and Flora Norris advanced, grim, like a close-up, her hand extended with its fingers hung like icicles.

—Now Daphne, this all comes to us sooner or later, you know, and we have to bear it, haven't we?

Daphne did not answer. She was tearing the giant roses to shreds and casting the petals in the face of Flora Norris, each petal slicing the matron's skin so that blood flowed to make a real rose blossoming upon the screen that seemed not a screen any more, for hiding behind, though who could be looking and why, except God, who may or may not be at home. Ah, thought Daphne, what is matron going to tell me?

—Are you listening, Daphne? We all have to bear it.

Daphne looked slyly at her, and smiled, because she knew what Flora Norris was taking her behind a screen to tell her. It was death. You have to hide behind a screen to talk of death, the way you cover your face with a handkerchief, ashamed, to hide your crying. Daphne knew it was death, and her mother was dead, and she waited for the matron to tell her.

—Yes, Daphne, it comes to us all, and we must be very, very brave.

Why do I talk this way, like a parson, thought Flora Norris. I'm talking to a half-wit, a loony, though one doesn't use that term now, not officially. I don't think she can understand what I'm telling her, and it's almost morning tea time, and I'm dying on my feet for a cup of tea and a bun filled with cream. I seem to have had no sleep last night, with all that dancing to take charge of, and the fuss afterwards to get them back to their wards and undressed, and then, on my rounds, seeing the rouged and powdered women, unwashed, sitting up in bed like gargoyles, with the night running down their faces and a dream smearing their eyes. Oh hell.

—Daphne, there's a telegram to say your mother died last night. Peacefully. All is well.

The matron signalled to the nurse to be ready, in case. Daphne smiled gently, and danced the foxtrot, or was it the destiny or maxina that Francie said you dance with your heartbeats matching? Was it the maxina or destiny? Or foxtrot? Daphne could not remember. She knew it was some kind of dance but she could not remember; so she pushed the overpowering roses and the screen out of the way so God could see, and danced her dance, to music, up and down the office and then out the door while Flora Norris called

—Nurse! Nurse! Whatever are you thinking of? Get her, get her, she's desperate.

They grabbed Daphne, as she danced the last of the foxtrot, and not even picking up her dropped satin slipper, they hurried her to the mountain room where she sat alone, in the pouring rain, with no coat on, while her mother called anxiously from the door

—Daphne! Daphne! You'll get your death of cold. Come in out of the rain.

And then her mother sang the song they all knew, Francie and Daphne and Toby and Chicks; half-wailing it so that it seemed tragic and terrible

> *Come in you naughty bird*
> *the rain is pouring down*
> *what would your mother say*
> *if you stay there and drown?*
> *You are a very naughty bird*
> *you do not think of me,*
> *I'm sure I do not care,*
> *said the sparrow on the tree....*

They sat afraid and silent on the edge of a long form of leather, with no back rest, so that their backs ached; but continued to sit upright, staring ahead at the hard fire that burned brilliantly and coldly like a coloured glacier. No warmth came from the fireplace, and Toby and his father shivered, gazing past the heavy fire-guard to the flames leaping remotely and ineffectually behind their iron cage.

Toby spoke.

—It's cold, he said.

The old woman sitting next to him on the couch answered him.

—It's warm. There's that lovely fire, she said, pointing to the blaze.

She had come to visit her daughter, she said, she came every week and knew the routine and was used to the strangeness. She had beside her a brown paper bag full of cream cakes and a thermos flask filled with tea, made at home. She and Alfreda were going to have a picnic.

—We have a picnic every time I come, she said to Toby. Alfreda is so fond of these cakes and she likes tea made at home, instead of the hospital tea. You can understand that, can't you?

She spoke the last sentence to Bob who sat holding tight to the basket he and Toby had carried between them up the hill, fighting like children to carry it,

—Let me, no, let me. Why do you want to hold it?

—Well, why do *you* want to hold it?

—It's something to hold.

Their basket held a bag of oranges and bananas and a cake of chocolate.

—Yes, it's cold, Toby repeated.

The woman glanced curiously at him. She was going to remind them both, him and the old man with him, who seemed to be shivering yet sat muffled in that smart-looking tweed overcoat, that there was a lovely fire in front of them, and what more could they ask for on a cold day like this with the winter still hanging on?

—The winter seems to be hanging on, she said.

Toby said in a loud voice,

—*Yes, the winter is hanging on, its teeth are indrawn like the teeth of an eel and that is why it is hanging on. Whatever it swallows will never escape from the black coil of winter.*

The woman looked uncertain, and thought, It must be in the family. Some of these visitors, I've noticed, are queerer than the patients.

Bob said suddenly,

—Don't, Toby. For God's sake keep quiet. Don't say things out loud like that! Think of your poor mother!

The other visitors in the room had stopped talking and were watching Bob and Toby. And then the nurse brought Alfreda, and Alfreda's mother moved along for her daughter to sit beside her. Alfreda was a dwarf, three feet high.

—Hello, slut, the dwarf said, in a hoarse voice, and dived for the bag of cream cakes which she swallowed, one after the other, without stopping to talk, while her mother sat watching

her. When Alfreda had finished the cakes she held up the thermos flask.
—What's this?
—That's tea, her mother said. Real home-made tea. We'll have a cup, shall we?
—Go to blazes and keep your tea. What else have you brought?
—There's a new pair of pants for you, from Aunty Molly.
—Pants, pants, can't anyone think of anything else but pants? And when am I going home?

She leaned to her mother, her eyes intense, her face full of scorn. Her mother smiled,
—The doctor says quite soon, Alfreda.
—Oh, go to hell.

And Alfreda got up and went to the door and called for the nurse.
—What did you dress me up for visitors when it's only that old slut, she called. Let's out of here.

The nurse, who was never far away, took Alfreda back to her ward. Alfreda's mother picked up her bag and smiling cheerfully at Toby and Bob, she went, with the remains of her picnic, to the nurse at the door to be let out.

And Toby and his father sat waiting for the nurse to bring Daphne. Bob Withers, looking about the room at the groups of visitors and patients, each, seemingly, with its separate picnic, thought, Daphne won't be like them, anyway, she'll be different. She won't swear and go on, she'll be quite different. What shall I say to her? How did she take her mother's death, I wonder? Should I say something about that? Good Lord, no.

But what if she doesn't know me?

He leaned to Toby.
—I say, Toby.

Toby was sitting in a dream, it was a fit coming, he thought, and here of all places, but how could he stop it. He knew that he shouldn't have come, and *then the cattle in the paddocks and on the railway stations, drinking their blue-lined cups of tea; their eyes and faces, and their horns growing like ivory trees, what could he do to stop it; and then the eel that was winter swallowing up the leaves and colour, and if you put your hand or heart down the throat of winter to seize what had been taken, you would have your hand and heart torn to pieces. It was a fit coming on, Toby thought, and he hadn't had a fit for a long time, not for very long, it was a fit coming on and what about Daphne, and then there was his mother too, taking up so much space. And the things to sell, at the rubbish dump, not this rubbish dump or that rubbish dump but which one; yes, surely it was a fit coming on and who could stop it?*

—I say, Toby.

But Toby fell forward suddenly upon the floor, his body writhing in the old way, his eyes vanished inwards to nothing and his face like a heavy damson plum, and where was Amy Withers to say,

—Take your teeth out, Toby. Take your teeth out.

And lay him on the sofa and put a coat over him to keep him warm, and have a cup of tea for afterwards, and words that said,

—It will go away, Toby. It won't be for always, and you will grow out of them and be like other boys.

His father knelt down beside him, saying,

—Toby. Toby.

The bananas had fallen on the floor, with the oranges, and the cake of chocolate lay near the fire that must have been warm and they had not known it, for the chocolate twisted and writhed with a curious liquid life of its own. And the nurse from the door came quickly to Toby and took his teeth out and put them upon the mantelpiece, and taking a wooden stick wrapped in gauze, like a stick of marzipan, she thrust it inside Toby's mouth, and his mouth chewed violently upon it until the fit was over and he fell into a deep sleep, his face peaceful, still flushed, and his hands clasped around the bag, now empty, that they had carried and quarreled over because it was something to hold on to.

The nurse was calm.

—We see these every day, she said to Bob. Are you waiting for someone?

—My daughter, Daphne Withers, said Bob.

The nurse looked surprised.

—Oh, she said. Oh, I'll find out.

She went into the office and Bob could hear her telephoning.

She returned.

—Go through the door. The nurse will let you through.

—But what about Toby?

—I'm afraid he can't go, it wouldn't be advisable, it will be too late when he wakes.

—But I can't leave him here.

Bob Withers was afraid. He had heard of people disappearing inside these hospitals, and then, when they said they were visitors, no one would let them out, and no one believed them. Why, anything could happen in a hospital like this, after all, it was still the dark ages.

The nurse divined his fears. She saw many visitors panic.
—You need not worry, she said. Mr. Withers will be here when you return. You have to go through there to visit Daphne because she's a special.
—A what?
—A special.

To Bob Withers a special was some line of food or clothing put cheap in the shops on a Friday, for the people to buy.

The nurse led him past rows of old women in bed, sleeping, or perhaps dead, with their mouth open and their cheeks hollow, and he thought, So this is where they put the old people.

And they came to a small room with a barred window and two chairs and a small table with a vase of violets upon it, made of crepe paper, though Bob did not notice at first and stooped to smell them, thinking, They're in flower early, they must be hothouse.

The nurse watched him.
—They're artificial, she said. Don't they look real?

She offered Bob one of the chairs and left the room. Bob sat down. He had nothing to give Daphne. He hadn't brought the bag of bananas and oranges, and the chocolate had melted. How then, would he begin his conversation? He rehearsed to himself,
—Well Daphne, so they're going to make you better tomorrow. And then it will be all over.

What would be all over? He didn't quite know. As far as he was concerned everything was over, so what did it matter, and here he was, how strange, sitting in a loony cell with Lou's overcoat on that still smelt of bath salts.

He began again
—Hello Daphne. Or should it be Daffy? And why didn't they hurry? His heart was beating too quickly, he felt, and his hands were shaking, old age coming on, and he felt tired, very tired with nowhere to go because the home was dead now and the frost had got the early plums, and he remembered that he had hidden the girdle that Amy made pikelets on, away in the shed behind the gramophone and the old kitchen table, and could not bear any more to look upon it.

If Sister Dulling had not worn her starched uniform and veil flowing and white, though not bridal, she would have looked like a barmaid. She was broad and coarse with her pale red hair and a welter of uncomfortable fat on her body, so that she tried not to eat between meals, but smoked then, to keep her from feeling hungry; and while the nurses picked at sweets and cakes at morning and afternoon tea, Sister Dulling said,
—No thank you, I prefer not to.

Except for an occasional biscuit when the doctor came in for a cup of tea, and

—Is your tea right? Would you like more sugar? A little weaker, perhaps? she would say to the doctor, who sat on the best chair in the office and drank from the best cup, with red string tied around its handle, so as to distinguish from the patients' cups.

And while the doctor drank his tea and smiled his glory around the staff-room, Sister Dulling would find big words to use, difficult words from the Medical Dictionary or the Shorter Oxford Dictionary that she kept in the desk for reference in writing her daily reports and sounding impressive. Other times she used the words more suited to her as a barmaid in disguise, yet a nurse too, who could talk to and tame the wild people so that they followed and obeyed her and gave her presents—the stalk of a flower, an empty envelope, a shoelace, a picture torn from one of the magazines, of real people living in a real house where the doors and windows open, and you know where the key is, hanging on the nail in the scullery.

The afternoon that Bob and Toby Withers came to visit Daphne, Sister Dulling herself had dressed her patient, giving her a ward skirt and pullover, new stockings, her Christmas pants, kept ready and marked with white tape, and a hat with a wide brim, the only hat she could find in the clothes room, to cover Daphne's head in case her relatives felt afraid and startled at the baldness.

—A nice hat for you, Daphne. Makes you look like a film star.

Daphne in the dead room looked up at the nice hat, seeing only its brown verandah and straw-lined eaves and feeling the heaviness of snow that had fallen all night for years upon the brown roof. She felt safe under the hat. The rain could not fall and her mother would not have to be standing at the door and crying out,

—Come in you naughty bird, out of the rain.

Daphne smiled then, remembering she was a don't care sparrow, and threw the hat into the corner.

Sister Dulling clicked her tongue.

—Your father is waiting for you, she said. You wouldn't disappoint him would you? He has come in the train.

Come in the train? If you come in the train you are always disappointed because it never takes you where you would like it to go, it takes you on and on to the waste world of swamp and mai-mai, with all the people crouched inside to break the back of paradise. Trains take you to the end. My father is disappointed whether he sees me or not, because he is sitting in his hut on the swamp, with a licence to die held in his hand and his gun ready to fire at the first sign of peace. How the snow falls on my head. I think there will be a storm.

—Come Daphne.

Sister Dulling replaced the hat on Daphne's head and led her to the room where Bob Withers sat, afraid and tired, jigging his knee because it was something to do.

—I'll be in the next room, if you want me, said Sister, with her greet-the-visitor smile.

Daphne stood in one corner of the room and looked at the man sitting on the chair. His face was pale and grey as if he had walked through dust for many years so that it clung to the folds of his clothing and covered his shoes and settled in his hair to make it grey. He has been standing up in the sky, she thought. And is covered with cloud. He has been sweeping out a crumbling house of stone. He has no wife to sweep for him and wear an apron for the children to cling to and cry in when they are hurt. I wish, she thought, I wish he would find a brush and make his suit look clean. And polish his shoes. He sits there, dirty and grey and licking his lips and does not seem to speak.

Who is he? Is he waiting for me to speak?

Pressing her lips together she sat down on the floor, first removing her hat for the sake of courtesy, as she had been taught when the sun stayed early in the sky; and watched the face of the grey man. When she took off her hat and laid it down like a laced straw well to catch the storm from the cloud, she saw the man's mouth open and his face wrinkle, as if he would cry, the way her father's face had changed when he heard that Francie was burned, and came home and saw them all clinging together like the people in the story who stuck under a spell; though not dancing up and down the cobbles of a fairy street; but crying. And the grey man in the chair, at the same time that he changed his face to look like Daphne's father crying, called out,

—Don't. Oh my God, no!
and looked at where her hair had been. With his eyes popping wide and his face afraid.

Then he said,

—Daphne. Everything's going to be all right.

But Daphne knew he was talking to himself, telling himself not to worry, that everything would be all right, though it was strange how he had discovered her name, and knew her to look at, that she ought to have had hair. And she should have hair too. Oh yes Daphne thought, I should have long hair to comb like a mermaid. But I have no hair, the woman from the underworld has taken it, so I shall put my hat on to hide that I am bald, like a front lawn or a park in the city or a picnic ground.

She put her hat on, and the grey man smiled and said kindly,
>—Hello Daphne. My word, it's cold out. We haven't seen the last of winter.

Daphne smiled at him, he was so strange and grey like chalk.

He smiled back and smoothed his hands together.
>—It won't be long now, he said, before you're home.

Daphne suddenly spoke, in a loud voice that made the nurse peep in the door,
>—What's at home? Are Mum and Dad and Francie and Toby and Chicks at home?

The nurse withdrew and the grey man smoothed his hands again and licked his lips.
>—Yes, he said. They're all at home.
>—Say them, then. Say them.
>—You mean their names?
>—Say them, and tell me.

The grey man repeated the names over, Mum and Dad and Francie and Toby and Chicks.

Daphne listened and thought, He's a cheat. He says the names as if he had learned them, like mountains, Rimutaka, Tararua, Ruahine, Kaimanawa; or like the names of towns where wollen mills are built; Bradford, Leeds, Halifax, Huddersfield. He is in league with the woollen mills and the small rooms on the side of the mountain.
>—I hate you, she said. Go away. The snow is too heavy in falling and it falls criss-cross, like a tapestry, so go away.

She came forward and saw that the grey man was shivering.
>—Say the names, she said, as if you don't know them. Say them new and just born.

He repeated the names slowly in a tired voice—Mum, Dad, Toby, Francie, Chicks.

Then he walked towards the door. She followed him,
>—What's Dad doing? she asked.

He hesitated.
>—Your father's gardening, he said. The frost has got the seed potatoes.
>—What's Francie doing?
>—Oh, Francie. Well, Francie's away just now. At work. At Mawhinneys.
>—What's she doing?
>—Oh. Peeling potatoes, I think.
>—And what's Toby doing?
>—Selling his scraps. He's in his truck.

Bob Withers had grown more composed. He felt in a dream,

as if he were playing a fantastic parlour game and must make no mistake.

—And what is Chicks doing?

—She's playing with her dolls, dressing them and wheeling them up and down.

—We never had dolls, said Daphne. We had clothes-pegs, which were better. And what's Mum doing?

—Your mother, said Bob Withers, is making pikelets.

Then he put his hands over his face and went from the room, and the nurse, curious, watched him go down the corridor and be let through the place where the old women lay. He reached the room where he had left Toby. He expected to find the room gone or changed somehow, as if he had dreamed it, and no people sitting with baskets of food, eating cream cakes and drinking thermos tea; but everything was the same except that Toby was sitting by the fire, crouched over it. He looked blue and cold like a man leaning towards a glacier. He spoke of Daphne.

—How is she, Dad? You were quick. How does she find the life here? The nurse was telling me they play tennis and have dances.

Bob picked up the empty bag.

—Where's the fruit?

—I gave it to the nurse. Some of the patients have no visitors.

—We'd better go. We're late. I heard of someone who was locked up in a place like this, through being late.

—How's Daphne?

Toby stood up to go, and shivered with the cold of the mountain wind and his father glanced apprehensively at him.

—You're all right? he said.

—Did Daphne know you and talk to you? The nurse was telling me that some of them don't even know their own mother and father.

—Oh, Bob answered quickly, Daphne's not like that. She's different. She's not like the rest of these queer people. Different altogether, and talking sensibly.

—How does she look? Does her hair still fall over her face?

Bob laughed.

—Too right, and she's brushing it away. She reminded me of Chicks the way she brushes her hair out of her eyes.

—But the operation will make her even better?

—Of course.

And back in the small room, Daphne, being undressed and put early to bed ready for the next day was thinking, I think he told me a lie about my mother. I think she was washing clothes and darning socks and not making pikelets. And I think that man was my father, no matter how much he pretended to be no relation and didn't kiss me hello and bring me a bag of fruit and a cake of chocolate; he was my father and couldn't deceive me. And my mother is sitting at home now, with a handleless cup stuck in the heel of my brother's thick grey work-sock, and darning the hole, criss-cross criss-cross, the way snow falls like snipped white wool through an empty sky. And my mother is prodding the clothes that bubble in the copper, and feeding the fire underneath with sticks of apple-box and pine cones while the cat twines about her heavy varicose legs and her feet move like laden ships, burst at the side, on a forever journey across wood and concrete seas, where the only sails are sheets, pyjamas, underpants and towels, pegged up to slap the worn winter face of a snivelling sunlight.

All this, except that my mother is dead, and I die tomorrow when snow falls criss-cross criss-cross to darn the believed crevice of my world.

GUY DE MAUPASSANT/The Horla

MAR. 8. What a lovely day! I have spent all the morning lying on the grass in front of my house, under the enormous plantain tree which covers and shades and shelters the whole of it. I like this part of the country; I am fond of living here because I am attached to it by deep roots, the profound and delicate roots which attach a man to the soil on which his ancestors were born and died, to their traditions, their usages, their food, the local expressions, the peculiar language of the peasants, the smell of the soil, the hamlets, and to the atmosphere itself.

I love the house in which I grew up. From my windows I can see the Seine, which flows by the side of my garden, on the other side of the road, almost through my grounds, the great and wide Seine, which goes to Rouen and Havre, and which is covered with boats passing to and fro.

On the left, down yonder, lies Rouen, populous Rouen with its blue roofs massing under pointed Gothic towers. Innumerable are they, delicate or broad, dominated by the spire of the cathedral, full of bells, which sound through the blue air on fine mornings, sending their sweet and distant iron clang to me, their metallic sounds, now stronger and now weaker, according as the wind is strong or light.

What a delicious morning it was! About eleven o'clock, a

long line of boats drawn by a steam-tug, as big as a fly, and which scarcely puffed while emitting its thick smoke, passed my gate.

After two English schooners, whose red flags fluttered toward the sky, there came a magnificent Brazilian three-master; it was perfectly white and wonderfully clean and shining. I saluted it, I hardly know why, except that the sight of the vessel gave me great pleasure.

May 12. I have had a slight feverish attack for the last few days, and I feel ill, or rather I feel low-spirited.

Whence come those mysterious influences which change our happiness into discouragement, and our self-confidence into diffidence? One might almost say that the air, the invisible air, is full of unknowable Forces, whose mysterious presence we have to endure. I wake up in the best of spirits, with an inclination to sing in my heart. Why? I go down by the side of the water, and surdenly, after walking a short distance, I return home wretched, as if some misfortune were awaiting me there. Why? Is it a cold shiver which, passing over my skin, has upset my nerves and given me a fit of low spirits? Is it the form of the clouds, or the tints of the sky, or the colors of the surrounding objects which are so changeable, which have troubled my thoughts as they passed before my eyes? Who can tell? Everything that surrounds us, everything that we see without looking at it, everything that we touch without knowing it, everything that we handle without feeling it, everything that we meet without clearly distinguishing it, has a rapid, surprising, and inexplicable effect upon us and upon our organs, and through them on our ideas and on our being itself.

How profound that mystery of the Invisible is! We cannot fathom it with our miserable senses: our eyes are unable to perceive what is either too small or too great, too near to or too far from us; we can see neither the inhabitants of a star nor of a drop of water; our ears deceive us, for they transmit to us the vibrations of the air in sonorous notes. Our senses are fairies who work the miracle of changing that movement into noise, and by that metamorphosis give birth to music, which makes the mute agitation of nature a harmony. So with our sense of smell, which is weaker than that of a dog, and so with our sense of taste, which can scarcely distinguish the age of a wine!

Oh! If we only had other organs which could work other miracles in our favor, what a number of fresh things we might discover around us!

May 16. I am ill, decidedly! I was so well last month! I am feverish, horribly feverish, or rather I am in a state of feverish enervation, which makes my mind suffer as much as my body. I have without ceasing the horrible sensation of some danger threatening me, the apprehension of some coming misfortune or of approaching death, a presentiment which is, no doubt, an attack of some illness still unnamed, which germinates in the flesh and in the blood.

May 18. I have just come from consulting my medical man, for I can no longer get my sleep. He found that my pulse was high, my eyes dilated, my nerves highly strung, but no alarming symptoms. I must have a course of shower baths and of bromide of potassium.

May 25. No change! My state is really very peculiar. As the evening comes on, an incomprehensible feeling of disquietude seizes me, just as if night concealed some terrible menace toward me. I dine quickly, and then try to read, but I do not understand the words, and can scarcely distinguish the letters. Then I walk up and down my drawing-room, oppressed by a feeling of confused and irresistible fear, a fear of sleep and a fear of my bed.

About ten o'clock I go up to my room. As soon as I have entered I lock and bolt the door. I am frightened—of what? Up till the present time I have been frightened of nothing. I open my cupboards, and look under my bed; I listen—I listen—to what? How strange it is that a simple feeling of discomfort, of impeded or heightened circulation, perhaps the irritation of a nervous center, a slight congestion, a small disturbance in the imperfect and delicate functions of our living machinery, can turn the most light-hearted of men into a melancholy one, and make a coward of the bravest? Then, I go to bed, and I wait for sleep as a man might wait for the executioner. I wait for its coming with dread, and my heart beats and my legs tremble, while my whole body shivers beneath the warmth of the bedclothes, until the moment when I suddenly fall asleep, as a man throws himself into a pool of stagnant water in order to drown. I do not feel this perfidious sleep coming over me as I used to, but a sleep which is close to me and watching me, which is going to seize me by the head, to close my eyes and annihilate me.

I sleep—a long time—two or three hours perhaps—then a dream—no—a nightmare lays hold of me. I feel that I am in bed and asleep—I feel it and I know it—and I feel also that somebody is coming close to me, is looking at me, touching me, is getting onto my bed, is kneeling on my chest, is taking my neck between his hands and squeezing it—squeezing it with all his might in order to strangle me.

I struggle, bound by that terrible powerlessness which paralyzes us in our dreams; I try to cry out—but I cannot; I want to move—I cannot; I try, with the most violent efforts and out of breath, to turn over and throw off this being which is crushing and suffocating me—I cannot!

And then suddenly I wake up, shaken and bathed in perspiration; I light a candle and find that I am alone, and after that crisis, which occurs every night, I at length fall asleep and slumber tranquilly till morning.

June 2. My state has grown worse. What is the matter with me? The bromide does me no good, and the shower-baths have no effect whatever. Sometimes, in order to tire myself out, though I am fatigued enough already, I go for a walk in the forest of Roumare. I used to think at first that the fresh light and soft air, impregnated with the odor of herbs and leaves, would instill new life into my veins and impart fresh energy to my heart. One day I turned into a broad ride in the wood, and then I diverged toward La Bouille, through a narrow path, between two rows of exceedingly tall trees, which placed a thick, green, almost black roof between the sky and me.

A sudden shiver ran through me, not a cold shiver, but a shiver of agony, and so I hastened my steps, uneasy at being alone in the wood, frightened stupidly and without reason, at the profound solitude. Suddenly it seemed as if I were being followed, that somebody was walking at my heels, close, quite close to me, near enough to touch me.

I turned round suddenly, but I was alone. I saw nothing behind me except the straight, broad ride, empty and bordered by high trees, horribly empty; on the other side also it extended until it was lost in the distance, and looked just the same—terrible.

I closed my eyes. Why? And then I began to turn round on one heel very quickly, just like a top. I nearly fell down, and opened my eyes; the trees were dancing round me and the earth heaved; I was obliged to sit down. Then, ah! I no longer remembered how I had come! What a strange idea! What a strange, strange idea! I did not the least know. I started off to the right, and got back into the avenue which had led me into the middle of the forest.

June 3. I have had a terrible night. I shall go away for a few weeks, for no doubt a journey will set me up again.

July 2. I have come back, quite cured, and have had a most delightful trip into the bargain. I have been to Mont Saint-Michel, which I had not seen before.

What a sight, when one arrives as I did, at Avranches toward the end of the day! The town stands on a hill, and I was taken into the public garden at the extremity of the town. I uttered a cry of astonishment. An extraordinarily large bay lay extended before me, as far as my eyes could reach, between two hills which were lost to sight in the mist; and in the middle of this immense yellow bay, under a clear, golden sky, a peculiar hill rose up, somber and pointed in the midst of the sand. The sun had just disappeared, and under the still flaming sky stood out the outline of that fantastic rock, which bears on its summit a picturesque monument.

At daybreak I went to it. The tide was low, as it had been the night before, and I saw that wonderful abbey rise up before me as I approached it. After several hours' walking, I reached the enormous mass of rock which supports the little town, dominated by the great church. Having climbed the steep and narrow street, I entered the most wonderful Gothic building that has ever been erected to God on earth, large as a town, and full of low rooms which seem buried beneath vaulted roofs, and of lofty galleries supported by delicate columns.

I entered this gigantic granite jewel, which is as light in its effect as a bit of lace and is covered with towers, with slender belfries to which spiral staircases ascend. The flying buttresses raise strange heads that bristle with chimeras, with devils, with fantastic animals, with monstrous flowers, are joined together by finely carved arches, to the blue sky by day, and to the black sky by night.

When I had reached the summit, I said to the monk who accompanied me: "Father, how happy you must be here!" And he replied: "It is very windy, Monsieur"; and so we began to talk while watching the rising tide, which ran over the sand and covered it with a steel cuirass.

And then the monk told me stories, all the old stories belonging to the place—legends, nothing but legends.

One of them struck me forcibly. The country people, those belonging to the Mornet, declare that at night one can hear talking going on in the sand, and also that two goats bleat, one with a strong, the other with a weak voice. Incredulous people declare that it is nothing but the screaming of the sea birds, which occasionally resembles bleatings, and occasionally human lamentations; but belated fishermen swear that they have met an old shepherd, whose cloak-covered head they can never see, wandering on the sand, between two tides, round the little town placed so far out of the world. They declare he is guiding and walking before a he-goat with a man's face and a she-goat with a woman's face, both with white hair, who talk incessantly, quarreling in a strange language, and then suddenly cease talking in order to bleat with all their might.

"Do you believe it?" I asked the monk. "I scarcely know," he replied; and I continued: "If there are other beings besides ourselves on this earth, how comes it that we have not known it for so long a time, or why have you not seen them? How is it that I have not seen them?"

He replied: "Do we see the hundred-thousandth part of

what exists? Look here; there is the wind, which is the strongest force in nature. It knocks down men, and blows down buildings, uproots trees, raises the sea into mountains of water, destroys cliffs and casts great ships onto the breakers; it kills, it whistles, it sighs, it roars. But have you ever seen it, and can you see it? Yet it exists for all that."

I was silent before this simple reasoning. That man was a philosopher, or perhaps a fool; I could not say which exactly, so I held my tongue. What he had said had often been in my own thoughts.

July 3. I have slept badly; certainly there is some feverish influence here, for my coachman is suffering in the same way as I am. When I went back home yesterday, I noticed his singular paleness, and I asked him: "What is the matter with you, Jean?"

"The matter is that I never get any rest, and my nights devour my days. Since your departure, Monsieur, there has been a spell over me."

However, the other servants are all well, but I am very frightened of having another attack, myself.

July 4. I am decidedly taken again; for my old nightmares have returned. Last night I felt somebody leaning on me who was sucking my life from between my lips with his mouth. Yes, he was sucking it out of my neck as a leech would have done. Then he got up, satiated, and I woke up, so beaten, crushed, and annihilated that I could not move. If this continues for a few days, I shall certainly go away again.

July 5. Have I lost my reason? What has happened? What I saw last night is so strange that my head wanders when I think of it!

As I do now every evening, I had locked my door; then, being thirsty, I drank half a glass of water, and I accidentally noticed that the water-bottle was full up to the cut-glass stopper.

Then I went to bed and fell into one of my terrible sleeps, from which I was aroused in about two hours by a still more terrible shock.

Picture to yourself a sleeping man who is being murdered, who wakes up with a knife in his chest, a gurgling in his throat, is covered with blood, can no longer breathe, is going to die and does not understand anything at all about it—there you have it.

Having recovered my senses, I was thirsty again, so I lighted a candle and went to the table on which my water-bottle was. I lifted it up and tilted it over my glass, but nothing came out. It was empty! It was completely empty! At first I could not understand it at all; then suddenly I was seized by such a terrible feeling that I had to sit down, or rather fall into a chair! Then I sprang up with a bound to look about me; then I sat down again, overcome by astonishment and fear, in front of the transparent crystal bottle! I looked at it with fixed eyes, trying to solve the puzzle, and my hands trembled! Somebody had drunk the water, but who? I? I without any doubt. It could surely only be I? In that case I was a somnambulist—was living, without knowing it, that double, mysterious life which makes us doubt whether there are not two beings in us—whether a strange, unknowable, and invisible being does not, during our moments of mental and physical torpor, animate the inert body, forcing it to a more willing obedience than it yields to ourselves.

Oh! Who will understand my horrible agony? Who will understand the emotion of a man sound in mind, wide-awake, full of sense, who looks in horror at the disappearance of a little water while he was asleep, through the glass of a water-bottle! And I remained sitting until it was daylight, without venturing to go to bed again.

July 6. I am going mad. Again all the contents of my water-bottle have been drunk during the night; or rather I have drunk it!

But is it I? Is it I? Who could it be? Who? Oh! God! Am I going mad? Who will save me?

July 10. I have just been through some surprising ordeals. Undoubtedly I must be mad! And yet!

On July 6, before going to bed, I put some wine, milk, water, bread, and strawberries on my table. Somebody drank—I drank—all the water and a little of the milk, but neither the wine, nor the bread, nor the strawberries were touched.

On the seventh of July I renewed the same experiment, with the same results, and on July 8 I left out the water and the milk and nothing was touched.

Lastly, on July 9 I put only water and milk on my table, taking care to wrap up the bottles in white muslin and to tie down the stoppers. Then I rubbed my lips, my beard, and my hands with pencil lead, and went to bed.

Deep slumber seized me, soon followed by a terrible awakening. I had not moved, and my sheets were not marked. I rushed to the table. The muslin round the bottles remained intact; I undid the string, trembling with fear. All the water had been drunk, and so had the milk! Ah! Great God! I must start for Paris immediately.

July 12. Paris. I must have lost my head during the last few days! I must be the plaything of my enervated imagination, unless I am really a somnambulist, or I have been brought under the power of one of those influences—hypnotic suggestion, for example—which are known to exist, but have hitherto been inexplicable. In any case, my mental state bordered on madness, and twenty-four hours of Paris sufficed to restore me to my equilibrium.

Yesterday after doing some business and paying some visits, which instilled fresh and invigorating mental air into me, I wound up my evening at the Théâtre Français. A drama by Alexander Dumas the Younger was being acted, and his brilliant and powerful play completed my cure. Certainly solitude is dangerous for active minds. We need men around us who can think and can talk. When we are alone for a long time, we people space with phantoms.

I returned along the boulevards to my hotel in excellent spirits. Amid the jostling of the crowd I thought, not without irony, of my terrors and surmises of the previous week, because I believed, yes, I believed, that an invisible being lived beneath my roof. How weak our mind is; how quickly it is terrified and unbalanced as soon as we are confronted with a small, incomprehensible fact. Instead of dismissing the problem with: "We do not understand because we cannot find the cause," we immediately imagine terrible mysteries and supernatural powers.

July 14. Fête of the Republic. I walked through the streets, and the crackers and flags amused me like a child. Still, it is very foolish to make merry on a set date, by Government decree. People are like a flock of sheep, now steadily patient, now in ferocious revolt. Say to it: "Amuse yourself," and it amuses itself. Say to it: "Go and fight with your neighbor," and it goes and fights. Say to it: "Vote for the Emperor," and it votes for the Emperor; then say to it: "Vote for the Republic," and it votes for the Republic.

Those who direct it are stupid, too; but instead of obeying men they obey principles, a course which can only be foolish, ineffective, and false, for the very reason that principles are ideas which are considered as certain and unchangeable, whereas in this world one is certain of nothing, since light is an illusion and noise is deception.

July 16. I saw some things yesterday that troubled me very much.

I was dining at my cousin's, Madame Sablé, whose husband is colonel of the Seventy-sixth Chasseurs at Limoges. There were two young women there, one of whom had married a medical man, Dr. Parent, who devotes himself a great deal to nervous diseases and to the extraordinary manifestations which just now experiments in hypnotism and suggestion are producing.

He related to us at some length the enormous results obtained by English scientists and the doctors of the medical school at Nancy, and the facts which he adduced appeared to me so strange that I declared that I was altogether incredulous.

"We are," he declared, "on the point of discovering one of the most important secrets of nature, I mean to say, one of its most important secrets on this earth, for assuredly there are some up in the stars, yonder, of a different kind of importance. Ever since man has thought, since he has been able to express and write down his thoughts, he has felt himself close to a mystery which is impenetrable to his coarse and imperfect senses, and he endeavors to supplement the feeble penetration of his organs by the efforts of his intellect. As long as that intellect remained in its elementary stage, this intercourse with invisible spirits assumed forms which were commonplace though terrifying. Thence sprang the popular belief in the supernatural, the legends of wandering spirits, of fairies, of gnomes, of ghosts, I might even say the conception of God, for our ideas of the Workman-Creator, from whatever religion they may have come down to us, are certainly the most mediocre, the stupidest, and the most unacceptable inventions that ever sprang from the frightened brain of any human creature. Nothing is truer than what Voltaire says: 'If God made man in His own image, man has certainly paid Him back again.'

"But for rather more than a century, men seem to have had a presentiment of something new. Mesmer and some others have put us on an unexpected track, and within the last two or three years especially, we have arrived at results really surprising."

My cousin, who is also very incredulous, smiled, and Dr. Parent said to her: "Would you like me to try and send you to sleep, Madame?"

"Yes, certainly."

She sat down in an easy-chair, and he began to look at her fixedly, as if to fascinate her. I suddenly felt myself somewhat discomposed; my heart beat rapidly and I had a choking feeling in my throat. I saw that Madame Sablé's eyes were growing heavy, her mouth twitched, and her bosom heaved, and at the end of ten minutes she was asleep.

"Go behind her," the doctor said to me; so I took a seat behind her. He put a visiting-card into her hands, and said to her: "This is a looking-glass; what do you see in it?"

She replied: "I see my cousin."

"What is he doing?"

"He is twisting his mustache."

"And now?"

"He is taking a photograph out of his pocket."

"Whose photograph is it?"

"His own."

That was true, for the photograph had been given me that same evening at the hotel.

"What is his attitude in this portrait?"

"He is standing up with his hat in his hand."

She saw these things in that card, in that piece of white pasteboard, as if she had seen them in a looking-glass.

The young women were frightened, and exclaimed: "That is quite enough! Quite, quite enough!"

But the doctor said to her authoritatively: "You will get up at eight o'clock tomorrow morning; then you will go and call on your cousin at his hotel and ask him to lend you the five thousand francs which your husband asks of you, and which he will ask for when he sets out on his coming journey."

Then he woke her up.

On returning to my hotel, I thought over this curious *séance* and I was assailed by doubts, not as to my cousin's absolute and undoubted good faith, for I had known her as well as if she had been my own sister ever since she was a child, but as to a possible trick on the doctor's part. Had not he, perhaps, kept a glass hidden in his hand, which he showed to the young woman in her sleep at the same time as he did the card? Professional conjurers do things which are just as singular.

However, I went to bed, and this morning, at about half past eight, I was awakened by my footman, who said to me: "Madame Sablé has asked to see you immediately, Monsieur." I dressed hastily and went to her.

She sat down in some agitation, with her eyes on the floor, and without raising her veil said to me: "My dear cousin, I am going to ask a great favor of you."

"What is it, cousin?"

"I do not like to tell you, and yet I must. I am in absolute want of five thousand francs."

"What, you?"

"Yes, I, or rather my husband, who has asked me to procure them for him."

I was so stupefied that I hesitated to answer. I asked myself whether she had not really been making fun of me with Dr. Parent, if it were not merely a very well-acted farce which had been got up beforehand. On looking at her attentively, however, my doubts disappeared. She was trembling with grief, so painful was this step to her, and I was sure that her throat was full of sobs.

I knew that she was very rich and so I continued: "What! Has not your husband five thousand francs at his disposal? Come, think. Are you sure that he commissioned you to ask me for them? Are you absolutely sure?"

She hesitated for a few seconds, as if she were making a great effort to search her memory, and then she replied: "Yes—yes, I am quite sure of it."

"He has written to you?"

She hesitated again and reflected, and I guessed the torture of her thoughts. She did not know. She only knew that she was to borrow five thousand francs of me for her husband. So she told a lie.

"Yes, he has written to me."

"When, pray? You did not mention it to me yesterday."

"I received his letter this morning."

"Can you show it to me?"

"No; no—no—it contained private matters, things too personal to ourselves. I burned it."

"So your husband runs into debt?"

She hesitated again, and then murmured: "I do not know."

Thereupon I said bluntly: "I have not five thousand francs at my disposal at this moment, my dear cousin."

She uttered a cry, as if she were in pain and said: "Oh! oh! I beseech you, I beseech you to get them for me."

She got excited and clasped her hands as if she were praying to me! I heard her voice change its tone; she wept and sobbed, harassed and dominated by the irresistible order that she had received.

"Oh! oh! I beg you to—if you knew what I am suffering—I want them today."

I had pity on her: "You shall have them by and by, I swear to you."

"Oh! thank you! thank you! How kind you are."

I continued: "Do you remember what took place at your house last night?"

"Yes."

"Do you remember that Dr. Parent sent you to sleep?"

"Yes."

"Oh! Very well then; he ordered you to come to me this morning to borrow five thousand francs, and at this moment you are obeying that suggestion."

She considered for a few moments, and then replied: "But as it is my husband who wants them—"

For a whole hour I tried to convince her, but could not succeed, and when she had gone I went to the doctor. He was just going out, and he listened to me with a smile, and said: "Do you believe now?"

"Yes, I cannot help it."

"Let us go to your cousin's."

She was already resting on a couch, overcome with fatigue. The doctor felt her pulse, looked at her for some time with one hand raised toward her eyes, which she closed by degrees under the irresistible power of this magnetic influence. When she was asleep, he said:

"Your husband does not require the five thousand francs any longer! You must, therefore, forget that you asked your cousin to lend them to you, and, if he speaks to you about it, you will not understand him."

Then he woke her up, and I took out a pocketbook and said: "Here is what you asked me for this morning, my dear cousin." But she was so surprised, that I did not venture to persist; nevertheless, I tried to recall the circumstance to her, but she denied it vigorously, thought that I was making fun of her, and in the end, very nearly lost her temper.

There! I have just come back, and I have not been able to eat any lunch, for this experiment has altogether upset me.

July 19. Many people to whom I have told the adventure have laughed at me. I no longer know what to think. The wise man says: Perhaps?

July 21. I dined at Bougival, and then I spent the evening at a boatmen's ball. Decidedly everything depends on place and surroundings. It would be the height of folly to believe in the supernatural on the *Ile de la Grenouillière*.* But on the top of Mont Saint-Michel or in India, we are terribly under the influence of our surroundings. I shall return home next week.

July 30. I came back to my own house yesterday. Everything is going on well.

August 2. Nothing fresh; it is splendid weather, and I spend my days in watching the Seine flow past.

August 4. Quarrels among my servants. They declare that the glasses are broken in the cupboards at night. The footman accuses the cook, she accuses the needlewoman, and the latter accuses the other two. Who is the culprit? It would take a clever person to tell.

August 6. This time, I am not mad. I have seen—I have seen—I have seen!—I can doubt no longer—*I have seen it!*

I was walking at two o'clock among my rose-trees, in the full sunlight—in the walk bordered by autumn roses which are beginning to fall. As I stopped to look at a Géant de Bataille, which had three splendid blooms, I distinctly saw the stalk of one of the roses bend close to me, as if an invisible hand had bent it, and then break, as if that hand had picked it! Then the flower

---
* Frog-island.

raised itself, following the curve which a hand would have described in carrying it toward a mouth, and remained suspended in the transparent air, alone and motionless, a terrible red spot, three yards from my eyes. In desperation I rushed at it to take it! I found nothing; it had disappeared. Then I was seized with furious rage against myself, for it is not wholesome for a reasonable and serious man to have such hallucinations.

But was it a hallucination? I turned to look for the stalk, and I found it immediately under the bush, freshly broken, between the two other roses which remained on the branch. I returned home, then, with a much disturbed mind; for I am certain now, certain as I am of the alternation of day and night, that there exists close to me an invisible being who lives on milk and on water, who can touch objects, take them and change their places; who is, consequently, endowed with a material nature, although imperceptible to sense, and who lives as I do, under my roof—

August 7. I slept tranquilly. He drank the water out of my decanter, but did not disturb my sleep.

I ask myself whether I am mad. As I was walking just now in the sun by the riverside, doubts as to my own sanity arose in me; not vague doubts such as I have had hitherto, but precise and absolute doubts. I have seen mad people, and I have known some who were quite intelligent, lucid, even clear-sighted in every concern of life, except on one point. They could speak clearly, readily, profoundly on everything; till their thoughts were caught in the breakers of their delusions and went to pieces there, were dispersed and swamped in that furious and terrible sea of fogs and squalls which is called *madness.*

I certainly should think that I was mad, absolutely mad, if I were not conscious that I knew my state, if I could not fathom it and analyze it with the most complete lucidity. I should, in fact, be a reasonable man laboring under a hallucination. Some unknown disturbance must have been excited in my brain, one of those disturbances which physiologists of the present day try to note and to fix precisely, and that disturbance must have caused a profound gulf in my mind and in the order and logic of my ideas. Similar phenomena occur in dreams, and lead us through the most unlikely phantasmagoria, without causing us any surprise, because our verifying apparatus and our sense of control have gone to sleep, while our imaginative faculty wakes and works. Was it not possible that one of the imperceptible keys of the cerebral finger-board had been paralyzed in me? Some men lose the recollection of proper names, or of verbs, or of numbers, or merely of dates, in consequence of an accident. The localization of all the avenues of thought has been accomplished nowadays; what, then, would there be surprising in the fact that my faculty of controlling the unreality of certain hallucinations should be destroyed for the time being?

I thought of all this as I walked by the side of the water. The sun was shining brightly on the river and made earth delightful, while it filled me with love for life, for the swallows, whose swift agility is always delightful in my eyes, for the plants by the riverside, whose rustling is a pleasure to my ears.

By degrees, however, an inexplicable feeling of discomfort seized me. It seemed to me as if some unknown force were numbing and stopping me, were preventing me from going further and were calling me back. I felt that painful wish to return which comes on you when you have left a beloved invalid at home, and are seized by a presentiment that he is worse.

I, therefore, returned despite myself, feeling certain that I should find some bad news awaiting me, a letter or a telegram. There was nothing, however, and I was surprised and uneasy, more so than if I had had another fantastic vision.

August 8. I spent a terrible evening, yesterday. He does not show himself any more, but I feel that He is near me, watching me, looking at me, penetrating me, dominating me, and more terrible to me when He hides himself thus than if He were to manifest his constant and invisible presence by supernatural phenomena. However, I slept.

August 9. Nothing, but I am afraid.

August 10. Nothing; but what will happen tomorrow?

August 11. Still nothing. I cannot stop at home with this fear hanging over me and these thoughts in my mind; I shall go away.

August 12. Ten o'clock at night. All day long I have been trying to get away, and have not been able. I contemplated a simple and easy act of liberty, a carriage ride to Rouen—and I have not been able to do it. What is the reason?

August 13. When one is attacked by certain maladies, the springs of our physical being seem broken, our energies destroyed, our muscles relaxed, our bones to be as soft as our flesh, and our blood as liquid as water. I am experiencing the same in my moral being, in a strange and distressing manner. I have no longer any strength, any courage, any self-control, nor even any power to set my own will in motion. I have no power left to *will* anything, but some one does it for me and I obey.

August 14. I am lost! Somebody possesses my soul and governs it! Somebody orders all my acts, all my movements, all my thoughts. I am no longer master of myself, nothing except an enslaved and terrified spectator of the things which I do. I wish to go out; I cannot. *He* does not wish to; and so I remain, trembling and distracted in the armchair in which he keeps me sitting. I merely wish to get up and to rouse myself, so as to think that I am still master of myself: I cannot! I am riveted to my chair, and my chair adheres to the floor in such a manner that no force of mine can move us.

Then suddenly, I must, I *must* go to the foot of my garden to pick some strawberries and eat them—and I go there. I pick the strawberries and I eat them! Oh! my God! my God! Is there a God? If there be one, deliver me! save me! succor me! Pardon! Pity! Mercy! Save me! Oh! what sufferings! what torture! what horror!

August 15. Certainly this is the way in which my poor cousin was possessed and swayed, when she came to borrow five thousand francs of me. She was under the power of a strange will which had entered into her, like another soul, a parasitic and ruling soul. Is the world coming to an end?

But who is He, this invisible being that rules me, this unknowable being, this rover of a supernatural race?

Invisible beings exist, then! How is it, then, that since the beginning of the world they have never manifested themselves in such a manner as they do to me? I have never read anything that resembles what goes on in my house. Oh! If I could only leave it, if I could only go away and flee, and never return, I should be saved; but I cannot.

August 16. I managed to escape today for two hours, like a prisoner who finds the door of his dungeon accidentally open. I suddenly felt that I was free and that He was far away, and so I gave orders to put the horses in as quickly as possible, and I drove to Rouen. Oh! how delightful to be able to say to my coachman: "Go to Rouen!"

I made him pull up before the library, and I begged them to lend me Dr. Herrmann Herestauss's treatise on the unknown inhabitants of the ancient and modern world.

Then, as I was getting into my carriage, I intended to say: "To the railway station!" but instead of this I shouted—I did not speak, but I shouted—in such a loud voice that all the passers-by turned round: "Home!" and I fell back onto the cushion of my carriage, overcome by mental agony. He had found me out and regained possession of me.

August 17. Oh! What a night! what a night! And yet it seems to me that I ought to rejoice. I read until one o'clock in the morning! Herestauss, Doctor of Philosophy and Theogony, wrote the history and the manifestation of all those invisible beings which hover around man, or of whom he dreams. He describes their origin, their domains, their power; but none of them resembles the one which haunts me. One might say that man, ever since he has thought, has had a foreboding and a fear of a new being, stronger than himself, his successor in this world, and that, feeling him near, and not being able to foretell the nature of the unseen one, he has, in his terror, created the whole race of hidden beings, vague phantoms born of fear.

Having, therefore, read until one o'clock in the morning, I went and sat down at the open window, in order to cool my forehead and my thoughts in the calm night air. It was very pleasant and warm! How I should have enjoyed such a night formerly!

There was no moon, but the stars darted out their rays in the dark heavens. Who inhabits those worlds? What forms, what living beings, what animals are there yonder? Do those who are thinkers in those distant worlds know more than we do? What can they do more than we? What do they see which we do not? Will not one of them, some day or other, traversing space, appear on our earth to conquer it, just as formerly the Norsemen crossed the sea in order to subjugate nations feebler than themselves?

We are so weak, so powerless, so ignorant, so small—we who live on this particle of mud which revolves in liquid air.

I fell asleep, dreaming thus in the cool night air, and then, having slept for about three quarters of an hour, I opened my eyes without moving, awakened by an indescribably confused and strange sensation. At first I saw nothing, and then suddenly it appeared to me as if a page of the book, which had remained open on my table, turned over of its own accord. Not a breath of air had come in at my window, and I was surprised and waited. In about four minutes, I saw, I saw—yes I saw with my own eyes—another page lift itself up and fall down on the others, as if a finger had turned it over. My armchair was empty, appeared empty, but I knew that He was there, He, and sitting in my place, and that He was reading. With a furious bound, the bound of an enraged wild beast that wishes to disembowel its tamer, I crossed my room to seize Him, to strangle Him, to kill Him! But before I could reach it, my chair fell over as if somebody had run away from me. My table rocked, my lamp fell and went out, and my window closed as if some thief had been surprised and had fled out into the night, shutting it behind him.

So He had run away; He had been afraid; He, afraid of me!

So tomorrow, or later—some day or other, I should be able to hold him in my clutches and crush him against the ground! Do not dogs occasionally bite and strangle their masters?

August 18. I have been thinking the whole day long. Oh! yes, I will obey Him, follow His impulses, fulfill all His wishes, show myself humble, submissive, a coward. He is the stronger; but an hour will come.

August 19. I know, I know, I know all! I have just read the following in the *Revue du Monde Scientifique:* "A curious piece of news comes to us from Rio de Janeiro. Madness, an epidemic of madness, which may be compared to that contagious madness which attacked the people of Europe in the Middle Ages, is at this moment raging in the Province of San-Paulo. The frightened inhabitants are leaving their houses, deserting their villages, abandoning their land, saying that they are pursued, possessed, governed like human cattle by invisible, though tangible beings, by a species of vampire, which feeds on their life while they are asleep, and which, besides, drinks water and milk without appearing to touch any other nourishment.

"Professor Don Pedro Henriques, accompanied by several medical savants, has gone to the Province of San-Paulo, in order to study the origin and the manifestations of this surprising madness on the spot, and to propose such measures to the Emperor as may appear to him to be most fitted to restore the mad population to reason."

Ah! Ah! I remember now that fine Brazilian three-master which passed in front of my windows as it was going up the Seine, on the eighth of last May! I thought it looked so pretty, so white and bright! That Being was on board of her, coming from there, where its race sprang from. And it saw me! It saw my house, which was also white, and He sprang from the ship on to the land. Oh! Good heavens!

Now I know, I can divine. The reign of man is over, and He has come. He whom disquieted priests exorcised, whom sorcerers evoked on dark nights, without seeing him appear, He to whom the imaginations of the transient masters of the world lent all the monstrous or graceful forms of gnomes, spirits, genii, fairies, and familiar spirits. After the coarse conceptions of primitive fear, men more enlightened gave him a truer form. Mesmer divined him, and ten years ago physicans accurately discovered the nature of his power, even before He exercised it himself. They played with that weapon of their new Lord, the sway of a mysterious will over the human soul, which had become enslaved. They called it mesmerism, hypnotism, suggestion, I know not what. I have seen them diverting themselves like rash children with this horrible power! Woe to us! Woe to man! He has come, the—the—what does He call Himself—the—I fancy that He is shouting out His name to me and I do not hear Him—the—yes—He is shouting it out—I am listening—I cannot—repeat—it—Horla—I have heard—the Horla—it is He—the Horla—He has come!—

Ah! the vulture has eaten the pigeon, the wolf has eaten the lamb; the lion has devoured the sharp-horned buffalo; man has killed the lion with an arrow, with a spear, with gunpowder; but the Horla will make of man what man has made of the horse and of the ox: His chattel, His slave, and His food, by the mere power of His will. Woe to us!

But, nevertheless, sometimes the animal rebels and kills the man who has subjugated it. I should also like—I shall be able to— but I must know Him, touch Him, see Him! Learned men say that eyes of animals, as they differ from ours, do not distinguish as ours do. And my eye cannot distinguish this newcomer who is oppressing me.

Why? Oh! Now I remember the words of the monk at Mont Saint-Michel: "Can we see the hundred-thousandth part of what exists? Listen; there is the wind which is the strongest force in nature; it knocks men down, blows down buildings, uproots trees, raises the sea into mountains of water, destroys cliffs, and casts great ships onto the breakers; it kills, it whistles, it sighs, it roars—have you ever seen it, and can you see it? It exists for all that, however!"

And I went on thinking: my eyes are so weak, so imperfect, that they do not even distinguish hard bodies, if they are as transparent as glass! If a glass without quicksilver behind it were to bar my way, I should run into it, just like a bird which has flown into a room breaks its head against the windowpanes. A thousand things, moreover, deceive a man and lead him astray. How then is it surprising that he cannot perceive a new body which is penetrated and pervaded by the light?

A new being! Why not? It was assuredly bound to come! Why should we be the last? We do not distinguish it, like all the others created before us? The reason is, that its nature is more delicate, its body finer and more finished than ours. Our make-up is so weak, so awkwardly conceived; our body is encumbered with organs that are always tired, always being strained like locks that are too complicated; it lives like a plant and like an animal nourishing itself with difficulty on air, herbs, and flesh; it is a brute machine which is a prey to maladies, to malformations, to decay; it is broken-winded, badly regulated, simple and eccentric, ingeniously yet badly made, a coarse and yet a delicate mechanism, in brief, the outline of a being which might become intelligent and great.

There are only a few—so few—stages of development in this world, from the oyster up to man. Why should there not be one more, when once that period is accomplished which separates the successive products one from the other?

Why not one more? Why not, also, other trees with immense, splendid flowers, perfuming whole regions? Why not other elements besides fire, air, earth, and water? There are four, only four, nursing fathers of various beings! What a pity! Why should not there be forty, four hundred, four thousand! How poor everything is, how mean and wretched—grudgingly given, poorly invented, clumsily made! Ah! the elephant and the hippopotamus, what power! And the camel, what suppleness!

But the butterfly, you will say, a flying flower! I dream of one that should be as large as a hundred worlds, with wings whose shape, beauty, colors, and motion I cannot even express. But I see it—it flutters from star to star, refreshing them and perfuming them with the light and harmonious breath of its flight! And the people up there gaze at it as it passes in an ecstasy of delight!

What is the matter with me? It is He, the Horla who haunts me, and who makes me think of these foolish things! He is within me, He is becoming my soul; I shall kill Him!

August 20. I shall kill Him. I have seen Him! Yesterday I sat down at my table and pretended to write very assiduously. I knew quite well that He would come prowling round me, quite close to me, so close that I might perhaps be able to touch Him, to seize Him. And then—then I should have the strength of desperation; I should have my hands, my knees, my chest, my forehead, my teeth to strangle Him, to crush Him, to bite Him, to tear Him to pieces. And I watched for Him with all my overexcited nerves.

I had lighted my two lamps and the eight wax candles on my mantelpiece, as if, by this light I should discover Him.

My bed, my old oak bed with its columns, was opposite to me; on my right was the fireplace; on my left the door, which was carefully closed, after I had left it open for some time, in order to attract Him; behind me was a very high wardrobe with a looking-glass in it, which served me to dress by every day, and in which I was in the habit of inspecting myself from head to foot every time I passed it.

So I pretended to be writing in order to deceive Him, for He also was watching me, and suddenly I felt, I was certain, that He was reading over my shoulder, that He was there, almost touching my ear.

I got up so quickly, with my hands extended, that I almost fell. Horror! It was as bright as at midday, but I did not see myself in the glass! It was empty, clear, profound, full of light! But my figure was not reflected in it—and I, I was opposite to it! I saw the large, clear glass from top to bottom, and I looked at it with unsteady eyes. I did not dare advance; I did not venture to make a movement; feeling certain, nevertheless, that He was there, but that He would escape me again, He whose imperceptible body had absorbed my reflection.

How frightened I was! And then suddenly I began to see myself through a mist in the depths of the looking-glass, in a mist as it were, or through a veil of water; and it seemed to me as if this water were flowing slowly from left to right, and making my figure clearer every moment. It was like the end of an eclipse. Whatever hid me did not appear to possess any clearly defined outlines, but was a sort of opaque transparency, which gradually grew clearer.

At last I was able to distinguish myself completely, as I do every day when I look at myself.

I had seen Him! And the horror of it remained with me, and makes me shudder even now.

August 21. How could I kill Him, since I could not get hold of Him? Poison? But He would see me mix it with the water; and then, would our poisons have any effect on His impalpable body? No—no—no doubt about the matter. Then?—then?

August 22. I sent for a blacksmith from Rouen and ordered iron shutters of him for my room, such as some private hotels in Paris have on the ground floor, for fear of thieves, and he is going to make me a similar door as well. I have made myself out a coward, but I do not care about that!

September 10. Rouen, Hotel Continental. It is done; it is done—but is He dead? My mind is thoroughly upset by what I have seen.

Well then, yesterday, the locksmith having put on the iron shutters and door, I left everything open until midnight, although it was getting cold.

Suddenly I felt that He was there, and joy, mad joy took possession of me. I got up softly, and I walked to the right and left for some time, so that He might not guess anything; then I took off my boots and put on my slippers carelessly; then I fastened the iron shutters and going back to the door quickly I double-locked it with a padlock, putting the key into my pocket.

Suddenly I noticed that He was moving restlessly round me, that in His turn He was frightened and was ordering me to let Him out. I nearly yielded, though I did not quite, but putting my back to the door, I half opened it, just enough to allow me to go out backward, and as I am very tall, my head touched the lintel. I was sure that He had not been able to escape, and I shut Him up quite alone, quite alone. What happiness! I had Him fast. Then I ran downstairs into the drawing-room which was under my bedroom. I took the two lamps and poured all the oil onto the carpet, the furniture, everywhere; then I set fire to it and made my escape, after having carefully double-locked the door.

I went and hid myself at the bottom of the garden, in a clump of laurel bushes. How long it was! how long it was! Everything was dark, silent, motionless, not a breath of air and not a star, but heavy banks of clouds which one could not see, but which weighed, oh! so heavily on my soul.

I looked at my house and waited. How long it was! I already began to think that the fire had gone out of its own accord, or that He had extinguished it, when one of the lower windows gave way under the violence of the flames, and a long, soft, caressing sheet of red flame mounted up the white wall, and kissed it as high as the roof. The light fell on to the trees, the branches, and the leaves, and a shiver of fear pervaded them also! The birds awoke; a dog began to howl, and it seemed to me as if the day were breaking! Almost immediately two other windows flew into fragments, and I saw that the whole of the lower part of my house was nothing but a terrible furnace. But a cry, a horrible, shrill, heart-rending cry, a woman's cry, sounded through the night, and two garret windows were opened! I had forgotten the servants! I saw the terror-struck faces, and the frantic waving of their arms!

Then, overwhelmed with horror, I ran off to the village, shouting: "Help! help! fire! fire!" Meeting some people who were already coming on to the scene, I went back with them to see!

By this time the house was nothing but a horrible and magnificent funeral pile, a monstrous pyre which lit up the whole country, a pyre where men were burning, and where He was burning also, He, He, my prisoner, that new Being, the new Master, the Horla!

Suddenly the whole roof fell in between the walls, and a volcano of flames darted up to the sky. Through all the windows which opened on to that furnace, I saw the flames darting, and I reflected that He was there, in that kiln, dead.

Dead? Perhaps? His body? Was not his body, which was transparent, indestructible by such means as would kill ours?

If He were not dead? Perhaps time alone has power over that Invisible and Redoubtable Being. Why this transparent, unrecognizable body, this body belonging to a spirit, if it also had to fear ills, infirmities, and premature destruction?

Premature destruction? All human terror springs from that! After man the Horla. After him who can die every day, at any hour, at any moment, by any accident, He came, He who was only to die at his own proper hour and minute, because He had touched the limits of his existence!

No—no—there is no doubt about it—He is not dead. Then —then—I suppose I must kill *myself!*

III

NEUROSES

The neuroses represent those aberrations of the emotions which express themselves in bizarre behavior but are not accompanied by the disintegration of the personality. The neurotic can function in society, he can make decisions and reason, but he may be very badly handicapped nevertheless.

Neuroses range from very mild and occasional indispositions which affect almost everyone at some time or other, to profound and destructive emotional disorders which can end in completely incapacitating diseases or in suicide. The neurotic does not represent a stage between the normal and the psychotic. Neuroses are specific diseases, and they often represent as well the defense of a mind against psychoses.

Hysteria, anxiety neuroses, and obsessions and compulsions are the most familiar of the neuroses. Hysterical attacks may well be brought on by anxiety but they may differ completely from anxiety neuroses inasmuch as their symptoms are generally related to the trauma that triggered the disease. An anxiety neurosis is traceable to feelings of guilt and fear but it expresses itself typically in terms of constriction. The subject gasps for breath; he may have palpitations of the heart. His disease, if it should take on a physical form, will result in asthma or a heart attack or perhaps, as in Dreiser's story, a disease of the lung. Despite its specificity of form, the anxiety attack and the simple hysterical attack can at times be indistinguishable.

Hysterical attacks, unlike anxiety neuroses, may take many forms. A person may lose his power of speech or movement during a hysterical attack because of his repressed shame for something he once said or did. Or the hysteric may "compartmentalize" his ego by splitting his personality into two or more parts as in schizophrenia. These "split" personalities differ from those of the schizophrenic because they are each integrated and capable of functioning separately. This kind of neurosis produces the Jekyll and Hyde creature and the mirror image of Poe's "William Wilson."

Obsessive-compulsives indulge in acts because they cannot help themselves. They may gamble or steal or they may merely feel compelled to commit some absurdity such as repeating magic words at specified times of the day. Compulsive behavior has its roots in the same human emotions of guilt and fear, and like all neuroses it will continue to dominate the individual until its source is exposed, its mechanism made known and the conflict behind it resolved. Dostoevsky's "Gambler" and Gordin Raf's kleptomaniac both suffer from forms of an obsessive-compulsive neurosis: the similarity of the symptoms is obvious. And if Alan Nelson's little tale explores the problem of kleptomania somewhat flippantly, it also offers a clear explanation of psychoanalytic techniques in such cases; transference and projection are embodied in the symbolic gloves.

A. Hysteria and Anxiety

EDWARD A. STRECKER / "Functional" Sickness*

IN THIS explanatory discussion, I am compelled to use the word "functional" in its common but far too restricted sense. All human sickness is functional, that is, the organs and parts of the body do *not* perform their functions satisfactorily as they do in health. This is true, whether or not there is inflammation or destruction of the tissues of the brain, or any of the body organs or parts. However, "functional" is usually, albeit too narrowly, used in the sense of illness due to unsolved emotional conflicts. Of course, since the *whole* person is in the grip of the conflict, the body cannot do its job properly, just as it could not function as it should if there were a growth in the stomach or a tumor in the brain, instead of a serious mental conflict.

Using "functional" in this restricted way, for purposes of explanation, how is the psychiatrist able to identify a patient's symptoms as functional? Certainly not by the kind of symptoms. Headache, backache, nausea, vomiting, skin rash, indeed the whole list of the complaints patients make to their doctors appears in case histories routinely and indifferently, as to whether the pathology is in terms of actual tissue as in cirrhosis of the liver, or less concrete, but just as real, pathology hidden behind the portals of the unconscious psyche, perhaps a repressed sexual trauma of childhood.

As a medical student, I was told not to worry about how to distinguish symptoms, headache or what not, the organic (the professor called these "real") from the functional symptoms (the professor called these "imaginary"). I was informed that the organic or "real" symptoms could be seen and demonstrated, like, for instance, vomiting or a skin rash or blood in the stool. Conversely, the functional symptoms, or "imaginary" ones, were not demonstrable or objective. They were subjective. They were the things of which the patients complained, perhaps backache. The inference was that unless the doctor could "prove" the backache by some chemical, x-ray or other test, then it would be safer to assume that there was no backache. The patient was one of those queer "hypochondriacs," a creature of imaginary ailments, and nothing much could be done about it.

I have often reflected that if I had put the objective-subjective teaching into practice, I would have done irreparable harm

* Reprinted from Edward A. Strecker, *Basic Psychiatry* (New York: Random House, Inc., 1952), pp. 135-182.

to many hundreds of very sick patients. Of course, the whole idea was silly and archaic. In an anxiety or other neurosis, the rapidly beating heart, perhaps 140 beats per minute is just as real as if there were a diseased heart. And the vomitus can be seen just as plainly, whether it comes from a psychic rejection of pregnancy or from a liver toxemia in a pregnant woman. The skin may be as flaming red when it expresses a mental conflict as it is in scarlet fever. And so on.

I am glad, too, further to disbar from the precincts of real scientific thought the oft-repeated fallacy that the patient who has so-called organic disease is a much sicker person than the one who is *just* "functional." In the course of years of practice, I have seen many patients with severe psychoneuroses. Personally, I would prefer to have a so-called organic disease, even if moderately severe. For one thing, there is usually less suffering. The sharp lancinating pain of appendicitis is not pleasant, but I would accept it rather than undergo long-drawn-out and baffling anxiety and tension. Furthermore, even with considerable allowance made for a more intelligent attitude toward nervous illness, there are still many, far too many, blind spots of ignorance and even intolerance. It is still too often sadly true that if one can point to something that may be seen through a microscope or in a test tube or revealed by some test, then one is considered legitimately and "respectably" sick—otherwise not.

Finally, if there is any question remaining as to how sick a person may be functionally, let me say that occasionally, though rarely, a patient may die of a psychoneurosis. At least, they may become so depleted and vulnerable, as a result of very severe unsolved emotional conflicts, that there is no longer enough resistance to overcome some chance complicating illness.

Perhaps I may sum up what I have written by saying that sickness is sickness. Always, all of the patient is sick. Always does sickness upset and distort the functioning of the organs of the body. Perhaps the chief difference is that in organic disease, the disturbance of function is chiefly at the level of damage to the tissue of organs; in functional disease, unsolved mental conflicts are at fault.

It is true that usually the pathology of organic disease may be more definitely visualized and localized. But by no means is this constantly true. It is not so very unusual to find discrepancies between the diagnosis during life and the findings at autopsy. At autopsy there may be more extensive involvement of organs than was realized or the location may be somewhat different than was diagnosed. Occasionally, too, pathology may be revealed that was not even remotely suspected. Medicine is an art more than a science.

Where is the pathology of irreconcilable emotional conflicts, the pathology of the psyche, psychopathology? Of course, it is in every cell and recess of the body and mind of the patient. Perhaps the psychopathology can be more readily visualized as being located in that area of the human personality which is "not-conscious." Here is a deep, almost bottomless reservoir with many levels, containing some traces or remnants of everything that has happened to the individual in his lifetime and his reactions to these happenings, perhaps even only thoughts. Many psychoanalysts would regard this as a very minimum estimate of the material not easily accessible to conscious, deliberate thinking. They feel that they have demonstrated by plumbing the depths of the "not-conscious" mind that material may be recovered, easily identifiable as having its source while the individual was a foetus in the womb of the mother or even reaching back through many eons of time, into the dim, historically unrecorded experiences of primitive man.

In any event, there is a heavy line of demarcation, but not completely closed, between the conscious and "not-conscious" mind. The conscious mind is the mind of awareness. It is the mind that says, "Good morning" and "How are you?" It orients, places the person correctly as to time, place and identity, and its content is useful in ordinary business and social conversations. Even at this level, it frequently reaches down into the "not-conscious" for help in associating and elaborating ideas. It says and does many things, but, of itself, it is not able to view the deeper reasons for the saying and doing. Altogether, it is a shallow compartment.

The "not-conscious" mind is very deep with many levels. Superficially, there is a level from which, with a little effort, "forgotten" things can be reclaimed and brought into consciousness. Deeper, there are levels from which material can be brought into the open only with strong labors of recall. Then there are sensitive areas scattered throughout, from which seep through interesting little slips of speech and behavior, the significance of which is not realized by the person who makes them. From time to time, a patient says to me, with great emphasis, of his wife, "She is a very good woman." Or a wife of her husband, "He is such a considerate man." Fine, laudatory remarks, but the speakers are unaware of the fact that there was a paradox in the words of the statements and the deep, obviously regretful sighs that accompanied them. Every physician occasionally receives an unsigned check from a patient. Perhaps sometimes it is a not-conscious evaluation of the value placed by the patient on the services rendered.

Then there are many deep layers of "not-conscious" mental activity. These are tightly sealed compartments, but their coverings may be pried off, perhaps by delirium, anaesthesia, drugs, in

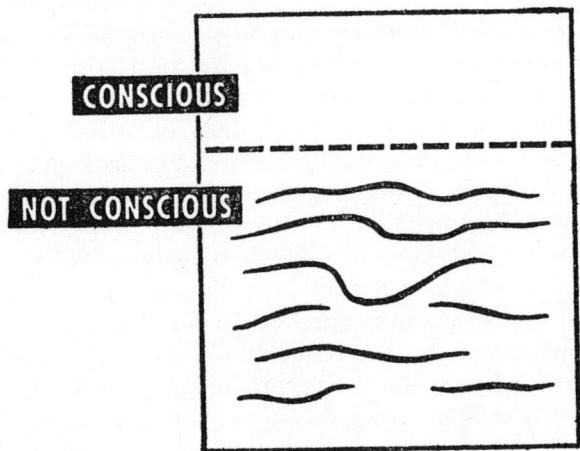

dream life and, as an important treatment technique, by the free association of psychoanalysis. And in every person's psyche, there are things in the subterranean depths which never come into the light of consciousness. Probably it is better that they do not.

It is scarcely necessary to validate the existence and operation of a "not-conscious" mind. In the outpourings of delirium (seemingly irrelevant babbling, but actually fraught with deep meaning); when inhibitions have been removed by an anaesthetic or by various drugs; in hypnosis, the waters of consciousness are stilled, and much flotsam and jetsam are churned up from the depths and revealed in the stream of unconscious thought and act.

In dreams, we walk in the valley of the unconscious. Often the things we "think" and "do" are very frightening. We may see strange people, including ourselves. Much of the dream content, many dream figures are adequately disguised. It is fortunate. Otherwise, our ego would be hopelessly belittled and shamed.

An added proof comes from the work of the psychotherapist and particularly the psychoanalyst, who by his skilled interpretation of the "random" unsupervised spoken thoughts of patients and their dreams, strips off many coverings of the hidden mental life, so that the patients may know themselves, the first step toward recovery.

Finally, perhaps I may borrow an analogy from the physical sciences. Anything that has once existed, even a scrap of paper, while it can be destroyed, cannot be effaced as though it had never been. By tearing it into bits, by burning it, by subjecting the ashes to heat, to acids and alkalies, by pressure, it can be changed so that it no longer can be recognized as the former scrap of paper, but always something remains. So, too, is it with a human experience, act, or even a thought.

The liver, a muscle or any organ of the body is composed of

cells that are chiefly instrumental in performing the function of the organ. They are bound together by connecting tissue. In the field of human behavior, perhaps we can accept the word "complexes" as a name for basic psychological "cells," promoters of conduct, good, bad, indifferent. Each one of us begins to imbibe complexes with our mother's milk, and early in our lives we soon accumulate a vast number of them. They concern all sorts of things—politics, religion, the length of women's skirts, marriage preferences, blondes, brunettes or redheads, baseball or golf. Indeed, anything under the sun. Less in our boasted logic and far more in our complexes are to be found the sources of our likes and dislikes, our loves and hates, our interests, our prejudices and intolerances, the fine things we do in our everyday lives and the ignoble and base ones.

The reasons we give for our interests and hobbies are usually high-sounding, plausible and fallacious. The range of human activities is limitless—collecting stamps, or coins (I mean old coins), voting the Republican or Democratic ticket, taking poor orphaned children to the circus, promoting parties to swell the fund for research and treatment of "polio," eating pistachio icecream. These things and many others are no less interesting, creditable and constructive, even though we do not know fully their derivations and inspirations. Actually we do not. The nucleus of the behavior drives which they activate and inspire in adult life were imbedded into our personalities when we were at our mothers' knees, long before we had enough intelligence even to know and recognize pros and cons, much less make decisions. I know enough about a certain great physician to realize that his decision to study medicine had the determining emotional motivation of the sorrow and distress of his adored mother at the death of his older sister of diabetes, when he was four years old. He has made valuable contributions to the treatment of diabetes. I know an intelligent man who spends considerable time and effort in promoting the idea that children should not be taught any prayers, even a simple "Now I lay me down to sleep" since, as he states, it damages their developing egos and will make them too dependent. Actually, I think his attitude was laid down in his childhood by his rigid and righteous, hell-and-damnation father: no music or dancing, no bright colors or laughter and long knee-racking hours spent in gloomy family prayers.

Many of our complexes lead us to satisfactory enough behavior. At its lowest rating, interestingly time-passing pursuits and avocations, at its highest, useful endeavors and occupations, philanthropies and perhaps the noblest, most unselfish and even saintly lives.

Every complex demands and must have its day in the Court of Human Behavior. In some shape or fashion, it *will* be heard, expressed in our everyday speech and actions. And, often, it may be expressed directly and easily enough. After all, there is nothing out of the way in collecting stamps or old coins, being a baseball fan or working for local option. At worst, sometimes enthusiasts in this or that movement become too enthusiastic and bore their friends. At social gatherings, I never discuss psychiatry unless I am convinced that the group earnestly desires to hear about it. Otherwise, I prefer to talk about sculpturing, the fourth dimension, the H bomb, or something about which I do not know anything.

There are two conditions which constitute a bar to the expression in conscious behavior of trends emanating from our unconscious complexes. The first condition is that the conscious recognition of the nature of the complex would be unpleasant and even shameful and repulsive to the total personality.

The second condition, which usually follows the first, is that the complex put into action would sin against the social code and bring down upon the head of the sinner the condemnation and retaliation of the herd, his fellow men. After all, the conscious behavior response to collecting stamps, or coins or even betting mildly on horse races is socially acceptable enough. To give rein in behavior to a strong latent homosexual drive or an incestuous desire of a son for his mother is not acceptable. Society would brand the transgressor as unclean—a moral leper. The law would seek to punish the offender.

Perhaps the appended diagram may serve to illustrate the situation:

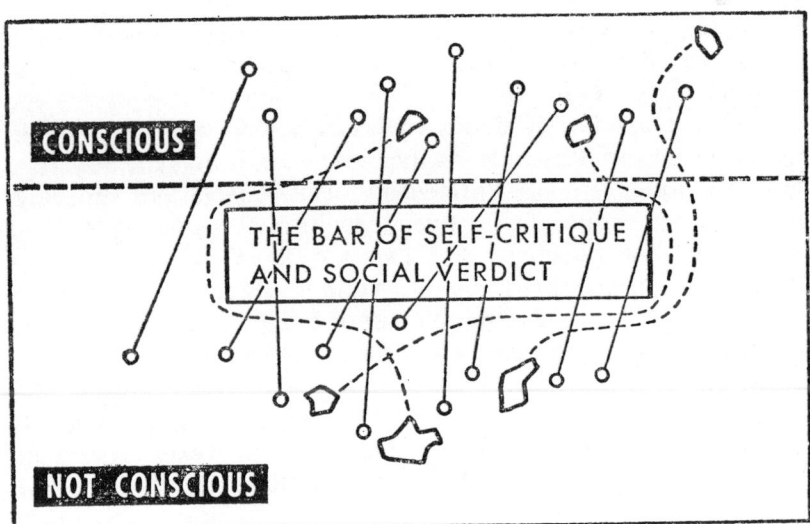

The small circles ₀°₀°₀° represent "normal" complexes. The conduct flowing from them is personally and socially acceptable. Therefore, they may appear in the stream of everyday conscious behavior, unchanged in form. The behavior resulting from the complexes ◇♡⌂ would be outlawed by the individual and by society. Therefore, seeking expression in unconsciousness, as they must, they are blocked by the bar of self-critique and the adverse social verdict, and they must be camouflaged ⌒○⌒ before they can appear in conscious behavior in passably acceptable form.

It may be repeated that every human being has complexes seeking expression in behavior, which, if uncensored and uninhibited, would be indicted at the bar of personal and social judgment. The unconscious psyche is the terrain upon which conflicts are fought and there are strong power drives from the ego with its self-preservative demands, from sex often socially unruly in its desires, from an unconscious but canny estimate of the balance between the amount of aggressiveness that the herd or society will accept.

It should be repeated, too, there is the Id, not only a powerful dynamo of energy, without which the human being would be pallid and ineffective, but also it is the source of instinctual demands asking for immediate gratification, irrespective of personal and social consequences. In one sense, the Id is primitive man, primitive in aggressive ego demands, in sex urges and in defiance of the herd social code. The opposite number to the Id, is the Superego, civilized, cultured man, containing among other things a conscience, capable of pronouncing adverse judgment upon "bad" behavior and stimulating "good" and even self-sacrificing, ideal and noble conduct. Naturally, the Superego closely scrutinizes Id behavior, recoils from, condemns and punishes its baser manifestations. Often it is too intolerant. The Ego is the referee, the arbiter. It strives to keep the Id within reasonable personal and social bounds. At the same time, it asks the Superego not to be too severe and unrelenting in its expectations and judgments. Not infrequently, the Ego is caught in the pincer movement between Id and Superego. The Ego, too, must maintain itself. It is the *person* as presented to public view, to his fellow men. Therefore it must not be either too blatant or too belittled. These, then, are the contending forces. This is the battleground. All human behavior, even ordinary everyday behavior, is the result of a compromise in the psyche. The vast majority are reasonably satisfactory compromises. But the fields of human conflict also are bestrewn with compromises, pathological, sick compromises which sacrifice some of the hold on reality, but as little as possible in the circumstances. Still something of mental health is relinquished.

Perhaps what has been said, I hope not at too great length, may be briefly summarized:

A. In addition to the conscious mind, there is a mind in every human being whose content and operations are beyond the horizons of consciousness.

B. This mind may be and actually often is the seat of extremely important pathology, psychopathology, determining human illness.

C. Such psychopathology results from irreconcilable drives, dictating opposing kinds of behavior.

D. Failing a reasonably satisfactory compromise, an impasse results. An irresistible force has encountered an immovable body. Such an impasse cannot continue. It would mean a psychological catastrophe, perhaps a major psychosis. However faulty it may be, a compromise must be found. Often some of the inner pressure is removed by changing or converting the emotional conflict into signs and symptoms, perhaps headache, nausea, vomiting, rapid beating of the heart and innumerable other symptoms, which are readily discoverable upon examination of the patient by the physician.

Human beings assailed by the forces of a severe mental conflict defend themselves as best they can. Naturally, they use those psychological weapons—mechanisms of defense—best adapted for each particular personality under assault. Each one of us utilizes some of them in miniature, in meeting the everyday problems of life and it is entirely normal for us to employ them in moderate amounts. For instance, some of us are given to a bit of rationalizing and use it expertly. A neighbor calls up inviting to an evening of bridge. We decline regretfully, pleading "a mean headache." We like bridge but the head does ache—and we *"can't stand that particular neighbor."* Fifteen minutes later, a friend we do like phones and we enthusiastically agree to go to the movies. The headache disappears. These mild self-deceptions or rationalizations are comparatively harmless. They even lubricate the wheels of complicated personal and social living.

On the other hand, a patient complains of abdominal pain, headache, nausea, vomiting, dizziness and colitis. As far as the sick woman is concerned, the illness *must be* within the framework of the symptoms. She makes the rounds of physicians seeking confirmation of her strong belief that she had some disease of her stomach or intestines—perhaps "a growth." In two of many such patients I have treated, the symptoms in one were a rationalization of the frustration and hostility resulting from lack of affection during childhood and practically rejection by her mother. In the other patient, the symptoms rationalized dissatisfaction with her husband and rebellion against sexual intercourse with him.

Rationalization and other mental mechanisms not only help shape the symptoms but effectively disguise them. In this way, the material of the mental conflict, the real reason for the symptoms, is excluded from the area of consciousness, where its recognition would belittle and shame the ego. Perhaps this simple diagram will illustrate the operation of the mechanism of rationalization:

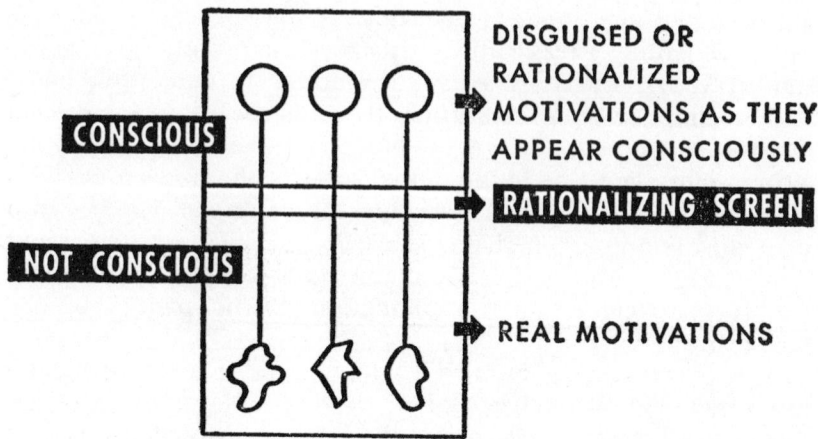

We would all like to know just how these transformations of mental conflicts into physical symptoms are accomplished. We do know how emotions influence the function of body tissues. We do know some of the passageways, the autonomic and ductless gland systems, certain parts of the brain and, indeed, we know that every tissue and cell of the body and notably the organs that bear the burden of the emotional conflict participate in the process.[1] A recent theory describes an "assemblage" of nerve brain cells, acting together by repeated, habitual behavior and becoming through frequent usage readily stimulated and capable of exciting the entire central nervous system into action, producing various forms of behavior.

As time goes on, we will acquire more accurate information. Incidentally, in passing it might be noted that even in the more concrete field of so-called physical disease, our knowledge is far from complete. For instance, we know only imperfectly the stages that occur between infection by the spirochete of syphilis and the end result which might be arteriosclerosis or locomotor ataxia or syphilis of any part of the body. We know, too, that tuberculosis is due to infection by the bacillus of Koch, but we

[1] *Organization of Behavior*, by D. O. Hebb. (John Wiley & Sons, Inc. New York, 1949.)

are far from knowing exactly why there are such varying end results: tuberculosis of the lungs, of bone and indeed of any organ or part of the body.

The basic mechanism of defense is *repression*. We ought to understand it readily enough since it has large areas in everyday normal life. It is not too difficult to "forget" a dental appointment or to pay the doctor's bill. I have found very few adults who remember as children having seen their parents in any of the stages of sexual love. Yet it is unlikely that the majority of children did not stumble into it, now and then. It is altogether probable that many childhood happenings fraught with deep emotional import would have confused and frightened our small egos. So they were repressed.

The repression which is a requisite in the production of functional illness is a much more serious consideration. It deals with conflict material which for the time being cannot be even remotely faced. Its mere approach to the periphery of consciousness is sufficient markedly to increase the patient's tension and anxiety. If it were suddenly illuminated by the floodlight of consciousness, there would be psychological panic and chaos. Such sensitive emotional material often dates back to childhood, perhaps early sexual trauma or the severe and damaging insult of being an unwanted and rejected child. Or a strong latent homosexuality. Or, as in war, the terrific emotional experiences of seeing scattered fragments of what a few moments before were whole, breathing, moving, talking, laughing fellow soldiers and friends. Or in civilian life, the sudden death of a beloved mother, the inconstancy of a lover, the sight of the infidelity of a husband or wife.

At first glance, repression would seem to be a psychological blessing. If things that are painful, belittling and shaming to remember can be wiped out of memory, relegated to the Nirvana of the forgotten, then they can no longer trouble us. Unfortunately, they do continue to trouble, often to the point of being instrumental in provoking illness. Emotionally highly charged material that is repressed because we cannot face it openly is not annihilated. It is merely submerged below the surface of consciousness. There it remains, an isolated sensitized focus of psychic unrest. The remembrance of the actual experience has been dislocated from the emotional matrix in which it was embedded. The molecule has been split and the emotional atom is sometimes spoken of as "free floating anxiety." It is inevitable that it should form attachments which often are symbolic representations of the original experience.

A young woman was markedly allergic to alcohol. The smell of any spiritous liquor like whiskey nauseated her, made her "catch" her breath, and the taste of liquor made her sick to her stomach with violent retching, long-continued vomiting, asthma-like gasping for air and feelings of suffocation. She avoided alcohol, which was simple enough, but she could scarcely avoid seeing people drink socially. And usually this made her feel very "uneasy" and tense. She knew of no reason why this should be so. She had no feeling about people drinking socially, and indeed she often envied their enjoyment and wished she could participate.

To cut a few corners, analytical probing of her psyche and removal of inhibition by sodium pentothal revealed that at about the age of six at least three times she had seen her mother in a drunken stupor, quite unconscious and breathing heavily and irregularly.

The case is nicely illustrative of repression. The child could not understand the dreadful situation intellectually. Therefore the psychic insult was all the more severe and damaging. She was desperate and terror-stricken because her frantic efforts to arouse her mother were unavailing. The experience could not be tolerated in conscious memory. It had to be repressed. The emotion which it had engendered became attached in consciousness to the "allergy" to alcohol and the whole train of symptoms, including asthmatic attacks.

The dissociation of thought and feeling produced by repression is scarcely conducive to mental health. Indeed, repression is a dangerous mental mechanism which paves the way for much functional sickness. It provides the favorable setting for the operation of other mechanisms of defense.

For instance, there is the very simple device of *regression*. Regression means to step backward, to utilize the weapons of childhood in attempting to meet and solve adult situations and problems. This is the area of sullenness, sulking and tears, of door slamming and fist pounding on tables, of temper tantrums, even of staged and artificial suicidal attempts. A few days ago I read in the public press the account of a husband who, sitting in an automobile, grew tired of waiting for his wife and expressed his frustration by crashing his fist through the windshield. He had to be taken to a hospital for treatment of severe lacerations. It did not solve his problem.

It is not adult behavior, even though a minimum of it is understandable and permissible in the life of every human being. It is said that a former President of the United States, when his will was thwarted, threw himself on the floor of one of the White House rooms and screamed and kicked like a child. True, his provocation was great, but the kicking and screaming did not accomplish his political objective. The patterns of these regressive techniques are laid down in childhood. Then they are much more logical. After all, a child's range of protest against the environment for what it considers unfair treatment is quite limited. In adult life the same childlike behavior is exhibited but it serves an unconscious complex. It may be an unconscious protest on the part of an immature husband that his wife is unwilling to be his mother, or by a child-wife that her husband is different from the father figure remaining in her psyche from her childhood. The angry vehemence and door-slamming of the husband "because" the breakfast eggs are overdone or the tears of the wife because her husband insists she return a hat which they cannot afford are merely the surface eruptions of emotional volcanoes whose real activities are deeply buried.

In some forms of "nervous" illness, the psychiatrist has difficulty in preventing the patient from putting him in the position of complete authority. The patient wants to be praised and petted, scolded and spanked. Least of all, unconsciously, does the patient want to grow up emotionally. Sometimes the physical symptoms of the neurosis are pitifully transparent—an assortment of discomforts and aches about which the patient unconsciously wants the doctor to show great concern, to rub them psychologically and make them well.

Projection and introjection or identification, its opposite number, are two interesting albeit somewhat dangerous mental mechanisms, commonly employed to escape the reality struggle of inner mental conflicts. They both have large and even mildly useful segments in average everyday life.

Projection removes the blame for things that go wrong, or "are not right," from our inner selves, where it belongs, and places it upon the environment. It does no great harm to blame the "fidgeting" of the caddy for a golf drive that foozled; the "poor" post-war materials for the paint that peeled off a few days after it was applied; the failure of the party upon the stupidity of the guests. We all do this sort of thing from time to time.

Classically, there is the automobile driver, often not too skillful, whose numerous accidents are always due to the "negligence" and even "homicidal mania" of the other drivers.

But there are deeper unconscious levels from which emerge less innocent behavior, behavior pressured by bias, prejudice and even bloody intolerance. And there are cesspools of projection. In one of John Steinbeck's short stories, a "poor white," is one of the ringleaders in the brutal lynching of a Negro. On his way home he ponders on his feeling of satisfaction, pleasant satiation as though he had eaten a fine, large meal. As he enters his cabin, his slatternly wife looks into his face and accuses him of having "had" a woman. In his room, he stares long and reflectively into a broken bit of mirror and concludes, "By God, I look as if I had a woman."

In sickness, both psychotic and psychoneurotic, projection

is frequently unconsciously employed as a defense mechanism. In a sense, it flings the "blame" as far as possible away from the inner core of real motivations into the outer world. Thus, the ego is not sullied.

As has been cited in the instance of a strong latent homosexual complex, the personality may accept, unconsciously, definite mental symptoms, hearing of defaming voices and fantastic "persecutions" in order to push out as far as possible the ego-shaming recognition of sexual love for the same sex.

I had a patient, now well, who had a whole host of psychosomatic symptoms referable to the genito-urinary area of the body. There was frequent urination, usually with discomfort, shooting pains in the sexual organs, sometimes "swelling" (which I was never able to verify), headache, fatigue. All these symptoms became markedly worse whenever he felt that his wife expected sex relations with him. At these times, he claimed, she was so "nervous" that she "worried" him. In the course of treatment, it became quite clear that the symptoms were the physical expressions of a defense mechanism, projection foci for a hidden-from-conscious-self, latent homosexuality.

If I may be permitted to indulge myself in another drawing, perhaps motivated by an erroneous belief that I have a talent for making ideas clear by diagrams, I would illustrate projection in this way:

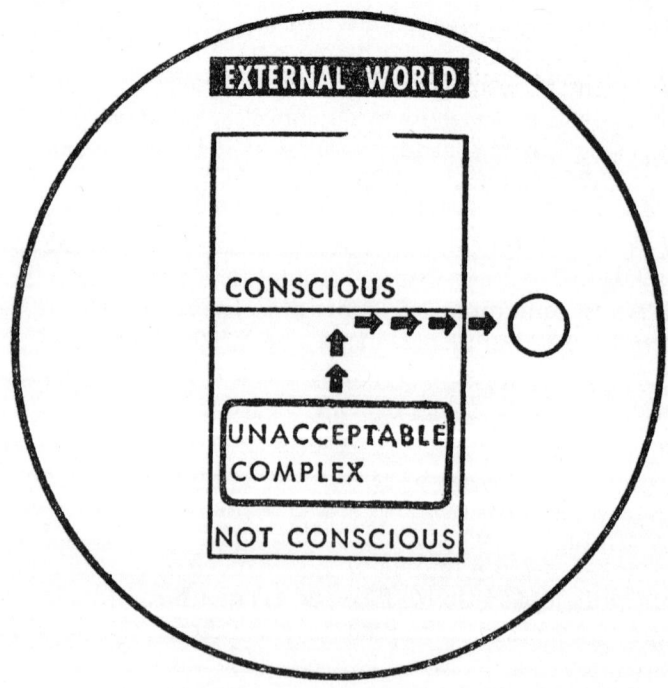

The unacceptable complex cannot face conscious recognition and is detoured into the environment, where it finds ego-saving, but false, explanations.

While I am at it, I might as well perpetrate another diagram, this time attempting to illustrate the workings of introjection or identification, which travels a path opposite from projection. In projection, when the ego is unable to face certain complexes, the personality disowns them, attempts to dislocate them and cast them into the environment, thus escaping self-blame. In identification, the personality, feeling the need of the strength of certain characteristics and qualities it does not possess, but prizes highly, attempts to seize them from the environment and incorporate them into self. That particular personality may then think and act as though the admired qualities really belonged to it. Actually, they do not belong; therefore the borrowed strength they are given is often false and does not endure.

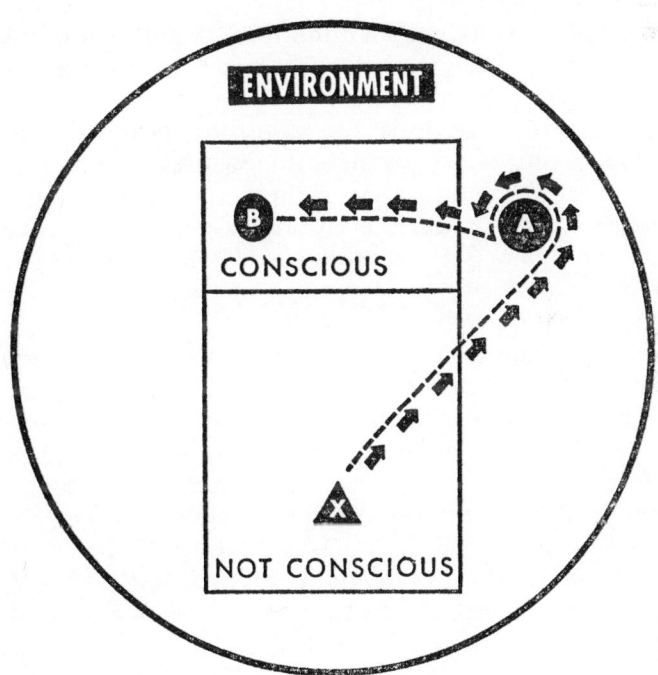

(X) represents some much desired quality for which the particular personality feels a great need, but does not possess, perhaps firmness and decisiveness.

(A) represents a strong expression of such qualities in some person in the environment. It need not be an actual living personage and often is a historical figure or even a fictional character.

The dotted line and arrows illustrate the mechanism of identifying and attempting to take over, as belonging to self. But (B) is not (A), and all too often in its ineffectual expression, it is revealed as a spurious psychological coin.

In its proper place, and kept within reasonable bounds, identification is extremely constructive. In childhood, the identification of the child with the parents, and the imitation that it stimulates, is the single most potent force for the development of personality and the building of emotional maturity. Always provided, of course, that the parents do not have feet of clay. Adolescent hero-worship, too, if not too mistakenly directed, helps to build sound personalities. In adult life we ally ourselves with various movements. Often our selection is unconsciously directed. The particular movement represents an ideal which alone we are too weak to accomplish. So, we identify ourselves with the purposive strength of leaders and numbers and gain personal strength in the identification.

In everyday living, identification enhances our pleasures and satisfactions. When we are really absorbed in a book or play, it is because we identify ourselves with one of the characters. We are so thrilled because it is "we" who do such brave and fine things. We would like to do them in real life.

The test of identification is the kind of action it produces. If it leads to behavior which, even though it be only very slightly, still does make us better and more effective in the right direction, capable of more satisfactory personal and social adjustments, then the identification is well worth-while. If it leads to inaction, if it is merely an escape from reality, then it is useless or worse. It is then much like the identification of a mental patient with Jesus Christ. He does nothing about it and merely sits in a corner of a mental hospital delusionally dreaming away his life.

It is not only a question with whom an identification is made but what in that figure is imitated. Is it the strengths or the weaknesses? The significant things or the trivia? Too frequently one sees rare opportunities to attain personality growth neglected. Among the official family and friends of a great President, a number of men and women profited psychologically by their contact with him. They imbibed of his strengths and of the sincerity of his desire to help the oppressed. They were not tempted by the President's flaws and faults. But then there were the others who identified with and imitated not the greatness of the man, but the manner and mannerisms of his speech and gestures—and the length of his cigarette holder. It was an unprofitable identification —imitation gone to seed. From the identification some of the weaklings gained false strength and confidence and a front of great importance, built on the sands of unconscious inferiority. One is reminded of the fly in Aesop's fable, perched on the wheel of the thundering chariot, observing the huge cloud of dust and remarking, "Lo, see what a cloud of dust *I* am raising."

Sometimes in the treatment of functional sickness, immature identifications occasion considerable difficulty. The psychiatrist in going over the life history has to help the patient topple over a long procession of figures, usually surrogates for the parents, with whom the patient has over-identified, and in weak and ineffectual ways. From them he has not borrowed strength but weakness. They serve to make it exceedingly difficult for him to understand the real meaning of his symptoms. Until they are cleared away, there is a stubborn barrier which blocks that necessary condition of recovery, growing up emotionally and adjusting to life as it is—"Know thyself."

In some degree, in each one of us, there are certain inconsistencies and contradictions in our everyday behavior. Often, our mental right hands do not know what our mental left hands are doing. Conduct quite opposed in character seems to flow from tightly insulated, logic-tight compartments in the unconscious. And never do the twain meet, except perhaps with psychiatric help. If we realized how paradoxical was our behavior it would be hypocrisy. Since we do not realize it at all consciously, and indeed become "hurt" or "angry" when someone calls attention to the inconsistency, it is *segregation,* one of the mechanisms of psychological defense. In its "normal" areas, but, too, in the shaping of a psychoneurosis, or even a psychosis, it is used freely to soften or evade the realities of mental conflict and to save the ego from belittling self-revealment.

Again there is Exhibit A, the "perfect" motor car driver, in reality anything but perfect, who damns and threatens other drivers on the road for the faults which he, himself, freely commits. And then there is the chap who campaigns earnestly for the closing of saloons on Sunday, but sips a cocktail at his club with evident enjoyment on the Sabbath. I am amused at several men I know who scrutinize candidates for membership in the somewhat exclusive club to which they belong with the utmost strictness. To pass their rigid tests, a man has to have a record rather better than Caesar demanded of his wife. It is amusing because their own records were not at all free from blots and they were lucky to get by the Entrance Committee. More seriously, there is the Sunday and Monday man. On Sunday, moved by the church services and a fine sermon, his heart really does overflow with love and mercy for his less fortunate fellow men. But on Monday, he is an aggressive, sharp and ruthless man, not dishonest, but certainly exacting the last ounce of each pound of a business deal. Or, the wealthy woman, wearing herself out in her earnest work in behalf of an organization devoted to improving the personal and social lot of domestic servants. Arriving home from the club meetings, she treats her own servants like dogs. At least she did in that remote area when there were still servants who could be treated like dogs.

There is the story of a Russian Countess, passionately devoted to grand opera. She suffered with the tragic figures and wept at their stage sufferings and distress. With her coachman and footman, she imperiously insisted that they remain at attention at their posts until the opera was over. One bitterly cold winter night, when she returned to the droshky, after having been racked with grief at the sad fate of the heroine of the opera, she found the servants at their posts in the correct postures—frozen to death.

Literature abounds in examples of segregation. Probably the most classical is Dr. Jekyll and Mr. Hyde.

In psychiatry, segregation is strikingly illustrated by the double personality sometimes seen in hysteria. For instance, in Janice X, personality "A" was quiet, gentle, neat, modest and altogether led an exemplary life. But, personality "B" was a noisy, coarse and flamboyant character, smeared over thickly with rouge and lipstick, given to participation in risqué situations and occasionally behaving on a level rather lower than that of the average prostitute. Of course, personalities "A" and "B" did not have even a bowing acquaintance with each other. No doubt "A" would have been shamed beyond expression at "B's" outrageous conduct and "B" would have labeled "A" as a psalm-singing, sniveling old maid.

A few years ago a man about forty years old came to me complaining of backache, headache, difficulty in concentration and great fatigue. No sufficient organic reason was found for the symptoms. In the course of a series of interviews, he said repeatedly and evidently believed that he was happily married to a "fine, good wife." Again and again he repeated that he loved his wife and two children very much. As the story of his life unfolded, another character appeared—a woman "friend." Again, with evident sincerity, he described this relationship as "a fine, platonic friendship." This woman, a widow, was a college graduate, Phi Beta Kappa, with a well-developed and able mind. Their intellectual interests were closely akin. Incidentally, she was thirty-seven years old to his forty, quite feminine in her manner and very attractive physically. Several times he let slip that she was not so capable and businesslike about "ordinary" things as was his wife. Even though my patient did not realize it for a long time, it soon became clear to me that the friendship was far from being solely on a platonic level. For one thing, by actual count, he spent more of the hours of the day with the widow than he did with his wife or anyone else. Love-making? Of course *not*—well, a little kissing and now and then "fondling." (My patient had some trouble with the selection of this word.) After all, they *were* close friends. Briefly, my patient was in love with the widow. Largely through his own increased understanding of self, he came to realize this. In all conscious honesty he had not realized it before. He had employed the ego-saving device of psychological segregation. It is a rather dangerous psychic fiction.

Often in treatment it is necessary to break down the dykes which shut off one conscious stream of segregated thinking from another that runs countercurrent. Observing and particularly feeling the incongruity, the patient arrives at a more mature evaluation and sounder adjustment.

Now for another diagram, this one to illustrate the workings of segregation. The conscious behavior does not express a satisfactory compromise between the demands of opposed complexes. They enter the conscious stream of thought and conduct separately and are acted out separately without recognition of **their incompatibility.**

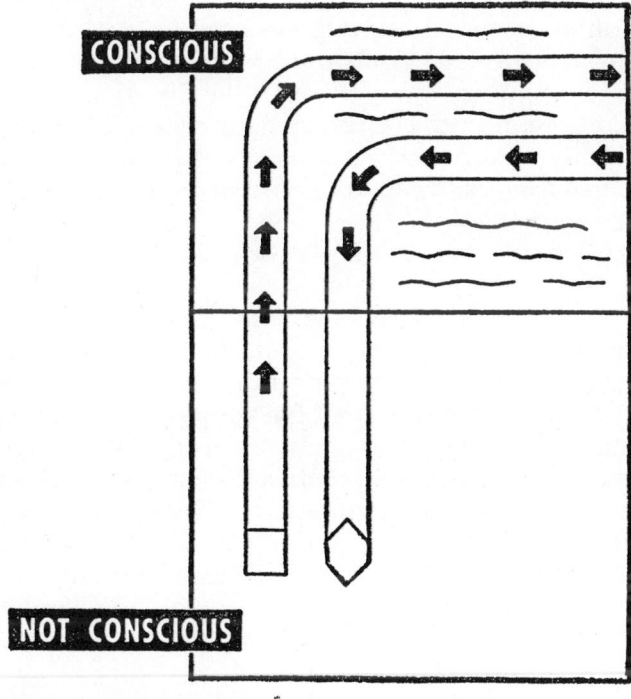

These, then, are some of the psychological stratagems and devices employed by the human psyche.

It is to be repeated that:

1. They are used in small amounts by even the most "normal" of us in the everyday business of personal and social life.

2. When beset by mental conflicts, strong opposing drives which cannot be effectively compromised, we fall back upon the second line of defense and evolve a psychoneurosis. The particular mechanisms of defense used are those which are peculiar to each given personality and have been tried out in everyday life. Each case of "nervous" illness differs from any other. One may contain a prominent area of regression or projection. Another, rationalization or identification or perhaps segregation, and so on. They all contain repressions. The clinical structure the psychiatrist sees, before he has opened up its hidden cellars and passageways, is largely determined by the markings of the personality which has built the structure.

3. The objective of the defense mechanism is to conceal motivations from conscious self and thus spare the ego from personal and social humiliation. The immediate gain is heavily offset by the penalty which must be paid in terms of functional sickness.

At best all these stratagems and devices are psychological crutches. Often, they are useful and serviceable for a time, but we would not choose to go through life on crutches.

What happens as a result of successful psychiatric treatment? I think it can be best expressed by saying that the patient attains some degree of *sublimation*. Sublimation means to purify or refine. In a psychic sense, it means the direction of the energy away from certain instincts, desires and tendencies into approved personal and social channels—rather than permitting them to flow unrestrictedly and harmfully into wasteful and even harmful and debasing channels.

Always, the patient who has secured fairly satisfactory adjustments as a result of treatment has accomplished something more than the mere disappearance of the neurotic symptoms. There is increased self-understanding. And there is some degree of sublimation. Probably not a great deal, but still some. Perhaps only an appreciation of the need for postponing immediate gratifications and a willingness to modify neurotic demands. A neurosis, though it is unconscious, and not deliberate, nevertheless is selfish in that it tends to sacrifice those in the environment—the family and others who are in close contact with the patient. If the treatment produces enough self-knowledge so that the person becomes more considerate of others, taking less and giving more, in other words, less selfish in behavior, then there is worthwhile sublimation. If treatment gives only relief from the neurotic symptoms, then it falls short of its proper goal. In my mind, it is axiomatic that unless the patient emerges from the treatment a better person than he or she was before, then the treatment has failed.

In history, both profane and sacred, there are innumerable examples of well-nigh complete and perfect sublimations. The prophets and saints, the great humanitarians, the unselfish benefactors of humanity, were men and women of flesh and blood. They, too, had drives which, unrestrained, would have led to selfish and even base conduct. The theologians would call them temptations. In any event, they subdued them and submerged them in the overwhelming love for their fellow men and their desire to help them. I am not suggesting that patients should expect anything similar from psychiatric treatment, or even strive for it. However, the study of the lives of these unselfishly great men and women does furnish good examples of the power of sublimation.

The various symptoms of functional sickness gather themselves into groups and are given separate names. These names are of interest chiefly to psychiatrists, and even psychiatrists have come to recognize that names are relatively unimportant. All the many signs and symptoms, psychosomatic, tensions, anxiety, fatigue, difficulty with concentration, fixation of interest on body sensations, obsessions, phobias and many others, are generously distributed throughout all the psychoneuroses. At most, the names indicate a preponderance of certain kinds of symptoms in this or that neurosis. And psychiatrists themselves do not wholly agree on classification. There are a number of lists and each one has some merit. Much more significant and valuable for treatment than the mere giving of a name to an illness is the thorough understanding of the personality of the person who is sick and a knowledge and appreciation of the important events in his life history.

"Sticks and stones can break my bones,
But names can never hurt me."

It is the environmental sticks and stones, the insults to the ego and the inner reactions to them which break the "bones" of the psyche—not the designation "anxiety neurosis" or "neurasthenia."

Personally, I think the simpler the classification, the better. If I cared to give names, the bulk of the functional illness I have seen could be grouped under one of the following designations:

A. Conversion Hysteria
B. Neurasthenia
C. Anxiety Neuroses
D. Obsessive-Compulsive Reactions

Conversion Hysteria is a very simple, childlike device. The patient escapes his mental conflict by the simple expedient of exchanging it (of course, unconsciously) for certain ego-protective symptoms, usually very gross symptoms, annihilation of whole functions, like paralysis, blindness, deafness, aphonia (loss of speech). Not very flatteringly, I have compared the mechanism of conversion hysteria to the habit of the trade rat. He takes something, often of value, like a watch or a piece of jewelry and leaves in its place something of no value, perhaps a pebble or a scrap of paper. The hysteric exchanges the mental conflict which he does not want, and which indeed would be a burden and trouble to his ego if he faced it consciously, for some symptom, perhaps hysterical blindness, deafness, paralysis, which, strange as it may seem, is of value to him, since he can and does regard it with satisfaction as the explanation of his illness. In this way, conversion hysteria does differ markedly from the other psychoneuroses. Once the conversion of the mental conflict into hysterical signs and symptoms is accomplished, the patient washes his psychological hands of the conflict, and regards his symptoms with amazing emotional complacency—even when the symptom is calamitous, like total blindness. In the other psychoneuroses, there is much unrest and anxiety from the inner psychic turmoil of unconscious, unsolved emotional conflicts.

Incidentally, soon in the history of his repeated attacks, the hysteric rarely fools anyone but himself—and almost never the psychiatrist. He or she has become blind or deaf or paralyzed and recovered sight, hearing or the function of walking too often—and too quickly. Nevertheless, it must be clearly understood, it is not faking or deliberate pretense. Hysteria is a definite and actual an illness as pneumonia.

World War I was replete with classical examples of conversion hysteria—the so-called "shell-shock" of the newspapers. As has been stated, they represented the unconscious psychological victory of the behavior demands of self-preservation over the duties, dangers and ideals of being a soldier. In my experience, often the symptoms were strikingly protective. Sometimes paralysis of both legs at the height of the charge against the enemy, deafness after being left in "no man's land" and listening for hours to the cries and groans of the wounded, blindness after seeing horrible death inflicted upon other soldiers by enemy fire. Frequently, the deafness and blindness were fortified by the wiping out of memory (amnesia) so that not only could the cries of the suffering wounded no longer be heard or mutilating destruction be seen, but no longer could they be remembered. Of course, not all the clinical examples of war conversion hysteria were so simple. For instance, in one group of soldiers, we were puzzled for a time by twisting, writhing, convulsive movements of their abdominal muscles. Later we learned that sometimes this followed the bayoneting of an enemy soldier through the belly.

While conversion hysteria is less common than formerly, yet there are still many examples to be found in civilian life.

A woman of middle age mistakenly suspected her husband of infidelity and particularly of an affair with a hypothetical "other woman." In her childhood she had had acute rheumatic fever

NEUROSES / *Edward A. Strecker* 463

which had left her heart very slightly impaired. Otherwise, she was a strong, healthy woman. One night, when her husband returned from a business conference, he found his wife in bed, gasping for breath and clutching wildly at her chest. He was frightened. It was a "heart attack." He summoned a physician, who examined the patient briefly, left some medicine, and said everything would be "all right." However, there were many more attacks, in fact, practically every time the husband had to go out at night. A noted heart specialist made thorough examinations and pronounced the heart in very satisfactory condition—"not the least thing to worry about." He suggested a psychiatrist. After a dozen interviews, the situation became quite clear to both psychiatrist and patient. In no wise were the "heart attacks" consciously planned. The patient was not aware of their underlying motivation. However, this motivation, the fear and unjustified suspicion that her husband was having an affair with another woman, leading to the hysterical subconscious wish to keep him closely tied to her side, was close enough to consciousness so that it was brought into the field of the patient's conscious appreciation without great difficulty. With the understanding of the situation, there came quite an emotional outburst with tears and a feeling of shame. Within the next few weeks there were several very minor attacks and then they disappeared. For several years there has not been any difficulty and the patient is definitely better adjusted and happier.

A sales engineer in a large exporting company did not get on well with his superior officer. He disliked him. Despised him would be more appropriate. At the same time he was a bit afraid of him. (During subsequent treatment, he realized that unconsciously J. reminded him of his father who had treated him very harshly during his childhood.) He disagreed thoroughly with J.'s business policies and often planned and even prepared "logical" arguments which would show J. his "mistakes." However, in the interviews with his superior, he acquitted himself very badly. His arguments were awkwardly phrased and ineffectively delivered. Always these conferences made him feel angry and humiliated. One day a rather important matter, about which he felt very strongly, was on the agenda for discussion the following morning. He spent most of the night in his apartment carefully preparing and marshalling his arguments. He awakened the next morning with a "sore" throat, and by the time he got to the office, he could not speak above an indistinct whisper. A laryngologist who examined him the same day said the minor degree of inflammation he found was not sufficient to account for the almost complete loss of speech. Normal, distinct speech did not return for almost three weeks.

A young divorcee, whose marriage had lasted less than a

year, chiefly because she contributed so little to it, fell "madly" in love with a man she had met in Reno and married him. After six months of "ideal happiness" she was no longer happy; in fact, she was very "miserable" and "nervous." I was called to see her by the family physician, who had been hurriedly summoned by the frightened husband because as they were retiring for the night, "Estelle screamed and fell to the floor paralyzed, just as she was getting into bed."

I examined the young woman about a week later. She was not able to walk a single step. Her legs were twisted in a grotesque position, crossed above the knees, rigid as though held in a vise. Clearly the condition was not explainable on the basis of any disease of the brain, spinal cord or nerves. Her general condition was excellent—good color, no fever, normal heart action. She did not seem at all upset emotionally and chatted amiably while I examined her. It was hysteria. Furthermore, it seemed fairly obvious that the "paralysis" was not only a symbolic, but an actual defense against sexual intercourse.

Even though the "paralysis" was removed readily enough by suggestion, and although I tried to fortify the "cure" by explanation derived from the material obtained from eight treatment periods (the patient was unwilling to continue) I did not feel I had accomplished much. True enough, she assured me I was a "wonderful" doctor, but then everything in her life was either "wonderful" or "ghastly."

Some years later, I learned that she had divorced her husband, married twice subsequently and that the fourth marriage was "on the rocks."

From the few interviews I had with the patient, including two pentothal interviews, came these few things: Estelle had been a "nervous child" given to hysterical "fits" when she could not have her own way. She loved her father and hated her mother. Why? "Mother punished me" (quite mildly, it proved) "but Daddy was wonderful, so gentle and considerate, and he never even scolded me"—"Probably it was a mistake to break off my first marriage. Jack was nice in many ways and in *one* way we were well suited" (this very coyly). "Bill" (her second husband) "was inconsiderate, rough and demanding"—"Well, yes, I might as well say so, I mean about sex." In a pentothal interview, she screamed, "I hate you, Bill, don't you dare touch me." And, so on.

In the brief case histories I have given may be found the warp and woof of hysteria.

Neurasthenia, and the anxiety reactions, are basically different from conversion hysteria. For one thing, the formation of the symptoms is much more intricate; the use of the mechanisms of defense is psychologically more skillful and far less obvious. Often the psychiatrist wanders through an unconsciously very cunningly contrived maze before he can find a way out for the patient. For instance, who at first glance would suspect that deep overconcern and anxiety on the part of a wife about her husband, frantic with real fear that a dreadful accident has occurred if he is ten minutes late in returning home, may consciously mask guilt feelings, which overlie an unconscious wish for his death? Or a husband's unconscious desire to be rid of a wife, perhaps because in his emotionally immature perspective she falls far short of his mother ideal with which he is still closely identified. Many conscious and unconscious layers of psychological insulation have to be peeled off before the truth, of which the patient is not even dimly aware, is revealed. Some interesting studies would seem to show that some mothers who constantly overfeed their children, not in the way of good mothers the world over, but literally stuffing them until the seams of their clothes are strained and their eyes begin to bulge—in reality are consciously compensating for inner guilt feelings, for not really wanting the child and not loving it sufficiently.

Another difference is that unlike conversion hysteria which emotionally tends to be a complacent, laissez-faire affair, there is in neurasthenia and the anxiety states marked emotional turmoil, often expressed as tormenting feelings of anxiety and experienced physically as tension. Known dangers, if they are severe enough, may drain our courage and strength, but it is the unknown that really grips our souls.

The psychosomatic signs and symptoms in neurasthenia and the anxiety neuroses tend to be less finished, less complete than in conversion hysteria. Usually total function, like walking or talking, seeing or hearing, are not abolished. More usual are partial symptoms, "muscular weakness," "spots" before the eyes, feelings of fullness in the ears, distressing heart sensations, shortness of breath, skin rashes and a host of others.

Studding the area of anxiety, arising out of unsolved emotional conflicts, and the psychological necessity of keeping them from breaking into consciousness, there are many and varied symptoms. In neurasthenia, fatigue, impaired concentration (which often patients in great alarm interpret falsely as memory failure), self-conscious and inferiority feelings, irritability, depression, phobias, etc. Many of these symptoms are repeated in the anxiety reactions, with perhaps more clearly defined segments or phobias. These fears are tied in consciousness to almost anything one can think of—open places, glass, dirt, fur, feathers. Painful as they are to the patient they serve to distract him from even more painful experiences, the recognition of the real nature and meaning of the phobias. They remind me of the trailing of the pretended broken wing by the mother bird as she tries to lead the chance observer away from the vicinity of her helpless young. Excepting that in the instance of the phobia, it is the sufferer who tries desperately to divert himself from the hidden nest of emotional conflict by some surface fear, perhaps claustrophobia.

In both neurasthenia and the anxiety states, innumerable psychosomatic symptoms appear, involving functional disturbances in every organ and part of the body. In the anxiety reactions startling anxiety crises may occur, sometimes with blanching pallor terrifically overacting heart and a sense of impending death. Or there may be nausea, vomiting, diarrhea, sweating, feelings of suffocation, dizziness and violent trembling. There could scarcely be plainer evidence of the bodily mirroring of disturbed inner emotions.

Neurasthenia, anxiety states and, indeed, all the psychoneuroses are compromises. Escapes? Yes. Retreats? Yes, but only to a line of defense, somewhere between everyday reality and a psychosis. Carefully they avoid the complete reality abandonment of a psychosis, with its extravagant and fantastic delusions, often spoken of as "insane." The psychoneuroses, all in all, represent the best compromise that a particular personality, besieged by mental conflict, can effect at any given time. The symptoms, I repeat, are the symbols of hidden conflict. To the ego and of the ego, they are the saving justification for being sick. The ego is able to point to the "heart," "stomach," and other symptoms and proclaim, "See, this is why and how I am sick."

The symptoms of a psychoneurosis are more than that. They represent, too, the battle being waged by the personality against the acceptance of the disabling illness.

There is a long antecedent interval of struggle inside the psyche, an attempt to adjust the differences between sharply divergent behavior demands. Then usually there is an insult from the environment, as in one of my patients who suddenly learned the sordid details of his wife's repeated infidelities. It was his Achilles' heel. I am inclined to think that all of us have a vulnerable spot, a psychological Achilles' heel. Usually these sensitive, more or less defenseless psychic areas can be traced back to deficits in the early child-mother, child-parent relationships. In any event, when this vulnerable place is wounded, frequently one may expect the appearance of symptoms. In the patient mentioned above, the first symptom was severe and frightening heart palpitation. So often the bodily symptoms in neurasthenia and anxiety states are the profiles of the physical pattern for "flight" or "fight" seen in frightened or infuriated animals.

Look at a cat, experimentally frightened in the laboratory by a fierce dog! It is obvious at once to anyone that something very moving is happening to the cat. Probably the consensus would be that the cat is desperately frightened and fighting mad. It is. There is every evidence of it. The back is arched, hair standing on end, pupils dilated. The cat is furiously spitting. Examinations show heart and blood vessels at the very peak of energetic functioning. Blood pressure is raised. Muscle metabolism is increased. Not only are the body organs and muscles receiving more blood, but the brain where quick decisions must be made is being richly supplied. Certain of the ductless glands and notably the adrenals share in the production of blood activity and pressure, probably even shortening the clotting time of the blood. If it is to be a fight to the finish, profuse bleeding might mean the difference between life and death. The liver stimulates the discharge of more sugar into the blood stream so that the muscles are adequately fueled for the mobilization of energy. Respiration is rapid. On the other hand, stomach and intestinal movements are decreased. Their functional activity would impede flight or fight.

With certain allowances and reservations, I think all this is somewhat akin to the situation in the body of the patient at certain stages of neurasthenic and anxiety reactions, the fighting stages. The allowances and reservations are largely in favor of the cat. For one thing, human beings *remember*. All too vividly, they remember the symptoms, the heart palpitation or what not, and remembering, the anxiety is increased. The way is paved for frequent recurrence of the symptoms. A vicious psychosomatic circle is set into operation. Furthermore, the problem of the cat is concrete—the menace of the fierce dog, the fear and anger, the necessity of escaping or fighting it out to a finish, the mobilization of the body forces and defenses best to accomplish this objective. But in the human being, with neurasthenia and anxiety states, the symptoms are so often the reanimation of childhood patterns, serious emotional trauma to the ego, repressed and dropped into the not-conscious mind.

There has been a long period of futile attempts to solve a problem, the origin of which is hidden from consciousness and the nature of which is not understood by the patient. The individual in the grip of a mental conflict senses that there is a psychological threat and more or less blindly fights against it. The symptoms appear and reappear with varying intensity.

Eventually, sooner or later, timed by the resistance of each particular personality, the tide of battle begins to go against the patient. There is fatigue—not muscular tiredness, but the fatigue of emotional wear and tear. The reflex reactions and sensations continue but the patient loses his aggressive attitude. His outer world shrinks and his inner world consists more and more of anxiety and residual sensations. The potential anxiety neurotic, and particularly the potential neurasthenic becomes increasingly introspective about his somatic sensations and brings into focus even normal sensations, usually disregarded, like the beat of the heart or the peristaltic waves of the stomach. He broods and ruminates over them, worries about them, ponders them. Often he endows them with dire significance, heart disease, an impending stroke, diabetes, cancer! It is at about this cross-section of his illness that he seeks medical help.

The analogy I have made might be objected to on the grounds that there are no fierce dogs in the world of humans. But there are. Even though they do not snarl and bite, yet they are fiercer and more dangerous than laboratory animals. And we are not so remote from the physiology of the cat but that on one level we respond in much the same way to fear.

From the pages of my records here are a few of many situations. They occur frequently in spite of the culture, refinements, material comforts and protections of modern life. These veneers are often stripped, exposing ugly, raw sores. The happiness and security of a woman, married and with two children, is in jeopardy, because a blackmailer threatens to reveal a serious mistake of her past to her husband. A young woman has real reason to fear that she is illegitimately pregnant and by a man of a different race and color. A wife in love with her husband, and for herself and her three children absolutely dependent upon him economically, has every reason to believe that her husband has attempted incestuous relations with a twelve-year-old daughter. An old couple, powerless to stay the increasingly serious delinquencies of an only son of seventeen, seemingly headed for a career in crime, prison and disgrace. These psychological dogs are fierce enough!

There are serious psychological threats within the framework of difficult home problems, sickness, particularly when chronic and hopeless, operations, and accidents and deprivations by death, all sorts of marital problems and sexual maladjustments, illicit relationships, insurmountable obstacles and frustrations in the love life.

Not that a serious insult from the environment is needed to precipitate a neurasthenic, anxiety or other neurosis. There may be merely something quite trivial or, indeed, nothing at all. The amour propre, the pride of the ego in maintaining psychological appearance may not be very great or the surface resistance may have been sapped by the severe and long-continued conflict behind the curtains of consciousness, a conflict more and more insistent upon some relief of inner pressure, demanding a compromise, even though it be a neurotic one. If at all possible, the ego "prefers" the saving grace of some face-saving occurrence. In this connection, it is interesting how often anxiety or neurasthenic symptoms follow close upon the heels of an uncomplicated illness like pneumonia, a simple fracture of a bone or a physiological process like normal childbirth.

Sometimes patients think their psychiatrists are not enough impressed by their symptoms, do not pay enough attention to them. The psychiatrist is impressed by the headache or backache or nausea or dizziness, but he is even more impressed by the necessity of discovering why the patient has these complaints. The answers are to be found in the long life history of the patient, and often in the area of childhood. Many of the answers are shrouded in the fogs of repression.

Obsessional thinking is "must" thinking, thinking which at least until its underlying sources have been uncovered is beyond the control of the person. However much he may consciously strive *not* to think of suicide or murder or serried rows of pine trees or what not, the thought persists and continues to dominate a large area of his thinking. Part, but only a small part, of the reason is simple enough. The very effort *not* to think of "it" defeats its own purpose. Often, if we make up our minds not to think of something, then that something is apt to knock all the more frequently and loudly at the door of memory. In pathological obsessional thinking, the reasons are deeper and more intricate.

Compulsive behavior is "must" behavior. It is behavior which, until its unconscious mainsprings have been revealed, must be carried out, even though the compulsive patient strives mightily to overcome the overmastering urge to do or not to do something. It may involve some simple act, to touch something or perhaps to refrain from touching it. Compulsions may be more serious, such as stealing (kleptomania) or setting fires (pyromania). In compulsive behavior, long and unbelievably involved and complicated rituals may be developed so that it may take the patient hours to get to bed at night or get up in the morning. Sometimes things which should be routine, like taking off the shoes or shaving or brushing the teeth, become the subject of endless pro and con inner psychic arguments. This is called "morbid indecision" and sometimes it may result literally in paralysis of action. I knew a man, who until he recovered, had to resort to the barber for shaving, since frequently for as much as a whole hour he would stand transfixed before his mirror, lathered shaving brush in hand, but unable to decide whether or not to apply it to his face.

Rarely is obsessional thinking directly translated into compulsive behavior. Indeed, sometimes it would seem as though the obsessional train of thought is a protection against carrying out the act. I have never known a true obsessive-compulsive patient, his mind occupied with fears of suicide, who actually took his own life.

On the other hand, unquestionably compulsive behavior is connected with various obsessions, which in turn are the cover-up or camouflage of repressed conflicts. Kleptomania often probably is the compulsive behavior expression of hidden sexual complexes. In the intelligent, middle-aged patient I cited, who was so obsessed by the number "13" that he was compelled to resort constantly to humiliating and ridiculous behavior, such as counting his steps and hopping over every thirteenth one—the real reason was the repressed complex of having been seduced in his boyhood by an ignorant, superstitious serving maid. In the woman who was made intensely sick to her stomach by the sight or odor of flowers, particularly roses, and who was compelled to walk long distances out of her way in order to avoid passing florist shops—the hidden reason was the repressed remembrance of her seduction and jilting by a faithless lover, who under promise to marry her, seduced her the last time he saw her, at which time he brought her a beautiful bunch of red roses.

Obsessions and compulsions are liberally distributed throughout the psychoses and psychoneuroses, but it is in the obsessive-compulsive neuroses that they come to their full flowering.

In this psychoneurosis, the psyche makes use of an ingenious combination of defensive mechanisms—displacement, substitution and symbolism.

A simple physical analogy is worth repeating. If into a tumbler flush filled with water, a stone is dropped, some of the water is displaced. The displaced water represents the emotional mental material which can no longer be contained in consciousness and must be displaced into the area of the "not remembered." The stone becomes the substitute for the displaced water and represents it. It is its symbol. Psychologically, it may be compared to the obsessions and compulsions which appear in consciousness as the symbols of repressed material.

Perhaps this diagram will be of some use in explaining the mechanisms at work in the production of an obsessive-compulsive psychoneurosis. The diagram will be used to illustrate the case of an interesting patient I treated.

$\boxed{E}\,\boxed{Em}$: Something which happened in the life of the individual, the experience and the emotional reaction it produced, once joined in consciousness. $\boxed{E}$ = The remembrance of the experiences displaced (repressed) into the "not conscious" mind.

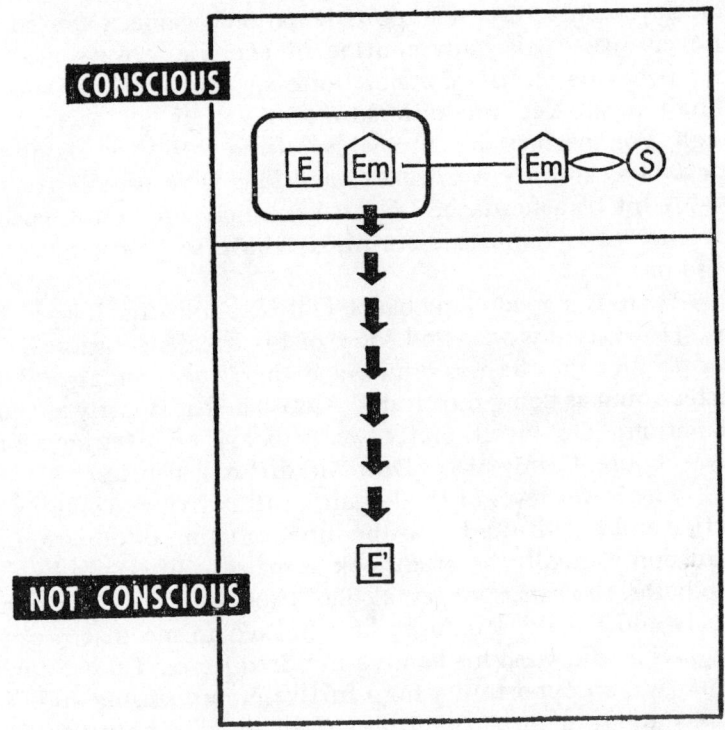

⌐Em⌐⊃Ⓢ: ⌐Em⌐ the unattached emotion (anxiety) becomes attached to Ⓢ the substitution for and the symbol of the displaced experience. It is often symbolized as obsessive thinking and compulsive behavior.

A.B., just turned forty-five, is a very successful man, but until recently he was very unhappy. He is married to a nice, intelligent, mature wife, and they have one child, a lovely little daughter. At one time in the course of treatment, he confided to me that he was "afraid" of the little girl, in fact, that he was afraid of all children. He felt ill-at-ease and somewhat insecure with them.

"But why should you feel that way?"—"Oh," he replied rather vaguely, "I don't think I really know. Sometimes I have a sort of feeling they can see through me."

The "front" of his personality he presented to the outside world was a good front. I am sure that even his intimate friends would have been surprised to learn with what slavish obsession and compulsion he worshiped at the altar of the complex of "clean, healthy living." Much of his behavior in this direction was carefully camouflaged and even usefully sublimated. For instance, earlier in his life he became a superb athlete, one of the five top-flight players in a certain important national game. Later in life, he never missed his daily routine of exercise, always vigorous. Other behavior facets were not quite so easily substantiated by rationalization. Yet, the rationalizations, all in all, were adroit enough. For instance, he invariably retired to bed at about nine o'clock. His carefully worded explanations were usually convincing—"A bit of a headache"—"An extremely important business conference early tomorrow morning. I have to be clear-headed." And so on.

He took a good many baths. Only he, and later I, knew how many. However, his wife and some of his friends occasionally observed to him that he was "quite a bather," or, jokingly, "There is such a thing as being too clean." Always he had a fairly adequate explanation: "Got myself pretty sweaty today," or "Messing around the warehouse. Grimy place. Dust and dirt of centuries."

The lower level of the "clean, healthy living" complex was secretive and ritualistic. It was the inner sanctum of obsession and compulsion. Actually, he often took as many as fifteen baths a day —tub baths, showers, sponges, alcohol rubs—most of them surreptitiously and hastily. Ruefully, he admitted to me that probably some days he did wash his hands a hundred times. Taking a drink of water was an opportunity for a furtive mouth-rinsing and, if no one was about, a throat gargling. (Incidentally, he never drank alcohol or used tobacco in any form.) There were many long rituals. The one which had to do with getting ready for bed at night was the most complicated. Its details were almost endless. It would require more pages than the publisher has available to describe the ritual. It was an orgy of cleanliness. Some of the high points were: 1) After bathing, a careful examination of the body surface with the aid of a mirror, and the rubbing of any "dirt" spots with a pledget of cotton dipped in alcohol. 2) The meticulous examination of the clothing to be worn the next day and a rubbing with cleansing fluid of those parts of the clothing which might come into contact with the body, particularly under the arms and the "crotch" (A.B. always emphasized "the crotch"). 3) The careful fashioning of two pieces of cotton, each about five inches long, which were soaked in Listerine, inserted into the inner folds of the groin and left there for five minutes. 4) The meticulous scrutiny of the top and bottom bed-sheets with a few drops of Listerine judiciously applied to any place that "didn't look quite clean." And so on.

The patient, badgered as he was, still retained a sense of humor and once smilingly told me how he had worked vigorously for several minutes on a bedclothes "spot" only to discover that it was a shadow cast by the edge of the bedlamp. Incidentally, A.B.

had good insight. He understood that his thinking and behavior were "illogical, ridiculous and fantastic," but at that cross-section he was powerless to inhibit it.

What repressions were there, so serious that it was necessary to keep the lid of obsessions, compulsions and elaborate ritual tightly clamped down to prevent their appearance in consciousness? Of course, there were many repressions, but one seemed to be directly determining. When A.B. was eight years old, an older brother (whom A.B. always feared and disliked) discovered him in the act of masturbation. The older brother took full advantage of the situation. There was quite a dramatic scene. The brother stigmatized A.B. as "unhealthy," "unclean," "filthy," "dirty," etc., etc., and threatened to expose him to the family. He made the little fellow get down on his knees and swear never to do *"it"* again and to promise to lead a "clean, healthy life." There are not enough adjectives to describe A.B.'s emotional state—fear, humiliation, shame, degradation.

Turning to the diagram, we are now at the cross-section when there was an actual experience, vividly and closely associated with a deep, emotional reaction, [E][Em]

CONSCIOUS

[E]
↓
―――――――――――――――――――――
↓
↓
↓
[E]

NOT CONSCIOUS

For two years following the experience, the older brother, in the words of A.B. "continued to hold it over my head"—"never let me forget it," "made me promise again and again," "kept me terrorized by intimating that after all he might have to tell my father and mother."

Then the brother went away from home to college. Soon after, A.B. managed to "forget" the experience. He could no longer tolerate the belittlement and shame of living with it in consciousness, so he repressed it. In the above diagram, the remembrance of the happening was displaced into the "not-conscious."

This then left suspended in consciousness the emotional reaction provoked by the original happening [Em] as so-called free floating anxiety.

It was psychologically mandatory that this emotionally sensitive material should become attached to something symbolic of what had been repressed. And so it did become attached to the complex ⓢ of "clean, healthy living" which could be tolerated in consciousness, even though it led to extreme obsessional thinking and bizarre compulsive behavior.

CONSCIOUS

NOT CONSCIOUS

I have sketched the psychological geography of the terrain upon which are erected the houses of "functional" sickness. Each house is built of and furnished with varying and carefully selected materials. In each instance, material and furnishings, the decor is that which the particular personality is familiar with and has found most useful in the small evasions of reality in so-called normal life. When faced with psychological crisis, the "functional" compromise to which we resort must be as secure and protective as possible.

Incidentally, the psychoneurosis has been called the great American disease. I do not know about that, but I do know that each year hundreds of thousands of people are rendered far less effective, in fact, partially disabled and made unhappy, by functional illness.

ERICH FROMM / Individual and Social Origins of Neurosis

THE HISTORY of science is a history of erroneous statements. Yet these erroneous statements which mark the progress of thought have a particular quality: they are productive. And they are not just *errors* either; they are statements, the truth of which is veiled by misconceptions, is clothed in erroneous and inadequate concepts. They are rational visions which contain the seed of truth, which matures and blossoms in the continuous effort of mankind to arrive at objectively valid knowledge about man and nature. Many profound insights about man and society have first found expression in myths and fairy tales, others in metaphysical speculations, others in scientific assumptions which have proven to be incorrect after one or two generations.

It is not difficult to see why the evolution of human thought proceeds in this way. The aim of any thinking human being is to arrive at the *whole* truth, to understand the *totality* of phenomena which puzzle him. He has only *one* short life and must want to have a vision of the truth about the world in this short span of time. But he could only understand this totality if his life span were identical with that of the human race. It is only in the process of historical evolution that man develops techniques of observation, gains greater objectivity as an observer, collects new data which are necessary to know if one is to understand the *whole*. There is a gap, then, between what even the greatest genius can visualize as the truth, and the limitations of knowledge which depend on the accident of the historical phase he happens to live in. Since we cannot live in suspense, we try to fill out this gap with the material of knowledge at hand, even if this material is lacking in the validity which the essence of the vision may have.

Every discovery which has been made and will be made has a long history in which the truth contained in it finds a less and less veiled and distorted expression and approaches more and more adequate formulations. The development of scientific thought is not one in which old statements are discarded as false and replaced by new and correct ones; it is rather a process of continuous *reinterpretation* of older statements, by which their true kernel is freed from distorting elements. The great pioneers of thought, of whom Freud is one, express ideas which determine the progress of scientific thinking for centuries. Often the workers in the field orient themselves in one of two ways; they fail to differentiate between the essential and the accidental, and defend rigidly the whole system of the master, thus blocking the process of reinterpretation and clarification; or they make the same mistake of failing to differentiate between the essential and the accidental, and equally rigidly fight against the old theories and try to replace them by new ones of their own. In both the orthodox and the rebellious rigidity, the constructive evolution of the vision of the master is blocked. The real task, however, is to reinterpret, to sift out, to recognize that certain insights had to be phrased and understood in erroneous concepts because of the limitations of thought peculiar to the historical phase in which they were first formulated. We may feel then that we sometimes understand the author better than he understood himself, but that we are only capable of doing so by the guiding light of his original vision.

This general principle, that the way of scientific progress is *constructive reinterpretation of basic visions* rather than repeating or discarding them, certainly holds true of Freud's theoretical formulations. There is scarcely a discovery of Freud which does not contain fundamental truths and yet which does not lend itself to an organic development beyond the concepts in which it has been clothed.

A case in point is Freud's theory on the origin of neurosis. I think we still know little of what constitutes a neurosis and less what its origins are. Many physiological, anthropological and sociological data will have to be collected before we can hope to arrive at any conclusive answer. What I shall do is to use Freud's view on the origin of neurosis as an illustration of the general principle which I have discussed, that reinterpretation is the constructive method of scientific progress.

Freud states that the *Oedipus complex* is justifiably regarded as the kernel of neurosis. I believe that this statement is the most fundamental one which can be made about the origin of neurosis, but I think it needs to be qualified and reinterpreted in a frame of reference different from the one Freud had in mind. What Freud meant in his statement was this: because of the sexual desire the little boy, let us say, has for his mother, he becomes the rival of his father, and the neurotic development consists in failure to cope with the anxiety rooted in this rivalry in a satisfactory way. I believe that Freud touched upon the most elementary root of neurosis in pointing to the conflict between the child and parental authority and the failure of the child to solve this conflict satisfactorily. But I do not think that this conflict is brought about essentially by the sexual rivalry, but that it results from the child's reaction to the pressure of parental authority, the child's fear of it and submission to it. Before I go on elaborating this point, I should like to differentiate between two kinds of authority. One is *objective,* based on the competency of the person in authority to function properly with respect to the task of guidance he has to perform. This kind of authority may be called *rational* authority. In contrast to it is what may be called *irrational* authority, which is based on the power which the authority has over those subjected to it and on the fear and awe with which the latter reciprocate.

It happens that, in most cultures, human relationships are greatly determined by irrational authority. People function in our society, as in most societies on the record of history, by becoming adjusted to their social role at the price of giving up part of their own will, their originality and spontaneity. While every human being represents the whole of mankind with all its potentialities, any functioning society is and has to be primarily interested in its self-preservation. The particular ways in which a society functions are determined by a number of *objective* economic and political factors, which are given at any point of historical development. Societies have to operate within the possibilities and limitations of their particular historical situation. In order that any society may function well, its members must acquire the kind of character which makes them *want* to act in the way they *have* to act as members of the society or of a special class within it. They have to *desire* what objectively is *necessary* for them to do. *Outer force* is to be replaced by *inner compulsion,* and by the particular kind of human energy which is channeled into character traits. As long as mankind has not attained a state of organization in which the interest of the individual and that of society are identical, the aims of society have to be attained at a greater or lesser expense of the freedom and spontaneity of the individual. This aim is performed by the process of child training and education. While education aims at the development of a child's potentialities, it has also the function of reducing his independence and freedom to the level necessary for the existence of that particular society. Although societies differ with regard to the extent to which the child must be impressed by irrational authority, it is always part of the function of child training to have this happen.

The child does not meet society directly at first; it meets it through the medium of his parents, who in their character structure and methods of education represent the social structure, who are the psychological agency of society, as it were. What, then, happens to the child in relationship to his parents? It meets through them the kind of authority which is prevailing in the particular society in which it lives, and this kind of authority tends to break his will, his spontaneity, his independence. But man is not born to be broken, so the child fights against the authority represented by his parents; he fights for his freedom not only *from* pressure but also for his freedom to be himself, a full-fledged human being, not an automaton. Some children are more successful than others; most of them are defeated to some extent in their fight for freedom. The ways in which this defeat is brought about are manifold, but whatever they are, the scars left from this defeat in the child's fight against irrational authority are to be found at the bottom of every neurosis. This scar is represented in a syndrome the most important features of which are: the weakening or paralysis of the person's originality and spontaneity; the weakening of the self and the substitution of a pseudo-self, in which the feeling of "I am" is dulled and replaced by the experience of self as the sum total of expectations others have about me; the substitution of autonomy by heteronomy; the fogginess, or, to use Dr. Sullivan's term, the "parataxic" quality of all interpersonal experiences.

My suggestion that the Oedipus complex be interpreted not as a result of the child's sexual rivalry with the parent of the same sex but as the child's fight with irrational authority represented by the parents does not imply, however, that the sexual factor does not play a significant role, but the emphasis is not on the incestuous wishes of the child and their necessarily tragic outcome, its original sin, but on the parents' prohibitive influence on the normal sexual activity of the child. The child's physical functions—first those of defecation, then his sexual desires and activities—are weighed down by moral considerations. The child is made to feel guilty with regard to these functions, and since the sexual urge is present in every person from childhood on, it becomes a constant source of the feeling of guilt. What is the function of this feeling of guilt? It serves to break the child's will and to drive it into submission. The parents use it, although unintentionally, as a means to make the child submit. There is nothing more effective in breaking any person than to give him the conviction of wickedness. The more guilty one feels, the more easily one submits because the authority has proven its own power by its right to accuse.

What appears as a feeling of guilt, is actually the fear of displeasing those of whom one is afraid. This feeling of guilt is the only one which most people experience as a moral problem, while the genuine moral problem, that of realizing one's potentialities, is lost from sight. Guilt is reduced to disobedience and is not felt as that which it is in a genuine moral sense, self-mutilation.

To sum up this point, it may be said that it is the defeat in the fight against authority which constitutes the kernel of the neurosis, and that not the incestuous wish of the child but the stigma connected with sex is one among the factors in breaking down his will. Freud painted a picture of the necessarily *tragic* outcome of a child's most fundamental wishes: his incestuous wishes are bound to fail and force the child into some sort of submission.

Have we not reason to assume that this hypothesis expresses in a veiled way Freud's profound pessimism with regard to any basic improvement in man's fate and his belief in the indispensable nature of irrational authority? Yet this attitude is only one part of Freud. He is at the same time the man who said that "from the time of puberty onward the human individual must devote himself to the great task of freeing himself from the parents"; he is the man who devised a therapeutic method the aim of which is the independence and freedom of the individual.

However, defeat in the fight for freedom does not always lead to neurosis. As a matter of fact, if this were the case, we would have to consider the vast majority of people as neurotics. What, then, are the specific conditions which make for the neurotic outcome of this defeat? There are some conditions which I can only mention: for example, one child may be broken more thoroughly than others, and the conflict between his anxiety and his basic human desires may, therefore, be sharper and more unbearable; or the child may have developed a sense of freedom and originality which is greater than that of the average person, and the defeat may thus be more unacceptable. But instead of enumerating other conditions which make for neurosis, I prefer to reverse the question and ask what the conditions are which are responsible for the fact that so many people do *not* become neurotic in spite of the failure in their personal fight for freedom. It seems to be useful at this point to differentiate between two concepts: that of defect and that of neurosis. If a person fails to attain freedom, spontaneity, a genuine experience of self, he may be considered to have a severe defect, provided we assume that freedom and spontaneity are the objective goals to be attained by every human being. If such a goal is not attained by the majority of members of any given society, we deal with the phenomenon of *socially patterned defect*. The individual shares it with many others; he is not aware of it as a defect, and his security is not threatened by the experience of being different, of being an outcast, as it were. What he may have lost in richness and in a genuine feeling of happiness is made up by the security of fitting in with the rest of mankind—*as he knows them*. As a matter of fact, his very defect may have been raised to a virtue by his culture and thus give him an enhanced feeling of achievement. An illustration is the feeling of guilt and anxiety which Calvin's doctrines aroused in men. It may be said that the person who is overwhelmed by a feeling of his own powerlessness and unworthiness, by the unceasing doubt of whether he is saved or condemned to eternal punishment, who is hardly capable of any genuine joy and has made himself into the cog of a machine which he has to serve, has a severe defect. Yet this very defect was culturally patterned; it was looked upon as particularly valuable, and the individual was thus protected from the neurosis which he would have acquired in a culture where the defect would give him a feeling of profound inadequacy and isolation.

Spinoza has formulated the problem of the socially patterned defect very clearly. He says: "Many people are seized by one and the same affect with great consistency. All his senses are so strongly affected by one object that he believes this object to be present even if it is not. If this happens while the person is awake, the person is believed to be insane. . . . But if the *greedy* person thinks only of money and possessions, the *ambitious* one only of fame, one does not think of them as being insane, but only as annoying; generally one has contempt for them. But *factually,* greediness, ambition, and so forth are forms of insanity, although usually one does not think of them as 'illness.' " These words were written a few hundred years ago; they still hold true, although the defect has been culturally patterned to *such* an extent now that it is not generally thought any more to be annoying or contemptuous. Today we come across a person and find that he acts and feels like an automaton; that he never experiences anything which is really his; that he experiences himself entirely as the person he thinks he is supposed to be; that smiles have replaced laughter, meaningless chatter replaced communicative speech; dulled despair has taken the place of genuine pain. Two statements can be made about this person. One is that he suffers from a defect of spontaneity and individuality which may seem incurable. At the same time it may be said that he does not differ essentially from thousands of others who are in the same position. With *most* of them, the cultural pattern provided for the defect saves them from the outbreak of neurosis. With *some,* the cultural pattern does not function, and the defect appears as a severe neurosis. The fact that in these cases the cultural pattern does not suffice to prevent the outbreak of a manifest neurosis is in most cases to be explained by the particular severity and structure of the individual conflicts. I shall not go into this any further. The point I want to stress is the necessity to proceed from the problem of the *origins of neurosis* to the problem of the *origins of the culturally patterned defect;* to the problem of the *pathology of normalcy.*

This aim implies that the psychoanalyst is not only concerned with the readjustment of the neurotic individual to his given society. His task must be also to recognize that the individual's ideal of normalcy may contradict the aim of the full realization of himself as a human being. It is the belief of the progressive forces in society that such a realization is possible, that the interest of society and of the individual need not be antagonistic forever. Psychoanalysis, if it does not lose sight of the human problem, has an important contribution to make in this direction. This contribution, by which it transcends the field of a medical specialty, was part of the vision which Freud had.

EDGAR ALLAN POE/William Wilson

> *What say of it? what say* CONSCIENCE *grim,*
> *That spectre in my path?*
> CHAMBERLAIN's Pharronida.

LET ME call myself, for the present, William Wilson. The fair page now lying before me need not be sullied with my real appellation. This has been already too much an object for the scorn—for the horror—for the detestation of my race. To the uttermost regions of the globe have not the indignant winds bruited its unparalleled infamy? Oh, outcast of all outcasts most abandoned!—to the earth art thou not forever dead? to its honors, to its flowers, to its golden aspirations?—and a cloud, dense, dismal, and limitless, does it not hang eternally between thy hopes and heaven?

I would not, if I could, here or today, embody a record of my later years of unspeakable misery and unpardonable crime. This epoch—these later years—took unto themselves a sudden elevation in turpitude, whose origin alone it is my present purpose to assign. Men usually grow base by degrees. From me, in an instant, all virtue dropped bodily as a mantle. From comparatively trivial wickedness I passed, with the stride of a giant, into more than the enormities of an Elah-Gabalus. What chance—what one event brought this evil thing to pass, bear with me while I relate. Death approaches; and the shadow which foreruns him has thrown a softening influence over my spirit. I long, in passing through the dim valley, for the sympathy—I had nearly said for the pity—of my fellow men. I would fain have them believe that I have been, in some measure, the slave of circumstances beyond human control. I would wish them to seek out for me, in the details I am about to give, some little oasis of *fatality* amid a wilderness of error. I would have them allow—what they cannot refrain from allowing—that, although temptation may have erewhile existed as great, man was never *thus*, at least, tempted before—certainly, never *thus* fell. And is it therefore that he has never thus suffered? Have I not indeed been living in a dream? And am I not now dying a victim to the horror and the mystery of the wildest of all sublunary visions?

I am the descendant of a race whose imaginative and easily excitable temperament has at all times rendered them remarkable; and, in my earliest infancy, I gave evidence of having fully inherited the family character. As I advanced in years it was more strongly developed; becoming, for many reasons, a cause of serious disquietude to my friends, and of positive injury to myself. I grew self-willed, addicted to the wildest caprices, and a prey to the most ungovernable passions. Weak-minded, and beset with constitutional infirmities akin to my own, my parents could do but little to check the evil propensities which distinguished me. Some feeble and ill-directed efforts resulted in complete failure on their part, and, of course, in total triumph on mine. Thenceforward my voice was a household law; and at an age when few children have abandoned their leading-strings, I was left to the guidance of my own will, and became, in all but name, the master of my own actions.

My earliest recollections of a school-life, are connected with a large, rambling, Elizabethan house, in a misty-looking village of England, where were a vast number of gigantic and gnarled trees, and where all the houses were excessively ancient. In truth, it was a dream-like and spirit-soothing place, that venerable old town. At this moment, in fancy, I feel the refreshing chilliness of its deeply-shadowed avenues, inhale the fragrance of its thousand shrubberies, and thrill anew with undefinable delight, at the deep hollow note of the church-bell, breaking, each hour, with sullen and sudden roar, upon the stillness of the dusky atmosphere in which the fretted Gothic steeple lay imbedded and asleep.

It gives me, perhaps, as much of pleasure as I can now in any manner experience, to dwell upon minute recollections of the school and its concerns. Steeped in misery as I am—misery, alas! only too real—I shall be pardoned for seeking relief, however slight and temporary, in the weakness of a few rambling details. These, moreover, utterly trivial, and even ridiculous in themselves, assume, to my fancy, adventitious importance, as connected with a period and a locality when and where I recognize the first ambiguous monitions of the destiny which afterward so fully overshadowed me. Let me then remember.

The house, I have said, was old and irregular. The grounds were extensive, and a high and solid brick wall, topped with a bed of mortar and broken glass, encompassed the whole. This prison-like rampart formed the limit of our domain; beyond it we saw but thrice a week—once every Saturday afternoon, when, attended by two ushers, we were permitted to take brief walks in a body through some of the neighboring fields—and twice during Sunday, when we were paraded in the same formal manner to the morning and evening service in the one church of the village. Of this church the principal of our school was pastor. With how deep a spirit of wonder and perplexity was I wont to regard him from our remote pew in the gallery, as, with step solemn and slow, he ascended the pulpit! This reverend man, with countenance so demurely benign, with robes so glossy and so clerically flowing, with wig so minutely powdered, so rigid and so vast,—could this be he who, of late, with sour visage, and in snuffy habiliments, administered, ferule in hand, the Draconian Laws of the academy? Oh, gigantic paradox, too utterly monstrous for solution!

At an angle of the ponderous wall frowned a more ponderous gate. It was riveted and studded with iron bolts, and surmounted with jagged iron spikes. What impressions of deep awe did it inspire! It was never opened save for the three periodical egressions and ingressions already mentioned; then, in every creak of its mighty hinges, we found a plenitude of mystery—a world of matter for solemn remark, or for more solemn meditation.

The extensive enclosure was irregular in form, having many capacious recesses. Of these, three or four of the largest constituted the play-ground. It was level, and covered with fine hard gravel. I well remember it had no trees, nor benches, nor any thing similar within it. Of couse it was in the rear of the house. In front lay a small parterre, planted with box and other shrubs, but through this sacred division we passed only upon rare occasions indeed—such as a first advent to school or final departure thence, or perhaps, when a parent or friend having called for us, we joyfully took our way home for the Christmas or Midsummer holydays.

But the house!—how quaint an old building was this!—to me how veritable a palace of enchantment! There was really no end to its windings—to its incomprehensible subdivisions. It was difficult, at any given time, to say with certainty upon which of its two stories one happened to be. From each room to every other there were sure to be found three or four steps either in ascent or descent. Then the lateral branches were innumerable—inconceivable—and so returning in upon themselves, that our most exact ideas in regard to the whole mansion were not very far different from those with which we pondered upon infinity. During the five years of my residence here, I was never able to ascertain with precision, in what remote locality lay the little sleeping apartment assigned to myself and some eighteen or twenty other scholars.

The school-room was the largest in the house—I could not help thinking, in the world. It was very long, narrow, and dismally low, with pointed Gothic windows and a ceiling of oak. In a remote and terror-inspiring angle was a square enclosure of eight or ten feet, comprising the *sanctum*, "during hours," of our principal, the Reverend Dr. Bransby. It was a solid structure, with massy door, sooner than open which in the absence of the "Dominie," we would all have willingly perished by the *peine forte et dure*. In other angles were two other similar boxes, far less reverenced, indeed, but still greatly matters of awe. One of these was the pulpit of the "classical" usher, one of the "English and mathematical." Interspersed about the room, crossing and recrossing in endless irregularity, were innumerable benches and desks, black, ancient, and time-worn, piled desperately with much bethumbed books, and so beseamed with initial letters, names at full length, grotesque figures, and other multiplied efforts of the knife, as to have entirely lost what little of original form might have been their portion in days long departed. A huge bucket with water stood at one extremity of the room, and a clock of stupendous dimensions at the other.

Encompassed by the massy walls of this venerable academy, I passed, yet not in tedium or disgust, the years of the third lustrum of my life. The teeming brain of childhood requires no external world of incident to occupy or amuse it; and the apparently dismal monotony of a school was replete with more intense excitement than my riper youth has derived from luxury, or my full manhood from crime. Yet I must believe that my first mental development had in it much of the uncommon—even much of the *outré*. Upon mankind at large the events of very early existence rarely leave in mature age any definite impression. All is gray shadow—a weak and irregular remembrance—an indistinct regathering of feeble pleasures and phantasmagoric pains. With me this is not so. In childhood I must have felt with the energy of a man what I now find stamped upon memory in lines as vivid, as deep, and as durable as the *exergues* of the Cathaginian medals.

Yet in fact—in the fact of the world's view—how little was there to remember! The morning's awakening, the nightly summons to bed; the connings, the recitations; the periodical half-holidays, and perambulations; the play-ground, with its broils, its pastimes, its intrigues;—these, by a mental sorcery long forgotten, were made to involve a wilderness of sensation, a world of rich incident, a universe of varied emotion, of excitement, the most passionate and spirit-stirring. "*Oh, le bon temps que ce siècle de fer!*"

In truth, the ardor, the enthusiasm, and the imperiousness of my disposition, soon rendered me a marked character among my schoolmates, and by slow, but natural gradations, gave me an ascendancy over all not greatly older than myself;—over all with a single exception. This exception was found in the person of a scholar, who, although no relation, bore the same christian and surname as myself;—a circumstance, in fact, little remarkable; for notwithstanding a noble descent, mine was one of those every-day appellations which seem, by prescriptive right, to have been, time out of mind, the common property of the mob. In this narrative I have therefore designated myself as William Wilson—a fictitious title not very dissimilar to the real. My namesake alone, of those who in school phraseology constituted "our set," presumed to compete with me in the studies of the class—in the sports and broils of the play-ground—to refuse implicit belief in my assertions, and submission to my will—indeed, to interfere with my arbitrary dictation in any respect whatsoever. If there is on earth a supreme and unqualified despotism, it is the despotism of a master-mind in boyhood over the less energetic spirits of its companions.

Wilson's rebellion was to me a source of the greatest embarrassment; the more so as, in spite of the bravado with which in public I made a point of treating him and his pretensions, I secretly felt that I feared him, and could not help thinking the equality which he maintained so easily with myself, a proof of his true superiority; since not to be overcome cost me a perpetual struggle. Yet this superiority—even this equality—was in truth acknowledged by no one but myself; our associates, by some unaccountable blindness, seemed not even to suspect it. Indeed, his competition, his resistance, and especially his impertinent and dogged interference with my purposes, were not more pointed than private. He appeared to be destitute alike of the ambition which urged, and of the passionate energy of mind which enabled me to excel. In his rivalry he might have been supposed actuated solely by a whimsical desire to thwart, astonish, or mortify myself; although there were times when I could not help observing, with a feeling made up of wonder, abasement, and pique, that he mingled with his injuries, his insults, or his contradictions, a certain most inappropriate, and assuredly most unwelcome *affectionateness* of manner. I could only conceive this singular behavior to arise from a consummate self-conceit assuming the vulgar airs of patronage and protection.

Perhaps it was this latter trait in Wilson's conduct, conjoined with our identity of name, and the mere accident of our having entered the school upon the same day, which set afloat the notion that we were brothers, among the senior classes in the academy. These do not usually inquire with much strictness into the affairs of their juniors. I have before said, or should have said, that Wilson was not, in a most remote degree, connected with my family. But assuredly if we *had* been brothers we must have been twins; for, after leaving Dr. Bransby's, I casually learned that my namesake was born on the nineteenth of January, 1813—and this is a somewhat remarkable coincidence; for the day is precisely that of my own nativity.

It may seem strange that in spite of the continual anxiety occasioned me by the rivalry of Wilson, and his intolerable spirit of contradiction, I could not bring myself to hate him altogether. We had, to be sure, nearly every day a quarrel in which, yielding me publicly the palm of victory, he, in some manner, contrived to make me feel that it was he who had deserved it; yet a sense of pride on my part, and a veritable dignity on his own, kept us always upon what are called "speaking terms," while there were many points of strong congeniality in our tempers, operating to awake in me a sentiment which our position alone, perhaps, prevented from ripening into friendship. It is difficult, indeed, to define, or even to describe, my real feelings toward him. They formed a motley and heterogeneous admixture;—some petulant animosity, which was not yet hatred, some esteem, more respect, much fear, with a world of uneasy curiosity. To the moralist it will be necessary to say, in addition, that Wilson and myself were the most inseparable companions.

It was no doubt the anomalous state of affairs existing between us, which turned all my attacks upon him, (and there were many, either open or covert) into the channel of banter or practical joke (giving pain while assuming the aspect of mere fun) rather than into a more serious and determined hostility. But my endeavors on this head were by no means uniformly successful, even when my plans were the most wittily concocted; for my namesake had much about him, in character, of that unassuming and quiet austerity which, while enjoying the poignancy of its own jokes, has no heel of Achilles in itself, and absolutely refuses to be laughed at. I could find, indeed, but one vulnerable point, and that, lying in a personal peculiarity, arising, perhaps, from constitutional disease, would have been spared by any antagonist less at his wit's end than myself;—my rival had a weakness in the facial or guttural organs, which precluded him from raising his voice at any time *above a very low whisper*. Of this defect I did not fail to take what poor advantage lay in my power.

Wilson's retaliations in kind were many; and there was one form of his practical wit that disturbed me beyond measure. How his sagacity first discovered at all that so petty a thing would vex me, is a question I never could solve; but having discovered, he habitually practised the annoyance. I had always felt aversion to my uncourtly patronymic, and its very common, if not plebian prænomen. The words were venom in my ears; and when, upon the day of my arrival, a second William Wilson came also to the academy, I felt angry with him for bearing the name, and doubly disgusted with the name because a stranger bore it, who would be the cause of its two-fold repetition, who would be constantly in my presence, and whose concerns, in the ordinary routine of the school business, must inevitably, on account of the detestable coincidence, be often confounded with my own.

The feeling of vexation thus engendered grew stronger with every circumstance tending to show resemblance, moral or physical, between my rival and myself. I had not then discovered the remarkable fact that we were of the same age; but I saw that we were of the same height, and I perceived that we were even singularly alike in general contour of person and outline of feature. I was galled, too, by the rumor touching a relationship, which had grown current in the upper forms. In a word, nothing could more seriously disturb me, (although I scrupulously concealed such disturbance), than any allusion to a similarity of mind, person, or condition existing between us. But, in truth, I had no reason to believe that (with the exception of the matter of relationship, and in the case of Wilson himself), this similarity had even been made a subject of comment, or even observed at all by our schoolfellows. That *he* observed it in all its bearings, and as fixedly as I, was apparent; but that he could discover in such circumstances so fruitful a field of annoyance, can only be attributed, as I said before, to his more than ordinary penetration.

His cue, which was to perfect an imitation of myself, lay both in words and in actions; and most admirably did he play his part. My dress it was an easy matter to copy; my gait and general manner were without difficulty, appropriated; in spite of his constitutional defect, even my voice did not escape him. My louder tones were, of course, unattempted, but then the key,—it was identical; *and his singular whisper, it grew the very echo of my own.*

How greatly this most exquisite portraiture harassed me (for it could not justly be termed a caricature), I will not now venture to describe. I had but one consolation—in the fact that the imitation, apparently, was noticed by myself alone, and that I had to endure only the knowing and strangely sarcastic smiles of my namesake himself. Satisfied with having produced in my bosom the intended effect, he seemed to chuckle in secret over the sting he had inflicted, and was characteristically disregardful of the public applause which the success of his witty endeavors might have so easily elicited. That the school, indeed, did not feel his design, perceive its accomplishment, and participate in his sneer, was, for many anxious months, a riddle I could not resolve. Perhaps the *gradation* of his copy rendered it not so readily perceptible; or, more possibly, I owed my security to the masterly air of the copyist, who, disdaining the letter (which in a painting is all the obtuse can see), gave but the full spirit of his original for my individual contemplation and chagrin.

I have already more than once spoken of the disgusting air of patronage which he assumed toward me, and of his frequent officious interference with my will. This interference often took the ungracious character of advice; advice not openly given, but hinted or insinuated. I received it with a repugnance which gained strength as I grew in years. Yet, at this distant day, let me do him the simple justice to acknowledge that I can recall no occasion when the suggestions of my rival were on the side of those errors or follies so usual to his immature age and seeming inexperience; that his moral sense, at least, if not his general talents and worldly wisdom, was far keener than my own; and that I might, to-day, have been a better and thus a happier man, had I less frequently rejected the counsels embodied in those meaning whispers which I then but too cordially hated and too bitterly despised.

As it was I at length grew restive in the extreme under his distasteful supervision, and daily resented more and more openly, what I considered his intolerable arrogance. I have said that, in the first years of our connection as schoolmates, my feelings in regard to him might have been easily ripened into friendship; but, in the latter months of my residence at the academy, although the intrusion of his ordinary manner had, beyond doubt, in some measure, abated, my sentiments, in nearly similar proportion, partook very much of positive hatred. Upon one occasion he saw this, I think, and afterward avoided, or made a show of avoiding me.

It was about the same period, if I remember aright, that, in an altercation of violence with him, in which he was more than usually thrown off his guard, and spoke and acted with an openness of demeanor rather foreign to his nature, I discovered, or fancied I discovered, in his accent, in his air, and general appearance, a something which first startled, and then deeply interested me, by bringing to mind dim visions of my earliest infancy—wild, confused, and thronging memories of a time when memory herself was yet unborn. I cannot better describe the sensation which oppressed me, than by saying that I could with difficulty shake off the belief of my having been acquainted with the being who stood before me, at some epoch very long ago—some point of the past even infinitely remote. The delusion, however, faded rapidly as it came; and I mention it at all but to define the day of the last conversation I there held with my singular namesake.

The huge old house, with its countless sub-divisions, had several large chambers communicating with each other, where slept the greater number of the students. There were, however (as must necessarily happen in a building so awkwardly planned), many little nooks or recesses, the odds and ends of the structure; and these the economic ingenuity of Dr. Bransby had also fitted up as dormitories; although, being the merest closets, they were capable of accommodating but a single individual. One of these small apartments was occupied by Wilson.

One night, about the close of my fifth year at the school, and immediately after the altercation just mentioned, finding every one wrapped in sleep, I arose from bed, and, lamp in hand, stole through a wilderness of narrow passages, from my own bedroom to that of my rival. I had long been plotting one of those ill-natured pieces of practical wit at his expense in which I had hitherto been so uniformly unsuccessful. It was my intention, now, to put my scheme in operation and I resolved to make him feel the whole extent of the malice with which I was imbued. Having reached his closet, I noiselessly entered, leaving the lamp, with a shade over it, on the outside. I advanced a step and listened to the sound of his tranquil breathing. Assured of his being asleep, I returned, took the light, and with it again approached the bed. Close curtains were around it, which, in the prosecution of my plan, I slowly and quietly withdrew, when the bright rays fell vividly upon the sleeper, and my eyes at the same moment, upon his countenance. I looked;—and a numbness, an iciness of feeling instantly pervaded my frame. My breast heaved, my knees tottered, my whole spirit became possessed with an abjectless yet intolerable horror. Gasping for breath, I lowered the lamp in still nearer proximity to the face. Were these—*these* the lineaments of William Wilson? I saw, indeed, that they were his, but I shook as if with a fit of ague, in fancying they were not. What *was* there about them to confound me in this manner? I gazed;—while my brain reeled with a multitude of incoherent thoughts. Not thus he appeared—assuredly not *thus*—in the vivacity of his waking hours. The same name! the same contour of person! the same day of arrival at the academy! And then his dogged and meaningless imitation of my gait, my voice, my habits, and my manner! Was it, in truth, within the bounds of human possibility, that *what* I *now saw* was the result, merely, of the habitual practise of this sarcastic imitation? Awestricken, and with a creeping shudder, I extinguished the lamp, passed silently from the chamber, and left, at once, the halls of that old academy, never to enter them again.

After a lapse of some months, spent at home in mere idleness, I found myself a student at Eton. The brief interval had been sufficient to enfeeble my remembrance of the events at Dr. Bransby's, or at least to effect a material change in the nature of the feelings with which I remembered them. The truth—the tragedy —of the drama was no more. I could now find room to doubt the evidence of my senses; and seldom called up the subject at all but with wonder at the extent of human credulity, and a smile at the vivid force of the imagination which I hereditarily possessed. Neither was this species of skepticism likely to be diminished by the character of the life I led at Eton. The vortex of thoughtless folly into which I there so immediately and so recklessly plunged, washed away all but the froth of my past hours, ingulfed at once every solid or serious impression, and left to memory only the veriest levities of a former existence.

I do not wish, however, to trace the course of my miserable profligacy here—a profligacy which set at defiance the laws, while it eluded the vigilance of the institution. Three years of folly, passed without profit, had but given me rooted habits of vice, and added, in a somewhat unusual degree, to my bodily stature, when, after a week of soulless dissipation, I invited a small party of the most dissolute students to a secret carousal in my chambers. We met at a late hour of the night; for our debaucheries were to be faithfully protracted until morning. The wine flowed freely, and there were not wanting other and perhaps more dangerous seductions; so that the gray dawn had already faintly appeared in the east while our delirious extravagance was at its height. Madly flushed with cards and intoxication, I was in the act of insisting upon a toast of more than wonted profanity, when my attention was suddenly diverted by the violent, although partial, unclosing of the door of the apartment, and by the eager voice of a servant from without. He said that some person, apparently in great haste, demanded to speak with me in the hall.

Wildly excited with wine, the unexpected interruption rather delighted than surprised me. I staggered forward at once, and a few steps brought me to the vestibule of the building. In this low and small room there hung no lamp; and now no light at all was admitted, save that of the exceedingly feeble dawn which made its way through the semi-circular window. As I put my foot over the threshold, I became aware of the figure of a youth about my own height, and habited in a white kerseymere morning frock, cut in the novel fashion of the one I myself wore at the moment. This the faint light enabled me to perceive; but the features of his face I could not distinguish. Upon my entering, he strode hurriedly up to me, and, seizing me by the arm with a gesture of petulant impatience, whispered the words "William Wilson" in my ear.

I grew perfectly sober in an instant.

There was that in the manner of the stranger, and in the tremulous shake of his uplifted finger, as he held it between my eyes and the light, which filled me with unqualified amazement; but it was not this which had so violently moved me. It was the pregnancy of solemn admonition in the singular, low, hissing utterance; and, above all, it was the character, the tone, *the key,* of those few, simple, and familiar, yet *whispered* syllables, which came with a thousand thronging memories of by-gone days, and struck upon my soul with the shock of a galvanic battery. Ere I could recover the use of my senses he was gone.

Although this event failed not of a vivid effect upon my disordered imagination, yet was it evanescent as vivid. For some weeks, indeed, I busied myself in earnest inquiry, or was wrapped in a cloud of morbid speculation. I did not pretend to disguise from my perception the identity of the singular individual who thus perseveringly interfered with my affairs, and harassed me with his insinuated counsel. But who and what was this Wilson? —and whence came he?—and what were his purposes? Upon neither of these points could I be satisfied—merely ascertaining, in regard to him, that a sudden accident in his family had caused his removal from Dr. Bransby's academy on the afternoon of the day in which I myself had eloped. But in a brief period I ceased to think upon the subject, my attention being all absorbed in a contemplated departure for Oxford. Thither I soon went, the uncalculating vanity of my parents furnishing me with an outfit and annual establishment, which would enable me to indulge at will in the luxury already so dear to my heart—to vie in profuseness of expenditure with the haughtiest heirs of the wealthiest earldoms in Great Britain.

Excited by such appliances to vice, my constitutional temperament broke forth with redoubled ardor, and I spurned even the common restraints of decency in the mad infatuation of my revels. But it were absurd to pause in the detail of my extravagance. Let it suffice, that among spendthrifts I out-Heroded Herod, and that, giving name to a multitude of novel follies, I added no brief appendix to the long catalogue of vices then usual in the most dissolute university of Europe.

It could hardly be credited, however, that I had, even here, so utterly fallen from the gentlemanly estate, as to seek acquaintance with the vilest arts of the gambler by profession, and, having become an adept in his despicable science, to practice it habitually as a means of increasing my already enormous income at the expense of the weak-minded among my fellow-collegians. Such, nevertheless, was the fact. And the very enormity of this offence against all manly and honorable sentiment proved, beyond doubt, the main if not the sole reason of the impunity with which it was committed. Who, indeed, among my most abandoned associates, would not rather have disputed the clearest evidence of his senses, than have suspected of such courses, the gay, the frank, the generous William Wilson—the noblest and most liberal commoner at

Oxford—him whose follies (said his parasites) were but the follies of youth and unbridled fancy—whose errors but inimitable whim—whose darkest vice but a careless and dashing extravagance?

I had been now two years successfully busied in this way, when there came to the university a young *parvenu* nobleman, Glendenning—rich, said report, as Herodes Atticus—his riches, too, as easily acquired. I soon found him of weak intellect, and, of course, marked him as a fitting subject for my skill. I frequently engaged him in play, and contrived, with the gambler's usual art, to let him win considerable sums, the more effectually to entangle him in my snares. At length, my schemes being ripe, I met him (with the full-intention that this meeting should be final and decisive) at the chambers of a fellow-commoner (Mr. Preston), equally intimate with both, but who, to do him justice, entertained not even a remote suspicion of my design. To give this a better coloring, I had contrived to have assembled a party of some eight or ten, and was solicitously careful that the introduction of cards should appear accidental, and originate in the proposal of my contemplated dupe himself. To be brief upon a vile topic, none of the low finesse was omitted, so customary upon similar occasions, that it is a just matter for wonder how any are still found so besetted as to fall its victim.

We had protracted our sitting far into the night, and I had at length effected the manœuvre of getting Glendenning as my sole antagonist. The game, too, was my favorite *écarté*. The rest of the company, interested in the extent of our play, had abandoned their own cards, and were standing around us as spectators. The *parvenu*, who had been induced by my artifices in the early part of the evening, to drink deeply, now shuffled, dealt, or played, with a wild nervousness of manner for which his intoxication, I thought, might partially, but could not altogether account. In a very short period he had become my debtor to a large amount, when, having taken a long draught of port, he did precisely what I had been coolly anticipating—he proposed to double our already extravagant stakes. With a well-feigned show of reluctance, and not until after my repeated refusal had seduced him into some angry words which gave a color of *pique* to my compliance, did I finally comply. The result, of course, did but prove how entirely the prey was in my toils: in less than an hour he had quadrupled his debt. For some time his countenance had been losing the florid tinge lent it by the wine; but now, to my astonishment, I perceived that it had grown to a pallor truly fearful. I say, to my astonishment. Glendenning had been represented to my eager inquiries as immeasurably wealthy; and the sums which he had as yet lost, although in themselves vast, could not, I supposed, very seriously annoy, much less so violently affect him. That he was overcome by the wine just swallowed, was the idea which most readily presented itself; and, rather with a view to the preservation of my own character in the eyes of my associates, than from any less interested motive, I was about to insist, peremptorily, upon a discontinuance of the play, when some expressions at my elbow from among the company, and an ejaculation evincing utter despair on the part of Glendenning, gave me to understand that I had effected his total ruin under circumstances which, rendering him an object for the pity of all, should have protected him from the ill offices even of a fiend.

What now might have been my conduct it is difficult to say. The pitiable condition of my dupe had thrown an air of embarrassed gloom over all; and, for some moments, a profound silence was maintained, during which I could not help feeling my cheeks tingle with the many burning glances of scorn or reproach cast upon me by the less abandoned of the party. I will even own that an intolerable weight of anxiety was for a brief instant lifted from my bosom by the sudden and extraordinary interruption which ensued. The wide, heavy folding doors of the apartment were all at once thrown open, to their full extent, with a vigorous and rushing impetuosity that extinguished, as if by magic, every candle in the room. Their light in dying, enabled us just to perceive that a stranger had entered, about my own height, and closely muffled in a cloak. The darkness, however, was not total; and we could only feel *that* he was standing in our midst. Before any one of us could recover from the extreme astonishment into which this rudeness had thrown all, we heard the voice of the intruder.

"Gentlemen," he said, in a low, distinct, and never-to-be-forgotten *whisper* which thrilled to the very marrow of my bones, "gentlemen, I made no apology for this behavior, because in thus behaving, I am fulfilling a duty. You are, beyond doubt, uninformed of the true character of the person who has to-night won at *écarté* a large sum of money from Lord Glendenning. I will therefore put you upon an expeditious and decisive plan of obtaining this very necessary information. Please to examine, at your leisure, the inner linings of the cuff of his left sleeve, and the several little packages which may be found in the somewhat capacious pockets of his embroidered morning wrapper."

While he spoke, so profound was the stillness that one might have heard a pin drop upon the floor. In ceasing, he departed at once, and as abruptly as he had entered. Can I—shall I describe my sensations? Must I say that I felt all the horrors of the damned? Most assuredly I had little time for reflection. Many hands roughly seized me upon the spot, and lights were immediately reproduced. A search ensued. In the lining of my sleeve were found all the court cards essential in *écarté,* and in the pockets of my wrapper, a number of packs, facsimiles of those used at our sittings, with the single exception that mine were of the species called, technically, *arrondées*; the honors being slightly convex at the ends, the lower cards slightly convex at the sides. In this disposition, the dupe who cuts, as customary, at the length of the pack, will invariably find that he cuts his antagonist an honor; while the gambler, cutting at the breadth, will, as certainly, cut nothing for his victim which may count in the records of the game.

Any burst of indignation upon this discovery would have affected me less than the silent contempt, or the sarcastic composure, with which it was received.

"Mr. Wilson," said our host, stooping to remove from beneath his feet an exceedingly luxurious cloak of rare furs, "Mr. Wilson, this is your property." (The weather was cold; and, upon quitting my own room, I had thrown a cloak over my dressing wrapper, putting it off upon reaching the scene of play.) "I presume it is supererogatory to seek here (eyeing the folds of the garment with a bitter smile) for any farther evidence of your skill. Indeed, we have had enough. You will see the necessity, I hope, of quitting Oxford—at all events, of quitting instantly my chambers."

Abased, humbled to the dust as I then was, it is probable that I should have resented this galling language by immediate personal violence, had not my whole attention been at the moment arrested by a fact of the most startling character. The cloak which I had worn was of a rare description of fur; how rare, how extravagantly costly, I shall not venture to say. Its fashion, too, was of my own fantastic invention; for I was fastidious to an absurd degree of coxcombry, in matters of this frivolous nature. When, therefore, Mr. Preston reached me that which he had picked up upon the floor, and near the folding-doors of the apartment, it was with an astonishment nearly bordering upon terror, that I perceived my own already hanging on my arm, (where I had no doubt unwittingly placed it,) and that the one presented me was but its exact counterpart in every, in even the minutest possible particular. The singular being who had so disastrously exposed me, had been muffled, I remembered, in a cloak; and none had been worn at all by any of the members of our party, with the exception of myself. Retaining some presence of mind, I took the one offered me by Preston; placed it, unnoticed, over my own; left the apartment with a resolute scowl of defiance; and, next morning ere dawn of day, commenced a hurried journey from Oxford to the continent, in a perfect agony of horror and of shame.

I fled in vain. My evil destiny pursued me as if in exultation, and proved, indeed, that the exercise of its mysterious dominion had as yet only begun. Scarcely had I set foot in Paris, ere I had fresh evidence of the detestable interest taken by this Wilson in my concerns. Years flew, while I experienced no relief. Villain! —at Rome, with how untimely, yet with how spectral an officiousness, stepped he in between me and my ambition! at Vienna, too —at Berlin—and at Moscow! Where, in truth, had I *not* bitter cause to curse him within my heart? From his inscrutable tyranny did I at length flee, panic-stricken, as from a pestilence; and to the very ends of the earth *I fled in vain.*

And again, and again, in secret communion with my own spirit, would I demand the questions "Who is he?—whence came he?—and what are his objects?" But no answer was there found. And now I scrutinized, with a minute scrutiny, the forms, and the methods, and the leading traits of his impertinent supervision. But even here there was very little upon which to base a conjecture. It was noticeable, indeed, that, in no one of the multiplied instances in which he had of late crossed my path, had he so crossed it except to frustrate those schemes, or to disturb those actions, which, if fully carried out, might have resulted in bitter mischief. Poor justification this, in truth, for an authority so imperiously assumed! Poor indemnity for natural rights of self-agency so pertinaciously, so insultingly denied!

I had also been forced to notice that my tormentor, for a very long period of time, (while scrupulously and with miraculous dexterity maintaining his whim of an identity of apparel with myself,) had so contrived it, in the execution of his varied interference with my will, that I saw not, at any moment, the features of his face. Be Wilson what he might, *this,* at least, was but the veriest of affectation, or of folly. Could he, for an instant, have supposed that, in my admonisher at Eton—in the destroyer of my honor at Oxford,—in him who thwarted my ambition at Rome, my revenge at Paris, my passionate love at Naples, or what he falsely termed my avarice in Egypt,—that in this, my arch-enemy and evil genius, I could fail to recognize the William Wilson of my school-boy days,—the name-sake, the companion, the rival,—the hated and dreaded rival at Dr. Bransby's? Impossible!—But let me hasten to the last eventful scene of the drama.

Thus far I had succumbed supinely to this imperious dominion. The sentiment of deep awe with which I habitually regarded the elevated character, the majestic wisdom, the apparent omnipresence and omnipotence of Wilson, added to a feeling of even terror, with which certain other traits in his nature and assumptions inspired me, had operated, hitherto, to impress me with an idea of my own utter weakness and helplessness, and to suggest an implicit, although bitterly reluctant submission to his arbitrary will. But, of late days, I had given myself up entirely to wine; and its maddening influence upon my hereditary temper rendered me more and more impatient of control. I began to murmur,—to hesitate,—to resist. And was it only fancy which induced me to believe that, with the increase of my own firmness, that of my tormentor underwent a proportional diminution? Be this as it may, I now began to feel the inspiration of a burning hope, and at length nurtured in my secret thoughts a stern and desperate resolution that I would submit no longer to be enslaved.

It was at Rome, during the Carnival of 18—, that I attended a masquerade in the palazzo of the Neapolitan Duke Di Broglio. I had indulged more freely than usual in the excesses of the wine-table; and now the suffocating atmosphere of the crowded rooms irritated me beyond endurance. The difficulty, too, of forcing my way through the mazes of the company contributed not a little to the ruffling of my temper; for I was anxiously seeking (let me not say with what unworthy motive) the young, the gay, the beautiful wife of the aged and doting Di Broglio. With a too unscrupulous confidence she had previously communicated to me the secret of the costume in which she would be habited, and now, having caught a glimpse of her person, I was hurrying to make my way into her presence. At this moment I felt a light hand placed upon my shoulder, and that ever-remembered, low, damnable *whisper* within my ear.

In an absolute phrenzy of wrath, I turned at once upon him who had thus interrupted me, and seized him violently by the collar. He was attired, as I had expected, in a costume altogether similar to my own; wearing a Spanish cloak of blue velvet, begirt about the waist with a crimson belt sustaining a rapier. A mask of black silk entirely covered his face.

"Scoundrel!" I said, in a voice husky with rage, while every syllable I uttered seemed as new fuel to my fury; "scoundrel! impostor! accursed villain! you shall not—you *shall not* dog me unto death! Follow me, or I stab you where you stand!"—and I broke my way from the ball-room into a small ante-chamber adjoining, dragging him unresistingly with me as I went.

Upon entering, I thrust him furiously from me. He staggered against the wall, while I closed the door with an oath, and commanded him to draw. He hesitated but for an instant; then, with a slight sigh, drew in silence, and put himself upon his defence.

The contest was brief indeed. I was frantic with every species of wild excitement, and felt within my single arm the energy and power of a multitude. In a few seconds I forced him by sheer strength against the wainscotting, and thus, getting him at mercy, plunged my sword, with brute ferocity, repeatedly through and through his bosom.

At that instant some person tried the latch of the door. I hastened to prevent an intrusion, and then immediately returned to my dying antagonist. But what human language can adequately portray *that* astonishment, *that* horror which possessed me at the spectacle then presented to view? The brief moment in which I averted my eyes had been sufficient to produce, apparently, a material change in the arrangements at the upper or farther end of the room. A large mirror,—so at first it seemed to me in my confusion—now stood where none had been perceptible before; and as I stepped up to it in extremity of terror, mine own image, but with features all pale and dabbled in blood, advanced to meet me with a feeble and tottering gait.

Thus it appeared, I say, but was not. It was my antagonist —it was Wilson, who then stood before me in the agonies of his dissolution. His mask and cloak lay, where he had thrown them, upon the floor. Not a thread in all his raiment—not a line in all the marked and singular lineaments of his face which was not, even in the most absolute identity, *mine own!*

It was Wilson; but he spoke no longer in a whisper, and I could have fancied that I myself was speaking while he said:

"You have conquered, and I yield. Yet henceforward art thou also dead—dead to the World, to Heaven, and to Hope! In me didst thou exist—and, in my death, see by this image, which is thine own, how utterly thou hast murdered thyself."

THEODORE DREISER / The Hand

I

DAVIDSON COULD distinctly remember that it was between two and three years after the grisly event in the Monte Orte Range—the sickening and yet deserved end of Mersereau, his quondam partner and fellow adventurer—that anything to be identified with Mersereau's malice toward him, and with Mersereau's probable present existence in the spirit world, had appeared in his life.

He and Mersereau had worked long together as prospectors, investors, developers of property. It was only after they had struck it rich in the Klondike that Davidson had grown so much more apt and shrewd in all commercial and financial matters, whereas

Mersereau had seemed to stand still—not to rise to the splendid opportunities which then opened to him. Why, in some of these later deals it had not been possible for Davidson even to introduce his old partner to some of the moneyed men he had to deal with. Yet Mersereau had insisted, as his right, if you please, on being 'in on' everything—everything!

Take that wonderful Monte Orte property, the cause of the subsequent horror. He, Davidson—not Mersereau—had discovered or heard of the mine, and had carried it along, with old Besmer as a tool or decoy—Besmer being the ostensible factor—until it was all ready for him to take over and sell or develop. Then it was that Mersereau, having been for so long his partner, demanded a full half—a third, at least—on the ground that they had once agreed to work together in all these things.

Think of it! And Mersereau growing duller and less useful and more disagreeable day by day, and year by year! Indeed, toward the last he had threatened to expose the trick by which jointly, seven years before, they had possessed themselves of the Skyute Pass Mine; to drive Davidson out of public and financial life, to have him arrested and tried—along with himself, of course. Think of that!

But he had fixed him—yes, he had, damn him! He had trailed Mersereau that night to old Besmer's cabin on the Monte Orte, when Besmer was away. Mersereau had gone there with the intention of stealing the diagram of the new field, and had secured it, true enough. A thief he was, damn him! Yet, just as he was making safely away, as he thought, he, Davidson, had struck him cleanly over the ear with that heavy rail-bolt fastened to the end of a walnut stick, and the first blow had done for him.

Lord, how the bone above Mersereau's ear had sounded when it cracked! And how bloody one side of that bolt was! Mersereau hadn't had time to do anything before he was helpless. He hadn't died instantly, though, but had turned over and faced him, Davidson, with that savage, scowling face of his and those blazing, animal eyes.

Lying half propped up on his left elbow, Mersereau had reached out toward him with that big, rough, bony right hand of his—the right with which he always boasted of having done so much damage on this, that, and the other occasion—had glared at him as much as to say:

'Oh, if I could only reach you just for a moment before I go!'

Then it was that he, Davidson, had lifted the club again. Horrified as he was, and yet determined that he must save his own life, he had finished the task, dragging the body back to an old fissure behind the cabin and covering it with branches, a great pile of pine fronds, and as many as one hundred and fifty boulders, great and small, and had left his victim. It was a sickening sight, but it had to be.

Then, having finished, he had slipped dismally away, like a jackal, thinking of that hand in the moonlight, held up so savagely, and that look. Nothing might have come of that either, if he hadn't been inclined to brood on it so much, on the fierceness of it.

No, nothing had happened. A year had passed, and if anything had been going to turn up it surely would have by then. He, Davidson, had gone first to New York, later to Chicago, to dispose of the Monte Orte claim. Then, after two years, he had returned here to Mississippi, where he was enjoying comparative peace. He was looking after some sugar property which had once belonged to him, and which he was now able to reclaim and put in charge of his sister as a home against a rainy day. He had no other.

But that body back there! That hand uplifted in the moonlight—to clutch him if it could! Those eyes!

II—June, 1905

Take that first year, for instance, when he had returned to Gatchard in Mississippi, whence both he and Mersereau had originally issued. After looking after his own property he had gone out to a tumble-down estate of his uncle's in Issaqueena County —a leaky old slope-roofed house where, in a bedroom on the top floor, he had had his first experience with the significance or reality of the hand.

Yes, that was where first he had really seen it pictured in that curious, unbelievable way; only who would believe that it was Mersereau's hand? They would say it was an accident, chance, rain dropping down. But the hand had appeared on the ceiling of that room just as sure as anything, after a heavy rainstorm—it was almost a cyclone—when every chink in the old roof had seemed to leak water.

During the night, after he had climbed to the room by way of those dismal stairs with their great landing and small glass oil-lamp he carried, and had sunk to rest, or tried to, in the heavy, wide, damp bed, thinking, as he always did those days, of the Monte Orte and Mersereau, the storm had come up. As he had listened to the wind moaning outside he had heard first the scratch, scratch, scratch, of some limb, no doubt, against the wall —sounding, or so it seemed in his feverish unrest, like some one penning an indictment against him with a worn, rusty pen.

And then, the storm growing worse, and in a fit of irritation and self-contempt at his own nervousness, he had gone to the window, but just as lightning struck a branch of the tree nearest the window and so very near him, too—as though some one, something, was seeking to strike him— (Mersereau?) and as though he had been lured by that scratching. God! He had retreated, feeling that it was meant for him.

But that big, knotted hand painted on the ceiling during the night! There it was, right over him when he awoke, outlined or painted as if with wet, gray white-wash against the wretched but normally pale blue of the ceiling when dry. There it was—a big, open hand just like Mersereau's as he had held it up that night—huge, knotted, rough, the fingers extended as if tense and clutching. And, if you will believe it, near it was something that looked like a pen—an old, long-handled pen—to match that scratch, scratch, scratch!

'Huldah,' he had inquired of the old black mammy who entered in the morning to bring him fresh water and throw open the shutters, 'what does that look like to you up there—that patch on the ceiling where the rain came through?'

He wanted to reassure himself as to the character of the thing he saw—that it might not be a creation of his own feverish imagination, accentuated by the dismal character of this place.

' 'Pears t' me mo' like a big han' 'an anythin' else, Marse Davi'son,' commented Huldah, pausing and staring upward. 'Mo' like a big fist, kinda. Dat air's a new drip come las' night, I reckon. Dis here ole place ain' gonna hang togethah much longah, less'n some repairin' be done mighty quick now. Yassir, dat air's a new drop, sho's yo' bo'n, en it come on'y las' night. I hain't never seed dat befo'.'

And then he had inquired, thinking of the fierceness of the storm:

'Huldah, do you have many such storms up this way?'

'Good gracious, Marse Davi'son, we hain't seed no such blow en—en come three years now. I hain't seed no sech lightnin' en I doan' know when.'

Wasn't that strange, that it should all come on the night, of all nights, when he was there? And no such other storm in three years!

Huldah stared idly, always ready to go slow and rest, if possible, whereas he had turned irritably. To be annoyed by ideas such as this! To always be thinking of that Monte Orte affair! Why couldn't he forget it? Wasn't it Mersereau's own fault? He never would have killed the man if he hadn't been forced to it.

And to be haunted in this way, making mountains out of molehills, as he thought then! It must be his own miserable fancy —and yet Mersereau had looked so threateningly at him. That glance had boded something; it was too terrible not to.

Davidson might not want to think of it, but how could he stop? Mersereau might not be able to hurt him any more, at least not on this earth; but still, couldn't he? Didn't the appearance of this hand seem to indicate that he might? He was dead, of course. His body, his skeleton, was under that pile of rocks and stones, some of them as big as washtubs. Why worry over that, and after two years? And still——

That hand on the ceiling!

III—*December, 1905*

Then, again, take that matter of meeting Pringle in Gatchard just at that time, within the same week. It was due to Davidson's sister. She had invited Mr. and Mrs. Pringle in to meet him one evening, without telling him that they were spiritualists and might discuss spiritualism.

Clairvoyance, Pringle called it, or seeing what can't be seen with material eyes, and clairaudience, or hearing what can't be heard with material ears, as well as materialization, or ghosts, and table-rapping, and the like. Table-rapping—that damned tap-tapping that he had been hearing ever since!

It was Pringle's fault, really. Pringle had persisted in talking. He, Davidson, wouldn't have listened, except that he somehow became fascinated by what Pringle said concerning what he had heard and seen in his time. Mersereau must have been at the bottom of that, too.

At any rate, after he had listened, he was sorry, for Pringle had had time to fill his mind full of those awful facts or ideas which had since harassed him so much—all that stuff about drunkards, degenerates, and weak people generally being followed about by vile, evil spirits and used to effect those spirits' purposes or desires in this world. Horrible!

Wasn't it terrible? Pringle—big, mushy creature that he was, sickly and stagnant like the springless pool—insisted that he had even seen clouds of these spirits about drunkards, degenerates, and the like, in street-cars, on trains, and about vile corners at night. Once, he said, he had seen just one evil spirit—think of that!—following a certain man all the time, at his left elbow—a dark, evil, red-eyed thing, until finally the man had been killed in a quarrel.

Pringle described their shapes, these spirits, as varied. They were small, dark, irregular clouds, with red or green spots somewhere for eyes, changing in form and becoming longish or round like a jellyfish, or even like a misshapen cat or dog. They could take any form at will—even that of a man.

Once, Pringle declared, he had seen as many as fifty about a drunkard who was staggering down a street, all of them trying to urge him into the nearest saloon, so that they might reëxperience in some vague way the sensation of drunkenness, which at some time or other they themselves, having been drunkards in life, had enjoyed!

It would be the same with a drug fiend, or indeed with any one of weak or evil habits. They gathered about such an one like flies, their red or green eyes glowing—attempting to get something from them, perhaps, if nothing more than a little sense of their old earth-life.

The whole thing was so terrible and disturbing at the time, particularly that idea of men being persuaded or influenced to murder, that he, Davidson, could stand it no longer, and got up and left. But in his room upstairs he meditated on it, standing before his mirror. Suddenly—would he ever forget it?—as he was taking off his collar and tie, he had heard that queer tap, tap, tap, right on his dressing-table or under it, and for the first time, which, Pringle said, ghosts made when table-rapping in answer to a call, or to give warning of their presence.

Then something said to him, almost as clearly as if he heard it:

'This is me, Mersereau, come back at last to get you! Pringle was just an excuse of mine to let you know I was coming, and so was that hand in that old house, in Issaqueena County. It was mine! I will be with you from now on. Don't think I will ever leave you!'

It had frightened and made him half sick, so wrought up was he. For the first time he felt cold chills run up and down his spine—the creeps. He felt as if some one were standing over him— Mersereau, of course—only he could not see or hear a thing, just that faint tap at first, growing louder a little later, and quite angry when he tried to ignore it.

People did live, then, after they were dead, especially evil people—people stronger than you, perhaps. They had the power to come back, to haunt, to annoy you if they didn't like anything you had done to them. No doubt Mersereau was following him in the hope of revenge, there in the spirit world, just outside this one, close at his heels, like that evil spirit attending the other man whom Pringle had described.

IV—*February, 1906*

Take that case of the hand impressed on the soft dough and plaster of Paris, described in an article that he had picked up in the dentist's office out there in Pasadena—Mersereau's very hand, so far as he could judge. How about that for a coincidence, picking up the magazine with that disturbing article about psychic materialization in Italy, and later in Berne, Switzerland, where the scientists were gathered to investigate that sort of thing? And just when he was trying to rid himself finally of the notion that any such thing could be!

According to that magazine article, some old crone over in Italy—spiritualist, or witch, or something—had got together a crowd of experimentalists or professors in an abandoned house on an almost deserted island off the coast of Sardinia. There they had conducted experiments with spirits, which they called materialization, getting the impression of the fingers of a hand, or of a whole hand and arm, or of a face, on a plate of glass covered with soot, the plate being locked on a small safe in the center of a table about which they sat!

He, Davidson, couldn't understand, of course, how it was done, but done it was. There in that magazine were half a dozen pictures, reproductions of photographs of a hand, an arm and a face—or part of one, anyhow. And if they looked like anything, they looked exactly like Mersereau's! Hadn't Pringle, there in Gatchard, Mississippi, stated spirits could move anywhere, over long distances, with the speed of light? And would it be any trick for Mersereau to appear there at Sardinia, and then engineer this magazine into his presence, here in Los Angeles? Would it? It would not. Spirits were free and powerful *over there*, perhaps.

There was not the least doubt that these hands, these partial impressions of a face, were those of Mersereau. Those big knuckles! That long, heavy, humped nose and that big jaw! Whose else could they be?—they were Mersereau's, intended, when they were made over there in Italy, for him, Davidson, to see later here in Los Angeles. Yes, they were! And looking at that sinister face reproduced in the magazine, it seemed to say, with Mersereau's old coarse sneer:

'You see? You can't escape me! I'm showing you how much alive I am over here, just as I was on earth. And I'll get you yet, even if I have to go farther than Italy to do it!'

It was amazing, the shock he took from that. It wasn't just that alone, but the persistence and repetition of this hand business. What could it mean? Was it really Mersereau's hand? As for the face, it wasn't all there—just the jaw, mouth, cheek, left temple, and a part of the nose and eye; but it was Mersereau's, all right. He had gone clear over there into Italy somewhere, in a lone house on an island, to get this message of his undying hate back to him. Or was it just spirits, evil spirits, bent on annoying him because he was nervous and sensitive now?

v—*October, 1906*

Even new crowded hotels and new buildings weren't the protection he had at first hoped and thought they would be. Even there you weren't safe—not from a man like Mersereau. Take that incident there in Los Angeles, and again in Seattle, only two months ago now, when Mersereau was able to make that dreadful explosive or crashing sound, as if one had burst a huge paper bag full of air, or upset a china-closet full of glass and broken everything, when as a matter of fact nothing at all had happened. Finding that it was nothing—or Mersereau—he was becoming used to it now; but other people, unfortunately, were not.

He would be—as he had been that first time—sitting in his room perfectly still and trying to amuse himself, or not to think, when suddenly there would be that awful crash. It was astounding! Other people heard it, of course. They had in Los Angeles. A maid and a porter had come running the first time to inquire, and he had had to protest that he had heard nothing. They couldn't believe it at first, and had gone to other rooms to look. When it happened the second time, the management had protested, thinking it was a joke he was playing; and to avoid the risk of exposure he had left.

After that he could not keep a valet or nurse about him for long. Servants wouldn't stay, and managers of hotels wouldn't let him remain when such things went on. Yet he couldn't live in a house or apartment alone, for there the noises and atmospheric conditions would be worse than ever.

vi—*June, 1907*

Take that last old house he had been in—but never would be in again!—at Anne Haven. There he actually visualized the hand—a thing as big as a washtub at first, something like smoke or shadow in a black room moving about over the bed and everywhere. Then, as he lay there, gazing at it spellbound, it condensed slowly, and he began to feel it. It was now a hand of normal size—there was no doubt of it in the world—going over him softly, without force, as a ghostly hand must, having no real physical strength, but all the time with a strange, electric, secretive something about it, as if it were not quite sure of itself, and not quite sure that he was really there.

The hand, or so it seemed—God!—moved right up to his

neck and began to feel over that as he lay there. Then it was that he guessed just what it was that Mersereau was after.

It was just like a hand, the fingers and thumb made into a circle and pressed down over his throat, only it moved over him gently at first, because it really couldn't do anything yet, not having the material strength. But the intention! The sense of cruel, savage determination that went with it!

And yet, if one went to a nerve specialist or doctor about all this, as he did afterward, what did the doctor say? He had tried to describe how he was breaking down under the strain, how he could not eat or sleep on account of all these constant tappings and noises; but the moment he even began to hint at his experiences, especially the hand or the noises, the doctor exclaimed:

'Why, this is plain delusion! You're nervously run down, that's all that ails you—on the verge of pernicious anæmia, I should say. You'll have to watch yourself as to this illusion about spirits. Get it out of your mind. There's nothing to it!'

Wasn't that just like one of these nerve specialists, bound up in their little ideas of what they knew or saw, or thought they saw?

VII—*November, 1907*

And now take this very latest development at Battle Creek recently where he had gone trying to recuperate on the diet there. Hadn't Mersereau, implacable demon that he was, developed this latest trick of making his food taste queer to him—unpalatable, or with an odd odor?

He, Davidson, knew it was Mersereau, for he felt him beside him at the table whenever he sat down. Besides, he seemed to hear something—clairaudience was what they called it, he understood; he was beginning to develop that, too, now! It was Mersereau, of course, saying in a voice which was more like a memory of a voice than anything real—the voice of some one you could remember as having spoken in a certain way, say, ten years or more ago:

'I've fixed it so you can't eat any more, you——'

There followed a long list of vile expletives, enough in itself to sicken one.

Thereafter, in spite of anything he could do to make himself think to the contrary, knowing that the food was all right, really, Davidson found it to have an odor or a taste which disgusted him, and which he could not overcome, try as he would. The management assured him that it was all right, as he knew it was—for others. He saw them eating it. But he couldn't—had to get up and leave, and the little he could get down he couldn't retain, or it wasn't enough for him to live on. God, he would die, this way! Starve, as he surely was doing by degrees now.

And Mersereau always seeming to be standing by. Why, if it weren't for fresh fruit on the stands at times, and just plain, fresh-baked bread in bakers' windows, which he could buy and eat quickly, he might not be able to live at all. It was getting to that pass!

VIII—*August, 1908*

That wasn't the worst, either, bad as all that was. The worst was the fact that under the strain of all this he was slowly but surely breaking down, and that in the end Mersereau might really succeed in driving him out of life here—to do what, if anything, to him there? What? It was such an evil pack by which he was surrounded, now, those who lived just on the other side and hung about the earth, vile, debauched creatures, as Pringle had described them, and as Davidson had come to know for himself, fearing them and their ways so much, and really seeing them at times.

Since he had come to be so weak and sensitive, he could see them for himself—vile things that they were, swimming before his gaze in the dark whenever he chanced to let himself be in the dark, which was not often—friends of Mersereau, no doubt, and inclined to help him just for the evil of it.

For this long time now Davidson had taken to sleeping with the light on, wherever he was, only tying a handkerchief over his eyes to keep out some of the glare. Even then he could see them— queer, misshapen things, for all the world like wavy, stringy jelly-fish or coils of thick, yellowish-black smoke, moving about, changing in form at times, yet always looking dirty or vile, somehow, and with those queer, dim, reddish or greenish glows for eyes. It was sickening!

IX—*October, 1908*

Having accomplished so much, Mersereau would by no means be content to let him go. Davidson knew that! He could talk to him occasionally now, or at least could hear him and answer back, if he chose, when he was alone and quite certain that no one was listening.

Mersereau was always saying, when Davidson would listen to him at all—which he wouldn't often—that he would get him yet, that he would make him pay, or charging him with fraud and murder.

'I'll choke you yet!' The words seemed to float in from somewhere, as if he were remembering that at some time Mersereau had said just that in his angry, savage tone—not as if he heard it; and yet he was hearing it, of course.

'I'll choke you yet! You can't escape! You may think you'll die a natural death, but you won't, and that's why I'm poisoning your food to weaken you. You can't escape! I'll get you, sick or well, when you can't help yourself, when you're sleeping. I'll choke you, just as you hit me with that club. That's why you're always seeing and feeling this hand of mine! I'm not alone. I've nearly had you many a time already, only you have managed to wriggle out so far, jumping up, but some day you won't be able to—see? Then——'

The voice seemed to die away at times, even in the middle of a sentence, but at the other times—often, often—he could hear it completing the full thought.

Sometimes he would turn on the thing and exclaim: 'Oh, go to the devil!' or, 'Let me alone!' or, 'Shut up!' Even in a closed room and all alone, such remarks seemed strange to him, addressed to a ghost; but he couldn't resist at times, annoyed as he was. Only he took good care not to talk if any one was about.

It was getting so that there was no real place for him outside of an asylum, for often he would get up screaming at night—he had to, so sharp was the clutch on his throat—and then always, wherever he was, a servant would come in and want to know what was the matter. He would have to say that it was a nightmare—only the management always requested him to leave after the second or third time, say, or after an explosion or two. It was horrible!

He might as well apply to a private asylum or sanatorium now, having all the money he had, and explain that he had delusions—delusions! Imagine!—and ask to be taken care of. In a place like that they wouldn't be disturbed by his jumping up and screaming at night, feeling that he was being choked, as he was, or by his leaving the table because he couldn't eat the food, or by his talking back to Mersereau, should they chance to hear him, or by the noises when they occurred.

They could assign him to a special nurse and a special room, if he wished—only he didn't wish to be too much alone. They could put him in charge of some one who would understand all these things, or to whom he could explain. He couldn't expect ordinary people, or hotels catering to ordinary people, to put up with him any more. Mersereau and his friends made too much trouble.

He must go and hunt up a good place somewhere where

they understood such things, or at least tolerated them, and explain, and then it would all pass for the hallucinations of a crazy man—though, as a matter of fact, he wasn't crazy at all. It was all too real, only the average or so-called normal person couldn't see or hear as he could—hadn't experienced what he had.

x—*December, 1908*

'The trouble is, Doctor, that Mr. Davidson is suffering from the delusion that he is pursued by evil spirits. He was not committed here by any court, but came of his own accord about four months ago, and we let him wander about here at will. But he seems to be growing worse, as time goes on.

'One of his worst delusions, Doctor, is that there is one spirit in particular who is trying to choke him to death. Dr. Major, our superintendent, says he has incipient tuberculosis of the throat, with occasional spasmodic contractions. There are small lumps or calluses here and there as though caused by outside pressure and yet our nurse assures us that there is no such outside irritation. He won't believe that; but whenever he tries to sleep, especially in the middle of the night, he will jump up and come running out into the hall, insisting that one of these spirits, which he insists are after him, is trying to choke him to death. He really seems to believe it, for he comes out coughing and choking and feeling at his neck as if some one has been trying to strangle him. He always explains the whole matter to me as being the work of evil spirits, and asks me not to pay any attention to him unless he calls for help or rings his call-bell; and so I never think anything more of it now unless he does.

'Another of his ideas is that these same spirits do something to his food—put poison in it, or give it a bad odor or taste, so that he can't eat it. When he does find anything he can eat, he grabs it and almost swallows it whole, before, as he says, the spirits have time to do anything to it. Once, he says, he weighed more than two hundred pounds, but now he only weighs one hundred and twenty. His case is exceedingly strange and pathetic, Doctor!

'Dr. Major insists that it is purely a delusion; that so far as being choked is concerned, it is the incipient tuberculosis, and that his stomach trouble comes from the same thing; but by association of ideas, or delusion, he thinks some one is trying to choke him and poison his food, when it isn't so at all. Dr. Major says that he can't imagine what could have started it. He is always trying to talk to Mr. Davidson about it, but whenever he begins to ask him questions, Mr. Davidson refuses to talk, and gets up and leaves.

'One of the peculiar things about his idea of being choked, Doctor, is that when he is merely dozing he always wakes up in time, and has the power to throw it off. He claims that the strength of these spirits is not equal to his own when he is awake, or even dozing, but when he's asleep their strength is greater and that then they may injure him. Sometimes, when he has had a fright like this, he will come out in the hall and down to my desk there at the lower end, and ask if he mayn't sit there by me. He says it calms him. I always tell him yes, but it won't be five minutes before he'll get up and leave again, saying that he's being annoyed, or that he won't be able to contain himself if he stays any longer, because of the remarks being made over his shoulder or in his ear.

'Often he'll say: "Did you hear that, Miss Liggett? It's astonishing, the low, vile things that man can say at times!" When I say, "No, I didn't hear," he always says, "I'm so glad!"'

'No one has ever tried to relieve him of this by hypnotism, I suppose?'

'Not that I know of, Doctor. Dr. Major may have tried it. I have only been here three months.'

'Tuberculosis is certainly the cause of the throat trouble, as Dr. Major says, and as for the stomach trouble, that comes from the same thing—natural enough under the circumstances. We may have to resort to hypnotism a little later. I'll see. In the mean time you'd better caution all who come in touch with him never to sympathize, or even to seem to believe in anything he imagines is being done to him. It will merely encourage him in his notions. And get him to take his medicine regularly; it won't cure, but it will help. Dr. Major has asked me to give special attention to his case, and I want the conditions as near right as possible.'

'Yes, sir.'

XI—*January, 1909*

The trouble with these doctors was that they really knew nothing of anything save what was on the surface, the little they had learned at a medical college or in practice—chiefly how certain drugs, tried by their predecessors in certain cases, were known to act. They had no imagination whatever, even when you tried to tell them.

Take that latest young person who was coming here now in his good clothes and with his car, fairly bursting with his knowledge of what he called psychiatrics, looking into Davidson's eyes so hard and smoothing his temples and throat—massage, he called it—saying that he had incipient tuberculosis of the throat and stomach trouble, and utterly disregarding the things which he, Davidson, could personally see and hear! Imagine the fellow trying to persuade him, at this late date, that all that was wrong with him was tuberculosis; that he didn't see Mersereau standing right beside him at times, bending over him, holding up that hand and telling him how he intended to kill him yet—that it was all an illusion!

Imagine saying that Mersereau couldn't actually seize him by the throat when he was asleep, or nearly so, when Davidson himself, looking at his throat in the mirror, could see the actual finger-prints—Mersereau's—for a moment or so afterward. At any rate, his throat was red and sore from being clutched, as Mersereau of late was able to clutch him! And that was the cause of these lumps. And to say, as they had said at first, that he himself was making them by rubbing and feeling his throat, and that it was tuberculosis!

Wasn't it enough to make one want to quit the place? If it weren't for Miss Liggett and Miss Koehler, his private nurse, and their devoted care, he would. That Miss Koehler was worth her weight in gold, learning his ways as she had, being so uniformly kind, and bearing with his difficulties so genially. He would leave her something in his will.

To leave this place and go elsewhere, though, unless he could take her along, would be folly. And anyway, where else would he go? Here at least were other people, patients with him—people who weren't convinced as were these doctors that all that he complained of was mere delusion. Imagine! Old Rankin, the lawyer, for instance, who had suffered untold persecution from one living person and another, mostly politicians, was convinced that his, Davidson's, troubles were genuine, and liked to hear about them, just as did Miss Koehler. These two did not insist, as the doctors did, that he had slow tuberculosis of the throat, and could live a long time and overcome his troubles if he would. They were merely companionable at such times as Mersereau would give him enough peace to be sociable.

The only real trouble, though, was that he was growing so weak from lack of sleep and food—his inability to eat the food which his enemy bewitched and to sleep at night on account of the choking—that he couldn't last much longer. The new physician whom Dr. Major had called into consultation in regard to his case was insisting that along with his throat trouble he was suffering from acute anæmia, due to long undernourishment, and that only a solution of strychnin injected into the veins would help him. But as to Mersereau poisoning his food—not a word would he hear. Besides, now that he was practically bedridden, not able to jump up as freely as before, he was subject to a veritable storm of bedevilment at the hands of Mersereau. Not only could he see—especially toward evening, and in the very early hours of the morning—Mersereau hovering about him like a black shadow, a great, bulky shadow—yet like him in outline, but he could feel his enemy's hand moving over him. Worse, behind or about him he often saw a veritable cloud of evil creatures, companions or tools of Mersereau's, who were there to help him and who kept swimming about like fish in dark waters, and seemed to eye the procedure with satisfaction.

When food was brought to him, early or late, and in whatever form, Mersereau and they were there, close at hand, as thick as flies, passing over and through it in an evident attempt to spoil it before he could eat it. Just to see them doing it was enough to poison it for him. Besides, he could hear their voices urging Mersereau to do it.

'That's right—poison it!'
'He can't last much longer!'
'Soon he'll be weak enough so that when you grip him he will really die!'

It was thus that they actually talked—he could hear them.

He also heard vile phrases addressed to him by Mersereau, the iterated and reiterated words 'murderer' and 'swindler' and 'cheat,' there in the middle of the night. Often, although the light was still on, he saw as many as seven dark figures, very much like Mersereau's, although different, gathered close about him—like men in consultation—evil men. Some of them sat upon his bed, and it seemed as if they were about to help Mesereau to finish him, adding their hands to his.

Behind them again was a complete circle of all those evil, swimming things with green and red eyes, always watching—helping, probably. He had actually felt the pressure of the hand to grow stronger of late, when they were all there. Only, just before he felt he was going to faint, and because he could not spring up any more, he invariably screamed or gasped a choking gasp and held a finger on the button which would bring Miss Koehler. Then she would come, lift him up, and fix his pillows. She also always assured him that it was only the inflammation of his throat, and rubbed it with alcohol, and gave him a few drops of something internally to ease it.

After all this time, and in spite of anything he could tell them, they still believed, or pretended to believe, that he was suffering from tuberculosis, and that all the rest of this was delusion, a phase of insanity!

And Mersereau's skeleton still out there on the Monte Orte!

And Mersereau's plan, with the help of others, of course, was to choke him to death; there was no doubt of that now; and yet they would believe after he was gone that he had died of tuberculosis of the **throat**. Think of that!

XII—*Midnight of February 10, 1909*

The Ghost of Mersereau (*bending over Davidson*): 'Softly! Softly! He's quite asleep! He didn't think we could get him—that I could! But this time—yes. Miss Koehler is asleep at the end of the hall and Miss Liggett can't come, can't hear. He's too weak now. He can scarcely move or groan. Strengthen my hand, will you! I will grip him so tight this time that he won't get away! His cries won't help him this time! He can't cry as he once did! Now! Now!'

A Cloud of Evil Spirits (*swimming about*): 'Right! Right! Good! Good! Now! Ah!'

Davidson (*waking, choking, screaming, and feebly striking out*): 'Help! Help! H-e-l-p! Miss—Miss——H—e—l—p!'

Miss Liggett (*dozing heavily in her chair*): 'Everything is still. No one restless. I can sleep.' (*Her head nods.*)

The Cloud of Evil Spirits: 'Good! Good! Good! His soul at last! Here it comes! He couldn't escape this time! Ah! Good! Good! Now!'

Mersereau (*to Davidson*): 'You murderer! At last! At last!'

XIII—*3 A.M. of February 10, 1909*

Miss Koehler (*at the bedside, distressed and pale*): 'He must have died some time between one and two, Doctor. I left him at one o'clock, comfortable as I could make him. He said he was feeling as well as could be expected. He's been very weak during the last few days, taking only a little gruel. Between half-past one and two I thought I heard a noise, and came to see. He was lying just as you see here, except that his hands were up to his throat, as if it were hurting or choking him. I put them down for fear they would stiffen that way. In trying to call one of the other nurses just now, I found that the bell was out of order, although I know it was all right when I left, because he always made me try it. So he may have tried to ring.'

Dr. Major (*turning the head and examining the throat*): 'It looks as if he had clutched at his throat rather tightly this time, I must say. Here is the mark of his thumb on this side and of his four fingers on the other. Rather deep for the little strength he had. Odd that he should have imagined that some one else was trying to choke him, when he was always pressing at his own neck! Throat tuberculosis is very painful at times. That would explain the desire to clutch at his throat.'

Miss Liggett: 'He was always believing that an evil spirit was trying to choke him, Doctor.'

Dr. Major: 'Yes, I know—association of ideas. Dr. Scain and I agree as to that. He had a bad case of chronic tuberculosis of the throat, with accompanying malnutrition, due to the effect of the throat on the stomach; and his notion about evil spirits pursuing him and trying to choke him was simply due to an innate tendency on the part of the subconscious mind to join things together—any notion say, with any pain. If he had had a diseased leg, he would have imagined that evil spirits were attempting to saw it off, or something like that. In the same way the condition of his throat affected his stomach, and he imagined that the spirits were doing something to his food. Make out a certificate showing acute tuberculosis of the esophagus as the cause, with delusions of persecution as his mental condition. While I am here we may as well look in on Mr. Baff.'

B. Obsessions and Compulsions

GORDIN RAF / A Case of Kleptomania

SELDOM DOES the psychiatrist have the opportunity of analysing and finding out what is lying behind that impulsive act which manifests itself in a pathological need of stealing, kleptomania. The act seems to be an apparently purposive one, requiring, outwardly, coordination and skill in the execution so that responsibility seems implied. But evidently the degree of discrimination found in the person after the act makes it difficult to accept the fact that the author of what is termed the crime, when acting under the pressure of the impulse, is not responsible for his act. Forensically, little attention has been paid to the psychopathological character of the kleptomaniac. In general, these individuals are treated as criminals, their case being considered of minor importance. The case of kleptomania described here, therefore, may contribute to the understanding of the psychological mechanism of this impulsive act, offering interest from the medical as well as from the forensic aspects.

A male patient, born in 1904, was, in 1949, sentenced to imprisonment for what was termed thefts. No notice was taken by the Court of the preliminary statement of a psychiatrist that the thefts, consisting of women's handbags or purses only, were the acts of a kleptomaniac. It will here be made clear that this was no case of ordinary theft.

During the course of approximately six months (December 1948-May 1949), there had occurred to him, temporarily, bursts of uncontrollable desire to appropriate women's handbags or purses. Such appropriations had been carried out on nine occasions in a department store. It was never a question of bags offered for sale, but always of a handbag belonging to some woman visiting the store, leaving the bag for a moment unwatched. The impulse to take the handbag, regularly, began with a sudden feeling of restlessness, and of sexual excitement and erection. The need of taking was irresistible, dulling momentarily his senses, and only when digging into the handbag did the sexual tension become relieved. Sometimes ejaculation followed too. After the occurrence he dimly realized the possible consequences of his action, but when the impulse reappeared, this insight was of no significance, and he acted as blindly as before. He never kept the bags after the "digging" but threw them away immediately, without further thought.

He was caught in the act only on the occasion of the ninth appropriation. At the investigation he, himself, told of eight earlier similar occurrences, being unable to give details. He clearly remembered only a sudden throbbing in his head and the sexual excitement irresistibly forcing him to take and dig into the handbag and then the immediate release he felt when the act was over. To him the whole thing was inexplicable. His personal financial standing was good, the value of his property was great and he had a very well paid and regular job. The amount of money taken from the handbags was trifling, as was stated in Court, neither was he certain whether he had, in fact, taken money or not. Upon request and without knowing the amounts involved, he, however, paid for all the damage done.

In the Court the matter was never cleared up. He was simply sent to prison for "nine thefts." That was in 1950. He stayed in prison until 1951 and was then released on probation. Almost a year went by without anything happening, but in August 1952, one day, when making purchases in the Market Square he, being in some way tense, was suddenly seized by the same irresistible impulse. He saw a woman's shopping bag on a stand, and at the top of the open bag was a red purse. Again he felt the throbbing in his head and the sexual excitement and a blind impulse again forced him to take the purse and dig into it. He then slowly, as in a haze, walked away, the purse still in his hand. Being surrounded by the market people, he had not gone further than some few yards before being caught. Upon request he immediately gave back the purse. Police investigations followed again. He admitted his "silly" action, without being able to explain what had prompted it. This time he began realizing that there was something wrong in him, and he himself suggested that he should see a doctor. He also mentioned that after the war, he had felt himself as strangely tired and mentally changed in some way. He had, by reason of exceptional external circumstances been under severe strain since 1947.

The man came into my care immediately after this last appropriation. To him, the whole matter was a complete mystery. His case was analysed psychologically and the analysis was carried out in three weeks. It has to be underlined that the method used is *psychobiological analysis*. The method of the psychoanalytical school, of which I do not approve, I consider mostly artificial psychological construction which has neither developed into an understandable psychology nor has it understood the scientific character of *Freud's* research. Psychobiology recognizes the importance of experiences in early childhood in determinating the further growth of the personality, but knows that important dynamic factors are also to be found in other periods and phases of life. Psychobiologically, the analysis of a person's past is made in order to understand the original personality behaviour and its development. This point of view, psychologically, includes constitutional as well as environmental factors.

In the analysis, the kleptomania problem was solved as follows:

The patient is an individual, who is constituted in a one-sided way, where the mental needs and the need of outward action are great, whereas the animal needs, particularly the sexual need, are minor in extent. This disproportion is evident from the story of his life.

> He is the only child. Environmental disturbing factors during childhood are not to be found. During adolescense, no sexual problems evinced themselves. In this respect, he matured late. Not until his seventeenth year did he notice any phenomena connected with sexuality and then only because the phenomenon of erection worried him. The off-hand explanation of an Army doctor that the cause of this was insufficient hygiene has been an adequate explanation to him until to-day, even though he is a married man with a grown up child. For decades, he has kept this "irritation" under control by thorough cleaning every third day, never passing that limit. He still speaks of this irritation without connecting it with the same phenomenon in coitus. In this respect he shows an infantilism and a strange limitation in the understanding of his emotional life. A further example may be mentioned. When taking part in shooting competitions, he prepared himself, regularly, on the previous evening by sexual intercourse in order to get rid of the competition tension. To him, *coitus has evidently always been more of an instinctive release from strain than any ordinary and conscious sexual need.* Before marriage he had no erotic experiences and

after marrying, the mere thought of other women simply never entered his mind. During the war, in the Army, he was a good companion in every other respect, but the men's rough talk and their affairs with women never touched him. By nature he is an ascetic, and, as the years went by, he, less and less, indulged in sexual intercourse. He does not smoke or drink alcohol.

As contrasted with the limitation of his emotional life, his need of mental and outward action is disproportionately large. He is a qualified builder, always working, building, planning buildings, keeping account of everything, making small technical improvements, showing in his work and interests the accuracy of a robot, with an exceptional good memory and a technical mind. The following brief summary of his social activities can be mentioned.

At the age of thirteen, during the war of 1918, he, as a volunteer, was engaged in the Army, working as a messenger and guard. After finishing his regular service he, for many years, stayed as a workman in building enterprises. Later he went through a technical school and was then employed by the State, without interruption until 1947. His duties included, in the beginning, the supervision and planning of building work and repairs. Later he assumed prime responsibility for large projects and the erection of new buildings. When war broke out in 1939, he, as extra work, had to see to the arrangements of bomb-shelters and of temporary military hospitals in a large district. After the war, he, in addition to his peace-time work, had to do a lot of re-arrangements. To this came during the war 1941-1944 the building of shelters, stores and all Staff buildings, the foundation, planning and building of about fifty military hospitals, all of which he was in charge. When working, he, as a person, was always balanced and he did his work perfectly.

He belonged to the Civil Guard from its foundation in 1917 until its end, as Sports Director, Auditor, Member of the Staff and, finally, as local Commander. He went through a course of instruction and became, during the war, an officer. He belonged to at least nine patriotic associations as a member, or as secretary or treasurer. He was an honorary member of the State's Building Association. After the war he worked in companies and building enterprises as a member of the board, as manager and so on.

He was a passionate collector, for the sake of collecting only. He collected coins, medals, commemorative coins, old weapons, such as guns, pistols, swords, ammunition, and stamps. Other spare-time hobbies were gardening, the history of the old capital and its fortifications and of old maps connected with that.

Being employed by the State, he in the turmoil after the war in 1944, little by little, was forced to devote himself to his work and duties to such an extent that his private life slowly decreased into non-existence. There was no time left for hobbies, rest or relaxation. During the first part of 1945 he, by order, obtained a wide responsibility for a report, concerning certain State buildings, of which the ground plans as well as a tremendous number of details had to be carried out by himself. When this extensive task was finished, he, in the summer of that year, for the first time, felt that something had gone wrong with his health. He felt a strange tiredness, especially in his legs, his memory worsened and a peculiar sensation began to trouble him. He could not stand the sight of a bright red colour because it always gave him the uncanny feeling as of some danger threatening him.

He now spent a short time in hospital. The tiredness in his legs could not be explained. *At this time, there was no insight that this was a symptom, psychosomatic in nature, indicating mental tiredness and exhaustion. It indicated that the border of his mental resistibility was reached and the troublesome red colour represented symbolically, too, the danger signal of his psychic organism.* But, not being aware of the meaning of the symptoms, he, after a short holiday, plunged into his work. The feeling of tiredness never left him entirely and his mental capacity was not the same as before. Then there came, in the years 1947-1948, a trial, in which he acted as witness and accused. After long and trying investigations he was acquitted, however. Immediately he recommenced his work. But from December 1948 until Spring 1949 he underwent a second trial, this time accused of offences committed during the last part of the war and subsequently, and thus during circumstances which were exceptional. *And just during this period of tension and utmost strain through tiring investigations, all the nine handbag appropriations took place.*

In this connection it may be mentioned that the patient's sexual life, at the same time had come to a complete stop, because his wife became an invalid as an aftermath of a long illness. He wanted to spare her and, without further thought, gave the whole thing up, devoting himself, instinctively, still more to his work. *Thus, at the same time as his mental exhaustion and the strain upon him increased, the trial and the pressing investigations demanding utmost mental activity, his main route of release from tension, the sexual intercourse, was blocked up. And so the tremendous mental tension exploded in a series of impulsive acts which clearly shows the nature of a substitute for the damned up psychic tension and the blocked up route to sexual release.*

Psychologically, taking the women's handbags are symbolic acts, in which the handbag represents the woman's genitals, and in which the sexual tension is relieved only after the patient has been able to dig into the bag (sexual activity). But the tension finding release in the symbolic act is not only ordinary erotic tension. In a broader sense, mental tension had always in this emotionally undifferentiated person, sought release, instinctively, the way biologically given by Nature, i. e. through coitus. And as this way, by reason of external circumstances and the patient's personal attitude in this respect, was no longer available, the tension increased and warning symptoms of mental exhaustion appeared. These warning symptoms were not, however, understood, and, slowly the border of the patient's psychic resistibility was reached, without his being conscious of it. Then, unfavourable external circumstances increased the strain to the bursting point and the psychic high tension found its temporary release in a short-circuit reaction, in which this tension combined with the blocked up sexual impulse detached itself from the personality control, and, the patient being in a state of impaired consciousness, led to an impulsive and symbolic act, which repeated itself.

The fact that the patient, when in my care, for the first time, got to know the connection between his mental exhaustion and the kleptomania symptom, also explains the single relapse in the autumn of 1952, *which, thus, occurred before the treatment.* When, in 1950, he was sent to prison, he first thought of suicide. Then he began to stupefy himself with work. This was made possible because nobody in the prison would look upon him as a criminal. He was allowed to move about freely and to do the work he wanted. Immediately, he was involved in the prison's building plans, drawing and planning buildings, supervising the work and repairs. One of his actions at this time may serve as an obvious example of his lack of perspective and of the discrepancy between his emotional passivity and the strong need of outward action. He was, as a person, offended at the way the prisoners were treated and with the bad conditions often seen in the prison. At the same time however, he eagerly was on the search, as suggested by the board, for a means of diminishing the possibilities of escape. His solution (of which he is still proud) was to minimize the window area in the cells to the utmost. By this he, without further thought, minimized the prisoner's possibilities of ventilation and of getting day-light into the cells.

As a summing up, when in 1951, he was released on probation, he was as exhausted as before. But immediately he recommenced his building work. In addition, at home, there was more work waiting. He had to look after his own house and had to take care of his invalid wife, doing most of her work too. There was no time left for rest and, little by little, he again became tense, reaching without knowing it the limit of his resisting power, and then the discharge came in the same manner as we have mentioned already.

Referring to the treatment I, in the autumn of 1952, stated in Court, (a) that the patient, without knowing it, was suffering from a lingering and long mental exhaustion, the tension of which had discharged itself by means of sexual tension into an impusive and symbolic act, kleptomania, which had to be regarded as a mental illness, (b) that during the acts, he, being in a state of impaired consciousness, had had no possibility of choice or preventing his actions, and not having had the appropriate treatment and thereby the insight into his illness, had had no possibility of preventing the single and last act of kleptomania, of which he is now accused, (c) which implies that he is *not responsible* for his action, and (d) that he, through the treatment had come to understand the motives of his acts and the factors which had contributed to it, and that he had now every possibility of recovery.

In this country a person, offending against the law, is considered as "not responsible for his deed, if suffering from actual insanity or a known mental illness".—In practice, however, only the obviously abnormal are declared not responsible. By routine, as in the case described here, the patient was put into prison for "nine thefts", no notice being taken by the Court of the preliminary medical statement, that this was a case of kleptomania, which is a *pathological need* of taking things. The last and single offence is, by routine, too, considered as a relapse into the crime.

The final sentence has not yet been passed by the High Court. The psychiatrists not capable of psychological analysis find it difficult to accept the fact that this man, in other respects ordinary, when acting under the pressure of his impulse, was not responsible for his action. The official psychiatric statement, finally asked for by the Court, is a voluminous report, showing a deplorable psychological incompetence and a richness of self-contradictions which makes it valueless if the question is of dispensing justice.

As regards my analysis of the case and the result of the treatment my standpoint is clear. I find it wrong that the patient, by reason of actions caused by mental illness, should be sentenced to imprisonment. The handling of a patient suffering from kleptomania, the psychological mechanism of which has been cleared up and understood by the patient, is a case for medical care and not a forensic case. Here is a question, in the case described here, not of a crime but of a mental illness and even if the patient does not show symptoms of insanity, he, during the moment of the impulsive act, was as irresponsible for his action as any psychotic person. A mental illness is not cured by putting the individual into prison, as is proved here by the "relapse". In addition, experience has proved the statement made by myself in Court, *two and a half years ago,* that the patient had every possibility of recovering after getting the appropriate treatment, to be right. Recovery has, after the treatment, progressed with no kind of complications right to the present day. The patient has proved his insight into the treatment by changing entirely his mode of life and simplifying his life in a way which enables him to get rest and relaxation and to preserve his mental balance.

SIGMUND FREUD / Dostoevsky and Parricide

FOUR FACETS may be distinguished in the rich personality of Dostoevsky: the creative artist, the neurotic, the moralist and the sinner. How is one to find one's way in this bewildering complexity?

The creative artist is the least doubtful: Dostoevsky's place is not far behind Shakespeare. *The Brothers Karamazov* is the most magnificent novel ever written; the episode of the Grand Inquisitor, one of the peaks in the literature of the world, can hardly be valued too highly. Before the problem of the creative artist analysis must, alas, lay down its arms.

The moralist in Dostoevsky is the most readily assailable. If we seek to rank him high as a moralist on the plea that only a man who has gone through the depths of sin can reach the highest summit of morality, we are neglecting a doubt that arises. A moral man is one who reacts to temptation as soon as he feels it in his heart, without yielding to it. A man who alternately sins and then in his remorse erects high moral standards lays himself open to the reproach that he has made things too easy for himself. He has not achieved the essence of morality, renunciation, for the moral conduct of life is a practical human interest. He reminds one of the barbarians of the great migrations, who murdered and did penance for it, till penance became an actual technique for enabling murder to be done. Ivan the Terrible behaved in exactly this way; indeed this compromise with morality is a characteristic Russian trait. Nor was the final outcome of Dostoevsky's moral strivings anything very glorious. After the most violent struggles to reconcile the instinctual demands of the individual with the claims of the community, he landed in the retrograde position of submission both to temporal and spiritual authority, of veneration both for the Tsar and for the God of the Christians, and of a narrow Russian nationalism—a position which lesser minds have reached with smaller effort. This is the weak point in that great personality. Dostoevsky threw away the chance of becoming a teacher and liberator of humanity and made himself one with their gaolers. The future of human civilization will have little to thank him for. It seems probable that he was condemned to this failure by his neurosis. The greatness of his intelligence and the strength of his love for humanity might have opened to him another, an apostolic, way of life.

To consider Dostoesvky as a sinner or a criminal rouses violent opposition, which need not be based upon a philistine assessment of criminals. The real motive for this opposition soon becomes apparent. Two traits are essential in a criminal: boundless egoism and a strong destructive urge. Common to both of these, and a necessary condition for their expression, is absence of love, lack of an emotional appreciation of (human) objects. One at once recalls the contrast to this presented by Dostoevsky—his great need of love and his enormous capacity for love, which is to be seen in manifestations of exaggerated kindness and caused him to love and to help where he had a right to hate and to be revengeful, as, for example, in his relations with his first wife and her lover. That being so, it must be asked why there is any temptation to reckon Dostoevsky among the criminals. The answer is that it comes from his choice of material, which singles out from all others violent, murderous and egoistic characters, thus pointing to the existence of similar tendencies within himself, and also from certain facts in his life, like his passion for gambling and his possible confession to a sexual assault upon a young girl.[1] The contradiction is resolved by the realization that Dostoevsky's very strong destructive instinct, which might easily have made him a criminal, was in his actual life directed mainly against his own person (inward instead of outward) and thus found expression as masochism and a sense of guilt. Nevertheless, his personality

---

[1] See the discussion of this in Fülöp-Miller and Eckstein (1926). Stefan Zweig (1920) writes: 'He was not halted by the barriers of bourgeois morality; and no one can say exactly how far he transgressed the bounds of law in his own life or how much of the criminal instincts of his heroes was realized in himself.' For the intimate connection between Dostoevsky's characters and his own experiences, see René Fülöp-Miller's remarks in the introductory section of Fülöp-Miller and Eckstein (1925), which are based upon N. Strakhov [1921].—[The topic of a sexual assault on an immature girl appears several times in Dostoevsky's writings—especially in the posthumous *Stavrogin's Confession* and *The Life of a Great Sinner*.]

retained sadistic traits in plenty, which show themselves in his irritability, his love of tormenting and his intolerance even towards people he loved, and which appear also in the way in which, as an author, he treats his readers. Thus in little things he was a sadist towards others, and in bigger things a sadist towards himself, in fact a masochist—that is to say the mildest, kindliest, most helpful person possible.

We have selected three factors from Dostoevsky's complex personality, one quantitative and two qualitative: the extraordinary intensity of his emotional life, his perverse innate instinctual disposition, which inevitably marked him out to be a sado-masochist or a criminal, and his unanalysable artistic gift. This combination might very well exist without neurosis; there are people who are complete masochists without being neurotic. Nevertheless, the balance of forces between his instinctual demands and the inhibitions opposing them (plus the available methods of sublimation) would even so make it necessary to classify Dostoevsky as what is known as an 'instinctual character'. But the position is obscured by the simultaneous presence of neurosis, which, as we have said, was not in the circumstances inevitable, but which comes into being the more readily, the richer the complication which has to be mastered by the ego. For neurosis is after all only a sign that the ego has not succeeded in making a synthesis, that in attempting to do so it has forfeited its unity.

How then, strictly speaking, does his neurosis show itself? Dostoevsky called himself an epileptic, and was regarded as such by other people, on account of his severe attacks, which were accompanied by loss of consciousness, muscular convulsions and subsequent depression. Now it is highly probable that this so-called epilepsy was only a symptom of his neurosis and must accordingly be classified as hystero-epilepsy—that is, as severe hysteria. We cannot be completely certain on this point for two reasons—firstly, because the anamnestic data on Dostoevsky's alleged epilepsy are defective and untrustworthy, and secondly, because our understanding of pathological states combined with epileptiform attacks is imperfect.

To take the second point first. It is unnecessary here to reproduce the whole pathology of epilepsy, for it would throw no decisive light on the problem. But this may be said. The old *morbus sacer* is still in evidence as an ostensible clinical entity, the uncanny disease with its incalculable, apparently unprovoked convulsive attacks, its changing of the character into irritability and aggressiveness, and its progressive lowering of all the mental faculties. But the outlines of this picture are quite lacking in precision. The attacks, so savage in their onset, accompanied by biting of the tongue and incontinence of urine and working up to the dangerous *status epilepticus* with its risk of severe self-injuries, may, nevertheless, be reduced to brief periods of *absence,* or rapidly passing fits of vertigo or may be replaced by short spaces of time during which the patient does something out of character, as though he were under the control of his unconscious. These attacks, though as a rule determined, in a way we do not understand, by purely physical causes, may nevertheless owe their first appearance to some purely mental cause (a fright, for instance) or may react in other respects to mental excitations. However characteristic intellectual impairment may be in the overwhelming majority of cases, at least *one* case is known to us (that of Helmholtz) in which the affliction did not interfere with the highest intellectual achievement. (Other cases of which the same assertion has been made are either disputable or open to the same doubts as the case of Dostoevsky himself.) People who are victims of epilepsy may give an impression of dullness and arrested development just as the disease often accompanies the most palpable idiocy and the grossest cerebral defects, even though not as a necessary component of the clinical picture. But these attacks, with all their variations, also occur in other people who display complete mental development and, if anything, an excessive and as a rule insufficiently controlled emotional life. It is no wonder in these circumstances that it has been found impossible to maintain that 'epilepsy' is a single clinical entity. The similarity that we find in the manifest symptoms seems to call for a functional view of them. It is as though a mechanism for abnormal instinctual discharge had been laid down organically, which could be made use of in quite different circumstances—both in the case of disturbances of cerebral activity due to severe histolytic or toxic affections, and also in the case of inadequate control over the mental economy and at times when the activity of the energy operating in the mind reaches crisis-pitch. Behind this dichotomy we have a glimpse of the identity of the underlying mechanism of instinctual discharge. Nor can that mechanism stand remote from the sexual processes, which are fundamentally of toxic origin: the earliest physicians described coition as a minor epilepsy, and thus recognized in the sexual act a mitigation and adaptation of the epileptic method of discharging stimuli.[2]

The 'epileptic reaction', as this common element may be called, is undoubtedly at the disposal of the neurosis whose essence it is to get rid by somatic means of amounts of excitation which it cannot deal with psychically. Thus the epileptic attack becomes a symptom of hysteria and is adapted and modified by it just as it is by the normal sexual process of discharge. It is therefore quite right to distinguish between an organic and an 'affec-

[2] [Cf. Freud's earlier paper on hysterical attacks (1909a), *Standard Ed.*, 9, 234.]

tive' epilepsy. The practical significance of this is that a person who suffers from the first kind has a disease of the brain, while a person who suffers from the second kind is a neurotic. In the first case his mental life is subjected to an alien disturbance from without, in the second case the disturbance is an expression of his mental life itself.

It is extremely probable that Dostoevsky's epilepsy was of the second kind. This cannot, strictly speaking, be proved. To do so we should have to be in a position to insert the first appearance of the attacks and their subsequent fluctuations into the thread of his mental life; and for that we know too little. The descriptions of the attacks themselves teach us nothing and our information about the relations between them and Dostoevsky's experiences is defective and often contradictory. The most probable assumption is that the attacks went back far into his childhood, that their place was taken to begin with by milder symptoms and that they did not assume an epileptic form until after the shattering experience of his eighteenth year—the murder of his father.[3] It would be very much to the point if it could be established that they ceased completely during his exile in Siberia, but other accounts contradict this.[4]

The unmistakable connection between the murder of the father in *The Brothers Karamazov* and the fate of Dostoevsky's own father has struck more than one of his biographers, and has led them to refer to 'a certain modern school of psychology'. From the standpoint of psycho-analysis (for that is what is meant), we are tempted to see in that event the severest trauma and to regard Dostoevsky's reaction to it as the turning-point of his neurosis. But if I undertake to substantiate this view psycho-analytically, I shall

[3] See René Fülöp-Miller (1924). [Cf. also the account given by Aimée Dostoevsky (1921) in her life of her father.] Of especial interest is the information that in the novelist's childhood 'something terrible, unforgettable and agonizing' happened, to which the first signs of his illness were to be traced (from an article by Suvorin in the newspaper *Novoe Vremya*, 1881, quoted in the introduction to Fülöp-Miller and Eckstein, 1925, xlv). See also Orest Miller (1921, 140): 'There is, however, another special piece of evidence about Fyodor Mikhailovich's illness, which relates to his earliest youth and brings the illness into connection with a tragic event in the family life of his parents. But, although this piece of evidence was given to me orally by one who was a close friend of Fyodor Mikhailovich, I cannot bring myself to reproduce it fully and precisely since I have had no confirmation of this rumour from any other quarter.' Biographers and scientific research workers cannot feel grateful for this discretion.

[4] Most of the accounts, including Dostoevsky's own, assert on the contrary that the illness only assumed its final, epileptic character during the Siberian exile. Unfortunately there is reason to distrust the autobiographical statements of neurotics. Experience shows that their memories introduce falsifications which are designed to interrupt disagreeable causal connections. Nevertheless, it appears certain that Dostoevsky's detention in the Siberian prison markedly altered his pathological condition. Cf. Fülöp-Miller (1924, 1186).

have to risk the danger of being unintelligible to all those readers who are unfamiliar with the language and theories of psychoanalysis.

We have one certain starting-point. We know the meaning of the first attacks from which Dostoevsky suffered in his early years, long before the incidence of the 'epilepsy'. These attacks had the significance of death: they were heralded by a fear of death and consisted of lethargic, somnolent states. The illness first came over him while he was still a boy, in the form of a sudden, groundless melancholy, a feeling, as he later told his friend Soloviev, as though he were going to die on the spot. And there in fact followed a state exactly similar to real death. His brother Andrey tells us that even when he was quite young Fyodor used to leave little notes about before he went to sleep, saying that he was afraid he might fall into this deathlike sleep during the night and therefore begged that his burial should be postponed for five days. (Fülöp-Miller and Eckstein, 1925, lx.)

We know the meaning and intention of such deathlike attacks.[5] They signify an identification with a dead person, either with someone who is really dead or with someone who is still alive and whom the subject wishes dead. The latter case is the more significant. The attack then has the value of a punishment. One has wished another person dead, and now one *is* this other person and is dead oneself. At this point psycho-analytical theory brings in the assertion that for a boy this other person is usually his father and that the attack (which is termed hysterical) is thus a self-punishment for a death-wish against a hated father.

Parricide, according to a well-known view, is the principal and primal crime of humanity as well as of the individual. (See my *Totem and Taboo*, 1912-13.) It is in any case the main source of the sense of guilt, though we do not know if it is the only one: researches have not yet been able to establish with certainty the mental origin of guilt and the need for expiation. But it is not necessary for it to be the only one. The psychological situation is complicated and requires elucidation. The relation of a boy to his father is, as we say, an 'ambivalent' one. In addition to the hate which seeks to get rid of the father as a rival, a measure of tenderness for him is also habitually present. The two attitudes of mind combine to produce identification with the father; the boy wants to be in his father's place because he admires him and wants to be like him, and also because he wants to put him out of the way. This whole development now comes up against a powerful obstacle. At a certain moment the child comes to understand that

---

[5] [The explanation was already given by Freud in a letter to Fliess of February 8, 1897 (Freud, 1950a, Letter 58).]

an attempt to remove his father as a rival would be punished by him with castration. So from fear of castration—that is, in the interests of preserving his masculinity—he gives up his wish to possess his mother and get rid of his father. In so far as this wish remains in the unconscious it forms the basis of the sense of guilt. We believe that what we have here been describing are normal processes, the normal fate of the so-called 'Oedipus complex'; nevertheless it requires an important amplification.

A further complication arises when the constitutional factor we call bisexuality is comparatively strongly developed in a child. For then, under the threat to the boy's masculinity by castration, his inclination becomes strengthened to diverge in the direction of femininity, to put himself instead in his mother's place and take over her role as object of his father's love. But the fear of castration makes *this* solution impossible as well. The boy understands that he must also submit to castration if he wants to be loved by his father as a woman. Thus both impulses, hatred of the father and being in love with the father, undergo repression. There is a certain psychological distinction in the fact that the hatred of the father is given up on account of fear of an *external* danger (castration), while the being in love with the father is treated as an *internal* instinctual danger, though fundamentally it goes back to the same external danger.

What makes hatred of the father unacceptable is *fear* of the father; castration is terrible, whether as a punishment or as the price of love. Of the two factors which repress hatred of the father, the first, the direct fear of punishment and castration, may be called the normal one; its pathogenic intensification seems to come only with the addition of the second factor, the fear of the feminine attitude. Thus a strong innate bisexual disposition becomes one of the preconditions or reinforcements of neurosis. Such a disposition must certainly be assumed in Dostoevsky, and it shows itself in a viable form (as latent homo-sexuality) in the important part played by male friendships in his life, in his strangely tender attitude towards rivals in love and in his remarkable understanding of situations which are explicable only by repressed homosexuality, as many examples from his novels show.

I am sorry, though I cannot alter the facts, if this exposition of the attitudes of hatred and love towards the father and their transformations under the influence of the threat of castration seems to readers unfamiliar with psycho-analysis unsavoury and incredible. I should myself expect that it is precisely the castration complex that would be bound to arouse the most general repudiation. But I can only insist that psycho-analytic experience has put these matters in particular beyond the reach of doubt and has taught us to recognize in them the key to every neurosis. This key, then, we must apply to our author's so-called epilepsy. So alien to our consciousness are the things by which our unconscious mental life is governed!

But what has been said so far does not exhaust the consequences of the repression of the hatred of the father in the Oedipus complex. There is something fresh to be added: namely that in spite of everything the identification with the father finally makes a permanent place for itself in the ego. It is received into the ego, but establishes itself there as a separate agency in contrast to the rest of the content of the ego. We then give it the name of super-ego and ascribe to it, the inheritor of the parental influence, the most important functions. If the father was hard, violent and cruel, the super-ego takes over those attributes from him and, in the relations between the ego and it, the passivity which was supposed to have been repressed is re-established. The super-ego has become sadistic, and the ego becomes masochistic—that is to say, at bottom passive in a feminine way. A great need for punishment develops in the ego, which in part offers itself as a victim to Fate, and in part finds satisfaction in ill-treatment by the super-ego (that is, in the sense of guilt). For every punishment is ultimately castration and, as such, a fulfilment of the old passive attitude towards the father. Even Fate is, in the last resort, only a later projection of the father.

The normal processes in the formation of conscience must be similar to the abnormal ones described here. We have not yet succeeded in fixing the boundary line between them. It will be observed that here the largest share in the outcome is ascribed to the passive component of repressed femininity. In addition, it must be of importance as an accidental factor whether the father, who is feared in any case, is also especially violent in reality. This was true in Dostoevsky's case, and we can trace back the fact of his extraordinary sense of guilt and of his masochistic conduct of life to a specially strong feminine component. Thus the formula for Dostoevsky is as follows: a person with a specially strong innate bisexual disposition, who can defend himself with special intensity against dependence on a specially severe father. This characteristic of bisexuality comes as an addition to the components of his nature that we have already recognized. His early symptoms of deathlike attacks can thus be understood as a father-identification on the part of his ego, which is permitted by his super-ego as a punishment. 'You wanted to kill your father in order to be your father yourself. Now you *are* your father, but a dead father'—the regular mechanism of hysterical symptoms. And further: 'Now your father is killing *you.*' For the ego the death symptom is a satisfaction in phantasy of the masculine wish and at the same time a masochistic satisfaction; for the super-ego it is a punitive satisfaction—that is, a sadistic satisfaction. Both of them, the ego and the super-ego, carry on the role of father.

To sum up, the relation between the subject and his father-object, while retaining its content, has been transformed into a relation between the ego and the super-ego—a new setting on a fresh stage. Infantile reactions from the Oedipus complex such as these may disappear if reality gives them no further nourishment. But the father's character remained the same, or rather, it deteriorated with the years, and thus Dostoevsky's hatred for his father and his death-wish against that wicked father were maintained. Now it is a dangerous thing if reality fulfils such repressed wishes. The phantasy has become reality and all defensive measures are thereupon reinforced. Dostoevsky's attacks now assumed an epileptic character; they still undoubtedly signified an identification with his father as a punishment, but they had become terrible, like his father's frightful death itself. What further content they had absorbed, particularly what sexual content, escapes conjecture.

One thing is remarkable: in the aura of the epileptic attack, one moment of supreme bliss is experienced. This may very well be a record of the triumph and sense of liberation felt on hearing the news of the death, to be followed immediately by an all the more cruel punishment. We have divined just such a sequence of triumph and mourning, of festive joy and mourning, in the brothers of the primal horde who murdered their father, and we find it repeated in the ceremony of the totem meal.[6] If it proved to be the case that Dostoevsky was free from his attacks in Siberia, that would merely substantiate the view that they were his punishment. He did not need them any longer when he was being punished in another way. But that cannot be proved. Rather does this necessity for punishment on the part of Dostoevsky's mental economy explain the fact that he passed unbroken through these years of misery and humiliation. Dostoevsky's condemnation as a political prisoner was unjust and he must have known it, but he accepted the undeserved punishment at the hands of the Little Father, the Tsar, as a substitute for the punishment he deserved for his sin against his real father. Instead of punishing himself, he got himself punished by his father's deputy. Here we have a glimpse of the psychological justification of the punishments inflicted by society. It is a fact that large groups of criminals want to be punished. Their super-ego demands it and so saves itself the necessity for inflicting the punishment itself.[7]

---

[6] See *Totem and Taboo* [(1912-13), Section 5 of Essay IV, *Standard Ed.*, 13, 140].
[7] [Cf. 'Criminals from a Sense of Guilt', the third essay in Freud's 'Some Character-Types Met with in Psycho-Analytic Work' (1916d), *Standard Ed.*, 14, 332.]

Everyone who is familiar with the complicated transformation of meaning undergone by hysterical symptoms will understand that no attempt can be made here to follow out the meaning of Dostoevsky's attacks beyond this beginning.[8] It is enough that we may assume that their original meaning remained unchanged behind all later accretions. We can safely say that Dostoevsky never got free from the feelings of guilt arising from his intention of murdering his father. They also determined his attitude in the two other spheres in which the father-relation is the decisive factor, his attitude towards the authority of the State and towards belief in God. In the first of these he ended up with complete submission to his Little Father, the Tsar, who had once performed with him in *reality* the comedy of killing which his attacks had so often represented in *play*. Here penitence gained the upper hand. In the religious sphere he retained more freedom: according to apparently trustworthy reports he wavered, up to the last moment of his life, between faith and atheism. His great intellect made it impossible for him to overlook any of the intellectual difficulties to which faith leads. By an individual recapitulation of a development in world-history he hoped to find a way out and a liberation from guilt in the Christ ideal, and even to make use of his sufferings as a claim to be playing a Christ-like role. If on the whole he did not achieve freedom and became a reactionary, that was because the filial guilt, which is present in human beings generally and on which religious feeling is built, had in him attained a super-individual intensity and remained insurmountable even to his great intelligence. In writing this we are laying ourselves open to the charge of having abandoned the impartiality of anlysis and of subjecting Dostoevsky to judgements that can only be justified from the partisan standpoint of a particular *Weltanschauung*. A conservative would take the side of the Grand Inquisitor and would judge Dostoevsky differently. The objection is just; and one can only say in extenuation that Dostoevsky's decision has every appearance of having been determined by an intellectual inhibition due to his neurosis.

It can scarcely be owing to chance that three of the masterpieces of the literature of all time—the *Oedipus Rex* of Sophocles, Shakespeare's *Hamlet* and Dostoevsky's *The Brothers Karamazov* —should all deal with the same subject, parricide. In all three,

---

[8] The best account of the meaning and content of his attacks was given by Dostoevsky himself, when he told his friend Strakhov that his irritability and depression after an epileptic attack were due to the fact that he seemed to himself a criminal and could not get rid of the feeling that he had a burden of unknown guilt upon him, that he had committed some great misdeed, which oppressed him. (Fülöp-Miller, 1924, 1188.) In self-accusations like these psycho-analysis sees signs of a recognition of 'psychical reality', and it endeavours to make the unknown guilt known to consciousness.

moreover, the motive for the deed, sexual rivalry for a woman, is laid bare.

The most straightforward is certainly the representation in the drama derived from the Greek legend. In this it is still the hero himself who commits the crime. But poetic treatment is impossible without softening and disguise. The naked admission of an intention to commit parricide, as we arrive at it in analysis, seems intolerable without analytic preparation. The Greek drama, while retaining the crime, introduces the indispensable toning-down in a masterly fashion by projecting the hero's unconscious motive into reality in the form of a compulsion by a destiny which is alien to him. The hero commits the deed unintentionally and apparently uninfluenced by the woman; this latter element is however taken into account in the circumstance that the hero can only obtain possession of the queen mother after he has repeated his deed upon the monster who symbolizes the father. After his guilt has been revealed and made conscious, the hero makes no attempt to exculpate himself by appealing to the artificial expedient of the compulsion of destiny. His crime is acknowledged and punished as though it were a full and conscious one—which is bound to appear unjust to our reason, but which psychologically is perfectly correct.

In the English play the presentation is more indirect; the hero does not commit the crime himself; it is carried out by someone else, for whom it is not parricide. The forbidden motive of sexual rivalry for the woman does not need, therefore, to be disguised. Moreover, we see the hero's Oedipus complex, as it were, in a reflected light, by learning the effect upon him of the other's crime. He ought to avenge the crime, but finds himself, strangely enough, incapable of doing so. We know that it is his sense of guilt that is paralysing him; but, in a manner entirely in keeping with neurotic processes, the sense of guilt is displaced on to the perception of his inadequacy for fulfilling his task. There are signs that the hero feels this guilt as a super-individual one. He despises others no less than himself: 'Use every man after his desert, and who should 'scape whipping?'

The Russian novel goes a step further in the same direction. There also the murder is committed by someone else. This other person, however, stands to the murdered man in the same filial relation as the hero, Dmitri; in this other person's case the motive of sexual rivalry is openly admitted; he is a brother of the hero's, and it is a remarkable fact that Dostoevsky has attributed to him his own illness, the alleged epilepsy, as though he were seeking to confess that the epileptic, the neurotic, in himself was a parricide. Then, again, in the speech for the defence at the trial, there is the famous mockery of psychology—it is a 'knife that cuts both ways':[9] a splendid piece of disguise, for we have only to reverse it in order to discover the deepest meaning of Dostoevsky's view of things. It is not psychology that deserves the mockery, but the procedure of judicial enquiry. It is a matter of indifference who actually committed the crime; psychology is only concerned to know who desired it emotionally and who welcomed it when it was done.[10] And for that reason all of the brothers, except the contrasted figure of Alyosha, are equally guilty—the impulsive sensualist, the sceptical cynic and the epileptic criminal. In *The Brothers Karamazov* there is one particularly revealing scene. In the course of his talk with Dmitri, Father Zossima recognizes that Dmitri is prepared to commit parricide, and he bows down at his feet. It is impossible that this can be meant as an expression of admiration; it must mean that the holy man is rejecting the temptation to despise or detest the murderer and for that reason humbles himself before him. Dostoevsky's sympathy for the criminal is, in fact, boundless; it goes far beyond the pity which the unhappy wretch has a right to, and reminds us of the 'holy awe' with which epileptics and lunatics were regarded in the past. A criminal is to him almost a Redeemer, who has taken on himself the guilt which must else have been borne by others. There is no longer any need for one to murder, since *he* has already murdered; and one must be grateful to him, for, except for him, one would have been obliged oneself to murder. That is not kindly pity alone, it is identification on the basis of similar murderous impulses—in fact, a slightly displaced narcissism. (In saying this, we are not disputing the ethical value of this kindliness.) This may perhaps be quite generally the mechanism of kindly sympathy with other people, a mechanism which one can discern with especial ease in this extreme case of a guilt-ridden novelist. There is no doubt that this sympathy by identification was a decisive factor in determining Dostoevsky's choice of material. He dealt first with the common criminal (whose motives are egotistical) and the political and religious criminal; and not until the end of his life did he come back to the primal criminal, the parricide, and use him, in a work of art, for making his confession.

The publication of Dostoevsky's posthumous papers and of his wife's diaries has thrown a glaring light on one episode in his

[9] [In the German (and in the original Russian) the simile is 'a stick with two ends'. The 'knife that cuts both ways' is derived from Constance Garnett's English translation. The phrase occurs in Book XII, Chapter X, of the novel.]
[10] [A practical application of this to an actual criminal case is to be found in Freud's comments on the Halsmann Case (1931d), p. 251 below, where *The Brothers Karamazov* is again discussed.]

life, namely the period in Germany when he was obsessed with a mania for gambling (cf. Fülöp-Miller and Eckstein, 1925), which no one could regard as anything but an unmistakable fit of pathological passion. There was no lack of rationalizations for this remarkable and unworthy behaviour. As often happens with neurotics, Dostoevsky's sense of guilt had taken a tangible shape as a burden of debt, and he was able to take refuge behind the pretext that he was trying by his winnings at the tables to make it possible for him to return to Russia without being arrested by his creditors. But this was no more than a pretext and Dostoevsky was acute enough to recognize the fact and honest enough to admit it. He knew that the chief thing was gambling for its own sake—*le jeu pour le jeu*.[11] All the details of his impulsively irrational conduct show this and something more besides. He never rested until he had lost everything. For him gambling was a method of self-punishment as well. Time after time he gave his young wife his promise or his word of honour not to play any more or not to play any more on that particular day; and, as she says, he almost always broke it. When his losses had reduced himself and her to the direst need, he derived a second pathological satisfaction from that. He could then scold and humiliate himself before her, invite her to despise him and to feel sorry that she had married such an old sinner; and when he had thus unburdened his conscience, the whole business would begin again next day. His young wife accustomed herself to this cycle, for she had noticed that the one thing which offered any real hope of salvation—his literary production—never went better than when they had lost everything and pawned their last possessions. Naturally she did not understand the connection. When his sense of guilt was satisfied by the punishments he had inflicted on himself, the inhibition upon his work became less severe and he allowed himself to take a few steps along the road to success.[12]

What part of a gambler's long-buried childhood is it that forces its way to repetition in his obsession for play? The answer may be divined without difficulty from a story by one of our younger writers. Stefan Zweig, who has incidentally devoted a study to Dostoevsky himself (1920), has included in his collection of three stories *Die Verwirrung der Gefühle* [*Confusion of Feelings*] (1927) one which he calls 'Vierundzwanzig Stunden aus dem

---

[11] 'The main thing is the play itself,' he writes in one of his letters. 'I swear that greed for money has nothing to do with it, although Heaven knows I am sorely in need of money.'
[12] 'He always remained at the gaming tables till he had lost everything and was totally ruined. It was only when the damage was quite complete that the demon at last retired from his soul and made way for the creative genius.' (Fülöp-Miller and Eckstein, 1925, lxxxvi.)

Leben einer Frau' ['Four-and-Twenty Hours in a Woman's Life']. This little masterpiece ostensibly sets out only to show what an irresponsible creature woman is, and to what excesses, surprising even to herself, an unexpected experience may drive her. But the story tells far more than this. If it is subjected to an analytical interpretation, it will be found to represent (without any apologetic intent) something quite different, something universally human, or rather something masculine. And such an interpretation is so extremely obvious that it cannot be resisted. It is characteristic of the nature of artistic creation that the author, who is a personal friend of mine, was able to assure me, when I asked him, that the interpretation which I put to him had been completely strange to his knowledge and intention, although some of the details woven into the narrative seemed expressly designed to give a clue to the hidden secret.

In this story, an elderly lady of distinction tells the author about an experience she has had more than twenty years earlier. She has been left a widow when still young and is the mother of two sons, who no longer need her. In her forty-second year, expecting nothing further of life, she happens, on one of her aimless journeyings, to visit the Rooms at Monte Carlo. There, among all the remarkable impressions which the place produces, she is soon fascinated by the sight of a pair of hands which seem to betray all the feelings of the unlucky gambler with terrifying sincerity and intensity. These hands belong to a handsome young man—the author, as though unintentionally, makes him of the same age as the narrator's elder son—who, after losing everything, leaves the Rooms in the depth of despair, with the evident intention of ending his hopeless life in the Casino gardens. An inexplicable feeling of sympathy compels her to follow him and make every effort to save him. He takes her for one of the importunate women so common there and tries to shake her off; but she stays with him and finds herself obliged, in the most natural way possible, to join him in his apartment at the hotel, and finally to share his bed. After this improvised night of love, she exacts a most solemn vow from the young man, who has now apparently calmed down, that he will never play again, provides him with money for his journey home and promises to meet him at the station before the departure of his train. Now, however, she begins to feel a great tenderness for him, is ready to sacrifice all she has in order to keep him and makes up her mind to go with him instead of saying goodbye. Various mischances delay her, so that she misses the train. In her longing for the lost one she returns once more to the Rooms and there, to her horror, sees once more the hands which had first excited her sympathy: the faithless youth had gone back to his play. She reminds him of his promise, but, obsessed by his passion, he calls her a spoil-sport, tells her to go, and flings back the money with which she has tried to rescue him. She hurries away in deep mortification and learns later that she has not succeeded in saving him from suicide.

The brilliantly told, faultlessly motivated story is of course complete in itself and is certain to make a deep effect upon the reader. But analysis shows us that its invention is based fundamentally upon a wishful phantasy belonging to the period of puberty, which a number of people actually remember consciously. The phantasy embodies a boy's wish that his mother should herself initiate him into sexual life in order to save him from the dreaded injuries caused by masturbation. (The numerous creative works that deal with the theme of redemption have the same origin.) The 'vice' of masturbation is replaced by the addiction to gambling;[13] and the emphasis laid upon the passionate activity of the hands betrays this derivation. Indeed, the passion for play is an equivalent of the old compulsion to masturbate; 'playing' is the actual word used in the nursery to describe the activity of the hands upon the genitals. The irresistible nature of the temptation, the solemn resolutions, which are nevertheless invariably broken, never to do it again, the stupefying pleasure and the bad conscience which tells the subject that he is ruining himself (committing suicide)—all these elements remain unaltered in the process of substitution. It is true that Zweig's story is told by the mother, not by the son. It must flatter the son to think: 'if my mother only knew what dangers masturbation involves me in, she would certainly save me from them by allowing me to lavish all my tenderness on her own body'. The equation of the mother with a prostitute, which is made by the young man in the story, is linked up with the same phantasy. It brings the unattainable woman within easy reach. The bad conscience which accompanies the phantasy brings about the unhappy ending of the story. It is also interesting to notice how the *facade* given to the story by its author seeks to disguise its analytic meaning. For it is extremely questionable whether the erotic life of women is dominated by sudden and mysterious impulses. On the contrary, analysis reveals an adequate motivation for the surprising behaviour of this woman who had hitherto turned away from love. Faithful to the memory of her dead husband, she had armed herself against all similar attractions; but—and here the son's phantasy is right—she did not, as a mother, escape her quite unconscious transference of love on to

---

[13] [In a letter to Fliess of December 22, 1897, Freud suggested that masturbation is the 'primal addiction', for which all later addictions are substitutes (Freud, 1950a, Letter 79).]

her son, and Fate was able to catch her at this undefended spot.

If the addiction to gambling, with the unsuccessful struggles to break the habit and the opportunities it affords for self-punishment, is a repetition of the compulsion to masturbate, we shall not be surprised to find that it occupied such a large space in Dostoevsky's life. After all, we find no cases of severe neurosis in which the auto-erotic satisfaction of early childhood and of puberty has not played a part; and the relation between efforts to suppress it and fear of the father are too well known to need more than than a mention.[14]

ALAN NELSON/The Shopdropper

"I'M A klepto-kleptomaniac, Doctor." Dr. Manly J. Departure, bursting with vitamins and energy after his year's leave of absence, gazed with professional cordiality at the angular young man across the desk who was kneading preposterously long fingers and scowling.

"Well, that's not too serious, Mr. Flint," Dr. Departure replied, permitting himself an affable chuckle. "There seems to be a lot of kleptomania going around this season. As for the stuttering . . ."

Mr. Flint did not smile.

"Not kleptomania, Doctor. *Klepto*-kleptomania." The young man continued to massage his fingers as though smoothing out invisible wrinkles. "I steal only from other kleptomaniacs, he said earnestly."

Dr. Departure's chuckle dribbled away.

"If I understand you," Dr. Departure began very slowly, "you have a pathological impulse to steal. But instead of stealing from department stores as does the normal kleptom . . . rather, the *usual* kleptomaniac, you feel impelled to steal the things other kleptomaniacs have already stolen?"

"That's right," the man answered. "I sneak into their rooms when they're out. They're getting harder and harder to find, too. Of course it's all stuff I have no particular use for. Look!"

He reached down, hauled up a bulky paper sack and handed it across the desk. Dr. Departure opened it and extracted, among other things, an egg beater, a plastic thimble, a pencil sharpener, a bottle of permanent wave lotion and an ocarina.

[14] Most of the views which are here expressed are also contained in an excellent book by Jolan Neufeld (1923).

"I just . . . just can't help myself, Doctor." Flint flexed his long lean fingers, frowned at them, then looked up once more at the doctor. "This urge I get—it's irresistible. And getting worse all the time. You've got to help me."

Dr. Departure laid the bag down and began running his finger over the small brass clock his wife had given him for Christmas; it always steadied him to focus his attention a moment or so on the little instrument ticking off the dollars like a taxi meter. Presently he lifted his eyes and studied the man: thin pallid face, a shaving cut over the adam's apple, conservative dresser. Nothing remarkable except his preoccupation with those very long fingers.

"Just a few routine questions, first," Dr. Departure said, picking up a pencil.

Flint, it turned out, was 37, graduated from high school, employed as an insurance clerk, unmarried. All very usual.

At the end of the hour the doctor arose and smiled reassuringly.

"Shall we say Tuesday at 10?" he said, seeing Flint to the door.

Shortly before 10 the following Tuesday, as Dr. Departure stepped out of the elevator to keep his appointment with Flint, he bumped into his brother-in-law, Dr. Bert Schnappenhocker, a tall, assertive psychiatrist with aggressive front teeth and iron gray hair, who specialized in rich divorcees, and whose very presence in the office adjoining his own caused Departure a kind of permanent, bristling hostility. If it weren't for the fact he was Emily's brother . . .

"Glad to see you back, Manly," Schnappenhocker boomed in that loathsome, hearty voice. "How'd they treat you at the asylum?"

"It was a rest home," Dr. Departure replied coldly, moving down the hall toward his own office.

"Well, if you begin to feel shaky again, feel free to drop in. Professional discount, of course." He laughed raucously and pounded Departure on the shoulder. "By the way, did I tell you I'm speaking before the Institute of Psychiatry banquet next month? Hope you can make it."

Quack! Dr. Departure muttered angrily, closing the door against Schnappenhocker's imbecilic and tuneless whistle outside. Then, shaking off his irritation, he called Flint in from the waiting room.

"Now!" he began brightly, after Flint seated himself and placed another bulky paper sack down beside the desk. "Now, about this . . . this kleptomania." He refused to utter that ridiculous word *klepto-kleptomania*. Since Flint's first visit, he'd been unable to find anything in the literature to cover the problem, but at length he reassured himself the thing wasn't as weird as it first appeared; after all, kleptomania was kleptomania, no matter who it was you stole from—possibly this man's case might be a little more complicated, that was all.

"I'd like you to start at the beginning, if you will, Mr. Flint, and tell me how this problem got started."

Flint looked troubled and poked the trinket-filled bag with his foot.

"It's the gloves," he said. "Never had any trouble until I started wearing the gloves. Then I began having this urge to snatch things off department store counters. Didn't take two weeks, though, until I couldn't get any kicks out of that any more. Then I started on the kleptos. . . ."

Dr. Departure smiled and felt the problem begin to unravel right then and there. So typical, this childish process of blaming inanimate objects for our own defects. Just last night his little niece had accused her rag doll of shattering the vase.

"Where are these gloves?" he inquired kindly.

Flint lifted his hands above the desk.

"I have them on," he said.

Dr. Departure blinked, leaned forward and gazed at the long, pink hands with the wrinkled knuckles, tapering fingers and well cared-for finger nails. They were as naked as billiard balls.

"I don't see any gloves," the doctor said in a moment.

"I know," Flint replied evenly. "They're invisible."

Ah, the pieces are beginning to fall into place, Dr. Departure thought. A case of guilt projection complicated by delusionary ideas. Ten to one there will be some flights of fantasy involving sorcery showing up soon.

"Where did you get these . . . these gloves?" he asked in a soft persuasive voice.

"I bought them from a gypsy who bought them from a three-fingered Brazilian witch doctor named Bessie."

"And where did the witch doctor get them?"

"She brewed them out of a stunted guayule bush that had been struck twice by lightning and injected three times with the blood of an insane virgin."

"And what was the . . . the purpose of these gloves?"

"To make it easier for the witch doctor's son to steal pigeon eggs." Flint looked away with troubled eyes. "The gloves are defective though. They're too strong."

This could go on forever, Dr. Departure thought sadly. If I ask him why he simply doesn't take the gloves off, he'll say he can't get them off.

"The worst of it is, Doctor—I can't get them off. See?"

Flint raised one hand, plucked futilely at the pink skin with the thumb and forefinger of the other. Suddenly, he leaned across the desk confidentially. "There's only one way they'll come off, Doctor."

"And what's that?"

"First I have to find a witch doctor who ranks as high in *his* community as Bessie does in hers. That's you."

"Now, just a moment!" Dr. Departure protested huffily.

From his pocket Flint whipped a piece of paper and a small box of white powder which he laid before the doctor.

"Then I have to get you to sprinkle this powder over the gloves while saying these words and making a gesture like this. After that I can peel them right off."

"Please!" Dr. Departure said firmly, holding up his hand. He'd had quite enough of invisible gloves—except, of course, in a symbolic sense.

"Let me tell *you* how to get those . . . those invisible gloves off." He paused, polished his glasses, cleared his throat and glanced oratorically at the ceiling. "First, what do the gloves represent? Nothing more than . . ."

For a solid hour, Dr. Departure probed, prodded and pronounced. He spoke eloquently on phobias; on fantasies; on fixations; and the little brass clock jumped when he pounded the table for emphasis. Flint watched and listened intently, then at last when Dr. Departure paused to wipe his forehead and glance significantly at his watch, he leaned forward.

"That's all very well, Doctor," he said. "But are you, or are you not, going to cast this spell?"

These things take time, Dr. Departure told himself wearily. Time and patience . . .

"Because if you're not," Flint continued, half rising from the chair. "I'm going some place else. There's another man down the hall here. A Dr. Schnapp . . . Schnappen . . ."

Hastily, Dr. Departure motioned the man back into the chair. Every time he'd lost a patient to Dr. Schnappenhocker, his brother-in-law through some fantastic freak of luck had been able to clear up the problem in practically no time. The crowing that went on afterwards was unbearable. The man had even written up one case for the *American Journal*.

Dr. Departure looked distastefully at the box of powder and studied the words on the slip of paper. Well, if he had to demonstrate the impotence of spell casting, he had to—that was all.

"If I cast this . . . this spell," he finally said, trying to get a deeper meaning into the words, "will you promise to really *try* to remove these imaginary gloves—shed them like you would so much dead skin—skin you no longer need?"

"Yes! Yes!" Flint agreed eagerly.

"EEDO! QUEEDO! SKIZZO LIBIDO!" Dr. Departure intoned, sprinkling powder over Flint's outstretched hands and making a certain gesture with his own. Then he sat back and smiled indulgently.

"Thanks!" Flint breathed gratefully. Then with a *zip-snick-snap!* he deftly peeled a transparent rubbery glove from each hand quite as if he were shedding so much dead skin, and tossed them both on the desk. In amazement, Dr. Departure gazed at this tiny mound of sheer limp rubber that had collapsed his psychological house of cards with such a nasty little plop.

"This should cover the fee," Flint was saying happily, placing three twenties on the blotter. "And thanks again." He went out, slamming the door.

Dr. Departure closed his eyes a moment and listened to the tick of the brass clock. Of course the man could be perpetrating an elaborate practical joke. It was even possible that that loud-mouth charlatan, that hand holder of rich nymphomaniacs, that psychoanalytical peeping tom, Dr. Schnappenhocker had put him up to it. No, on second thought it couldn't have been a practical joke. No one—not even Bert Schnappenhocker himself—would be willing to pay $25 an hour for that meager pleasure.

He picked up one glove and examined it. It was inside out now—peeling it off had done that—but both sides seemed practically the same. Never had he touched anything so wonderfully soft and delicate, so light and completely transparent! He turned it over and over. It had no more body than a cobweb, yet it was as resilient as a rubber girdle. He put his fingers into it tentatively. Remarkable how snug and comfortable it was! He pulled it completely on. Why you scarcely knew it was there! He picked up the other glove, pulled it on too. . . .

The reason I can't get these gloves off, Dr. Departure told himself the next day staring at his fingers, is that the rubber sticks so close to the skin I can't get a good grip on it. If only I had longer finger nails.

The door opened suddenly and through it popped the beaming face of Dr. Schnappenhocker.

"Morning, Manly!" he boomed. "Just out drumming up a little business and right off I thought of you." He laughed heartily.

"Don't you ever knock?" Dr. Departure growled.

"No offense, Doctor. Thought I'd leave you a program for next month's Institute banquet. Did I tell you I was guest speaker?" He dropped a folder on the chair and disappeared.

Dr. Departure turned his attention back to the gloves. It *was* odd he couldn't get them off. Very odd. Not that this bothered him particularly—they were so snug and light you scarcely knew you had them on. Tonight he'd get Emily to peel them off. It *was* a bit disconcerting, though, not to be able to do it yourself.

Of course he'd had no impulse toward kleptomania—absolutely none at all. He smiled to himself. As a matter of fact—if you permitted yourself such a wild thought—it was just the other way around. Last night he'd left a book on the bus and this morning he'd misplaced his favorite pipe in the coffee shop. Odd. Very odd.

His eyes drifted to the two sacks of stolen articles Flint had left. Have to return *those,* he told himself—not good to have them lying around. He scooped up the bags and pawing through them discovered from price tags that most of them came from Snow Brothers' Department Store. It was lunch time; he'd drop them off right now.

A pre-inventory sale was raging in Snow Brothers'; its aisles throbbed with a squirming horde of women shoppers, and Dr. Departure, hugging two paper sacks, burrowed his way determinedly toward the accommodation desk.

It was in Women's Purses that the whim suddenly seized him. He fought it off. It returned—more powerfully, more insistently—and in a moment it swelled into a wild, unreasoning, clamoring urge that made his fingers tingle and his whole body quiver.

He found himself edging over to a counter, reaching into the sack he carried. His breathing came faster as he removed the first article his fingers touched—a windshield wiper. Furtively, he looked about. No one was watching. With a quick darting motion he sneaked the wiper between two leather bags on the counter. Then glancing nervously about once more, he hurried away with a pounding heart, feeling an odd tingling triumph.

"Opposite of kleptomania—that's what you have!" Mrs. Departure was accusing her husband in a loud hysterical voice two weeks later at dinner time. She was a large resolute woman with steely eyes and sensible shoes. At the moment, however, she was considerably unstrung. "You're an *un*-kleptomaniac, and you've *got* to do something about it!"

"And I tell you it's these damn gloves!" the doctor shouted pacing back and forth. His dinner lay cold and untouched. His hair was rumpled. His eyes glittered with strange lights. His hands had a strange plucking motion one against the other.

"You shoplifter . . . I mean . . . you shopdropper!" Her long, usually solid jaw quivered with anguish. "Sneaking into department stores, leaving trinkets all over the place. My blue vase! The pruning shears! Almost the entire silverware set! Even your little brass clock! All gone!"

"It's the gloves, I tell you!" Vainly he tugged, plucked and snatched at his finger tips. "I put them on backwards. Inside out! ... Damn! If I could only get a grip on them!"

"And today the public library called again," she cried shrilly. "Not a day passes but what you sneak three or four of your own books onto their shelves!"

"Well, if you'd helped me get these things off that first night like I asked you to, maybe I wouldn't be in this fix!"

"But this evening!" Mrs. Departure's lips twitched, her voice shrilled ever higher. "On the bus—that was the last straw! I saw you with my own eyes! The way you sneaked that man's wallet out of his pocket, stuffed it with four of your own dollar bills, then put it back! I tell you, Manly, you've got to see some one!"

"And I tell you there's nothing wrong with me! It's the gloves! When Flint skinned them off, it turned them inside out. They're on backwards! Can't you get that through your head!" He jammed a cigarette in his mouth.

"Gloves! Gloves! Gloves! I tell you for the hundredth time you haven't any gloves on!"

"Where *is* that cigarette lighter," Dr. Departure growled, slapping his pockets. "I had it right in my vest this morning."

"The question is," she said, laughing a bit hysterically and throwing back the flaps of his coat, "where is your vest? ... Manly, I might as well tell you—I've already made an appointment for you. Tomorrow."

She dug in her purse and handed him a card.

"Schnappenhocker!" he screamed.

"Bert was really very nice about it."

"I will *not* go to that revolting brother of yours," Dr. Departure shrieked, turning a shiny purple. "Not even if he was the last doctor on earth! That pompous witch doctor! That ..." Suddenly in mid-sentence he let out his breath and stared into space a moment, a pleased and reflective expression beginning to relax his face. Witch doctor? There was still a little powder left. ... Why hadn't he thought of palming the gloves off on Bert before? That loud mouth wit-snapper was always trying on other people's garments for a laugh—ladies' hats, little boys' bow ties, Dr. Departure's own rather conservative rain shoes. The man simply couldn't *resist* a pair of rubber gloves!

"You will go," his wife was saying in a low vibrant voice.

"Most certainly I will go!" Dr. Departure replied in an equally vibrant voice, the sweet smile of anticipation growing on his face.

Never were doctor and patient ever happier to see one another than the following day when Dr. Departure entered the softly shaded inner sanctum of Dr. Bert Schnappenhocker. Dr. Schnappenhocker beamed at his rival with the undisguised eagerness of an anatomy student about to dissect an especially interesting species of tailless amphibia, while Dr. Departure gazed back with the smirky innocence of one all set to administer an emotional hot-foot. For two full minutes they wrung each other's hands.

"Well!" Dr. Schnappenhocker finally said heartily, impatient to make the initial incision. "Emily tells me you have a little problem."

"I hate to bother you with it, really," Dr. Departure replied, trying to keep from grinning.

For almost an hour Dr. Departure allowed his brother-in-law to worm the whole unlikely story out of him, then finally when he gave the instructions and pushed the little box of white powder across the desk, he watched Schnappenhocker shake his head with a coy gesture of hopelessness and settle back in his chair.

"Manly, old man," Schnappenhocker said. "Another six months of absolute rest and quiet ought to do it for you. Maybe eight. You owe it to Emily, you know. *And* to yourself." He reached for the telephone.

Dr. Departure was prepared for this. Wild lights shining from his eyes—or what he *hoped* were wild lights—he leapt from the chair, seized the copper letter opener and leaned across the desk breathing hard.

"Are you going to cast that spell or aren't you!" he shouted, digging the opener into the mahogany desk top.

Dr. Schnappenhocker blinked apprehensively.

"Sure, Manly. Sure!" he placated. "I'll cast the spell, *then* I'll make your reservation." He picked up the box of powder and glanced nervously at the slip of paper.

"EEDO! SQUEEDO! SKIZZO LIBIDO!"

With a *zip-snick-snap!* Dr. Departure peeled off the glove from the left hand. Then, as he fumbled with the right hand, an agonizing decision suddenly leapt out at him: should he make a shoplifter out of his brother-in-law, or a shopdropper? Should he leave the gloves right side out or wrong side out? Each alternative offered such dazzling possibilities that for a moment Dr. Departure felt himself almost torn in two by the exquisite but mutually exclusive choices. Then the answer came to him. What if he left one glove right side out, the other wrong side out . . . ?

"Why Bert!" Mrs. Departure said, opening the door to her brother Dr. Schnappenhocker a week later. "Come on in!"

"I can't," Dr. Schnappenhocker replied, handing her a cardboard carton filled with assorted articles. "Just thought I'd drop these off. They're a few more things Manly deposited in my office when he was . . . well, before I cured him."

Mrs. Departure took the carton.

"I must say you're a miracle man, Bert. Just one treatment and now he's as fit as a fiddle."

"It was nothing," Schnappenhocker said, backing down the steps nervously. There was a tenseness about his eyes and he kept jerking at the ends of his fingers.

Mrs. Departure closed the door and returned to the dining room where her husband was wolfing down a tremendous dinner.

"That was Bert," she explained. "With another carton of junk. You know, I'm worried about the man. He keeps bringing all this stuff over here insisting it's yours, but it all belongs to him! Here's his fountain pen, his copper letter opener, even his appointment book! And what makes it even stranger," she went on, shaking her head, "every time he deposits a load, he manages to sneak off with an armful of *our* stuff!"

She went to the window and peeked through the Venetian blinds. "Look at him out there! Unscrewing the nozzle of the hose! Why, the man's turning into a human pack rat!"

"Probably been working too hard on that speech," Dr. Departure said, beaming and helping himself to another pork chop. "Always knew Schnappenhocker would crack up someday."

FËDOR DOSTOEVSKY/The Gambler

I CONFESS it was disagreeable to me. Though I had made up my mind that I would play, I had not proposed to play for other people. It rather threw me out of my reckoning, and I went into the gambling saloon with very disagreeable feelings. From the first glance I disliked everything in it. I cannot endure the flunkeyishness of the newspapers of the whole world, and especially our Russian papers, in which, almost every spring, the journalists write articles upon two things: first, on the extraordinary magnificence and luxury of the gambling saloons on the Rhine, and secondly, on the heaps of gold which are said to lie on the tables. They are not paid for it; it is simply done from distinterested obsequiousness. There was no sort of magnificence in these trashy rooms, and **not** only were there no piles of gold lying on the table, but there was hardly any gold at all. No doubt some time, in the course of the season, some eccentric person, either an Englishman or an Asiatic of some sort, a Turk, perhaps (as it was that summer), would suddenly turn up and lose or win immense sums; all the others play for paltry guldens, and on an average there is very little money lying on the tables.

As soon as I went into the gambling saloon (for the first time in my life), I could not for some time make up my mind to play. There was a crush besides. If I had been alone, even then, I believe I should soon have gone away and not have begun playing. I confess my heart was beating and I was not cool. I knew for certain, and had made up my mind long before, that I should not leave Roulettenburg unchanged, that some radical and fundamental change would take place in my destiny; so it must be and so it would be. Ridiculous as it may be that I should expect so much for myself from roulette, yet I consider even more ridiculous the conventional opinion accepted by all that it is stupid and absurd to expect anything from gambling. And why should gambling be worse than any other means of making money—for instance, commerce? It is true that only one out of a hundred wins, but what is that to me?

In any case I determined to look about me first and not to begin anything in earnest that evening. If anything did happen that evening it would happen by chance and be something slight, and I staked my money accordingly. Besides, I had to study the game; for, in spite of the thousand descriptions of roulette which I had read so eagerly, I understood absolutely nothing of its working until I saw it myself.

In the first place it all struck me as so dirty, somehow, morally horrid and dirty. I am not speaking at all of the greedy, uneasy faces which by dozens, even by hundreds, crowd round the gambling tables. I see absolutely nothing dirty in the wish to win as quickly and as much as possible. I always thought very stupid the answer of that fat and prosperous moralist, who replied to some one's excuse "that he played for a very small stake," "So much the worse, it is such petty covetousness." As though covetousness were not exactly the same, whether on a big scale or a petty one. It is a matter of proportion. What is paltry to Rothschild is wealth to me, and as for profits and winnings, people, not only at roulette, but everywhere, do nothing but try to gain or squeeze something out of one another. Whether profits or gains are nasty is a different question. But I am not solving that question here. Since I was myself possessed by an intense desire of winning, I felt as I went into the hall all this covetousness, and all this covetous filth if you like, in a sense congenial and convenient. It is most charming when people do not stand on ceremony with one another, but act openly and aboveboard. And, indeed, why deceive oneself? Gambling is a most foolish and imprudent pursuit! What was particularly ugly at first sight, in all the rabble round the roulette table, was the respect they paid to that pursuit, the solemnity and even reverence with which they all crowded round the tables. That is why a sharp distinction is drawn here between the kind of game that is *mauvais genre* and the kind that is permissible to well-bred people. There are two sorts of gambling: one the gentlemanly sort: the other the plebian, mercenary sort, the game played by all sorts of riff-raff. The distinction is sternly observed here, and how contemptible this distinction really is! A gentleman may stake, for instance, five or ten louis d'or, rarely more; he may, however, stake as much as a thousand francs if he is very rich; but only for the sake of the play, simply for amusement, that is, simply to look on at the process of winning or of losing, but must on no account display an interest in winning. If he wins, he may laugh aloud, for instance; may make a remark to one of the bystanders; he may even put down another stake, and may even double it, but solely from curiosity, for the sake of watching and calculating the chances, and not from the plebian desire to win. In fact, he must look on all gambling, roulette, *trente et quarante,* as nothing else than a pastime got up entirely for his amusement. He must not even suspect the greed for gain and the shifty dodges on which the bank depends.

It would be extremely good form, too, if he should imagine that all the other gamblers, all the rabble, trembling over a gulden, were rich men and gentlemen like himself and were playing simply for their diversion and amusement. This complete ignorance of reality and innocent view of people would be, of course, extremely aristocratic. I have seen many mammas push forward their daughters, innocent and elegant misses of fifteen and sixteen, and, giving them some gold coins, teach them how to play. The young lady wins or loses, invariably smiles and walks away, very well satisfied. Our General went up to the table with solid dignity; a flunkey rushed to hand him a chair, but he ignored the flunkey; he, very slowly and deliberately, took out his purse, very slowly and deliberately took three hundred francs in gold from his purse, staked them on the black, and won. He did not pick up his winnings, but left them on the table. Black turned up again; he didn't pick up his winnings that time either; and when, the third time, red turned up, he lost at once twelve hundred francs. He walked away with a smile and kept up his dignity. I am positive he was raging inwardly, and if the stake had been two or three times as much he would not have kept up his dignity but would have betrayed his feelings. A Frenchman did, however, before my eyes, win and lose as much as thirty thousand francs with perfect gaiety and no sign of emotion. A real gentleman should not show excitement even if he loses his whole fortune. Money ought to be so much below his gentlemanly dignity as to be scarcely worth noticing. Of course, it would have been extremely aristocratic not to notice the sordidness of all the rabble and all the surroundings. Sometimes, however, the opposite pose is no less aristocratic—to notice—that is, to look about one, even, perhaps, to stare through a lorgnette at the rabble; though always taking the rabble and the sordidness as nothing else but a diversion of a sort, as though it were a performance got up for the amusement of gentlemen. One may be jostled in that crowd, but one must look about one with complete conviction that one is oneself a spectator and that one is in no sense part of it. Though, again, to look very attentively is not quite the thing; that, again, would not be gentlemanly because, in any case, the spectacle does not deserve much, or close, attention. And, in fact, few spectacles do deserve a gentleman's close attention. And yet it seemed to me that all this was deserving of very close attention, especially for one who had come not only to observe it, but sincerely and genuinely reckoned himself as one of the rabble. As for my hidden moral convictions, there is no place for them, of course, in my present reasonings. Let that be enough for the present. I speak to relieve my conscience. But I notice one thing: that of late it has become horribly repugnant to me to test my thoughts and actions by any moral standard whatever. I was guided by something different. . . .

The rabble certainly did play very sordidly. I am ready to believe, indeed, that a great deal of the most ordinary thieving goes on at the gambling table. The croupiers who sit at each end of the table look at the stakes and reckon the winnings; they have a great deal to do. They are rabble, too! For the most part they are French. However, I was watching and observing, not with the object of describing roulette. I kept a sharp look-out for my own sake, so that I might know how to behave in the future. I noticed, for instance, that nothing was more common than for some one to stretch out his hand and snatch what one had won. A dispute would begin, often an uproar, and a nice job one would have to find witnesses and to prove that it was one's stake!

At first it was all an inexplicable puzzle to me. All I could guess and distinguish was that the stakes were on the numbers, on odd and even, and on the colours. I made up my mind to risk a hundred guldens of Polina Alexandrovna's money. The thought that I was not playing for myself seemed to throw me out of my reckoning. It was an extremely unpleasant feeling, and I wanted to be rid of it as soon as possible. I kept feeling that by beginning for Polina I should break my own luck. Is it impossible to approach the gambling table without becoming infected with superstition? I began by taking out five friedrichs d'or (fifty gulden) and putting them on the even. The wheel went round and thirteen turned up—I had lost. With a sickly feeling I staked another five friedrichs d'or on red, simply in order to settle the matter and go away. Red turned up. I staked all the ten friedrichs d'or—red turned up again. I staked all the money again on the same, and again red turned up. On receiving forty friedrichs d'or I staked twenty upon the twelve middle figures, not knowing what would come of it. I was paid three times my stake. In this way from ten friedrichs d'or I had all at once eighty. I was overcome by a strange, unusual feeling which was so unbearable that I made up my mind to go away. It seemed to me that I should not have been playing at all like that if I had been playing for myself. I staked the whole eighty friedrichs d'or, however, on even. This time four turned up; another eighty friedrichs d'or was poured out to me, and, gathering up the whole heap of a hundred and sixty friedrichs d'or, I set off to find Polina Alexandrovna.

They were all walking somewhere in the park and I only succeeded in seeing her after supper. This time the Frenchman was not of the party, and the General unbosomed himself. Among other things he thought fit to observe to me that he would not wish to see me at the gambling tables. It seemed to him that it would compromise him if I were to lose too much: "But even if you were to win a very large sum I should be compromised, too," he added significantly. "Of course, I have no right to dictate your actions, but you must admit yourself . . ." At this point he broke off, as his habit was. I answered, drily, that I had very little money, and so I could not lose very conspicuously, even if I did play. Going upstairs to my room I succeeded in handing Polina her winnings, and told her that I would not play for her another time.

"Why not?" she asked, in a tremor.

"Because I want to play on my own account," I answered, looking at her with surprise; "and it hinders me."

"Then you still continue in your conviction that roulette is your only escape and salvation?" she asked ironically.

I answered very earnestly, that I did; that as for my confidence that I should win, it might be absurd; I was ready to admit it, but that I wanted to be let alone.

Polina Alexandrovna began insisting I should go halves with her in to-day's winnings, and was giving me eighty friedrichs d'or, suggesting that I should go on playing on those terms. I refused the half, positively and finally, and told her that I could not play for other people, not because I didn't want to, but because I should certainly lose.

"Yet I, too," she said, pondering, "stupid as it seems, am building all my hopes on roulette. And so you must go on playing, sharing with me, and—of course—you will."

At this point she walked away, without listening to further objections.

Yet all yesterday she did not say a single word to me about playing, and avoided speaking to me altogether. Her manner to me remained unchanged: the same absolute carelessness on meeting me; there was even a shade of contempt and dislike. Altogether she did not care to conceal her aversion; I noticed that. In spite of that she did not conceal from me, either, that I was in some way necessary to her and that she was keeping me for some purpose. A strange relation had grown up between us, incomprehensible to me in many ways when I considered her pride and haughtiness with every one. She knew, for instance, that I loved her madly, even allowed me to speak of my passion; and, of course, she could not have shown greater contempt for me than by allowing me to speak of my passion without hindrance or restriction. It was as much as to say that she thought so little of my feelings that she did not care in the least what I talked about to her and what I felt for her. She had talked a great deal about her own affairs before, but had never been completely open. What is more, there was this peculiar refinement in her contempt for me: she would know, for instance, that I was aware of some circumstance in her life, or knew of some matter that greatly concerned her, or she would tell me herself something of her circumstances, if to forward her objects she had to make use of me in some way, as a slave or an errand-boy; but she would always tell me only so much as a man employed on her errands need know, and if I did not know the whole chain of events, if she saw herself how worried and anxious I was over her worries and anxieties, she never deigned to comfort me by giving me her full confidence as a friend; though she often made use of me for commissions that were not only troublesome, but dangerous, so that to my thinking she was bound to be open with me. Was it worth her while, indeed, to trouble herself about my feelings, about my being worried, and perhaps three times as much worried and tormented by her anxieties and failures as she was herself?

I knew of her intention to play roulette three weeks before. She had even warned me that I should have to play for her, and it would be improper for her to play herself. From the tone of her words, I noticed even then that she had serious anxieties, and was not actuated simply by a desire for money. What is money to her for its own sake? She must have some object, there must be some circumstance at which I can only guess, but of which so far I have no knowledge. Of course, the humiliation and the slavery in which she held me might have made it possible for me (it often does) to question her coarsely and bluntly. Seeing that in her eyes I was a slave and utterly insignificant, there was nothing for her to be offended at in my coarse curiosity. But the fact is, that though she allowed me to ask questions, she did not answer them, and sometimes did not notice them at all. That was the position between us.

A great deal was said yesterday about a telegram which had been sent off four days before, and to which no answer had been received. The General was evidently upset and preoccupied. It had, of course, something to do with Granny. The Frenchman was troubled, too. Yesterday, for instance, after dinner, they had a long, serious talk. The Frenchman's tone to all of us was unusually high and mighty, quite in the spirit of the saying: "Seat a pig at table and it will put its feet on it." Even with Polina he was casual to the point of rudeness; at the same time he gladly took part in the walks in the public gardens and in the rides and drives into the country. I had long known some of the circumstances that bound the Frenchman to the General: they had made plans for establishing a factory together in Russia; I don't know whether their project had fallen through, or whether it was being discussed. Moreover, I had by chance come to know part of a family secret. The Frenchman had actually, in the previous year, come to the General's rescue, and had given him thirty thousand roubles to make up a deficit of Government monies missing when he resigned his duties. And, of course, the General is in his grip; but now the principal person in the whole business is Mlle. Blanche; about that I am sure I'm not mistaken.

What is Mlle. Blanche? Here among us it is said that she is a distinguished Frenchwoman, with a colossal fortune and a mother accompanying her. It is known, too, that she is some sort of relation of our *marquis,* but a very distant one: a cousin, or something of the sort. I am told that before I went to Paris, the Frenchman and Mlle. Blanche were on much more ceremonious, were, so to speak, on a more delicate and refined footing; now their acquaintance, their friendship and relationship, was of a rather coarse and more intimate character. Perhaps our prospects seemed to them so poor that they did not think it very necessary to stand on ceremony and keep up appearances with us. I noticed even the day before yesterday how Mr. Astley looked at Mlle. Blanche and her mother. It seemed to me that he knew them. It even seemed to me that our Frenchman had met Mr. Astley before.

Mr. Astley, however, is so shy, so reserved and silent, that one can be almost certain of him—he won't wash dirty linen in public. Anyway, the Frenchman barely bows to him and scarcely looks at him, so he is not afraid of him. One can understand that, perhaps, but why does Mlle. Blanche not look at him either? Especially when the *marquis* let slip yesterday in the course of conversation —I don't remember in what connection—that Mr. Astley had a colossal fortune and that he—the *marquis*—knew this for a fact; at that point Mlle. Blanche might well have looked at Mr. Astley. Altogether the General was uneasy. One can understand what a telegram announcing his aunt's death would mean!

Though I felt sure Polina was, apparently for some object, avoiding a conversation with me, I assumed a cold and indifferent air: I kept thinking that before long she would come to me of herself. But both to-day and yesterday I concentrated my attention principally on Mlle. Blanche. Poor General! He is completely done for! To fall in love at fifty-five with such a violent passion is a calamity, of course! When one takes into consideration the fact that he is a widower, his children, the ruin of his estate, his debts, and, finally, the woman it is his lot to fall in love with. Mlle. Blanche is handsome. But I don't know if I shall be understood if I say that she has a face of the type of which one might feel frightened. I, anyway, have always been afraid of women of that sort. She is probably five-and-twenty. She is well grown and broad, with sloping shoulders; she has a magnificent throat and bosom; her complexion is swarthy yellow. Her hair is as black as India ink, and she has a tremendous lot of it, enough to make two ordinary coiffures. Her eyes are black with yellowish whites; she has an insolent look in her eyes; her teeth are very white; her lips are always painted; she smells of musk. She dresses effectively, richly and with *chic,* but with much taste. Her hands and feet are exquisite. Her voice is a husky contralto. Sometimes she laughs, showing all her teeth, but her usual expression is a silent and impudent stare— before Polina and Marya Filippovna, anyway (there is a strange rumour that Marya Filippovna is going back to Russia). I fancy that Mlle. Blanche has had no sort of education. Possibly she is not even intelligent; but, on the other hand, she is striking and she is artful. I fancy her life has not passed without adventures. If one is to tell the whole truth, it is quite possible that the *marquis* is no relation of hers at all, and that her mother is not her mother. But there is evidence that in Berlin, where we went with them, her mother and she had some decent acquaintances. As for the *marquis* himself, though I still doubt his being a *marquis,* yet the fact that he is received in decent society—among Russians, for instance, in Moscow, and in some places in Germany—is not open to doubt. I don't know what he is in France. They say he has a château.

I thought that a great deal would have happened during this fortnight, and yet I don't know if anything decisive has been said between Mlle. Blanche and the General. Everything depends on our fortune, however; that is, whether the General can show them plenty of money. If, for instance, news were to come that Granny were not dead, I am convinced that Mlle. Blanche would vanish at once. It surprises and amuses me to see what a gossip I've become. Oh! how I loathe it all! How delighted I should be to drop it all, and them all! But can I leave Polina, can I give up spying round her? Spying, of course, is low, but what do I care about that?

I was interested in Mr. Astley, too, to-day and yesterday. Yes, I am convinced he's in love with Polina. It is curious and absurd how much may be expressed by the eyes of a modest and painfully chaste man, moved by love, at the very time when the man would gladly sink into the earth rather than express or betray anything by word or glance. Mr. Astley very often meets us on our walks. He takes off his hat and passes by, though, of course, he is dying to join us. If he is invited to do so, he immediately refuses. At places where we rest—at the Casino, by the bandstand, or before the fountain—he always stands somewhere not far from our seat; and wherever we may be—in the park, in the wood, or on the Schlangenberg—one has only to glance round, to look about one, and somewhere, either in the nearest path or behind the bushes, Mr. Astley's head appears. I fancy he is looking for an opportunity to have a conversation with me apart. This morning we met and exchanged a couple of words. He sometimes speaks very abruptly. Without saying "good-morning," he began by blurting out—

"Oh, Mlle. Blanche! . . . I have seen a great many women like Mlle. Blanche!"

He paused, looking at me significantly. What he meant to say by that I don't know. For on my asking what he meant, he shook his head with a sly smile, and added, "Oh, well, that's how it is. Is Mlle. Pauline very fond of flowers?"

"I don't know; I don't know at all," I answered.

"What? You don't even know that!" he cried, with the utmost amazement.

"I don't know; I haven't noticed at all," I repeated, laughing.

"H'm! That gives me a queer idea."

Then he shook his head and walked away. He looked pleased, though. We talked the most awful French together.

To-day has been an absurd, grotesque, ridiculous day. Now it is eleven o'clock at night. I am sitting in my little cupboard of a room, recalling it. It began with my having to go to roulette to play for Polina Alexandrovna. I took the hundred and sixty friedrichs d'or, but on two conditions: first, that I would not go halves —that is, if I won I would take nothing for myself; and secondly, that in the evening Polina should explain to me why she needed to win, and how much money. I can't, in any case, suppose that it is simply for the sake of money. Evidently the money is needed, and as quickly as possible, for some particular object. She promised to explain, and I set off. In the gambling hall the crowd was awful. How insolent and how greedy they all were! I forced my way into the middle and stood near the croupier; then I began timidly experimenting, staking two or three coins at a time. Meanwhile, I kept quiet and looked on; it seemed to me that calculation meant very little, and had by no means the importance attributed to it by some players. They sit with papers before them scrawled over in pencil, note the strokes, reckon, deduce the chances, calculate, finally stake and—lose exactly as we simple mortals who play without calculations. On the other hand, I drew one conclusion which I believe to be correct: that is, though there is no system, there really is a sort of order in the sequence of casual chances—and that, of course, is very strange. For instance, it happens that after the twelve middle numbers come the twelve later numbers; twice, for instance, it turns up on the twelve last numbers and passes to the twelve first numbers. After falling on the twelve first numbers, it passes again to numbers in the middle third, turns up three or four times in succession on numbers between thirteen and twenty-four, and again passes to numbers in the last third; then, after turning up two numbers between twenty-five and thirty-six, it passes to a number among the first twelve, turns up once again on a number among the first third, and again passes for three strokes in succession to the middle numbers; and in that way goes on for an hour and a half or two hours. One, three and two—one, three and two. It's very amusing. One day or one morning, for instance, red will be followed by black and back again almost without any order, shifting every minute, so that it never turns up red or black for more than two or three strokes in succession. Another day, or another evening, there will be nothing but red over and over again, turning up, for instance, more than twenty-two times in succession, and so for a whole day. A great deal of this was explained to me by Mr. Astley, who spent the whole morning at the tables, but did not once put down a stake.

  As for me, I lost every farthing very quickly. I staked straight off twenty friedrichs d'or on even and won, staked again and again won, and went on like that two or three times. I imagine I must have had about four hundred friedrichs d'or in my hands in about five minutes. At that point I ought to have gone away, but a strange sensation rose up in me, a sort of defiance of fate, a desire to challenge it, to put out my tongue at it. I laid down the largest stake allowed—four thousand gulden—and lost it. Then, getting hot, I pulled out all I had left, staked it on the same number, and lost again, after which I walked away from the table as though I were stunned. I could not even grasp what had happened to me, and did not tell Polina Alexandrovna of my losing till just before dinner. I spent the rest of the day sauntering in the park.

At dinner I was again in an excited state, just as I had been three days before. The Frenchman and Mlle. Blanche were dining with us again. It appeared that Mlle. Blanche had been in the gambling hall that morning and had witnessed my exploits. This time she addressed me, it seemed, somewhat attentively. The Frenchman set to work more directly, and asked me: Was it my own money I had lost? I fancy he suspects Polina. In fact, there is something behind it. I lied at once and said it was.

The General was extremely surprised. Where had I got such a sum? I explained that I had begun with ten friedrichs d'or, that after six or seven times staking successfully on equal chances I had five or six hundred gulden, and that afterwards I had lost it all in two turns.

All that, of course, sounded probable. As I explained this I looked at Polina, but I could distinguish nothing from her face. She let me lie, however, and did not set it right; from this I concluded that I had to lie and conceal that I was in collaboration with her. In any case, I thought to myself, she is bound to give me an explanation, and promised me this morning to reveal something.

I expected the General would have made some remark to me, but he remained mute; I noticed, however, signs of disturbance and uneasiness in his face. Possibly in his straitened circumstances it was simply painful to him to hear that such a pile of gold had come into, and within a quarter of an hour had passed out of, the hands of such a reckless fool as me.

I suspect that he had a rather hot encounter with the Frenchman yesterday. They were shut up together talking for a long time. The Frenchmen went away seeming irritated, and came to see the General again early this morning—probably to continue the conversation of the previous day.

Hearing what I had lost, the Frenchman observed bitingly, even spitefully, that one ought to have more sense. He added—I don't know why—that though a great many Russians gamble,

Russians were not, in his opinion, well qualified even for gambling.

"In my mind," said I, "roulette is simply made for Russians."

And when at my challenge the Frenchman laughed contemptuously, I observed that I was, of course, right, for to speak of the Russians as gamblers was abusing them far more than praising them, and so I might be believed.

"On what do you base your opinion?" asked the Frenchman.

"On the fact that the faculty of amassing capital has, with the progress of history, taken a place—and almost the foremost place—among the virtues and merits of the civilized man of the West. The Russian is not only incapable of amassing capital, but dissipates it in a reckless and unseemly way. Nevertheless we Russians need money, too," I added, "and consequently we are very glad and very eager to make use of such means as roulette, for instance, in which one can grow rich all at once, in two hours, without work. That's very fascinating to us; and since we play badly, recklessly, without taking trouble, we usually lose!"

"That's partly true," observed the Frenchman complacently.

"No, it is not true, and you ought to be ashamed to speak like that of your country," observed the General, sternly and impressively.

"Allow me," I answered. "I really don't know which is more disgusting: Russian unseemliness or the German faculty of accumulation by honest toil."

"What an unseemly idea!" exclaimed the General.

"What a Russian idea!" exclaimed the Frenchman.

I laughed; I had an intense desire to provoke them.

"Well, I should prefer to dwell all my life in a Kirgiz tent," I cried, "than bow down to the German idol."

"What idol?" cried the General, beginning to be angry in earnest.

"The German faculty for accumulating wealth. I've not been here long, but yet all I have been able to observe and verify revolts my Tatar blood. My God! I don't want any such virtue! I succeeded yesterday in making a round of eight miles, and it's all exactly as in the edifying German picture-books: there is here in every house a *vater* horribly virtuous and extraordinarily honest—so honest that you are afraid to go near him. I can't endure honest people whom one is afraid to go near. Every such German *vater* has a family, and in the evening they read improving books aloud. Elms and chestnut trees rustle over the house. The sun is setting; there is a stork on the roof, and everything is extraordinarily practical and touching. . . . Don't be angry, General; let me tell it in a touching style. I remember how my father used to read similar books to my mother and me under the lime-trees in the garden. . . . So I am in a position to judge. And in what complete bondage and submission every such family is here. They all work like oxen and all save money like Jews. Suppose the *vater* has saved up so many gulden and is reckoning on giving his son a trade or a bit of land; to do so, he gives his daughter no dowry, and she becomes an old maid. To do so, the youngest son is sold into bondage or into the army, and the money is added to the family capital. This is actually done here; I've been making inquiries. All this is done from nothing but honesty, from such intense honesty that the younger son who is sold believes that he is sold from nothing but honesty: and that is the ideal when the victim himself rejoices at being led to the sacrifice. What more? Why, the elder son is no better off: he has an Amalia and their hearts are united, but they can't be married because the pile of gulden is not large enough. They, too, wait with perfect morality and good faith, and go to the sacrifice with a smile. Amalia's cheeks grow thin and hollow. At last, in twenty years, their prosperity is increased; the gulden have been honestly and virtuously accumulating. The *vater* gives his blessing to the forty-year-old son and his Amalia of thirty-five, whose chest has grown hollow and whose nose has turned red. . . . With that he weeps, reads them a moral sermon, and dies. The eldest son becomes himself a virtuous *vater* and begins the same story over again. In that way, in fifty or seventy years, the grandson of the first *vater* really has a considerable capital, and he leaves it to his son, and he to his, and he to his, till in five or six generations one of them is a Baron Rothschild or goodness knows who. Come, isn't that a majestic spectacle? A hundred or two hundred years of continuous toil, patience, intelligence, honesty, character, determination, prudence, the stork on the roof! What more do you want? Why, there's nothing loftier than that; and from that standpoint they are beginning to judge the whole world and to punish the guilty; that is, any who are ever so little unlike them. Well, so that's the point: I would rather waste my substance in the Russian style or grow rich at roulette. I don't care to be Goppe and Co. in five generations. I want money for myself, and I don't look upon myself as something subordinate to capital and necessary to it. I know that I have been talking awful nonsense, but, never mind, such are my convictions."

"I don't know whether there is much truth in what you have been saying," said the General thoughtfully, "but I do know you begin to give yourself insufferable airs as soon as you are permitted to forget yourself in the least . . ."

As his habit was, he broke off without finishing. If our General began to speak of anything in the slightest degree more important than his ordinary everyday conversation, he never finished his sentences. The Frenchman listened carelessly with rather wide-open eyes; he had scarcely understood anything of what I had said. Polina gazed with haughty indifference. She seemed not to hear my words, or anything else that was said that day at table. . . .

It is a year and eight months since I looked at these notes, and only now in sadness and dejection it has occurred to me to read them through. So I stopped then at my going to Homburg. My God! With what a light heart, comparatively speaking, I wrote those last lines! Though not with a light heart exactly, but with a sort of self-confidence, with undaunted hopes! Had I any doubt of myself? And now more than a year and a half has passed, and I am, to my own mind, far worse than a beggar! Yes, what is being a beggar? A beggar is nothing! I have simply ruined myself! However, there is nothing I can compare myself with, and there is no need to give myself a moral lecture! Nothing could be stupider than moral reflections at this date! Oh, self-satisfied people, with what proud satisfaction these prattlers prepare to deliver their lectures! If only they knew how thoroughly I understand the loathsomeness of my present position, they would not be able to bring their tongues to reprimand me. Why, what, what can they tell me that I do not know? And is that the point? The point is that—one turn of the wheel, and all will be changed, and those very moralists will be the first (I am convinced of that) to come up to congratulate me with friendly jests. And they will not all turn away from me as they do now. But, hang them all! What am I now? Zero. What may I be to-morrow? To-morrow I may rise from the dead and begin to live again! There are still the makings of a man in me.

I did, in fact, go to Homburg then, but . . . afterwards I went to Roulettenburg again, and to Spa. I have even been in Baden, where I went as valet to the councillor Gintse, a scoundrel, who was my master here. Yes, I was a lackey for five whole months! I got a place immediately after coming out of prison. (I was sent to prison in Roulettenburg for a debt I made here.) Some one, I don't know who, paid my debt—who was it? Was it Mr. Astley? Polina? I don't know, but the debt was paid; two hundred thalers in all, and I was set free. What could I do? I entered the service of this Gintse. He is a young man and frivolous, he liked to be idle, and I could read and write in three languages. At first I went into his service as a sort of secretary at thirty guldens a month; but I ended by becoming a regular valet: he had not the means to keep a secretary; and he lowered my wages; I had nowhere to go, I remained—and in that way became a lackey by my own doing. I had not enough to eat or to drink in his service, but on the other hand, in five months I saved up seventy gulden. One evening in Baden, however, I announced to him that I intended parting from him; the same evening I went to roulette. Oh, how my heart beat! No, it was not money that I wanted. All that I wanted then was that next day all these Gintses, all these *ober-kellners,* all these magnificent Baden ladies—that they might be all talking about me, repeating my story, wondering at me, admiring me, praising me, and doing homage to my new success. All these are childish dreams and desires, but . . . who knows, perhaps I should meet Polina again, too, I should tell her, and she would see that I was above all these stupid ups and downs of fate. . . . Oh, it was not money that was dear to me! I knew I should fling it away to some Blanche again and should drive in Paris again for three weeks with a pair of my own horses, costing sixteen thousand francs. I know for certain that I am not mean; I believe that I am not even a spendthrift—and yet with what a tremor, with what a thrill at my heart, I hear the croupier's cry: *trente-et-un, rouge, impair et passe,* or: *quatre, noir, pair et manque!* With what avidity I look at the gambling table on which louis d'or, friedrichs d'or and thalers lie scattered: on the piles of gold when they are scattered from the croupier's shovel like glowing embers, or at the piles of silver a yard high that lie round the wheel. Even on my way to the gambling hall, as soon as I hear, two rooms away, the clink of the scattered money I almost go into convulsions.

Oh! that evening, when I took my seventy gulden to the gambling table, was remarkable too. I began with ten gulden, staking them again on *passe.* I have a prejudice in favour of *passe.* I lost. I had sixty gulden left in silver money; I thought a little and chose *zéro.* I began staking five gulden at a time on *zéro;* at the third turn the wheel stopped at *zéro;* I almost died of joy when I received one hundred and seventy-five gulden; I had not been so delighted when I won a hundred thousand gulden. I immediately staked a hundred gulden on *rouge*—it won; the two hundred on *rouge*—it won; the whole of the four hundred on *noir*—it won; the whole eight hundred on *manque*—it won; altogether with what I had before it made one thousand seven hundred gulden and that—in less than five minutes! Yes, at moments like that one forgets all one's former failures! Why, I had gained this by risking more than life itself, I dared to risk it, and—there I was again, a man among men.

I took a room at the hotel, locked myself in and sat till three o'clock counting over my money. In the morning I woke up, no longer a lackey. I determined the same day to go to Homburg: I had not been a lackey or been in prison there. Half an hour before my train left, I set off to stake on two hazards, no more, and lost fifteen hundred florins. Yet I went to Homburg all the same, and I have been here for a month. . . .

I am living, of course, in continual anxiety. I play for the tiniest stakes, and I keep waiting for something, calculating, standing for whole days at the gambling table and watching the play; I even dream of playing—but I feel that in all this, I have, as it were, grown stiff and wooden, as though I had sunk into a muddy swamp. I gather this from my feeling when I met Mr. Astley. We had not seen each other since that time, and we met by accident. This was how it happened: I was walking in the gardens and reckoning that now I was almost without money, but that I had fifty gulden—and that I had, moreover, three days before paid all I owed at the hotel. And so it was possible for me to go once more to roulette—if I were to win anything, I might be able to go on playing; if I lost I should have to get a lackey's place again, if I did not come across Russians in want of a tutor. Absorbed in these thoughts, I went my daily walk, across the park and the forest in the adjoining principality.

Sometimes I used to walk like this for four hours at a time, and go back to Homburg hungry and tired. I had scarcely gone out of the gardens into the park, when suddenly I saw on one of the seats Mr. Astley. He saw me before I saw him, and called to me. I sat down beside him. Detecting in him a certain dignity of manner, I instantly moderated my delight; though I was awfully delighted to see him.

"And so you are here! I thought I should meet you," he said to me. "Don't trouble yourself to tell me your story; I know, I know all about it; I know every detail of your life during this last year and eight months."

"Bah! What a watch you keep on your old friends!" I answered. "It is very creditable in you not to forget. . . . Stay, though, you have given me an idea. Wasn't it you bought me out of prison at Roulettenburg where I was imprisoned for debt for two hundred gulden? Some unknown person paid it for me."

"No, oh, no; it was not I who bought you out when you were in prison at Roulettenburg for a debt of two hundred gulden. But I knew that you were imprisoned for a debt of two hundred gulden."

"Then you know who did pay my debt?"

"Oh, no, I can't say that I know who bought you out."

"Strange; I don't know any of our Russians; besides, the

Russians here, I imagine, would not do it; at home in Russia the Orthodox may buy out other Orthodox Christians. I thought it must have been some eccentric Englishman who did it as a freak."

Mr. Astley listened to me with some surprise. I believe he had expected to find me dejected and crushed.

"I am very glad, however, to find that you have quite maintained your independence of spirit and even your cheerfulness," he pronounced, with a rather disagreeable air.

"That is, you are chafing inwardly with vexation at my not being crushed and humiliated," I said, laughing.

He did not at once understand, but when he understood, he smiled.

"I like your observations: I recognize in those words my clever, enthusiastic and, at the same time, cynical old friend; only Russians can combine in themselves so many opposites at the same time. It is true, a man likes to see even his best friend humiliated; a great part of friendship rests on humiliation. But in the present case I assure you that I am genuinely glad that you are not dejected. Tell me, do you intend to give up gambling?"

"Oh, damn! I shall give it up at once as soon as I . . ."

"As soon as you have won back what you have lost! Just what I thought; you needn't say any more—I know—you have spoken unawares, and so you have spoken the truth. Tell me, have you any occupation except gambling?"

"No, none. . . ."

He began cross-examining me. I knew nothing. I scarcely looked into the newspapers, and had literally not opened a single book all that time.

"You've grown rusty," he observed. "You have not only given up life, all your interests, private and public, the duties of a man and a citizen, your friends (and you really had friends)— you have not only given up your objects, such as they were, all but gambling—you have even given up your memories. I remember you at an intense and ardent moment of your life; but I am sure you have forgotten all the best feelings you had then; your dreams, your most genuine desires now do not rise above *pair, impair, rouge, noir,* the twelve middle numbers, and so on, I am sure!"

"Enough, Mr. Astley, please, please don't remind me," I cried with vexation, almost with anger, "let me tell you, I've forgotten absolutely nothing; but I've only for a time put everything out of my mind, even my memories, until I can make a radical improvement in my circumstances; then . . . then you will see, I shall rise again from the dead!"

"You will be here still in ten years' time," he said. "I bet you I shall remind you of this on this very seat, if I'm alive."

"Well, that's enough," I interrupted impatiently; "and to

prove to you that I am not so forgetful of the past, let me ask: where is Miss Polina now? If it was not you who got me out of prison, it must have been her doing. I have had no news of her of any sort since that time."

"No, oh no, I don't believe she did buy you out. She's in Switzerland now, and you'll do me a great favour if you leave off asking about Miss Polina," he said resolutely, and even with some anger.

"That means that she has wounded you very much!" I laughed with displeasure.

"Miss Polina is of all people deserving of respect the very best, but I repeat—you will do me a great favour if you cease questioning me concerning Miss Polina. You never knew her: and her name on your lips I regard as an insult to my moral feelings."

"You don't say so! you are wrong, however; besides, what have I to talk to you about except that, tell me that? Why, all our memories really amount to that! Don't be uneasy, though; I don't want to know your private secret affairs. . . . I am only interested, so to say, in Miss Polina's external affairs. That you could tell me in a couple of words."

"Certainly, on condition that with those two words all is over. Miss Polina was ill for a long time; she's ill even now. For some time she stayed with my mother and sister in the north of England. Six months ago, her grandmother—you remember that madwoman?—died and left her, personally, a fortune of seven thousand pounds. At the present time Miss Polina is travelling with the family of my married sister. Her little brother and sister, too, were provided for by their grandmother's will, and are at school in London. The General, her stepfather, died a month ago in Paris of a stroke. Mlle. Blanche treated him well, but succeeded in getting possession of all he received from the grandmother. . . . I believe that's all."

"And De Grieux? Is not he travelling in Switzerland, too?"

"No, De Grieux is not travelling in Switzerland: and I don't know where De Grieux is; besides, once for all, I warn you to avoid such insinuations and ungentlemanly coupling of names, or you will certainly have to answer for it to me."

"What! in spite of our friendly relations in the past?"

"Yes, in spite of our friendly relations in the past."

"I beg a thousand pardons, Mr. Astley. But allow me, though: there is nothing insulting or ungentlemanly about it; I am not blaming Miss Polina for anything. Besides—a Frenchman and a Russian young lady, speaking generally—it's a combination, Mr. Astley, which is beyond your or my explaining or fully comprehending."

"If you will not mention the name of De Grieux in company with another name, I should like you to explain what you mean by the expression of 'the Frenchman and the Russian young lady.' What do you mean by that 'combination'? Why the Frenchman exactly and why the Russian young lady?"

"You see you are interested. But that's a long story, Mr. Astley. You need to understand many things first. But it is an important question, however absurd it may seem at first sight. The Frenchman, Mr. Astley, is the product of a finished beautiful tradition. You, as a Briton, may not agree with this; I, as a Russian, do not either, from envy maybe; but our young ladies may be of a different opinion. You may think Racine artificial, affected and perfumed; probably you won't even read him. I, too, think him artificial, affected and perfumed—from one point of view even absurd; but he is charming, Mr. Astley, and, what is more, he is a great poet, whether we like it or not. The national type of Frenchman, or, rather, of Parisian, had been moulded into elegant forms while we were still bears. The revolution inherited the traditions of the aristocracy. Now even the vulgarest Frenchman has manners, modes of address, expressions and even thoughts, of perfectly elegant form, though his own initiative, his own soul and heart, have had no part in the creation of that form; it has all come to him through inheritance. Well, Mr. Astley, I must inform you now that there is not a creature on the earth more confiding, and more candid, than a good, clean and not too sophisticated Russian girl. De Grieux, appearing in a peculiar rôle, masquerading, can conquer her heart with extraordinary ease; he has elegance of form, Mr. Astley, and the young lady takes this form for his individual soul, as the natural form of his soul and his heart, and not as an external garment, which has come to him by inheritance. Though it will greatly displease you, I must tell you that Englishmen are for the most part awkward and inelegant, and Russians are rather quick to detect beauty, and are eager for it. But to detect beauty of soul and originality of character needs incomparably more independence and freedom than is to be found in our women, above all in our young ladies—and of course ever so much more experience. Miss Polina—forgive me, the word is spoken and one can't take it back—needs a long, long time to bring herself to prefer you to the scoundrel De Grieux. She thinks highly of you, becomes your friend, opens all her heart to you; but yet the hateful scoundrel, the base and petty money-grubber, De Grieux, will still dominate her heart. Mere obstinacy and vanity, so to say, will maintain his supremacy, because at one time this De Grieux appeared to her with the halo of an elegant marquis, a disillusioned liberal, who is supposed to have ruined himself to help her family and her frivolous stepfather. All these shams have been discovered later on. But the fact that they have been discovered makes no difference:

anyway, what she wants is the original De Grieux—that's what she wants! And the more she hates the present De Grieux the more she pines for the original one, though he existed only in her imagination. You are a sugar-boiler, Mr. Astley."

"Yes, I am a partner in the well-known firm, Lovel & Co."

"Well, you see, Mr. Astley, on one side—a sugar-boiler, and on the other—Apollo Belvedere; it is somewhat incongruous. And I am not even a sugar-boiler; I am simply a paltry gambler at roulette, and have even been a lackey, which I think Miss Polina knows very well, as I fancy she has good detectives."

"You are exasperated, and that is why you talk all this nonsense," Mr. Astley said coolly, after a moment's thought. "Besides, there is nothing original in what you say."

"I admit that! But the awful thing is, my noble friend, that however stale, however hackneyed, however farcical my statements may be—they are nevertheless true! Anyway, you and I have made no way at all!"

"That's disgusting nonsense . . . because, because . . . let me tell you!" Mr. Astley, with flashing eyes, pronounced in a quivering voice, "let me tell you, you ungrateful, unworthy, shallow and unhappy man, that I am come to Homburg expressly at her wish, to see you, to have a long and open conversation with you and to tell her everything—what you are feeling, thinking, hoping, and . . . what you remember!"

"Is it possible? Is it possible?" I cried, and tears rushed in streams from my eyes.

I could not restrain them. I believe it was the first time it happened in my life.

"Yes, unhappy man, she loved you, and I can tell you that, because you are—a lost man! What is more, if I were to tell you that she loves you to this day—you would stay here just the same! Yes, you have destroyed yourself. You had some abilities, a lively disposition, and were not a bad fellow; you might have even been of service to your country, which is in such need of men, but— you will remain here, and your life is over. I don't blame you. To my mind all Russians are like that, or disposed to be like that. If it is not roulette it is something similar. The exceptions are very rare. You are not the first who does not understand the meaning of work (I am not talking of your peasantry). Roulette is a game pre-eminently for the Russians. So far you've been honest and preferred serving as a lackey to stealing. . . . But I dread to think what may come in the future. Enough, good-bye! No doubt you are in want of money? Here are ten louis d'or from me. I won't give you more, for you'll gamble it away in any case. Take it and good-bye! Take it!"

"No, Mr. Astley, after all you have said."

"Ta—ake it!" he cried. "I believe that you are still an honourable man, and I give it as a true friend gives to another friend. If I were sure that you would throw up gambling, leave Homburg and would return to your own country, I would be ready to give you at once a thousand pounds to begin a new career. But I don't give you a thousand pounds: I give you only ten louis d'or just because a thousand pounds and ten louis d'or are just the same to you now; it's all the same—you'll gamble it away. Take it and good-bye."

"I will take it if you will let me embrace you at parting."

"Oh, with pleasure!"

We embraced with sincere feeling, and Mr. Astley went away.

No, he is wrong! If I was crude and silly about Polina and De Grieux, he was crude and hasty about Russians. I say nothing of myself. However . . . however, all that is not the point for the time: that is all words, words, and words, deeds are what are wanted! Switzerland is the great thing now! To-morrow . . . Oh, if only it were possible to set off to-morrow! To begin anew, to rise again. I must show them. . . . Let Polina know that I still can be a man. I have only to . . . But now it's too late—but to-morrow . . . oh, I have a presentiment and it cannot fail to be! I have now fifteen louis d'or, and I have begun with fifteen gulden! If one begins carefully . . . and can I, can I be such a baby! Can I fail to understand that I am a lost man, but—can I not rise again! Yes! I have only for once in my life to be prudent and patient and—that is all! I have only for once to show will power and in one hour I can transform my destiny! The great thing is will power. Only remember what happened to me seven months ago at Roulettenburg just before my final failure. Oh! it was a remarkable instance of determination: I had lost everything then, everything. . . . I was going out of the Casino, I looked, there was still one gulden in my waistcoat pocket: "Then I shall have something for dinner," I thought. But after I had gone a hundred paces I changed my mind and went back. I staked that gulden on *manque* (that time it was on *manque*), and there really is something peculiar in the feeling when, alone in a strange land, far from home and from friends, not knowing whether you will have anything to eat that day—you stake your last gulden, your very last! I won, and twenty minutes later I went out of the Casino, having a hundred and seventy gulden in my pocket. That's a fact! That's what the last gulden can sometimes do! And what if I had lost heart then? What if I had not dared to risk it? . . .

To-morrow, to-morrow it will all be over!

67457